Key to 1:250 000 Maps, atlas pages 18-143

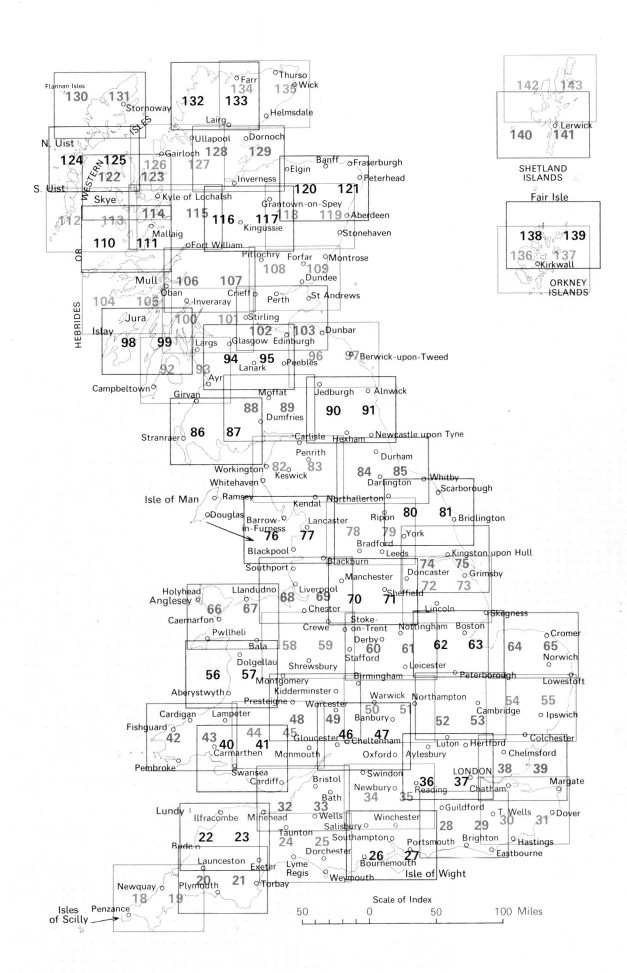

Ordnance Survey
ROAD ATLAS
of Great Britain

O|S
Ordnance Survey
ROAD ATLAS
of Great Britain

Ordnance Survey

Temple Press

TEMPLE · PRESS
NEWNES·BOOKS

Temple Press was founded in the 1890s, and soon became the leading publisher of transport journals and books — *The Motor Manual*, first published in 1903, reached 36 editions while the Temple Press Book of the Model T Ford which appeared in 1912 was an early motoring bestseller, with more than 150,000 copies sold. Newnes was founded in 1881 by Sir George Newnes, whose company purchased Country Life in 1897 and Collingridge in 1927. Today Country Life Books, Collingridge and Temple Press books are all published by Newnes Books.

First published 1983 by

Ordnance Survey   and   Temple Press
Romsey Road   an imprint of Newnes Books
Maybush   84/88 The Centre
Southampton SO9 4DH   Feltham
                                 Middlesex TW13 4BH

Copyright © Crown Copyright 1983

Second Impression 1983

The representation in this atlas of a road is no evidence of the existence of a right of way.

ISBN 0 600 35054 1

Printed in Great Britain

Contents

6 The National Grid

7 Ordnance Survey 1:50 000 Scale Maps

8 National Parks, Forest Parks and
  Long-distance Paths

9 Motoring Information

10 Route Planning Maps

16 Mileages between Selected Towns

17 Legend to 1:250 000 Scale Maps

18 **Ordnance Survey 1:250 000 Maps**
  for key see front endpaper

144 London Through Routes

145 Central London

153 Town Through Route Maps

160 Street Index to Central London Maps

164 Index to 1:250 000 Scale Maps

Front endpaper
Distances between Principal Towns
Key to 1:250 000 Maps, atlas pages 18-143
Back endpaper
Road Signs

The National Grid

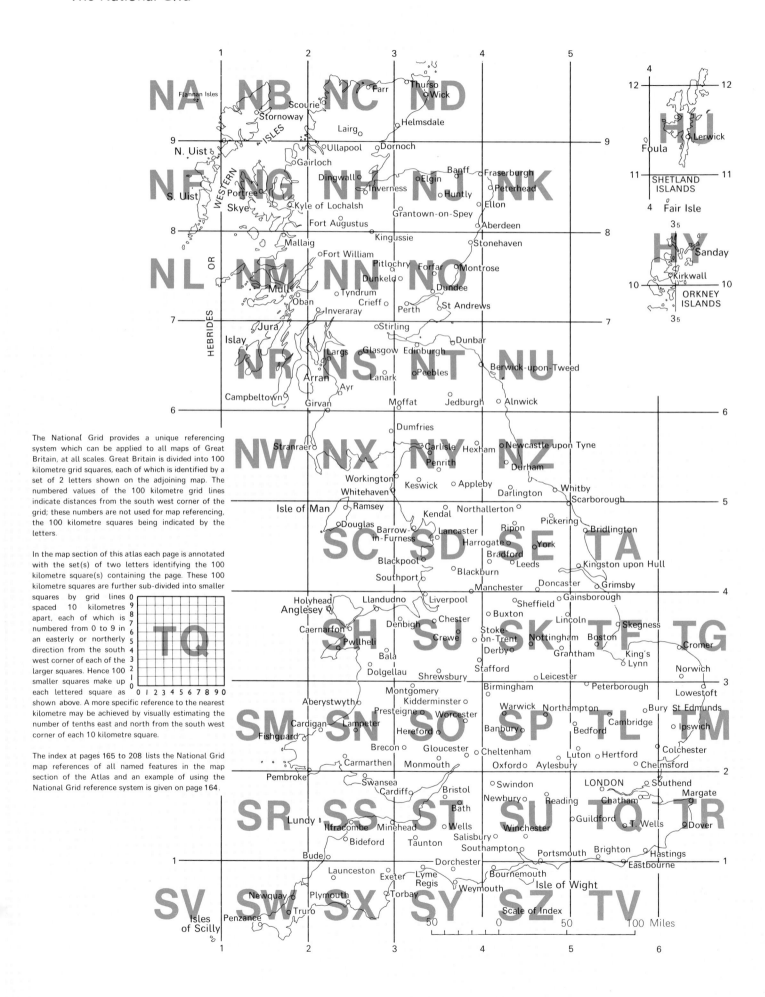

The National Grid provides a unique referencing system which can be applied to all maps of Great Britain, at all scales. Great Britain is divided into 100 kilometre grid squares, each of which is identified by a set of 2 letters shown on the adjoining map. The numbered values of the 100 kilometre grid lines indicate distances from the south west corner of the grid; these numbers are not used for map referencing, the 100 kilometre squares being indicated by the letters.

In the map section of this atlas each page is annotated with the set(s) of two letters identifying the 100 kilometre square(s) containing the page. These 100 kilometre squares are further sub-divided into smaller squares by grid lines spaced 10 kilometres apart, each of which is numbered from 0 to 9 in an easterly or northerly direction from the south west corner of each of the larger squares. Hence 100 smaller squares make up each lettered square as shown above. A more specific reference to the nearest kilometre may be achieved by visually estimating the number of tenths east and north from the south west corner of each 10 kilometre square.

The index at pages 165 to 208 lists the National Grid map references of all named features in the map section of the Atlas and an example of using the National Grid reference system is given on page 164.

Key to Ordnance Survey 1:50 000 Scale Maps
See page 153 for notes on this sheet map series

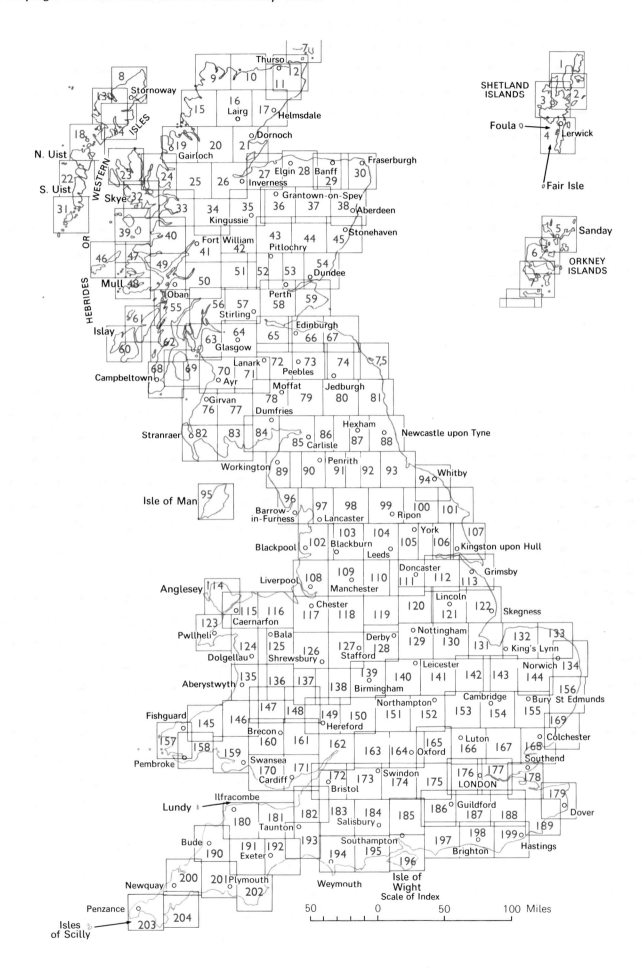

SHETLAND ISLANDS

Foula

Fair Isle

Lerwick

Sanday

ORKNEY ISLANDS

Stornoway

N. Uist

S. Uist

WESTERN ISLES

Skye

Mull

Islay

HEBRIDES OR

Campbeltown

Isle of Man

Anglesey

Pwllheli

Dolgellau

Aberystwyth

Fishguard

Pembroke

Newquay

Penzance

Isles of Scilly

Thurso

Lairg

Helmsdale

Dornoch

Gairloch

Elgin

Banff

Fraserburgh

Inverness

Grantown-on-Spey

Aberdeen

Kingussie

Stonehaven

Fort William

Pitlochry

Dundee

Oban

Perth

Stirling

Glasgow

Edinburgh

Lanark

Peebles

Moffat

Jedburgh

Ayr

Dumfries

Girvan

Stranraer

Carlisle

Hexham

Newcastle upon Tyne

Workington

Penrith

Whitby

Barrow-in-Furness

Lancaster

Ripon

York

Kingston upon Hull

Blackpool

Blackburn

Leeds

Doncaster

Grimsby

Liverpool

Manchester

Lincoln

Chester

Skegness

Caernarfon

Nottingham

Bala

Derby

King's Lynn

Shrewsbury

Stafford

Leicester

Norwich

Birmingham

Cambridge

Bury St Edmunds

Northampton

Brecon

Hereford

Luton

Colchester

Oxford

Swansea

Southend

Cardiff

Swindon

LONDON

Bristol

Guildford

Dover

Ilfracombe

Lundy

Salisbury

Southampton

Brighton

Hastings

Bude

Taunton

Exeter

Weymouth

Isle of Wight

Plymouth

Scale of Index

50   0   50   100 Miles

7

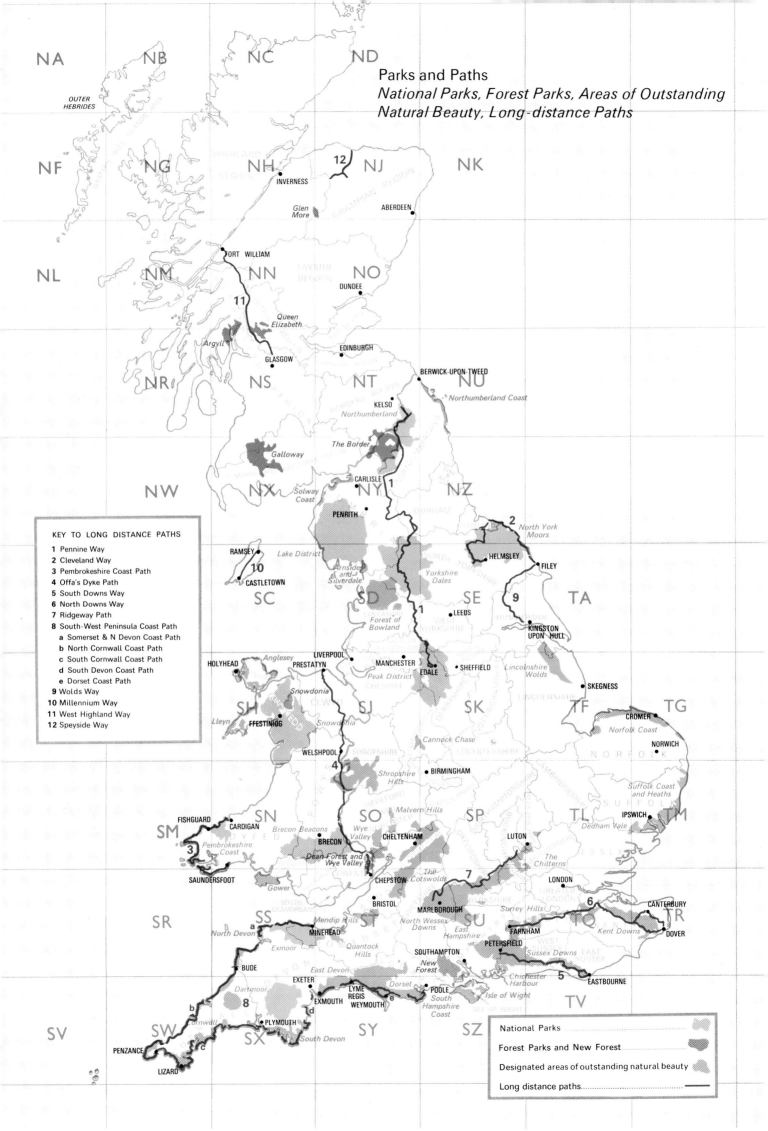

Parks and Paths
National Parks, Forest Parks, Areas of Outstanding Natural Beauty, Long-distance Paths

NA   NB   NC   ND

NF   NG   NH   NJ   NK
OUTER HEBRIDES

NL   NM   NN   NO

NR   NS   NT   NU

NW   NX   NY   NZ

SC   SD   SE   TA

SH   SJ   SK   TF   TG

SN   SO   SP   TL   TM

SM   SR   SS   ST   SU   TQ   TR

SV   SW   SX   SY   SZ   TV

KEY TO LONG DISTANCE PATHS
1 Pennine Way
2 Cleveland Way
3 Pembrokeshire Coast Path
4 Offa's Dyke Path
5 South Downs Way
6 North Downs Way
7 Ridgeway Path
8 South-West Peninsula Coast Path
   a Somerset & N Devon Coast Path
   b North Cornwall Coast Path
   c South Cornwall Coast Path
   d South Devon Coast Path
   e Dorset Coast Path
9 Wolds Way
10 Millennium Way
11 West Highland Way
12 Speyside Way

National Parks
Forest Parks and New Forest
Designated areas of outstanding natural beauty
Long distance paths

Cities and towns labelled: INVERNESS, ABERDEEN, Glen More, FORT WILLIAM, DUNDEE, Queen Elizabeth, Argyll, EDINBURGH, GLASGOW, BERWICK-UPON-TWEED, Northumberland Coast, KELSO, Northumberland, The Border, Galloway, CARLISLE, PENRITH, North York Moors, HELMSLEY, FILEY, RAMSEY, Lake District, CASTLETOWN, Arnside and Silverdale, Yorkshire Dales, LEEDS, Forest of Bowland, SKEGNESS, Lincolnshire Wolds, LIVERPOOL, PRESTATYN, MANCHESTER, SHEFFIELD, EDALE, Peak District, HOLYHEAD, Anglesey, CROMER, Snowdonia, Norfolk Coast, NORWICH, FFESTINIOG, Lleyn, WELSHPOOL, Cannock Chase, Suffolk Coast and Heaths, Shropshire Hills, BIRMINGHAM, IPSWICH, FISHGUARD, CARDIGAN, Brecon Beacons, Malvern Hills, Dedham Vale, Wye Valley, CHELTENHAM, LUTON, The Chilterns, Pembrokeshire Coast, BRECON, Dean Forest and Wye Valley, CHEPSTOW, The Cotswolds, MARLBOROUGH, LONDON, SAUNDERSFOOT, Gower, BRISTOL, North Wessex Downs, Surrey Hills, CANTERBURY, Mendip Hills, MINEHEAD, East Hampshire, FARNHAM, Kent Downs, DOVER, North Devon, Exmoor, Quantock Hills, SOUTHAMPTON, PETERSFIELD, Sussex Downs, BUDE, East Devon, New Forest, Chichester Harbour, EASTBOURNE, EXETER, Dartmoor, LYME REGIS, Dorset, POOLE, EXMOUTH, WEYMOUTH, South Hampshire Coast, Isle of Wight, PENZANCE, Cornwall, PLYMOUTH, South Devon, LIZARD

Motoring Information

WEATHER FORECASTS

Bedford area (40 mile radius)	01-246 8099
Belfast area	0232 8091
Birmingham area	021-246 8091
Bristol area (including	0272 8091
Weston-Super-Mare)	0793 8091
Cardiff area	0222 8091
Devon and Cornwall	0392 8091
Edinburgh area	031-246 8091
Essex coast	01-246 8096
Glasgow area	041-246 8091
Kent coast	01-246 8098
Lancashire Merseyside Greater Manchester and Cheshire	061-246 8091
Leeds Bradford and Huddersfield area	0532 8091
London area	01-246 8091
	0483 8091
Norfolk and Suffolk	0473 8091
North East England	0632 8091
North Lincs Retford and South Humberside	0522 8091
North Wales coast from Conwy to Chester	061-246 8093
Nottingham Leicester and Derby area	0602 8091
Sheffield area (20 mile radius)	0742 8091
Southern Hampshire and Isle of Wight (including coastal area between Poole harbour and Chichester)	0703 8091
South West Midlands	0452 8091
Sussex coast	01-246 8097
Thames Valley	0734 8091

WEATHER CENTRES

For personal advice call the Meteorological Office

London	01-836 4311
Glasgow	041-248 3451
Manchester	061-832 6701
Newcastle	0632 26453
Nottingham	0602 384092
Southampton	0703 28844

RADIO INFORMATION

B.B.C. National Radio gives frequent road and weather information. The frequencies used are:-

		kHz/metres	MHz
Radio 1	M.W.	1053/285 V.H.F.	88-91
		1089/275	88-91
		1485/202	88-91
Radio 2	M.W.	693/433	88-91
		909/330	88-91
Radio 4	L.W.	200/1500	92-95
(Aberdeen)	M.W.	1449/207	92-95
(Carlisle)		1485/202	92-95
(London)		720/417	92-95
(Plymouth)		774/388	92-95
(Redruth)		756/397	92-95
(Tyneside)		603/498	92-95
Radio Scotland		810/370	
		858/513	97-100
Radio Wales		657/457	
		882/340	
Radio Cymru			92-97

TRAVEL INFORMATION

The information given covers roads within:-

Birmingham (50 mile radius)	021-246 8021
Coventry	(0203) 8021
Hereford	(0432) 8021
Bristol (70 mile radius)	(0272) 8021
Bournemouth	(0202) 8021
Cheltenham	(0242) 8021
Gloucester	(0452) 8021
Southampton	(0703) 8021
Swindon	(0793) 8021
Liverpool (50 mile radius)	051-246 8021
Blackburn	(0254) 8021
Blackpool	(0253) 8021
Manchester	061-246 8021
London (70 mile radius)	01-246 8021
Bishop's Stortford	(0279) 8021
Brighton	(0273) 8021
Chelmsford	(0245) 8021
Colchester	(0206) 8021
Guildford	(0483) 8021
High Wycombe	(0494) 8021
Luton	(0582) 8021
Medway	(0634) 8021
Oxford	(0865) 8021
Portsmouth	(0705) 8021
Reading	(0734) 8021
Royal Tunbridge Wells	(0892) 8021
Southend-on-Sea	(0702) 8021
N E England & Lake District	
Newcastle upon Tyne	(0632) 8021
Middlesbrough	((0642) 8021
Scotland	
Edinburgh	031-246 8021
Glasgow	041-246 8021
Sheffield (30 mile radius)	(0742) 8021
Bradford	(0274) 8021
Doncaster	(0302) 8021
Huddersfield	(0484) 8021
Leeds	(0532) 8021
South Wales	
Cardiff	(0222) 8021
Newport	(0633) 0821
Motorways	01-246 8031
Rail (London and Inter City)	01-246 8030
Sea	01-246 8032
Air	01-246 8033

LOCAL RADIO

I.L.R.

	kHz/metres	MHz
1 North Sound (Aberdeen)	M.W. 1035/290 V.H.F. 96·9	
2 West Sound (Ayr)	1035/290	96·2
(Girvan)	1035/290	97·1
3 B R M B Radio (Birmingham)	1152/261	94·8
4 2 C R (Bournemouth)	828/362	97·2
5 Pennine Radio (Bradford)	1278/235	96·0
6 Radio West (Bristol)	1260/238	96·3
7 Saxon Radio (Bury St. Edmunds)	1251/240	96·3
8 C B C (Cardiff)	1359/221	96·0
9 Mercia Sound (Coventry)	1359/220	95·9
10 Radio Tay (Dundee)	1161/258	95·8
(Perth)	1584/189	96·4
11 Radio Forth (Edinburgh)	1548/194	96·8
12 Devon Air Radio (Exeter)	666/450	95·8
(Torbay)	954/314	95·1
13 Radio Clyde (Glasgow)	1152/261	95·1
14 Severn Sound (Gloucester & Cheltenham)	774/388	95·0
15 Radio Wyvern (Hereford)	954/314	95·8
(Worcester)	1350/196	96·2
16 Moray Firth Radio (Inverness)	1107/271	95·9
17 Radio Orwell (Ipswich)	1170/257	97·1
18 Radio Aire (Leeds)	828/362	94·6
19 Centre Radio (Leicester)	1260/238	97·1
20 Radio City (Liverpool)	1548/194	96·7
21 Capital Radio (London)	1548/194	95·8
22 London Broadcasting Co.	1152/261	97·3
23 Chiltern Radio (Luton)	828/362	97·5
(Bedford)	792/380	95·5
24 Piccadily Radio (Manchester)	1152/261	97·0
25 Radio Trent (Nottingham)	999/301	96·2
26 Hereward Radio (Peterborough)	1332/225	95·7
27 Plymouth Sound	1152/261	96·0
28 Radio Victory (Portsmouth)	1170/257	95·0
29 Radio 210 (Reading)	1431/210	97·0
30 Radio Hallam (Sheffield)	1548/194	95·2
(Rotherham)	1548/194	95·9
31 Essex Radio (Southend)	1431/210	95·3
(Chelmsford)	1359/220	96·4
32 Swansea Sound	1170/257	95·1
33 Wiltshire Radio (Swindon)	1161/258	96·4
(West Wilts)	936/321	97·4
34 Radio Tees (Teesside)	1170/257	95·0
35 Metro Radio (Tyne & Wear)	1152/261	97·0
36 Beacon Radio (Wolverhampton & Black Country)	990/303	97·2
37 Marcher Sound/Sain-Y-Gororau (Wrexham & Deeside)	1260/238	95·4

LOCAL RADIO

Local radio stations giving road and weather reports

B.B.C.	kHz/metres	MHz
1 Radio Sussex	M.W. 1485/202 V.H.F. 95·3	
	1161/258	95·3
2 Radio Bristol	1548/194	95·5
	1584/189	95·5
3 Radio Cambridgeshire	1026/292	96·0
	1449/207	96·0
4 Radio Cornwall (Redruth)	630/476	95·2
	630/476	96·4
(Bodmin)	657/457	97·3
5 Radio Cumbria	756/397	95·6
	1458/206	95·6
6 Radio Cleveland	1548/194	95·8
	1548/194	96·6
7 Radio Derby	1116/269	96·5
	1116/269	94·2
8 Radio Devon (Barnstaple)	801/375	97·5
(Exeter)	990/303	97·0
(Plymouth)	855/351	97·5
(Torbay)	1458/206	97·5
9 Radio Furness	837/358	96·1
10 Radio Humberside	1485/202	96·9
11 Radio Lancashire	858/351	96·4
12 Radio Leeds	774/388	92·4
13 Radio Leicester	837/358	95·1
14 Radio Lincolnshire	1368/219	94·9
15 Radio London	1458/206	94·9
16 Radio Manchester	1458/206	95·1
17 Radio Medway	1035/290	96·7
18 Radio Merseyside	1485/202	95·8
19 Radio Newcastle	1458/206	95·4
	1458/206	96·3
20 Radio Norfolk	873/344	96·1
	855/351	96·1
21 Radio Northampton	1107/271	96·6
22 Radio Nottingham	1521/197	95·4
23 Radio Oxford	1485/202	95·2
24 Radio Sheffield	1035/290	97·4
	1035/290	88·6
25 Radio Solent	999/300	96·1
	1359/221	96·1
26 Radio Stoke-on-Trent	1503/200	94·6
27 Radio WM (West Midlands)	1458/206	95·6
	828/362	95·6
28 Radio York	666/450	90·2
	666/450	97·2
ISLE OF MAN		
1 Manx Radio	219/1368	96·9
	219/1368	89·0

Route
Planning Maps

Abb's Head
emouth

Berwick-upon-Tweed

A1
A697
Alnwick
A1068
Amble-by-the-Sea
Ashington
Morpeth
Bedlington
A1696
Blyth
Whitley Bay
Newcastle upon Tyne
Tynemouth
A69
South Shields
Gateshead
onsett
A692
Sunderland
A691
Seaham
A68
A690
Durham
A1(M)
A19
Bishop Auckland
A689
Hartlepool
arnard Castle
A688
A68
Stockton -on-Tees
Middlesbrough
A174
A66
Darlington
Guisborough
A171
Whitby
Scotch Corner
A172
A1
A19
A684
Northallerton
A169
A171
Thirsk
A170
Pickering
Scarborough
A61
A168
Malton
Filey
Ripon
A64
A165
 kipton
A59
A61
A1
Harrogate
Knaresborough
A166
Great Driffield
Bridlington
A658
York
A59
A1079
A163
Beverley
A165
ighley
A64
Wetherby
A19
Market Weighton
adford
LEEDS
A6120
Selby
A163
A1079
Kingston upon Hull
alifax
M62
Castleford
Howden
A63
A1033
Withernsea
Dewsbury
M62
Goole
Humber Bridge
Pontefract
Huddersfield
Wakefield
Thorne
A18
Scunthorpe
A15
Immingham
dham
A61
A638
Grimsby
HESTER
A629
Barnsley
Doncaster
M180
Brigg
A18
A1031
A628
Rotherham
M18
A159
A46
A16
Louth
Glossop
A57
Bawtry
Market Rasen
A57
SHEFFIELD
A631
Gainsborough
Mablethorpe
Buxton
Worksop
A1
A156
A158
A52
Skegness
Chesterfield
A60
Lincoln
A623
A6
A614
A57
Mansfield
A46
Horncastle
A16
Leek
Matlock
A38
A15
A153
Ripley
Newark-on-Trent
A617
A607
Sleaford
A1121
Boston
Ashbourne
A610
Nottingham
A1
Hunstanton
A149
Wells-next-the-Sea
A148
Cromer
A52
A52
Grantham
A17
THE WASH
Fakenham
North Walsham
A140
A149
ttoxeter
A6
A453
A151
Spalding
King's Lynn
A148
A1065
A1067
Burton upon Trent
A6006
Melton Mowbray
A15
A16
A1101
East Dereham
A47
Swaffham
Norwich
Caister-on-Sea
A515
Ashby-de-la-Zouch
A50
Loughborough
Wisbech
A1122
A10
A1122
Great Yarmouth
chfield
A453
Oakham
A606
Stamford
A47
Downham Market
A134
A11
Acle
A47
Brownhills
Leicester
A47
A43
Peterborough
March
A1075
Wymondham
A146
Lowestoft
Walsall
A5
Hinckley
A6
Market Harborough
A6003
Corby
A605
Oundle
A141
A142
A1065
Bungay
A1116
Beccles
Nuneaton
A427
Kettering
Thrapston
Chatteris
Ely
A1066
Diss
A12
RMINGHAM
Rugby
M69
Wellingborough
A604
Huntingdon
A142
A11
Thetford
A143
omsgrove
Coventry
M45

NORTH SEA

Flamborough Head

River Humber

Spurn Head

Yarmouth Roads

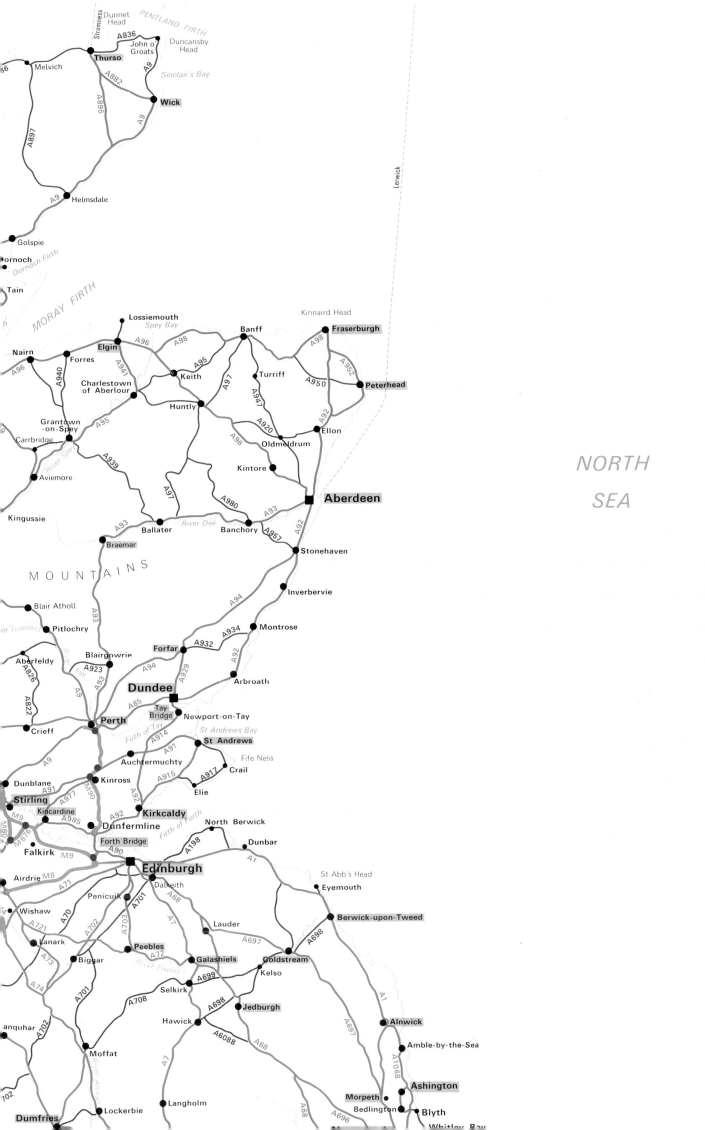

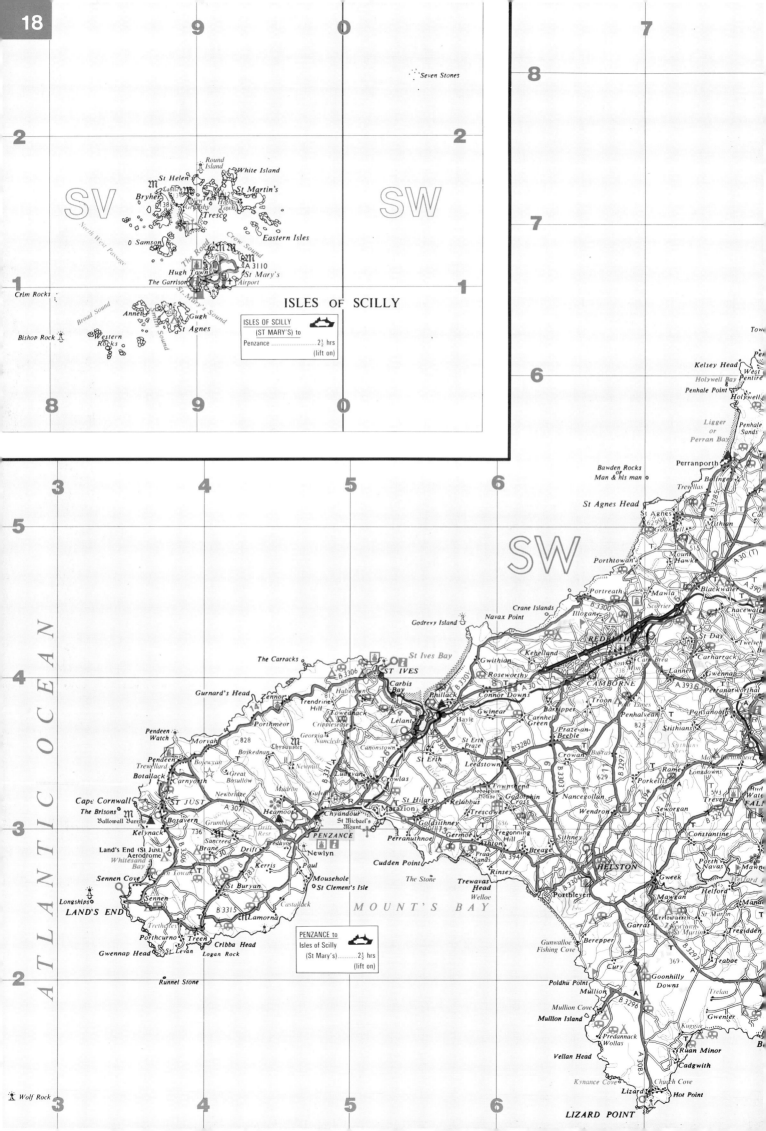

ISLES OF SCILLY

Inset top-left (Isles of Scilly):

Seven Stones

SV · SW

Round Island · White Island · St Helen · St Martin's · Bryher · Tean · Higher Town · Tresco · New Grimsby · Old Grimsby · Eastern Isles · North West Passage · 0 Samson · Crow Sound · The Road · A 3110 · Hugh Town · St Mary's · Airport · The Garrison · St Mary's Sound · Crim Rocks · Broad Sound · Annet · Gugh · St Agnes · St Mary's Sound · Bishop Rock · Western Rocks

ISLES OF SCILLY
(ST MARY'S) to
Penzance .... 2½ hrs
(lift on)

Main map:

ATLANTIC OCEAN

SW

Seven Stones

Kelsey Head · West Pentire · Holywell Bay · Penhale Point · Holywell · Ligger or Perran Bay · Penhale Sands · Bawden Rocks or Man & his man · Perranporth · Trevellas · Bolingey · St Agnes Head · St Agnes · Goonbell · Mithian · Mount Hawke · Porthtowan · Blackwater · Portreath · Mawla · Scorrier · Chacewater · Crane Islands · Illogan · St Day · Twelveheads · Godrevy Island · Navax Point · Gwithian · Kehelland · REDRUTH · Carn Brea · Carharrack · Gwennap · The Carracks · St Ives Bay · Roseworthy · Lanner · St Ives Bay · Phillack · Connor Downs · CAMBORNE · Troon · Penhallean · Ponsanooth · St Ives · Carbis Bay · Hayle · Gwinear · Barripper · Praze-an-Beeble · Stithians · Gurnard's Head · Zennor · Halsetown · Lelant · Carnhell Green · Gwithian · Crowan · Trendrine Hill · Towednack · Gwinear · St Erth Praze · Leedstown · Porthmeor · Cripplesease · Canonstown · St Erth · Nancegollan · Porkellis · Londowns · Pendeen Watch · Morvah · Georgia · Nancledra · River Hayle · Townshend · Wendron · Trevena · Chysauster · Newmill · Ludgvan · Godolphin House · FALMOUTH · Pendeen · Trewellard · Bojewyan · Boskednan · Great Bosullow · Crowlas · St Hilary · Godolphin Cross · Seworgan · Botallack · Carnyorth · Newbridge · Madron · Gulval · Relubbus · Trescowe · Constantine · Cape Cornwall · ST JUST · A 307 · Heamoor · Marazion · Tregew · Porth Navas · The Brisons · Bosavern · Grumbla · PENZANCE · Chyandour · St Michael's Mount · Goldsithney · Germoe · Tregonning Hill · Sithney · Helford · Ballowall Barrow · Kelynack · Sancreed · Brane · Drift · Newlyn · Perranuthnoe · Ashton · Breage · HELSTON · Gweek · Land's End (St Just) Aerodrome · Whitesand Bay · Drift Resr · Paul · Cudden Point · Praa Sands · Rinsey · Porthleven · Mawgan · Helford · Sennen Cove · Carn Towan · Kerris · Mousehole · St Clement's Isle · The Stone · Trewavas Head · Welloe · Trelowarren · St Martin · Tregidden · Longships · Sennen · St Buryan · MOUNT'S BAY · Gunwalloe Fishing Cove · Berepper · Garras · Newtown-in-St Martin · LAND'S END · Lamorna · Castallack · Gweer · Trethewey · Treen · Cribba Head · Cury · Traboe · Porthcurno · St Levan · Logan Rock · Poldhu Point · Mullion · Goonhilly Downs · Trelan · Gwennap Head · Runnel Stone · Mullion Cove · Mullion Island · Gwenter · Predannack Wollas · Kuggar · Vellan Head · Ruan Minor · Cadgwith · Church Cove · Wolf Rock · Kynance Cove · Lizard · Hot Point · LIZARD POINT

PENZANCE to
Isles of Scilly
(ST MARY'S) ....2½ hrs
(lift on)

8   9   0   1   2

Rumps Point
Pentire Point
New Polzeath
Gulland Rock
Padstow Bay
Port Isaac Bay
Port Isaac
Portgaverne
Portquin
Port Quin Bay
Polzeath
Trebetherick
Tradizzick
Rock
St Minver
St Endellion
Trelights
Pendoggett
Tregeare Rounds
Camelford
Helstone
St Teath
Crowdy Reservoir
Lewannick
Laneast
Trewen
River Inny
Polyphant
Altarnun
Trebartha
North Hill

TREVOSE HEAD
Qules
Constantine Bay
Trevornick
Trevone
Padstow
Crugmeer
St Merryn
Shop
Little Petherick
Chapel Amble
St Kew
St Kew Highway
Tudy
Michaelstow
St Breward
Row
Garrow Tor
Brown Willy
1377
Codda
Bolventor
BODMIN MOOR
Kilmar Tor
Henwood
Rilla Mill
Upper Cross
Coad's Green
Coradon Hill
Darite

Gunver Head
Park Head
Bedruthan Steps
Porthcothan Bay
Trenance
Penrose
St Ervan
Rumford
Tredinnick
St Issey
Trevanson
Wadebridge
Egloshayle
St Mabyn
Blisland
Temple
880
912
Maldenwell
Warleggan
924
Common Moor
The Butlers
Minions
Trethevy Quoit
Tremar
St Ive
Merrymeet

Mawgan Porth
Berry's Point
Watergate Bay
Vale or Lanherne
St Mawgan
Mawgan or Lanherne
Talskiddy
Tregurrian
Newquay Aerodrome
St Wenn
St Breock Downs
Ruthernbridge
Nanstallon
St Lawrence
Withiel
Rosenannon
Cardinham
Mount
Les
St Neot
Dobwalls
LISKEARD
Menheniot

Newquay
NEWQUAY
Crantock
St Columb Minor
Colan
Mountjoy
Trebudannon
St Columb Major
Castle an Dinas
Victoria
Belowda
Roche
Bilberry
Lanivet
BODMIN
Bodmin Road Sta
East Taphouse
Braddock
St Pinnock
St Keyne
Trewidland
Herodsfoot

Cubert
Crantock
Trevarren
Kestle Mill
St Columb Road
Fraddon
Indian Queens
St Dennis
Henbarrow
Bugle
Stenalees
Penwithick
Lanlivery
Luxulyan
LOSTWITHIEL
Boconnoc
Bocaddon
Sandplace
Duloe
Widegates
St Martin
Downderry

St Newlyn East
Newlyn Downs
Summercourt
Mitchell
Brighton
Whitemoor Down
Nanpean
Foxhole
Carthew
Trethurgy
St Blazey
Tywardreath
Par
Golant
Penpoll
Lerryn
Lanreath
Muchlarnick
Pelynt
Morval
LOOE

Rejerrah
Goonhavern
Zelah
St Allen
Carland Cross
Ladock
New Mills
St Stephen
Coombe
St Mewan
Trewoon
ST AUSTELL
Boscoppa
Polgooth
Charlestown
Porthpean
Polkerris
Menabilly
FOWEY
Polruan
Lansallos
Pencarrow Head
Polperro
Talland Bay
St George's or Looe Island

Trispen
Zabuloe
Shortlanesend
Tresillian
St Erme
Probus
Grampound Road
Grampound
Creed
Sticker
Polmassick
St Ewe
Pentewan
Mevagissey Bay
Gribbin Head
St Austell Bay
SX

Kenwyn
Merther
TRURO
St Clement
Trewarthenick
Tregony
Trevarrick
Ruan Lanihorne
Lamorran
Mevagissey
Portmellon
Chapel Point

Kea
Malpas
Old Kea
Playing Place
St Michael Penkevil
Philleigh
Veryan
Portloe
Portholland
Boswinger
Penare
Gorran Haven
St Michael Caerhays
Veryan Bay
Dodman Point

Feock
Trelissick
Mylor Bridge
Trewithian
Rosevine
Gerrans
Portscatho
Greeb Point
Nare Head
Gerrans Bay
Carne

Flushing
St Mawes
Castle
Pendennis Point
Zone Point
Bohortha
Falmouth Bay

Rosemullion Head
Anthony-in-Meneage
Nare Point
Porthallow
Porthoustock
Manacle Point
St Keverne
The Manacles
Head

ENGLISH CHANNEL

3   2   1   0   9   8

Penzance inset

Kennels
Trevaylor
Trevaylor
Kenegie
Hotel
Rosemorran
Tregar
Tremearne
Bone
Tolver
Pleming
Gulval
Ponjou
Longrock
Hospl
Sch
Heamoor
Chyandour
Trevarrack
Trythogga
Boscathnoe Resr
Rosehill
Hospl
Lesingey Round
Castle Horneck
Muse
Dock Memorial
Wherry Town
Pier
PENZANCE
48
Cressars
Western Cressar
Ryemar
Trereife
The Gear
NEWLYN
Gwavas
Ordnance Survey Tidal Observatory
Lake
Trewarveneth
Chyenhal
Chywoone Grove
Skilly

VEHICLE FERRY
FROM PENZANCE TO
Isles of Scilly 2¾ hrs

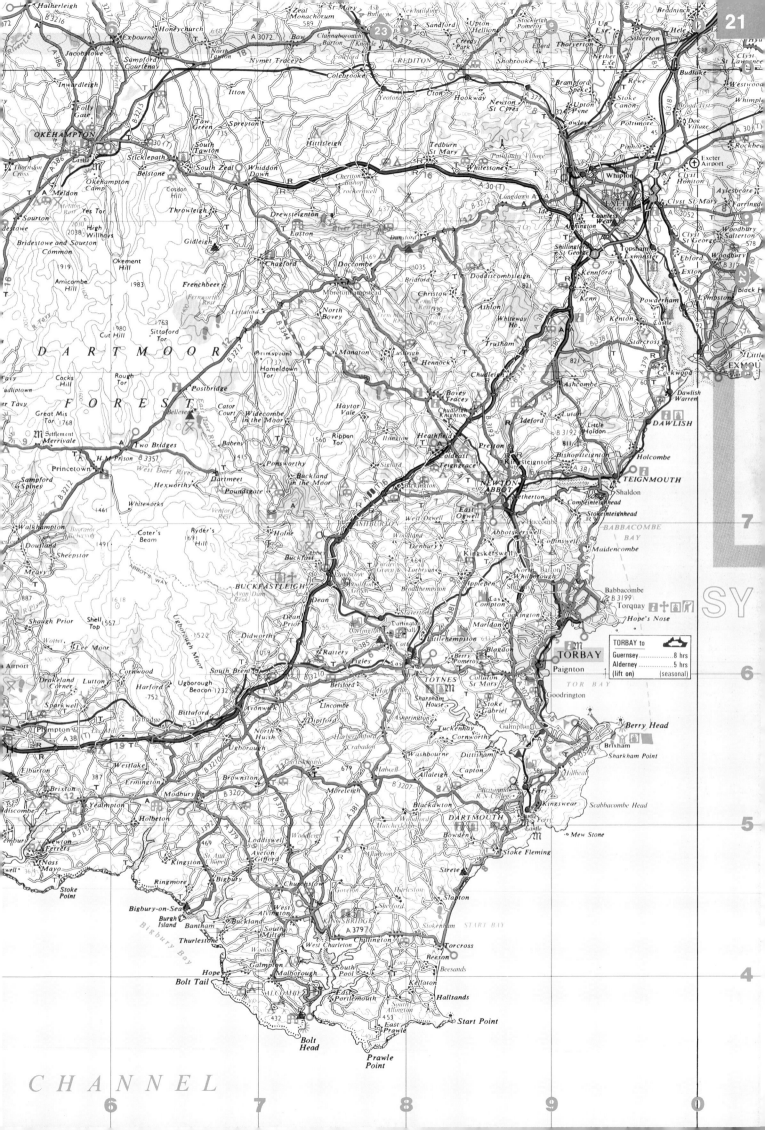

BRISTOL CHANNEL

ILFRACOMBE

LUNDY
North West Point
466
South West Point
Rat Island

Bull Point
Lee 675
Rockham Bay
Morte Point 451
Mortehoe
Woolacombe
Morte Bay
688

Baggy Point
Pickwell
Croyde Bay
North Buckland
Georgeham
Croyde 518
Knowle
Saunton
Pippa
Braunton
Hear
Punc

Braunton Toll
Braunton Burrows
Bideford Bar

BARNSTAPLE

OR

BIDEFORD BAY

Westward Ho!
Appledore
Instow
Bickleto
NORTHAM
Tapeley
Westleigh
Horwoo
Abbotsham
BIDEFORD
Woodtown
Alverdis
Fairy Cross
Landcross
Littleham
Weare Gifford
Monkleigh

Frithelstock
GRE
TOR
Little Torrington

HARTLAND POINT
Titchberry
Windbury Point
Stoke
Hartland
Clovelly
Hartland Quay
564
Clovelly Dykes
Buck's Mills
Milford
Philham
Dyke
Buck Cross
Elmscott
Woolfardisworthy
710
Parkham
Parkham Ash 709
Buckland Brewer

South Hole
Melbury
Knaps Longpeak
Welcombe
771
Ashmansworthy
East Putford
West Putford
Stibb Cross
Langtree
Gooseham
Eastcott
Dinworthy 708
Peters irland
512
Youlstone
Bulkworthy
Winswe
Morwenstow
734
Bradworthy
Abbots Bickington
Newton St Petrock
Higher Sharpnose Point
Shop
Woodford 656
Upper Tamar Lake
Sulcombe
Milton Damerel
Lower Sharpnose Point
Lower Tamar Lakes
Soldon Cross
Shebbear
560
Coombe
Kilkhampton
Alfardisworthy
Holsworthy Beacon
Thornbury
Buckland Filleigh
Stibb
A39
B3254
571
Chilsworthy
Bradford
Crookbury
Sheepwash
Holsworthy
Black Torrington
574
BUDE BAY
Poughill
STRATTON
Grimscott
HOLSWORTHY
13
Bude Haven
Flexbury
Launcells
Pancrasweek
Highampton
467
BUDE
A3072
BAY
Marhamchurch
Bridgerule
Pyworthy 531
Hollacombe
Graddon Moor 632
216
Widemouth Bay
Coppathorne
440
R Deer
Halwill Junction
Dizzard Point
632
Halwill
Beaworthy
449
Poundstock
Whitstone
Clawton
Tregole 544
20
Week St Mary
North Tamerton
Quoditch
St Gennys
Trewint
18
Cambeak
Jacobstow
Telcott
Lana
Ashwater
Eworthy
Germansweek
Crackington Haven
Wainhouse Corner
543
Clubworthy
West Curry 598
Luffincott
14
85·2
South Wheatley
Northcott
Chapmans Well Virginstow
Boscastle
Lesnewth
Otterham
Warbstow
Bennacott
Brazacott
Boyton
East Panson
Bratton Clovelly
841
Canworthy Water
St Giles on the Heath
Trevalga
641
North Petherwin
Polapit Tamar
Broadwoodwidger
Castle
Tintagel Head
Bossiney
Tremaine
Yeolmbridge
Werrington
Thrushelton
Tintagel
Hallworthy
Davidstow
Tremail
Trenglos
Tresmeer
Egloskerry
Langore
Cross Green
Stowford
Lewdow
1009
Treknow
Trewarmett
Tregeare
Red Down
St Stephens
464
Portgate
Start Point
Trewen
LAUNCESTON
Lifton
Tinhay
Coryton
Delabole
14
St Clether
Laneast
Tregadillett
Castle
PORT
Lawhitton
Marystow
Chillaton
Trelill
Cumelford
River Inny
Trewen
South Petherwin
Lewannick
Kelly
Black
North Brent
Port Isaac Bay
Helstone
St Teath
Rough Tor 1377
Altarnun
Polyphant
Bradstone
Milton Abbot
Portgaverne
Treligga Rounds
Michaelst
727
Garrow Tor 527
Brown Willy 1206
Codda
Letant
Dunterton
384
Trefill
11
Garrow Tor
Codda
1082

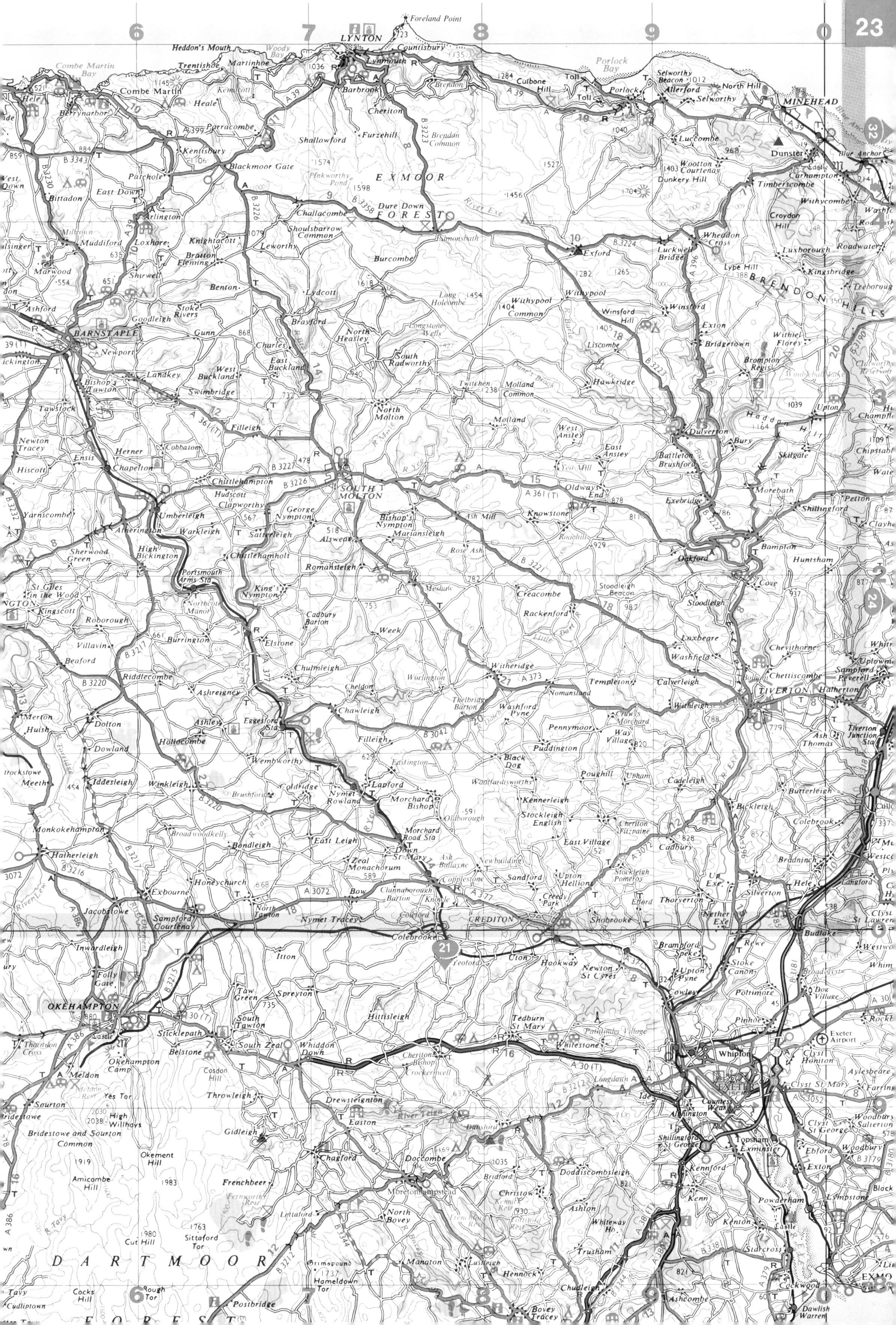

Foreland Point
LYNTON
Heddon's Mouth
Woody Bay
Countisbury
Combe Martin Bay
Trentishoe
Martinhoe
Lynmouth
Porlock Bay
Culbone Hill
Selworthy Beacon
Allerford
North Hill
Hele
Combe Martin
Kemacott
Barbrook
Brendon
Porlock
Selworthy
MINEHEAD
Berrynarbor
Heale
Cheriton
Parracombe
Shallowford
Furzehill
Brendon Common
Luccombe
Dunster
Blue Anchor
Kentisbury
Blackmoor Gate
EXMOOR
Wootton Courtenay
Dunkery Hill
Carhampton
Patchole
Pinkworthy Pond
Timberscombe
West Down
East Down
Bittadon
Arlington
Challacombe
Dure Down
FOREST
River Exe
Withycombe
Croydon Hill
Loxhore
Muddiford
Shoulsbarrow Common
Simonsbath
Exford
Luckwell Bridge
Wheddon Cross
Luxborough
Roadwater
Knightacott
Leworthy
Marwood
Bratton Fleming
Burcombe
Lype Hill
Kingsbridge
Shirwell
BRENDON HILLS
Benton
Lydcott
Long Holcombe
Withypool Common
Withypool
Treborough
Ashford
Goodleigh
Stoke Rivers
Brayford
Winsford Hill
Winsford
BARNSTAPLE
Gunn
Longstone Wells
Exton
Withiel Florey
Newport
Charles
North Heasley
Liscombe
Bridgetown
Brompton Regis
East Buckland
South Radworthy
Landkey
West Buckland
Bishop's Tawton
Swimbridge
Twitchen
Molland Common
Hawkridge
Tawstock
North Molton
Upton
Filleigh
Molland
West Anstey
Dulverton
Bury
Newton Tracey
Cobbaton
East Anstey
Skilgate
Herner
Ensis
Chapelton
Battleton
Brushford
Hiscott
Yeo Mill
Chittlehampton
SOUTH MOLTON
Oldways End
Morebath
Hudscott
Clapworthy
Exebridge
Petton
Shillingford
Yarnscombe
Umberleigh
George Nympton
Bishop's Nympton
Ash Mill
Knowstone
Warkleigh
Atherington
Satterleigh
Mariansleigh
Alswear
Sherwood Green
High Bickington
Chittlehamholt
Rose Ash
Roachill
Oakford
Bampton
Huntsham
Romansleigh
Portsmouth Arms Sta
St Giles in the Wood
Meshaw
Creacombe
Stoodleigh Beacon
Cove
King's Nympton
Northcote Manor
Kingscott
Roborough
Cadbury Barton
Rackenford
Stoodleigh
Burrington
Week
Loxbeare
Villavin
Elstone
Little Dart
Chevithorne
Beaford
Washfield
Riddlecombe
Chulmleigh
Worlington
Witheridge
Sampford Peverell
Templeton
Calverleigh
Cheldon
Ashreigney
Thelbridge Barton
Nomansland
TIVERTON
Halberton
Merton
Huish
Chawleigh
Dolton
Ashley
Eggesford Sta
Washford Pyne
Cruwys Morchard
Withleigh
Tiverton Junction Sta
Dowland
Pennymoor
Way Village
Ash Thomas
Hollocombe
Filleigh
Puddington
Wembworthy
Eastington
Black Dog
Poughill
Upham
Cadeleigh
Iddesleigh
Meeth
Winkleigh
Coldridge
Lapford
Woolfardisworthy
Butterleigh
Brushford
Nymet Rowland
Morchard Bishop
Kennerleigh
Bickleigh
Oldborough
Stockleigh English
Cheriton Fitzpaine
Colebrook
Monkokehampton
Broadwoodkelly
Morchard Road Sta
Bondleigh
East Leigh
East Village
Cadbury
Hatherleigh
Down St Mary
Zeal Monachorum
Ash Bullayne
Newbuilding
Bradninch
Copplestone
Sandford
Upton Hellions
Stockleigh Pomeroy
Honeychurch
Clannaborough Barton
Knowle
Hele
Langford
Exbourne
Bow
Creedy Park
Up Exe
Silverton
Jacobstowe
North Tawton
Efford
Thorverton
Sampford Courtenay
Nymet Tracey
Colebrooke
Coleford
CREDITON
Shobrooke
Nether Exe
Bradlake
Inwardleigh
Yeoford
Uton
Hookway
Brampford Speke
Rewe
Itton
Newton St Cyres
Stoke Canon
Broadclyst
Folly Gate
Upton Pyne
Taw Green
Spreyton
Cowley
Poltimore
Dog Village
OKEHAMPTON
South Tawton
Hittisleigh
Pinhoe
Castle
Tedburn St Mary
Pathfinder Village
Exeter Airport
Thornton Cross
Sticklepath
Whiddon Down
South Zeal
Belstone
Cheriton Bishop
Whitestone
Whipton
Clyst Honiton
Okehampton Camp
Crockernwell
Meldon
Cosdon Hill
Longdown
Ide
EXETER
Aylesbeare
Clyst St Mary
Sourton
Yes Tor
Throwleigh
Drewsteignton
Countess Wear
Alphington
Bridestowe
High Willhays
River Teign
Clyst St George
Woodbury Salterton
Bridestowe and Sourton Common
Gidleigh
Easton
Dunsford
Shillingford St George
Topsham
Exminster
Ebford
Woodbury
Okement Hill
Chagford
Doccombe
Doddiscombsleigh
Kennford
Exton
Amicombe Hill
Frenchbeer
Bridford
Kenn
Fernworthy Resr
Moretonhampstead
Christow
Lympstone
Powderham
Lettaford
North Bovey
Kennick Resr
Tottiford Resr
Ashton
Whiteway Ho
Kenton
Cut Hill
Sittaford Tor
Trusham
Starcross
DARTMOOR
Grimspound
Manaton
Lustleigh
Hennock
Hameldown Tor
Chudleigh
Ashcombe
Cockwood
Tavy
Cudliptown
Cocks Hill
Rough Tor
Postbridge
Bovey Tracey
Dawlish Warren
EXMOUTH
FOREST

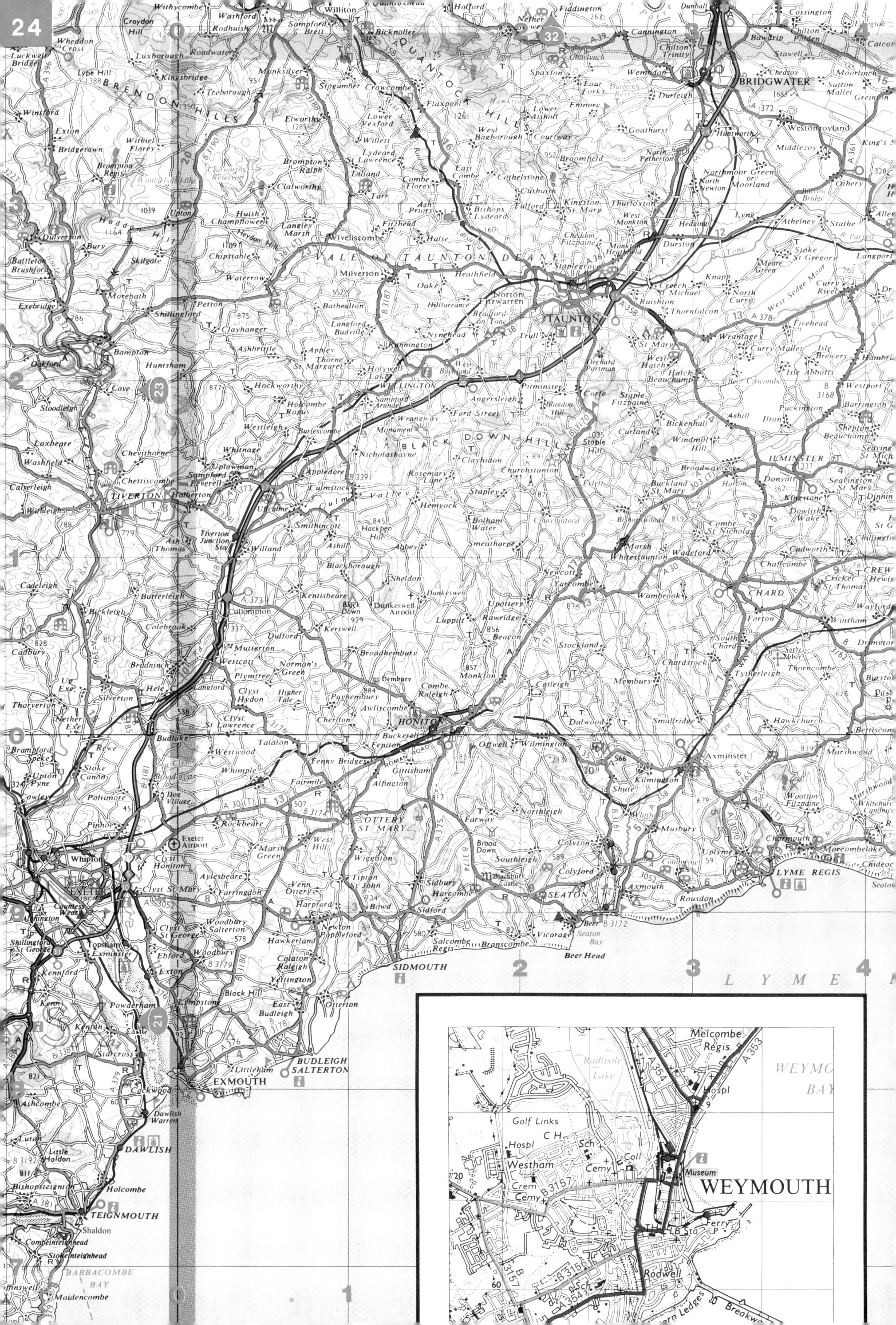

BRENDON HILLS

VALE OF TAUNTON DEANE

QUANTOCK HILLS

BRIDGWATER

TAUNTON

WELLINGTON

TIVERTON

BLACK DOWN HILLS

ILMINSTER

CHARD

HONITON

OTTERY ST MARY

EXETER

Exeter Airport

AXMINSTER

LYME REGIS

SIDMOUTH

BUDLEIGH SALTERTON

EXMOUTH

DAWLISH

TEIGNMOUTH

BABBACOMBE BAY

SEATON

Beer Head

Seaton Bay

LYME BAY

WEYMOUTH

Melcombe Regis

Radipole Lake

Westham

Golf Links

WEYMOUTH BAY

Rodwell

PORTSMOUTH to

PORTSMOUTH to	
Le Havre	5½ hrs
Guernsey	6½-7 hrs
St Malo	8½-10 hrs
Jersey	9-9½ hrs
Cherbourg	4-6½ hrs
	(seasonal)

SPITHEAD

SOLENT

C H A N N E L

WARLINGHAM 37 Biggin Hill Knockholt Pound Otford 30 Ryarsh New Hythe Aylesford Abbey Eccles

Whyteleafe Tatsfield Chevening Sevenoaks Knole Borough Green Offham East Barming MAIDSTONE

CATERHAM Woldingham Westerham Brasted Chart Ide Hill SEVENOAKS Ivy Hatch Plaxtol Mereworth West Peckham Mereworth Castle Nettlestead

Godstone Oxted Limpsfield Crockham Hill Toy Hill Sevenoaks Weald Shipbourne Hadlow East Peckham Neilstead Green Yalding Hunton Linton Chart Sutton

Bletchingley Tandridge Hurst Green Marlpit Hill Four Elms Penshurst Sta Leigh TONBRIDGE Whetsted Paddock Wood Marden Staplehurst

South Nutfield Redhill & Heliport Godstone Sta Crowhurst Blindley Heath Edenbridge Castle Hever Chiddingstone Causeway Hildenborough Higham Wood Golden Green Tudeley Five Oaks Green Collier Street Milebush

Horley Smallfield Newchapel Lingfield Marsh Green Chiddingstone Penshurst Bidborough Southborough Mayfield Brenchley Horsmonden Curtisden Green

Burstow Felbridge Dormansland Markbeech Cowden Sta Fordcombe Speldhurst Pembury Lamberhurst Goudhurst Cranbrook Common

Capthorne Crawley Down East Grinstead Felcourt Cowden Blackham Ashurst Langton Green ROYAL TUNBRIDGE WELLS Bayham Abbey Bells Yew Green Scotney Castle Kilndown Cranbrook Hartley

Pound Hill Turner's Hill Sunnyside Ashurstwood Hartfield Withyham Friar's Gate Groombridge Eridge Green Frant Wadhurst Cousley Wood Bedgebury Forest Flimwell Iden Green

Selsfield Common Forest Row Saint Hill Coleman's Hatch Upper Hartfield Eridge Sta Boarshead Three Leg Cross Hawkhurst The Moor Four

West Hoathly Sharpthorne Wych Cross ASHDOWN FOREST CROWBOROUGH Mark Cross Tidebrook Stonegate Ticehurst Salehurst Bodiam Castle

Balcombe Highbrook Ardingly Horsted Keynes Chelwood Gate Nutley Rotherfield Mayfield Witherenden Hill Etchingham Robertsbridge Vinehall Street Cripp's Corner

Paxhill Park Lindfield Danehill Fairwarp High Hurstwood Five Ashes Burwash Bateman's Oxley's Green Brightling Mountfield Staplecross

HAYWARDS HEATH Sheffield Park Sta Fletching Maresfield Hadlow Down Cross in Hand Broadoak Cade Street Burwash Common Dallington Netherfield Whatlington

Scaynes Hill Newick Buxted Uckfield Blackboys HEATHFIELD Little London Punnett's Town Rushlake Green Netherfield BATTLE

Wivelsfield Chailey Ridgewood Framfield Waldron Horam Warbleton Ponts Green Penhurst Catsfield Beauport Park

BURGESS HILL Wivelsfield Green South Street Little Horsted Isfield Vine's Cross Foul Mile Bodle Street Green Ashburnham Place Ninfield Crowhurst Hollington

Hurstpierpoint Ditchling Plumpton Green Spithurst Barcombe Cross Shortgate East Hoathly Chiddingly Cowbeech Herstmonceux Windmill Hill Boreham Street Lunsford's Cross

Keymer East Chiltington Barcombe Hamsey Ringmer Laughton Whitesmith Golden Cross Hellingly Mugham Down Hooe Sidley

Clayton Westmeston Plumpton Cooksbridge Offham Little Hill Glyndebourne Ripe Horsebridge HAILSHAM Wartling Little Common BEXHILL

Ditchling Beacon Mount Harry South Malling LEWES Glynde Upper Dickers Priory Royal Greenwich Observatory Castle Pevensey

Patcham Stanmer Coldean Falmer Iford Beddingham West Firle Selmeston Arlington Polegate Hankham Westham St L

Moulsecoomb Kingston near Lewes Rodmell Firle Beacon Berwick Wilmington Folkington Stone Cross Langney Pevensey Bay

BRIGHTON Bevendean Woodingdean Southease Tarring Neville Alciston Willingdon Hampden Park Langney Point

Kemp Town Ovingdean Telscombe Saltdean South Heighton Alfriston Jevington Willingdon Hill

Rottingdean Peacehaven Piddinghoe Denton Bishopstone East Blatchington Lullington Willington Hill

NEWHAVEN SEAFORD Westdean Friston Jevington EASTBOURNE

The Long Man East Dean

NEWHAVEN to Dieppe .... 4 hrs

BEACHY HEAD

TV

ENGLISH CHANNEL

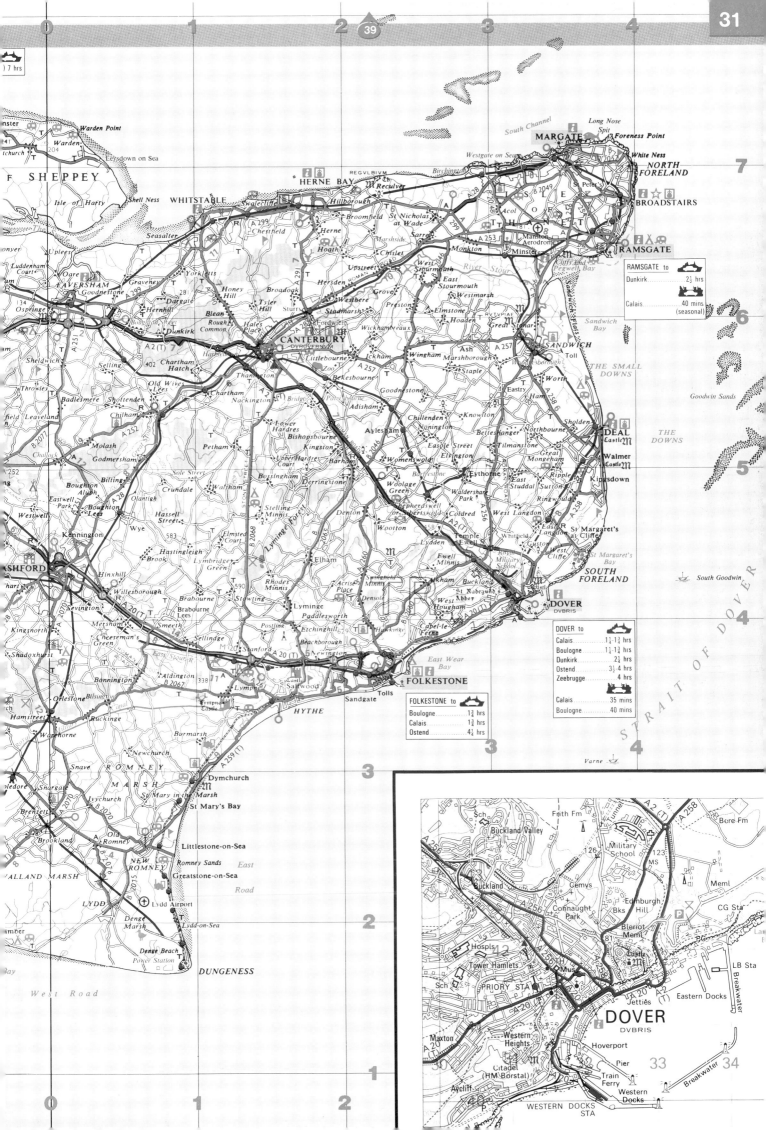

) 7 hrs

Warden Point
Warden
204
Leysdown on Sea
Isle of Harty
Shell Ness
Seasalter
F SHEPPEY
WHITSTABLE
Swalecliffe
HERNE BAY
Reculver
REGVLBIVM
Chestfield
Broomfield
Hillborough
St Nicholas
at Wade
Herne
Hoath
Marshside
Chislet
West
Stourmouth
East
Stourmouth
River Stour
Birchington
Westgate on Sea
MARGATE
Long Nose
Spit
Foreness Point
White Ness
NORTH
FORELAND
ISLE
Acol
BROADSTAIRS
B 2049
OF
Manston
Aerodrome
St Peter's
THANET
Minster
RAMSGATE

FAVERSHAM
Goodnestone
Ospringe
Uplees
Luddenham
Court
Oare
Graveney
Hernhill
Boughton Street
Dunkirk
A2(T)
Sheldwich
Selling
Throwley
Badlesmere
Leaveland
Molash
Chilham
Shottenden
Godmersham
Chalock
Boughton
Aluph
Eastwell
Park
Boughton
Lea
Westwell
Kennington
ASHFORD
Hinxhill
Sevington
Willesborough
Kingsnorth
Shadoxhurst
Mersham
Cheeseman's
Green
Bonnington
Orlestone
Hamstreet
Warehorne
Ruckinge

Yorkletts
Honey
Hill
Daggate
Blean
Rough
Common
Hales
Place
Tyler
Hill
Sturry
Broadoak
CANTERBURY
DVROVERNVM
Fordwich
Wickhambreaux
Littlebourne
Ickham
Thanington
Chartham
Hatch
Old Wives
Lees
Chartham
Nackington
Bridge
Patrixbourne
Bekesbourne
Zoo
Lower
Hardres
Bishopsbourne
Kingston
Upper Hardres
Court
Bossingham
Barham
Derringtone
Petham
Waltham
Crundale
Sole Street
Hassell
Street
Stelling
Minnis
Lyminge Forest
Denton
Hastingleigh
Brook
Elmsted
Court
Lymbridges
Green
Rhodes
Minnis
Acrise
Place
Elham
Stowting
Lyminge
Brabourne
Brabourne
Lees
Smeeth
Sellindge
Postling
Paddlesworth
Etchinghill
Beachborough
Stanford
Newington
Aldington
Lympne
Saltwood
Sandgate
HYTHE
Burmarsh
Newchurch
ROMNEY
MARSH
Snave
Dymchurch
St Mary in the Marsh
St Mary's Bay
Ivychurch
Brenzett
Brookland
Old
Romney
NEW
ROMNEY
Littlestone-on-Sea
Romney Sands
Greatstone-on-Sea
Lydd
WALLAND MARSH
Lydd Airport
Lydd-on-Sea
Denge
Marsh
Denge Beach
Power Station
DUNGENESS
West Road

Westbere
Grove
Preston
Stodmarsh
Hersden
Upstreet
Westmarsh
Elmstone
Hoaden
Great Stonar
Ash
Wingham
Marshborough
Staple
Woodnesborough
SANDWICH
Toll
Sandwich
Flats
Sandwich
Bay
Goodnestone
Chillenden
Nonington
Knowlton
Eastry
Ham
Worth
THE SMALL
DOWNS
Goodwin Sands
Aylesham
Womenswold
Barfrestone
Eastle Street
Elvington
Eythorne
Tilmanstone
Betteshanger
Northbourne
Sholden
Great
Mongeham
DEAL
Castle
Walmer
Castle
Kingsdown
THE
DOWNS
Woolage
Green
Shepherdswell
or Sibertswold
Coldred
East
Studdal
Waldershare
Park
Sutton
Ripple
Ringwould
Denton
Wootton
Lydden
Temple
Ewell
Fwell
Minnis
Ewell
West Langdon
East
Langdon
St Margaret's
at Cliffe
Whitfield
Guston
St Margaret's
Bay
Cliffe
St Margaret's
Bay
Royal
Military
School
SOUTH
FORELAND
South Goodwin
STRAIT OF DOVER
Alkham
Buckland
St Radegund's
Abbey
West
Hougham
Capel-le-
Ferne
DOVER
DVBRIS
East Wear
Bay
FOLKESTONE
Varne

RAMSGATE to
Dunkirk .... 2½ hrs
Calais .... 40 mins
(seasonal)

DOVER to
Calais .... 1¼–1¾ hrs
Boulogne .... 1¼–1¾ hrs
Dunkirk .... 2¼ hrs
Ostend .... 3½–4 hrs
Zeebrugge .... 4 hrs
Calais .... 35 mins
Boulogne .... 40 mins

FOLKESTONE to
Boulogne .... 1¾ hrs
Calais .... 1¾ hrs
Ostend .... 4¼ hrs

Dover inset:
Frith Fm
A2(T)
A258
Bere Fm
Buckland Valley
Tunnel
Military
School
MS
126
123
Buckland
A256
Gemys
Connaught
Park
Edinburgh
Hill
Bleriot
Meml
Meml
CG Sta
Hospls
Tower Hamlets
Castle
Mus
P
PRIORY STA
Sch
Maxton
Western
Heights
Aycliff
Citadel
(HM Borstal)
A20
Hoverport
Pier
Train
Ferry
Western
Docks
WESTERN DOCKS
STA
Eastern Docks
Jetties
LB Sta
Breakwater
DOVER
DVBRIS
Breakwater
33
34
30

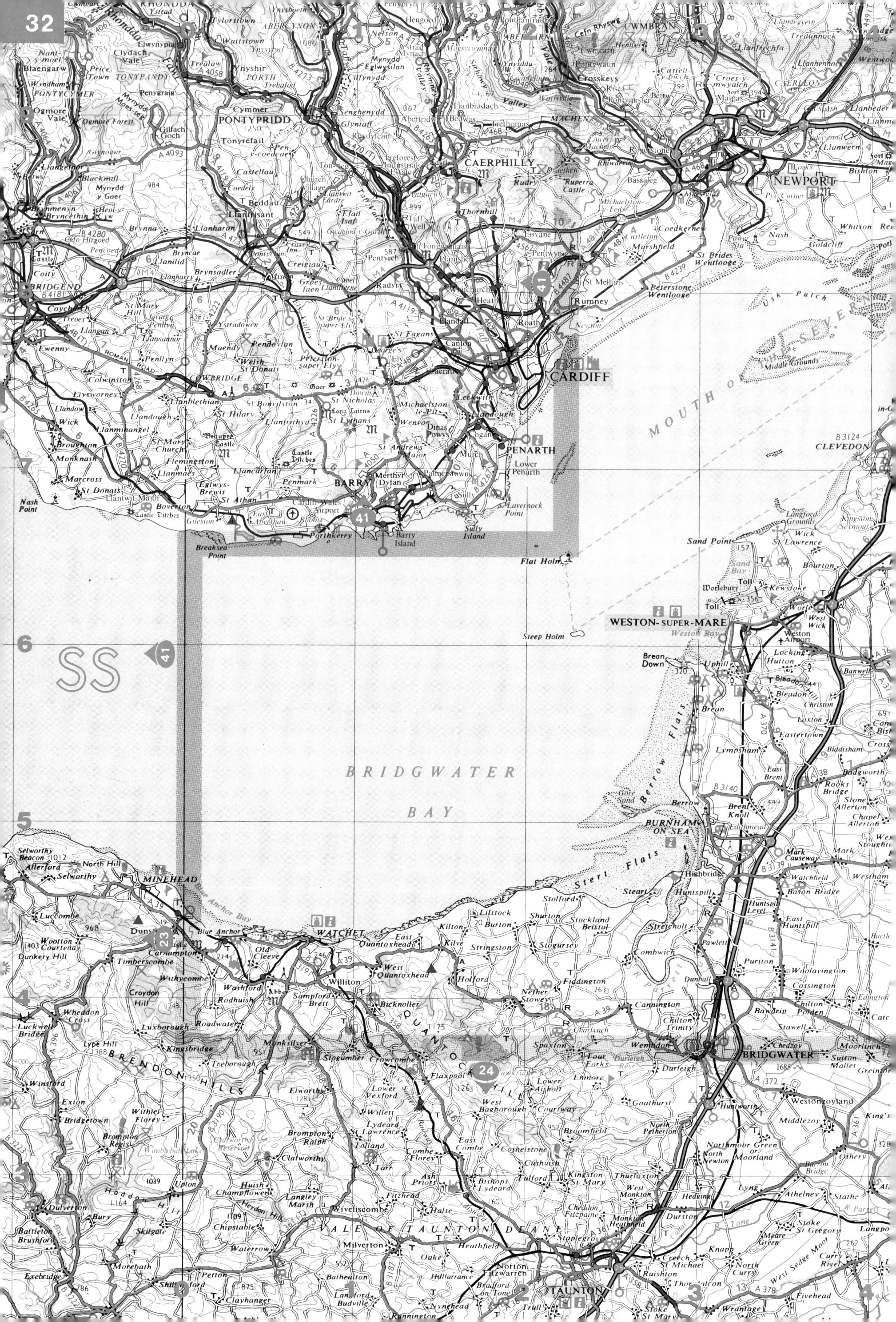

MOUTH OF THE SEVERN

CARDIFF
NEWPORT
PENARTH
BARRY
CAERPHILLY
PONTYPRIDD
BRIDGEND
COWBRIDGE

CLEVEDON
WESTON-SUPER-MARE
Weston Bay
Sand Point
Sand Bay
Brean Down
Berrow Flats
BURNHAM-ON-SEA
Brent Knoll
Stert Flats

Flat Holm
Steep Holm

BRIDGWATER BAY

SS

MINEHEAD
Blue Anchor Bay
WATCHET
Blue Anchor
Dunster
Carhampton
Williton
BRENDON HILLS
QUANTOCK HILLS

BRIDGWATER

VALE OF TAUNTON DEANE
TAUNTON

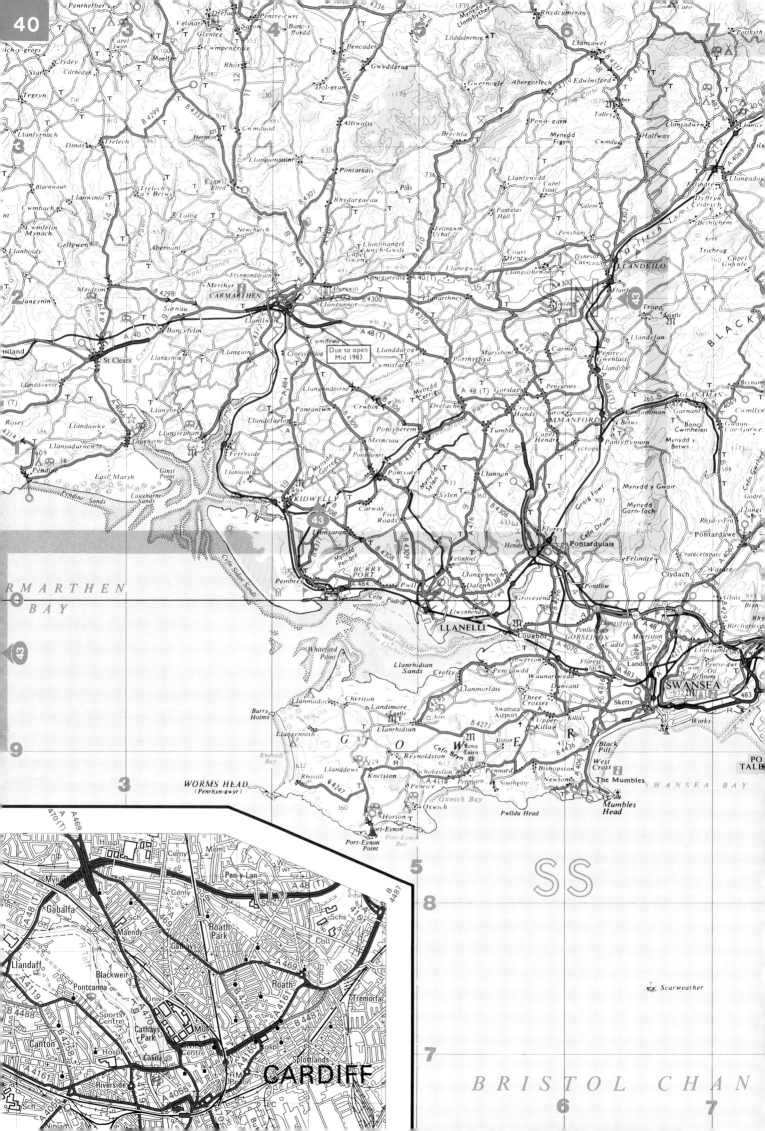

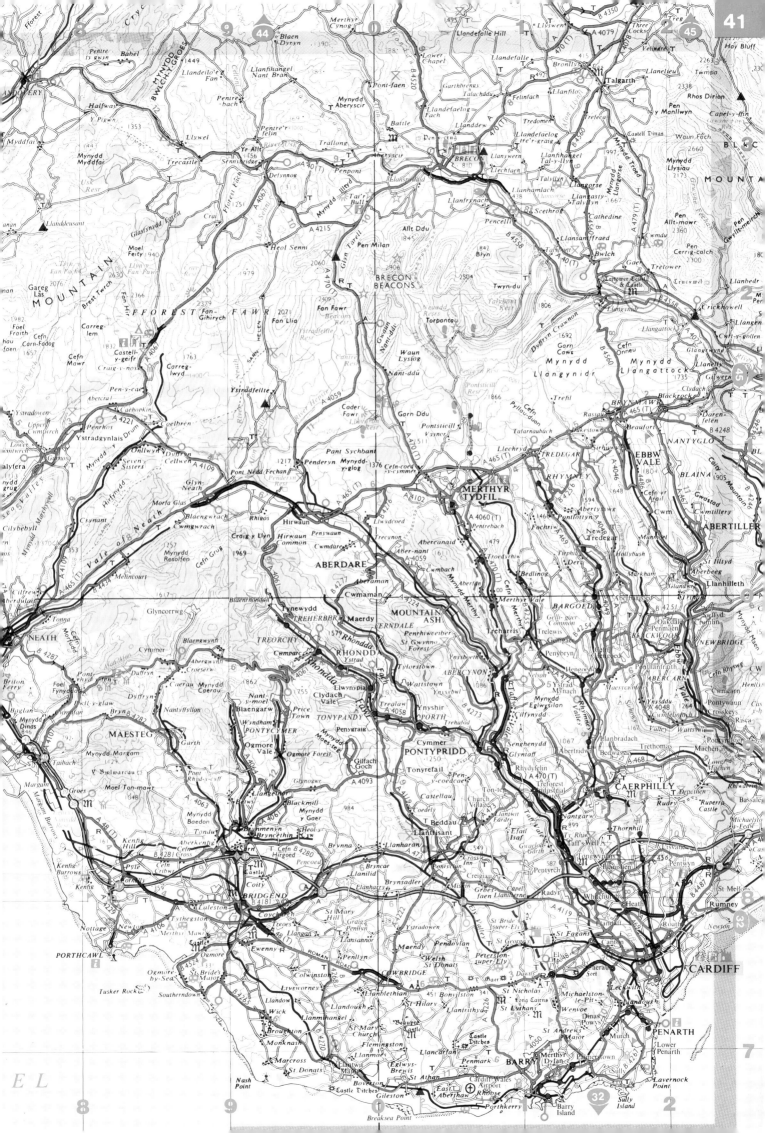

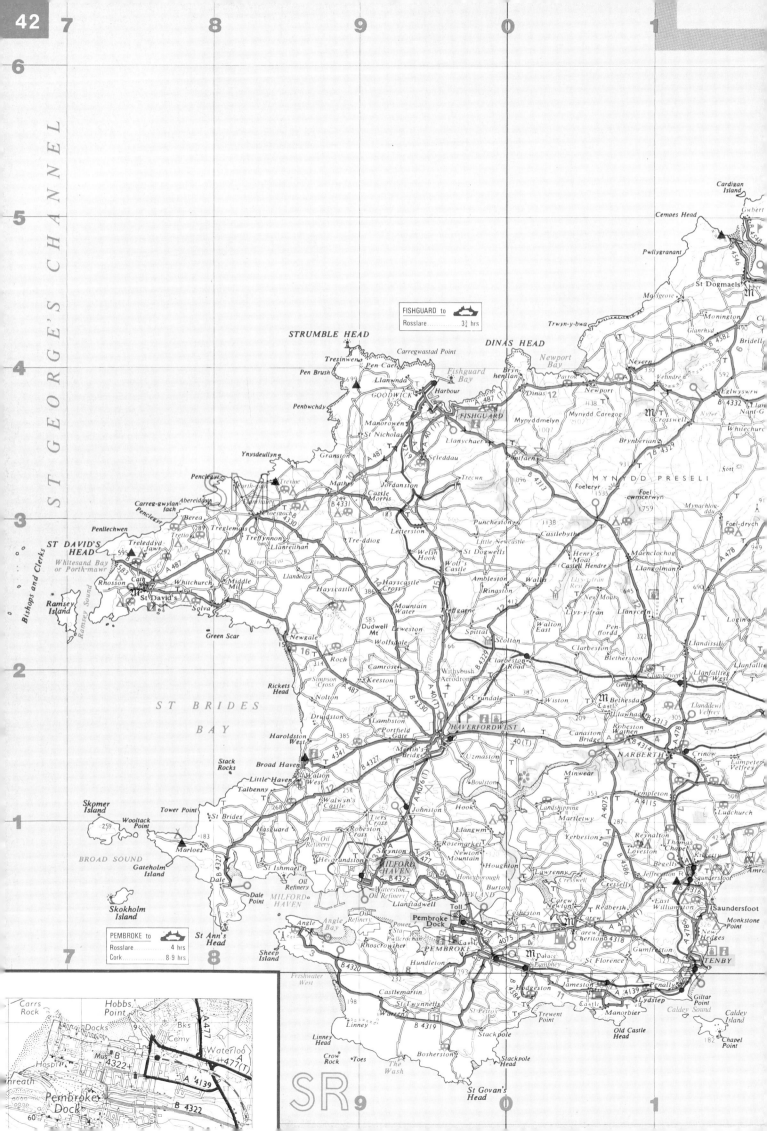

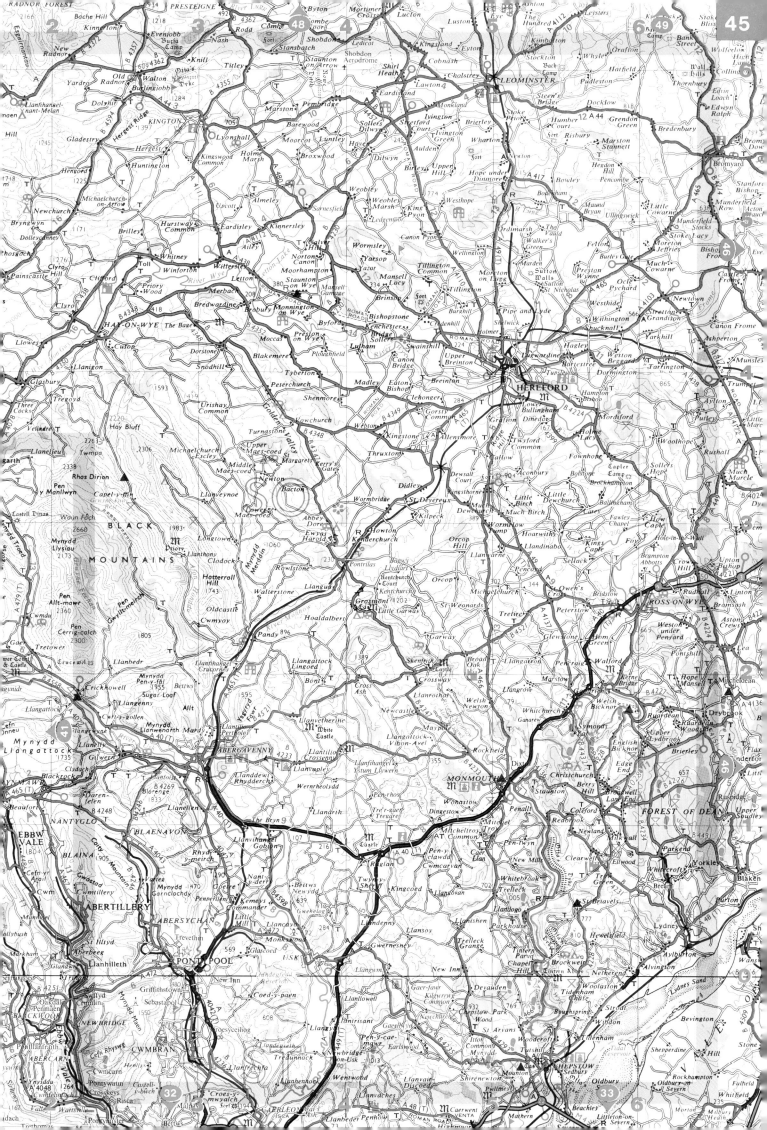

WORCESTER

GREAT MALVERN

LEDBURY

ROSS-ON-WYE

FOREST OF DEAN

EVESHAM

TEWKESBURY

CHELTENHAM

CHARLTON KINGS

GLOUCESTER

STROUD

NAILSWORTH

CIRCENSTER
CORINIVM

TETBURY

DROITWICH

Due to open
Late 1983

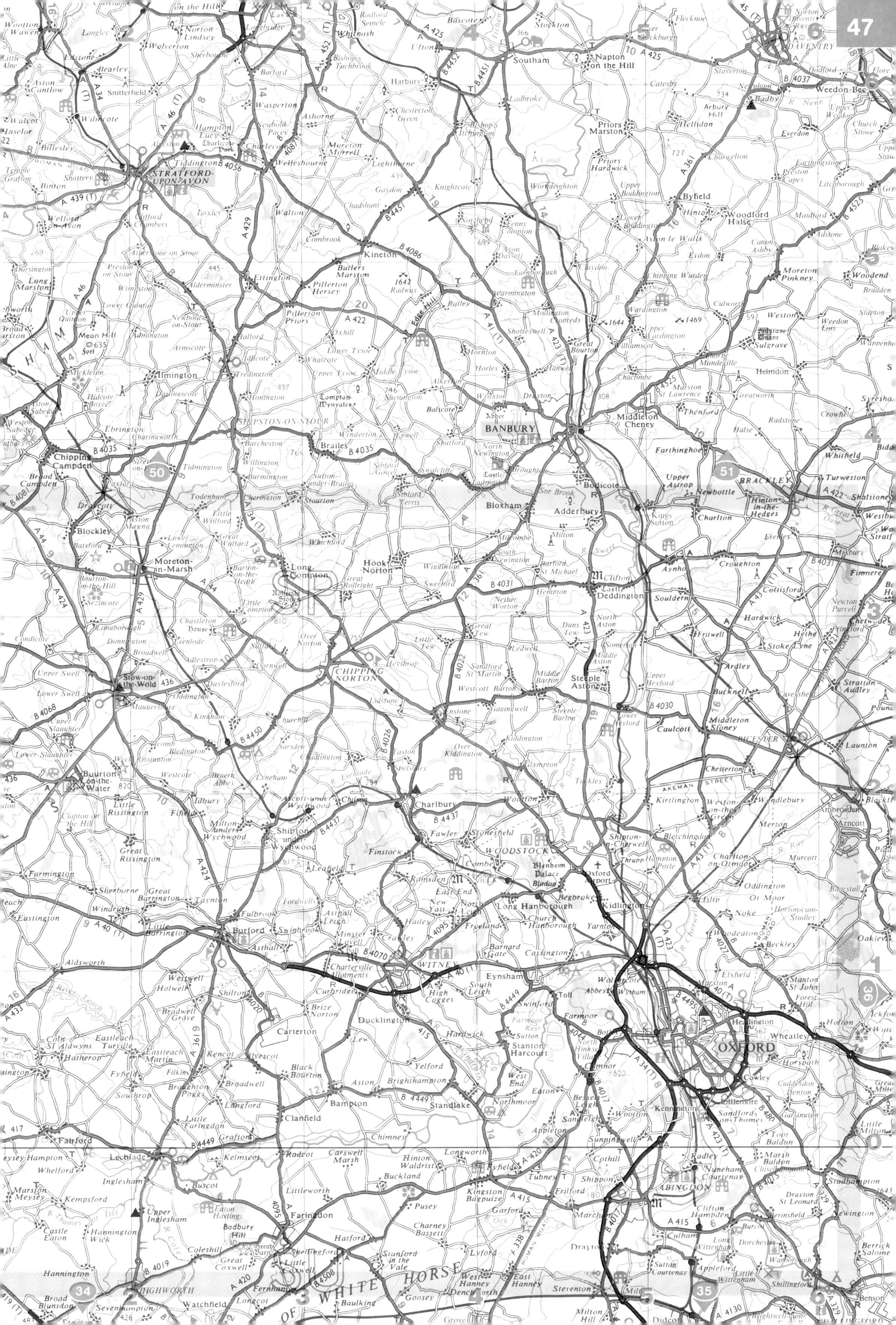

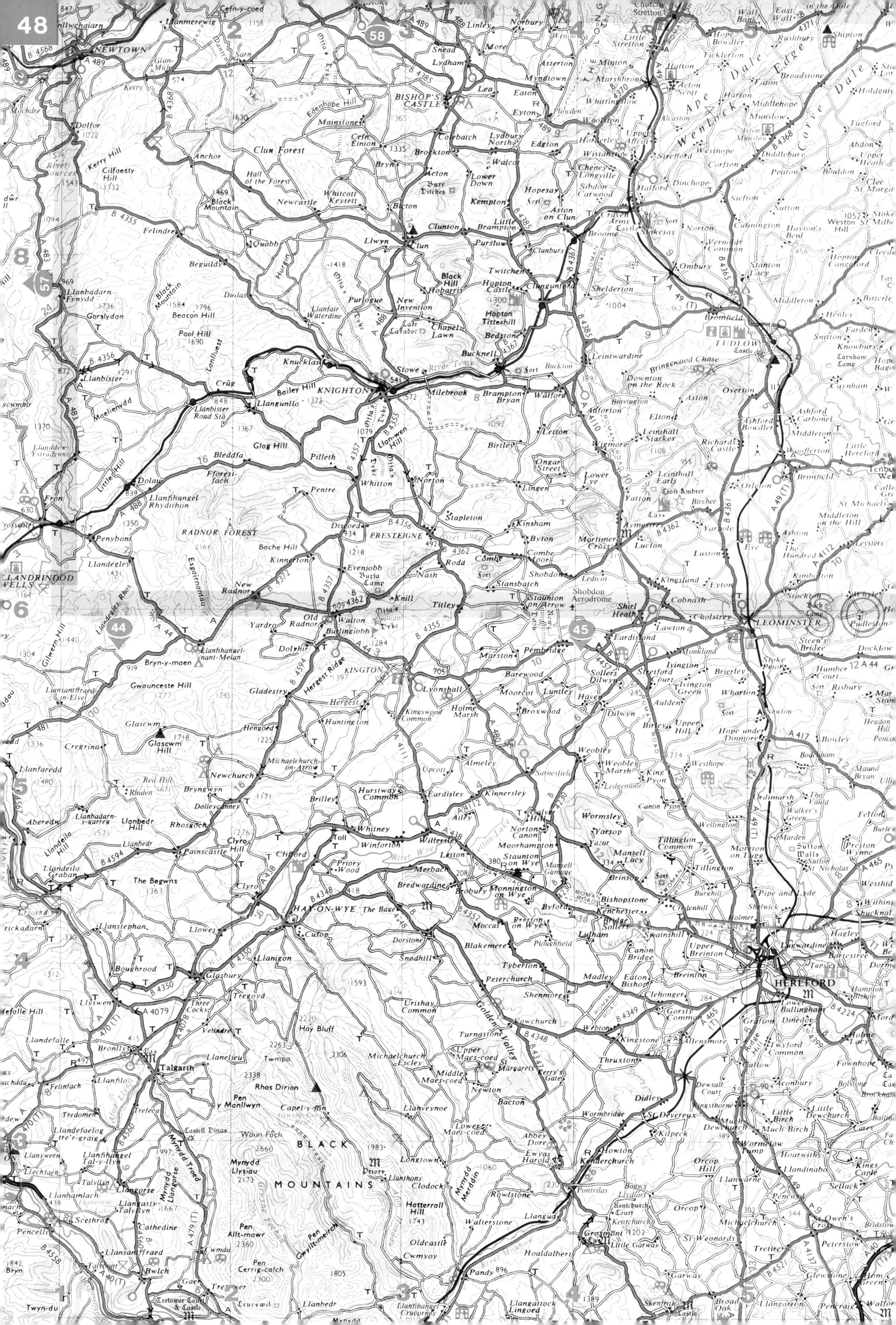

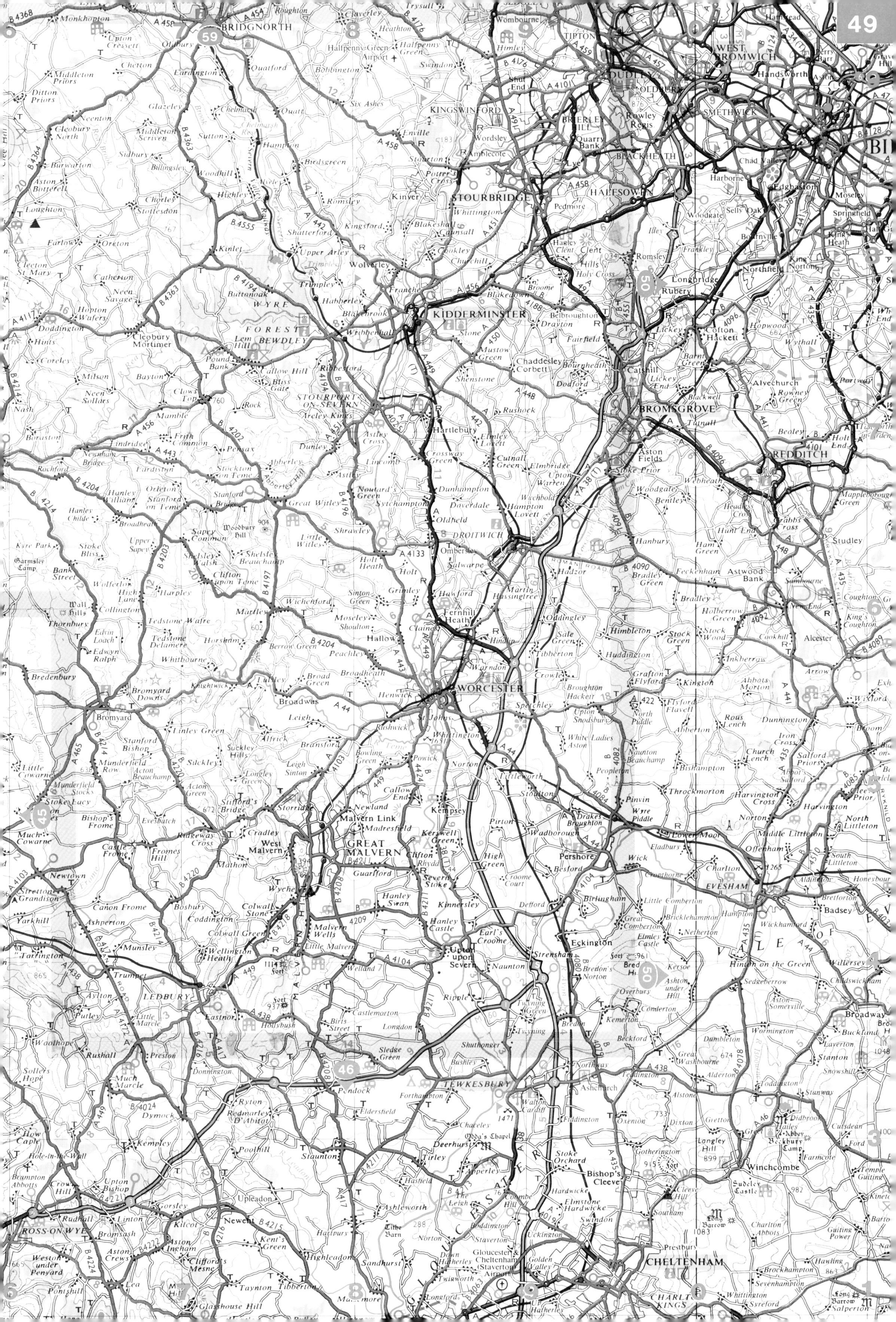
BRIDGNORTH
KIDDERMINSTER
STOURBRIDGE
HALESOWEN
DUDLEY
WEST BROMWICH
SMETHWICK
OLDBURY
KINGSWINFORD
BROMSGROVE
REDDITCH
DROITWICH
WORCESTER
GREAT MALVERN
LEDBURY
TEWKESBURY
CHELTENHAM
ROSS-ON-WYE
EVESHAM
Pershore
Bromyard
BEWDLEY
STOURPORT-ON-SEVERN
WYRE FOREST
Cleobury Mortimer
Winchcombe
Bishop's Cleeve
Upton upon Severn
Malvern Link
West Malvern
Malvern Wells
Newent
Alcester
Studley
Edgbaston
Harborne
Northfield
Longbridge
Rubery
Blackheath
Brierley Hill
Rowley Regis
Tipton
Wombourne
Himley
Kinver
Wolverley
Hartlebury
Ombersley
Hallow
Kempsey
Eckington
Strensham
Bredon
Ashchurch
Deerhurst
Tirley
Staunton
Kempley
Dymock
Much Marcle
Upton Bishop
Linton
Weston under Penyard
Clifford's Mesne
Highleadon
Sandhurst
Hartpury
Ashleworth
Prestbury
Charlton Kings
Sudeley Castle
VALE OF EVESHAM
GLOUCESTER
59
50
45
46
7
8
9
0
1

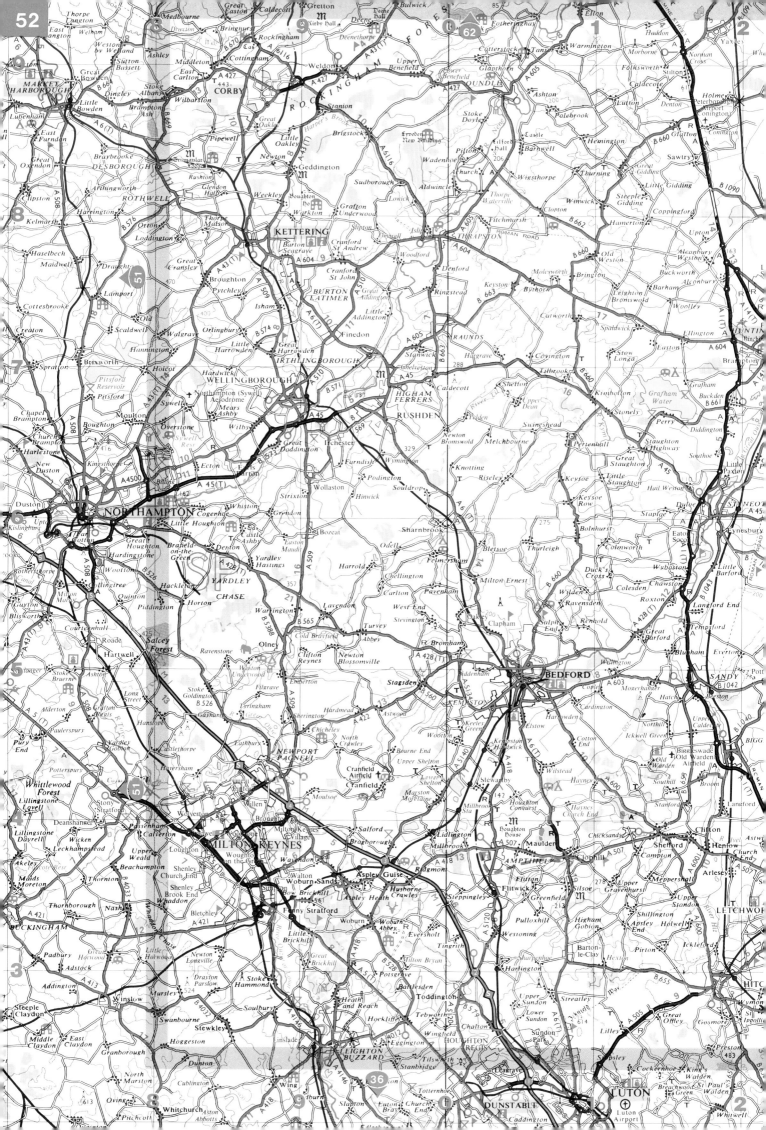

Southery Fens
Methwold Fens
Queen's Ground
Mundford
Shropham
Great Hockham
Puddledock
Brandon Creek
Feltwell
East Wretham
Eccles Road
Wilby
Brandon Bank
Feltwell Anchor
Castle
Grime's Graves
Harling Road Sta
Larling
Quidenham
Weeting
Santon Downham
Hockwold Fens
Hockwold cum Wilton
Burnt Fen
Croxton
Bridgham
East Harling
Kenninghall
Lakenheath Sta
Brandon
Brandon Park
Wangford Fen
Shippea Hill Sta
Brettenham
North Lopham
Lakenheath
Thetford Warren
THETFORD
Priory
Prickwillow
Wangford Warren
South Lopham
Queen Adelaide
Rushford
Garboldisham
The Delph
Lakenheath Warren
Kenny Hill
Gasthorpe
Middle Fen
Elveden
Euston
Blo Norton
Great Fen
Mildenhall Fen
Eriswell
Barnham
Coney Weston
Hopton
Stuntney
Thelnetham
Market Weston
Redgrave
Beck Row
Holywell Row
Hinderclay
Broad Hill
Barningham
Little Fakenham
Isleham Fen
Thistley Green
Rickinghall
Botesdale
West Row
Mildenhall
Hepworth
Priory
Isleham
Worlington
Honington
Sapiston
Wattisfield
Soham
Barton Mills
Bardwell
Stanton
Soham Mere
Icklingham
Troston
Ixworth Thorpe
Freckenham
Fordham
Tuddenham
Ampton
Walsham le Willows
Gislingham
Wicken
Ingham
Great Livermere
New River
Lackford
West Stow
Culford
Ixworth
Langham
Four Ashes
Fordham Abbey
Chippenham
Herringswell
Cavenham
Flempton
Little Fen
Timworth Green
Badwell Ash
Westhorpe
Landwade
Kennett
Hengrave
Great Ashfield
Stowlangtoft
Wyverstone
Burwell
Snailwell
Icknield Way
Fornham All Saints
Fornham St Martin
Great Barton
Hunston
Wyverstone Street
Pakenham
Stanton Street
Bacton
Exning
Kentford
Risby
Earl's Green
Higham
Thurston
Norton
Swaffham Prior
Moulton
Westley
BURY ST EDMUNDS
Haughley Green
Newmarket Heath
Gazeley
Little Saxham
Tostock
Elmswell
Ward Green
Swaffham Bulbeck
NEWMARKET
Denham Castle
Barrow
Great Saxham
Blackthorpe
Beyton
Woolpit
Wetherden
Old Newton
Horringer
Ickworth House
Kingshall Street
Hessett
Haughley
Ashley
Dalham
Denham
Rushbrooke
Rougham Green
Drinkstone
Cheveley
Dunstall Green
Sicklesmere
Drinkstone Green
Harleston
Stowupland
Chevington
Little Welnetham
Bradfield St George
Stetchworth
Saxon Street
Ousden
Hargrave
Great Welnetham
Rattlesden
Woodditton
Hawstead
Bradfield St Clare
Gedding
Poystreet Green
Dullingham
Ditton Green
Upend
Kirtling
Lidgate
Whepstead
Chedburgh
Bradfield Combust
Felsham
Buxhall
Great Finborough
Combs Ford
Combs
Six Mile Bottom
Westley Waterless
Depden Green
Rede
Burrough Green
Kirtling Green
Thorns
Wickhambrook
Great Green
High Street Green
Needham Market
Brinkley
Cowlinge
Clopton Green
Wickham Street
Brockley Green
Lawshall
Cockfield
Thorpe Green
Brettenham
Battisford Tye
Battisford
Weston Colville
Great Bradley
Carlton
Denston
Hawkedon
Stansfield
Hartest
Shimpling Street
Thorpe Morieux
Charles Tye
Ringshall
Weston Green
Little Bradley
Stradishall
Cross Green
West Wratting
Boxted
Shimpling
Alpheton
Preston St Mary
Hitcham
Wattisham
Ringshall Stocks
Balsham
Thurlow
Stanstead
Bridge Street
Kettlebaston
Great Bricett
West Wickham
Barnardiston
Hundon
Lavenham
Bildeston
Nedging Tye
Offton
Great Wratting
Poslingford
Glemsford
Kentwell Hall
Brent Eleigh
Monks Eleigh
Naughton
Withersfield
Horseheath
Chilton Street
Cavendish
Chelsworth
Semer
Linton
Kedington
Milden
Whatfield
Elmsett
Bartlow
HAVERHILL
Clare
Long Melford
Acton
Little Waldingfield
Lindsey
Shudy Camps
Castle Camps
Sturmer
Wixoe
Stoke by Clare
Foxearth
Great Waldingfield
Kersey
Helions Bumpstead
Ashen
Ovington
Belchamp St Paul
Borley
The Heath
Edwardstone
HADLEIGH
Ashdon
Church End
Steeple Bumpstead
Birdbrook
Ridgewell
Belchamp Otten
SUDBURY
Groton
Belchamp Walter
Bulmer
Great Cornard
Newton
Boxford
Chapelend Way
Little Yeldham
Middleton
Layham
Sewards End
Hempstead
Stambourne
Great Yeldham
Gestingthorpe
Bulmer Tye
Assington
Polstead
Raydon
Radwinter
Great Henny
Twinstead
Holton St Mary
Toppesfield
Wimbish
Cornish Hall End
Great Sampford
Wickham St Paul
Lamarsh
Stoke-by-Nayland
Wimbish Green
Gainsford End
Castle Hedingham
Great Maplestead
Alphamstone
Nayland
Higham
Thorington Street
Howlett End
Debden
Howe Street
Little Maplestead
Little Sampford
Sible Hedingham
Pebmarsh
Bures
Stratford St Mary
Dedham
Little Horkesley
Boxted
Langham
Debden Green
Finchingfield
Mount Bures
Thaxted
Little Bardfield
Wethersfield
Blackmore End
HALSTEAD
Wormingford
Great Horkesley
Blacksmith's Corner
Great Bardfield
Colne Engaine
Wakes Colne
Gosfield
Chappel
Ardleigh
Shalford
Beazley End
Earls Colne
Colne Valley
Fordham
West Bergholt
Duton Hill
Lindsell
High Garrett
Greenstead Green
Mile End
Bardfield Saling
Shalford Green
Great Easton
Fordstreet
Crockleford Heath
Great Saling
Bocking Churchstreet
Eight Ash Green
Bran End
Great Tey
Aldham
COLCHESTER
Molehill Green
Butcher's Pasture
Stebbing
Panfield
Bocking
BRAINTREE
Stisted
Beacon End
Stanway
Little Easton
Marks Tey
Wivenhoe Cross
Old Heath
GREAT DUNMOW
Churchend
Rayne
Coggeshall
Copford Green
WIVENHOE
Little Dunmow
Shrub End
Takeley
Bannister Green
Easthorpe
Blackheath
Black Notley
Feering
Layer de la Haye
Rowhedge
Felsted
Silver End
Fingringhoe

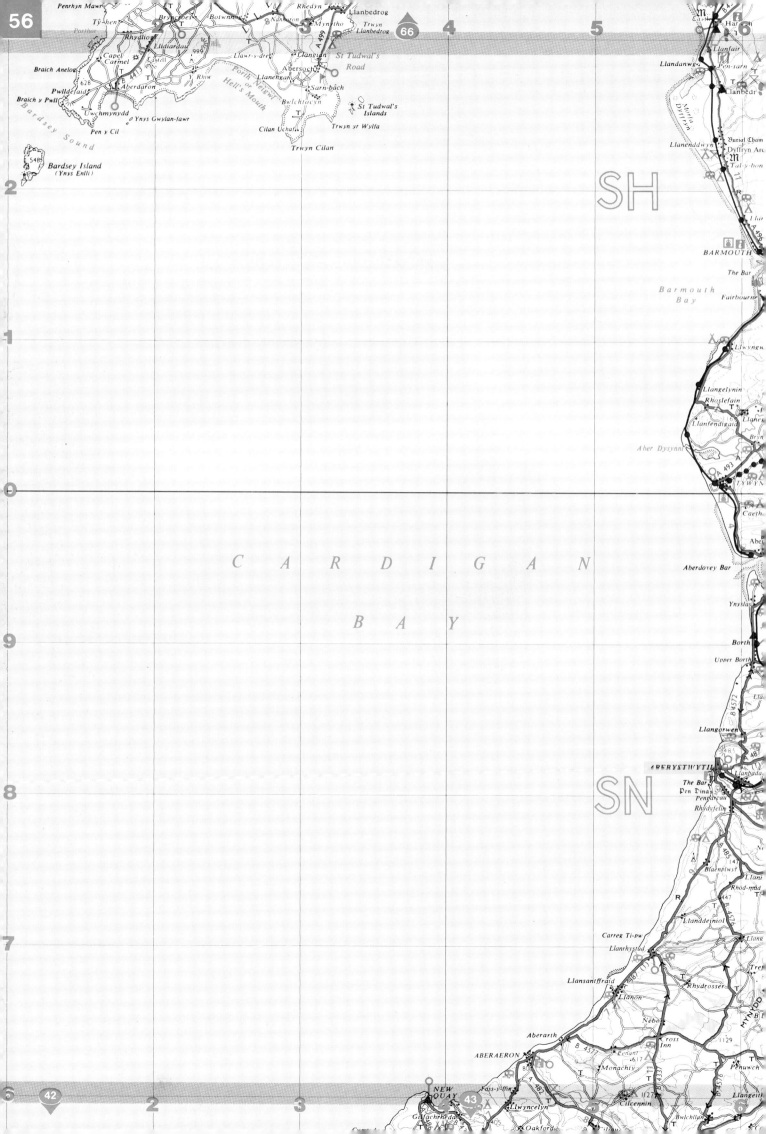

C A R D I G A N

B A Y

Bardsey Sound

Bardsey Island
(Ynys Enlli)

Penrhyn Mawr
Tŷ-hen
Rhydlios
Llidiardau
Capel Carmel
Braich Anelog
Pwlldefaid
Braich y Pwll
Uwchmynydd
Pen y Cil
Ynys Gwylan-fawr
Aberdaron
Rhiw
Bryncroes
Botwnnog
Nanhoron
Mynytho
Llangian
Abersoch
Llanengan
Sarn-bach
Bwlchtocyn
St Tudwal's Islands
Cilan Uchaf
Trwyn yr Wylfa
Trwyn Cilan
Rhedyn
Llanbedrog
Trwyn Llanbedrog
Llanfor-y-drel
Porth Neigwl or Hell's Mouth
St Tudwal's Road

SH

SN

Harlech
Llanfair
Llandanwg
Pen-sarn
Llanbedr
Morfa Dyffryn
Llanenddwyn
Dyffryn Ardudwy
Tal-y-bont
BARMOUTH
The Bar
Barmouth Bay
Fairbourne
Llwyngwril
Llangelynin
Rhoslefain
Llanfendigaid
Aber Dysynni
TYWYN
Aberdovey Bar
Ynyslas
Borth
Upper Borth
Llangorwen
ABERYSTWYTH
Llanbadarn
The Bar
Pen Dinas
Penparcau
Rhydyfelin
Blaenplwyf
Rhod-mad
Llanddeiniol
Carreg Ti-pw
Llanrhystud
Llansantffraid
Llanon
Nebo
Aberarth
ABERAERON
Monachty
Cross Inn
Penuwch
NEW QUAY
Foss-y-ffin
Llwyncelyn
Gilfachrheda
Cileennin
Bwlchllan
Oakford

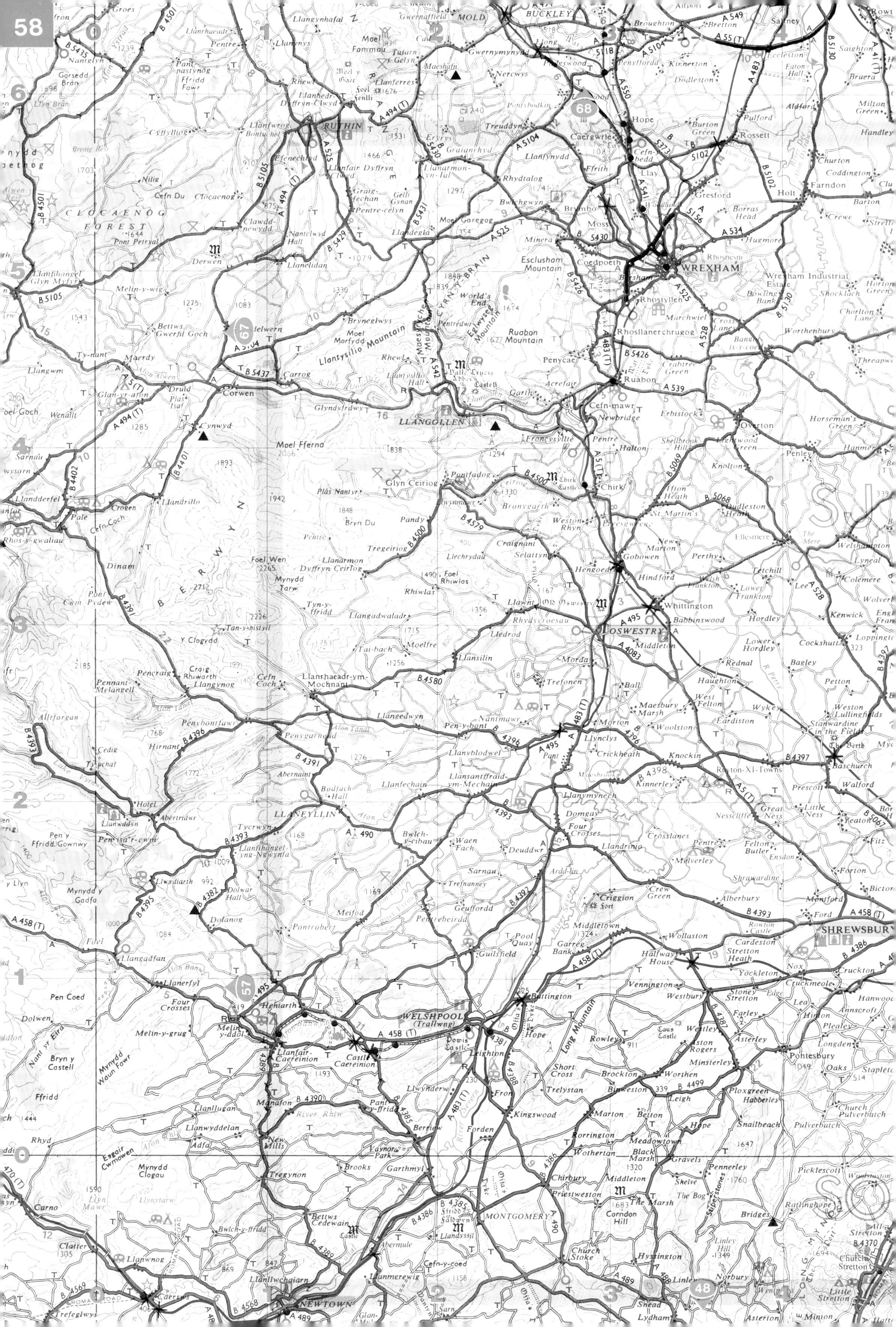

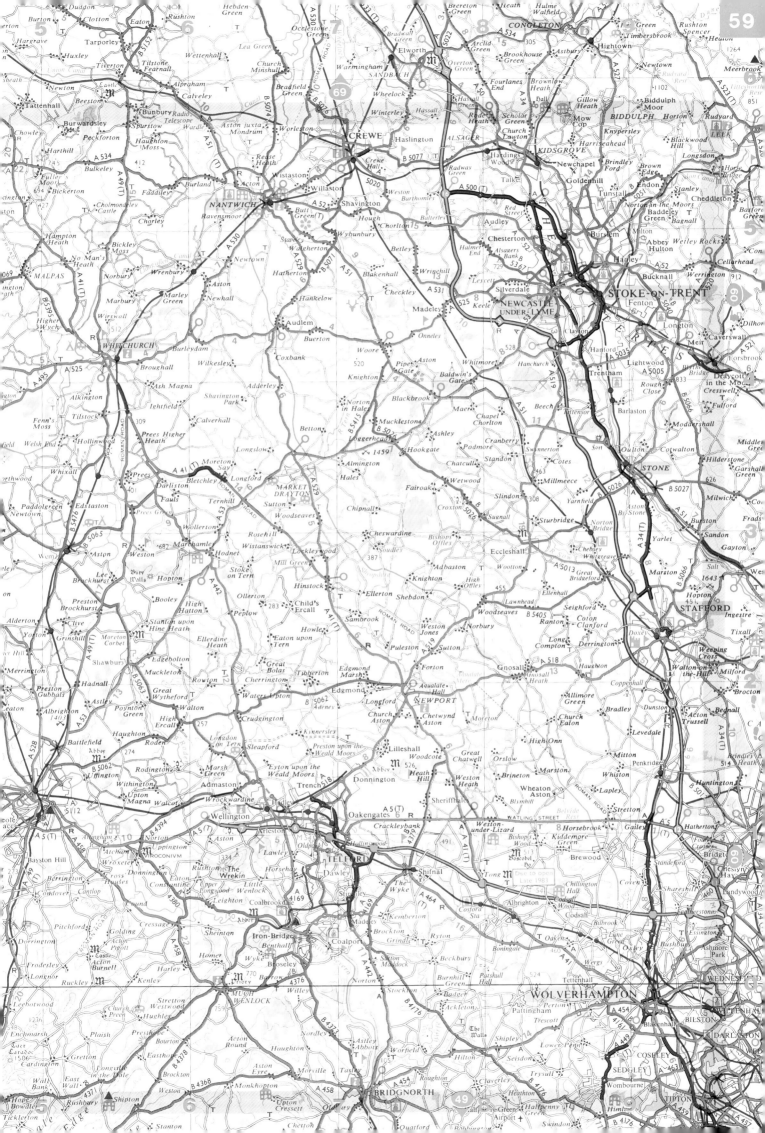

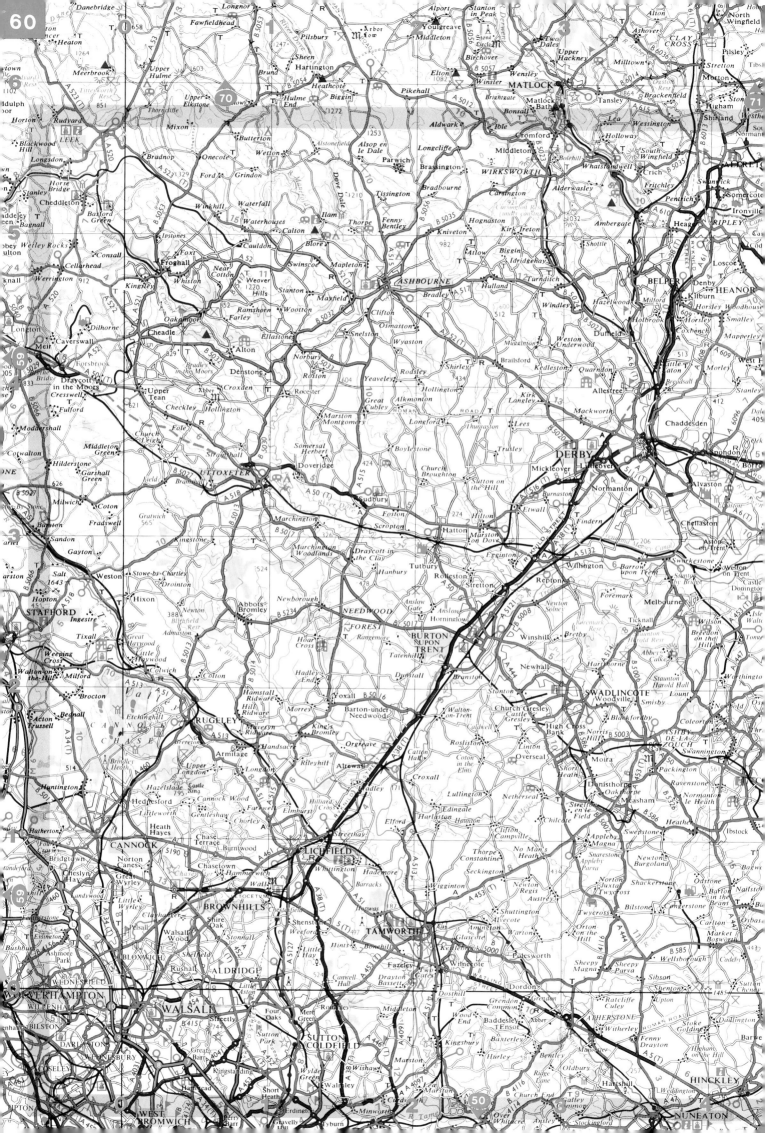

MANSFIELD WOODHOUSE
MANSFIELD
Skegby
SUTTON IN ASHFIELD
KIRKBY IN ASHFIELD
Huthwaite
Stanton Hill
Teversal
Pleasley
New Clipstone
Old Clipstone
Forest Town
Rainworth
Bilsthorpe
Kneesall
Eakring
Kersall
Ompton
Ossington
Maplebeck
Winkburn
Kirklington
Farnsfield
Blidworth
Ravenshead
Haywood Oaks
Edingley
Halam
Southwell
Normanton
Upton
Averham
Staythorpe
Hockerton
Kelham
North Muskham
South Muskham
Holme
Langford
Winthorpe
NEWARK ON TRENT
Collingham
Swinderby
Thurlby
Auburn
Bassingham
Norton Disney
Stapleford
Carlton-le-Moorland
Caunton
Norwell
Norwell Woodhouse
Cromwell
Brough
Coddington
Balderton
Farndon
Rolleston
Fiskerton
Thurgarton
Bleasby
East Stoke
Thorpe
Elston
Syerston
Flintham
Cotham
Hawton
Barnby in the Willows
Stragglethorpe
Fenton
Claypole
Stubton
Brandon
Caythorpe
Beckingham
Brant Broughton
Hough-on-the-Hill
Carlton Scroope
Hougham
Marston
Foston
Allington
Sedgebrook
Great Gonerby
GRANTHAM
Barrowby
Harlaxton
Denton
Woolsthorpe
Belvoir
Castle
Knipton
Harston
Stathern
Eaton
Branston
Croxton Kerrial
Croxton Park
Waltham on the Wolds
Stonesby
Sproxton
Buckminster
Stainby
North Witham
Coston
Sewstern
Gunby
South Witham
Wymondham
Edmondthorpe
Market Overton
Teigh
Barrow
Greetham
Ashwell
Cottesmore
Langham
Burley
Exton
Whitwell
OAKHAM
Catmose
Braunston
Egleton
Brooke
Upper Hambleton
Manton
Preston
Ridlington
Wing
Pilton
Lyndon
North Luffenham
Edith Weston
South Luffenham
Morcott
Barrowden
Seaton
Harringworth
Lyddington
Stoke Dry
Caldecott
Thorpe by Water
Great Easton
Bringhurst
Drayton
Medbourne
Slawston
Hallaton
Horninghold
Blaston
Stockerston
Glooston
Cranoe
Tur Langton
Church Langton
Thorpe Langton
Welham
East Langton
Shangton
Noseley
Goadby
Carlton Curlieu
Illston on the Hill
Rolleston
East Norton
Wardley
URPINGHAM
Bisbrooke
Glaston
Ayston
Ridlington
Belton
Allexton
Tugby
Skeffington
Billesdon
Loddington
Launde Abbey
Tilton on the Hill
Halstead
Cold Newton
Lowesby
Marefield
Owston
Withcote
Knossington
Cold Overton
Somerby
Pickwell
Whissendine
Ashwell
Barleythorpe
Burrough on the Hill
Twyford
Burrough
Thorpe Satchville
Great Dalby
Little Dalby
Ashby Folville
Gaddesby
Barsby
South Croxton
Queniborough
Rearsby
Thrussington
Ratcliffe on the Wreake
Sileby
Rotherby
Hoby
Frisby on the Wreake
Asfordby
Kirby Bellars
Burton Lazars
Great Dalby
MELTON MOWBRAY
Stapleford
Saxby
Freeby
Thorpe Arnold
Asfordby Hill
Ragdale
Walton on the Wolds
Seagrave
Barrow upon Soar
Quorndon
Quorn
Mountsorrel
Rothley
Cropston
Thurcaston
Anstey
Birstall
Wanlip
Syston
Barkby
Thurmaston
Beeby
Humberstone
Scraptoft
Thurnby
Bushby
Evington
Stoughton
Houghton on the Hill
Keyham
Hungarton
Baggrave Hall
Quenby Hall
Beeby
LEICESTER
RATAE
OADBY
WIGSTON
Knighton
Aylestone
Glen Parva
Blaby
South Wigston
Countesthorpe
Whetstone
Kilby
Newton Harcourt
Great Glen
Burton Overy
Carlton Curlieu
Kibworth Harcourt
Kibworth Beauchamp
Smeeton Westerby
Saddington
Fleckney
Arnesby
Peatling Magna
Willoughby Waterleys
Shearsby
Bruntingthorpe
Peatling Parva
Primethorpe
Broughton Astley
Sutton in the Elms
Cosby
Enderby
Narborough
Huncote
Croft
Stoney Stanton
Sapcote
Sharnford
Aston Flamville
Burbage
Elmesthorpe
Earl Shilton
Barwell
Kirkby Mallory
Peckleton
Desford
Newbold Verdon
Thurlaston
Kirkby Muxloe
Leicester Forest East
Braunstone
Glenfield
Glen Parva
Kirby Fields
Ratby
Groby
Field Head
Markfield
Thornton
Bagworth
Stanton under Bardon
Newtown Linford
Cropston
Bradgate
Swithland
Woodhouse Eaves
Woodhouse
Mountsorrel
COPT OAK
CHARNWOOD FOREST
Nanpantan
Woodthorpe
LOUGHBOROUGH
Thorpe Acre
Hathern
Long Whatton
Diseworth
Kegworth
EAST MIDLANDS AIRPORT
Sutton Bonington
Normanton on Soar
Zouch
Stanford on Soar
Cotes
Wymeswold
Burton on the Wolds
Rempstone
Costock
East Leake
West Leake
Kingston on Soar
Gotham
Bunny
Bradmore
Ruddington
Keyworth
Widmerpool
Wysall
Willoughby on the Wolds
Upper Broughton
Nether Broughton
Old Dalby
Grimston
Saxelbye
Asfordby
Wartnaby
Ab Kettleby
Holwell
Scalford
Scarrington
Hose
Long Clawson
Harby
Goadby Marwood
Eastwell
Eaton
Stathern
Plungar
Barkestone-le-Vale
Redmile
Bottesford
Muston
Langar
Granby
Sutton
Elton
Whatton
Aslockton
Orston
Thoroton
Hawksworth
Scarrington
Car Colston
Screveton
Flawborough
Kilvington
Alverton
Staunton
Sibthorpe
Shelton
Kneeton
Hoveringham
Caythorpe
Gunthorpe
East Bridgford
Shelford
Stoke Bardolph
Burton Joyce
Lowdham
Gonalston
Epperstone
Woodborough
Calverton
Oxton
Halloughton
Lambley
ARNOLD
NOTTINGHAM
CARLTON
Radcliffe on Trent
Bingham
Saxondale
Cropwell Butler
Tithby
Cropwell Bishop
Colston Bassett
Kinoulton
Hickling
Long Clawson
Colston Bassett
Owthorpe
Clipston
Cotgrave
Normanton-on-the-Wolds
Stanton-on-the-Wolds
Plumtree
Tollerton
Edwalton
WEST BRIDGFORD
Nottingham Airport
Ruddington
Bassingfield
Gamston
Wilford
BEESTON
Chilwell
Attenborough
Toton
Bramcote
STAPLEFORD
Sandiacre
Risley
Breaston
LONG EATON
Sawley
Thrumpton
Barton in Fabis
Clifton
Trowell
Nuthall
Kimberley
Awsworth
Cossall
Bilborough
Strelley
Wollaton
EASTWOOD
Watnall
Brinsley
Underwood
Annesley
Annesley Woodhouse
Newstead
Abbey
Linby
Papplewick
HUCKNALL
Hucknall Airfield
Bulwell
Bestwood
SHERWOOD FOREST

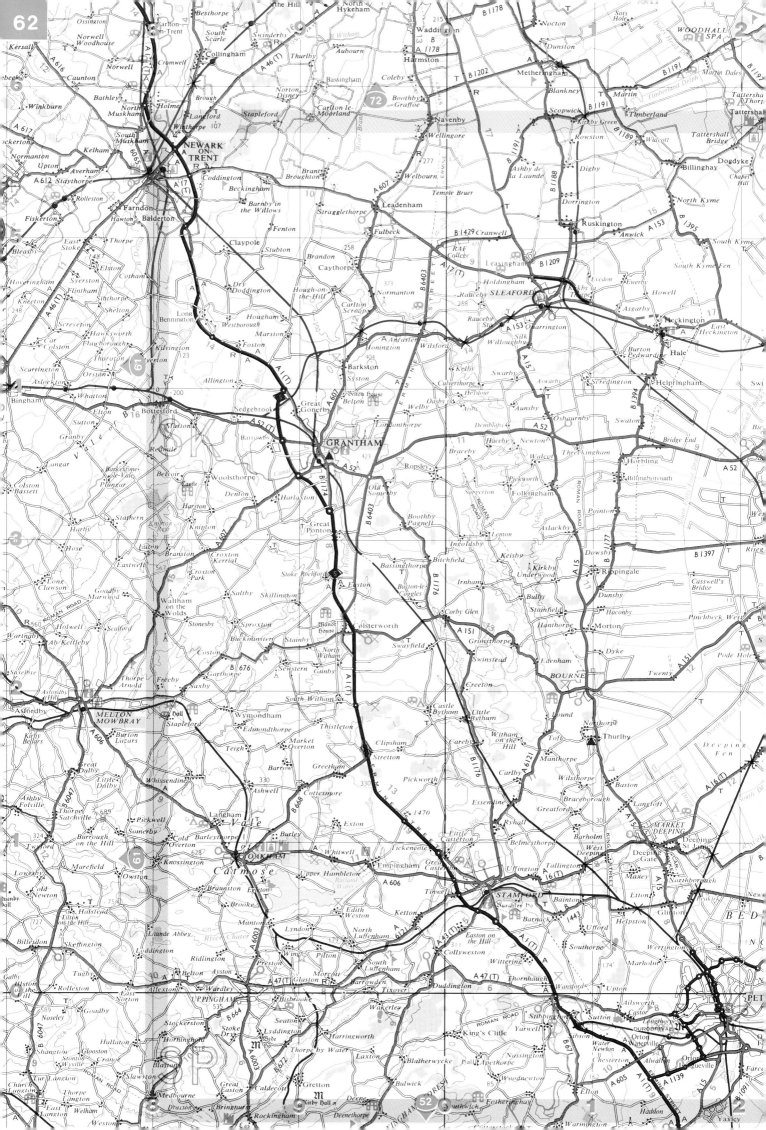

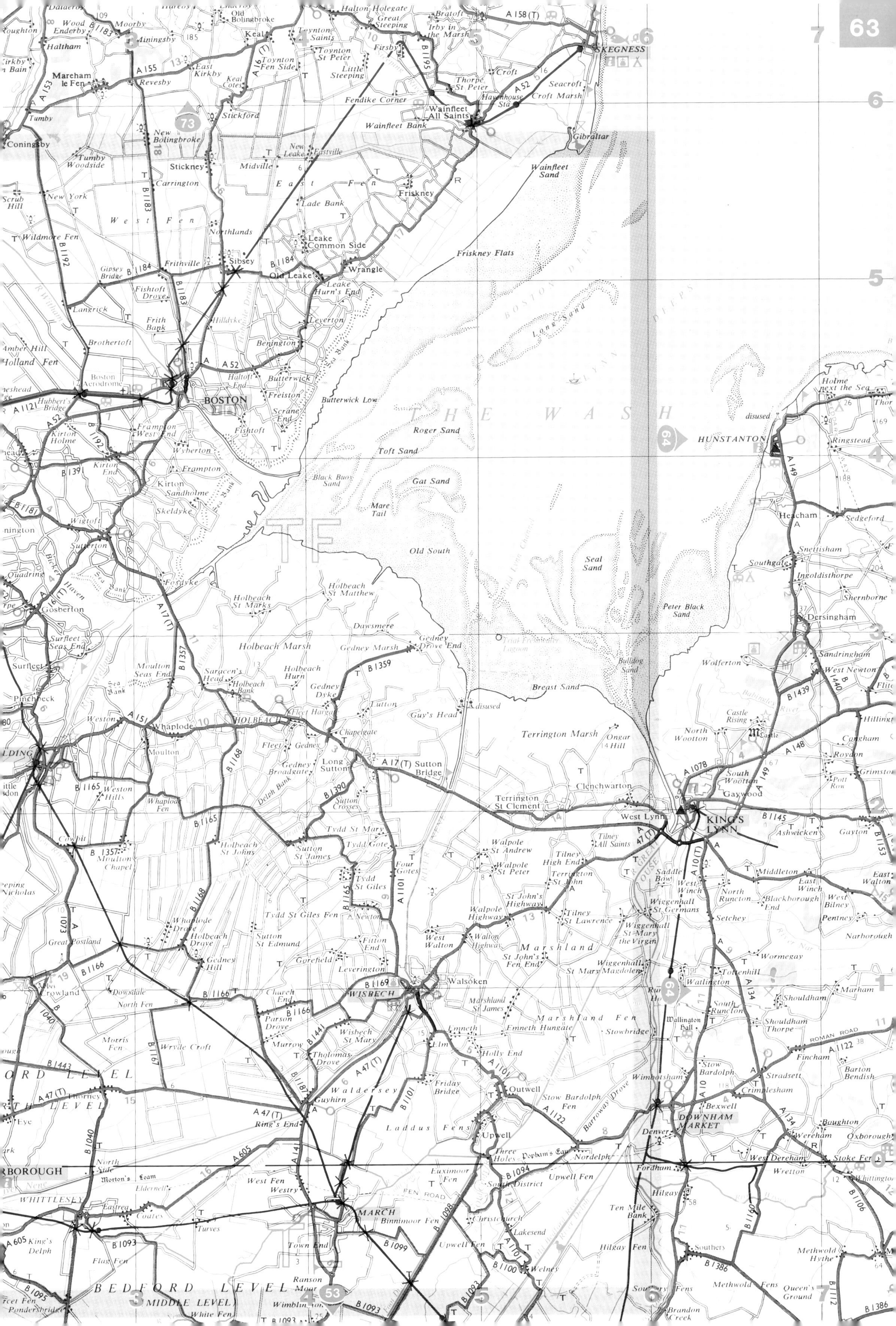

Halton Holegate
Great Steeping
Bratoft
Irby in the Marsh
Wood Enderby
Moorby
Old Bolingbroke
Keal
Toynton All Saints
Toynton St Peter
Toynton Fen Side
Firsby
Little Steeping
Haltham
Miningsby
East Kirkby
Keal Cotes
Mareham le Fen
Revesby
SKEGNESS
Thorpe St Peter
Croft
Seacroft
Croft Marsh
Havenhouse Sta
Fendike Corner
Wainfleet All Saints
Wainfleet Bank
Tumby
Stickford
New Bolingbroke
Coningsby
Gibraltar
Tumby Woodside
Stickney
New Leake
Eastville
Midville
Carrington
Wainfleet Sand
East Fen
Friskney
Scrub Hill
New York
West Fen
Lade Bank
Northlands
Wildmore Fen
Leake Common Side
Friskney Flats
Gipsey Bridge
Frithville
Sibsey
Old Leake
Wrangle
Leake Hurn's End
Fishtoft Drove
Langrick
Hilldyke
Leverton
Frith Bank
Brothertoft
Benington
BOSTON DEEPS
Long Sand
Amber Hill
Holland Fen
Boston Aerodrome
Haltoft End
Butterwick
Freiston
Hubbert's Bridge
BOSTON
Scrane End
Butterwick Low
Frampton West End
THE WASH
Kirton Holme
Fishtoft
Roger Sand
Wyberton
Kirton End
Frampton
Toft Sand
HUNSTANTON
Holme next the Sea
Ringstead
disused
Kirton
Sandholme
Black Buoy Sand
Gat Sand
Skeldyke
Mare Tail
Wigtoft
Heacham
Sedgeford
Sutterton
TF
Old South
Snettisham
Southgate
Ingoldisthorpe
Quadring
Seal Sand
Fosdyke
Holbeach St Matthew
Holbeach St Marks
Shernborne
Gosberton
Peter Black Sand
Dersingham
Dawsmere
Surfleet Seas End
Holbeach Marsh
Gedney Marsh
Gedney Drove End
Sandringham
Surfleet
Moulton Seas End
Saracen's Head
Holbeach Hurn
Bulldog Sand
Wolferton
West Newton
Sea Bank
Holbeach Bank
Gedney Dyke
Breast Sand
Pinchbeck
Lutton
disused
Castle Rising
Weston
Whaplode
HOLBEACH
Fleet Hargate
Guy's Head
Terrington Marsh
Ongar Hill
North Wootton
Congham
SPALDING
Moulton
Fleet
Gedney
Chapelgate
Roydon
Long Sutton
Sutton Bridge
Gedney Broadgate
South Wootton
Grimston
Weston Hills
Whaplode Fen
Sutton Crosses
Clenchwarton
Gaywood
Terrington St Clement
West Lynn
KING'S LYNN
Ashwicken
Gayton
Cowbit
Moulton Chapel
Holbeach St Johns
Tydd St Mary
Tydd Gote
Sutton St James
Tilney All Saints
Walpole St Andrew
Walpole St Peter
Tilney High End
Terrington St John
Middleton
East Winch
Four Gotes
Tydd St Giles
Saddle Bow
West Winch
North Runcton
Blackborough End
West Bilney
Pentney
Walpole Highway
St John's Highway
Tilney St Lawrence
Wiggenhall St Germans
Wiggenhall St Mary the Virgin
Setchey
Tydd St Giles Fen
Newton
Whaplode Drove
Holbeach Drove
Great Postland
Sutton St Edmund
Fitton End
West Walton
Walton Highway
Marshland
St John's Fen End
Wiggenhall St Mary Magdalen
Narborough
Wormegay
Gorefield
Leverington
Gedney Hill
Crowland
Dowsdale
North Fen
Church End
WISBECH
Walsoken
Tottenhill
Watlington
Marham
Shouldham
Marshland St James
Marshland Fen
Emneth Hungate
Stowbridge
Parson Drove
Wisbech St Mary
Emneth
South Runcton
Wallington Hall
Shouldham Thorpe
Morris Fen
Wryde Croft
Murrow
Tholomas Drove
Elm
Holly End
ROMAN ROAD
Fincham
Barton Bendish
BEDFORD LEVEL
Friday Bridge
Outwell
Wimbotsham
Stow Bardolph
Stradsett
Crimplesham
NORTH LEVEL
Thorney
Eye
Guyhirn
Waldersey
Stow Bardolph Fen
Bexwell
DOWNHAM MARKET
Ring's End
Laddus Fens
Upwell
Denver
Wereham
Boughton
Oxborough
Three Holes
Popham's Eau
Nordelph
West Dereham
Stoke Ferry
PETERBOROUGH
North Side
Morton's Leam
West Fen
Westry
Euximoor Fen
South District
Upwell Fen
Fordham
Wretton
Whittington
Eldernell
FEN ROAD
Hilgay
WHITTLESEY
Eastrea
Coates
Turves
MARCH
Binnimoor Fen
Christchurch
Ten Mile Bank
King's Delph
Flag Fen
Town End
Upwell Fen
Lakesend
Hilgay Fen
Southery
Methwold Hythe
Welney
Ranson Moor
Southery Fens
Methwold Fens
Queen's Ground
Pondersbridge
MIDDLE LEVEL
Wimblington
White Fen
Brandon Creek

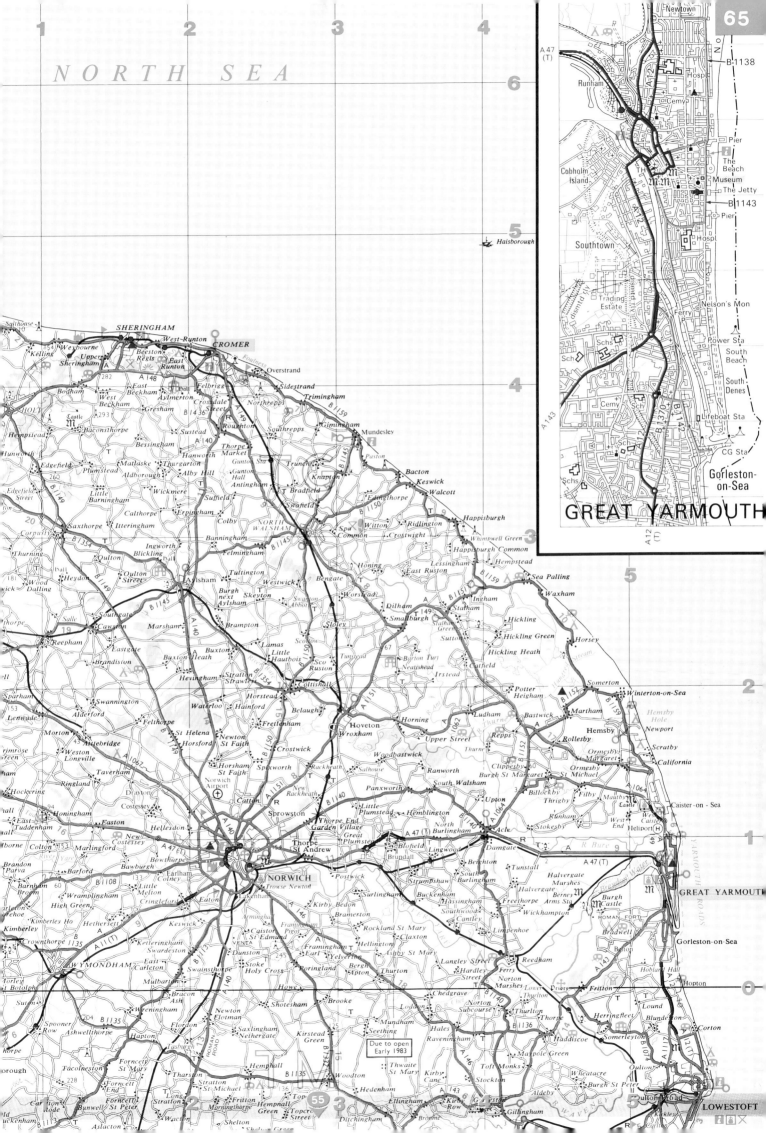

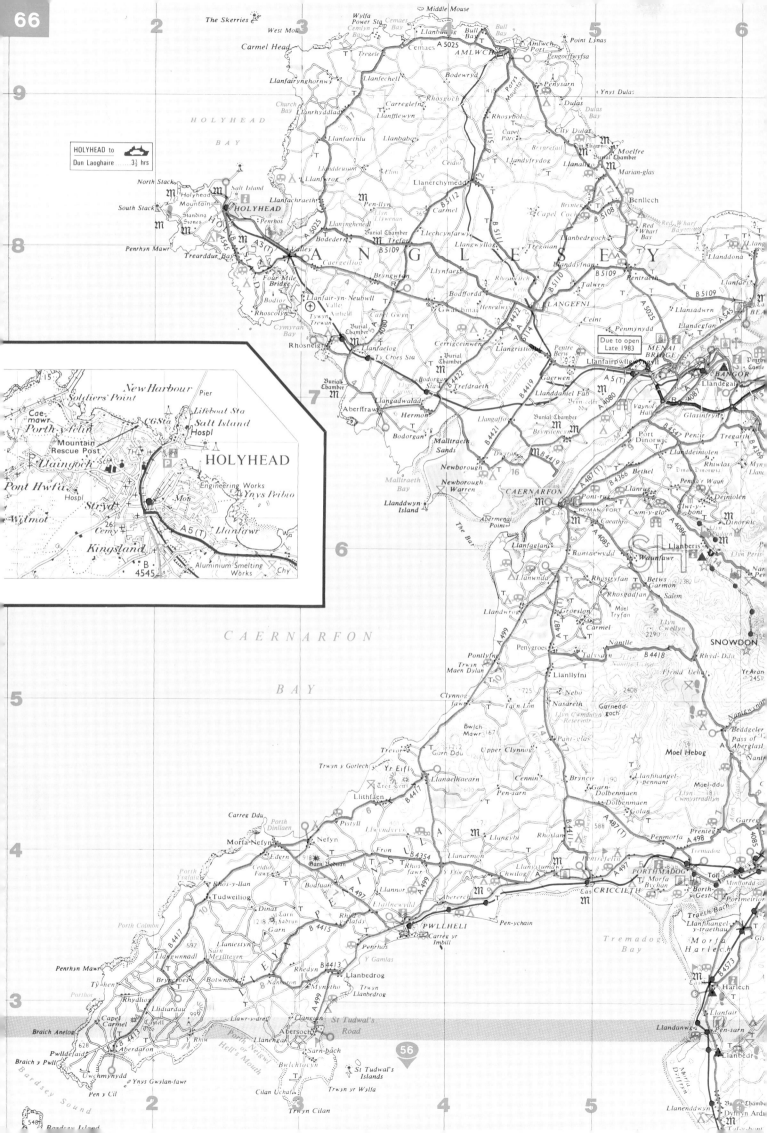

9

West Hoyle Bank

Welsh Channel

Point of Ayr (disused)

Great Ormes Head (Pen-y-Gogarth)
Toll
LLANDUDNO
A 546
Little Ormes Head
Penrhyn-side
Penrhyn Bay
Rhos-on-Sea
Puffin Island
Penmon
CONWY BAY
Llandrillo-yn-Rhos
Degawny
COLWYN BAY
Llysfaen
Old Colwyn
PRESTATYN
Talacre
Gronant
RHYL A 548
Gwespyr
Llanasa
Kinmel Bay
Meliden
A 547
Gwaenysgor
Gop Hill
Trelawnyd
Rhuddlan
Dyserth
Moel Hiraddug
Whitford
A 5151
Cwm
Dutchman Bank
PENMAENMAWR
CONWY
Dwygyfylchi
Conwy Sands
Tywyn
Llandudno Junction
Mochdre
Colwyn Bay
Penmaenrhos
Abergele Roads Towyn
Pensarn
ABERGELE
Gwrych Castle
A 55 (T)
St George
Dinorben
A 547
Pengwern
Bodelwyddan
St Asaph Llanelwy
A 55 (T)
Rhuallt
Pen-y-cefn
B 5429
Caerwys
MENAI
Traeth Lafan
van Sands
LLANFAIRFECHAN
Llanfairfechan
Aber
Henryd
Tal-y-cafn
A 470 (T)
B 5106
B 5381
Bryn-y-maen
Llanelian-yn-Rhos
Dolwen
Betws-yn-Rhos
Dawn
Moelfre Isaf
Moelfre Uchaf
ROMAN ROAD
Llanfair Talhaiarn
Trefnant
Plas-yn-Cefn
Llannerch Hall
Bodfari
Graig
A 541
Due to open Late 1983
Aber Falls
Moel Wnion
Llanllechid
Rachub
FOEL-FRAS
Drosgl
Drum
Rowen
Tyn-y-groes
Graig
Eglwysbach
Gell
Mwdwl Eithin
Llangernyw
Llannefydd
Henllan
B 5382
B 5382
DENBIGH
Las
Llangwyfan
Llandyrnog
BETHESDA
CARNEDD LLEWELYN
Dolgarrog
Llanbedr-y-cennin
Tal-y-Bont
Rhos-y-mawr
A 548
Llansannan
Tan-y-fron
Gwaenynog
Groes
A 543
B 5429
A 525
Llanrhaeadr
Pentre
Llangynhafal
Llandynog
CARNEDD DAFYDD
Llanddoged
Trefriw
Pandy Tudur
A 548
Gwytherin
Bylchau
B 5435
Nantglyn
Gorsedd Bran
Pant-pastynog
Rhewl
Llanynys
Llanfwrog
Efenechtyd
Ruthin
A 5 (T)
LLANRWST
Melin-y-coed
Moel Seisiog
Moel Llyn
Llyn Alwen
Bryn Trillyn
Llyn Aled
Llyn Bran
Mynydd Hiraethog
Cefn Du
Clocaenog
CLOCAENOG FOREST
Llanfwrog
GLYDER FAWR
Capel Curig
Pont Cyfyng
Swallow Falls
Oaklands
BETWS-Y-COED
Nebo
Capel Garmon
Alwen
Hafod-Dinbych
Nilig
Derwen
Llanelidan
A 4086
Carnedd Moel-siabod
Pont-y-pant
Mynydd Cribau
Fairs Glen
Glan Conwy
Capel Garmon
A 543
Pentrefoelas
Rhydlydan
Cerrigydrudion
Llanfihangel Glyn Myfyr
Melin-y-wig
Dolwyddelan
Penmachno
A 5 (T)
Pentrefoelas
Cefnbrith
Glasfryn
B 5105
Bettws Gwerfil Goch
Gwyddelwern
A 470 (T)
Moel Penamnen
Pen y Bedw
Ysbyty Ifan
Garn Prys
Ty-mawr
A 5104
Maerdy
Rhiwbryfdir
Tanygrisiau
BLAENAU FFESTINIOG
Glanaber Terrace
Llyn Conwy
B 4407
Gylchedd
Carnedd y Filiast
Gellinedd
Llangwm
Ty-nant
A 5 (T)
Druid
Corwen
Moelwyn Mawr
Migneint
A 4212
Carnedd Iago
Arenig Fach
Fron-goch
Glan-yr-afon
Foel Goch
Wenallt
A 494 (T)
Plas Isaf
Cynwyd
Moel Ferna
A 496
FFESTINIOG
Maentwrog
A 470 (T)
Graig Wen
B 4391
Cwm Prysor
Cefn-ddwysarn
Sarnau
Rhiwlas
Llandderfel
Pale
Cefn-coch
Crogen
Llandrillo
Llanfor
BALA
Rhos-y-gwaliau
B 4402
Dinam
Foel Wen
Gellilydan
Craig Cyfynys
Trawsfynydd
A 4212
Moel Llyfnant
Craig yr Hyrddod
Moel Ysgyfarnogod
Rhinog Fawr
Moel y Feidiog
Mynydd Bryn-llech
Llanuwchllyn
Llangower
Pont Pydew
B 4391
Roman Steps
Bronaber
A 470 (T)
Mynydd Bach
Foel Figenau
Foel y Geifr
Craig Rhiwarth
Pennant Melangell
Llangynog
Rhobell Fawr
CAMBRIAN
Dyrysgol
Arddu
Aran Benllyn
Ty-nant
Hirnant
B 4391
Cefndeuddwr
Ganllwyd
B 4403
Y Lletr
Llanfachreth
Rhydymain
A 494 (T)
Penygarnedd
Llanrhaeadr-ym-Mochnant

57

58

68

MOUNTAINS
BERWYN

7 8 9 0 1

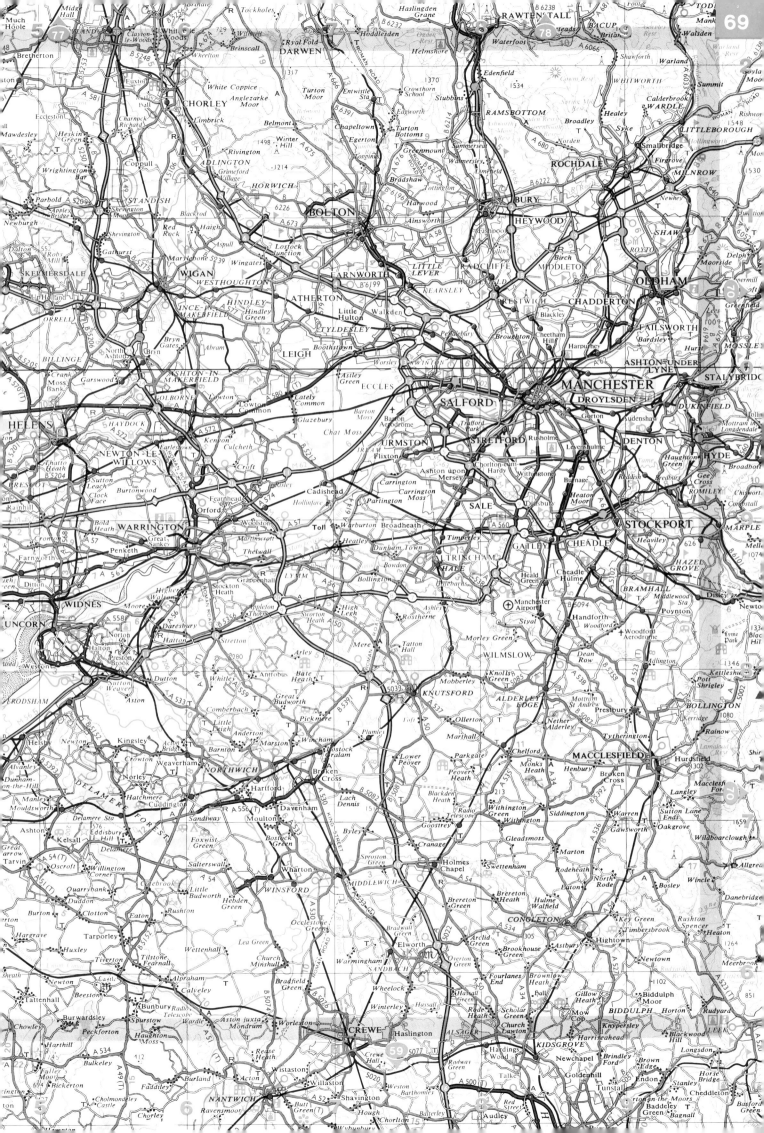

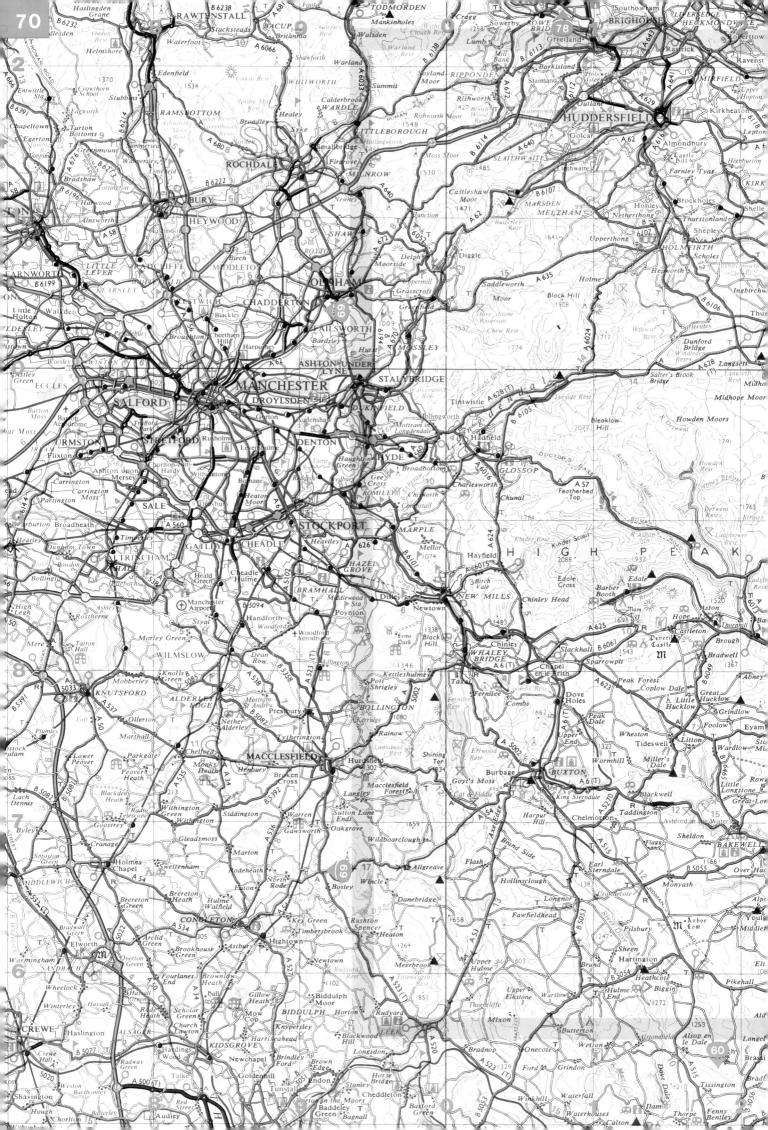

DEWSBURY
WAKEFIELD
NORMANTON
FEATHERSTONE
PONTEFRACT
KNOTTINGLEY
Snaith
Rawcliffe
Gowdall
Pollington
Ossett
Horbury
Middlestown
Netherton
Crigglestone
Walton
Wintersett
Ryhill
Crofton
Sharlston
Ackworth Moor Top
Badsworth
Womersley
Little Smeaton
Kirk Smeaton
Walden Stubbs
Norton
Campsall
Burghwallis
Askern
Fenwick
Sykehouse
Fishlake
Thorne
Moorends
Thorne Waste or Moors
Hatfield
Stainforth
Kirk Bramwith
Thorpe in Balne
HEMSWORTH
South Elmsall
South Kirkby
South Hiendley
Kinsley
ROYSTON
Carlton
Clayton West
High Hoyland
West Bretton
Kexbrough
Cawthorne
DENBY DALE
Upper Denby
BARNSLEY
Gawber
Ardsley
DARFIELD
CUDWORTH
Grimethorpe
Great Houghton
Brierley
Hooton Pagnell
Brodsworth
Hickleton
Thurnscoe
Goldthorpe
Marr
ADWICK LE STREET
BENTLEY
Arksey
DONCASTER
Edenthorpe
Armthorpe
Dunscroft
Hatfield Woodhouse
Hatfield Moors
Cantley
Bessacarr
Branton
Auckley
Blaxton
Wroot
Finningley
Silkstone
Hoyland Swaine
Silkstone Common
DODWORTH
WORSBROUGH
PENISTONE
Oxspring
Thurgoland
Wentworth Castle
Pilley
Birdwell
WOMBWELL
Jump
Brampton
Tankersley
HOYLAND NETHER
Elsecar
Wortley
STOCKSBRIDGE
Deepcar
Bolsterstone
Ewden Village
High Green
Chapeltown
Wentworth
Thorpe Hesley
WATH UPON DEARNE
Bolton upon Dearne
MEXBOROUGH
SWINTON
CONISBROUGH
Barnburgh
Sprotbrough
High Melton
Cadeby
Warmsworth
New Edlington
Loversall
New Rossington
Rossington
Hooton Roberts
Ravenfield
RAWMARSH
Thrybergh
Wharncliffe Side
Grenoside
Oughtibridge
Ecclesfield
Dalton
ROTHERHAM
Bramley
Braithwell
Stainton
MALTBY
Tickhill
Bawtry
Harworth
Austerfield
Misson
Scaftworth
Everton
Scrooby
Mattersey
Wiseton
Worrall
Low Bradfield
Tinsley
Wickersley
Whiston
Hooton Levitt
Roche Abbey
Firbeck
Oldcotes
Ranskill
Stannington
SHEFFIELD
Catcliffe
Treeton
Thurcroft
Laughton en le Morthen
Dinnington
Langold
Letwell
Blyth
Torworth
High Neb
Fulwood
Handsworth
Aughton
Ulley
Aston
Woodhouse
Todwick
Kiveton Park
Anston
Gildingwells
Woodsetts
Carlton in Lindrick
Barnby Moor
Sutton
Hathersage
Beighton
Hackenthorpe
Gleadless Townend
Mosborough
Wales
Harthill
Thorpe Salvin
Shireoaks
Rhodesia
WORKSOP
Ranby
Babworth
EAST RETFORD
Grove
Dore
Beauchief
Norton
Greenhill
Coal Aston
Eckington
Killamarsh
Totley
Dronfield Woodhouse
DRONFIELD
Renishaw
Barlborough
Clowne
Whitwell
Hodthorpe
Elkesley
Gamston
Eaton
Nether Padley
Froggatt
Holmesfield
Unstone
West Handley
Apperknowle
Creswell
Welbeck Abbey
Clumber Park
West Drayton
Curbar
Common Side
Barlow
Whittington
STAVELEY
Newbold
Brimington
CHESTERFIELD
Holbeck
Norton
Carburton
Bothamsall
Haughton
Bevercotes
West Markham
Baslow
Cutthorpe
Old Brampton
Calow
Duckmanton
Shuttlewood
Elmton
Whaley
BOLSOVER
Nether Langwith
Cuckney
Thoresby Hall
Walesby
Pilsley
Chatsworth House
Edensor
Wadshelf
Holymoorside
Hasland
Arkwright Town
Carr Vale
Scarcliffe
Upper Langwith
Church Warsop
Meden Vale
Budby
Kirton
Egmanton
Walton
Temple Normanton
Palterton
WARSOP
Edwinstowe
Boughton
Ollerton
Wellow
Laxton
Beeley
Rowsley
Wingerworth
Grassmoor
Glapwell
Shirebrook
New Houghton
Ompton
New Tupton
North Wingfield
Pleasley
MANSFIELD WOODHOUSE
Old Clipstone
New Clipstone
Kneesall
Stanton in Peak
Two Dales
Upper Hackney
Ashover
CLAY CROSS
Pilsley
Hardwick Hall
Teversal
Forest Town
Kersall
Eakring
Birchover
Milltown
Stretton
Tibshelf
MANSFIELD
Skegby
Bilsthorpe
Maplebeck
Wensley
Winster
MATLOCK
Morton
Stanton Hill
Tansley
Brackenfield
Stonebroom
Huthwaite
SUTTON IN ASHFIELD
Winkburn
Bonsall
Matlock Bath
Higham
Shirland
Westhouses
Rainworth
Kirklington
Lea
Wessington
Holloway
South Normanton
KIRKBY IN ASHFIELD
Blidworth
Farnsfield
Hockerton
Edingley
Normanton
Upton
Cromford
Middleton
South Wingfield
Whatstandwell
Crich
Pinxton
Annesley Woodhouse
Ravenshead
Haywood Oaks
Halam
WIRKSWORTH
ALFRETON
Swanwick
Somercotes
Selston
Annesley
Newstead Abbey
Southwell
Carsington
Alderwasley
Fritchley
Pentrich
Ironville
Bagthorpe
New Brinsley
Linby
Papplewick
Oxton
Halloughton
Fiskerton
Hognaston
Kirk Ireton
Ambergate
Heage
RIPLEY
Thurgarton

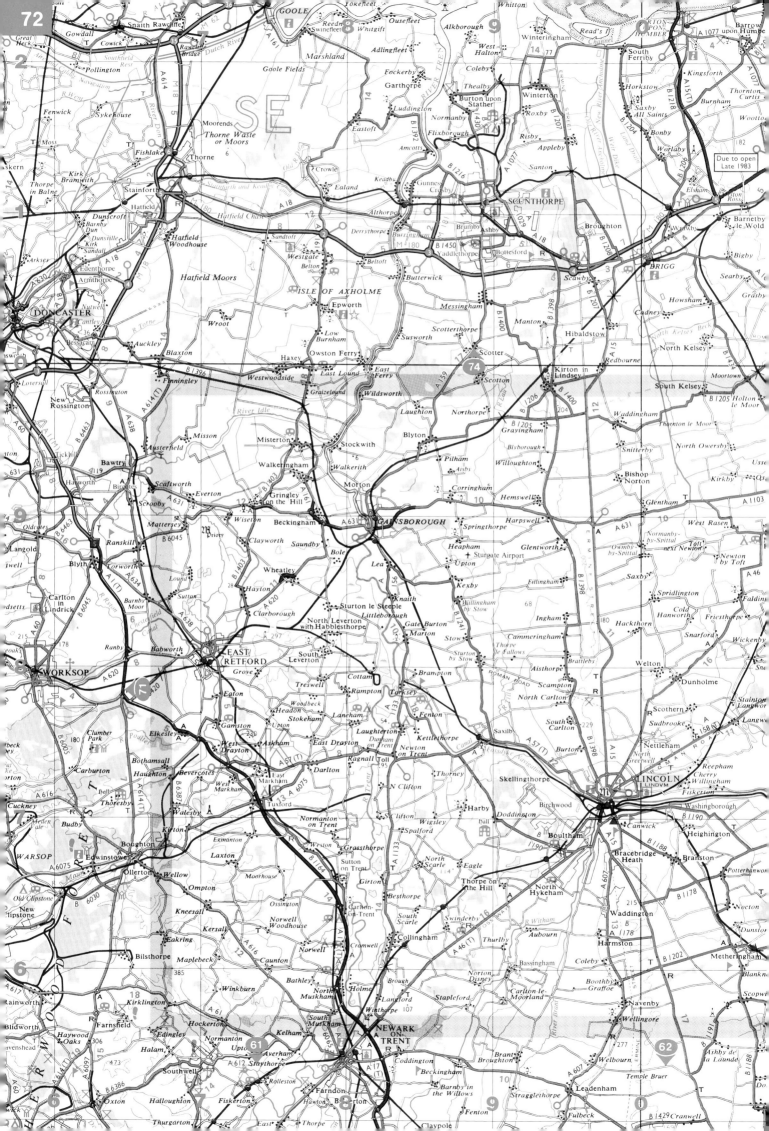

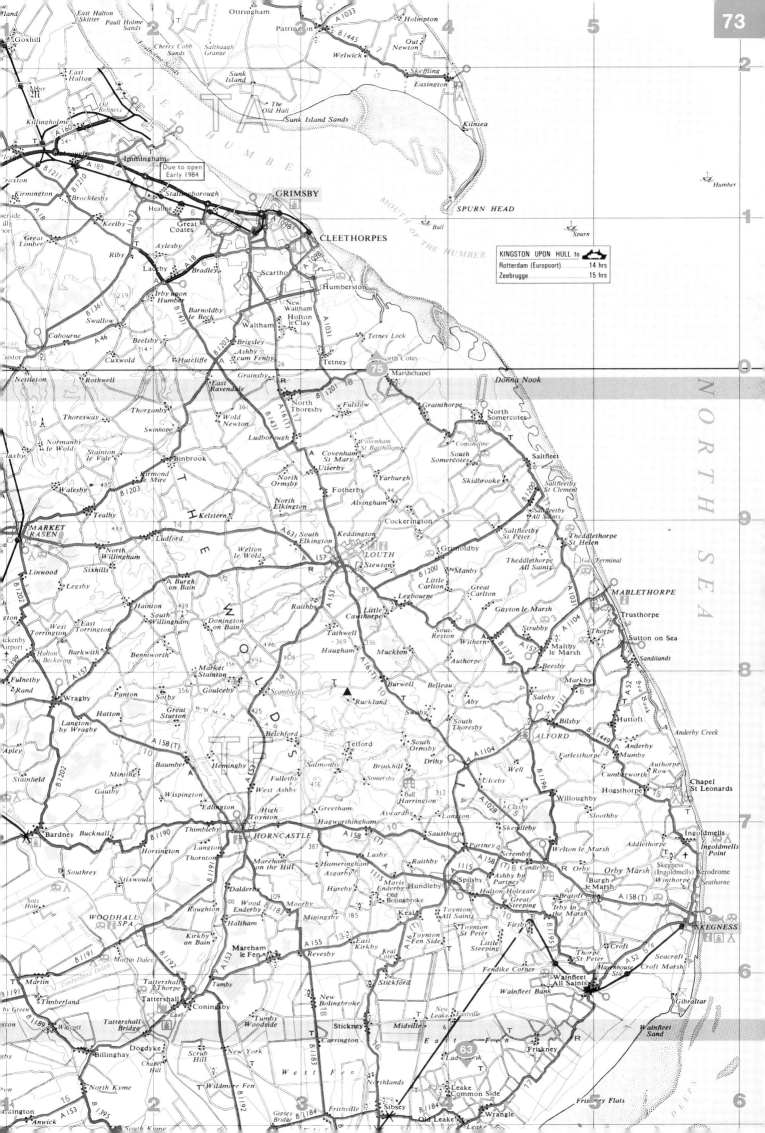

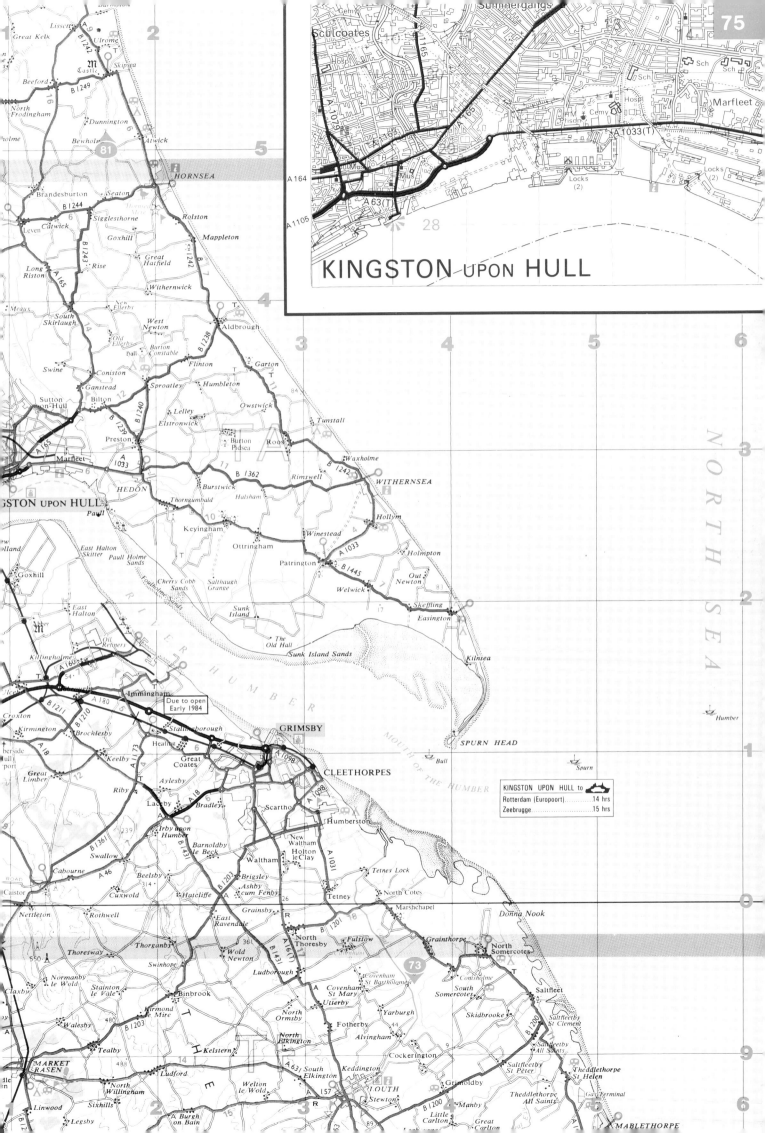

SC

IRISH SEA

NX

POINT OF AYRE

Rue Point
The Ayres
Cranstal
The Lhen
Dhowin
Bride
Jurby West
Jurby Head
Jurby East
Shellag Point
Ballasalla
Aerodrome
Sandygate
St Judes
Regaby
The Cronk
A14
St Judes
Dhoor
A17
Silby
A13
The Curragh's
A3
RAMSEY BAY
Orrisdale Head
Ballaugh
Churchtown
Cronk Sumark
RAMSEY
A9
Port e Vullen
Cronk y Voddy
Glen Auldyn
Maughold
Ravensdale
Maughold Head
Kirk Michael
Ballajora
Slieau Dhoo
Port Mooar
Gob y Deigan
Ballacarnane Beg
Barregarrow
Druidale
North Barrule
Corrany
Knocksharry
Clagh Ouyr
Port Cornaa
Cronk-y-Voddy
Druidale
SNAEFELL
Dhoon
St Patrick's Isle
Ballagyr
Lambfell Moar
B10
Bulgham Bay
Castle
Colden
King Orry's Grave
PEEL
Ballig
A1
St John's
Baldwin
Laxey
Laxey Head
Contrary Head
Sheau Ruy
B21
Ballacannell
Patrick
A30
B22
Laxey Bay
A27
Baldrine
ISLE   OF   MAN
Baldrine
Dalby Point
Glenmaye
Crosby
Clay Head
Hillberry
Dalby
Foxdale
Glen Vine
Union Mills
Onchan
Port Groudle
Garth
Eairy
Braaid
N'arbyl Bay
South Barrule
Close Clark
St Mark's
Quine's Hill
Onchan Head
Stroin Vuigh
Ronague
Newtown
DOUGLAS
Little Ness
Douglas Bay
Ballamodha
Port Soderick
Douglas Head
Fleshwick Bay
Colby
Ballabeg
Ballasalla
Santon Head
Bradda Head
Bradda
Port Erin
Isle of Man (Ronaldsway) Airport
The Howe
Creigneish
CASTLETOWN
Derbyhaven
Port St Mary
St Michael's Island
Calf of Man
Langness
SPANISH HEAD
Dreswick Point
Chicken Rock

DOUGLAS to	
Heysham	3¾ hrs
Liverpool	4 hrs
Seasonal	
Fleetwood	3 hrs
Belfast	4½ hrs
Dublin	4½ hrs
Ardrossan	6 hrs

82
Prior Park
Dunnerdale
Broughton Mill
Stoneside Hill
Hycemoor
Bootle Sta
Bootle
Bootle Fell
Duddon Bridge
Broughton in Furness
Annaside
Black Combe
970
A595 (T)
Hallthwaites
Foxfield
Grizebeck
Whitbeck
The Green
Kirkby-in-Furness
Whicham
Silecroft
MILLOM
Souterate
Kirksanton
Askam and Furness
Ireleth
Pennington
Haverigg
Lindal in Furness
DALTON-IN-FURNESS
Stainton with Adgarley
Newton
Walney Airfield
Furness Abbey
BARROW-IN-FURNESS
North Scale
Leece
Vickerstown
Biggar
Rampside
Tummer Hill Scar
Roa Island
Sheep Island
Piel Island
South End
Piel Bar
BL
BLA

68

HEYSHAM to
Douglas .... 3¾ hrs

FLEETWOOD to
Douglas .... 3 hrs
(seasonal)

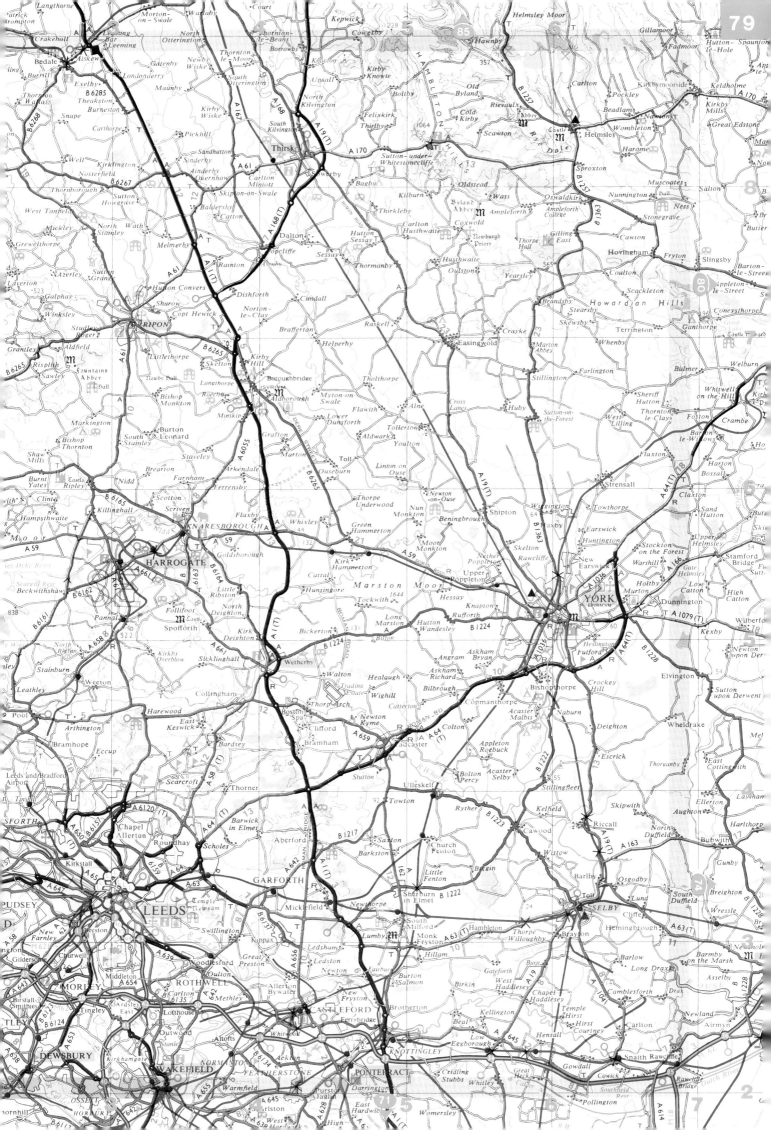

NORTH SEA

WHITBY

Saltwick Bay
Abbey
Stainsacre
Sneaton
Hawsker
Ugglebarnby
Sneatonthorpe
Raw
Fylingthorpe
Ness Point or
North Cheek
Robin Hood's Bay
A 171
B 1416
R
Ravenscar
Old Peak or
South Cheek

959
Burn Howe
Rigg
Fylingdales Moor
Staintondale

Cloughton
Newlands
Cloughton Wyke
Cloughton
Harwood
Dale
Burniston
Cromer Point
Langdale
End
Silpho
656
Scalby Ness
Rocks
Toll
SCALBY
Hackness
A 165
Castle
Everley
SCARBOROUGH
Sawdon
Ayton
Irton
Black Rocks
Hutton
Buscel
Eastfield
Osgodby
Cayton Bay
Ebberston
Snainton
Brompton
Seamer
Cayton
The Wyke
Wykeham
B 1261
Lebberston
A 170
Gristhorpe
FILEY
Yedingham
Willerby
Flixton
Folkton
R Hertford
A 1039
Filey Bay
Staxton
Muston
Sherburn
Ganton
Hunmanby
Holiday Camp
East-Heslerton
Fordon
Reighton
Sands
A 64 (T)
West
Heslerton
Reighton
Speeton
Crab Rocks
Wintringham
Wold
Newton
B 1229
Foxholes
Burton Fleming
Bempton
Holiday
Camp
Butterwick
Willy
Howe
Grindale
FLAMBOROUGH
HEAD
Helperthorpe
Weaverthorpe
Thwing
Flamborough
West
Lutton
Boynton
Sewerby
Duggleby
Kirby
Grindalythe
B 1253
Rudston
BRIDLINGTON
Langtoft
B 1254
Sledmere
Kilham
Carnaby
Hilderthorpe
Haisthorpe
BRIDLINGTON
Ruston
Parva
Burton Agnes
BAY
Harpham
Fraisthorpe
B 1252
Lowthorpe
TA
Fridaythorpe
Wetwang
Garton-on-
the-Wolds
A 166
Nafferton
Gransmoor
Barmston
Huggate
Tibthorpe
GREAT
DRIFFIELD
Lissett
A 9
Ulrome
Wansford
Great Kelk
Kirkburn
B 1242
North
Dalton
Skerne
Foston
on the
Wolds
Skipsea
Bainton
Brigham
Beeford
Watton
Hutton
Cranswick
Rotsea
North
Frodingham
Dunnington
Bewholme
Atwick
Middleton-on-
the-Wolds
Hempholme
B 1246
Kilnwick
Lund
Burshill
HORNSEA
Holme on
the Wolds
Beswick
Brandesburton
Seaton
South Dalton
Lockington
Aike
B 1244
Sigglesthorne
Rolston
Scorborough
Arram
Leven
Catwick
Goxhill
Mappleton
Etton
Rise
Goodmanham
Cherry
Burton
Routh
Long
Riston
Great
Hatfield
Market Weighton
Tickton
Withernwick
A 1079 (T)
A 165

NX

SC

SOLWAY

Kirkbean
Cault
Southerness
Southerness Point
ipped Scaur
Mote of Mark
Rockcliffe
Castlehill Point
est 5 Island

Skinburness
Silloth
Lees Scar Lighthouse
Beckfoot
Peltho
Mawbray
Dubmill Point
Allonby
Allonby Bay
Westnewton
Crosscanonby
Crosby
Allerby
Hayton
Aspatria

Whitrigg
Newton Arlosh
Kirkbride
Kirkbampton
Abbeytown
Wedholme Flow
Aikton
Wiggonby
Baldwinholme
Great Orton
Little Orton
Dundraw
Lessonhall
Waverton
Wigton
West Curthwaite
Blencogo
Blendogo
Bromfield
Red Dial
Westward
Rosley
Welton
Langrigg
Mealsgate
Boltongate
Plumbland
Blennerhasset
Bothel
Whitrigg
Ireby
Caldbeck
Hesket Newmarket
Torpenhow
Fell Side
Nether Row
Millhouse
High Pike
Mosedale

MARYPORT
Dearham
Flimby
Broughton Moor
Dovenby
Broughton
Seaton
Camerton
Brigham
Bridgefoot
Papcastle
Embleton
Dubwath
Bassenthwaite
Great Calva
Knott
SKIDDAW FOREST
SKIDDAW
Saddleback or Blencathra
Scales

WORKINGTON
Clifton
Greysouthen
Eaglesfield
Deanscales
COCKERMOUTH
Lorton
Lord's Seat
Thornthwaite
Latrigg
Threlkeld
Moss Bay
Harrington
Branthwaite
Dean
Pardshaw
Ullock
Mockerkin
Grisedale Pike
Braithwaite
KESWICK
Stair
Causey Pike
Derwent Water
Dowthwaitehead
Great Dodd

Distington
Gilgarran
Pica
Asby
Lamplugh
Loweswater
Loweswater Fell
Brackenthwaite Fell
Derwent Fells
Little Town
High Seat
Watendlath
Great Seat

Lowca
Moresby
Parton
WHITEHAVEN
Moresby Parks
Arlecdon
Frizington
Kirkland
Murton Fell
Crummock Water
Newlands Pass
Grange
High Stile
Rosthwaite
Helvellyn

St Bees Head
Rottington
Sandwith
Cleator Moor
Cleator
Ennerdale Bridge
Great Borne
Ennerdale Water
Red Pike
High Stile
Buttermere
Buttermere Fell
Borrowdale
Borrowdale Fells
Wythburn Fells
Ullscarf
Dunmail Raise
Seat Sandal

St Bees
EGREMONT
Grike
Lank Rigg
Ennerdale Fell
Pillar
Scoat Fell
Black Sail Pass
Seathwaite
Hay Stacks
Great Gable
Glaramara
High White Stones

Nethertown
Haile
Caw Fell
Haycock
Kirk Fell
Sty Head
Great End
Stake Pass
Langdale Pikes
Rydal
Grasmere

Beckermet
Braystones
Calder Bridge
Seatallan
Wasdale Head
Lingmell
Scafell Pike
Chapel Stile
Elterwater
Little Langdale
AMBLESIDE
Clappersgate

Sellafield Sta
Gosforth
Nether Wastdale
The Screes
Wast Water
Burnmoor Tarn
COPELAND FOREST
CUMBRIAN MOUNTAINS
Hardknott Pass
Wrynose Pass
Skelwith Bridge

Seascale
Santon Bridge
Boot
Outward Bound Mountain Sch
Beckfoot
Eskdale
ROMAN FORT
Cockley Beck
FURNESS FELLS
Holmrook
Drigg
Eskdale Green
Harter Fell
Outgate
Hawkshead

Ravenglass
Muncaster Castle
Woodend
Devoke Water
THE OLD MAN OF CONISTON
Coniston
Bowmanstead
Kokoarrah
Waberthwaite
Ulpha Fell
Whitfell
Ulpha
Stickle Pike
Caw
Seathwaite
Torver
GRIZEDALE FOREST
Satterthwaite

Hycemoor
Bootle Sta
Corney
Prior Park
Stoneside Hill
Dunnerdale
Broughton Mills
Woodland Fell
Water Yeat
Selker Bay
Bootle
Bootle Fell
Black Combe
Duddon Bridge
Broughton in Furness
Dluwith
Oxen Park
Colton
Rusland
Finsthwaite
Hallthwaites
Foxfield
Grizebeck
Lowick
Spark Bridge
Newby Bridge

NORTH SEA

JARROW
Jarrow Slake

NEWCASTLE UPON TYNE to
Esbjerg .... 18-21 hrs
Bergen .... 19½-24 hrs

Seasonal
Gothenburg .... 24-28 hrs
Stavanger .... 17½-22 hrs
Oslo .... 26-32 hrs

GREENOCK
PORT GLASGOW
HELENSBURGH
DUMBARTON
CLYDEBANK
PAISLEY
RENFREW
GLASGOW
COATBRIDGE
RUTHERGLEN
BEARSDEN
KIRKINTILLOCH
KILSYTH
CUMBER
MOTHERW
HAMILTON
EAST KILBRIDE
BARRHEAD
JOHNSTONE
ELDERSLIE
NEILSTON
BEITH
KILWINNING
IRVINE
KILMARNOCK
NEWMILNS
DARVEL
GALSTON
GREENHOLM
TROON
PRESTWICK
New Prestwick
AYR
KILBIRNIE
Lochwinnoch
STEWARTON
FENWICK
CUMNOCK
HOLMHEAD
AUCHINLECK
MUIRKIRK

CAMPSIE FELLS
Carron Valley Forest
KILPATRICK HILLS
Strathblane Hills
Whitelee Forest

Inchmurrin
Balloch
Alexandria
Bonhill
Killearn
Dumgoyne
Strathblane
Blanefield
Milngavie
Bishopbriggs
Lennoxtown
Milton of Campsie
Mollinsburn
Bishopton
Erskine
Drumchapel
Govan
Pollokshaws
Thornliebank
Clarkston
Busby
Newton Mearns
Eaglesham
Waterfoot
Carmunnock
Cambuslang
Uddingston
Bothwell
Bellshill
Stonefield
High Blantyre
Strathaven
Beith
Gateside
Dalry
Dunlop
Stewarton
Fenwick
Waterside
Kilmaurs
Crosshouse
Gatehead
Hurlford
Galston
Sorn
Mauchline
Tarbolton
Failford
Symington
Monkton
Alloway
Dalrymple

101
93
88

Kincardine
DUNFERMLINE
Aberdour
BURNTISLAND
Pettycur
Inchkeith
Airth
Blair Cas
Valleyfield
Crossford
Low Torry
Torryburn
CULROSS
Power Station
Longannet Point
Charlestown
Limekilns
Rosyth
INVERKEITHING
Hillend
Dalgety Bay
St Colme Ho
Inchcolm
Oxcars
Torwood
Larbert
Stenhousemuir
GRANGEMOUTH
BO'NESS
Grangepans
Carriden
Muirhouses
Blackness
Camelon
FALKIRK
Bonnybridge
High Bonnybridge
Greenhill
Glen Village
Redding
Reddingmuirhead
Brightons
Shieldhill
Maddiston
California
Linlithgow Bridge
LINLITHGOW
Philpstoun
Old Philpstoun
Whitecross
Champany
The Binns
Hopetoun
QUEENSFERRY
North Queensferry
Forth Road Bridge
Inch Garvie
Forth Br
Toll
Dalmeny
Cramond Island
Barnbougle Castle
Granton
Cramond
Black Rocks
Leith
EDINBURGH
Newton
Dundas Castle
Kirkliston
Edinburgh Airport Ingliston
Gogar
Corstorphine
Newbridge
Ratho Station
Ratho
Winchburgh
Ecclesmachan
Uphall
Broxburn
Burnside
Bridgend
Loan
Standburn
Avonbridge
Slamannan
Binniehill
Limerigg
Jawcraig
Westfield
Torphichen Preceptory
Cairnpapple
Dechmont
Uphall Station
BATHGATE
Boghall
LIVINGSTON
Livingston Village
Dedridge
East Calder
Kirknewton
Balerno
Currie
Bonnington
Wilkieston
Long Hermiston
Juniper Green
Colinton
Craiglockhart
Morningside
Braid Hills
Liberton
Craigmillar
Duddingston
Arthur's Seat
Gilmerton
Kaimes
Fairmilehead
Straiton
LOANHEAD
Bilston
Roslin
Polton
Rosewell
Milton Bridge
Auchendinny
PENICUIK
Carrington
Longriggend
Black Loch
ARMADALE
Whiteside
Blackridge
Westrigg
Forrestfield
Seafield
Blackburn
East Whitburn
Bellsquarry
Polbeth
WHITBURN
Harthill
Eastfield
Kirk of Shotts
Salsburgh
Newhouse
Longridge
Stoneyburn
Addiewell
West Calder
Breich
Fauldhouse
Greenburn
Shotts
Stane
Dykehead
Hartwood
Allanton
Bonkle
Newmains
WISHAW
Waterloo
Bogside
Castlehill
Law
Carluke
Yieldshields
Dalserf
Rosebank
Roadmeetings
Kilcadzow
Braidwood
Netherburn
Crossford
Cartland
Hazelbank
Nemphlar
Auchenheath
Kirkfieldbank
LANARK
New Lanark
Kirkmuirhill
Ravenstruther
Carstairs
Carstairs Junction
Pettinain
Carnwath
Libberton
Newbigging
Walston
Elsrickle
Candy Mill
Ewe Hill
Skirling
Biggar
Thankerton
Quothquan
Shieldhill
Symington
Coulter
Wiston
Lamington
Roberton
Douglas Water
Rigside
Uddington
Douglas
Hawksland
Brocketsbrae
Broken Cross Muir
Tinto
Tinto Hills
Hendreys Course
Woolfords Cottages
Cobbinshaw Resr
Rootpark
Forth
Auchengray
Tarbrax
Braehead
West Mains
Dunsyre
Black Mount
Dolphinton
Romannobridge
Mountain Cross
Blyth Bridge
Castlecraig
Drochil Castle
Broughton Heights
Broughton
Drumelzier
Dawyck
Stobo
Tinnis Castle
Bellspool
PENTLAND HILLS
White Craig
Byrehope Mount
Bleak Law
Mendick Hill
West Linton
Carlops
Newhall
Auchencorth Moss
Leadburn
Howgate
The Mount
Scald Law
Silverburn
Black Hill
Harlaw Resr
Threipmuir Resr
Glencorse Resr
Bavelaw Castle
Woodhouselee
Allermuir Hill
Harperrig Resr
Bore Stane
Crosswood Resr
Cowdenburn
Waterheads
Halmyre Mains
Wether Law
Eddleston
Milkieston Rings
Cringletie
Craigie Hill
Black Meldon
White Meldon
Neidpath Castle
PEEBLES
Glentress Forest
Glentress
Kings Muir
Cardrona
Cardrona Forest
Dunslair Heights
Hallyne
Kirkton Manor
Cademuir Hill
Trahenna Hill
Whitelaw Hill
Preston Law
Hundleshope Heights
Stob Law
Dun Rig
Posso
Goseland Hill
Culter Fell
Common Law
Blakehope Head
Glenlood Hill
Stanhope
Taberon Law
Dollar Law
Black Law
Pykestone Hill
Horse Hope Hill
Crook Inn
Hearthstane
Tweedsmuir
Glenwhappen Rig
Glenmuck Height
Broad Law
Talla Reservoir
Talla Linnfoots
Meggethead
Cappercleuch
Rodono Hotel
Tibbie Shiels Inn
The Wiss
Dryhope
Mountbenger
Deer Law
Lochcraig Head
Craigmaid
Clyde Law
Cape Law
White Coomb
Herman Law
Ramsey Knowe
Ettrick
Ramseycleuch
Tushielaw Inn
Glenbreck
Duncangill Head
Culter Cleuch Shank
Broad Hill
Startup Hill
Dungavel Hill
Scaur Hill
Robertson Law
Backstane Hill
Pagie Hill
Auchensaugh Hill
Middle Muir
Crawfordjohn
Glespin
Common Hill
Abington
Drake Law
Kirkton
Crawford
Tewsgill Hill
Camps Water
White Hill
Spango Hill
Rake Law
Wellgrain Dod
Elvanfoot
Wedder Dod
Leadhills
Dun Law
Braehead
Bankend
Happendon
Howgate Hill
Douglas Water
Blackhope Scar
Black Knowe Head
Deuchar Law
Blake Muir
Wallace's Hill
Glen Ho
LOWTHER
NT
FIRTH

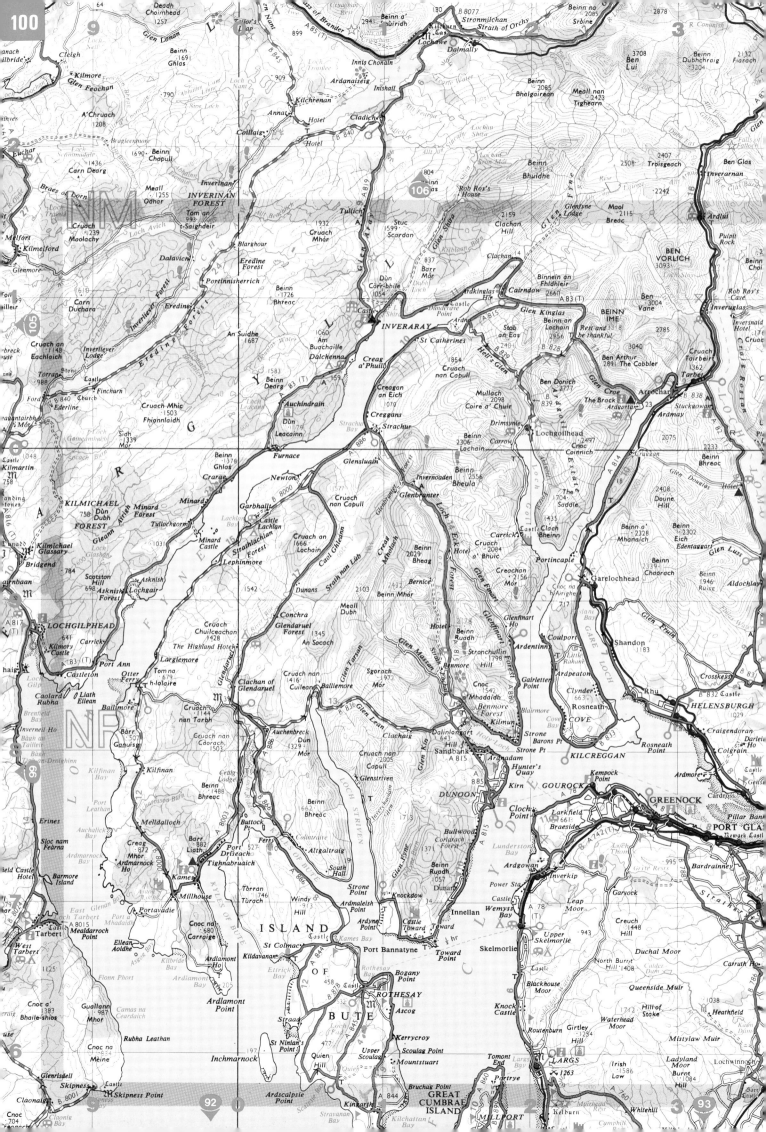

Glenalmond
Buchanty
Methven
Pitcairngreen
Almondbank
Luncarty
Scone Palace
Old Scone
New Scone
Huntingtower
Tibbermore
PERTH
Bridgend
Kinnoull Hill
St Fillans
Comrie
Dalginross
Ochtertyre
Hosh
Gilmerton
Monzie
CRIEFF
KEILLOUR FOREST
Madderty
St David's
Clathy
Findo Gask
Aberdalgie
Forteviot
Forgandenny
Bridge of Earn
Muthill
Drummond Castle
FOREST OF GLENARTNEY
Dalchruin
Ben Clach
Strathallan Cas
AUCHTERARDER
Dunning
Aberuthven
Kincardine Castle
Gleneagles Sta
Blackford
Braes of Ogilvie
Greenloaning
Braco
Glen Eagles
Common of Dunning
Glendevon Forest
Glendevon
Milnathort
KINROSS
LOCH LEVEN
Kinbuck
Ashfield
Sheriff Muir
Doune
Deanston
DUNBLANE
BRIDGE OF ALLAN
Blairlogie
ALVA
TILLICOULTRY
DOLLAR
Blairingone
Powmill
Crook of Devon
Cleish Hills
BLAIRADAM FOREST
Kelty
Menstrie
Causewayhead
Tullibody
Cambus
New Sauchie
Coalsnaughton
Devonside
Forest Mill
STIRLING
Cambuskenneth
St Ninians
Bannockburn
ALLOA
Clackmannan
Saline
Gargunnock
Touch Hills
Cowie
Kincardine
Airth
Blairhall
Carnock
Oakley
DUNFERMLINE
Crossford
Charlestown
Limekilns
Rosyth
INVERKEITHING
North Queensferry
Carron Valley Forest
DUNIPACE
DENNY
Larbert
Stenhousemuir
GRANGEMOUTH
BO'NESS
FALKIRK
Bonnybridge
Carriden
Blackness
QUEENSFERRY
Kilsyth Hills
KILSYTH
Cumbernauld
LINLITHGOW
Philpstoun
Winchburgh
Kirkliston
Edinburgh Airport
Ratho
Uphall
Broxburn
Dechmont
Torphichen
Westfield
Avonbridge
Slamannan
Armadale
BATHGATE
LIVINGSTON
East Calder
Whitburn
Blackburn
KIRKINTILLOCH
COATBRIDGE
AIRDRIE
Calderbank
Chapelhall
Newhouse
Holytown
Shotts
Harthill
Fauldhouse
Stoneyburn
Addiewell
West Calder
Breich
MOTHERWELL
Newmains
Allanton
Bellsquarry
Kirknewton
Balerno

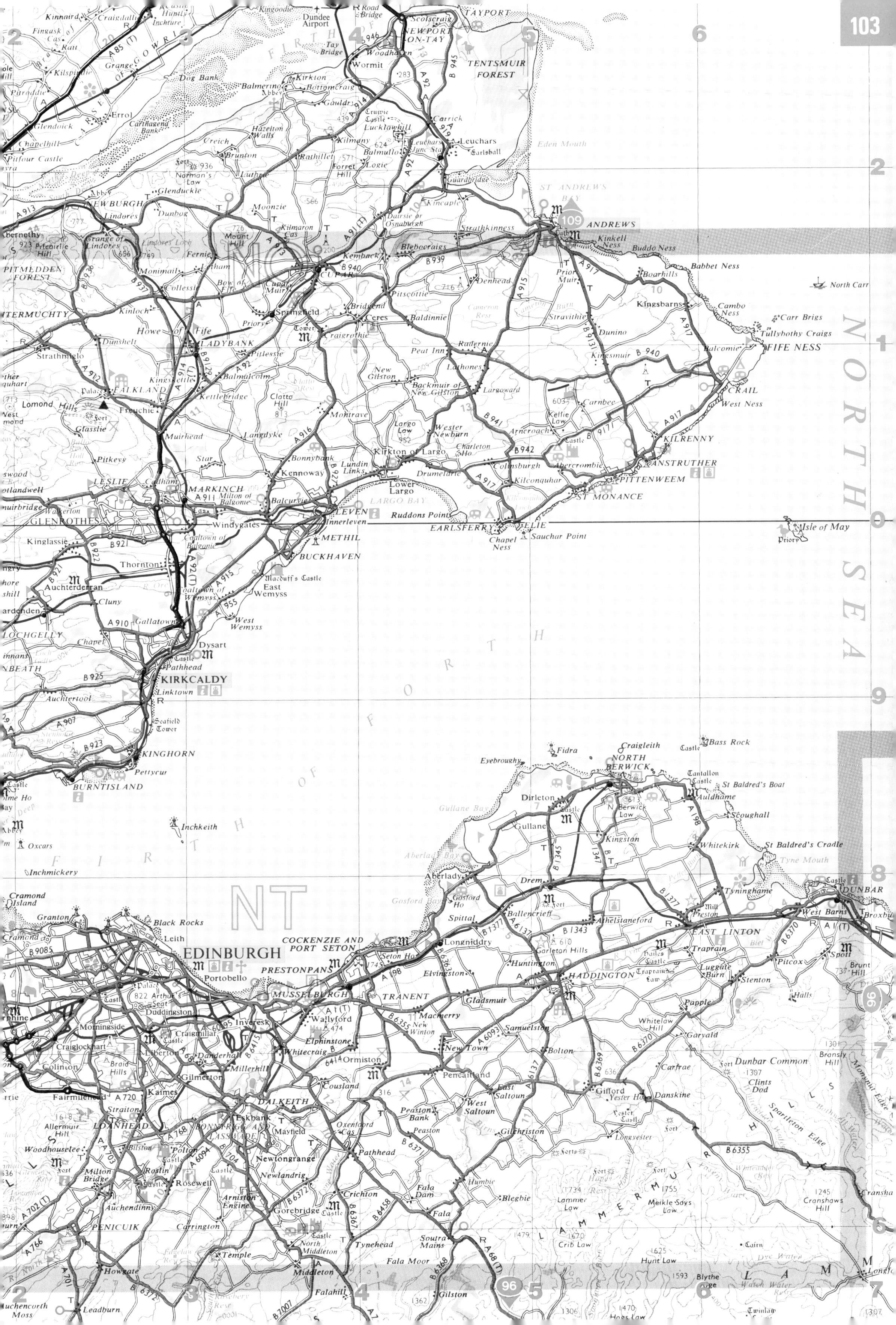
TAYPORT
NEWPORT-ON-TAY
Dundee Airport
Tay Bridge
Wormit
Woodhaven
TENTSMUIR FOREST
FIRTH OF TAY
Kinnaird
Inchture
Errol
Glendoick
Balmerino
Kirkton
Gauldry
Leuchars
Guardbridge
Eden Mouth
ST ANDREWS BAY
ST ANDREWS
Kinkell Ness
Buddo Ness
Babbet Ness
North Carr
Kingsbarns
Cambo Ness
Carr Brigs
Tullybothy Craigs
FIFE NESS
Balcomie
CRAIL
West Ness
KILRENNY
ANSTRUTHER
PITTENWEEM
ST MONANCE
ELIE
EARLSFERRY
Chapel Ness
Sauchar Point
Isle of May
NORTH SEA
NEWBURGH
Lindores
Pitmedden Forest
AUCHTERMUCHTY
Collessie
CUPAR
Kemback
Blebocraigs
Strathkinness
Denhead
Pitscottie
Ceres
Craigrothie
Springfield
Priory
LADYBANK
Pitlessie
FALKLAND
Lomond Hills
Freuchie
Kettlebridge
Largoward
Carnbee
Arncroach
Kirkton of Largo
LEVEN
Lundin Links
Lower Largo
Largo Bay
Ruddons Point
Colinsburgh
Kilconquhar
Kennoway
MARKINCH
LESLIE
GLENROTHES
Windygates
Innerleven
METHIL
BUCKHAVEN
East Wemyss
West Wemyss
Thornton
Kinglassie
Auchterderran
Cluny
LOCHGELLY
Gallatown
Dysart
Pathhead
KIRKCALDY
Linktown
Seafield Tower
KINGHORN
Pettycur
BURNTISLAND
Inchkeith
Oxcars
Inchmickery
Cramond Island
FIRTH OF FORTH
Fidra
Eyebroughy
NORTH BERWICK
Craigleith
Bass Rock
Tantallon Castle
St Baldred's Boat
Auldhame
Scoughall
Dirleton
Gullane
Gullane Bay
Kingston
Whitekirk
St Baldred's Cradle
Tyne Mouth
Aberlady Bay
Aberlady
Drem
Tyninghame
DUNBAR
West Barns
Broxburn
Gosford Bay
Athelstaneford
EAST LINTON
Traprain
Spott
Pitcox
Stenton
Luggate Burn
HADDINGTON
Longniddry
COCKENZIE AND PORT SETON
PRESTONPANS
Seton Ho
Elvingston
Gladsmuir
TRANENT
Macmerry
Samuelston
Bolton
Garvald
Whitelaw Hill
Papple
Dunbar Common
Clints Dod
Spartleton Edge
Carfrae
Gifford
Yester Ho
Danskine
Longyester
LAMMERMUIR HILLS
Lammer Law
Crib Law
Hunt Law
Meikle Says Law
Cranshaws Hill
Blythe Edge
Monynut Edge
Pencaitland
East Saltoun
West Saltoun
Gilchriston
Humbie
Blegbie
Fala
Fala Dam
Fala Moor
Soutra Mains
Gilston
Falahill
EDINBURGH
Granton
Black Rocks
Leith
Portobello
Arthur's Seat
Duddingston
MUSSELBURGH
Inveresk
Wallyford
Elphinstone
Whitecraig
Ormiston
Cousland
Craigmillar
Liberton
Danderhall
Millerhill
Gilmerton
DALKEITH
Eskbank
Mayfield
Newtongrange
Newlandrig
Pathhead
Crichton
Tynehead
Gorebridge
Arniston Engine
Carrington
Temple
North Middleton
Middleton
Morningside
Craiglockhart
Colinton
Braid Hills
Fairmilehead
Kaimes
Straiton
LOANHEAD
BONNYRIGG AND LASSWADE
Bilston
Polton
Roslin
Rosewell
Milton Bridge
Auchendinny
PENICUIK
Howgate
Leadburn
Woodhouselee
NO
NT

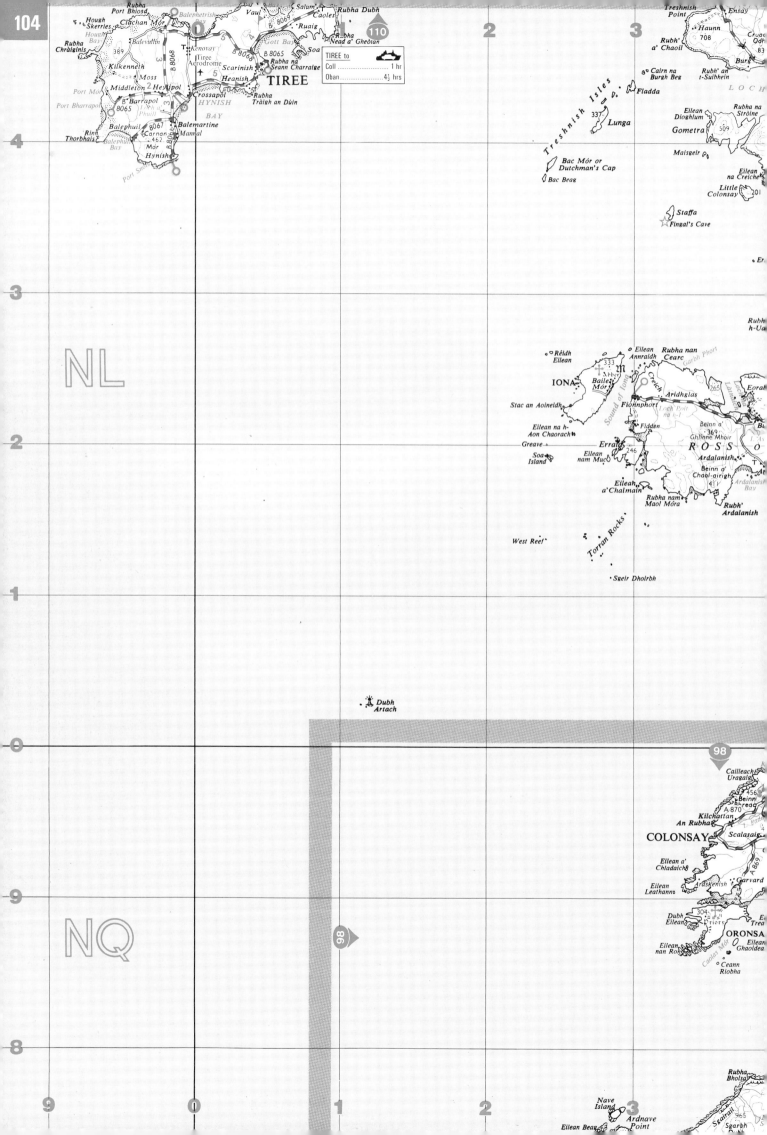

TIREE

TIREE to
Coll .... 1 hr
Oban .... 4½ hrs

Rubha
Port Bhiosd
Hough
Skerries
Clachan Mór
Balephetrish
Vaul
Salum
Caoles
Rubha Dubh
Treshnish
Point
Ensay
Haunn
708
Cruac
Odh
Hough
Bay
Rubha
Chràiginis
Balevullin
389
Kenovay
Tiree
Aerodrome
B 8069
Ruaig
Soa
Rubha
Nead a' Gheòtan
110
Rubh'
a' Chaoil
Rubh' an
t-Suibhein
Burg
Kilkenneth
Moss
Middleton
Heylipol
B 8065
Scarinish
Heanish
Rubha na
Seann Charraige
Gott Bay
Cairn na
Burgh Beg
Eilean
Dioghlum
Rubha an
Stròine
Port Mòr
B'Barrapol
8065
Crossapol
HYNISH
BAY
Rubha
Tràigh an Dùin
Fladda
Lunga
337
Gometra
509
Port Bharrapol
Balephuil
8067
Carnan
462
Mór
Hynish
Balemartine
Mannal
Bac Mór or
Dutchman's Cap
Maisgeir
Eilean
na Creiche
Rinn
Thorbhais
Balephuil
Bay
Port Sn
Bac Beag
Little
Colonsay
201
Staffa
Fingal's Cave

Treshnish Isles

LOCH

Er

NL

Rèidh
Eilean
Eilean
Annraidh
Rubha nan
Cearc
Garbh Phort
Rubh
h-Ua
Abbey
333
IONA
Baile
Mór
Creich
Aridhglas
265
Eoral
Stac an Aoineidh
Fionnphort
Loch Pòit
na h-I
Eilean na h-
Aon Chaorach
Fidden
Beinn a'
369
Ghlinne Mhòir
ROSS O
Greave
Errald
Eilean
nam Muc
246
Ardalanish
Beinn a'
Chaol-airigh
Soa
Island
Eileah
a' Chalmain
Rubha nam
Maol Mòra
Rubh'
Ardalanish
Ardalanish
Bay
West Reef
Torran Rocks
Sgeir Dhoirbh

Dubh
Artach

98

NQ

98

Dubh
Artach

Cailleach
Uragaig
456
Beinn
Bhreac
Kilchattan
A 870
An Rubha
COLONSAY
Scalasaig
Eilean a'
Chladaich
Eilean
Leathanno
Ardskenish
Garvard
Dubh
Eileann
304
Priory
Eilean
nan Ron
Caolas Mòr
ORONSA
Eilean
Ghaoidea
Ceann
Riobha

Rubha
Bholsa

Nave
Island
Ardnave
Point
Sgeir
Sgarbh
965
Eilean Beag

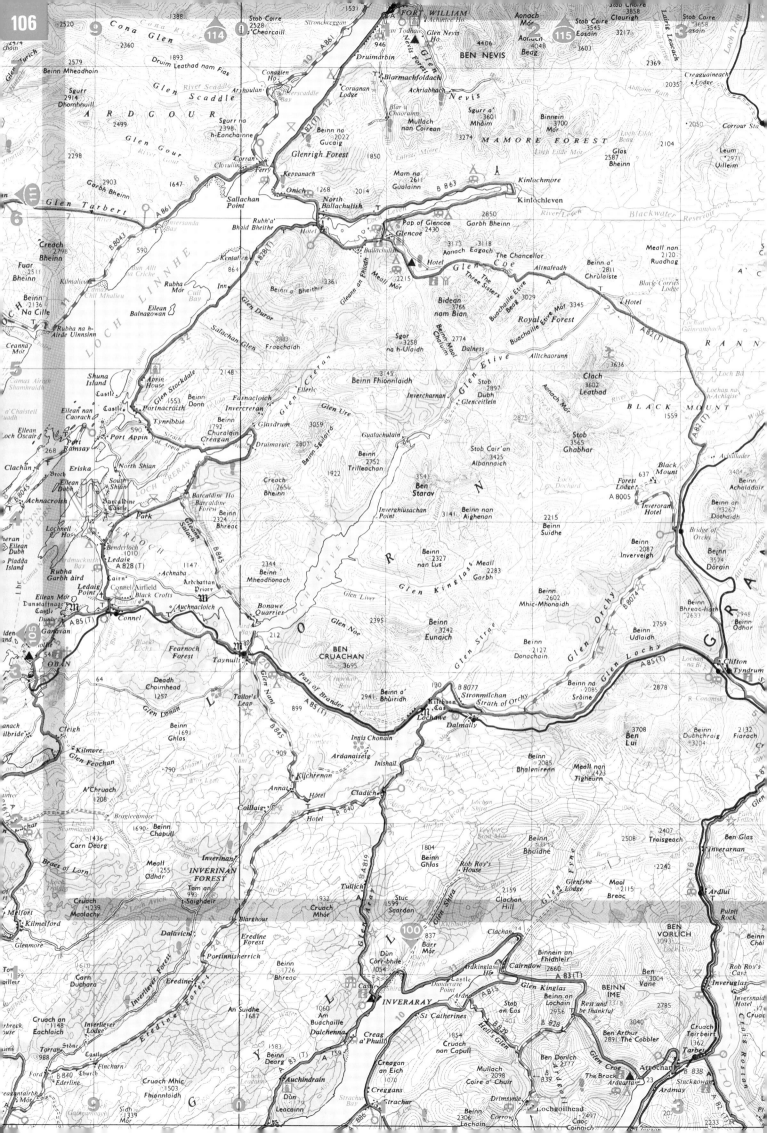

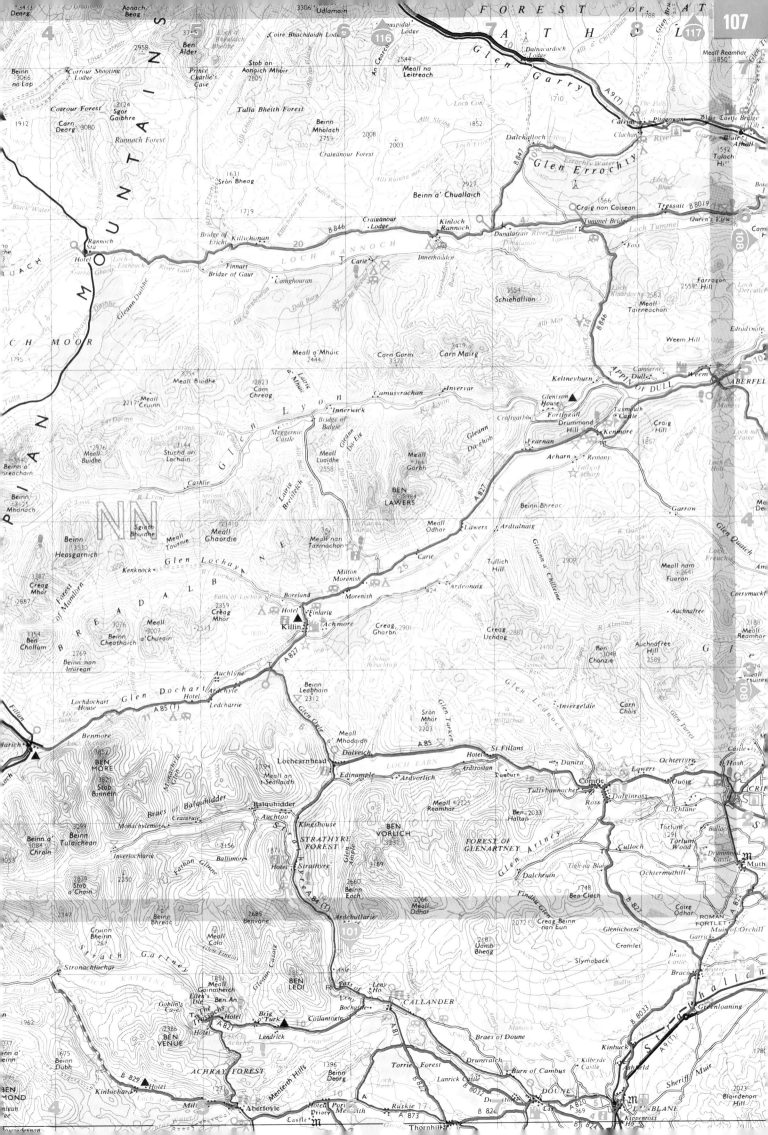

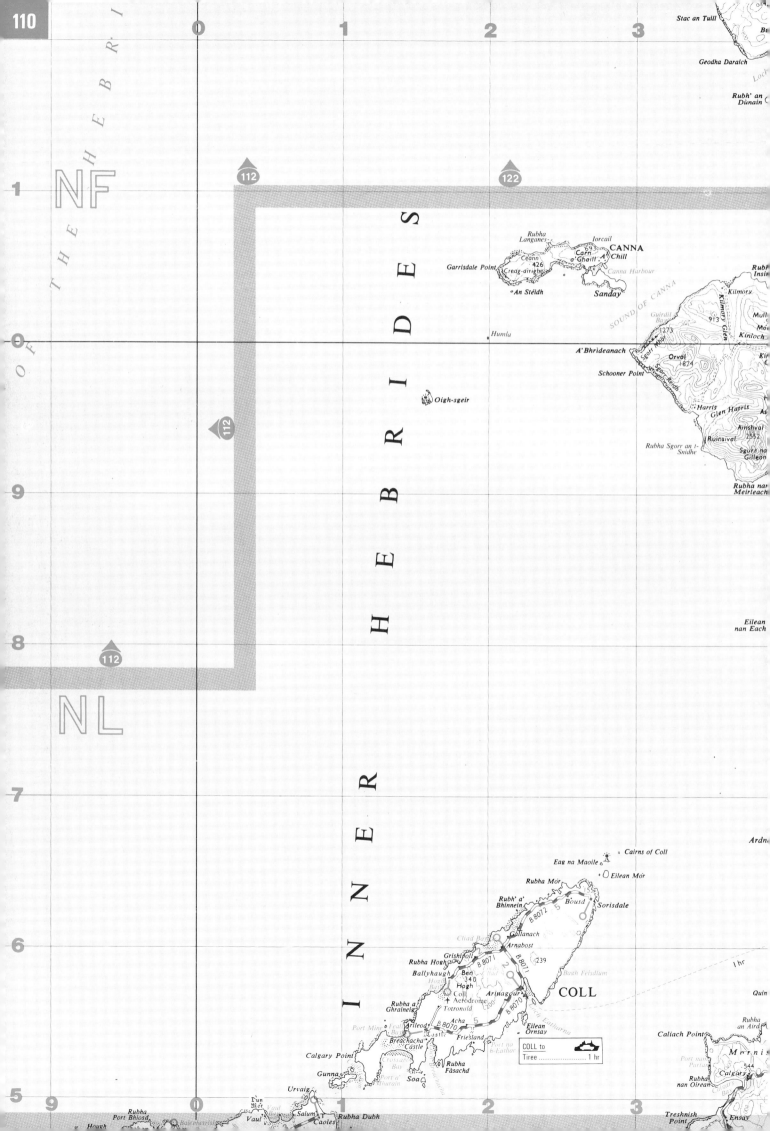

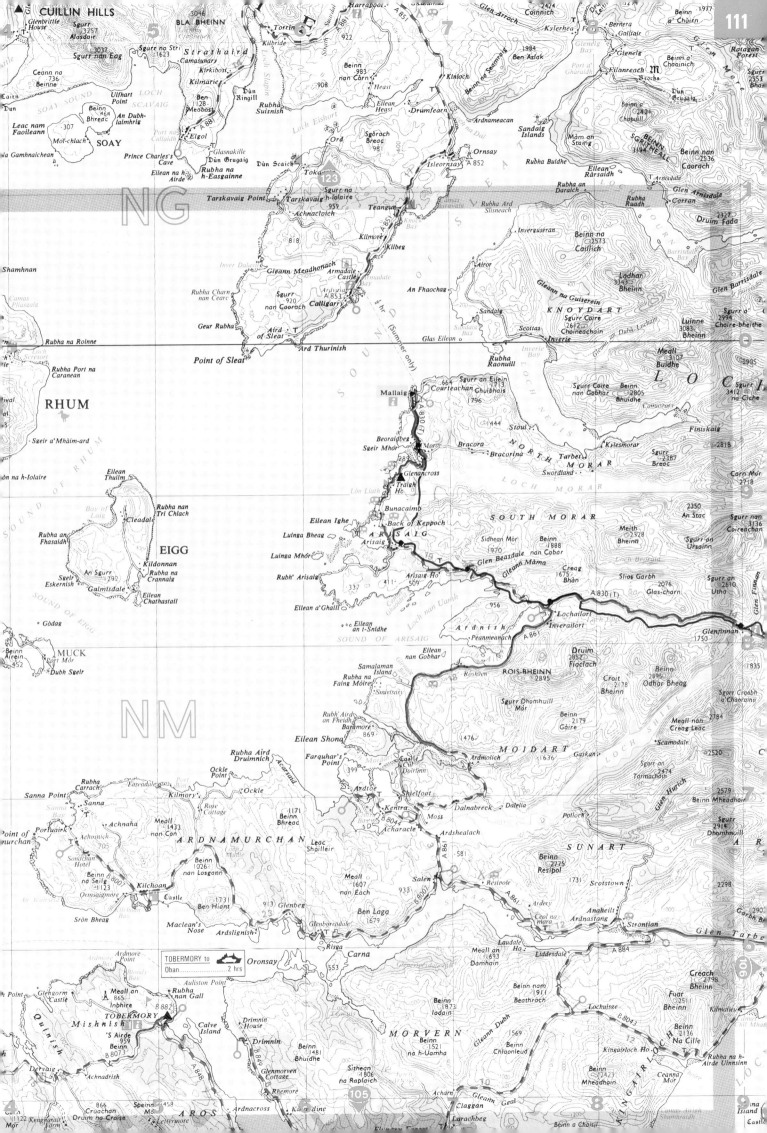

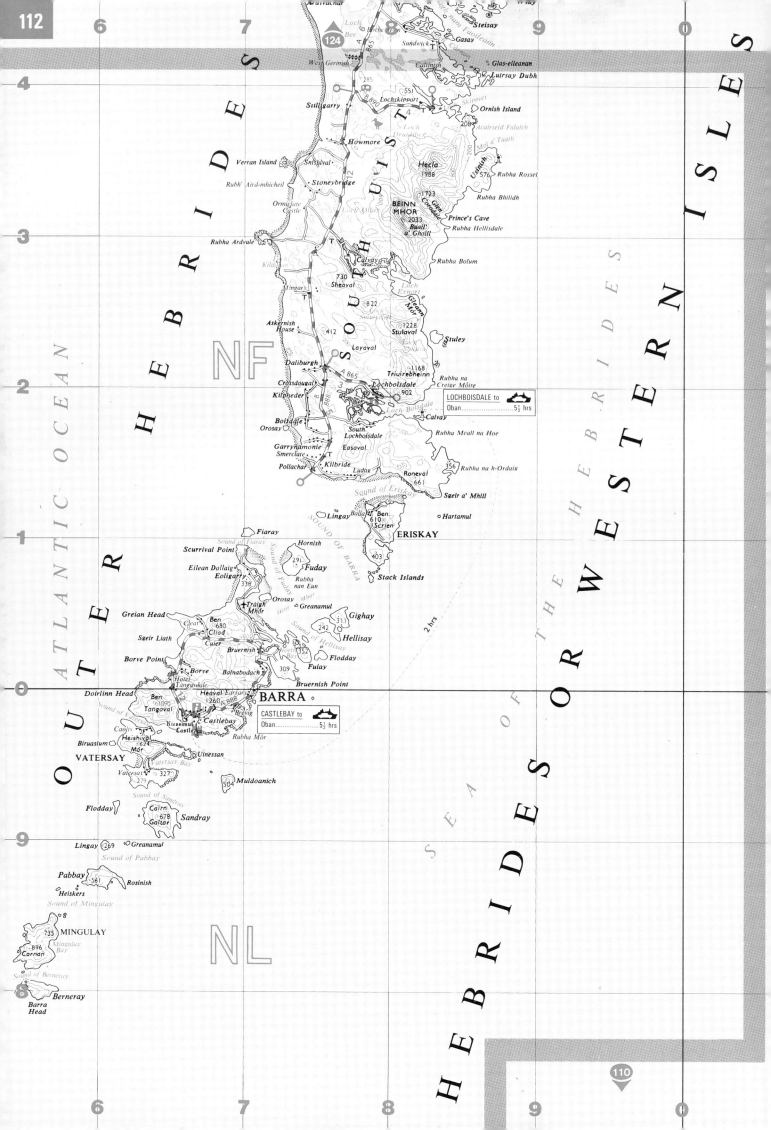

OUTER HEBRIDES OR WESTERN ISLES

ATLANTIC OCEAN

HEBRIDES

SOUTH UIST

NF

Aravachar
Steisay
Loch Bee
124
Sandwick
Gasay
West Gerinish
Caitinish
Glas-elleanan
Luirsay Dubh

551
Stilligarry
Lochskiport
Skinport
Ornish Island
285
Acairseid Falaich
208

Howmore
Loch Druidibeg

Verran Island
Snishival
Hecla
1988
Usinish
Rubha Rossel
576
Rubh' Aird-mhicheil
Stoneybridge
1723
Rubha Bhilidh

Ormiclate Castle
Loch Ollay
BEINN MHOR
2033
Gleann Coradale
Prince's Cave
Buall' a' Ghoill
Rubha Hellisdale

Rubha Ardvule
Kildanan
Calvay
730
Sheaval
Rubha Bolum

Tingary
T
Loch Eynort
Gleann Mor

822
Loch Snigisclett
Askernish House
412
1228
Stulaval
Stuley

Daliburgh
Layaval
1168

Crossdougal
A 865
Triuirebheinn
Rubha na Creige Moire

Kilpheder
Lochboisdale
902
LOCHBOISDALE to
Oban..............5½ hrs

Boisdale
Orosay
South Lochboisdale
Calvay
Rubha Meall na Hoe

Garrynamonie
Smerclate
Easaval
Roneval
661
356
Rubha na h-Ordaig

Pollachar
Kilbride
Ludag
Sgeir a' Mhill

Sound of Eriskay
Rubha Mol na Hoe

Lingay
Balla
Ben Scrien
610
Hartamul

ERISKAY

Fiaray
Hornish
Scurrival Point
291
Fuday
403
Stack Islands
Eilean Dallaig
Eoligarry
338
Rubha nan Eun

Orosay Mhor
Traigh Mhor
Greanamul
Gighay
Greian Head
Ben Cliad
680
242
31J
Hellisay
Sgeir Liath
Cuier
352
Borve Point
Bruernish
Floddday
Fulay
Borve
Balnabadach
309
Bruernish Point
Hotel Tangasdale
Doirlinn Head
Heaval Earsary
1260
BARRA
Ben Tangoval
1090
Brevig
CASTLEBAY to
Oban..............5½ hrs
Caolis
Kissimul Castle
Castlebay
Heishival Mor
624
Rubha Mor
Biruaslum
Uinessan
VATERSAY
Vatersay Bay
Muldoanich
504
Vatersay
279
327

Sound of Sandray
Floddday
Cairn Galtar
678
Sandray

Lingay
269
Greanamul
Sound of Pabbay

Pabbay
561
Rosinish
Heiskers
Sound of Mingulay

NL

MINGULAY
735
Mingulay Bay
896
Carnan

Sound of Berneray
Berneray
Barra Head

SEA OF THE HEBRIDES

2 hrs

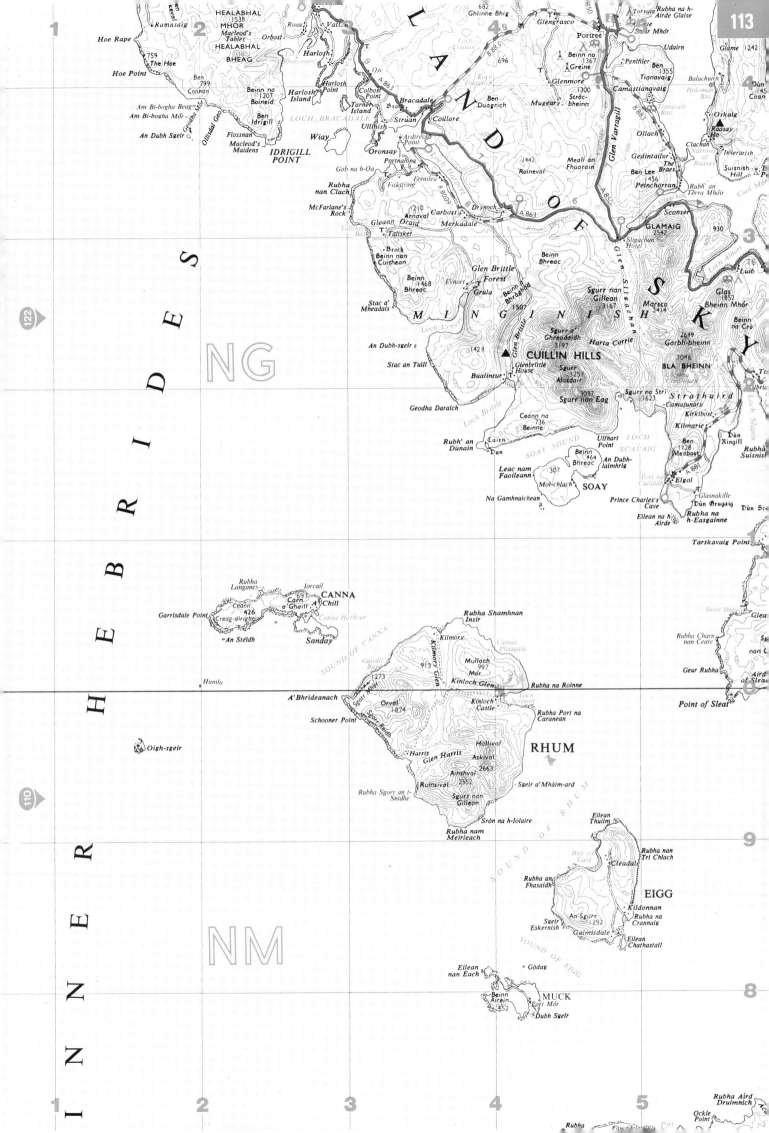

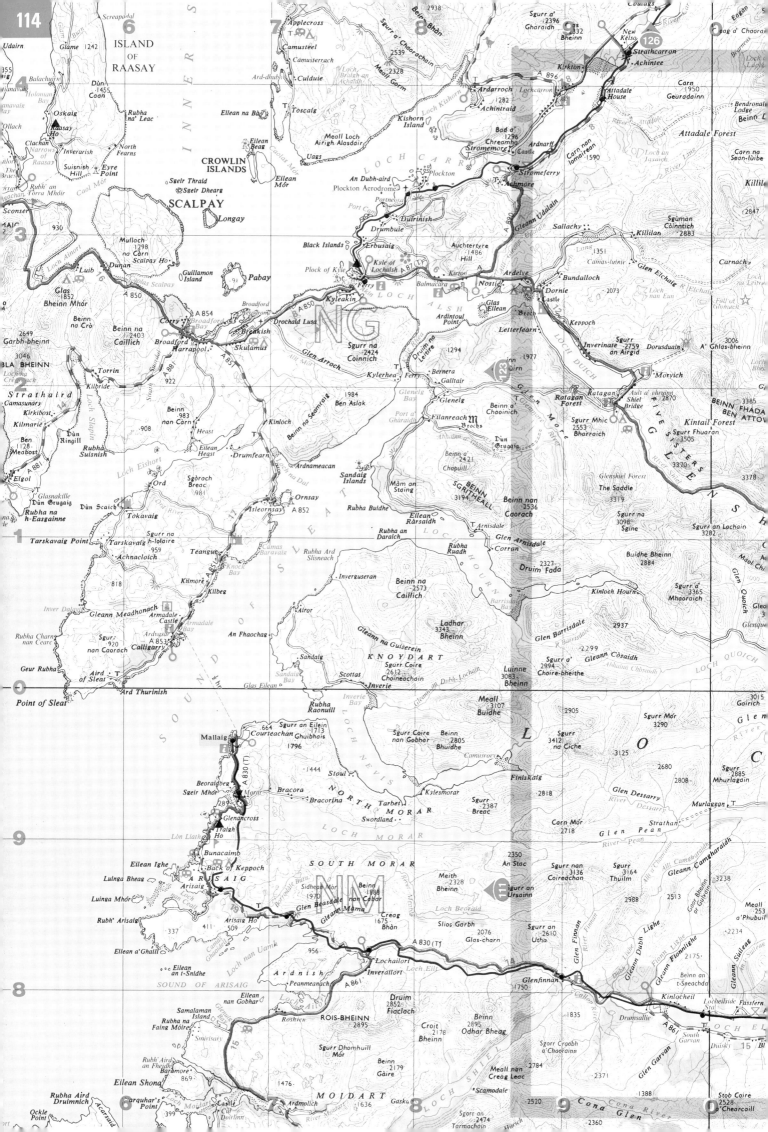

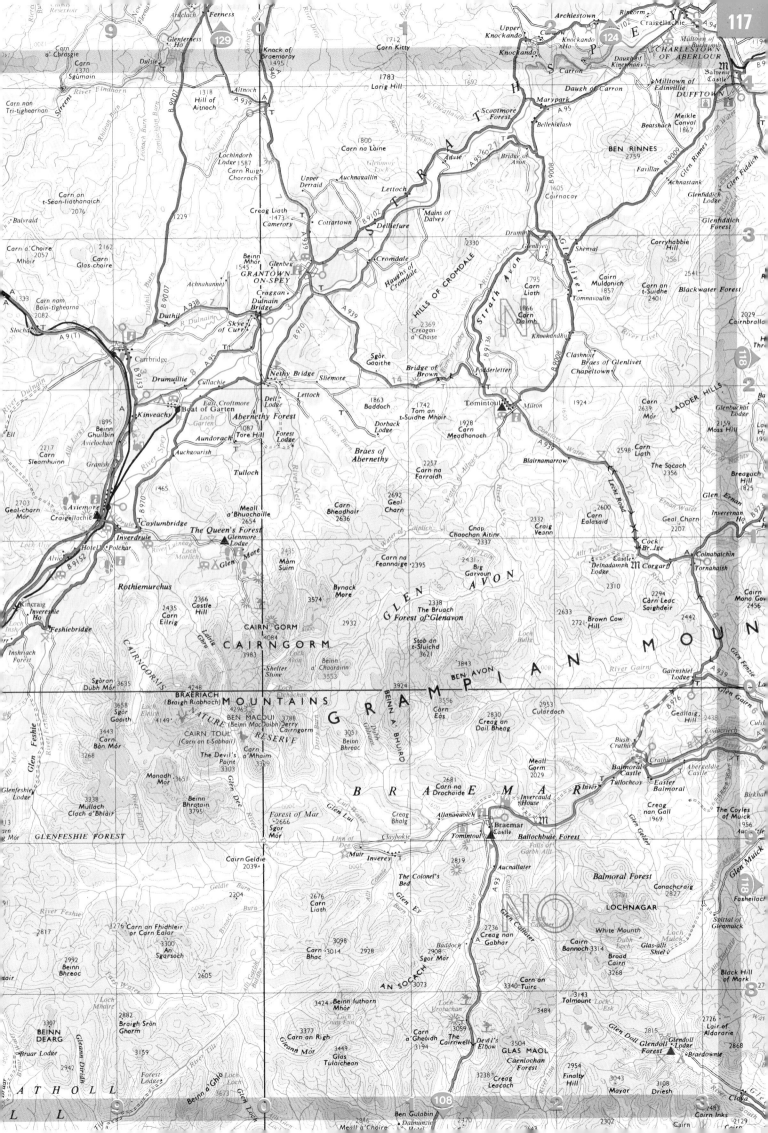

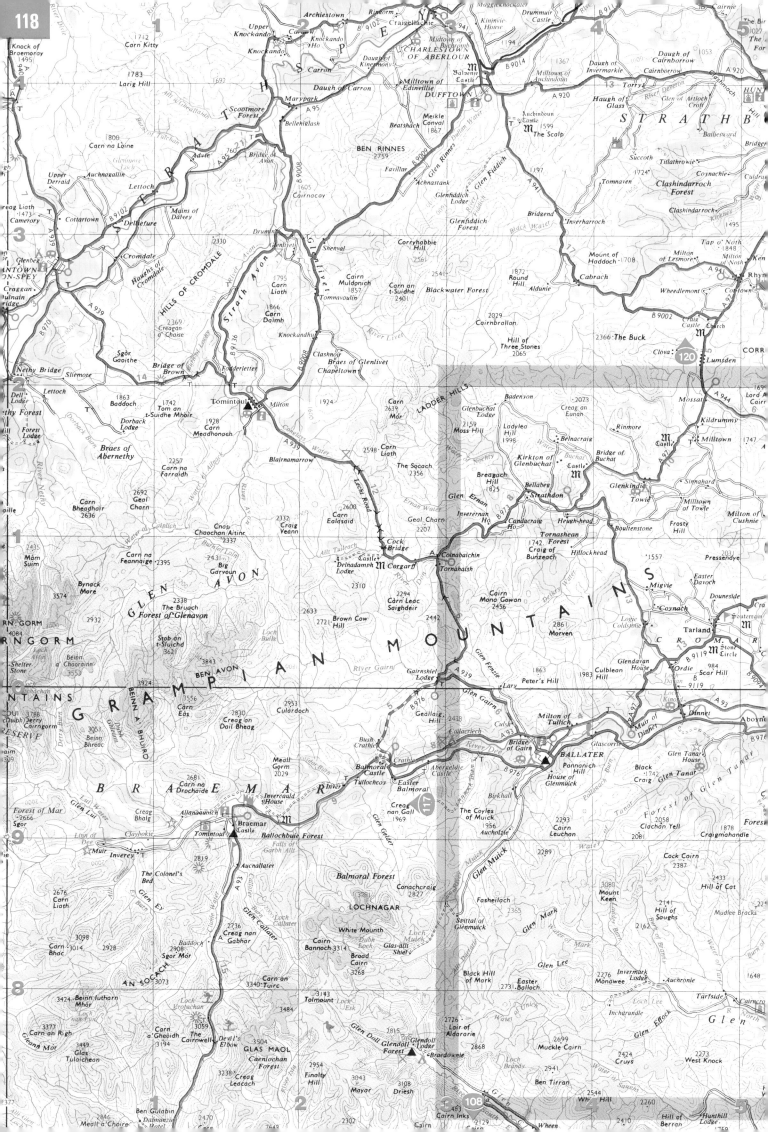

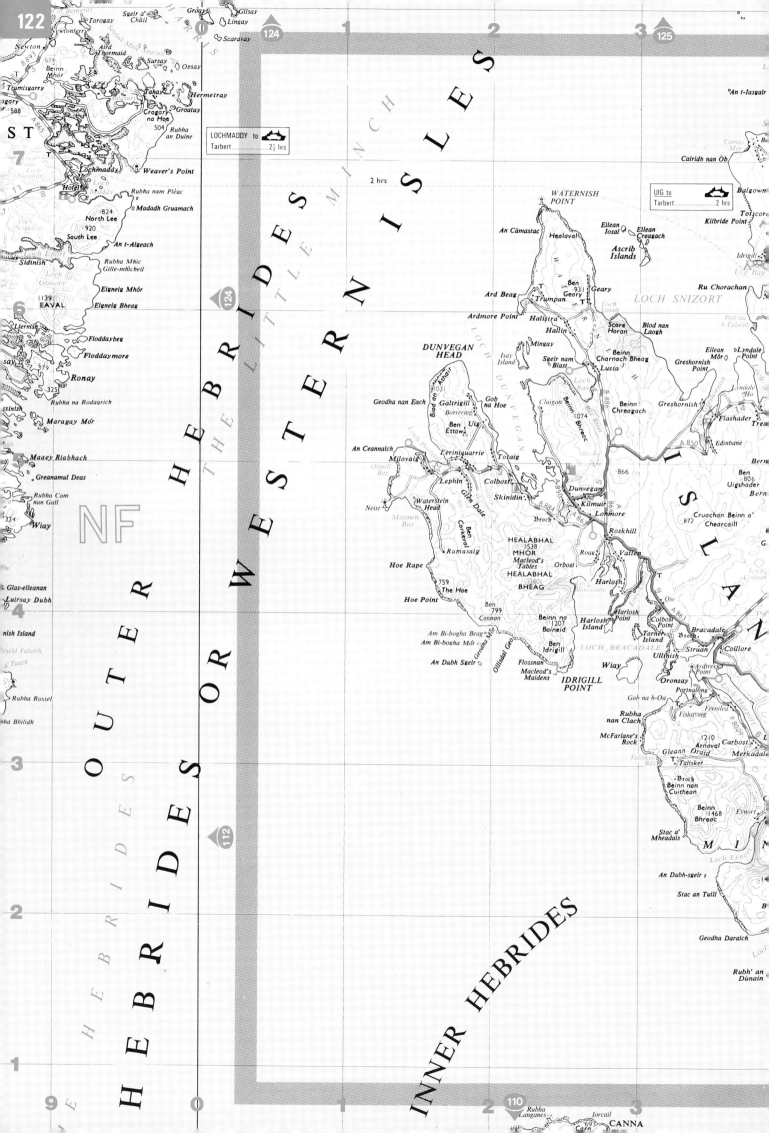

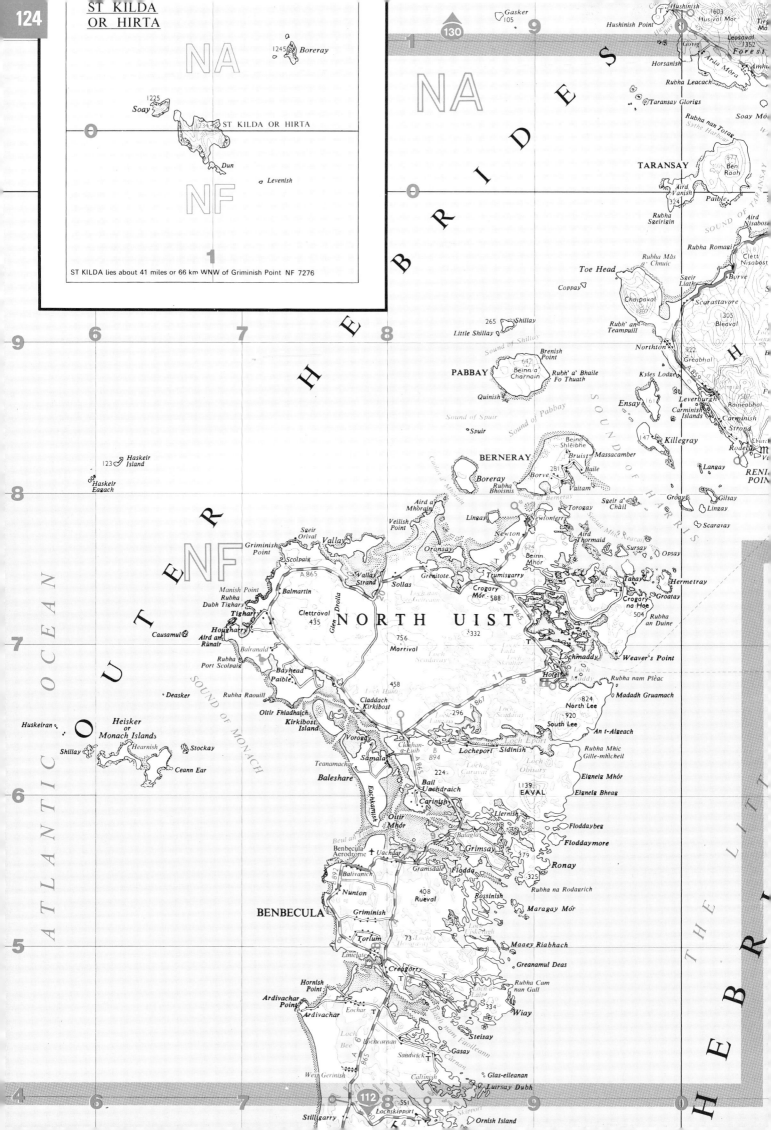

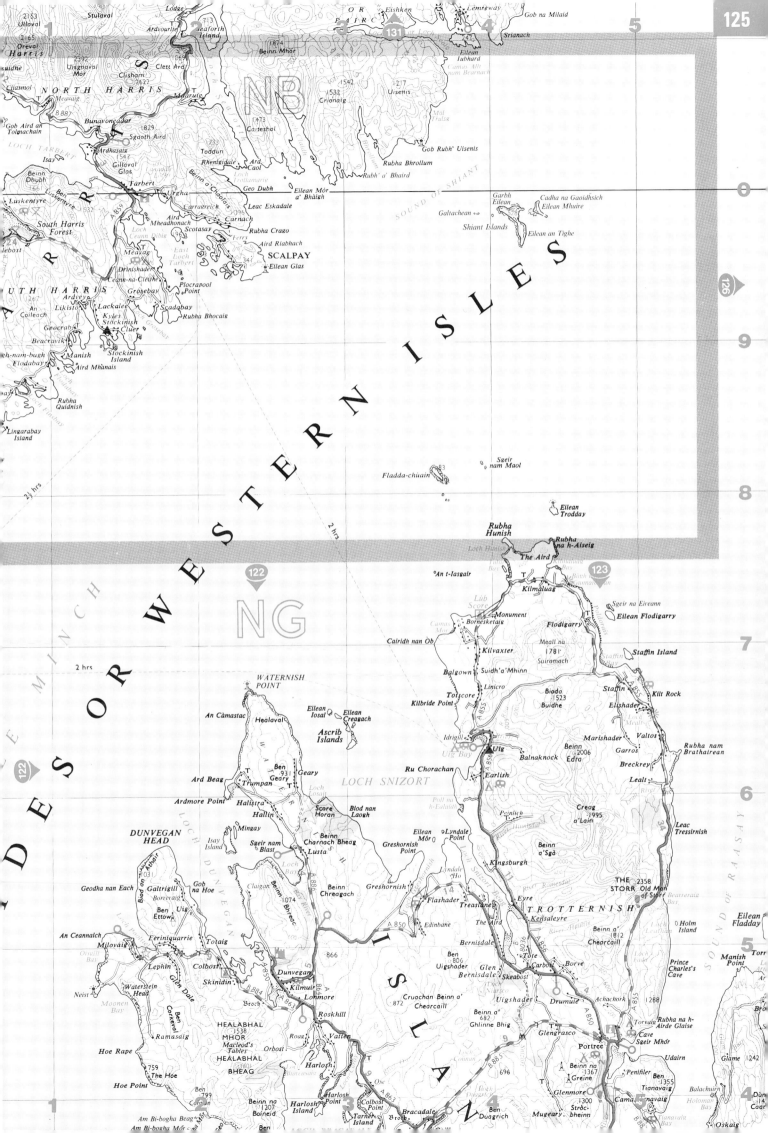

OR PAIRC
131
Eishken
Lemreway
Gob na Milaid
Srianach
Eilean Iubhard
Camas Allt nam Bearnach
Gob Rubh' Uisenis
Rubha Bhrollum
Rubh' a' Bhaird

North Harris
Uig

2153 Ullaval
2165 Oreval
Harris
Clisham 2622
Stulaval
Ardvourlie
Seaforth Island
Beinn Mhor
1874
NB
1542
1532 Crionaig
1217
Uisenis
Mol Truisg

Cliasmol
Uisgnaval Mor
B887
Meavaig
1829
Sgaoth Aird
NORTH HARRIS
Madruig
713
1473 Cartashal
733

Gob Aird an Tolmachain
Bunavoneadar
Ardhasaig
Gillaval Glos
Toddun
Rhenigidale
Ard Caol
Geo Dubh
Gob Rubh' Uisenis

Isay
Beinn Dhubh
1166
Ben Luskentyre
1532
Tarbert
Urgha
Aird a' Chaolais
Eilean Mór a' Bhàigh
SOUND OF SHIANT

Loch Tarbert
A859
Aird Mheadhonach
Carragreich
Leac Eskadale
Carnach
Garbh Eilean
578
Cadha na Gaoidhsich
Eilean Mhuire

Luskentyre
South Harris Forest
Scotasay
Rubha Crago
Galtachean
Shiant Islands
Eilean an Tighe

Ferry
24
lebost
1267
Meavag
Drinishader
Ceann-na-Cleithe
East Loch Tarbert
Aird Riabhach
SCALPAY
Eilean Glas

WESTERN
ISLES

UTH HARRIS
An Coileach
Ardvey
Likisto
Lackalee
Kyles Stockinish
Cluer
Grosebay
Rubha Bhocaig
Scadabay

Geocrab
Beacravik
Stockinish Island
h-nam-bugh Flodabay
Manish
Aird Mhanais

Rubha Quidnish

Lingarabay Island

2½ hrs
Fladda-chùain
83
Sgeir nam Maol

2 hrs
Eilean Trodday

Rubha Hunish
Rubha na h-Aiseig
The Aird

122
NG

An t-Iasgair
Loch Hunish
Kilmaluag
123

Lùb Score
Monument
Bornesketaig
Flodigarry
Sgeir na Eireann
Eilean Flodigarry

Cairidh nan Òb
Kilvaxter
Meall na 1781 Suiramach
Staffin Island

WATERNISH POINT
Balgown
Suidh'a'Mhinn
Linicro
Totscore
Kilbride Point
Idrigill
Bioda 1523 Buidhe
Staffin
Elishader
Kilt Rock

An Càmastac
Healaval
Eilean Iosal
Eilean Creagach
Ascrib Islands
Ru Chorachan
Uig Bay
Uig
Balnaknock
Beinn 2006 Edra
Marishader
Garros
Valtos
Breckrey
Rubha nam Brathairean

Ben 931 Geary
Geary
Earlish
Peinlich
Lealt

Ard Beag
Trumpan
LOCH SNIZORT
Creag a'Lain 1995
Leac Tressirnish

Ardmore Point
Halistra
Hallin
Score Horan
Blod nan Laogh
Eilean Mór
Lyndale Point
Beinn a'Sgà

DUNVEGAN HEAD
Mingay
Beinn Charnach Bheag
Lusta
Greshornish Point
Kingsburgh
THE STORR 2358 Old Man of Storr
Sound of Raasay

Isay Island
Sgeir nam Biast
Greshornish
Lyndale Ho
TROTTERNISH
Eilean Fladday

Geodha nan Each
Galtrigill
Borreraig
Gob na Hoe
Claigan
Beinn Chreagach
Flashader
Treaslane
Eyre
Bearreraig Bay

Ben Ettow
Uig
Beinn Bhreac 1074
866
A850
Edinbane
The Aird
Kensaleyre
Beinn a' 1812 Chearcaill
Holm Island

An Ceannalch
Feriniquarrie
Totaig
Bernisdale
Tote
Borve
Prince Charles's Cave

Milovaig
Lephin
Colbost
Dunvegan
Ben 806 Uigshader
Glen Bernisdale
Skeabost
Carbost
Drumuie
Achachork
A855 1288
Manish Point

Neist
Waterstein Head
Skinidin
Kilmuir
Lonmore
Cruachan Beinn a' Chearcaill 872
Uigshader
Torvaig
Rubha na h-Airde Glaise
Cave
Glame 1242

Moonen Bay
Ben Corkeval
Glen Dale
Roskhill
Beinn a' 682 Ghlinne Bhig
Glengrasco
Sgeir Mhor

HEALABHAL MHOR 1538
Macleod's Tables
Roag
Vatten
Harlosh
Ose
Portree
Beinn na 1367 Greine
Udairn

HEALABHAL BHEAG 1601
759 The Hoe
Ben 799 Conan
Harlosh Island
Harlosh Point
Colbost Point
Bracadale
Ben Duagrich
Glenmore
1300
Penifiler
Ben Tianavaig 1355
Balachuirn

Hoe Rape
Hoe Point
Am Bi-bogha Beag
Am Bi-bogha Mór
Beinn na Boineid
Tarner Island
Ben Mugeary
Ben Stròc-bheinn
Cama svaig
Holoman Bay
Oskaig

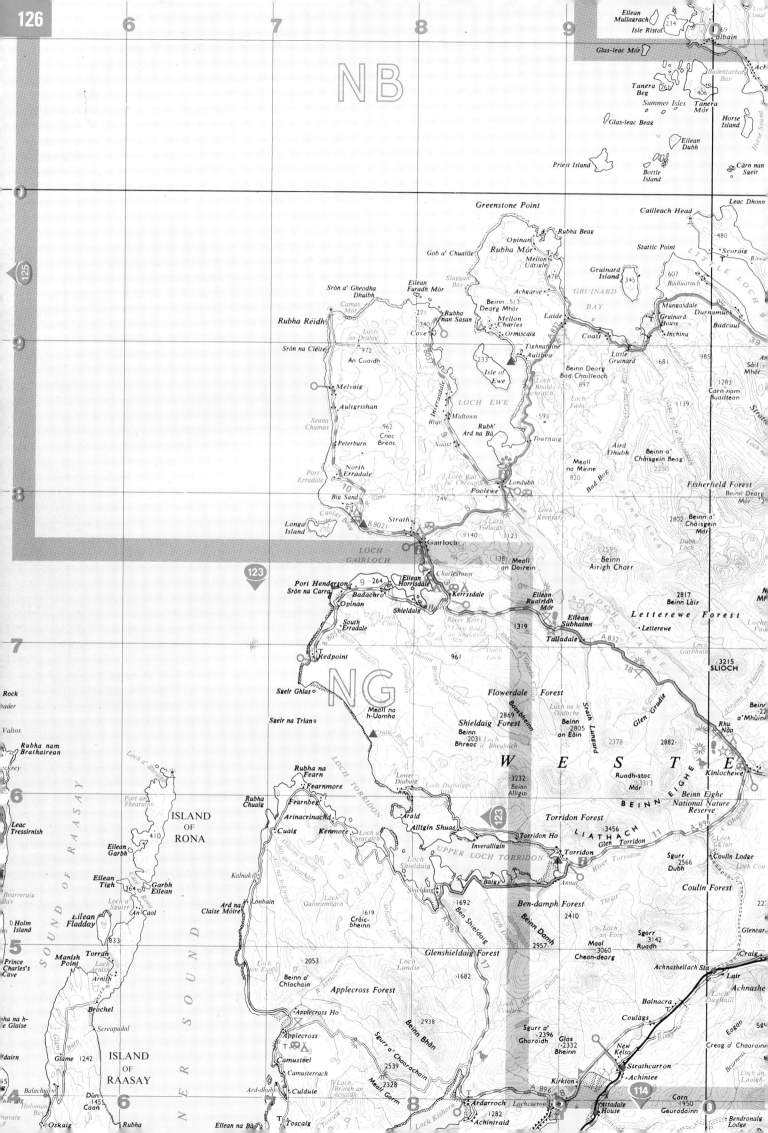

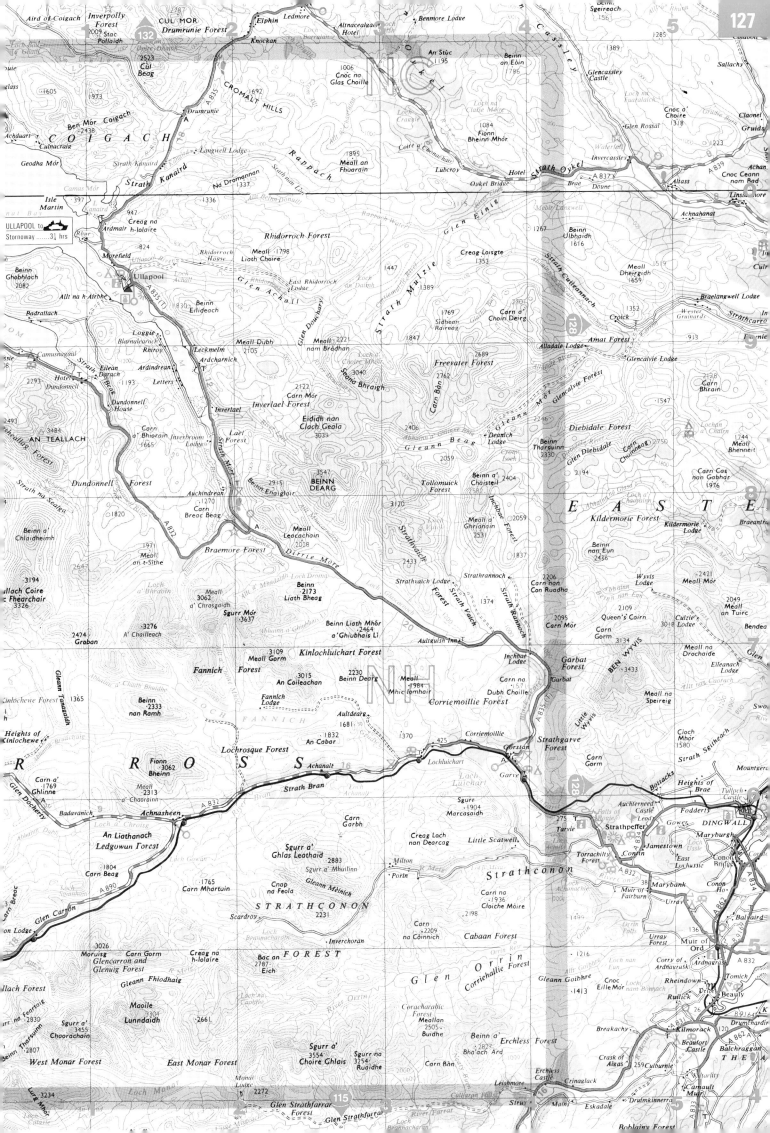

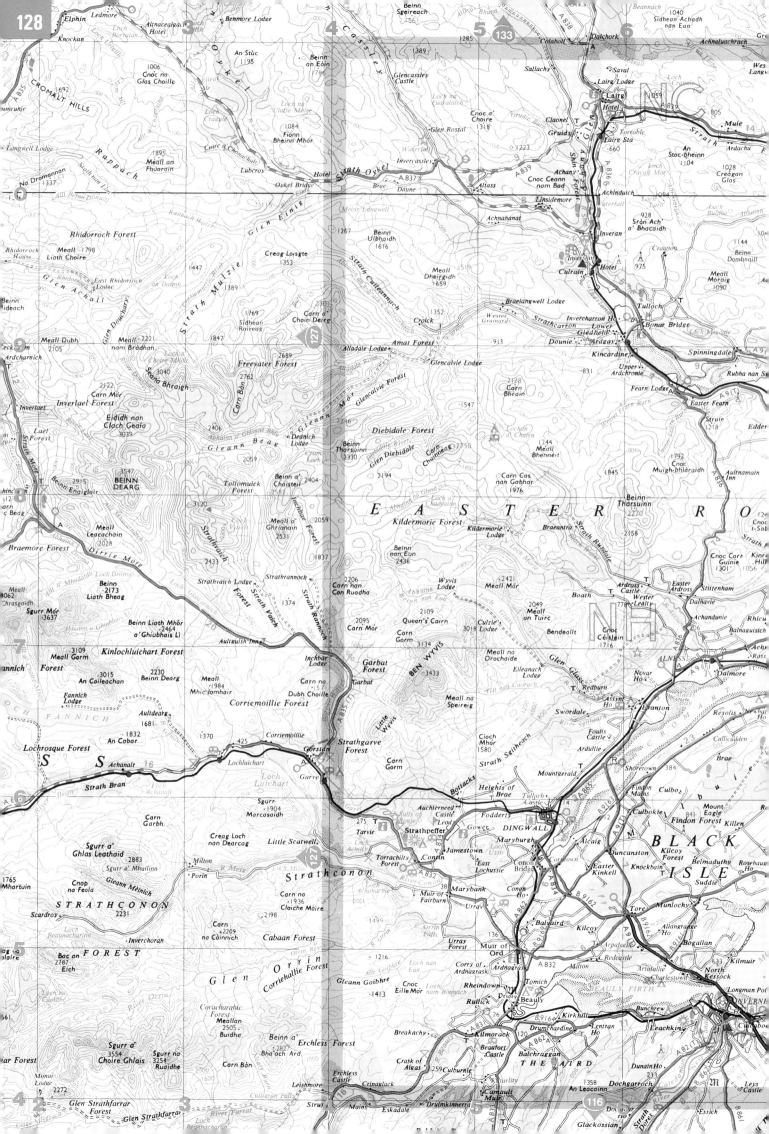

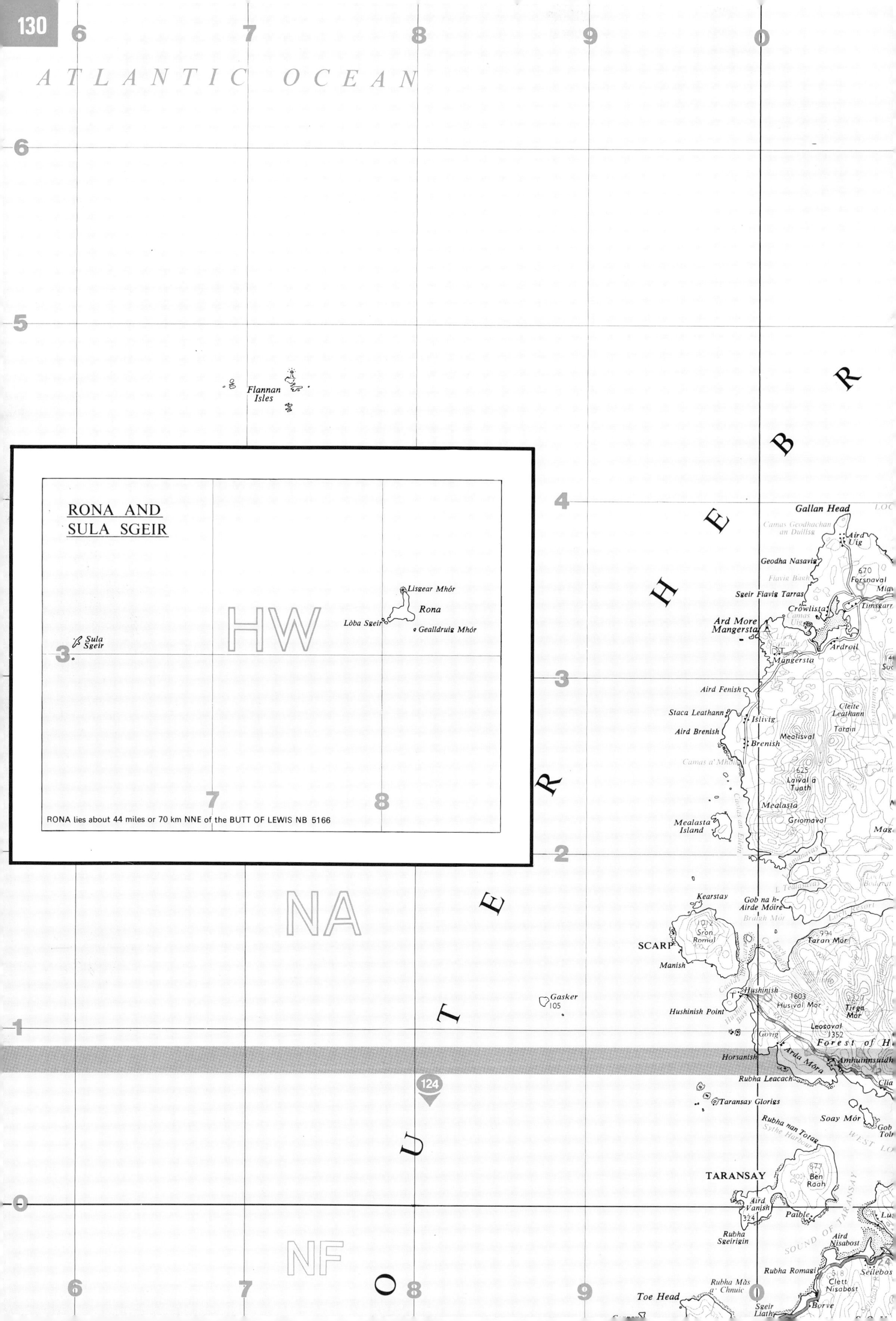

6   7   8   9   0

A T L A N T I C   O C E A N

6

6

5

5

Flannan Isles

R

4

Gallan Head
LOC

Camas Geodhachan an Duilisg
Aird Uig

Geodha Nasavig

670
Forsnaval
Mia

Sgeir Fiavig Tarras

Flavig Bask

Crowlista
Timsgarr

Camas Uig

**RONA AND
SULA SGEIR**

HW

Lisgear Mhór

Rona

Lòba Sgeir
Gealldruig Mhór

*Ard More
Mangersta*

Ardroil

Mangersta

*Sula
Sgeir*

3

3

Aird Fenish

Staca Leathann
Islivig

*Cleite
Leathann*

Aird Brenish
Mealisval
Tataun

Brenish

R

Camas a' Mhòil

625
*Laival a
Tuath*

Mealasta

*Mealasta
Island*

Griomaval
Mag

7   8

2

2

RONA lies about 44 miles or 70 km NNE of the BUTT OF LEWIS NB 5166

E

Kearstay

*Gob na h-
Airde Móire*

Braigh Mòr

NA

1032
*Sròn
Romul*

994
Taran Mór

SCARP

Manish

T
Hushinish

1603
Husival Mór

2227
*Tirga
Mór*

Hushinish Point

Hushinish Bay

Leosoval
1352

Gòvig
Forest of H

1

1

T

Gasker
105

Horsanish

Arda Móra
Amhuinnsuidh

Rubha Leacach
Clia

124

Taransay Gloriss

U

Rubha nan Tòrag
Soay Mór
*Gob
Tolr*

Skye Harbour

WEST LO

0

0

TARANSAY

877
*Ben
Raah*

*Aird
Vanish*
324

Paible
Lu

NF

*Rubha
Sgeirigin*

*Aird
Nisabost*

SOUND OF TARANSAY

*Rubha Màs
a' Chnuic*

Rubha Romasi
Sèilebos

*Clett
Nisabost*

6   7   8   9   0

Toe Head
Borve

*Sgeir
Liath*

BUTT OF LEWIS

ISLE OF LEWIS

NB

NG

THE MINCH

Cladach an Eilein
Five Penny Ness
Eoropie
Port of Ness
Lionel
Habost
Cross Sands
Aird Dell
Port Skigersta
Dell
NESS
Glen Cross
Skigersta
Meall Geal
Toa Galson
A 857
Cuiashader
Cladach Cuiashader
Galson
Roinn a'
Bhuic
Ben Dell
Cellar Head
Five Penny
Borve
Rubha Bhlanisgaidh
Cladach Dibadale
Rubha Leathann
Shader
Sguinean nan
Creagan Briste
Aird Barvas
Stejnaclet
Ballantrushal
520
Diaval
Rubli a' Bhiogair
Rinn Druim Tallig
Labost
Brue
Barvas
Arnol
813
Muirneag
New
Tolsta
North
Tolsta
Tolsta Head
Bragar
A 858
Beinn
Bragar
Gleann Mòr Barvas
A 857
Port nam Bothaig
Shawbost
Dalbeg
19
Gleann Bhruhadail
Glen
Tolsta
Dalmore
Port Bun a' Ghlinne
Garenin
Gress
Campay
Carloway
857
12
Creag Fhraoch
Floday
Little
Bernera
Creag
Mhòr
Kirivick
955
Beinn
Mholach
Back
Coll
Sgeir Leathann
Harsgeir
Hacklete
Pabay
Mòr
Tobson
Tolsta Chaolais
Upper
Coll
Coll
Sands
Vatisker Point
Tiumpan
Head
BROAD BAY
Portnaguran
Vacsay
Breaclete
GREAT
BERNERA
Hacklete
Breasclete
Sròn Ruadh
LOCH A TUATH
Portvoller
Portvoller Bay
Aird
Reef
Vula
Mòr
Kirkibost
Barraglom
Keava
Newmarket
Melbost
Sands
STORNOWAY
Shulishader
Sheshader
Floday
Vula Beag
Crulivig
Eilean
Kearstay
Callanish
Laxdale
Stornoway
Aerodrome
Melbost
Garrabost
Rubha na Greine
Geshader
Standing
Stones
Stone Circle
Garynahine
Lews
Castle
Sandwick
AIGNISH EYE PENINSULA
Rubha nam Bàirneach
Linshader
A 858
Eitshal
A 866
Knock
Bayble
Bayble Bay
Teahaval
890
Holm
Gob
Shilldinish
288
Bayble Hill
Rubh' Dubh
Enaclete
Achmore
Arnish Moor
Stac Shuardail
Chicken
Head
Beinn
adhonach
Rubh'a'
Bhàigh Uaine
Eilean
Orasaidh
STORNOWAY to
Ullapool...........3¾ hrs
Leurbost
Grimshader
Ben
Casgro
Raerinish Point
Rubh' Dubh
Roineval
Crossbost
Ranish
Soval
Lodge
Barkin Isles
Tabhaidh Mhòr
Balallan
Laxay
Keose
Eilean
Chaluim
Chille
Eilean Orasaidh
Shiltenish
Kershader
Caversta
Cromore
Eilean Thòraidh
Habost
Marvig
B 8060
Kintarvie
Arivruaich
Molasgair
Seaforth
Head
Calbost
Rubha na
Creige Mòire
Aird an
Troin
Glenside
Rubha Iosal
Gravir
A 859
Sithean
an Airgid
PARK
OR
PAIRC
Orinsay
Lemreway
Gob na
Milaid
Kebock Head
Eishken
Beinn
a' Bhoth
Liuthaid
Aline
Lodge
Stulaval
Ardvourlie
Seaforth
Island
Eilean
Iubhard
Sèanach
TARBERT to
Uig............2 hrs
Lochmaddy............2½ hrs
Beinn Mhòr
NORTH HARRIS
Clisham
2622
Meavaig
Maaruig
Crionaig
125
Uisenis
Uisenis
Bunavoneadar
Caiteshal
Ardhasaig
Sgaoth Aird
Toddun
Gob Rubh'
Uisenis
Gillaval
Glas
Rhenigidale
Ard
Caol
Rubha Bhrollum
Tarbert
Rubh' a' Bhaird
Urgha
Geo Dubh
Eilean Mòr
a' Bhàigh
Carragreich
Leac Eskadale
Ardvie
Mheadhonach
Scotasay
Carnach
Aird Crago
South Harris
Forest
Meavag
Aird Riabhach
SCALPAY
Drinishader
East
Loch
Tarbert
Terry
Eilean Glas
Plocrapool
Ceann-na-Cleithe

Stornoway inset:
Newmarket
Sch
New Valley
Laxdale
Maryhill
A 857
Monument
Hospl
Coultregrein
Marybank
Goat
Hill
STORNOWAY
Lews Castle
College
Moss End
A 859
Aird a'
Chleirich
A 866
Cemys

STACK SKERRY & SULE SKERRY

HX

Sule Skerry

O Stack Skerry

NB

2

6

Stack Skerry lies about 32 miles or 50 km N of WHITEN HEAD NC5068

THE MINCH

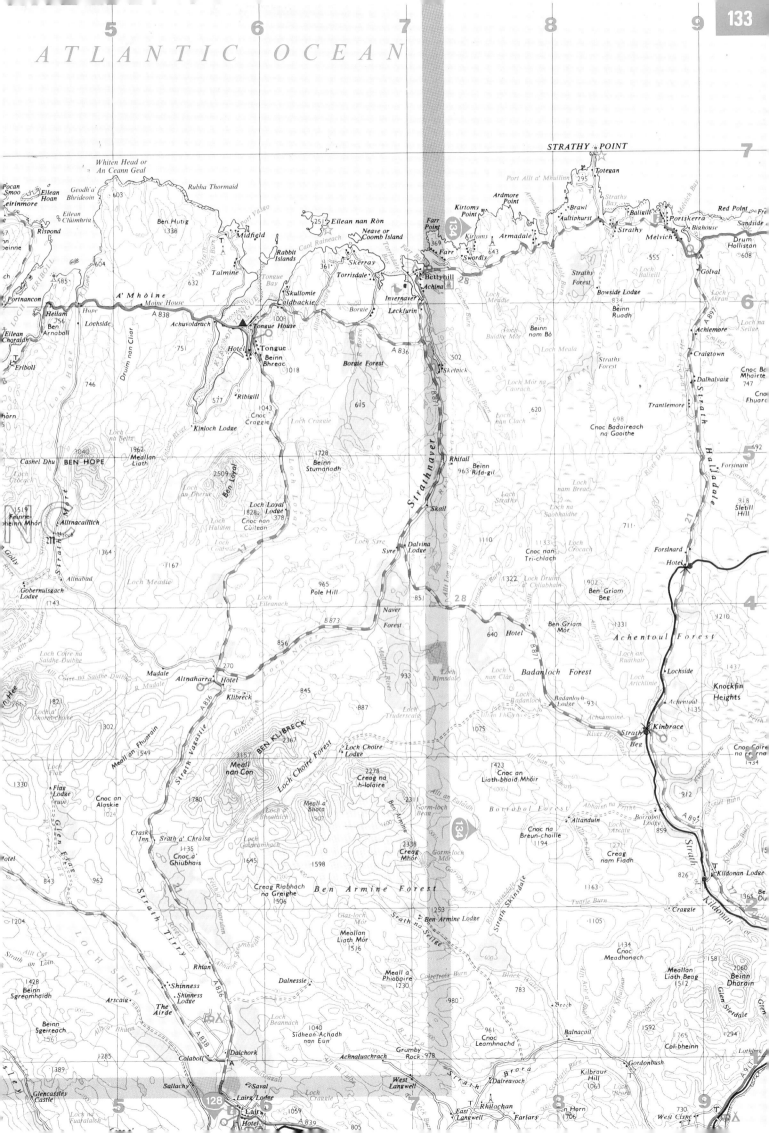

O C E A N

DUNNET HEAD

Langaton Point
Red Head
Mell Head
Uppertown
Netherton
Island of Stroma
Muckle Skerry
Pentland Skerries

DUNCANSBY HEAD

SCRABSTER to
Stromness............... 2 hrs
Thorshavn (Faroes)..13 hrs
(seasonal)

Briga Head
Burifa Hill
Dunnet Hill
Brough
The Thirl
Hunspow
Ham
Scarfskerry
Point
Scarfskerry
Rattar
Men of Mey
Tang Head
St John's Point
Castle of Mey
Mey
Gills
Canisbay
Gills Bay
Huna
Hotel
John o' Groats
Stacks of Duncansby
Boars of Duncansby

Brims Ness
Spear Head
Holborn Head
Clett
Thurso Bay
Clardon Head
Clardon
The Spur
Castlehill
Castletown
Greenland
Barrock
Inkstack
Brabster
Worth Hill
Wife Geo
Skirza
Skirza Head
Ness Head
Freswick
Freswick Bay

Chapel
Crosskirk
Forss Ho
Bridge of Forss
Scrabster
THURSO
Murkle
Olrig Ho
Tain
Lochend
Slickly
Alterwall
Reaster
Auckengill
Nybster
Brough Head

Achreamie
Newlands of Geise
Westfield
Geise
Weydale
Hilliclay
Durran
Bowermadden
Lyth
Sortat
Keiss
Mireland
Tang Head

Shebster
Forsie
Lieurary
Buckies
Achingills
Sordale
Stemster Knockdee
Bowertower
Barrock Ho
How
Hastigrow
Killimster

Broubster
Calder Mains
Braal Castle
Roadside
Clayock
Stemster Ho
Halcro
North Watten
Kirk
Ackergill Tower
Noss Head

Shurrery
Brawlbin
Scotscalder Sta
Olgrinmore
Dorrery
Halkirk
Georgemas Junc Sta
Banniskirk Ho
Harpsdale
Loch Watten
Reiss
Winless
Sealky Head
Staxigoe

Blàr Dearg
Spittal
Backlass
Watten
Bilbster
Wick Airport
Ackergill
North Head

Westerdale
Mybster
Tormsdale
Stirkoke Ho
Milton
WICK
Wick Bay

Strathmore Lodge
Beinn Chàiteag
Lochmore Cott
Hill of Rangag
Stemster Hill
Badlipster
Tannach
Newton
Whiterow
South Head
Castle of Old Wick
Hempriggs Ho
Helman Head

Lochdhu Hotel
Dalnawillan Lodge
Coire na Beinne
Achavanich
Cnoc an Earrannaiche
Camster
Grey Cairns
Hill of Oliclett
Thrumster
Sarclet
Sarclet Head

Ben Alisky
Cnocan Conachreag
Crofts of Benachielt
Rumster Forest
Roster
Bruan
Whaligoe
Ulbster

Houstry
Smerral
Latheronwheel Ho
Latheron
Latheronwheel
Forse Ho
Swiney
Forse
Lybster
Stone Rows
Clyth
Halberry Head

Braemore
Dunbeath
Dunbeath Bay
Dunbeath Castle

Scaraben
Meall na Caorach
Ramscraigs
Knockally
Borgue
Newport
An Dùn
Ceann Leathad nam Bò
Langwell Ho
Berriedale
Boch-ailean

Wag
Langwell Forest
Aultibea
Ousdale
Ord Point
Helmsdale

N O R T H   S E A

Coghill Loch
Holbornhead
Cairn
Scrabster
Scrabster Ho
LB Sta
Thurso Bay
Castle (remains of)
CG Lookout
Mountain Rescue Post
Pennyland
Castle (ruin)
Thurso
THURSO
Ormlie
Oldfield Ho
Hospl
Weir

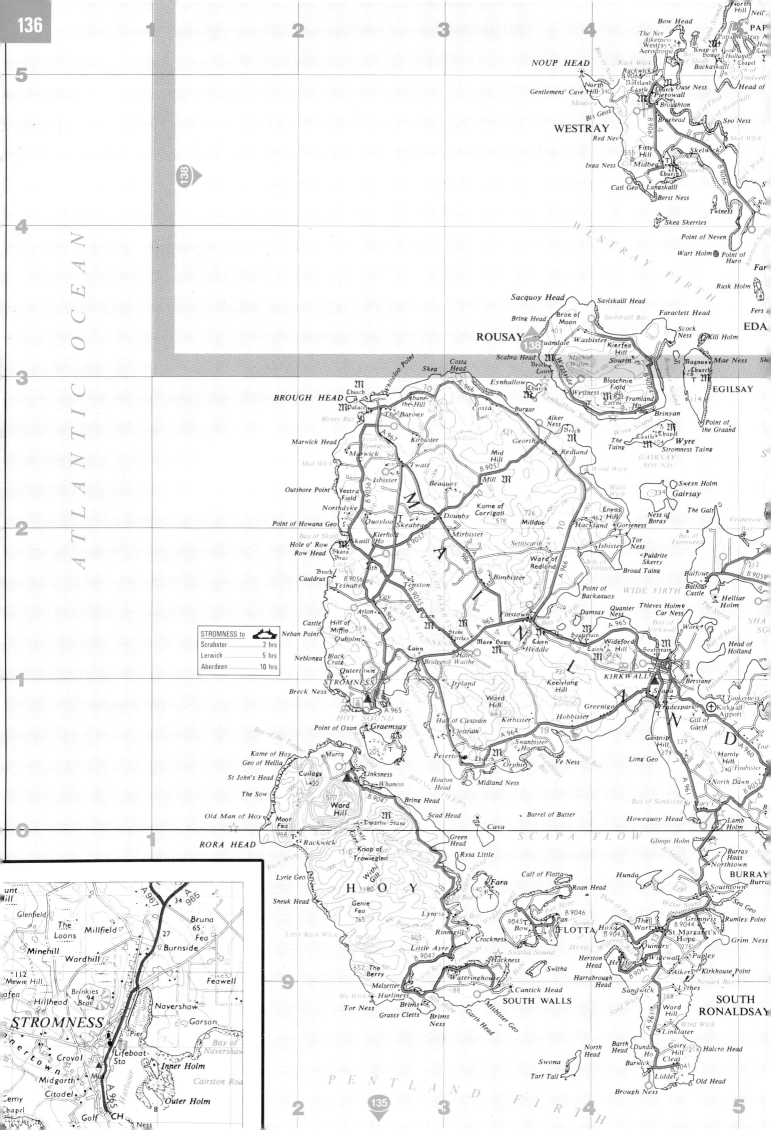

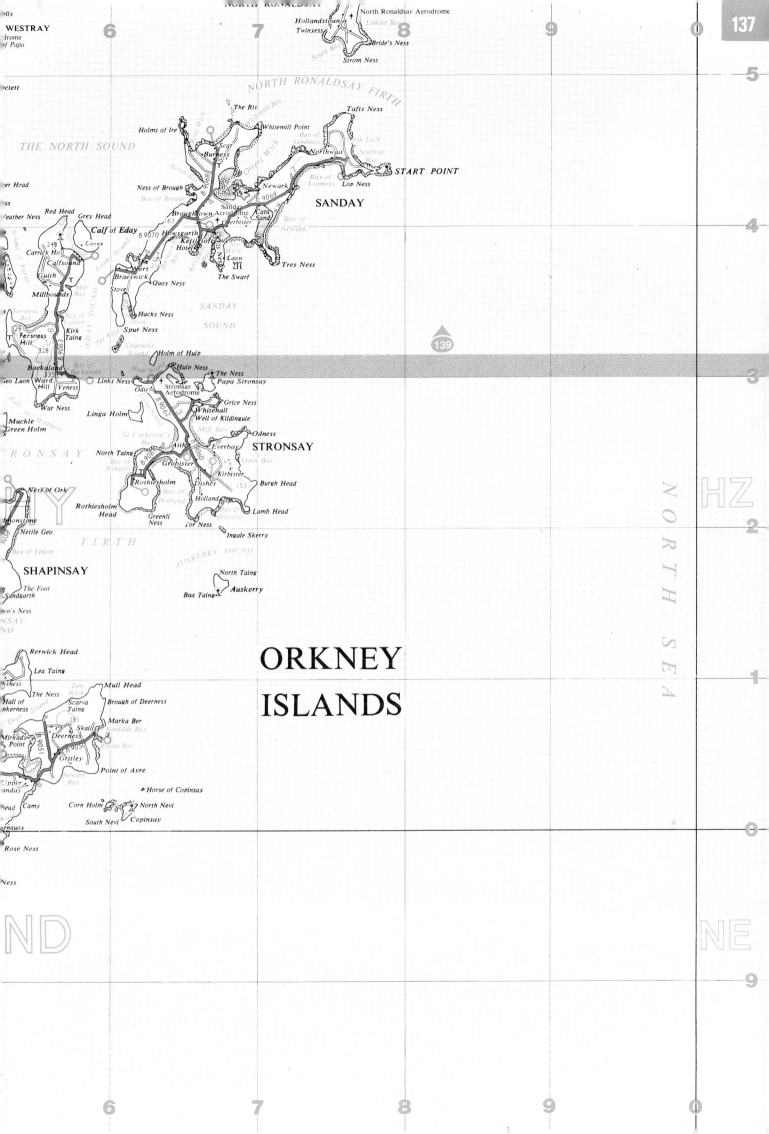

WESTRAY
drome
of Papa

NORTH RONALDSAY
Hollandstoun
Twinyess
North Ronaldsay Aerodrome
Linklet Bay
Bride's Ness
South Bay
Strom Ness

NORTH RONALDSAY FIRTH

THE NORTH SOUND

The Riv
Whitemill Bay
Holms of Ire
Whitemill Point
Tafts Ness
Scar
Bay of
Sandauoy
North Loch
Burness
Northwaa
Scuthvie
Bay
START POINT
Ness of Brough
Newark
Bay of
Lopness
Lop Ness
Bay of Brough
Sanday
Broughtown Aerodrome
Overbister
Cata
Sand
SANDAY
Calf of Eday
Howsgarth
Kettletoft
Hotel
Wick
Cairn
Cairns
Bay of
Newark
Red Head
Grey Head
Weather Ness
Carrick Ho
Calfsound
The
Wort
Braeswick
Quoy Ness
The Swarf
Tres Ness
Guith
Stove
Millbounds
Mill
Bay
Hacks Ness
SANDAY
Fersness
Bay
Spur Ness
SOUND
Fersness
Hill
Kirk
Taing
Spurness
Sound
Holm of Huip
Backaland
Huip Ness
Holm of Huip
Geo Luon Ward
Hill
Veness
Links Ness
The Ness
Papa Stronsay
Odie
Stronsay
Aerodrome
War Ness
Linga Holm
Grice Ness
Whitehall
Well of Kildinguie
Muckle
Green Holm
Mill Bay
Odness
STRONSAY
North Taing
Aith
Everbay
Bay of
Bomasty
Grobister
Odin Bay
STRONSAY
Kirbister
Rothiesholm
Dishes
Burgh Head
Ness of Ork
Holland
Rothiesholm
Head
Bay of
Holland
Greenli
Ness
Tor Ness
Lamb Head
Monstone
Nettle Geo
Bay of Linton
Ingale Skerry
FIRTH
AUSKERRY SOUND
North Taing
SHAPINSAY
Auskerry
Baa Taing
The Foot
Sandgarth
co's Ness

ORKNEY
ISLANDS

Rerwick Head
Lea Taing
Mull Head
Den
Wick
The Ness
Brough of Deerness
Hall of
nkerness
Scarva
Taing
Marka Ber
Mirkady
Point
Deerness
Skaill
Sandside Bay
Gritley
Roana Bay
Point of Ayre
Upper
anday
Horse of Copinsay
Camy
Corn Holm
North Nevi
South Nevi
Copinsay
nquoy
Rose Ness

Ness

NORTH SEA
HZ
NE

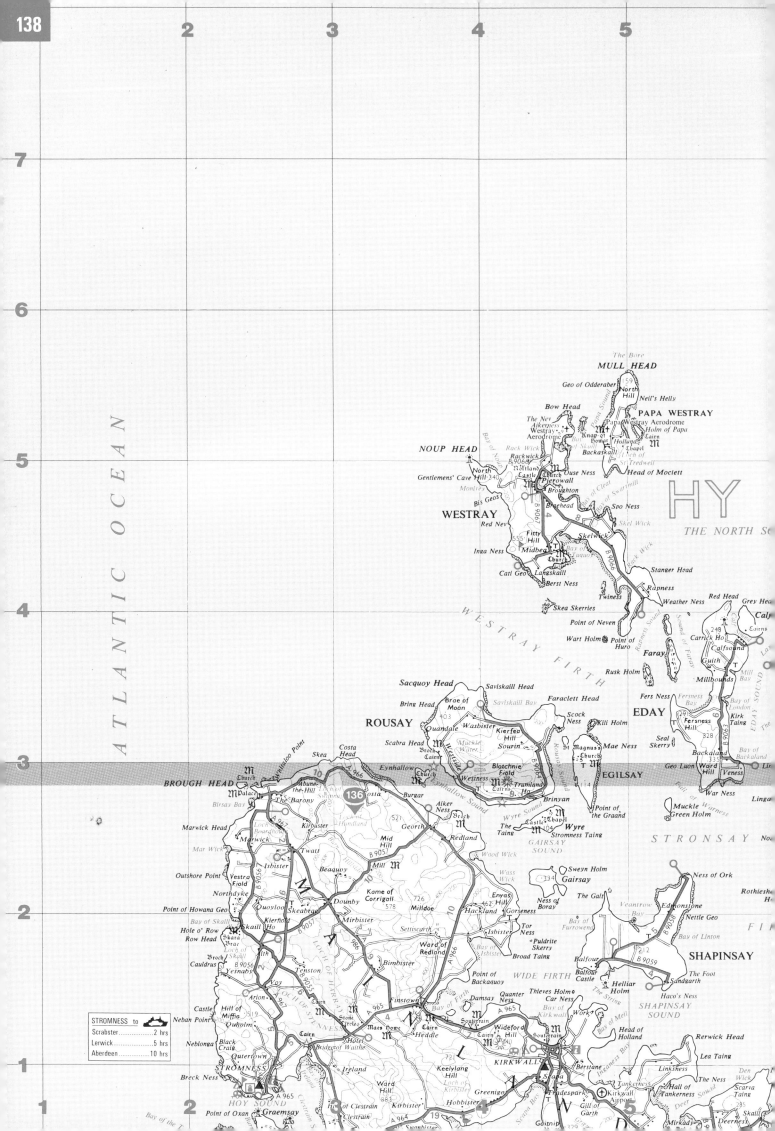

ATLANTIC OCEAN

MULL HEAD
The Bore
Geo of Odderaber
North
Hill
159
Neil's Helly
Bow Head
PAPA WESTRAY
The Nev
Aikerness
Westray
Aerodrome
Papa Westray Aerodrome
Holm of Papa
Knap of Howar
Cairn
Holland
Chapel
NOUP HEAD
Rack Wick
Backaskaill
Loch of St Tredwell
Chapel
St Tredwell
Rackwick
B 9064
Netland
Castle
Church
Ouse Ness
Head of Moclett
North
Gentlemens' Cave Hill 340
Hill
Pierowall
Broughton
Bay of Swartmill
Spo Ness

HY
THE NORTH So

Monivey
Brachead
Bay of Swartmill
WESTRAY
Bis Geos
B 9067
Red Nev
Fitty
Hill
555
Midbea
Skelwick
Skel Wick
Rack Wick
Inga Ness
Midbea
Church
Bay of Tuquoy
B 9066
Stanger Head
Catl Geo
Langskaill
Berst Ness
Rapness
Twiness
Weather Ness
Red Head
Grey Hea
Skea Skerries
Caly
WESTRAY FIRTH
Point of Neven
Cairns
248
Carrick Ho
Wart Holm
Point of Huro
Calfsound
Faray
Rusk Holm
Guith
Millbounds
Mill Bay
Sacquoy Head
Saviskaill Head
Fers Ness
Fersness Bay
Bay of London
Bring Head
Brae of Moan
403
Saviskaill Bay
Faraclett Head
Scock Ness
Kili Holm
EDAY
Fersness Hill
328
29
B 9063
Kirk Taing
ROUSAY
Quandale
Wasbister
Kierfea Hill
Sourin
Muckle Water
St Magnus Church
Mae Ness
Seal Skerry
Backaland
335
Bay of Backaland
Scabra Head
Broch Cairn
Wetsdale
Blotchnie Field
Geo Luon
Ward Hill
Lir
Veness
BROUGH HEAD
Church
Skea
Costa Head
Eynhallow
Church
Westness
Cairns
Trumland Ho
EGILSAY
War Ness
Fall of Warness
Swilliloo Point
Abune-the-Hill
Costa
Eynhallow Sound
Brinyan
Wyre Sound
Point of the Graand
Muckle Green Holm
Linga
Palace
The Barony
Burgar
Aiker Ness
Broch
The Taing
Castle
Chapel
Wyre
Stromness Taing
STRONSAY
No
Birsay Bay
Lochend
Loch of Hundland
521
Georth
Redland
GAIRSAY SOUND
Marwick Head
Kirbuster
Mid Hill
Wood Wick
Sweyn Holm
Ness of Ork
Marwick
B 9057
Mill
Wass Wick
334
Gairsay
Rothieshe
Mar Wick
Twatt
Beaquoy
The Galt
Outshore Point
Vestra Fiold
B 9057
Kame of Corrigall
578
726
Milldoe
Enyas Hill
462
Gorseness
Ness of Boray
Edmonstone
Nettle Geo
FI
Northdyke
B 9056
Quoyloo
Skeabrae
Dounby
Hackland
Tor Ness
Bay of Furrowend
B 9058
Bay of Linton
Point of Howana Geo
Kierfiold
Mirbister
Settiscarth
Isbister
Puldrite Skerry
212
SHAPINSAY
Bay of Skaill
Skaill Ho
B 9057
986
Ward of Redland
Bay of Isbister
Broad Taing
Balfour
Balfour Castle
B 9059
Hole o' Row
Row Head
Skara Brae
Tith
Bimbister
A 966
Point of Backaquoy
WIDE FIRTH
Helliar Holm
The Foot
Sandgarth
Cauldrus
Yesnaby
B 9056
Voy
Tenston
Cairn
Quanter Ness
Damsay
Bay of Kirkwall
SHAPINSAY SOUND
Arion
A 965
Finstown
Bay of Firth
Thieves Holmo
Car Ness
Work
Haco's Ness
Castle
Hill of Miffia 519
Stone Circle
Cairn
Heddle
Wideford Hill 240
Southtown
Rerwick Head
Neban Point
Ouholm
Maes Howe
A 965
Southtown
Berstane
Lea Taing
Neblonga
Black Craig
Bridge of Waithe
Cairn
KIRKWALL
Ingness Bay
Linksness
The Ness
Outertown
Ireland
721
Keelylang Hill
Greenigoe
Scapa
Tankerness
Den Wick
Scarva Taing
STROMNESS
Ward Hill 883
Kirbister
Hobbister
Tradespark
Kirkwall Airport
Hall of Tankerness
285
Skaill
Breck Ness
HOY SOUND
Graemsay
Point of Oxan
Ho of Clestrain
Cairn
A 964
Gill of Garth
Gaitnip
Deer Sound
Deerness
Bay of the T
Clestrain
Swanbister
379

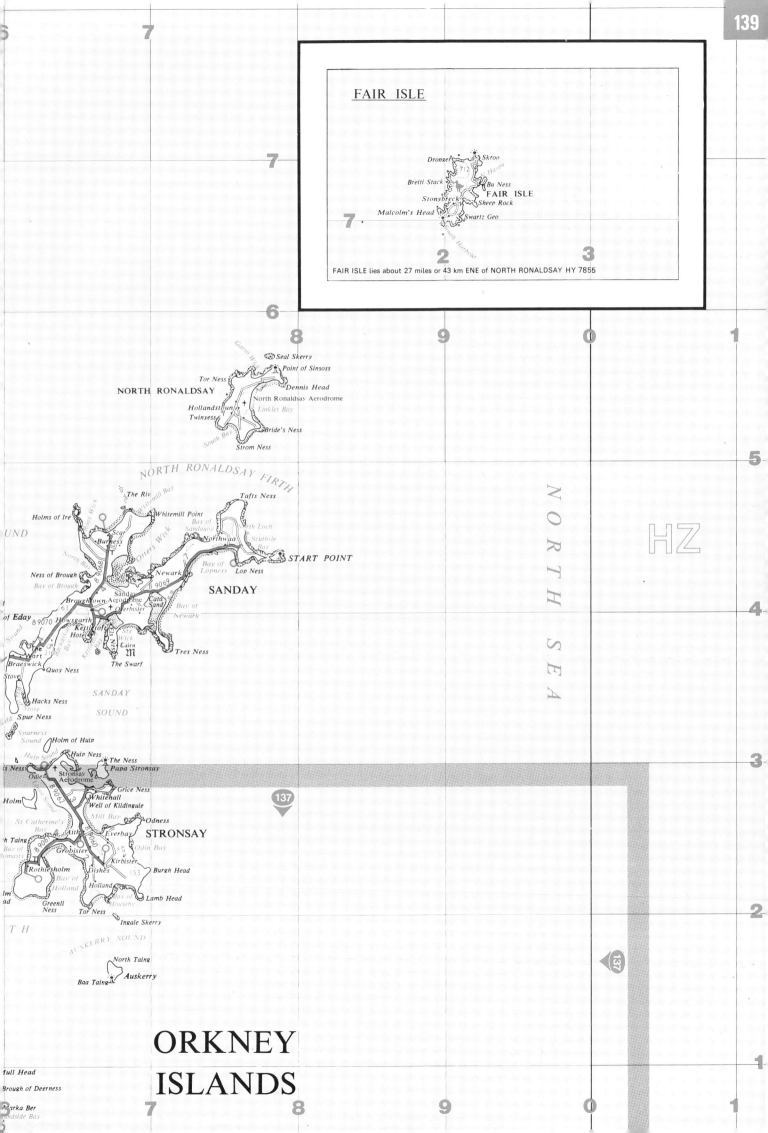

FAIR ISLE

Dronger
Skroo
N Haven
Breiti Stack
Bu Ness
Stonybreck
FAIR ISLE
Sheep Rock
Malcolm's Head
Swartz Geo
South Harbour

FAIR ISLE lies about 27 miles or 43 km ENE of NORTH RONALDSAY HY 7855

Seal Skerry
Point of Sinsoss
Garso Wick
Tor Ness
Dennis Head
NORTH RONALDSAY
North Ronaldsay Aerodrome
Hollandstoun
Linklet Bay
Twinyess
Bride's Ness
South Bay
Strom Ness

NORTH RONALDSAY FIRTH

The Riv
Whitemill Bay
Tafts Ness
Holms of Ire
Whitemill Point
Bay of
Sandquoy
North Loch
Scar
Northwaa
Scuthvie
SOUND
Burness
Bay
Otters Wick
START POINT
Ness of Brough
Newark
Bay of
Lop Ness
Bay of Brough
Lopness
B 9068
SANDAY
of Eday
Broughtown Aerodrome
Cata
Bay of
B 9070
Sanday
Sand
Newark
Howsgarth
Overbister
Kettletoft
Hotel
Sty
Wick
The
Cairn
Wort
Tres Ness
Braeswick
The Swarf
Stove
Quoy Ness
Hacks Ness
SANDAY
Stove
Spur Ness
SOUND
Spurness
Sound
Holm of Huip
Huip Sound
Huip Ness
The Ness
Ness
Papa Stronsay
Odie
Stronsay
Aerodrome
Grice Ness
Holm
Whitehall
Well of Kildinguie
St Catherine's
Mill Bay
Bay
Odness
h Taing
Ith
Everbay
STRONSAY
Bay of
Grobister
Odin Bay
mast
Kirbister
Rothiesholm
Dishes
Burgh Head
Bay of
Holland
Holland
Bay of
Housby
Lamb Head
Greenli
Ness
Tor Ness
m
Ingale Skerry
d

T H

AUSKERRY SOUND
North Taing
Baa Taing
Auskerry

ORKNEY
ISLANDS

Mull Head
Brough of Deerness
arka Ber
ndside Bay

NORTH SEA

HZ

137

137

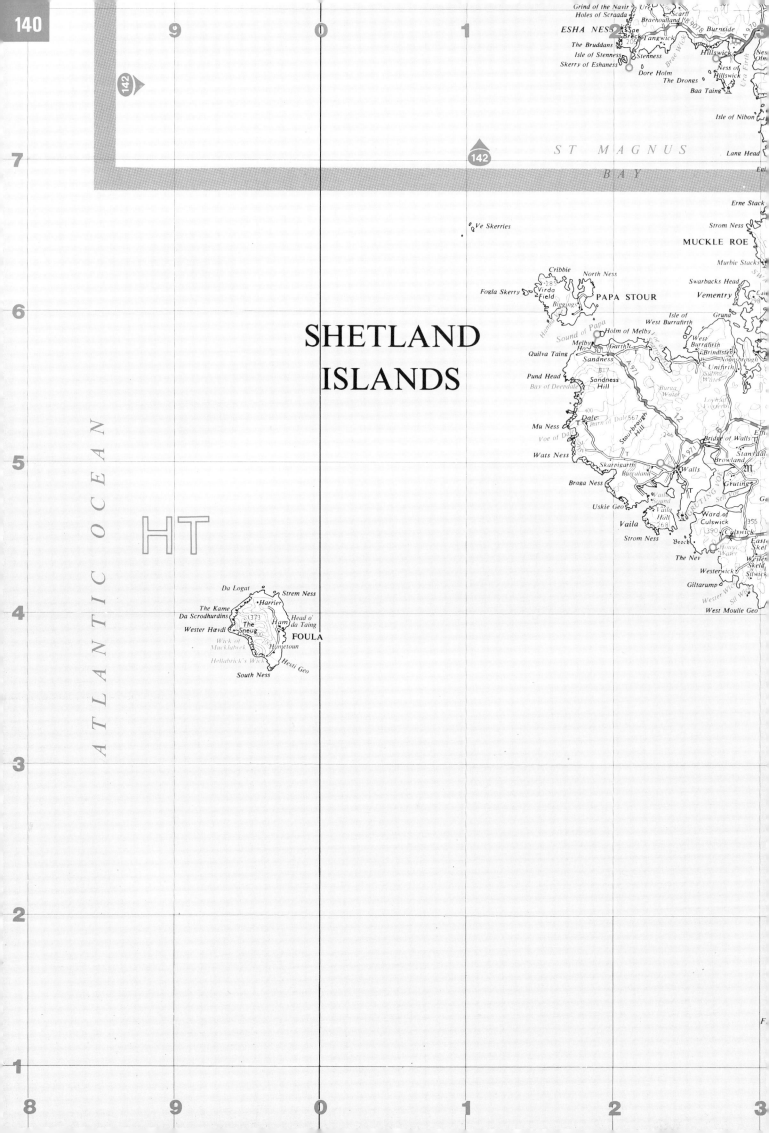

SHETLAND
ISLANDS

ATLANTIC OCEAN

HT

ESHA NESS
Grind of the Navir · Ure
Holes of Scraada · Scarff
Brae · Brachoulland · A 9078 · Burnside
Skae · Breck · Tangwick · A 970
The Bruddans · Stenness · Hillswick
Isle of Stenness · Stenness · Ness of Hillswick
Skerry of Eshaness · Dore Holm · The Drongs · Ura Firth
Baa Taing · Isle of Nibon

ST MAGNUS
142
BAY
Lang Head

Erne Stack
Strom Ness
MUCKLE ROE
Murbie Stacks
Ve Skerries
Cribbie · North Ness · Swarbacks Head · Vementry
Fogla Skerry · Virda Field · PAPA STOUR · Gruna
Biggings · Isle of West Burrafirth · West Burrafirth
Sound of Papa · Holm of Melby · Brindister
Melby Ho · Garth · Noonsbrough
Quilva Taing · Sandness · Unifirth · Sulma Water
Pund Head · Sandness Hill · Bursa Water
Bay of Deepdale · B17
Loch of Grunnafirth
Dale · Stourbrough Hill · 567 · Bridge of Walls
Mu Ness · Burn of Dale · 246 · Stansdal · Browland
Wats Ness · Skarpigarth · A 971 · Walls · Gruting
Braga Ness · Burgaland · GRUTING VOE
Uskie Geo · Vaila Sound · Ward of Culswick · 355
Vaila · Vaila Hall · 390 · Culswick
Strom Ness · Broch · East Skel
The Nev · Water · Wester Skeld · Silwick
Westerwick
Giltarump · Wester Wick · West Moulie Geo

Da Logat · Strem Ness
The Kame · Harrier
Da Scrodhurdins · 373 · Head o' da Taing
Wester Hævdi · The Sneug · Ham · FOULA
Wick of Mucklabek · Hametoun
Hellabrick's Wick · Hesti Geo
South Ness

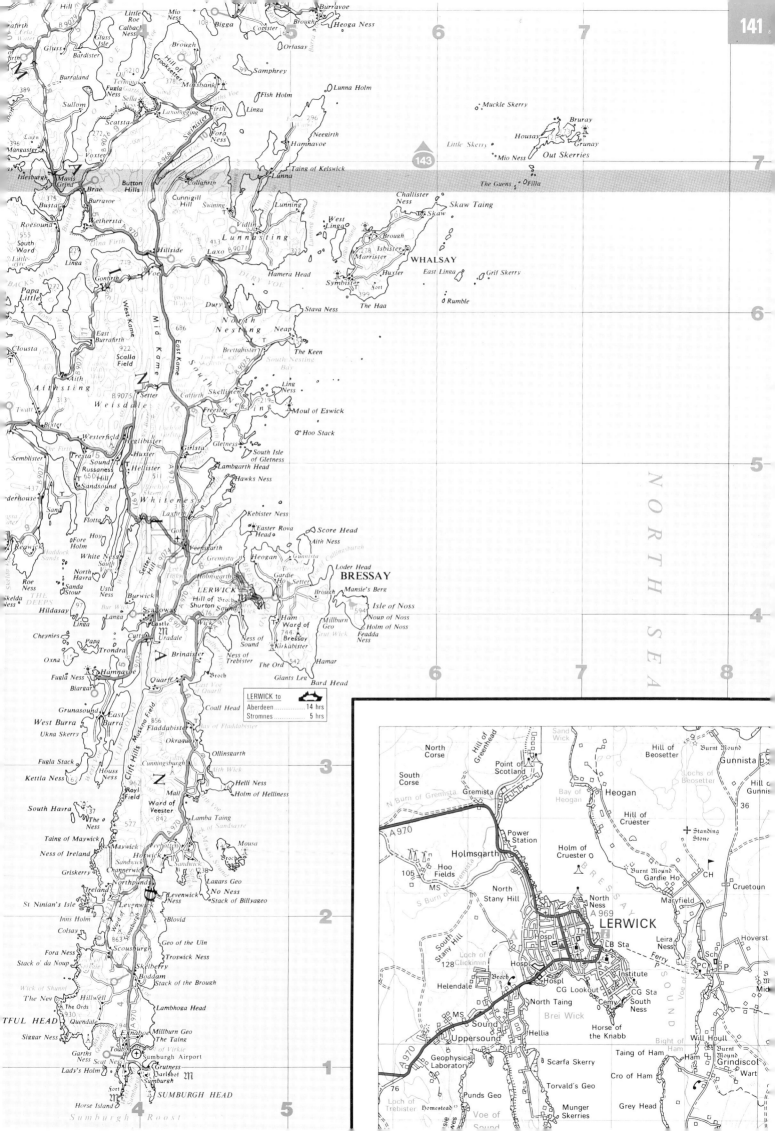

LERWICK to
Aberdeen .... 14 hrs
Stromnes .... 5 hrs

NORTH SEA

WHALSAY

BRESSAY

LERWICK

SUMBURGH HEAD

HO

ATLANTIC OCEAN

HT

1

0

9

8

7

6

5

Isle of Fethala
Garmus Taing
Uyea
Burrier Wick
The Breck
Fugla Ness
South Wick
Hevdadale Head
Erga Field
564
North Roe
Lang Clodie Wick
644
Beorgs of Skelberry
Gruna Stack
Turls Head
North Roe
River Water
The Faither
Muckle Ossa
351 Kettligill Head
Heillia
740
Housetter
Ockran Head
Burries Ness
475
Man o' Scord
Ronas Hill
Collafirth
Colla
South Head
Heylor
567
The Clifts
Voe
Ollaberry
Faan Hill
Whalwick Taing
Hamnavoe
Head of Stanshi
Ure
Scarff
Burnside
Urafirth
Grind of the Navir
Braehoulland
Fela Water
Gluss
Bardiste
Holes of Scraada
ESHA NESS
Soe
Breck Tangwick
Hillswick
Ness of Olnesfirth
Burraland
The Bruddans
Stenness
Ness of Hillswick
389
Isle of Stenness
Dore Holm
Baa Tains
Sullom
Skerry of Eshaness
The Drongs
Isle of Nibon
396
Cairn
Mangaster
ST MAGNUS
Lang Head
Egilsay
Islesburgh
Mavis Grind
BAY
Erne Stack
Bustar
140 Ve Skerries
Strom Ness
Roesound
855
South Ward
MUCKLE ROE
Murbie Stacks
Little
Linga
Cribbie
North Ness
Swarbacks Head
Papa
Little
Forla Skerry
Virda Field
Biggings
PAPA STOUR
Vementry
Isle of
West Burrafirth
Gruna
SHETLAND
Sound of Papa
Holm of Melby
West Burrafirth
Clousta
Melby
Garthe
Brindister
Noonsbrough
Quilva Taing
Sandness
Unifirth
ISLANDS
Pund Head
Sandness Hill
Aithsting
Bay of Deepdale
Twatt
Dale
567
Bixter
Mu Ness
Stourbrough Hill
246
Bridge of Walls
Wes
Wats Ness
Stansdale
Browland
Semblister
Tresta
Skarpigearth
Walls
Gruting
Braga Ness
Garderhouse
Uskie Geo

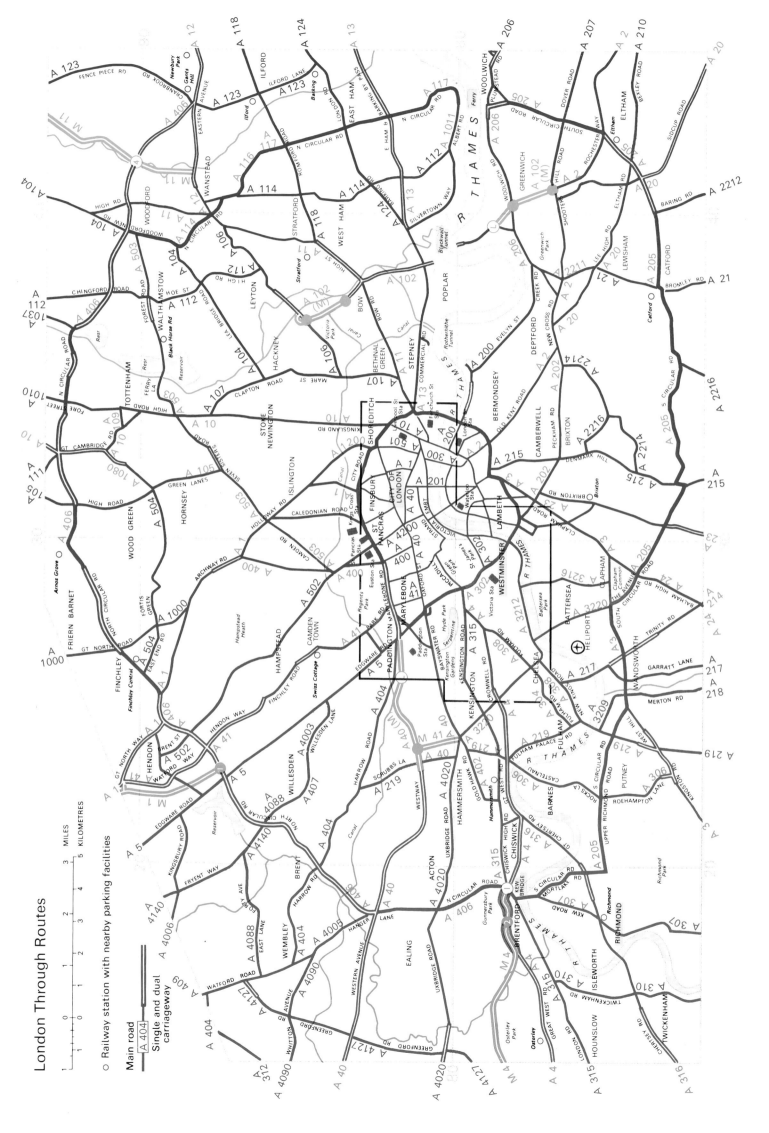

London Through Routes

○ Railway station with nearby parking facilities

Main road **A 404**

Single and dual carriageway

Central London

Key to Central London Map Pages

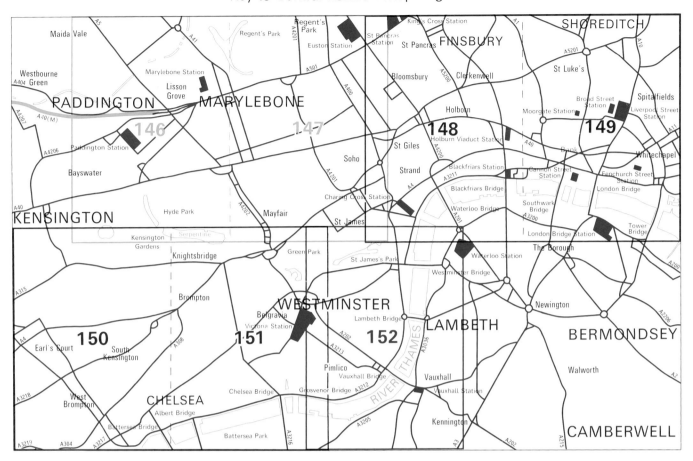

For Complete Street Index see pages 160 to 163

LEGEND

Map Scale 1:10 000

ROUTE RESTRICTIONS	RESTRICTIONS D'ITINERAIRE	FAHRBAHN-BESCHRÄNKUNGEN
(Some may not apply at all times or to all vehicles)	(Il se peut que certaines ne soient pas applicables à toutes les heures ou à tous les véhicules)	(z.T. nicht ganzzeitig bzw. für alle Fahrzeuge in Kraft)
Main Roads and Bus Routes	Route principale et ligne d'autobus	Hauptstrassen und Busweg
One way traffic routes	Voie de circulation en sens unique	Einbahnstrassen
No access in direction shown	Pas d'accès dans la direction indiquée	In angezeigter Richtung keine Zufahrt

TOURIST INFORMATION	RENSEIGNEMENTS TOURISTIQUES DIVERS	ALLGEMEINE TOURISTENANGABEN
Selected places of interest	Endroits d'un intérêt touristique particulier	Ausgesuchte Örte von Interesse für Touristen

Royal Academy of Arts

Horse Guards

i	Information Centre	Bureau de renseignements	Auskunftsstelle
	Railway Station	Gare	Bahnhof
⊖	Underground Station	Gare de Metro	Untergrundbahnhof
	Bus/Coach Station	Gare d'autobus/d'autocar	Busbahnhof
P	Parking	Parking	Parkplatz
✚	Casualty Station	Centre médical pour accidentés	Unfallstation

The lines on this map form part of the National Grid and are spaced at 1 kilometre intervals.
The representation on this map of a road track or path is no evidence of the existence of a right of way.
Compiled from Ordnance Survey 1:10 000 material and revised for significant changes 1981.

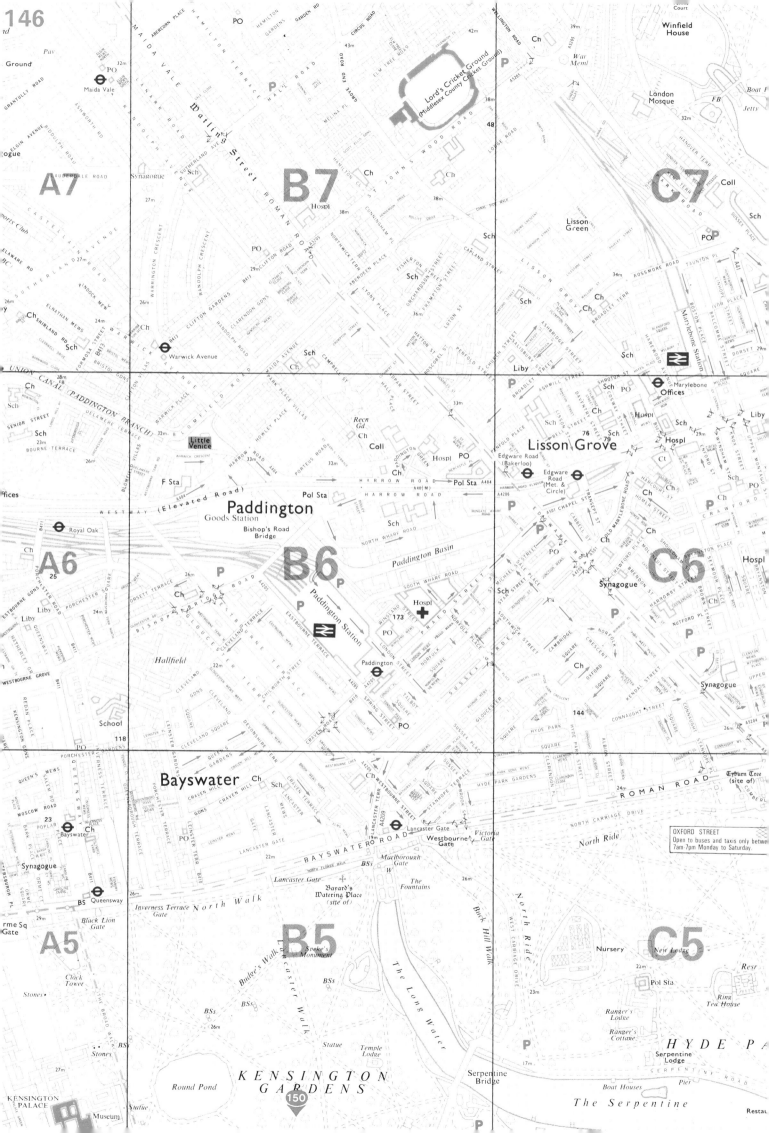

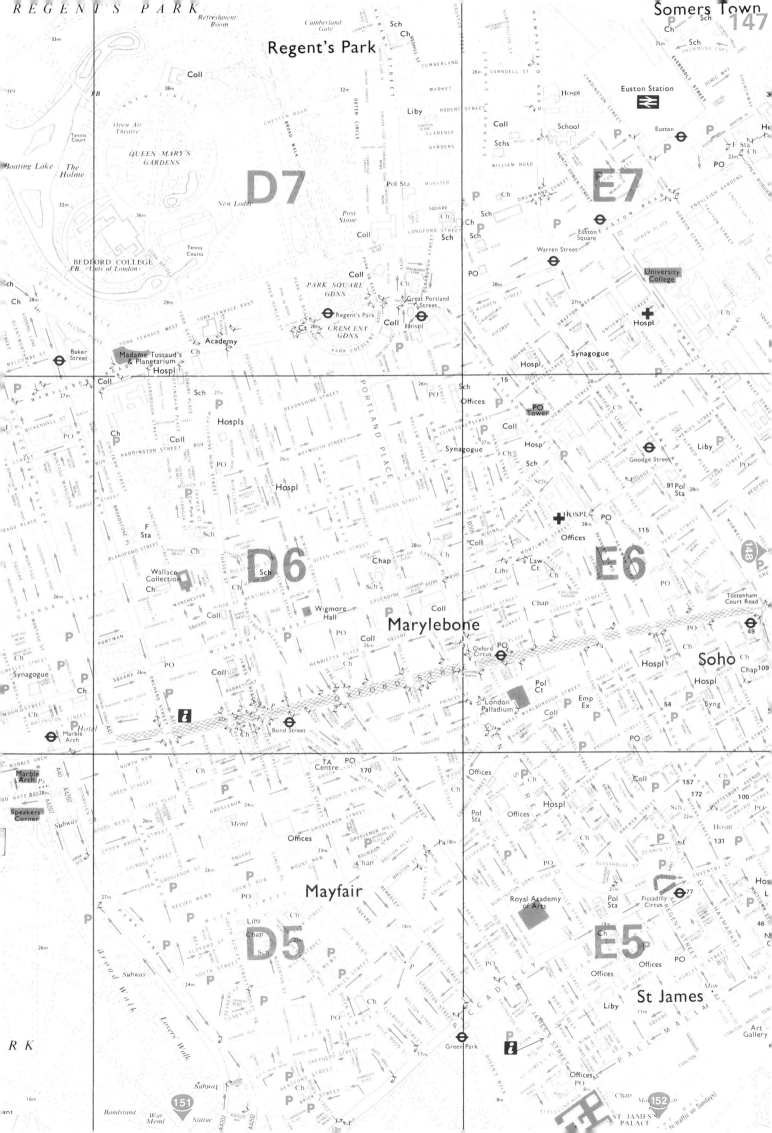

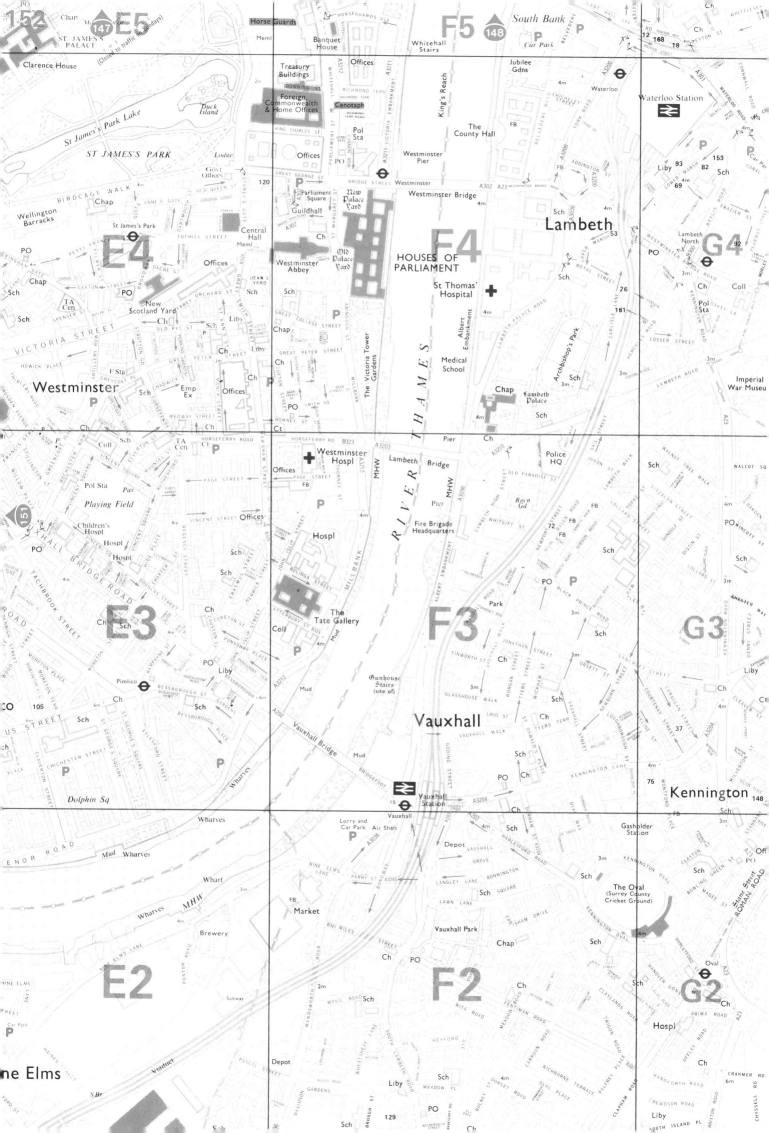

Town Through Route Maps

Aberdeen	*page* 121	Leeds	*page* 155
Ardrossan and Saltcoats	92	Leicester	156
Birmingham and Smethwick	157	Lerwick	141
Blackpool	155	Liverpool	68
Bournemouth	158	Manchester and Salford	156
Brighton and Hove	28	Middlesbrough and Stockton-on-Tees	155
Bristol	158	Newcastle upon Tyne	154
Cambridge	158	Pembroke Dock	42
Cardiff	40	Penzance and Newlyn	19
Coventry	157	Plymouth	159
Dover	31	Portsmouth	159
Dundee	154	Ramsgate	39
Edinburgh	97	Sheffield	156
Exeter	159	Southampton	159
Felixstowe	55	Stornoway	131
Glasgow	154	Stranraer	86
Gloucester	158	Stromness	136
Great Yarmouth	65	Swansea	158
Holyhead	66	Thurso	135
Inverness	129	Jarrow	91
Ipswich	158	Weymouth	24
Kingston-upon-Hull	75	Wolverhampton	157

2·centimetres to 1 kilometre   (one grid square)

2   1   0 Kilometres 1   2   3

1   0 Miles 1   2

1 kilometre = 0·6214 mile   1 mile = 1·6093 kilometres

These town centre maps are taken from Ordnance Survey Landranger series maps, reproduced to show principal features and routes and best used in conjunction with local direction indications.

The Landranger series is the 20th century successor to the famous 'One Inch' maps, which were first published in 1801. The 204 Landranger maps cover the whole of Great Britain, the area on each being about 620 square miles. The sheet maps are easily recognisable by their magenta covers.

Rights of way are marked on the maps of England and Wales, which are ideal for walking and through the wealth of detail are useful for local journeys and exploration by car or motorcycle. More than 100 types of topographical detail are shown, including contours, footpaths, streams, woods, crags, buildings, stately homes, ancient monuments, bus and coach stations, and selected camping and caravan sites, parking places and viewpoints.

The Ordnance Survey keeps the Landranger series as up to date as possible – major changes are shown on reprints and as soon as there is significant overall change on a sheet a new edition is produced.

When Landranger maps were introduced in the 1970s at the scale of 1:50 000 (about $1\frac{1}{4}$ inches to 1 mile) they were generally photographic enlargements of One Inch maps, brought up to date and presented in a new format. By the early 1980s, however, almost two-thirds of the maps in the series had been redrawn after revision and issued as Second Series Landranger maps; the rest of the maps will have been converted to Second Series style by the end of the decade. A key to the Landranger series appears on page 7 of this atlas.

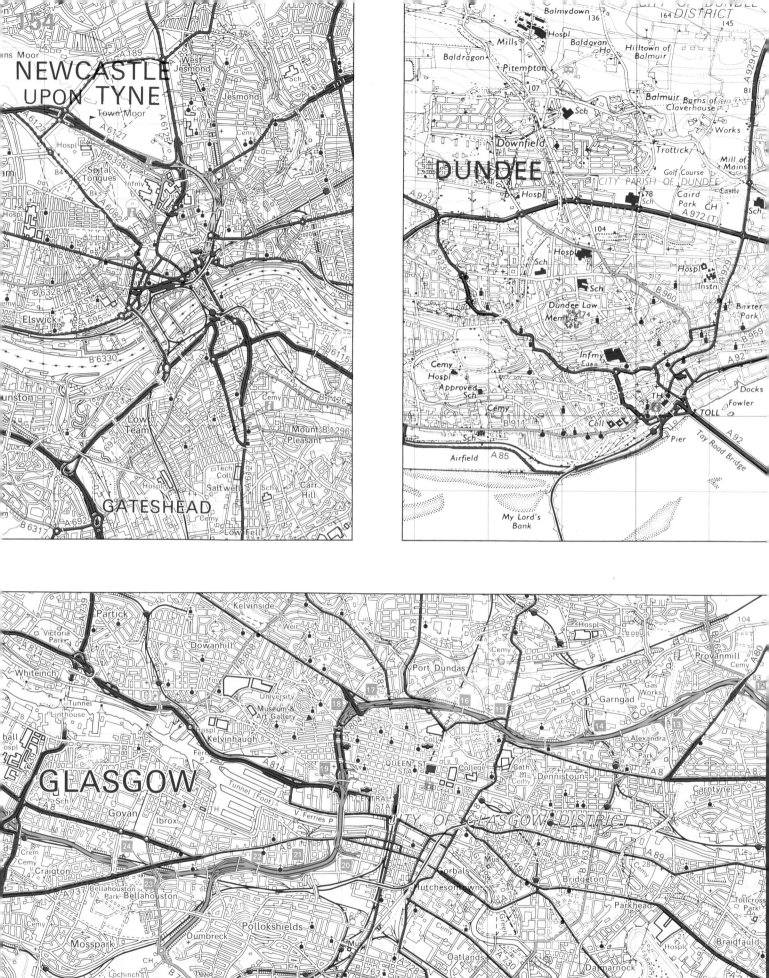

154

NEWCASTLE UPON TYNE

GATESHEAD

DUNDEE

GLASGOW

RUTHERGLEN

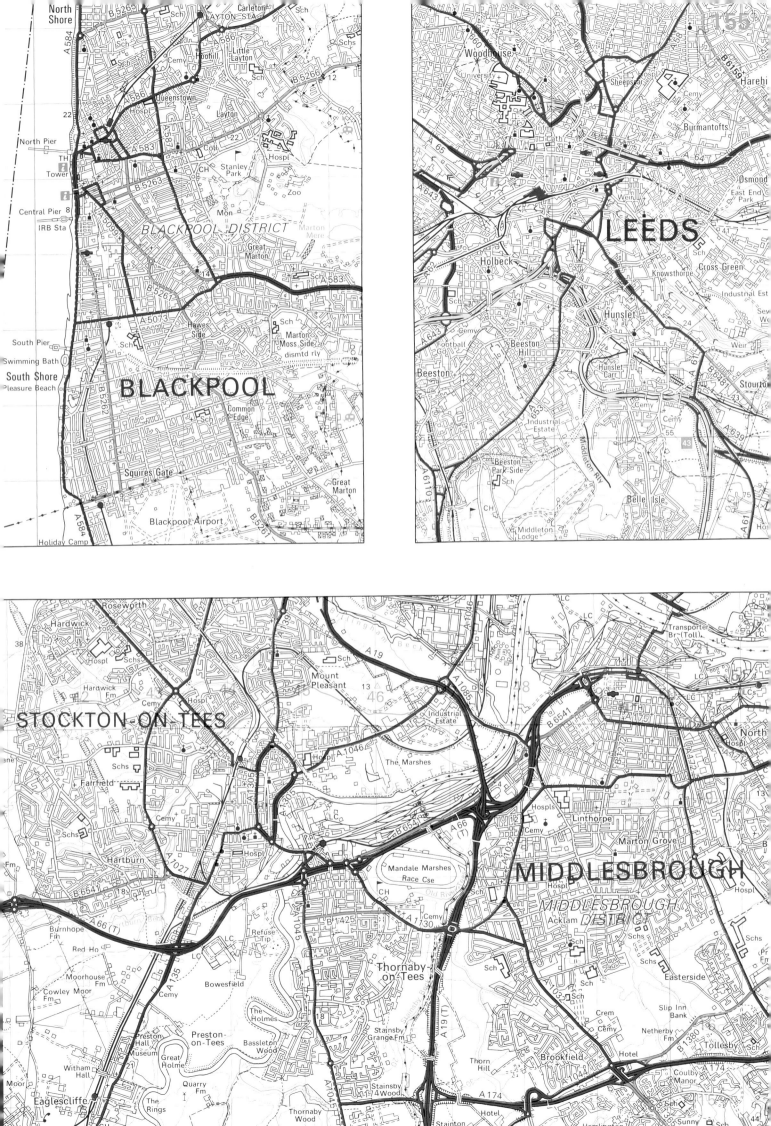

SALFORD

MANCHESTER

MANCHESTER DISTRICT

SHEFFIELD DISTRICT

SHEFFIELD

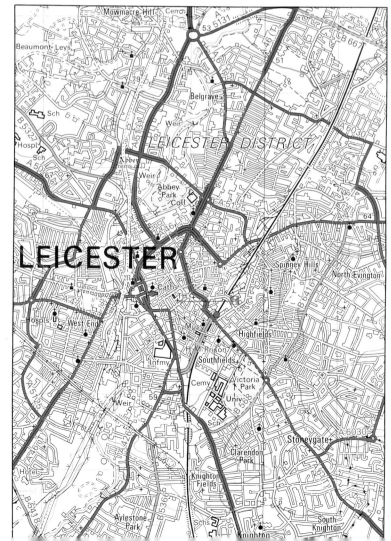

LEICESTER DISTRICT

LEICESTER

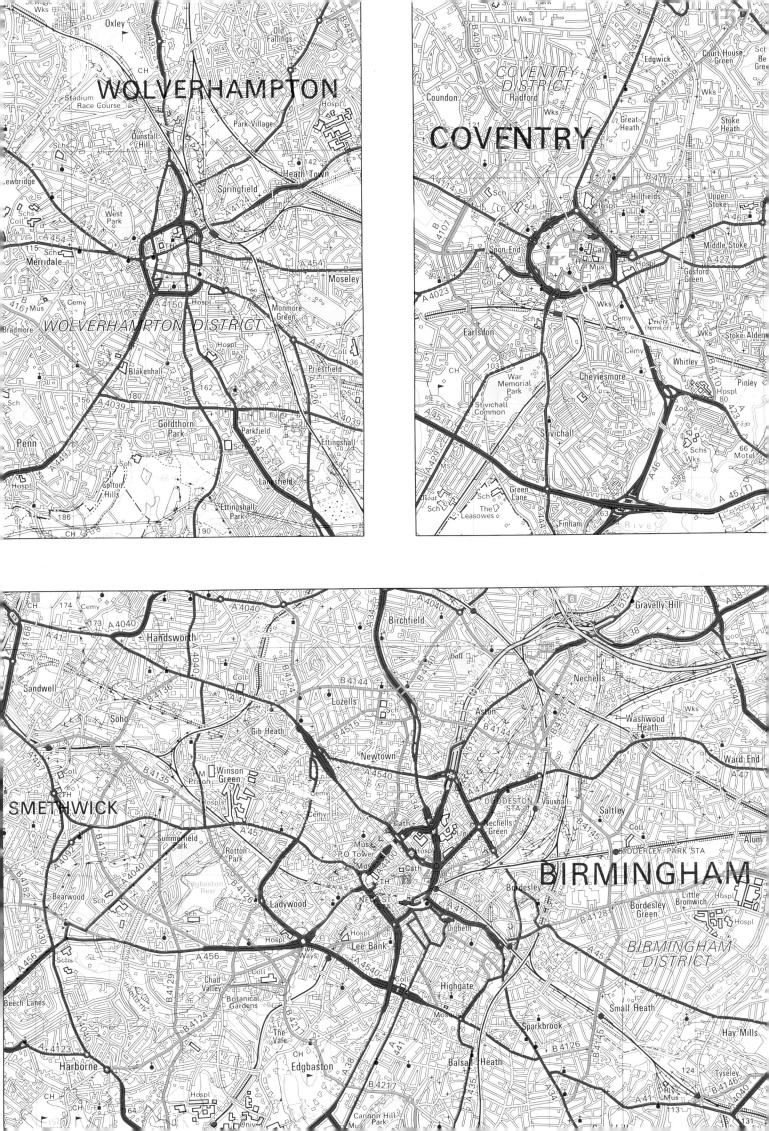

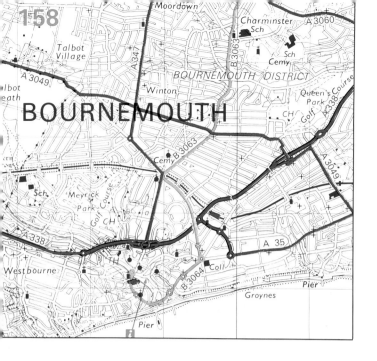

BOURNEMOUTH

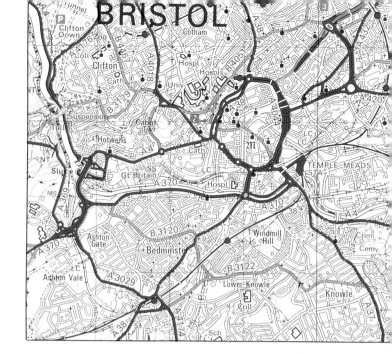

BRISTOL

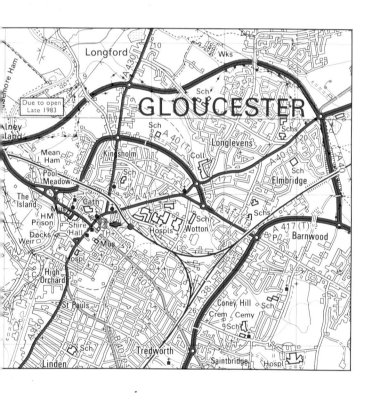

GLOUCESTER

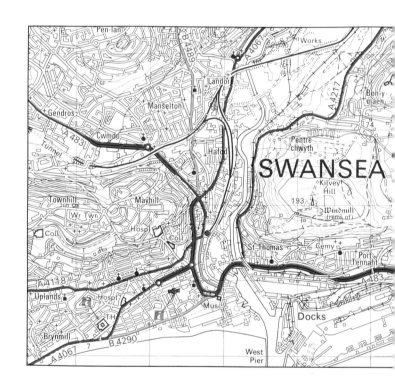

SWANSEA

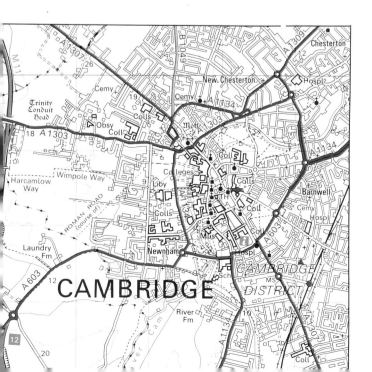

CAMBRIDGE

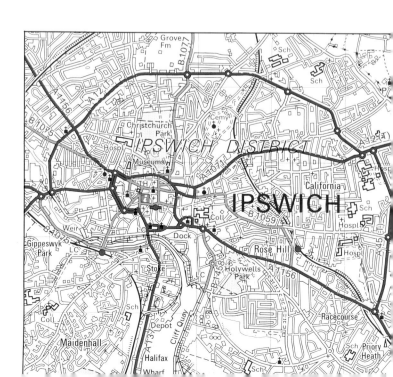

IPSWICH

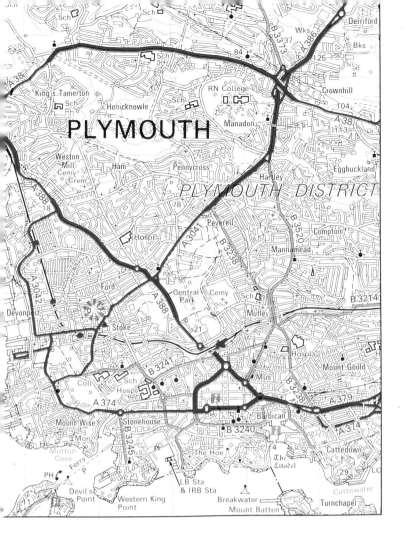

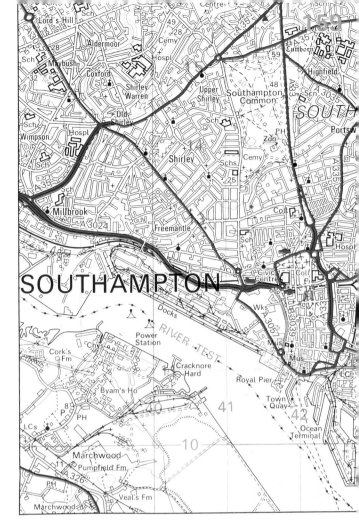

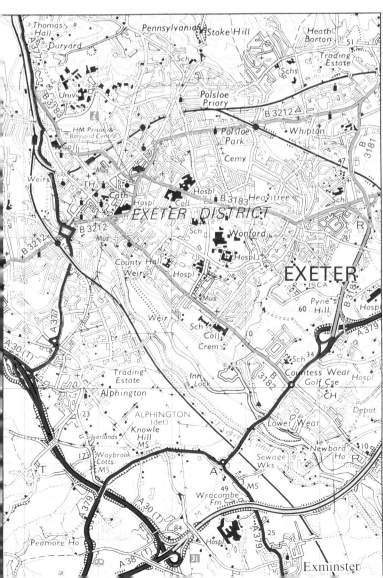

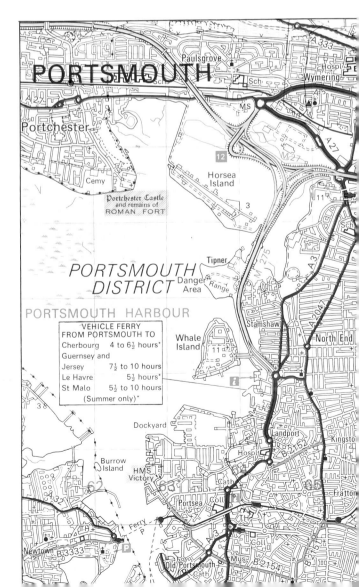

L

Lackington Street 149 H6
Lambeth High Street 152 F3
Lambeth Mews 152 F3
Lambeth Palace Road 152 F4
Lambeth Road 152 G4
Lambeth Walk 152 F3
Lamb's Buildings 149 H7
Lamb's Conduit Passage 148 F6
Lamb's Conduit Street 148 F7
Lamb's Passage 149 H7
Lamb Street 149 J6
Lamont Road 150 B2
Lamont Road Passage 150 B2
Lanark Place 146 B7
Lanark Road 146 B7
Lancashire Court 147 D5
Lancaster Gate 146 B5
Lancaster Mews 146 B5
Lancaster Place 148 F5
Lancaster Terrace 146 B5
Lancelot Place 151 C4
Lancing Street 147 E7
Landon Place 151 C4
92 Lanfranc Street 152 G4
Langham Place 147 D6
Langham Street 147 D6
Langley Court 148 F5
Langley Lane 152 F2
Langley Street 148 F6
Langton Close 148 F7
Langton Street 150 B2
Lansdowne Row 147 D5
Lansdowne Terrace 148 F7
Lauderdale Road 146 A7
Laud Street 152 F3
93 Launcelot Street 152 G4
Launceston Place 150 B4
Laurence Pountney Hill 149 H5
Laurence Pountney Lane 149 H5
Laverton Mews 150 A3
Laverton Place 150 A3
Lavington Street 149 G5
Lawn Lane 152 F2
Lawrence Lane 149 H6
Lawrence Street 150 C2
Laxton Place 147 D7
Laystall Street 148 G7
Leadenhall Place 149 J6
Leadenhall Street 149 J6
Leake Court 152 F4
Leake Street 152 F4
Leather Lane 148 G6
Lecky Street 150 B3
Leeke Street 148 F7
Lees Place 147 D5
Leicester Court 148 E5
Leicester Place 147 E5
Leicester Square 147 E5
Leicester Street 147 E5
Leigh Street 148 F7
Leinster Gardens 146 B6
Leinster Mews 146 B5
Leinster Place 146 B5
Leinster Terrace 146 B5
Leman Street 149 J6
Lennox Gardens 151 C4
Lennox Gardens Mews 151 C3
Leonard Street 149 H7
Leopards Court 148 G6
Leverett Street 151 C3
Lever Street 149 H7
Lewisham Street 152 E4
Lexham Gardens 150 A3
Lexham Gardens Mews 150 A4
Lexham Mews 150 A4
Lexham Walk 150 A4
Lexington Street 147 E5
Leyden Street 149 J6
Ligonier Street 149 J7
Lilestone Street 146 C7
Lillie Road 150 A2
Lillie Yard 150 A2
Limerston Street 150 B2
Lime Street 149 J6
94 Lime Street Passage 149 J6
Lincoln's Inn Fields 148 F6
Lincoln Street 151 C3
Lindsey Street 149 G6
Linhope Street 146 C7
Lisle Street 147 E5
Lisson Grove 146 C6
Lisson Street 146 C6
Litchfield Street 148 E5
Little Albany Street 147 D7
Little Argyll Street 147 E6
Little Britain 149 H6
Little Chester Street 151 D4
95 Little College Lane 149 H5
Little College Street 152 F4
Little George Street 152 E4
Little Marlborough Street 147 E6
Little New Street 148 G6
Little Portland Street 147 E6
Little Russell Street 148 F6
Little Sanctuary 152 E4
Little Smith Street 152 E4
Little Somerset Street 149 J6
Little St James's Street 147 E5
Little Titchfield Street 147 E6
Little Trinity Lane 149 H5
Liverpool Street 149 J6
Livonia Street 147 E6
Lizard Street 149 H7
Lloyd Baker Street 148 G7
Lloyd's Avenue 149 J6
Lloyd Square 148 G7
Lloyd's Row 148 G7
Lloyd Street 148 G7
Lodge Road 146 B7
Logan Mews 150 A3
Logan Place 150 A3
Lollard Place 152 G3
Lollard Street 152 G3
Lomard Court 148 G6
Lombard Lane 148 G6
Lombard Street 149 H6
Lombardy Place 146 A5
London Bridge Street 149 H5
London Mews 146 B6
London Street 149 J5
London Street 146 B6
London Wall 149 H6
Long Acre 148 F6
Longford Street 147 D7
Long Lane 149 G6
Longmoore Street 151 E3
96 Long's Court 148 E5
Long Street 149 J7
Long Yard 148 F7
Lord North Street 152 F4
Lords Hill Road 146 A6
Lordship Place 150 C2
Lorne Court 148 G7
Lothbury 149 H6
Lots Road 150 B2
Loughborough Street 152 F3
Lovat Lane 149 J5
Love Lane 149 H6
Lower Belgrave Street 151 D4
103 Milroy Walk 148 G5

Lower Grosvenor Place 151 D4
Lower James Street 147 E5
Lower John Street 147 E5
Lower Marsh 152 G4
Lower Newport Street 148 E5
97 Lower Robert Street 148 F5
Lower Sloane Street 151 D3
Lower Thames Street 149 J5
Lowndes Close 151 D4
Lowndes Place 151 D4
Lowndes Square 151 C4
Lowndes Street 151 D4
Loxham Street 148 F7
Lucan Place 151 C3
98 Ludgate Broadway 148 G6
Ludgate Circus 148 G6
99 Ludgate Court 148 G6
Ludgate Hill 148 G6
Ludgate Square 148 G6
Ludlow Street 149 H7
Luke Street 149 J7
Lumley Court 148 F5
Lumley Street 147 D6
Lupus Street 151 D3
Lupus Street 151 E3
Luscombe Way 152 F2
Luton Street 146 B7
Luxborough Street 147 D6
Lyall Mews 151 D4
Lyall Mews West 151 D4
Lyall Street 151 D4
Lygon Place 151 D4
Lyons Place 146 B7

M

Mabledon Place 148 E7
Macclesfield Road 149 H7
100 Macclesfield Street 147 E5
Mac Farren Place 147 D7
Macklin Street 148 F6
Mackworth Street 147 E7
Maddox Street 147 D5
Magdalen Street 149 J5
Magee Street 152 G2
Maida Avenue 146 B7
Maida Vale 146 B7
Maiden Lane 148 F5
Malet Place 147 E7
Malet Street 147 E6
Mallord Street 150 B2
Mallory Street 146 C7
Mallow Street 149 H7
Malta Street 149 H7
Maltravers Street 148 G5
Manchester Mews 147 D6
Manchester Square 147 D6
Manchester Street 147 D6
Mandeville Place 147 D6
Manette Street 147 E6
101 Manningford Close 148 G7
Manresa Road 150 C3
Mansell Street 149 J6
Mansfield Mews 147 D6
Mansfield Street 147 D6
Mansion House Place 149 H6
Mansion House Street 149 H6
Manson Mews 150 B3
Manson Place 150 B3
Maple Place 147 E6
Maple Street 147 E6
Marble Arch 147 C5
Marchmont Street 148 F7
Margaret Court 147 E6
Margaret Street 147 E6
Margaretta Terrace 150 C2
Margery Street 148 G7
Market Court 147 E6
Market Mews 147 D5
Market Place 147 E6
Markham Square 151 C3
Markham Street 151 C3
Mark Lane 149 J5
Mark Street 149 J7
Marlborough Road 147 E5
Marlborough Street 150 C3
Marloes Road 150 A4
Marshall Street 147 E6
Marsham Street 152 E3
Martin Lane 149 H5
Martlett Court 148 F6
Mart Street 148 F5
Marylebone High Street 147 D6
Marylebone Lane 147 D6
Marylebone Mews 147 D6
Marylebone Passage 147 E6
Marylebone Road 147 C6
Marylebone Street 147 D6
Marylee Way 152 F3
Mason's Arms Mews 147 D5
Mason's Place 149 H7
Mason's Yard 147 E5
Matthew Parker Street 152 E4
Maunsel Street 152 E3
106 Mays Court 148 F5
Mayfair Place 147 D5
Mays Court 148 F5
107 Mc Auley Close 152 G4
Mcleod's Mews 150 A3
Meadow Mews 152 F2
Meadow Place 152 F2
Meadow Road 152 F2
Mead Row 152 G4
Meard Street 147 E5
Mecklenburgh Place 148 F7
Mecklenburgh Square 148 F7
Medway Street 152 E4
Meek Street 150 B2
Melbourne Place 148 F6
Melbury Place 146 C7
Melcombe Place 146 C6
Melcombe Street 147 D7
Melina Place 146 B7
Melon Place 150 A4
Melton Street 147 E7
102 Memel Court 149 H7
Memel Street 149 H7
Mepham Street 149 H5
Mercer Street 148 F6
Meredith Street 148 G7
Merrington Road 150 A2
Meymott Street 148 G5
Micawber Street 149 H7
Micklethwaite Road 150 A2
Middlesex Street 149 J6
Middle Street 149 H6
Middle Temple Lane 148 G5
Middleton Buildings 147 E6
Middle Yard 149 J5
103 Midford Place 147 E7
Midhope Street 148 F7
Midland Road 148 F7
Milborne Grove 150 B3
Miles Street 152 F2
Milk Street 149 H6
Millman Mews 148 F7
Millman Street 148 F7
Mills Court 149 J7
Mill Street 147 E5
Milman's Street 150 B2
Milner Street 151 C3
103 Milroy Walk 148 G5

Milton Street 149 H6
Milverton Street 152 G3
Mincing Lane 149 J5
Minera Mews 151 D3
Minories 149 J5
Mitchell Street 149 H7
Mitre Court 149 H6
Mitre Street 149 J6
Molyneux Street 146 C6
Moncorvo Close 150 C4
Monck Street 152 E4
Monkwell Square 149 H6
Monmouth Street 148 F6
Montagu Close 149 H5
Montague Street 148 F6
Montague Street 149 H6
Montagu Mansions 147 C6
Montagu Mews North 147 C6
Montagu Mews South 147 C6
Montagu Mews West 147 C6
Montagu Place 147 C6
Montagu Row 147 C6
Montagu Square 147 C6
Montagu Street 147 C6
Montclare Street 149 J7
Montford Place 152 G3
Montpelier Place 151 C4
Montpelier Square 151 C4
Montpelier Street 151 C4
Montpelier Terrace 151 C4
Montpelier Walk 151 C4
Montreal Place 148 F5
Montrose Place 151 D4
Monument Street 149 H5
Moore Street 151 C3
Moorfields 149 H6
Moorfields Highwalk 149 H6
Moorgate 149 H6
Moor Lane 149 H6
104 Moor Place 149 H6
Moor Street 147 E6
Mora Street 149 H7
Moravian Close 150 B2
Moreland Street 149 G7
Moreton Place 152 E3
Moreton Street 152 E3
Moreton Terrace 152 E3
105 Moreton Terrace Mews Nth 152 E3
Moreton Terrace Mews Sth 152 E3
Morgan's Lane 149 J5
Morley Street 152 G4
Morpeth Terrace 151 E3
Mortimer Market 147 E7
Mortimer Street 147 E6
Morton Mews 150 A3
Morwell Street 148 E6
Moscow Place 146 A5
Moscow Road 146 A5
Mossop Street 151 C3
Motcomb Street 151 D4
Mount Mills 149 H7
Mount Pleasant 148 G7
Mount Row 147 D5
Mount Street 147 D5
Moxon Street 147 D6
Mulberry Walk 150 B2
Mulready Street 146 C7
Mundy Street 149 J7
Munster Square 147 D7
Murphy Street 152 G4
Muscovy Street 149 J5
Museum Street 148 F6
Myddelton Passage 148 G7
Myddelton Square 148 G7
Myddelton Street 148 G7

N

Nantes Passage 149 J6
Nassau Street 147 E6
Navarre Street 149 J7
Neal Street 148 F6
Neal's Yard 148 F6
Neathouse Place 151 E3
Nelson Passage 149 H7
Netherton Grove 150 B2
Netley Street 147 E7
Nevern Place 150 A3
Nevern Road 150 A3
Nevern Square 150 A3
Neville Street 150 B3
Neville Terrace 150 B3
New Bond Street 147 D5
New Bridge Street 148 G6
New Broad Street 149 J6
Newburgh Street 147 E6
New Burlington Mews 147 E5
New Burlington Place 147 E5
New Burlington Street 147 E5
Newbury Street 149 H6
Newcastle Close 148 G6
Newcastle Place 146 B6
106 Newcastle Row 148 G7
New Cavendish Street 147 D6
New Change 149 H6
107 New Charles Street 149 H7
New Compton Street 148 E6
New Coventry Street 147 E5
New Fetter Lane 148 G6
Newgate Street 149 G6
New Gaulston Street 149 J6
Newham Terrace 152 G4
New Inn Broadway 149 J7
New Inn Street 149 J7
New Inn Yard 149 J7
New London Street 149 J6
Newman Passage 147 E6
Newman's Row 148 F6
Newman Street 147 E6
New North Place 149 J7
New North Road 149 H7
New North Street 148 F7
New Oxford Street 148 F6
Newport Court 148 E5
Newport Place 148 E5
New Quebec Street 147 C6
New Row 148 F5
New Square 148 F6
New Street 149 J6
New Street Square 148 G6
Newton Street 148 F6
New Turn Stile 148 F6
New Union Street 149 H6
Nicholas Lane 149 H5
Nicholson Street 149 G5
Nile Street 149 H7
Nine Elms Lane 151 E2
Noble Street 149 H6
Noel Street 147 E6
Norfolk Crescent 146 C6
Norfolk Place 146 B6
Norfolk Row 152 F3
Norfolk Square 146 B6
Norfolk Square Mews 146 B6
Norman Street 149 H7
Norris Street 147 E5
Northampton Buildings 148 G7
Northampton Road 148 G7
Northampton Square 149 H7
North Audley Street 147 D5
North Bank 146 C7
Northburgh Street 149 G7

North Carriage Drive 146 C5
Northcourt 147 E6
North Crescent 147 E6
North End Road 150 A2
North Gower Street 147 E7
Northington Street 148 F7
North Mews 148 F7
North Row 147 D5
North Tenter Street 149 J6
North Terrace 150 C4
Northumberland Alley 149 J6
Northumberland Avenue 148 F5
Northumberland Street 148 F5
North Wharf Road 146 B6
Northwick Close 146 B7
Northwick Terrace 146 B7
Norton Folgate 149 J6
Norwich Street 148 G6
Nottingham Court 148 F6
Nottingham Place 147 D6
Nottingham Street 147 D6
Nutford Place 146 C6

O

Oakden Street 152 G3
Oakey Lane 152 G4
Oakfield Street 150 B2
114 Oakley Gardens 151 C2
Oakley Street 150 C2
Oak Tree Road 146 C7
Oat Lane 149 H6
Observatory Gardens 150 A4
Offley Road 152 G2
Ogle Street 147 E6
Old Bailey 148 G6
Old Bargehouse Alley 148 G5
Old Barrack Yard 151 D4
Old Bond Street 147 E5
Old Broad Street 149 J6
Old Brompton Road 150 B3
Old Burlington Street 147 E5
Old Castle Street 149 J6
115 Old Cavendish Street 147 D6
Old Church Street 150 B2
Old Compton Street 147 E6
Old Court Place 150 A4
Old Gloucester Street 148 F6
Old Jewry 149 H6
Old Marylebone Road 146 C6
Old Nichol Street 149 J7
Old North Street 148 F6
Old Paradise Street 152 F3
Old Park Lane 147 D5
Old Pye Street 152 E4
Old Quebec Street 147 C6
Old Queen Street 152 E4
108 Old Seacoal Lane 148 G6
Old South Lambeth Road 152 F2
Old Square 148 G6
Old Street 149 H7
Oliver's Yard 149 H7
Olympia Yard 146 A5
Omeara Street 149 H5
Ongar Road 150 A2
Onslow Gardens 150 B3
Onslow Mews 150 B3
Onslow Mews East 150 B3
Onslow Square 150 B3
Onslow Street 148 G7
Orange Street 147 E5
109 Orange Yard 147 E6
Oratory Lane 150 B3
Orchardson Street 146 B7
Orchard Street 147 D6
Orde Hall Street 148 F6
Orme Court 146 A5
Orme Court Mews 146 A5
Orme Lane 146 A5
Orme Square 146 A5
Ormond Close 148 F6
Ormonde Gate 151 C3
Ormond Mews 148 F7
Ormond Yard 147 E5
Orsett Mews 146 A6
Orsett Street 152 F3
Orsett Terrace 146 B6
Osbert Street 152 E3
Osnaburgh Street 147 D7
Osnaburgh Terrace 147 D7
Ossington Buildings 147 D6
Ossulston Street 148 E7
Osten Mews 150 A4
Outer Circle 147 C7
Oval Place 152 F2
Oval Way 152 F2
Ovington Gardens 151 C4
Ovington Mews 151 C4
Ovington Square 151 C4
Ovington Street 151 C3
111 Owen's Court 148 G7
112 Owen's Row 148 G7
Oxendon Street 147 E5
Oxford Circus 147 E6
Oxford Circus Avenue 147 E6
113 Oxford Court 149 H5
Oxford Square 146 C6
Oxford Street 147 D6

P

Padbury Court 149 J7
Paddington Green 146 B6
Paddington Street 147 D6
Page Street 152 E3
Paget Street 148 G7
Pakenham Street 148 F7
Palace Avenue 150 A4
Palace Gate 150 B4
Palace Green 146 A5
Palace Street 151 E4
Palfrey Place 152 F2
Palissy Street 149 J7
Pall Mall 147 E5
Pall Mall East 148 E5
Pall Mall Place 147 E5
Palmer Street 152 E4
Pancras Lane 149 H6
Panton Street 147 E5
Panyer Alley 149 H6
Paradise Walk 151 C2
Pardon Street 149 G7
Paris Garden 148 G5
Park Close 151 C4
Park Crescent 147 D7
Park Crescent Mews East 147 D7
Park Crescent Mews West 147 D7
Parker Mews 148 F6
Parker Street 148 F6
Parkgate Road 151 C2
Park Lane 147 D5
Park Place 147 E5
Park Place Villas 146 B6
Park Road 146 C7
Park Square East 147 D7
Park Square Mews 147 D7
120 Park Square West 147 D7

Park Street 147 D5
Park Street 149 H5
Park Walk 150 B2
Park West Place 146 C6
Parliament Street 152 F4
Parry Street 152 F2
Pascal Street 152 E2
Passmore Street 151 D3
Paternoster Row 149 H6
Paternoster Square 149 G6
Pater Street 150 A4
Paton Street 149 H7
Paul Street 149 J7
Paultons Square 150 B2
Paultons Street 150 B2
Paveley Street 146 C7
Pavilion Road 151 C4
Pavilion Street 151 C4
Peabody Avenue 151 D3
Pearman Street 152 G4
Pear Place 152 G4
Pear Tree Court 148 G7
Pear Tree Street 149 H7
Peerless Street 149 H7
Pegasus Place 152 G2
Pelham Crescent 150 C3
Pelham Place 150 C3
Pelham Street 150 C3
Pelter Street 149 J7
114 Pemberton Row 148 G6
Pembroke Close 151 D4
Pembroke Mews 150 A4
Pembroke Road 150 A3
Pembroke Square 150 A4
Pembroke Villas 150 A3
Pembroke Walk 150 A3
Penfold Place 146 C6
Penfold Street 146 B7
Pennant Mews 150 A3
Penton Rise 148 F7
Penywern Road 150 A3
Pepys Street 149 J5
Percival Street 148 G7
Percy Circus 148 F7
Percy Mews 147 E6
Percy Passage 147 E6
115 Percy Street 147 E6
Perkins Rents 152 E4
Perry's Place 147 E6
Petersham Lane 150 B4
Petersham Mews 150 B4
Petersham Place 150 B4
Peter's Hill 149 H5
Peter's Lane 148 G6
Peter Street 147 E5
Peto Place 147 D7
Petty France 152 E4
Petyt Place 150 C2
Petyward 151 C3
Phene Street 151 C2
Philbeach Gardens 150 A3
Phillimore Gardens 150 A4
Phillimore Place 150 A4
Phillimore Walk 150 A4
Philpot Lane 149 J5
Phipp Street 149 J7
Phoenix Place 148 F7
Phoenix Road 147 E7
Phoenix Street 148 E6
Piccadilly 147 E5
Piccadilly Arcade 147 E5
Piccadilly Circus 147 E5
Piccadilly Place 147 E5
Pickard Street 149 G7
Pickering Mews 146 A6
Pickering Place 147 E5
Pickle Herring Street 149 J5
Picton Place 147 D6
Pilgrim Street 148 G6
Pimlico Road 151 D3
Pindar Street 149 J6
Pindock Mews 146 A7
Pine Street 148 G7
Pitfield Street 149 J7
Pitt's Court 149 J5
Pitt's Head Mews 147 D5
Pitt Street 150 A4
Platina Street 149 H7
Playhouse Yard 148 G6
Pleydell Street 148 G6
Plough Place 148 G6
Plough Yard 149 J7
Plumber's Place 148 G7
Plumtree Court 148 G6
Plympton Place 146 C7
Plympton Street 146 C7
Poets' Corner 152 F4
Poland Street 147 E6
Pollen Street 147 E6
Pollitt Drive 146 B7
Pomell Way 149 J6
Pond Place 150 C3
Ponsonby Place 152 E3
Ponsonby Terrace 152 E3
Ponton Road 152 E2
Pont Street 151 C4
Pont Street Mews 151 C4
Pooles Buildings 148 G7
Poppins Court 148 G6
118 Porchester Gardens 146 A5
Porchester Gardens Mews 146 A6
Porchester Mews 146 A6
Porchester Place 146 C6
Porchester Road 146 A6
Porchester Square 146 A6
Porchester Terrace 146 B5
Porchester Terrace North 146 A6
Porter Street 147 C6
Porteus Road 146 B6
Portland Mews 147 E6
Portland Place 147 D6
Portman Close 147 D6
Portman Mews South 147 D6
Portman Square 147 D6
Portman Street 147 D6
Portpool Lane 148 G6
Portsea Mews 146 C6
Portsea Place 146 C6
Portsmouth Street 148 F6
Portsoken Street 149 J6
Portugal Street 148 F6
Potters' Fields 149 J5
Poultry 149 H6
Powis Place 148 F7
Praed Mews 146 B6
Praed Street 146 B6
Pratt Walk 152 F3
Prescot Street 149 J6
President Street 149 H7
Price's Street 148 G5
Prideaux Place 148 F7
Prima Road 152 G2
Primrose Hill 148 G6
Primrose Street 149 J6
Prince Albert Road 146 C7
Prince Consort Road 150 B4
Princelet Street 149 J6
Prince of Wales Terrace 150 A4
Princes Arcade 147 E5
Princes Gardens 150 B4
Prince's Gate Mews 150 B4
120 Princes Mews 152 E4
Prince's Mews 152 F4

Princes Place 147 E5
Princes Street 147 D6
Prince's Street 149 H6
Princeton Street 148 F6
Printer Street 148 G6
Priory Walk 150 B3
Procter Street 148 F6
Providence Court 147 D5
Provost Street 149 H7
Pudding Lane 149 H5
Puddle Dock 148 G5
Puma Court 149 J6
Pump Court 148 G6

Q

Quadrant Arcade 147 E5
Quaker Street 149 J7
Quebec Mews 147 D6
Queen Anne Mews 147 D6
Queen Anne's Gate 152 E4
Queen Anne Street 147 D6
Queenhithe 149 H5
Queensberry Place 150 B3
Queensborough Mews 146 B5
Queensborough Passage 146 B5
Queensborough Way 150 B3
Queensbury Mews West 150 B3
Queensbury Way 150 B3
Queen's Elm Square 150 B3
Queen's Gardens 146 B5
Queen's Gate 150 B4
Queen's Gate Gardens 150 B4
Queen's Gate Mews 150 B4
Queen's Gate Place 150 B4
Queen's Gate Place Mews 150 B4
Queen's Gate Terrace 150 B4
Queens Mews 146 A5
Queen Square 148 F6
Queen Square Place 148 F6
Queenstown Road 151 D2
Queen Street 149 H5
Queen Street Place 149 H5
Queens Walk 147 E5
Queensway 146 A5
Queen Victoria Street 149 H5

R

Radley Mews 150 A4
Radnor Mews 146 B6
Radnor Place 146 C6
Radnor Street 149 H7
Radnor Walk 151 C3
Railway Approach 149 H5
Railway Place 149 J5
Rainsford Street 146 C6
Ralston Street 151 C3
Ramillies Place 147 E6
Ramillies Street 147 E6
Rampayne Street 152 E3
Randall Road 152 F3
Randall Row 152 F3
Randolph Avenue 146 A7
Randolph Crescent 146 B7
Randolph Mews 146 B7
Randolph Road 146 B7
Ranelagh Grove 151 D3
Ranelagh Road 152 E3
Rangoon Street 149 J6
Ranston Street 146 C7
Raphael Street 151 C4
Rathbone Place 147 E6
Rathbone Street 147 E6
Raven Road 152 F3
Ravey Street 149 J7
Rawlings Street 151 C3
122 Rawsthorne Place 148 G7
Rawstorne Street 148 G7
Ray Street 148 G7
Redan Place 146 A6
Redburn Street 151 C2
Redchurch Street 149 J7
Redcliffe Gardens 150 A2
Redcliffe Mews 148 G6
Redcliffe Place 150 B2
Redcliffe Road 150 B2
Redcliffe Square 150 A3
Redcliffe Street 150 A2
Redcross Way 149 H5
Redesdale Street 151 C3
Redfield Lane 150 A3
123 Redfield Mews 150 A3
Redhill Street 147 D7
Red Lion Court 148 G6
Red Lion Square 148 F6
Red Lion Street 148 F6
Red Place 147 D5
Reece Mews 150 B3
Reeves Mews 147 D5
Regency Street 152 E3
Regent Place 147 E5
Regent Square 148 F7
Regent Street 147 E5
Regnart Buildings 147 E7
Relton Mews 151 C4
Rembrandt Close 151 D3
Remnant Street 148 F6
Rennie Street 148 G5
Reston Place 150 B4
Rex Place 147 D5
Rhoda Street 149 J7
Richardson's Mews 147 E7
Richard's Place 151 C3
Richbell Place 148 F6
Richborne Terrace 152 F2
Richmond Buildings 147 E6
Richmond Mews 147 E6
Richmond Terrace 152 F4
Richmond Terrace Mews 152 F4
Rickett Street 150 A2
Ridgemount Gardens 147 E6
Ridgmount Place 147 E6
Ridgmount Street 147 E6
Riding House Street 147 E6
Rifle Court 152 G2
Riley Street 150 B2
125 Rising Sun Court 149 H6
Rita Road 152 F2
River Street 148 G7
Rivington Place 149 J7
Rivington Street 149 J7
Robert Adam Street 147 D6
Robert Close 146 B7
126 Roberts Mews 151 D4
127 Robert's Place 148 G7
Robert Street 147 D7
Robert Street 148 F5
Robinson Street 151 C2
Rochelle Street 149 J7
Rochester Mews 152 E4
Rochester Row 152 E3
Rochester Street 152 E4
128 Rochester Walk 149 H5
Rodmarton Street 147 D6
Roger Street 148 F7
Roland Gardens 150 B3
Roland Way 150 B3
Rolls Buildings 148 G6
Rolls Passage 148 G6

Romilly Street 147 E5
Romney Street 152 F4
Rood Lane 149 J5
Ropemaker Street 149 H6
Rosary Gardens 150 B3
Roscoe Street 149 H7
Rose Alley 149 H5
Rose and Crown Court 149 H6
Rose and Crown Yard 147 E5
Roseberry Square 148 G7
Rosebery Avenue 148 G7
Rosemoor Street 151 C3
Rose Street 148 F5
129 Rosetta Close 152 F2
Rosoman Street 148 G7
Rossmore Road 146 C7
Rotherham Walk 149 H5
Roupell Street 148 G5
Rowington Close 146 A6
Roxby Place 150 A2
Royal Arcade 147 E5
Royal Avenue 151 C3
130 Royal Exchange Avenue 149 H6
Royal Exchange Buildings 149 H6
Royal Hospital Road 151 C3
Royal Mint Street 149 J5
Royal Opera Arcade 147 E5
Royal Street 152 F4
Rugby Street 148 F7
131 Rupert Court 147 E5
Rupert Street 147 E5
Russell Court 147 E5
Russell Place 152 E3
Russell Square 148 F6
Russell Street 148 F5
Russia Row 149 H6
Rutherford Street 152 E3
132 Rutland Garden Mews 151 C4
Rutland Gardens 151 C4
Rutland Gate 150 C4
133 Rutland Gate Mews 151 C4
Rutland Mews East 150 C4
Rutland Mews South 151 C4
Rutland Street 150 C4
Ryder Court 147 E5
Ryder Street 147 E5
Ryder Yard 147 E5
Rysbrack Street 151 C4

S

Sackville Street 147 E5
Saffron Hill 148 G6
Saffron Street 148 G6
Sage Way 148 F7
Sail Street 152 F4
St Alban's Grove 150 A4
St Alban's Mews 146 B6
St Alban's Street 147 E5
St Alphage Garden 149 H6
St Alphage Highwalk 149 H6
St Andrew's Hill 148 G6
St Andrew's Place 147 D7
St Andrew Street 148 G6
St Anne's Court 147 E6
St Ann's Lane 152 E4
St Ann's Street 152 E4
St Anselm's Place 147 D5
St Barnabas Street 151 D3
St Botolph Street 149 J6
St Bride's Avenue 148 G6
St Bride's Passage 148 G6
St Bride Street 148 G6
St Chad's Place 148 F7
St Chad's Street 148 F7
St Christopher's Place 147 D6
St Clare Street 149 J6
St Cross Street 148 G6
St Dunstan's Alley 149 J5
St Dunstan's Hill 149 J5
St Dunstan's Lane 149 J5
St George's Drive 151 E3
St George's Lane 149 H5
St George's Square 152 E3
St George Street 147 D5
St Giles High Street 148 E6
St Giles Place 148 E6
St Helena Street 148 G7
St Helen's Place 149 J6
St James's Market 147 E5
St James's Place 147 E5
St James's Row 148 G7
St James's Square 147 E5
St James's Street 147 E5
St James's Walk 148 G7
St John's Lane 148 G6
St John's Square 148 G7
St John Street 148 G7
St John's Wood Road 146 B7
St Katherine's Row 149 J5
St Katherine's Way 149 J5
St Leonard's Terrace 151 C3
St Loo Avenue 151 C2
St Luke's Street 150 C3
St Margaret Street 152 F4
St Mark's grove 150 A2
St Mark Street 149 J6
St Martin's Court 147 E6
St Martin's Lane 148 F5
St Martin's Le Grand 148 H6
St Martin's Place 148 F5
St Martin's Street 148 E5
St Mary at Hill 149 J5
St Mary Avenue 149 J6
St Mary's Terrace 146 B6
135 St Matthew Street 152 E4
St Michael's Alley 149 H6
St Michael's Street 146 C6
St Olave's Court 149 H6
St Olave's Gardens 152 G3
St Oswald's Place 152 F3
St Oswulf Street 152 E3
St Paul's Church Yard 149 H6
136 St Peter's Alley 149 H6
St Petersburgh Mews 146 A5
St Petersburgh Place 146 A5
St Swithin's Lane 149 H5
St Thomas Street 149 H5
St Vincent Street 147 D6
Salamanca Place 152 G3
Salamanca Street 152 G3
Salem Road 146 A5
Sale Place 146 C6
Salisbury Court 148 G6
Salisbury Place 146 C6
Salisbury Square 148 G6
Salisbury Street 146 C7
Samford Street 146 C7
Sancroft Street 152 G3
Sandell Street 152 G4
Sandland Street 148 F6
Sandwich Street 148 F7
Sandy's Row 149 J6
Sanswalk 148 G7
Saunders Street 152 G3
Savage Gardens 149 J5
Saville Row 147 E5
Savona Street 151 E2
Savoy Court 148 F5
Savoy Hill 148 F5
Savoy Place 148 F5
Savoy Row 148 F5

Savoy Steps 148 F5
Savoy Street 148 F5
Savoy Walk 148 F5
Scala Street 147 E6
Scarborough Street 149 J6
Scarsdale Place 150 A4
Scarsdale Villas 150 A4
Sclater Street 149 J7
137 Scotswood Street 148 G7
Scott Ellis Gardens 146 B7
Scrutton Street 149 J7
Seacoal Lane 148 G6
Seaford Street 148 F7
Seagrave Road 150 A3
Seaton Place 147 E7
Sebastian Street 148 G7
Secker Street 148 G5
Sedding Street 151 D3
Seddon Street 148 F7
Sedlescombe Road 150 A2
Sedley Place 147 D6
Seething Lane 149 J5
Sekforde Street 148 G7
Sellon Mews 152 G3
Selwood Place 150 B3
Selwood Terrace 150 B3
Semley Place 151 D3
Senior Street 146 A6
138 Serjeants' Inn 148 G6
Serle Street 148 F6
Serpentine Road 146 C5
Seville Street 151 C4
Seward Street 149 H7
Seymour Mews 147 D6
Seymour Place 146 C6
Seymour Street 147 C6
Seymour Walk 150 B2
139 Shacklewell Street 149 J7
Shad Thames 149 J5
Shaftesbury Avenue 147 E5
Shaftesbury Mews 150 A4
Shafto Mews 151 C4
Shakomb Street 150 B2
Shaver's Place 147 E5
Shawfield Street 151 C3
Sheba Street 149 J7
Sheffield Street 148 F6
Sheffield Terrace 150 A5
Shelton Street 148 F6
Shepherd Close 147 D5
Shepherdess Place 149 H7
Shepherdess Walk 149 H7
Shepherd Market 147 D5
Shepherds Place 147 D5
Shepherd Street 147 D5
Sheraton Street 147 E6
Sherbourne Lane 149 H5
Sherlock Mews 147 D6
Sherwood Street 147 E5
Shillibeer Place 146 C6
Shirland Road 146 A7
Shoe Lane 148 G6
Shoreditch High Street 149 J7
Shorter Street 149 J5
Shorts Gardens 148 F6
Shouldham Street 146 C6
Shroton Street 146 C6
Sicilian Avenue 148 F6
Siddons Lane 147 C7
Sidford Place 152 G4
Sidmouth Street 148 F7
Sidney Close 150 B3
Silbury Street 149 H7
Silk Street 149 H6
Silver Place 147 E5
Singer Street 149 H7
142 Sise Lane 149 H6
Skin Market Place 149 H5
143 Skinner Place 151 D3
Skinners Lane 149 H5
Skinner Street 148 G7
Slaidburn Street 150 B2
Sleaford Stream 152 E2
Slingsby Place 148 F5
Sloane Avenue 151 C3
Sloane Court East 151 D3
Sloane Court West 151 D3
Sloane Gardens 151 D3
Sloane Square 151 D3
Sloane Street 151 C3
Sloane Terrace 151 D3
Smallbrook Mews 146 B6
Smart's Place 148 F6
Smithfield Street 148 G6
Smith's Court 147 E5
Smith Square 152 F4
Smith Street 151 C3
Smith Terrace 151 C3
Snowden Street 149 J7
Snow Hill 148 G6
Soho Square 147 E6
Soho Street 147 E6
Soley Mews 148 G7
Somers Crescent 146 C6
Southampton Buildings 148 G6
Southampton Place 148 F6
Southampton Row 148 F6
Southampton Street 148 F5
South Audley Street 147 D5
South Bolton Gardens 150 B3
South Carriage Drive 151 C4
South Crescent 147 E6
South Eaton Place 151 D3
South End 150 A4
South End Row 150 A4
South Island Place 152 G2
South Lambeth Road 152 F2
South Molton Lane 147 D6
South Molton Street 147 D6
South Parade 150 B3
South Place 149 H6
South Place Mews 149 H6
South Square 148 G6
South Street 147 D5
South Tenter Street 149 J5
South Terrace 150 C3
Southwark Bridge Road 149 H5
Southwark Street 149 H5
Southwell Gardens 150 A4
South Wharf Road 146 B6
Southwick Mews 146 B6
Southwick Place 146 C6
Southwick Street 146 C6
144 Southwick Yard 146 C6
145 Spafield Street 148 G7
Spanish Place 147 D6
Spear Mews 150 A3
Speedy Place 148 F7
Spencer Street 148 G7
Spenser Street 152 E4
Spital Square 149 J6
Sprimont Place 151 C3
Spring Gardens 148 F5
Spring Mews 147 C6
Spring Street 146 B6
Stables Way 152 G3
Stacey Street 148 E6
Stackhouse Street 151 C4
Stadium Street 150 B2
Stafford Place 151 E4
Stafford Street 147 E5
Stafford Terrace 150 A4

Staff Street 149 H7
Stag Place 151 E4
146 Stainer Street 149 H5
Staining Lane 149 H6
Stalbridge Street 146 C6
Stamford Street 148 G5
Stanbrook Court 147 E5
147 Standard Place 149 J7
Stanford Road 150 A4
Stanford Street 152 E3
Stanhope Gardens 150 B3
Stanhope Gate 147 D5
Stanhope Mews East 150 B3
Stanhope Mews South 150 B3
Stanhope Mews West 150 B3
Stanhope Place 146 C6
Stanhope Row 147 D5
Stanhope Street 147 E7
Stanhope Terrace 146 B5
Stanley Close 152 F2
148 Stannary Place 152 G3
Stannary Street 152 G3
149 Staple Inn 148 G6
Staple Inn Buildings 148 G6
Star Alley 149 J5
Starcross Street 147 E7
Star Street 146 C6
Star Yard 148 G6
Stationers' Hall Court 148 G6
Stephen Mews 147 E6
Stephenson Way 147 E7
Stephen Street 147 E6
Sterling Street 151 C4
Steward Street 149 J6
Stewart's Grove 150 C3
Steve Lane 149 H5
Stillington Street 152 E3
Stone Buildings 148 F6
Stonecutter Street 148 G6
Stoney Lane 149 J6
Stoney Street 149 H5
Store Street 147 E6
Storey's Gate 152 E4
Stourcliffe Street 146 C6
Strand 148 F5
Strand Lane 148 F5
Stratford Avenue 150 A4
Stratford Place 147 D6
Stratford Road 150 A4
Strathearn Place 146 C5
Stratton Street 147 D5
Streatham Street 148 F6
Strout's Place 149 J7
Strutton Gardens 152 E4
Strype Street 149 J6
150 Studio Place 151 C4
Stukeley Street 148 F6
Suffolk Lane 149 H5
Suffolk Place 147 E5
Suffolk Street 147 E5
Summers Street 148 G7
Sumner Place 150 B3
Sumner Place Mews 150 B3
Sumner Street 149 H5
151 Sunningdale Gardens 150 A4
Sun Street 149 J6
Sun Street Passage 149 J6
Surrey Street 148 F5
Sussex Gardens 146 B6
Sussex Mews East 146 B6
Sussex Mews West 146 B5
152 Sussex Place 146 B6
Sussex Place 146 B6
Sussex Place 146 C7
Sussex Square 146 B5
Sussex Street 151 D3
Sutherland Avenue 146 B7
Sutherland Avenue 146 A4
Sutherland Row 151 D3
Sutherland Street 151 D3
Sutton Row 147 E6
Swallow Passage 147 D6
Swallow Place 147 D6
Swallow Street 147 E5
Swanfield Street 149 J7
Swan Lane 149 H5
Swan Walk 151 C2
Swinton Place 148 F7
Swinton Street 148 F7
Sycamore Street 149 H7
Sydney Mews 150 B3
Sydney Place 151 C3
Sydney Street 150 C3
Symons Street 151 C3

T

Tabernacle Street 149 H7
Tachbrook Mews 151 E3
Tachbrook Street 152 E3
Tadema Road 150 B2
Talbot Square 146 B6
Talbot Yard 149 H5
Tallis Street 148 G5
Tamworth Street 150 A2
Tankerton Street 148 F7
153 Tanswell Street 152 G4
Taunton Mews 146 C7
Taunton Place 146 C7
Tavistock Place 148 F7
Tavistock Square 148 E7
Tavistock Street 148 F5
Taviton Street 147 E7
154 Tedworth Gardens 151 C3
Tedworth Square 151 C3
Telegraph Street 149 H6
Temple Avenue 148 G5
Temple Lane 148 G6
Temple Place 148 F5
Templeton Place 150 A3
Tenison Court 147 E5
Tenison Way 148 G5
Tenniel Close 146 A5
Tenterden Street 147 D6
Terminus Place 151 D4
Thackeray Street 150 A4
Thanet Street 148 F7
Thavie's Inn 148 G6
Thayer Street 147 D6
155 The Arches 148 F5
The Boltons 150 B3
The Broad Walk 146 A5
The Cut 148 G5
Theed Street 148 G5
The Little Boltons 150 B3
The Mall 147 E5
Theobald's Road 148 F6
The Parade 151 C2
The Sanctuary 152 E4
The Terrace 148 G6
The Vale 150 B2
Thirleby Road 152 E4
Thistle Grove 150 B3
Thoresby Street 149 H7
Thorndike Close 150 B2
Thorndike Street 152 E3
Thornhaugh Street 147 E7
Thornton Place 146 C6
Thrale Street 149 H5
Thrawl Street 149 J6
Threadneedle Street 149 H6

Three Kings Yard 147 D5
Three Nun Court 149 H6
Throgmorton Avenue 149 H6
Throgmorton Street 149 H6
Thurloe Close 150 C3
Thurloe Place 150 B3
Thurloe Place Mews 150 B3
Thurloe Square 150 B3
Thurloe Street 150 B3
Tilney Court 149 H7
Tilney Street 147 D5
Timber Street 149 H7
Tinworth Street 152 F3
157 Tisbury Court 147 E5
Titchborne Row 146 C6
Tite Street 151 C2
Tokenhouse Yard 149 H6
Tolmers Square 147 E7
Tomlinson Close 149 J7
Tompion Street 148 G7
Tonbridge Street 148 F7
Tooley Street 149 H5
Topaz Street 152 F3
Topham Street 148 G7
Tor Gardens 150 A4
Torrington Place 147 E7
Torrington Square 147 E7
Tothill Street 147 E6
Tottenham Court Road 147 E6
Tottenham Mews 147 E6
Tottenham Street 147 E6
Tower Bridge Approach 149 J5
Tower Bridge Road 149 J5
Tower Court 148 F6
Tower Hill 149 J5
158 Tower Street 149 H5
Toynbee Street 149 J6
Tradescant Road 152 F2
Trafalgar Square 148 F5
Transept Street 146 C6
Trebeck Street 147 D5
Trebovir Road 150 A3
Tregunter Road 150 B3
Trenchold Street 152 F2
Tresham Crescent 146 C7
159 Treveris Street 149 H5
Trevor Place 151 C4
Trevor Square 151 C4
Trevor Street 151 C4
Trigon Road 152 F2
Trinity Place 149 J5
Trinity Square 149 J5
Triton Square 149 H6
Trump Street 149 H6
Tryon Street 151 C3
Tudor Street 148 G5
Tufton Street 152 E4
Turks Row 151 C3
Turnagain Lane 148 G6
Turnmill Street 148 G6
Turpentine Lane 151 D3
Turville Street 149 J7
Tweezer's Alley 148 G5
Twyford Place 148 F6
Tyburn Way 147 C5
Tyers Street 152 F3
Tyers Terrace 152 F3
Tyne Street 149 J6
Tysoe Street 148 G7

U

Udall Street 152 E3
Ulster Place 147 D7
Undershaft 149 J6
Underwood Row 149 H7
Underwood Street 149 H7
160 Unicorn Passage 149 J5
Union Court 149 G5
Union Street 149 H5
Union Walk 149 J7
University Street 147 E7
Upbrook Mews 146 B6
Upper Belgrave Street 151 D4
Upper Berkeley Street 147 C6
Upper Brook Street 147 D5
Upper Cheyne Row 151 C2
Upper Grosvenor Street 147 D5
Upper Ground 148 G5
Upper Harley Street 147 D7
Upper James Street 147 E5
Upper John Street 147 E5
Upper Marsh 152 F4
Upper Montagu Street 146 C6
Upper Phillimore Gardens 150 A4
Upper St Martin's Lane 148 F5
Upper Tachbrook Street 152 E3
Upper Thames Street 148 G5
Upper Wimpole Street 147 D6
Upper Woburn Place 147 E7
Uverdale Road 150 B2

V

Vale Close 146 B7
Vandon Street 152 E4
Vandy Street 149 J7
Vane Street 152 E3
Vanston Place 150 A2
Varndell Street 147 E7
Vauxhall Bridge Road 152 E3
Vauxhall Cross 152 F2
Vauxhall Grove 152 F2
Vauxhall Street 152 F3
Vauxhall Walk 152 F3
Venables Street 146 C6
Vere Street 147 D6
Vernon Place 148 F6
Vernon Rise 148 F7
Vernon Square 148 F7
Vestry Street 149 H7
Viaduct Buildings 148 G6
Vicarage Gardens 146 A5
Vicarage Gate 150 A4
Victoria Embankment 148 F5
Victoria Grove 150 B4
Victoria Road 150 B4
Victoria Square 151 D4
Victoria Street 152 E4
Vigo Street 147 E5
Villiers Street 148 F5
Vincent Square 152 E3
Vincent Street 152 E3
Vine Court 149 J6
Vine Hill 148 G7
Vine Lane 149 J5
Vine Street 147 E5
Vinery Villas 146 C7
Vineyard Walk 148 G7
Vintners Place 149 H5
Virgil Place 146 C6
161 Virgil Street 152 F4
Virginia Road 149 J7
Viscount Street 149 H7

W

Warthman Street 148 G6
Wakefield Street 148 F7
Wakley Street 148 G7
Walberswick Street 152 F2
Walbrook 149 H5
Walcott Square 152 G3
Walham Grove 150 A2
Walker's Court 147 E5
Walmer Place 146 C6
Walmer Street 146 C6
Walnut Tree Walk 152 G3
Walpole Street 151 C3
Walton Close 152 F2
Walton Street 151 C4
Wandon Road 150 A2
Wandsworth Road 152 F2
Wansdown Place 150 A2
Wardens Grove 149 H5
Wardour Mews 147 E6
Wardour Street 147 E6
Wardrobe Place 149 G6
162 Wardrobe Terrace 148 G5
Warner Street 148 G7
Warner Yard 148 G7
Warren Mews 147 E7
Warren Street 147 E7
Warrington Crescent 146 B7
Warrington Gardens 146 B7
Warwick Avenue 146 B7
Warwick Court 148 F6
Warwick Crescent 146 B6
Warwick House Street 147 E5
Warwick Lane 149 G6
Warwick Place 146 B6
Warwick Road 150 A3
Warwick Row 151 D4
Warwick Square 148 G6
Warwick Square 151 E3
Warwick Square Mews 151 E3
Warwick Street 147 E5
Warwick Way 151 E3
Watergate 148 G5
Watergate Walk 148 F5
Waterloo Place 147 E5
Waterloo Road 152 G4
Waterloo Road 148 G5
Waterson Street 149 J7
Watling Court 149 H6
Watling Street 149 H6
Watson's Mews 146 C6
Waverton Street 147 D5
Weaver's Lane 149 J5
Weighhouse Street 147 D6
Weir's Passage 147 E7
Welbeck Street 147 D6
Welbeck Way 147 D6
Well Court 149 H6
Wellesley Terrace 149 H7
Wellington Road 146 C7
Wellington Row 149 J7
Wellington Square 151 C3
Wellington Street 148 F5
Wells Mews 147 E6
Wells Square 148 F7
Wells Street 147 E6
Wells Way 150 B4
Wentworth Street 149 J6
Wesley Street 147 D6
Westbourne Crescent 146 B5
Westbourne Gardens 146 A6
Westbourne Grove 146 A6
Westbourne Grove Terrace 146 A6
Westbourne Park Mews 146 A6
Westbourne Terrace 146 B5
Westbourne Terrace Mews 146 B6
Westbourne Terrace Road 146 B6
West Carriage Drive 146 C5
West Central Street 148 F6
West Cromwell Road 150 A3
165 West Eaton Place Mews 151 D3
Westgate Terrace 150 A2
West Halkin Street 151 D4
West Harding Street 148 G6
Westland Place 149 H7
166 West Mews 151 E3
Westminster Bridge Road 152 G4
Westminster Buildings 149 H6
Westmoreland Place 151 D3
Westmoreland Street 147 D6
Westmoreland Terrace 151 D3
Weston Street 149 J5
West Poultry Avenue 148 G6
West Road 151 C3
West Smithfield 148 G6
West Street 148 E6
West Tenter Street 149 J6
West Warwick Place 151 E3
Westway 146 B6
Wetherby Gardens 150 B3
Wetherby Mews 150 A3
Wetherby Place 150 B3
Weymouth Mews 147 D6
Weymouth Street 147 D6
Wharf Road 149 H7
Wharton Street 148 F7
Wheatley Street 147 D6
Wheatsheaf Lane 152 F2
167 Wheler Street 149 J7
Whetstone Park 148 F6
168 Whichcote Street 148 G5
Whidborne Street 148 F7
Whinsland Street 146 B6
Whiskin Street 148 G7
Whitby Street 149 J7
Whitcomb Court 147 E5
Whitcomb Street 147 E5
Whitechapel High Street 149 J6
Whitecross Place 149 H6
Whitecross Street 149 H7
Whitefriars Street 148 G6
169 Whitehall 148 F5
Whitehall Court 148 F5
Whitehall Gardens 148 F5
Whitehall Place 148 F5
White Hart Yard 149 H5
Whitehaven Street 146 C7
Whitehead's Grove 151 C3
170 White Horse Alley 148 G6
White Horse Street 147 D5
White Kennett Street 149 J6
White Lion Hill 149 H6
White Lion Yard 147 D5
White's Row 149 J6
Whitfield Place 147 E7
Whitfield Street 147 E6
Whitgift Street 152 F3
171 Whiting Street 152 G4
Whittington Alley 149 H6
Whittlesey Street 148 G5
Wickham Street 152 F3
Wicklow Street 148 F7
Widegate Street 149 J6
Wigmore Place 147 D6
Wigmore Street 147 D6
Wigton Place 152 G3
Wilbraham Place 151 D3
Wilcox Road 152 F2
Wild Court 148 F6

Wild Street 148 F6
Wilfred Street 151 E4
Wilkes Street 149 J6
William IV Street 148 F5
William Mews 151 C4
William Road 147 E7
William Street 151 C4
Willoughby Street 148 F6
Willow Place 152 E3
Willow Street 149 J7
Wilmington Square 148 G7
Wilmington Street 148 G7
Wilson Street 149 H6
151 Wilton Crescent 151 D4
Wilton Mews 151 D4
Wilton Place 151 D4
Wilton Road 151 E3
Wilton Row 151 D4
Wilton Street 151 D4
Wilton Terrace 151 D4
Wimpole Mews 147 D6
Wimpole Street 147 D6
Winchester Street 149 H5
Winchester Street 151 D3
Winchester Walk 149 H5
Wincott Street 152 G3
Windmill Row 152 G3
Windmill Street 147 E6
Windsor Terrace 149 H7
Wine Office Court 148 G6
172 Winnett Street 147 E5
Winsland Mews 146 B6
173 Winsland Street 146 B6
Winsley Street 147 E6
Winsor Place 152 E3
Winterton Place 150 B2
Withers Place 149 H7
Woburn Place 148 F7
Woburn Square 148 E7
Woburn Walk 148 E7
Woodbridge Street 148 G7
Woodfall Street 151 C3
Woodseer Street 149 J6
Woods Mews 147 D5
Woodstock Mews 147 D6
Woodstock Street 147 D6
Wood Street 149 H6
Wootton Street 148 G5
Worgan Street 152 F3
World's End Passage 150 B2
Wormwood Street 149 J6
Worship Street 149 J7
Wren Street 148 F7
Wright's Lane 150 A4
Wybert Street 147 E7
Wyclif Street 148 G7
Wynard Terrace 152 F3
Wyndham Mews 146 C6
Wyndham Place 146 C6
Wyndham Street 146 C6
Wyndham Yard 146 C6
Wynstay Gardens 150 A4
Wynyatt Street 148 G7
Wythburn Place 146 C6
Wyvil Road 152 F2

Y

Yardley Street 148 G7
Yarmouth Place 147 D5
Yeoman's Row 151 C4
York Bridge 147 D7
York Buildings 148 F5
York Gate 147 D7
York House Place 150 A4
York Place 148 F5
York Road 152 F4
York Street 147 C6
York Terrace East 147 D7
York Terrace West 147 D7
Young Street 150 A4

Z

Zoar Street 149 H5

Index to 1:250 000 Scale Maps

Content

The Index lists all the definitive names shown in the map section of the Atlas. For each entry the Atlas page number is listed and the National Grid map reference is given to the nearest kilometre of the feature to which the name applies.

For long linear features, such as the River Thames, more than one reference is given. For these multiple entries and where a name applies to more than one feature the County, Region or Island Area name is also given.

Abbreviations used in the Index to identify the nature of certain named features and abbreviations for Counties used in the Index are also listed.

Method of Listing Names

Names are listed alphabetically in the Index as they appear on the map. For example, 'Ashdown Forest' appears under 'A', while 'Forest of Bere' is under 'F'. Similarly, 'Beaulieu River' appears under 'B' but 'River Thames' is under 'R'. When the definite article precedes a name, the name appears first. Thus, 'The Wash' becomes 'Wash, The' and is listed under 'W'. An exception to this rule is made in the case of Gaelic and Welsh place names. These are listed under the initial letter of the Gaelic or Welsh definite article. For example, 'An Ceannaich' is listed under 'A', and 'Y Llethr' is listed under 'Y'.

Example Use of Index

To find Dorking refer to the name in the index and read off the reference 28TQ1649. The first number indicates that Dorking is shown on page 28. The remaining two letters and four figures signify that the town lies within the 100 kilometre square TQ (see diagram on page 6) and is 16 kilometres east and 49 kilometres north of the south west corner of the square. The 10 kilometre grid numbers '1' and '4' are shown on the edges of page 28 and the exact location of Dorking is found by estimating '6' tenths eastward from the grid line '1' and '9' tenths northwards from the grid line '4'. In the National Grid Reference system the Eastings (16 for Dorking) are always stated before the Northings (49 for Dorking).

Features can thus be located on the Atlas pages by referring to the page number and grid number only; the two letters are required for the full grid reference to locate a feature on any map which shows the National Grid.

List of County Names Showing Abbreviations Used in this Index

England

Avon	Avon
Bedfordshire	Beds.
Berkshire	Berks.
Buckinghamshire	Bucks.
Cambridgeshire	Cambs.
Cheshire	Ches.
Cleveland	Cleve.
Cornwall	Corn.
Cumbria	Cumbr.
Derbyshire	Derby.
Devon	Devon
Dorset	Dorset
Durham	Durham
East Sussex	E Susx
Essex	Essex
Gloucestershire	Glos.
Greater London	Gtr London
Greater Manchester	Gtr Mches.
Hampshire	Hants.
Hereford and Worcester	Here. and Worc.
Hertfordshire	Herts.
Humberside	Humbs.
Isle of Wight	I. of W.
Kent	Kent
Lancashire	Lancs.
Leicestershire	Leic.
Lincolnshire	Lincs.
Merseyside	Mers.
Norfolk	Norf.
North Yorkshire	N Yorks.
Northamptonshire	Northants.
Northumberland	Northum.
Nottinghamshire	Notts.
Oxfordshire	Oxon.
Shropshire	Shrops.
Somerset	Somer.
South Yorkshire	S Yorks.
Staffordshire	Staffs.
Suffolk	Suff.
Surrey	Surrey
Tyne and Wear	Tyne and Wear
Warwickshire	Warw.
West Midlands	W Mids
West Sussex	W Susx
West Yorkshire	W Yorks
Wiltshire	Wilts.

Wales

Clwyd	Clwyd
Dyfed	Dyfed
Gwent	Gwent
Gwynedd	Gwyn.
Mid Glamorgan	Mid Glam.
Powys	Powys
South Glamorgan	S Glam.
West Glamorgan	W Glam.

Other Areas

Isle of Man	I. of M.
Isles of Scilly	Is. of Sc.

Region and Islands Area Names
Scotland

Regions

Borders	Borders
Central	Central
Dumfries and Galloway	Dumf. and Galwy.
Fife	Fife
Grampian	Grampn.
Highland	Highld.
Lothian	Lothian
Strathclyde	Strath.
Tayside	Tays.

Islands areas

Orkney	Orkney
Shetland	Shetld.
Western Isles	W Isles

Abbreviations which are used in this Index to identify the nature of certain named features

ant.	Antiquity
chan.	Channel or arm of the sea
dist.	District or name of an area
is.	Island
mt.	Mountain, mount or hill
pt.	Point or headland on coast
sbk.	Sandbank

Abbas Combe

Alphington

A

Abbas Combe 25 ST 7022
Abberley 49 SO 7567
Abberley Hill 49 SO 7566
Abberton (Essex) 39 TM 0019
Abberton (Here. and Worc.) 50 SO 9953
Abberton Reservoir 39 TL 9818
Abberwick 91 NU 1213
Abbess Roding 37 TL 5711
Abbey 24 ST 1410
Abbey Brook 70 SK 1892
Abbey Burn 95 NS 9353
Abbeycwmhir 57 SO 0571
Abbey Dore 45 SO 3830
Abbey Head 87 NX 7343
Abbey Hulton 59 SJ 9148
Abbey St. Bathans 96 NT 7662
Abbeystead 77 SD 5654
Abbeytown 82 NY 1750
Abbey Wood 37 TQ 4779
Abbotrule 90 NT 6112
Abbots Bickington 22 SS 3813
Abbots Bromley 60 SK 0824
Abbotsbury 25 SY 5785
Abbotsford 96 NT 5034
Abbotsham 22 SS 4226
Abbotside Common 83 SD 8196
Abbotskerswell 21 SX 8569
Abbots Langley 36 TL 0902
Abbots Leigh 33 ST 5473
Abbotsley 53 TL 2256
Abbots Morton 50 SP 0255
Abbots Ripton 53 TL 2377
Abbot's Salford 50 SP 0650
Abbot's Way (ant.) 21 SX 6266
Abbotswood 26 SU 3722
Abbotts Ann 34 SU 3243
Abdon 48 SO 5786
Aber (Dyfed) 43 SN 4748
Aber (Gwyn.) 67 SH 6572
Aberaeron 56 SN 4562
Aberaman 41 SO 0101
Aberangell 57 SH 8409
Aberarder 116 NH 6225
Aberarder Forest 116 NN 4888
Aberargie 108 NO 1615
Aberarth 56 SN 4763
Aber-banc 43 SN 3541
Aberbargoed 41 SO 1500
Aberbeeg 41 SO 2102
Abercanaid 41 SO 0503
Abercarn 41 ST 2195
Abercegir 57 SH 8001
Aberchalder 115 NH 3403
Aberchalder Burn 116 NH 5618
Aberchalder Forest 115 NN 3499
Aberchirder 121 NJ 6252
Abercraf 41 SN 8212
Abercrombie 103 NO 5102
Abercych 43 SN 2441
Abercynon 41 ST 0894
Aberdalgie 108 NO 0720
Aberdare 41 SO 0002
Aberdaron 56 SH 1726
Aberdeen 119 NJ 9305
Aberdeen Airport 119 NJ 8712
Aberdour 102 NT 1885
Aberdovey Bar 56 SN 5994
Aberdulais 41 SS 7799
Aberdyfi 56 SN 6196
Aber Dysynni 56 SH 5603
Aberedw 44 SO 0747
Abereiddy 42 SM 7931
Abererch 66 SH 3936
Aber Falls 67 SH 6669
Aberfan 41 SO 0700
Aberfeldy 108 NN 8549
Aberffraw 66 SH 3568
Aberffrwd 57 SN 6878
Aberford 79 SE 4336
Aberfoyle 101 NN 5200
Abergavenny 45 SO 2914
Abergeldie Castle 117 NO 2895
Abergele 67 SH 9477
Abergele Roads 67 SH 9379
Abergorlech 43 SN 5833
Abergwesyn 44 SN 8552
Abergwili 43 SN 4421
Abergwynant 57 SH 6717
Abergwynfi 41 SS 8996
Abergynolwyn 57 SH 6706
Aberhosan 57 SN 8197
Aberkenfig 41 SS 8983
Aberlady 103 NT 4679
Aberlady Bay 103 NT 4581
Aberlemno 109 NO 5255
Aberllefenni 57 SH 7609
Abermenai Point 66 SH 4461
Abermeurig 43 SN 5655
Abermule 58 SO 1694
Abernaint 58 SJ 1221
Abernant (Dyfed) 43 SN 3423
Aber-nant (Mid Glam.) 41 SO 0103
Abernethy 108 NO 1816
Abernethy Forest 117 NH 9918
Abernyte 108 NO 2531
Aberporth 43 SN 2651
Aberporth Airfield 43 SN 2549
Aberscross 129 NC 7600
Abersoch 56 SH 3128
Abersychan 45 SO 2704
Abertillery 41 SO 2104
Abertridwr (Mid Glam.) 41 ST 1289
Abertridwr (Powys) 57 SJ 0319
Abertysswg 41 SO 1305
Aberuthven 108 NN 9715
Aberyscir 41 SN 9929
Aberystwyth 56 SN 5881
Abhainn a'Bhealaich 100 NM 9506
Abhainn a' Chadh' Bhuidhe 127 NH 1367
Abhainn a' Choilich 115 NH 0824
Abhainn a' Choire 132 NC 3526
Abhainn a' Gharbh Choire 123 NG 8769
Abhainn a' Ghiubhais Lì 127 NH 2471
Abhainn a' Ghlinne Bhig 123 NG 8217
Abhainn a' Ghlinne Bhig 127 NH 3484
Abhainn an Fhasaigh 126 NH 0267
Abhainn an Loin 132 NC 3241
Abhainn an t-Sratha' Chàrnaig 129 NH 7198
Abhainn an t-Srathain 132 NC 2362
Abhainn an t-Srath Chuileannaich 128 NH 4393
Abhainn Bearraray 130 NB 0514
Abhainn Beinn nan Eun 128 NH 4673
Abhainn Bràigh-horrisdale 123 NG 8167
Abhainn Bruachaig 127 NH 0763
Abhainn Cam Linne 106 NM 9723
Abhainn Chòsaidh 114 NG 9201
Abhainn Chuaig 123 NG 7256
Abhainn Crò Chlach 116 NH 6205
Abhainn Cuileig 127 NH 1776
Abhainn Dalach 106 NN 0341
Abhainn Deabhag 115 NH 2724
Abhainn Dearg 126 NG 8847
Abhainn Droma 127 NH 2276
Abhainn Dubh (Highld.) 123 NG 7851
Abhainn Dubh (Highld.) 127 NH 0657
Abhainn Duibhe 107 NN 4253
Abhainn Fionain 106 NM 9518
Abhainn Geiraha 131 NB 5150
Abhainn Ghlas 98 NR 3166
Abhainn Ghleann Iubharnadeal 98 NR 4570
Abhainn Mhòr (Strath.) 99 NR 7377
Abhainn Mhòr (Strath.) 99 NR 7571
Abhainn na Clach Airigh 132 NC 1420
Abhainn na Cuile 99 NR 8269
Abhainn na Frithe 134 NC 8226
Abhainn na Glasa 128 NH 4579
Abhainn Rath 106 NN 2868
Abhainn Sgeamhaidh 133 NC 5616
Abhainn Sithidh 115 NH 0624
Abhainn Srath na Sealga 127 NH 0780
Abhainn Thràil 126 NG 9153
A'Bhrideanach (pt.) 110 NM 2999
A' Bhuidheanach Bheag 116 NN 6677
Abingdon 47 SU 4997
Abinger Common 28 TQ 1145
Abington 95 NS 9323
Abington Pigotts 53 TL 3044
Ab Kettleby 61 SK 7223
Ablington 46 SP 1007
Abney 70 SK 1979
Aboyne 119 NO 5298
Abram 69 SD 6001
Abriachan 116 NH 5535
Abridge 37 TQ 4696
Abthorpe 51 SP 6446
Abune-the-Hill 136 HY 2928
Aby 73 TF 4178
Acairseid Falaich 112 NF 8537
Acarsaid 111 NM 5871
Acaster Malbis 79 SE 5845
Acaster Selby 79 SE 5741
Accrington 78 SD 7528
Acha 110 NM 1854
Achachork 123 NG 4746
Achaglachgach Forest 99 NR 8064
Achahoish 99 NR 7877
A' Chailleach (Highld.) (mt.) 127 NH 1371
A' Chailleach (Highld.) (mt.) 116 NH 6804
A' Chailleach Am Bodach (pt.) 132 NC 2473
Achairn Burn 135 ND 2949
Achalader (Tays.) 108 NO 1245
Achallader (Strath.) 106 NN 3244
Achaluachrach 133 NC 6709
Achanalt 127 NH 2561
Achanamara 99 NR 7887
Achandunie 128 NH 6472
Ach' an Todhair 106 NN 0972
Achany 128 NC 5601
Achany Glen 128 NC 5704
Achaphubuil 115 NN 0875
Acharacle 111 NM 6767
Acharn (Highld.) 111 NM 7050
Acharn (Tays.) 107 NN 7543
Acharosson Burn 100 NR 9376
Achath 119 NJ 7311
Achavanich 135 ND 1742
Achduart 127 NC 0403
Achentoul 134 NC 8733
Achentoul Forest 134 NC 8638
Achfary 132 NC 2939
Achgarve 126 NG 8893
Achiemore (Highld.) 132 NC 3667
Achiemore (Highld.) 134 NC 8958
A' Chill 110 NG 2705
Achiltibuie 126 NC 0208
Achina 133 NC 7060
Achinduich 128 NC 5800
Achingills 135 ND 1663
Achinhoan Head 92 NR 7617
Achintee (Highld.) 126 NG 9441
Achintraid 123 NG 8438
Achintree House 115 NN 1273
Achleck 105 NM 4145
A'Chleit (Highld.) (is.) 132 NC 0320
A'Chlèit (Island of Mull) 105 NM 4118
A'Chlèit (Strath.) (pt.) 92 NR 6841
Achlyness 132 NC 2452
Achmelvich 132 NC 0524
Achmelvich Bay 132 NC 0525
Achmore (Central) 107 NN 5832
Achmore (Highld.) 123 NG 8533
Achmore (Isle of Lewis) 131 NB 3129
Achnaba 106 NM 9436
Achnacarnin 132 NC 0431
Achnacarry 115 NN 1787
Achnacloish 111 NG 5908
Achnacroish 105 NM 8541
Achnadrish 111 NM 4551
Achnagarron 128 NH 6870
Achnaha 111 NM 4668
Achnahanat 128 NH 5198
Achnahannet 117 NH 9727
Achnasaul 115 NN 1589
Achnasheen 127 NH 1658
Achnashellach Forest 126 NH 0247
Achnastank 117 NJ 2733
Achosnich 111 NM 4467
A' Chràlaig 115 NH 0914
Achranich 105 NM 7047
Achray Forest 101 NN 5103
Achreamie 135 ND 0166
Achriabhach 106 NN 1468
Achriesgill 132 NC 2554
A'Chruach (Isle of Arran) 92 NR 9633
A'Chruach (Strath.) 106 NM 9021
A'Chruach (Strath.) 92 NR 6110
A'Chruach (Strath.) 92 NR 7630
A Chruach (Tays.) 107 NN 3756
Achurch 52 TL 0283
Achuvoldrach 133 NC 5659
Achvaich 129 NH 7194
Achvarasdal 134 NC 9864
Achvarasdal Burn 134 NC 9862
Ackergill 135 ND 3553
Ackergill Tower 135 ND 3554
Acklam (Cleve.) 85 NZ 4817
Acklam (N Yorks.) 80 SE 7861
Ackleton 59 SO 7798
Acklington 91 NU 2201
Ackton 79 SE 4121
Ackworth Moor Top 71 SE 4316
Acle 65 TG 3910
Acock's Green 50 SP 1383
Acol 31 TR 3067
Acomb 90 NY 9366
Aconbury 45 SO 5133
Acre 78 SD 7824
Acrefair 58 SJ 2743
Acrise Place 31 TR 1942
Acton (Ches.) 59 SJ 6253
Acton (Gtr London) 37 TQ 2080
Acton (Shrops.) 48 SO 3184
Acton (Suff.) 54 TL 8945
Acton Beauchamp 49 SO 6750
Acton Bridge 69 SJ 5975
Acton Burnell 59 SJ 5301
Acton Green 49 SO 6950
Acton Pigott 59 SJ 5402
Acton Round 59 SO 6395
Acton Scott 48 SO 4589
Acton Trussell 59 SJ 9317
Acton Turville 33 ST 8080
Adbaston 59 SJ 7627
Adber 25 ST 5920
Adderbury 47 SP 4635
Adderley 59 SJ 6639
Adderstone 97 NU 1330
Addiewell 102 NS 9962
Addingham 78 SE 0749
Addington (Bucks.) 51 SP 7428
Addington (Kent) 30 TQ 6659
Addlestone 36 TQ 0464
Addlethorpe 73 TF 5469
Adeney 59 SJ 6918
Adfa 57 SJ 0501
Adforton 48 SO 4071
Adisham 31 TR 2253
Adlestrop 47 SP 2427
Adlingfleet 74 SE 8421
Adlington (Ches.) 69 SJ 9180
Adlington (Lancs) 69 SD 6013
Admaston (Shrops.) 59 SJ 6313
Admaston (Staffs.) 60 SK 0423
Admington 50 SP 1945
Adstock 51 SP 7329
Adstone 51 SP 5951
Adventurers' Fen 53 TL 5668
Advie 117 NJ 1234
Adwell 36 SU 6899
Adwick le Street 71 SE 5308
Adwick upon Dearne 71 SE 4601
Adziel 121 NJ 9453
Ae Village 88 NX 9889
Affleck 121 NJ 8623
Affleck Castle (ant.) 109 NO 4938
Affpuddle 25 SY 8093
Afon Aeron 43 SN 5757
Afon Afan 41 SS 8195
Afon Aled 67 SH 9570
Afon Alwen 67 SJ 0244
Afon Banwy neu Einion 58 SJ 1307
Afon Bidno 57 SN 8584
Afon Biga 57 SN 8589
Afon Cain 58 SJ 1618
Afon Cefni 66 SH 4370
Afon Ceirw 67 SH 9247
Afon Cennen 43 SN 6318
Afon Cerist 57 SH 8416
Afon Claerwen 57 SN 8664
Afon Cledwen 67 SH 8762
Afon Clywedog 57 SN 8890
Afon Cothi 43 SN 6033
Afon Cynin 43 SN 2621
Afon Cywyn 43 SN 3114
Afon Ddu 67 SH 7464
Afon Duad 43 SN 3729
Afon Dugoed 57 SH 9012
Afon Dulas (Gwyn.) 57 SH 7508
Afon Dulas (Powys) 57 SN 7699
Afon Dulyn 67 SH 7267
Afon Dwyfach 66 SH 4746
Afon Dwyfor 66 SH 4941
Afon Dyfi 57 SH 8715
Afon Dysynni 57 SH 6206
Afon Eden 67 SH 7029
Afon Gamlan 57 SH 6924
Afon Glaslyn 66 SH 5941
Afon Gronw 43 SN 2119
Afon Gwy 45 ST 5398
Afon Gwydderig 41 SN 8431
Afon Honddu 45 SO 2925
Afon Leri 57 SN 6588
Afon Llafar 67 SH 8535
Afon Lliw 40 SS 5999
Afon Llugwy 67 SH 6860
Afon Llwchwr 40 SS 4996
Afon Llynfi 41 SO 1331
Afon Lwyd 57 SN 8590
Afon Machno 67 SH 7748
Afon Marteg 57 SN 9974
Afon Mawddach 57 SH 7220
Afon Mellte 41 SN 9209
Afon Mynwy 45 SO 4717
Afon Nyfer 42 SN 1237
Afon Porth-llwyd 67 SH 7365
Afon Rheidol 57 SN 6778
Afon Rhiw 57 SJ 0200
Afon Senni 41 SN 9224
Afon Syfynwy 42 SN 0324
Afon Taf 43 SN 2116
Afon Tanat 58 SJ 1424
Afon Teifi 43 SN 5346
Afon Trannon 57 SN 9890
Afon Troddi (River Trothy) 45 SO 4314
Afon Tryweryn 67 SH 8839
Afon Twrch (Dyfed) 43 SN 6445
Afon Twrch (Dyfed) 41 SN 7715
Afon Twrch (Powys) 57 SH 9714
Afon Twymyn 57 SN 8797
Afon Tywi 43 SN 6624
Afon Vyrnwy 58 SJ 1614
Afon Wnion 57 SH 8021
Afon Yscir 41 SN 9934
Afon Ystrad 67 SJ 0162
Afon Ystwyth 57 SN 6276
Afton Bridgend 88 NS 6212
Afton Resr. 88 NS 6304
Afton Water 88 NS 6307
Agden Resr. 71 SK 2592
Agglethorpe 78 SE 0886
A' Ghairbhe 126 NH 0158
A' Ghlas-bheinn 114 NH 0023
A' Ghoil 132 NC 3571
Aigas Forest 128 NH 4341
Aignish 131 NB 4832
Aike 74 TA 0445
Aiker Ness (Orkney) 136 HY 3826
Aikerness (Westray) 138 HY 4552
Aikers 136 ND 4590
Aiketgate 83 NY 4846
Aikton 82 NY 2753
Ailey 45 SO 3348
Ailsa Craig 86 NX 0199
Ailsworth 62 TL 1199
Ainderby Quernhow 79 SE 3480
Ainderby Steeple 84 SE 3392
Aingers Green 39 TM 1120
Ainsdale 68 SD 3111
Ainshval (mt.) 110 NM 3794
Ainstable 83 NY 5346
Ainsworth 69 SD 7610
Aintree 68 SJ 3798
Aira Force 83 NY 3920
Aird (Dumf. and Galwy.) 86 NX 0960
Aird (Isle of Lewis) 131 NB 5635
Aird (Strath.) 99 NM 7600
Aird a' Mhòrain 124 NF 8379
Aird an Rùnair 124 NF 6970
Aird an Troim 131 NB 2316
Aird Barvas 131 NB 3553
Aird Brenish 130 NA 9727
Aird Dell 131 NB 4761
Aird-dhubh 123 NG 7040
Aird Dhubh 126 NG 9382
Airde, The 133 NC 5313
Aird Fada 105 NM 4424
Aird Fenish 130 NA 9929
Aird Luing 105 NM 7406
Aird Mhànais 125 NG 1188
Aird Mheadhonach 125 NG 1998
Aird Nisabost 124 NG 0497
Aird of Coigach 132 NC 0711
Aird of Kinloch 105 NM 5228
Aird of Sleat 111 NG 5900
Aird Riabhach 125 NG 2396
Airdrie 101 NS 7665
Airdriehill 101 NS 7867
Airds Bay 106 NN 0032
Airds Moss 94 NS 5724
Aird, The (Highld.) (dist) 128 NH 5241
Aird, The, (Island of Skye) 123 NG 4052
Aird, The, (Island of Skye) 123 NG 4375
Aird Thormaid 124 NF 9276
Aird Uig 130 NB 0437
Aird Vanish 124 NF 9999
Aire and Calder Navigation (N Yorks.) 71 SE 5820
Aire and Calder Navigation (N Yorks.) 71 SE 6119
Airedale 78 SE 0345
Airie Hill 88 NX 6268
Airies 86 NW 9767
Airlie Castle 108 NO 2952
Airmyn 74 SE 7224
Airntully 108 NO 0935
Airor 111 NG 7205
Airth 102 NS 8987
Airton 78 SD 9059
Aisby (Lincs.) 72 SK 8792
Aisby (Lincs.) 62 TF 0138
Aiskew 79 SE 2788
Aislaby (Cleve) 85 NZ 4012
Aislaby (N Yorks.) 80 NZ 8508
Aislaby (N Yorks.) 80 SE 7785
Aisthorpe 72 SK 9479
Aith (Fetlar) 143 HU 6390
Aith (Orkney) 136 HY 2417
Aith (Shetld.) 141 HU 3455
Aith (Stronsay) 137 HY 6525
Aith Hope 136 ND 2989
Aith Ness 141 HU 5144
Aithsting (dist.) 141 HU 3455
Aith Voe (Shetld.) 141 HU 3458
Aith Voe (Shetld.) 141 HU 4328
Aith Wick 141 HU 4429
Aitnoch 117 NH 9839
Akeld 97 NT 9529
Akeley 51 SP 7037
Akeman Street (Bucks.) (ant.) 36 SP 7316
Akeman Street (Oxon.) (ant.) 47 SP 3213
Akenham 55 TM 1448
Akermoor Loch 89 NT 4020
Alavna Roman Fort (ant.) 82 NY 0437
Albaston 20 SX 4270
Alberbury 58 SJ 3514
Albourne 28 TQ 2616
Albrighton (Shrops.) 59 SJ 4918
Albrighton (Shrops.) 59 SJ 8103
Alburgh 55 TM 2786
Albury (Herts.) 37 TL 4324
Albury (Surrey) 28 TQ 0547
Alby Hill 65 TG 1934
Alcaig 128 NH 5657
Alcaston 48 SO 4587
Alcester 50 SP 0857
Alciston 29 TQ 5005
Alconbury 52 TL 1875
Alconbury Weston 52 TL 1777
Aldbar Castle (ant.) 109 NO 5757
Aldborough (Norf.) 65 TG 1834
Aldborough (N Yorks.) 79 SE 4065
Aldbourne 34 SU 2675
Aldbrough (Humbs.) 75 TA 2338
Aldbrough St. John 84 NZ 2011
Aldbury 36 SP 9612
Aldclune 108 NN 9064
Aldeburgh 55 TM 4656
Aldeburgh Bay 55 TM 4755
Aldeby 65 TM 4593
Aldenham 37 TQ 1198
Alderbury 26 SU 1827
Alderford 65 TG 1218
Alderholt 26 SU 1212
Alderley 33 ST 7690
Alderley Edge 69 SJ 8478
Aldermaston 35 SU 5965
Aldermaston Soke 36 SU 6263
Aldermaston Wharf 35 SU 6067
Alderminster 50 SP 2248
Aldershot 35 SU 8650
Alderton (Glos.) 46 SP 0033
Alderton (Northants.) 51 SP 7346
Alderton (Shrops.) 59 SJ 4923
Alderton (Suff.) 55 TM 3441
Alderton (Wilts.) 33 ST 8382
Alderwasley 60 SK 3153
Aldfield 79 SE 2669
Aldford 68 SJ 4159
Aldham 54 TL 9125
Aldingbourne 28 SU 9205
Aldingham 77 SD 2871
Aldington (Here. and Worc.) 50 SP 0644
Aldington (Kent) 31 TR 0736
Aldochlay 100 NS 3591
Aldreth 53 TL 4473
Aldridge 60 SK 0500
Aldringham 55 TM 4460
Aldsworth 47 SP 1509
Aldunie 121 NJ 3626
Aldwark (Derby.) 71 SK 2257
Aldwark (N Yorks.) 79 SE 4663
Aldwick 28 SZ 9199
Aldwincle 52 TL 0081
Aldworth 35 SU 5579
Aled Isat Resr. 67 SH 9159
Alemoor Loch 89 NT 4015
Ale Water (Borders) 89 NT 4317
Ale Water (Borders) 97 NT 8764
Alexandria 101 NS 3979
Alfardisworthy 22 SS 2911
Alfington 24 SY 1197
Alfold 28 TQ 0333
Alford (Grampn.) 119 NJ 5715
Alford (Lincs.) 73 TF 4575
Alford (Somer.) 25 ST 6032
Alfred's Tower 25 ST 7435
Alfreton 60 SK 4155
Alfrick 49 SO 7453
Alfriston 29 TQ 5103
Alhampton 25 ST 6234
Alhang (mt.) 88 NS 6400
Aline Lodge 131 NB 1911
Alkborough 74 SE 8721
Alkerton 50 SP 3743
Alkham 31 TR 2441
Alkington 59 SJ 5239
Alkmonton 60 SK 1838
Alladale Lodge 128 NH 4389
Alladale River 128 NH 4188
Allaleigh 21 SX 8053
Allanaquoich 117 NO 1191
Allangrange House 128 NH 6251
Allanton (Borders) 97 NT 8654
Allanton (Strath.) 95 NS 8457
Allan Water (Borders) 89 NT 4606
Allan Water (Central) 101 NN 7802
Allardice 119 NO 8174
All Cannings 34 SU 0661
Allendale Common 84 NY 8651
Allendale Town 83 NY 8455
Allenheads 84 NY 8645
Allensmore 45 SO 4635
Aller 24 ST 4029
Allerby 82 NY 0839
Aller Dean 97 NT 9847
Allerford 23 SS 9047
Allermuir Hill 103 NT 2266
Allerston 81 SE 8782
Allerthorpe 74 SE 7847
Allerton 68 SJ 3986
Allerton Bywater 79 SE 4127
Allestree 60 SK 3439
Allexton 62 SK 8100
Allgreave 70 SJ 9767
Allhallows 30 TQ 8377
Alligin Shuas 123 NG 8358
Allimore Green 59 SJ 8519
Allington (Lincs.) 62 SK 8540
Allington (Wilts.) 34 SU 0663
Allington (Wilts.) 34 SU 2039
Allithwaite 77 SD 3876
Allnabad 133 NC 4641
Alloa 102 NS 8893
Allonby 82 NY 0842
Allonby Bay 82 NY 0541
Alloway 93 NS 3318
All Saints South Elmham 55 TM 3482
All Stretton 58 SO 4395
Allt a'Bhunn 133 NC 4812
Allt Ach' a' Bhàthàich 134 NC 8116
Allt a' Chaoil-réidhe 116 NN 5175
Allt a' Chaorainn 114 NM 9587
Allt a' Chaoruinn (Highld.) 127 NC 2703
Allt a' Chireachain 107 NN 7872
Allt a' Choire Mhóir 127 NH 1968
Allt a' Chonais 127 NH 0548
Allt a'Choromaig 106 NM 9120
Allt a' Chraois 133 NC 4438
Allt à Gheallaidh 117 NJ 1238
Allt a' Ghiubhais 123 NG 7968
Allt Airigh-dhamh 134 NC 8238
Allt a' Mhadaidh 127 NH 2274
Allt a' Mhuilinn (Highld.) 134 NC 8312
Allt a' Mhuilinn (Tays.) 116 NN 7675
Alltan Dearg 133 NC 6359
Allt an Dùin 134 NC 8125
Allt an Ealaidh 133 NC 7027
Allt an Stacain 106 NN 1220
Allt an Tairbh 98 NR 5488
Allt an Tiaghaich 132 NC 1623
Allt an t-Srathain 123 NG 7155
Allt Arnan 106 NN 2918
Allt Bail 'a' Mhuilinn 107 NN 5743
Allt Beinn Dònuill 127 NH 2399
Allt Beitheach 111 NM 7551
Allt Beochlich 106 NN 0115
Allt Bhlàraidh 115 NH 3518
Allt Bhran 116 NN 7889
Allt Braglenmore 106 NM 9119
Allt Breinag 116 NH 4707
Allt Càm (Highld.) 116 NN 4477
Allt Càm (Highld.) 116 NN 5178
Allt Càm Ban 116 NH 5606
Allt Camgharaidh 114 NM 9788
Allt Camghouran 107 NN 5253
Allt Car 133 NC 4317
Allt Chaiseagail 133 NC 5810
Alltchaorunn 106 NN 1950
Allt Choire a' Bhalachain 115 NN 0995
Allt Chomhraig 116 NN 8197
Allt Chonoghlais 106 NN 3336
Allt Cinn-locha 99 NR 7879
Allt Coire a'Chaolain 106 NN 2048
Allt Coire an Eoin 106 NN 2172
Allt Coire Lain Oig 116 NN 5198
Allt Coire na Saigh Duibhe 133 NC 4736
Allt Con 107 NN 6967
Allt Conait 107 NN 5245
Allt Connie 117 NO 0786
Allt Crunachdain 116 NN 5291
Allt Cuaich 116 NN 6686
Allt Darrarie 118 NO 3181
Allt Dearg 129 NH 8246
Allt Dochard 106 NN 2045
Allt Doe 116 NH 4107
Allt Easach 106 NN 0642
Allt Eigheach 107 NN 4360
Allt Eileag 127 NC 3107
Allt Fearna 106 NN 1222
Allt Féith Thuill 107 NN 3872
Allt Fionn Ghlinne 106 NN 3122
Alltforgan 57 SH 9624
Allt Forsiescye 135 ND 0158
Allt Garbh 115 NH 1619
Allt Garbh-airigh 128 NH 6399
Allt Garbh Buidhe 117 NN 9981
Allt Gharbh Ghaig 116 NN 7682
Allt Ghlas 107 NN 5364
Allt Glas Choire 116 NN 7373
Allt Glas Dhoire 115 NN 3084
Allt Gleann Da-Eig 107 NN 5944
Allt Gleann nam Meann 101 NN 5114
Allt Gleann Udalain 123 NG 8629
Allt Glen Loch 108 NO 0071
Allt Goibhre 128 NH 4148
Allt Hallater 106 NN 1338
Allt Làire 115 NN 3175
Allt Lon a' Chuil 134 NC 7240
Allt Loraich 115 NN 3878
Allt Lorgy 117 NH 8716
Allt Lundie 115 NH 2807
Allt Madagain 116 NN 6298
Alltmawr 44 SO 0647
Allt Mhoille 106 NN 1031
Allt Mhucarnaich 127 NH 2678
Allt Mór (Highld.) 116 NH 7404
Allt Mór (Highld.) 117 NN 8295
Allt Mór (Island of Skye) 123 NG 7221
Allt Mór (Tays.) 107 NN 7453
Allt na Bogair 107 NN 5954
Alltnacaillich 133 NC 4645
Allt na Caim 107 NN 3763
Allt na Doire Gairbhe 114 NH 0328
Allt na Gile 98 NR 4778
Allt na Glaise 107 NN 5769
Allt na h-Airbhe 127 NH 1193
Allt na h-Eirigh 123 NG 7054
Allt na Lairige (Highld.) 106 NN 2872
Allt na Lairige (Strath.) 106 NN 2316
Allt na Lairige Móire 106 NN 1163
Allt na Lùibe 133 NC 6410
Allt na Muic 115 NH 2515
Allt nan Achaidhean 134 NC 7729
Allt nan Airighean 98 NR 3650
Allt nan Caorach 128 NH 5267
Allt nan Ramh 132 NC 2237
Allt Odhar 116 NH 5104
Allt Phocaichain 115 NH 3009
Allt Riabhach 115 NH 2219
Allt Riobain 107 NN 4530
Allt Ruighe nan Saorach 107 NN 6463
Allt Sleibh 107 NN 6566
Allt Smeòrail 134 NC 8511
Allt Srath a'Ghlinne 107 NN 6719
Allt Tolaghan 106 NN 2440
Allt Tuileach 117 NJ 2208
Allt Uisg an t-Sithein 116 NH 5921
Alltwalis 43 SN 4431
Alltwen 40 SN 7303
Allweston 25 ST 6614
Almeley 45 SO 3351
Almer 25 SY 9098
Almington 59 SJ 7034
Almondbank 108 NO 0626
Almondbury 70 SE 1614
Almondsbury 33 ST 6083
Alne 79 SE 4965
Alness 128 NH 6569
Alness Bay 128 NH 6367
Alnham 91 NT 9910
Alnmouth 91 NU 2410
Alnmouth Bay 91 NU 2510
Alnwick 91 NU 1912
Alphamstone 54 TL 8735
Alpheton 54 TL 8850
Alphington 21 SX 9190

Alport Auchineden Hill

Alport	70	SK 2164
Alpraham	69	SJ 5859
Alresford	39	TM 0621
Alrewas	60	SK 1715
Alsager	59	SJ 7955
Alsagers Bank	59	SJ 8048
Alsop en le Dale	60	SK 1655
Alston	83	NY 7146
Alstone	46	SO 9832
Alstonefield	60	SK 1355
Alston Moor	83	NY 7338
Alswear	23	SS 7222
Altandhu	132	NB 9812
Altanduin	134	NC 8025
Altarnun	19,20	SX 2281
Altass	128	NC 5000
Alterwall	135	ND 2865
Altgaltraig	100	NS 0473
Altham	78	SD 7632
Althorne	38	TQ 9098
Althorpe	74	SE 8309
Altnabreac Station	135	ND 0045
Altnacealgach Hotel	132	NC 2610
Altnafeadh	106	NN 2256
Altnaharra	133	NC 5635
Altofts	79	SE 3723
Alton (Derby.)	71	SK 3664
Alton (Hants.)	35	SU 7139
Alton (Staffs.)	60	SK 0742
Alton Pancras	25	ST 6902
Alton Priors	34	SU 1062
Alton Water Reservoir	55	TM 1536
Altrincham	69	SJ 7687
Altt Ddu	41	SO 0224
Alturlie Point	129	NH 7149
Altyre House	129	NJ 0254
Altyre Woods	129	NJ 0353
Alum Bay	26	SZ 3085
Alva	102	NS 8897
Alvanley	69	SJ 4973
Alvaston	60	SK 3933
Alvechurch	50	SP 0272
Alvecote	60	SK 2404
Alvediston	26	ST 9723
Alveley	49	SO 7584
Alverdiscott	23	SS 5225
Alverstoke	27	SZ 5998
Alverstone	27	SZ 5785
Alverton	61	SK 7942
Alves	129	NJ 1362
Alvescot	47	SP 2704
Alveston (Avon)	33	ST 6388
Alveston (Warw.)	50	SP 2256
Alvie	117	NH 8609
Alvingham	73	TF 3691
Alvington	45	SO 6000
Alwalton	62	TL 1395
Alwen Resr.	67	SH 9454
Alwinton	90	NT 9206
Alyth	108	NO 2448
Amat Forest	128	NH 4690
Am Balg (is.)	132	NC 1866
Ambergate	60	SK 3451
Amber Hill	63	TF 2346
Amberley (Glos.)	46	SO 8401
Amberley (W Susx)	28	TQ 0313
Am Bi-bogha Beag	122	NG 1938
Am Bi-bogha Mór	122	NG 1838
Amble-by-the-Sea	91	NU 2604
Amblecote	49	SO 8885
Ambleside	83	NY 3704
Ambleston	42	SN 0026
Ambrosden	47	SP 6019
Am Buachaille	100	NN 0507
Amcotts	74	SE 8514
Amersham	36	SU 9597
Amesbury	34	SU 1541
Am Fraoch Eilean	98	NR 4662
Amhainn na Clach Airigh	132	NC 1321
A' Mhoine (dist.)	133	NC 5160
Amhuinnsuidhe	124	NB 0408
Amicombe Hill	21	SX 5687
Amington	60	SK 2304
Amisfield Town	88	NY 0082
Amlwch	66	SH 4392
Amlwch Port	66	SH 4593
Ammanford	43	SN 6212
Amotherby	80	SE 7473
Ampfield	26	SU 3923
Ampleforth	79	SE 5878
Ampleforth College	79	SE 5978
Ampney Crucis	46	SP 0602
Ampney St. Mary	46	SP 0802
Ampney St. Peter	46	SP 0701
Amport	34	SU 2944
Ampthill	52	TL 0337
Ampton	54	TL 8671
Amroth	42	SN 1607
Amulree	108	NN 8936
An Acairseid	111	NM 4363
Anaheilt	111	NM 8162
An Cabar (mt.)	127	NH 2564
An Càmastac	122	NG 2365
An Caol	123	NG 6152
Ancaster	62	SK 9843
An Ceannaich	122	NG 1350
An Ceann Geal or Whiten Head	133	NC 4968
An Cearcall	107	NN 6270
Anchor	48	SO 1785
An Clachan	98	NR 2171
An Coileach (mt.)	125	NG 0892
An Coileachan (mt.)	127	NH 2468
An Coire	105	NM 8014
Ancroft	97	NT 9945
An Cruachan (Highld.)	115	NH 0935
An Cruachan (Jura)	99	NM 6900
Ancrum	96	NT 6224
Ancton	28	SU 9800
An Cuaidh	126	NG 7689
Anderby	73	TF 5275
Anderby Creek	73	TF 5575
Anderson	25	SY 8797
Anderton	69	SJ 6475
Andover	34	SU 3645
Andover Down	34	SU 3946
Andoversford	46	SP 0219
Andreas	76	SC 4199
An Dubh-aird	123	NG 7833
An Dubh-laimhrig	123	NG 4715
An Dubh Sgeir (Island of Skye)	122	NG 1936
An Dubh-sgeir (Island of Skye)	122	NG 3422
An Dubh-sgeir (Strath.)	92	NR 6655
An Dùn (pt.)	135	ND 1425
An Dùnan	98	NR 5773
An Fhaochag	111	NG 6903
An Garbh-eilean (is.)	132	NC 3373
An Gead Loch	115	NH 1038
Angersleigh	24	ST 1918
Angle	42	SM 8603
Angle Bay	42	SM 8802
Anglesey	66	SH 4279
Angle Tarn	83	NY 4114
Anglezarke Moor	69	SD 6317
Angmering	28	TQ 0704
Angram	79	SE 5148
Angram Common	83	SD 8499
Angram Reservoir	78	SE 0476
An Grianan (mt.)	132	NC 2662
Angry Brow (sbk.)	68	SD 3019
An Iola	106	NM 9747
Ankerville	129	NH 8174
Anlaby	74	TA 0328
An Lairig	116	NN 4977
An Leacainn	116	NH 5740
An Leàn-chàrn (mt.)	132	NC 4152
An Liathanach	127	NH 1257
Anmer	64	TF 7429
Annan	89	NY 1966
Annandale	89	NY 1292
Annaside	76	SD 0986
Annat (Highld.)	126	NG 8954
Annat (Strath.)	106	NN 0322
Annat Bay	126	NH 0397
Annathill	101	NS 7270
Anna Valley	34	SU 3444
Annbank	93	NS 4022
Annbank Station	93	NS 4024
Annesley	61	SK 5153
Annesley Woodhouse	61	SK 4953
Annet	18	SV 8608
Annet Burn	101	NN 6907
Annfield Plain	84	NZ 1551
Annick Water	93	NS 3843
Annie	101	NN 5810
Annochie	121	NJ 9342
Annscroft	58	SJ 4407
An Riabhachan (mt.)	115	NH 1133
An Rubha	98	NR 3594
An Sgarsoch (mt.)	117	NN 9383
An Sgurr	111	NM 4684
An Sleaghach	105	NM 7643
Ansley	50	SP 2991
Anslow	60	SK 2125
Anslow Gate	60	SK 2024
An Socach (Grampn.) (mt.)	117	NO 0980
An Socach (Highld.) (mt.)	132	NC 2558
An Socach (Strath.)	100	NS 0587
An Stac	111	NM 8689
An Stèidh (is.)	110	NG 2103
Anstey (Herts.)	53	TL 4032
Anstey (Leic.)	61	SK 5408
Anstiebury (ant.)	28	TQ 1543
An Stoc-bheinn	128	NC 6402
Anston	71	SK 5184
Anstruther	103	NO 5603
An Stùc (mt.)	132	NC 3409
An Stuchd	99	NR 7580
Ansty (Warw.)	50	SP 3983
Ansty (Wilts.)	26	ST 9526
Ansty (W Susx)	29	TQ 2923
An Suidhe (Highld.)	116	NH 8107
An Suidhe (Strath.)	100	NN 0007
An t-Aigeach (pt.)	124	NF 9364
An Teallach (mt.)	127	NH 0684
Anthill Common	27	SU 6412
Anthorn	89	NY 1958
An t-Iasgair (is.)	122	NG 3574
Antingham	65	TG 2533
Antonine Wall (Strath.) (ant.)	101	NS 5972
Antonine Wall (Strath.) (ant.)	101	NS 7677
Antony	20	SX 3954
An Torc or Boar of Badenoch	116	NN 6276
Antrobus	69	SJ 6479
An t-Sùileag	114	NN 0282
An Tunna	92	NR 9736
An Uidh	128	NH 6396
Anwick	62	TF 1150
Anwoth	87	NX 5856
Aoineadh Mór	105	NM 4919
Aonach air Chrith (mt.)	115	NH 0408
Aonach Beag (Highld.)	106	NN 1971
Aonach Beag (Highld.)	116	NN 4574
Aonach Buidhe	115	NH 0532
Aonach Eagach (mt.)	106	NN 1557
Aonach Mór (Highld.)	115	NN 1973
Aonach Mór (Strath.)	106	NN 2148
Aonach Shasuinn	115	NH 1718
Ape Dale	48	SO 4789
Apes Hall	53	TL 5590
Apethorpe	62	TL 0295
Apley	73	TF 1075
Apperknowle	71	SK 3878
Apperley	46	SO 8628
Appin House	106	NM 9349
Appin of Dull	107	NN 7948
Appleby (Humbs.)	74	SE 9414
Appleby in Westmorland	83	NY 6820
Appleby Magna	60	SK 3110
Appleby Parva	60	SK 3109
Applecross	123	NG 7144
Applecross Forest	123	NG 7647
Applecross House	123	NG 7145
Appledore (Devon)	22	SS 4630
Appledore (Devon)	24	ST 0614
Appledore (Kent)	30	TQ 9529
Appleford	47	SU 5293
Appleshaw	34	SU 3048
Appleton	47	SP 4401
Appleton-le-Moors	80	SE 7387
Appleton-le-Street	80	SE 7373
Appleton Roebuck	79	SE 5542
Appleton Thorn	69	SJ 6484
Appleton Wiske	85	NZ 3904
Appletreehall	90	NT 5117
Appletreewick	78	SE 0560
Appley	24	ST 0721
Appley Bridge	69	SD 5209
Appuldurcombe House (ant.)	27	SZ 5579
Apse Heath	27	SZ 5682
Apsley End	52	TL 1232
Apuldram	27	SU 8403
Aquae Sulis (ant.)	33	ST 7464
Aqualate Hall	59	SJ 7719
Aqualate Mere	59	SJ 7720
Araid	123	NG 7958
Aran Benllyn	57	SH 8523
Aran Fawddwy	57	SH 8422
Arbeadie	119	NO 6996
Arbirlot	109	NO 6040
Arboll	129	NH 8781
Arborfield	36	SU 7567
Arborfield Cross	36	SU 7666
Arborfield Garrison	36	SU 7665
Arbor Low (ant.)	70	SK 1663
Arbroath	109	NO 6340
Arbury Hill	51	SP 5358
Arbuthnott	119	NO 8074
Archiestown	120	NJ 2344
Arclid Green	69	SJ 7962
Ardachu	128	NC 6703
Ardalanish	104	NM 3618
Ardalanish Bay	104	NM 3717
Arda Móra	124	NB 0208
Ardanaiseig	106	NN 0824
Ardargie House Hotel	108	NO 0715
Ardarroch	123	NG 8339
Ard Beag	122	NG 2161
Ardbeg	98	NR 4146
Ard Caol	125	NB 2301
Ardcharnich	127	NH 1788
Ardchattan Priory (ant.)	106	NM 9734
Ardchiavaig	104	NM 3818
Ardchullarie More	101	NN 5813
Ardchyle	107	NN 5229
Ardclach	129	NH 9545
Ard-dhubh	123	NG 7040
Ardd-lin	58	SJ 2516
Ardechive	115	NN 1490
Ardeley	53	TL 3127
Ardelve	123	NG 8727
Arden	101	NS 3684
Ardencaple House	105	NM 7619
Arden Great Moor	85	SE 5193
Ardens Grafton	50	SP 1154
Ardentallan House	105	NM 8323
Ardentinny	100	NS 1887
Ardeonaig	107	NN 6635
Ardersier	129	NH 7854
Ardery	111	NM 7562
Ardessie	127	NH 0589
Ardfern	105	NM 8004
Ardgartan	100	NN 2702
Ardgay	128	NH 5990
Ardgay Station	128	NH 6090
Ardgoil Estate	100	NN 2200
Ardgoil Forest	100	NS 2198
Ardgour (dist.)	106	NM 9467
Ardgowan	100	NS 2072
Ardhasaig	125	NB 1202
Ardindrean	127	NH 1588
Ardingly	29	TQ 3429
Ardingly Resr.	29	TQ 3330
Ardington	34	SU 4388
Ardintoul Point	123	NG 8324
Ardivachar	124	NF 7445
Ardivachar Point	124	NF 7446
Ardkinglas House	100	NN 1710
Ardlair	121	NJ 5528
Ardlamont Bay	100	NR 9764
Ardlamont House	100	NR 9865
Ardlamont Point	100	NR 9963
Ardleigh	54	TM 0529
Ardleigh Reservoir	54	TM 0328
Ardler	108	NO 2641
Ardley	47	SP 5427
Ardlui	106	NN 3115
Ardlussa	99	NR 6487
Ardlussa Bay	99	NR 6588
Ardmaddy Castle	105	NM 7816
Ardmair	127	NH 1198
Ardmaleish Point	100	NS 0769
Ardmarnock Bay	100	NR 9072
Ardmarnock House	100	NR 9172
Ardmay	100	NN 2802
Ardmeanach (dist.)	105	NM 4327
Ardminish	92	NR 6448
Ardminish Bay	92	NR 6548
Ardmolich	111	NM 7172
Ardmore	132	NC 2051
Ardmore (Islay)	98	NR 4650
Ardmore (Strath.)	100	NS 3178
Ardmore Bay	111	NM 4659
Ard More Mangersta	130	NB 0032
Ardmore Point (Highld.)	132	NC 1651
Ardmore Point (Highld.)	134	NC 7666
Ardmore Point (Island of Mull)	111	NM 4759
Ardmore Point (Island of Skye)	122	NG 2159
Ardmore Point (Islay)	98	NR 4750
Ardmucknish Bay	106	NM 8837
Ard na Claise Móire	123	NG 6852
Ardnacross	111	NM 5449
Ardnacross Bay	92	NR 7625
Ardnadam	100	NS 1580
Ardnagrask	128	NH 5149
Ardnameacan	123	NG 7114
Ardnamurchan (dist.)	111	NM 5766
Ardnarff	114	NG 8935
Ardnastang	111	NM 8061
Ardnave	98	NR 2873
Ardnave Point	98	NR 2975
Ardneil Bay	93	NS 1847
Ardnish (dist.)	111	NM 7281
Ardno	100	NN 1408
Ardnoe Point	99	NR 7794
Ardo	121	NJ 8538
Ardoch	108	NO 0937
Ardoch Burn	101	NN 7405
Ardochy House	115	NH 2102
Ardo House	121	NJ 9221
Ardoyne	121	NJ 6527
Ardpatrick	99	NR 7560
Ardpatrick House	99	NR 7559
Ardpatrick Point	92	NR 7357
Ardpeaton	100	NS 2185
Ardrishaig	99	NR 8585
Ardroil	130	NB 0432
Ardrossan	93	NS 2342
Ardross Castle	128	NH 6174
Ardscalpsie Point	92	NS 0457
Ardshealach	111	NM 6967
Ardskenish	98	NR 3491
Ardsley	71	SE 3805
Ardsley East	79	SE 3024
Ardslignish	111	NM 5661
Ardtalla	98	NR 4654
Ardtalnaig	107	NN 7039
Ard Thurinish	111	NM 5999
Ardtoe	111	NM 6370
Ardtornish Point	105	NM 6942
Ardtreck Point	122	NG 3336
Ardtrostan	107	NN 6723
Ardtun	105	NM 4022
Arduaine	105	NM 7910
Ardullie	128	NH 5863
Ardvasar	111	NG 6303
Ardverikie Forest	116	NN 5081
Ardvey	125	NG 1292
Ardvorlich	107	NN 6322
Ardvourlie	131	NB 1810
Ardwell	86	NX 1045
Ardwell Point	86	NX 0644
Ardyne Burn	100	NS 1172
Ardyne Point	100	NS 0968
Areley Kings	49	SO 8070
Arenig Fach	67	SH 8241
Arenig Fawr	67	SH 8237
Argoed Mill	57	SN 9962
Argyll (dist.)	100	NM 9903
Aridhglas	104	NM 3123
Arileod	110	NM 1654
Arinacrinachd	123	NG 7458
Arinagour	110	NM 2257
Arion	136	HY 2514
Arisaig (Highld.)	111	NM 6686
Arisaig (Highld.) (dist.)	111	NM 6687
Arisaig House	111	NM 6984
Arivruaich	131	NB 2417
Arkendale	79	SE 3860
Arkengarthdale	84	NZ 0001
Arkengarthdale Moor	84	NY 9405
Arkesden	53	TL 4834
Ark Hill	109	NO 3542
Arkholme	77	SD 5871
Arkle (mt.)	132	NC 3046
Arkley	37	TQ 2296
Arks Edge	90	NT 7106
Arksey	71	SE 5706
Arkwright Town	71	SK 4270
Arlecdon	82	NY 0419
Arlesey	52	TL 1935
Arleston	59	SJ 6410
Arley (Ches.)	69	SJ 6780
Arley (Warw.)	50	SP 2890
Arlingham	46	SO 7010
Arlington (Devon)	23	SS 6140
Arlington (E Susx)	29	TQ 5407
Arlington (Glos.)	46	SP 1006
Armadale (Highld.)	134	NC 7864
Armadale (Lothian)	102	NS 9368
Armadale Bay (Highld.)	134	NC 7965
Armadale Bay (Island of Skye)	111	NG 6404
Armadale Burn	134	NC 7859
Armadale Castle	111	NG 6304
Armathwaite	83	NY 5046
Arminghall	65	TG 2504
Armitage	60	SK 0816
Armscote	50	SP 2444
Armthorpe	71	SE 6105
Arnabost	110	NM 2060
Arnaval (mt.)	122	NG 3431
Arncliffe	78	SD 9371
Arncliffe Cote	78	SD 9470
Arncott	36	SP 6117
Arncroach	103	NO 5105
Arndilly House	120	NJ 2946
Arne	26	SY 9788
Arnesby	51	SP 6192
Arnfield Brook	70	SK 0298
Arngask	102	NO 1310
Arnicle	92	NR 7138
Arnisdale	123	NG 8410
Arnish	123	NG 5948
Arnish Moor	131	NB 4030
Arniston Engine	103	NT 3462
Arnol	131	NB 3148
Arnold	61	SK 5745
Arnot Resr.	103	NO 2002
Arnprior	101	NS 6194
Arnside	77	SD 4578
Arnton Fell	90	NY 5295
Aros (dist.)	111	NM 5249
Aros Bay	98	NR 4652
Aros Mains	105	NM 5645
Aros River	105	NM 5145
Arpafeelie	128	NH 6150
Arrad Foot	77	SD 3080
Arram	74	TA 0344
Arrathorne	84	SE 2093
Arreton	27	SZ 5386
Arrington	53	TL 3250
Arrochar	100	NN 2904
Arrow	50	SP 0856
Arscaig	133	NC 5014
Artafallie	128	NH 6249
Artfield Fell	86	NX 2367
Arthington	79	SE 2644
Arthingworth	51	SP 7581
Arthog	57	SH 6414
Arthrath	121	NJ 9636
Arthur Seat (Cumbr.)	89	NY 4978
Arthur's Seat (Lothian)	103	NT 2872
Arthurstone	108	NO 2642
Artrochie	121	NK 0032
Arundel	28	TQ 0107
Arundel Park	28	TQ 0108
Arvhoulan	106	NN 0168
Asby	82	NY 0620
Ascog	100	NS 1063
Ascot	36	SU 9168
Ascott-under-Wychwood	47	SP 2918
Ascrib Islands	122	NG 3064
Asenby	79	SE 3975
Asfordby	61	SK 7018
Asfordby Hill	61	SK 7219
Asgarby (Lincs.)	62	TF 1145
Asgarby (Lincs.)	73	TF 3366
Asgog Bay	100	NR 9366
Asgog Loch	100	NR 9570
Ash (Kent)	30	TQ 5964
Ash (Kent)	31	TR 2958
Ash (Somer.)	25	ST 4720
Ash (Surrey)	35	SU 8950
Ashampstead	35	SU 5676
Ashbocking	55	TM 1654
Ashbourne	60	SK 1846
Ashbrittle	24	ST 0521
Ash Bullayne	23	SS 7704
Ashburnham Place	29	TQ 6914
Ashburton	21	SX 7569
Ashbury (Devon)	20	SX 5097
Ashbury (Oxon.)	34	SU 2685
Ashby	74	SE 9009
Ashby by Partney	73	TF 4266
Ashby Canal (Leic.)	60	SK 3801
Ashby Canal (Warw.)	50	SP 4191
Ashby cum Fenby	75	TA 2500
Ashby de la Launde	62	TF 0455
Ashby-de-la-Zouch	60	SK 3516
Ashby Folville	61	SK 7012
Ashby Magna	51	SP 5690
Ashby Parva	51	SP 5288
Ashby St. Ledgers	51	SP 5768
Ashby St. Mary	65	TG 3202
Ashchurch	46	SO 9233
Ashcombe	21	SX 9179
Ashcott	25	ST 4336
Ashdon	53	TL 5842
Ashdown Forest	29	TQ 4530
Asheldham	39	TL 9701
Ashen	54	TL 7442
Ashendon	36	SP 7014
Ash Fell	83	NY 7404
Ashfield (Central)	101	NN 7803
Ashfield (Suff.)	55	TM 2062
Ashfield Green	55	TM 2673
Ashford (Devon)	23	SS 5335
Ashford (Kent)	31	TR 0142
Ashford (Surrey)	36	TQ 0671
Ashford Bowdler	48	SO 5170
Ashford Carbonel	48	SO 5270
Ashford Hill	35	SU 5562
Ashford in the Water	70	SK 1969
Ashgill	94	NS 7849
Ashie Moor	116	NH 5931
Ashiestiel Hill	96	NT 4134
Ashill (Devon)	24	ST 0811
Ashill (Norf.)	64	TF 8804
Ashill (Somer.)	24	ST 3217
Ashingdon	38	TQ 8693
Ashington (Northum.)	91	NZ 2687
Ashington (W Susx)	28	TQ 1315
Ashintully Castle	108	NO 1061
Ashkirk	96	NT 4722
Ashleworth	46	SO 8125
Ashley (Cambs.)	54	TL 6961
Ashley (Ches.)	69	SJ 7784
Ashley (Devon)	23	SS 6411
Ashley (Glos.)	46	ST 9394
Ashley (Hants.)	26	SU 3831
Ashley (Northants.)	51	SP 7991
Ashley (Staffs.)	59	SJ 7536
Ashley Green	36	SP 9705
Ashley Heath	26	SU 1105
Ash Magna	59	SJ 5739
Ashmansworth	34	SU 4156
Ashmansworthy	22	SS 3317
Ash Mill	23	SS 7823
Ashmore	25	ST 9117
Ashmore Park	60	SJ 9602
Ashorne	50	SP 3057
Ashover	71	SK 3463
Ashow	50	SP 3170
Ashperton	49	SO 6441
Ashprington	21	SX 8157
Ash Priors	24	ST 1429
Ashreigney	23	SS 6213
Ashridge College	36	SP 9912
Ashtead	37	TQ 1858
Ash Thomas	23	ST 0010
Ashton (Ches.)	69	SJ 5069
Ashton (Corn.)	18	SW 6028
Ashton (Devon)	21	SX 8584
Ashton (Here. and Worc.)	48	SO 5164
Ashton (Northants.)	51	SP 7649
Ashton (Northants.)	52	TL 0588
Ashton Common	33	ST 8958
Ashton-in-Makerfield	69	SJ 5799
Ashton Keynes	46	SU 0494
Ashton under Hill	50	SO 9938
Ashton-under-Lyne	69	SJ 9399
Ashton upon Mersey	69	SJ 7792
Ashurst (Hants.)	26	SU 3310
Ashurst (Kent)	29	TQ 5038
Ashurst (W Susx)	28	TQ 1716
Ashurstwood	29	TQ 4236
Ashury (Oxon.)	34	SU 2685
Ashwater	20	SX 3895
Ashwell (Herts.)	53	TL 2639
Ashwell (Leic.)	62	SK 8613
Ashwellthorpe	65	TM 1397
Ashwick	33	ST 6447
Ashwicken	64	TF 7018
Ashworth Moor Resr.	69	SD 8315
Askam in Furness	76	SD 2177
Askern	71	SE 5613
Askernish House	112	NF 7323
Askerswell	25	SY 5292
Askett	36	SP 8105
Askham (Cumbr.)	83	NY 5123
Askham (Notts.)	72	SK 7374
Askham Bryan	79	SE 5548
Askham Richard	79	SE 5347
Askival (mt.)	111	NM 3995
Asknish	100	NR 9291
Asknish Forest	100	NR 9191
Askrigg	84	SD 9491
Askrigg Common	84	SD 9493
Askwith	78	SE 1648
Aslackby	62	TF 0830
Aslacton	55	TM 1591
Aslockton	61	SK 7440
Asloun	119	NJ 5414
Aspatria	82	NY 1442
Aspenden	53	TL 3528
Aspley Guise	52	SP 9436
Aspley Heath	52	SP 9334
Aspull	69	SD 6108
Asselby	74	SE 7127
Assich Forest	129	NH 8146
Assington	54	TL 9338
Assynt House	128	NH 5967
Astbury	69	SJ 8461
Astcote	51	SP 6753
Asterley	58	SJ 3707
Asterton	48	SO 3991
Asthall	47	SP 2811
Asthall Leigh	47	SP 3012
Astley (Here. and Worc.)	49	SO 7867
Astley (Shrops.)	59	SJ 5218
Astley (Warw.)	50	SP 3189
Astley Abbots	59	SO 7096
Astley Cross	49	SO 8069
Astley Green	69	SJ 7099
Astley Hall (ant.)	69	SD 5718
Aston (Berks.)	36	SU 7884
Aston (Ches.)	69	SJ 5578
Aston (Ches.)	59	SJ 6046
Aston (Derby.)	70	SK 1883
Aston (Here. and Worc.)	48	SO 4571
Aston (Herts.)	37	TL 2722
Aston (Oxon.)	47	SP 3302
Aston (Shrops.)	59	SJ 5228
Aston (Shrops.)	59	SJ 6109
Aston (Staffs.)	59	SJ 7540
Aston (S Yorks.)	71	SK 4685
Aston (W Mids)	50	SP 0789
Aston Abbotts	36	SP 8420
Aston Botterell	49	SO 6284
Aston-by-Stone	59	SJ 9131
Aston Cantlow	50	SP 1359
Aston Clinton	36	SP 8812
Aston Crews	46	SO 6723
Aston End	37	TL 2724
Aston Eyre	59	SO 6594
Aston Fields	50	SO 9669
Aston Flamville	51	SP 4692
Aston Ingham	46	SO 6823
Aston juxta Mondrum	59	SJ 6556
Aston le Walls	51	SP 4950
Aston Magna	47	SP 1935
Aston Munslow	48	SO 5186
Aston on Clun	48	SO 3981
Aston-on-Trent	60	SK 4129
Aston Resrs.	77	SD 6036
Aston Rogers	58	SJ 3406
Aston Rowant	36	SU 7299
Aston Sandford	36	SP 7507
Aston Somerville	50	SP 0438
Aston Subedge	50	SP 1341
Aston Tirrold	35	SU 5586
Aston Upthorpe	35	SU 5586
Astwick	52	TL 2138
Astwood	52	SP 9547
Astwood Bank	50	SP 0362
Aswarby (Lincs.)	62	TF 0639
Aswardby (Lincs.)	73	TF 3770
Atcham	59	SJ 5408
Athelington	55	TM 2170
Athelney	24	ST 3428
Athelstaneford	103	NT 5377
Atherfield Point	27	SZ 4478
Atherington	23	SS 5923
Atherstone	60	SP 3097
Atherstone on Stour	50	SP 2050
Atherton	69	SD 6703
Atholl (dist.)	107	NN 7872
Atlow	60	SK 2248
Attadale Forest	114	NG 9935
Attadale House	114	NG 9239
Attenborough	61	SK 5134
Attingham	59	SJ 5409
Attleborough (Norf.)	64	TM 0495
Attleborough (Warw.)	50	SP 3790
Attlebridge	65	TG 1216
Atwick	81	TA 1850
Atworth	33	ST 8565
Aubourn	72	SK 9262
Auchagallon	92	NR 8934
Auchalick Bay	100	NR 9074
Auchallater	117	NO 1588
Aucharnie	121	NJ 6341
Auchattie	119	NO 6994
Auchavan	108	NO 1969
Auchbraad	99	NR 8381
Auchenblae	119	NO 7278
Auchenbrack	88	NX 7696
Auchenbreck	100	NS 0281
Auchencairn	87	NX 7951
Auchencairn Bay	87	NX 8251
Auchencarroch	101	NS 4182
Auchen Castle (ant.)	89	NT 0603
Auchencorth Moss	95	NT 2055
Auchencrow	97	NT 8560
Auchendinny	103	NT 2561
Auchendores Resr.	100	NS 3572
Auchengray	95	NS 9953
Auchengruith	88	NS 8209
Auchenhalrig	121	NJ 3661
Auchenheath	95	NS 8043
Auchenreoch Loch	88	NX 8171
Auchensaugh Hill	95	NS 8527
Auchensoul	86	NX 2593
Auchentiber	93	NS 3647
Auchgourish	117	NH 9315
Auchindoun Castle (ant.)	121	NJ 3437
Auchindrain	100	NN 0303
Auchindrean	127	NH 1980
Auchineden Hill	101	NS 4980

Auchingilloch (mt.) ...94 NS 7035
Auchininna ...121 NJ 6446
Auchinleck (Dumf. and Galwy.) ...87 NX 4570
Auchinleck (Strath.) ...93 NS 5422
Auchinloch ...101 NS 6670
Auchintoul ...119 NJ 5316
Auchleuchries ...121 NK 0136
Auchleven ...121 NJ 6224
Auchlochan ...95 NS 8037
Auchlossan ...119 NJ 5701
Auchlunies ...119 NO 8999
Auchlyne ...107 NN 5129
Auchlyne West Burn ...107 NN 4830
Auchmacoy ...121 NJ 9930
Auchmillan ...93 NS 5129
Auchmithie ...109 NO 6744
Auchmuirbridge ...103 NO 2101
Auchmull ...119 NO 5874
Auchnacloich ...106 NM 9533
Auchnacree ...109 NO 4663
Auchnafree ...107 NN 8133
Auchnafree Hill ...107 NN 8030
Auchnagallin ...117 NJ 0533
Auchnagatt ...121 NJ 9341
Aucholzie ...118 NO 3490
Auchope Cairn ...90 NT 8819
Auchronie ...118 NO 4480
Auchterarder ...102 NN 9312
Auchterderran ...103 NT 2195
Auchterhouse ...108 NO 3337
Auchtermuchty ...103 NO 2311
Auchterneed ...128 NH 4959
Auchtertool ...103 NT 2190
Auchtertyre Hill ...123 NG 8329
Auchter Water ...95 NS 8754
Auchtitench Hill ...88 NS 7118
Auchtoo ...107 NN 5620
Auckengill ...135 ND 3764
Auckley ...71 SE 6501
Audenshaw ...69 SJ 9196
Audlem ...59 SJ 6543
Audley ...59 SJ 7950
Audley End (ant.) ...53 TL 5237
Audley End Station ...53 TL 5136
Auds ...121 NJ 6564
Aughton (Humbs.) ...74 SE 7038
Aughton (Lancs.) ...68 SD 3804
Aughton (Lancs.) ...77 SD 5467
Aughton (S Yorks.) ...71 SK 4586
Aughton Park ...68 SD 4106
Auld Darkney (mt.) ...109 NO 4266
Auldearn ...129 NH 9155
Aulden ...45 SO 4654
Auldhame ...103 NT 5984
Auldhouse ...94 NS 6250
Auldton Fell ...89 NT 1108
Aulich Burn ...107 NN 5961
Auliston Point ...111 NM 5457
Ault a' chruinn ...114 NG 9420
Aultanrynie ...132 NC 3436
Aultbea ...126 NG 8789
Aultdearg ...127 NH 2865
Aultgrishan ...126 NG 7485
Aultguish Inn ...127 NH 3570
Aultibea ...135 ND 0423
Aultiphurst ...134 NC 8065
Aultmore (Grampn.) ...121 NJ 4053
Aultmore (Grampn.) (dist.) ...121 NJ 4557
Ault-na-goire ...116 NH 5423
Aultnamain Inn ...128 NH 6681
Aulton ...121 NJ 6028
Aundorach ...117 NH 9716
Aunsby ...62 TF 0438
Auquhorthies ...121 NJ 8329
Auskerry (is.) ...137 HY 6716
Auskerry Sound ...137 HY 6618
Aust ...33 ST 5789
Austerfield ...71 SK 6594
Austrey ...60 SK 2906
Austwick ...78 SD 7668
Authorpe ...73 TF 3980
Authorpe Row ...73 TF 5373
Avebury ...34 SU 0969
Avebury (ant.) ...34 SU 1070
Aveley ...37 TQ 5680
Avening ...33 ST 8797
Averham ...61 SK 7654
Aveton Gifford ...21 SX 6947
Avielochan ...117 NH 9016
Aviemore ...117 NH 8912
Avington ...34 SU 3767
Avoch ...129 NH 6955
Avoch Bay ...129 NH 7054
Avon ...26 SZ 1498
Avonbridge ...102 NS 9072
Avon Castle ...26 SU 1303
Avon Dam Resr. ...21 SX 6765
Avon Dassett ...50 SP 4150
Avonmouth ...33 ST 5177
Avon Water ...94 NS 7143
Avon Wick ...21 SX 7158
Awbridge ...26 SU 3323
Awkley ...33 ST 5885
Awliscombe ...24 ST 1301
Awre ...46 SO 7008
Awsworth ...61 SK 4843
Axbridge ...33 ST 4254
Axe Edge ...70 SK 0370
Axford (Hants.) ...35 SU 6043
Axford (Wilts.) ...34 SU 2369
Axminster ...24 SY 2998
Axmouth ...24 SY 2591
Aylburton ...45 SO 6101
Ayle ...83 NY 7149
Aylesbeare ...24 SY 0391
Aylesbury ...36 SP 8213
Aylesby ...75 TA 2007
Aylesford ...30 TQ 7359
Aylesham ...31 TR 2352
Aylestone ...61 SK 5701
Aylmerton ...65 TG 1839
Aylsham ...65 TG 1926
Aylton ...49 SO 6537
Aymestrey ...45 SO 4265
Aynho ...47 SP 5133
Ayot St. Lawrence ...37 TL 1916
Ayot St. Peter ...37 TL 2115
Ayr ...93 NS 3321
Ayres, The ...76 NX 4303
Aysgarth ...78 SE 0088
Ayside ...77 SD 3983
Ayston ...62 SK 8601
Aythorpe Roding ...37 TL 5815
Ayton (Borders) ...97 NT 9260
Ayton (N Yorks.) ...81 SE 9884
Aywick (Yell) ...143 HU 5386
Ay Wick (Yell) ...143 HU 5486
Azerley ...79 SE 2574

B

Baa Taing (Auskerry) ...137 HY 6715
Baa Taing (Shetld.) ...142 HU 2774
Babbacombe ...21 SX 9365
Babbacombe Bay ...21 SX 9568
Babbet Ness ...103 NO 5914
Babbinswood ...58 SJ 3329
Babcary ...25 ST 5628
Babel ...41 SN 8235
Babell ...68 SJ 1574

Babeny ...21 SX 6775
Babingley River ...64 TF 6825
Babraham ...53 TL 5150
Babworth ...72 SK 6880
Bac an Eich ...127 NH 2249
Bac Beag (is.) ...104 NM 2337
Bach Camp (ant.) ...45 SO 5460
Bache Hill ...48 SO 2163
Bach Island ...105 NM 7726
Bachlag ...98 NR 4175
Back ...131 NB 4840
Backaland ...138 HY 5630
Backaskail Bay ...139 HY 6438
Backaskail ...138 HY 4850
Backbarrow ...77 SD 3584
Backfolds ...121 NK 0252
Backford ...68 SJ 3971
Backhill (Grampn.) ...121 NJ 7939
Backhill (Grampn.) ...121 NK 0039
Backhill of Clackriach ...121 NJ 9246
Backhill of Trustach ...119 NO 6397
Backies ...129 NC 8302
Backlass ...135 ND 2053
Backmuir of New Gilston ...103 NO 4308
Back of Keppoch ...111 NM 6587
Backstane Hill ...95 NS 9127
Backwater Reservoir ...108 NO 2560
Backwell ...33 ST 4868
Backworth ...91 NZ 2972
Bac Mòr or Dutchman's Cap ...104 NM 2438
Bacon End ...38 TL 6018
Baconsthorpe ...65 TG 1237
Bacton (Here. and Worc.) ...45 SO 3732
Bacton (Norf.) ...65 TG 3434
Bacton (Suff.) ...54 TM 0466
Bacup ...78 SD 8622
Bad a'Chreamha ...123 NG 8536
Badachro ...123 NG 7873
Badanloch Forest ...134 NC 7935
Badanloch Lodge ...134 NC 7933
Badavanich ...127 NH 1058
Bad Bog ...126 NG 9281
Badbury ...34 SU 1980
Badbury Hill ...47 SU 2694
Badbury Rings (ant.) ...26 ST 9602
Badby ...51 SP 5559
Badcall (Highld.) ...132 NC 1541
Badcall (Highld.) ...132 NC 2355
Badcall Bay ...132 NC 1541
Badcaul ...126 NH 0191
Baddeley Green ...59 SJ 9250
Baddesley Ensor ...60 SP 2798
Baddidarach ...132 NC 0923
Baddinsgill Reservoir ...95 NT 1255
Baddoch ...117 NO 1382
Baddoch (mt.) ...117 NO 0719
Badenoch (dist.) ...116 NN 7091
Badenscoth ...121 NJ 7038
Badentarbat Bay ...126 NC 0008
Badenyon ...118 NJ 3419
Badger ...59 SO 7699
Badgers Mount ...37 TQ 5061
Badgeworth (Glos.) ...46 SO 9019
Badgworth (Somer.) ...32 ST 3952
Badingham ...55 TM 3067
Badlesmere ...31 TR 0154
Badlipster ...135 ND 2049
Badluarach ...126 NG 9994
Badminton ...33 ST 8082
Badminton House ...33 ST 8082
Badmondisfield Hall (ant.) ...54 TL 7457
Badninish ...129 NH 7694
Badrallach ...127 NH 0691
Badsey ...50 SP 0743
Badsworth ...71 SE 4614
Badwell Ash ...54 TL 9969
Bagby ...79 SE 4680
Bagendon ...46 SP 0006
Bage, The ...45 SO 2943
Baggrave Hall ...61 SK 6909
Baggy Point ...22 SS 4140
Bagh an Tailleir (pt.) ...99 NR 8431
Bagh Feisdhun ...110 NM 2458
Bagh Loch an Ròin ...132 NC 1954
Bagh na Doide ...99 NR 6976
Bàgh nam Faoileann ...124 NF 8444
Bàgh nan Gunnaichean ...123 NG 4574
Bàgh Tigh-an-Droighinn ...99 NR 8579
Bagillt ...68 SJ 2175
Bagillt Bank (sbk.) ...68 SJ 2376
Baginton ...50 SP 3474
Baglan ...41 SS 7493
Bagley ...58 SJ 4027
Bagnall ...59 SJ 9250
Bagshot (Surrey) ...36 SU 9163
Bagshot (Wilts.) ...34 SU 3165
Bagshot Heath ...36 SU 9061
Bagthorpe (Norf.) ...64 TF 7932
Bagthorpe (Notts.) ...61 SK 4751
Bagworth ...61 SK 4408
Bagwy Llydiart ...45 SO 4427
Baildland Hill ...93 NS 2552
Baildon ...78 SE 1539
Baile ...122 NF 9381
Bailebeag ...116 NH 5018
Baile Boidheach ...99 NR 7473
Baile Mòr ...104 NM 2824
Bailey Hill ...48 SO 2472
Bailiesward ...121 NJ 4737
Baillieston ...101 NS 6764
Bail Uachdraich ...124 NF 8160
Bainbridge ...84 SD 9390
Bainton (Cambs.) ...62 TF 0906
Bainton (Humbs.) ...81 SE 9652
Bairnkine ...90 NT 6515
Bait or St. Mary's Island ...91 NZ 3575
Bakers End ...38 TL 3917
Baker Street ...38 TQ 6381
Bakewell ...70 SK 2168
Bala ...67 SH 9236
Balachurn ...122 NG 5540
Balaglas ...124 NF 8457
Bala Lake or Llyn Tegid ...67 SH 9033
Balallan ...131 NB 2920
Balbeg ...116 NH 4924
Balbeggie ...108 NO 1629
Balbegno Castle ...119 NO 6372
Balbithan ...119 NJ 7917
Balbithan House ...119 NJ 8018
Balblair ...129 NH 7066
Balcary Point ...87 NX 8249
Balchery ...129 NH 8182
Balchladich ...132 NC 0330
Balchraggan ...128 NH 5343
Balchrick ...132 NC 1960
Balcombe ...29 TQ 3130
Balcomie ...103 NO 6209
Balcurvie ...103 NO 3400
Balderhead Resr. ...84 NY 9118
Baldersby ...79 SE 3578
Balderstone ...77 SD 6332
Balderton ...62 SK 8151
Baldhu ...18 SW 7743
Baldinnie ...103 NO 4311
Baldock ...53 TL 2434
Baldoon Sands ...87 NX 4563
Baldrine ...76 SC 4281
Balduff Hill ...108 NO 2053
Baldwin ...76 SC 3581
Baldwinholme ...82 NY 3351
Baldwin's Gate ...59 SJ 7939

Bale ...64 TG 0136
Balemartine ...104 NL 9841
Balephetrish Bay ...104 NM 0047
Balephuil ...104 NL 9640
Balephuil Bay ...104 NL 9440
Balerno ...102 NT 1666
Baleshare (is.) ...124 NF 7861
Balevullin ...104 NL 9546
Balfield ...109 NO 5468
Balfour ...136 HY 4716
Balfour Castle ...136 HY 4716
Balfron ...101 NS 5488
Balgaveny ...121 NJ 6640
Balgavies ...109 NO 5351
Balgedie ...102 NO 1603
Balgonar ...102 NT 0293
Balgove ...121 NJ 8133
Balgowan ...116 NN 6394
Balgowan Point ...86 NX 1242
Balgown ...122 NG 3868
Balgray ...109 NO 4138
Balgray Reservoir ...93 NS 5157
Balgrochan ...101 NS 6278
Balgy ...123 NG 8454
Balhagardy ...121 NJ 7623
Balhary ...108 NO 2646
Baliasta ...143 HP 6009
Baligill ...134 NC 8566
Balintore (Highld.) ...129 NH 8675
Balintore (Tays.) ...108 NO 2859
Balintraid ...129 NH 7370
Balivanich ...124 NF 7755
Balkeerie ...108 NO 3244
Balkholme ...74 SE 7828
Balkissock ...86 NX 1381
Ball ...58 SJ 3026
Balla ...112 NF 7811
Ballabeg ...76 SC 2470
Ballacannell ...76 SC 4382
Ballacarnane Beg ...76 SC 3088
Ballachulish ...106 NN 0857
Ballageich Hill ...93 NS 5350
Ballagyr ...76 SC 2685
Ballajora ...76 SC 4790
Ballamodha ...76 SC 2773
Ballantrae ...86 NX 0382
Ballantrae Bay ...86 NX 0783
Ballantrushal ...131 NB 3753
Ballard Point ...26 SZ 0481
Ballasalla (I. of M.) ...76 SC 2870
Ballasalla (I. of M.) ...76 SC 3497
Ballater ...118 NO 3695
Ballaugh ...76 SC 3493
Ballechin ...108 NN 9353
Ballencleuch Law ...88 NS 9304
Ballencrieff ...103 NT 4878
Ball Hill ...34 SU 4263
Balliekine ...92 NR 8739
Balliemore (Strath.) ...105 NM 8228
Balliemore (Strath.) ...100 NS 0584
Ballig ...76 SC 2882
Ballikinrain Castle ...101 NS 5687
Ballimore (Central) ...100 NN 5217
Ballimore (Strath.) ...100 NR 9283
Ballimaby ...98 NR 2267
Ballindean ...108 NO 2529
Ballinger Common ...36 SP 9103
Ballingham ...45 SO 5731
Ballingry ...102 NT 1797
Ballinlick ...108 NN 9840
Ballinloan Burn ...108 NN 9442
Ballinluig ...108 NN 9852
Ballintuim ...108 NO 1054
Balloch (Highld.) ...129 NH 7346
Balloch (Strath.) ...101 NS 3981
Balloch (Tays.) ...107 NN 8419
Balloch (Tays.) ...108 NO 3557
Ballochan ...119 NO 5290
Ballochbuie Forest ...117 NO 1989
Balloch Castle ...101 NS 3983
Ballochroy ...92 NR 7252
Balloch, The (mt.) ...121 NJ 4648
Ballo Resr. ...28 SU 9926
Balls Cross ...28 SU 9826
Ballygown ...104 NM 4343
Ballygrant ...98 NR 3966
Ballyhaugh ...110 NM 1758
Ballymichael ...92 NR 9231
Balmacara Forest ...115 NH 3925
Balmacara ...114 NG 8127
Balmaclellan ...88 NX 6578
Balmacneil ...108 NN 9850
Balmae ...87 NX 6845
Balmaha ...101 NS 4290
Balmalcolm ...103 NO 3108
Balmanno Hill ...102 NO 1414
Balmartin ...124 NF 7273
Balmedie ...119 NJ 9617
Balmerino ...103 NO 3524
Balmerlawn ...26 SU 3003
Balmoral Castle ...117 NO 2595
Balmoral Forest ...117 NO 2587
Balmore ...101 NS 6073
Balmore Forest ...117 NH 3333
Balmullo ...103 NO 4220
Balmungie ...129 NH 7459
Balmurrie ...86 NX 2066
Balnabodach ...112 NF 7101
Balnacoil ...134 NC 8011
Balnacra ...126 NG 9746
Balnafoich ...116 NH 6835
Balnaglaic ...116 NH 4430
Balnaguard ...108 NN 9451
Balnaguard Burn ...108 NN 9249
Balnaguisich ...128 NH 6771
Balnahara ...105 NM 4534
Balnahard ...104 NR 4199
Balnakeil ...132 NC 3968
Balnakeil Bay ...132 NC 3869
Balnaknock ...123 NG 4162
Balnamoon ...109 NO 5463
Balnapaling ...129 NH 7969
Balquhidder ...107 NN 5320
Balranald ...124 NF 7169
Balsall Common ...50 SP 2377
Balscote ...47 SP 3841
Balsham ...53 TL 5850
Balta (is.) ...143 HP 6608
Baltasound (Unst) ...143 HP 6208
Balta Sound (Unst) ...143 HP 6508
Baltasound Aerodrome ...143 HP 6207
Balterley ...59 SJ 7550
Balthangie ...121 NJ 8351
Baltonsborough ...25 ST 5434
Balvaird ...128 NH 5744
Balvarran ...108 NO 0762
Balvenie Castle (ant.) ...121 NJ 3240
Balvicar ...100 NM 7616
Balvraid ...117 NH 8231
Bamber Bridge ...77 SD 5626
Bamburgh ...97 NU 1834
Bamff ...108 NO 2251
Bamford ...70 SK 2083
Bampton (Cumbr.) ...83 NY 5118
Bampton (Devon) ...23 SS 9522
Bampton (Oxon.) ...47 SP 3103
Bampton Common ...83 NY 4716
Banavie ...115 NN 1177
Banbury ...51 SP 4540
Banc Cwmhelen ...40 SN 6811
Banchory ...119 NO 6995

Banchory-Devenick ...119 NJ 9002
Banc Nant Rhys ...57 SN 9841
Bancyfelin ...43 SN 3218
Banc-y-ffordd ...43 SN 4037
Bandirran House ...108 NO 1930
Banff ...121 NJ 6863
Bangor ...66 SH 5872
Bangor-Is-coed ...58 SJ 3945
Banham ...54 TM 0688
Bank ...26 SU 2807
Bankend (Dumf. and Galwy.) ...88 NY 0268
Bankend (Strath.) ...95 NS 8033
Bankfoot ...108 NO 0635
Bankglen ...88 NS 5912
Bankhead (Grampn.) ...119 NJ 6608
Bankhead (Grampn.) ...119 NJ 8910
Bank Newton ...78 SD 9152
Banknock ...101 NS 7779
Banks (Cumbr.) ...90 NY 5664
Banks (Lancs.) ...68 SD 3820
Bankshill ...89 NY 1981
Banks Sands ...77 SD 3724
Bank Street ...49 SO 6362
Banningham ...65 TG 2129
Banniskirk House ...135 ND 1657
Bannister Green ...38 TL 6920
Bannockburn ...101 NS 8190
Ban Rubha ...105 NM 7106
Banstead ...37 TQ 2559
Bantham ...21 SX 6643
Banton ...101 NS 7479
Banwell ...32 ST 3959
Baosbheinn (mt.) ...123 NG 8765
Bapchild ...30 TQ 9363
Baramore ...111 NM 6474
Barassie ...93 NS 3232
Barbaraville ...129 NH 7472
Barber Booth ...70 SK 1184
Barbon ...77 SD 6282
Barbreck House ...105 NM 8306
Barbreck River ...105 NM 8306
Barbrook Reservoir ...71 SK 2777
Barbury Castle (ant.) ...34 SU 1476
Barby ...51 SP 5470
Barcaldine Castle (ant.) ...106 NM 9140
Barcaldine Forest ...106 NM 9741
Barcaldine House ...106 NM 9641
Barcheston ...50 SP 2639
Barclay Hill ...87 NX 7552
Barcombe ...29 TQ 4214
Barcombe Cross ...29 TQ 4216
Barcraigs Resr. ...93 NS 3857
Barden ...84 SE 1493
Barden Fell ...78 SE 0858
Barden Resrs. ...78 SE 0257
Bardfield Saling ...54 TL 6826
Bard Head ...141 HU 5135
Bardister ...142 HU 3577
Bardney ...73 TF 1169
Bardon Mill ...90 NY 7764
Bardowie ...101 NS 5873
Bardrainney ...100 NS 3372
Bardsea ...77 SD 3074
Bardsey ...79 SE 3643
Bardsey Island (Ynys Enlli) ...56 SH 1221
Bardsey Sound ...56 SH 1323
Bardsley ...69 SD 9201
Bardwell ...54 TL 9473
Barewood ...45 SO 3856
Barford (Norf.) ...65 TG 1007
Barford (Warw.) ...50 SP 2660
Barford St. John ...47 SP 4332
Barford St. Michael ...47 SP 4332
Barfrestone ...31 TR 2650
Bargatton Loch ...88 NX 6962
Bargoed ...41 SO 1500
Bargrennan ...86 NX 3476
Barham (Cambs.) ...52 TL 1375
Barham (Kent) ...31 TR 2050
Barham (Suff.) ...55 TM 1451
Bar Hill ...53 TL 3863
Barholm ...62 TF 0811
Barkby ...61 SK 6309
Barkestone-le-Vale ...61 SK 7734
Barkham ...36 SU 7866
Barking ...37 TQ 4785
Barking (Suff.) ...54 TM 0653
Barkingside ...37 TQ 4489
Barkisland ...78 SE 0419
Barkston (Lincs.) ...62 SK 9241
Barkston (N Yorks.) ...79 SE 4936
Barkway ...53 TL 3835
Barkwith ...73 TF 1681
Barlaston ...59 SJ 8938
Barlavington ...28 SU 9716
Barlborough ...71 SK 4777
Barlby ...79 SE 6334
Barlestone ...60 SK 4205
Barley (Herts.) ...53 TL 4038
Barley (Lancs.) ...78 SD 8240
Barleythorpe ...61 SK 8409
Barling ...38 TQ 9289
Barlow (Derby.) ...71 SK 3474
Barlow (N Yorks.) ...79 SE 6428
Barlow (Tyne and Wear) ...91 NZ 1560
Barmby Moor ...80 SE 7748
Barmby on the Marsh ...74 SE 6828
Barmekin Hill ...119 NJ 7207
Barmer ...64 TF 8133
Barmoor Castle ...97 NT 9939
Barmore Island ...99 NR 8771
Barmouth ...56 SH 6115
Barmouth Bay ...56 SH 5612
Barmpton ...84 NZ 3318
Barmack ...62 TF 0705
Barnacle ...50 SP 3884
Barnard Castle ...84 NZ 0516
Barnard Gate ...47 SP 4010
Barnardiston ...54 TL 7148
Barnbougle Castle (ant.) ...102 NT 1678
Barnburgh ...71 SE 4803
Barnby ...55 TM 4789
Barnby Dun ...71 SE 6109
Barnby in the Willows ...62 SK 8552
Barnby Moor ...72 SK 6684
Barnes ...37 TQ 2276
Barnet ...37 TQ 2395
Barnetby le Wold ...74 TA 0509
Barney ...64 TF 9932
Barnham (Suff.) ...54 TL 8779
Barnham (W Susx.) ...28 SU 9604
Barnham Broom ...65 TG 0807
Barnhead ...109 NO 6657
Barnhill ...129 NJ 1457
Barnhills ...86 NW 9871
Barnhourie (sbk.) ...82 NX 9350
Barningham (Durham) ...84 NZ 0810
Barningham (Suff.) ...54 TL 9676
Barnoldby le Beck ...75 TA 2303
Barnoldswick ...78 SD 8746
Barns Green ...28 TQ 1227
Barnsley (Glos.) ...46 SP 0705
Barnsley (S Yorks.) ...71 SE 3406
Barns Ness ...96 NT 7277
Barnstaple ...23 SS 5533
Barnstaple or Bideford Bay ...22 SS 3432
Barnston (Essex) ...38 TL 6519
Barnston (Mers.) ...68 SJ 2783
Barnt Green ...50 SP 0073

Barnton ...69 SJ 6374
Barnwell ...52 TL 0485
Barnwood ...46 SO 8518
Barochan House (ant.) ...101 NS 4168
Barons Point ...100 NS 2280
Barony, The ...136 HY 2527
Barr ...86 NX 2794
Barra (is.) ...112 NF 6801
Barra Castle ...121 NJ 7925
Barrachan ...86 NX 3649
Barrack ...121 NJ 8942
Barraer Fell ...86 NX 3761
Barraglom ...131 NB 1634
Barra Head ...112 NL 5579
Barrahormid ...99 NR 7184
Barrapol ...104 NL 9542
Barras ...119 NO 8580
Barrasford ...90 NY 9273
Barravullin ...105 NM 7907
Barr Castle (ant.) ...100 NS 3458
Barregarrow ...76 SC 3288
Barrel of Butter (is.) ...136 HY 3500
Barr Ganuisg ...100 NR 9280
Barr Glen ...92 NR 6936
Barrhead ...101 NS 5058
Barr Hill (Dumf. and Galwy.) ...88 NX 7781
Barrhill (Strath.) ...86 NX 2382
Barrington (Cambs.) ...53 TL 3949
Barrington (Somer.) ...24 ST 3918
Barripper ...18 SW 6338
Barrisdale Bay ...111 NG 8605
Barr Liath ...100 NR 9673
Barrmill ...93 NS 3651
Barr Mòr (Strath.) ...105 NM 8138
Barr Mòr (Strath.) ...100 NN 1312
Barrock ...135 ND 2571
Barrock House ...135 ND 2862
Barrow (Lancs.) ...77 SD 7338
Barrow (Leic.) ...62 SK 8815
Barrow (Shrops.) ...59 SJ 6500
Barrow (Somer.) ...25 ST 7231
Barrow (Suff.) ...54 TL 7663
Barroway Drove ...63 TF 5703
Barrowby ...62 SK 8736
Barrow Deep (lightship) ...39 TM 3004
Barrowden ...62 SK 9400
Barrowford ...78 SD 8538
Barrow Gurney ...33 ST 5267
Barrow-in-Furness ...76 SD 1969
Barrow Street ...25 ST 8430
Barrow upon Humber ...74 TA 0721
Barrow upon Soar ...61 SK 5717
Barrow upon Trent ...60 SK 3528
Barr Water ...92 NR 6836
Barry (S Glam.) ...41 ST 1168
Barry (Tays.) ...109 NO 5334
Barry Island ...41 ST 1166
Barry Links ...109 NO 5431
Barry Links Station ...109 NO 5433
Barsalloch Point ...86 NX 3441
Barsby ...61 SK 6911
Barsham ...55 TM 3989
Barston ...50 SP 2078
Bartestree ...45 SO 5641
Bar, The (Dyfed) ...56 SN 5780
Bar, The (Gwyn.) ...56 SH 4161
Bar, The (Gwyn.) ...56 SH 6014
Barth Head ...136 ND 4285
Barthol Chapel ...121 NJ 8134
Barthomley ...59 SJ 7652
Bartley ...26 SU 3012
Bartlow ...53 TL 5845
Barton (Cambs.) ...53 TL 4055
Barton (Ches.) ...58 SJ 4454
Barton (Devon) ...21 SX 9067
Barton (Glos.) ...46 SP 0925
Barton (Lancs.) ...77 SD 5136
Barton (Lancs.) ...68 SD 3509
Barton (N Yorks.) ...84 NZ 2208
Barton (Warw.) ...50 SP 1051
Barton Aerodrome ...69 SJ 7397
Barton Bendish ...64 TF 7105
Barton Hartshorn ...51 SK 6431
Barton in Fabis ...61 SK 5232
Barton in the Beans ...60 SK 3906
Barton-le-Clay ...52 TL 0831
Barton-le-Street ...80 SE 7274
Barton-le-Willows ...80 SE 7163
Barton Mills ...54 TL 7173
Barton Moss ...69 SJ 7397
Barton on Sea ...26 SZ 2493
Barton-on-the-Heath ...47 SP 2532
Barton Seagrave ...52 SP 8877
Barton Stacey ...34 SU 4340
Barton Stacey Camp ...35 SU 4343
Barton St. David ...25 ST 5431
Barton Turf ...65 TG 3522
Barton-under-Needwood ...60 SK 1818
Barton-Upon-Humber ...74 TA 0222
Barvas ...131 NB 3649
Barway ...53 TL 5475
Barwell ...50 SP 4496
Barwick in Elmet ...79 SE 3937
Baschurch ...58 SJ 4222
Bascote ...50 SP 4063
Basford Green ...60 SJ 9951
Bashall Eaves ...77 SD 6943
Bashley ...26 SZ 2496
Basildon ...38 TQ 7189
Basing ...35 SU 6652
Basingstoke ...35 SU 6352
Basingstoke Canal ...35 SU 8453
Baslow ...71 SK 2572
Bason Bridge ...32 ST 3445
Bassaleg ...32 ST 2787
Bassenthwaite ...82 NY 2332
Bassenthwaite Lake ...82 NY 2129
Bassett ...26 SU 4116
Bassingbourn ...53 TL 3344
Bassingfield ...61 SK 6137
Bassingham ...72 SK 9059
Bassingthorpe ...62 SK 9628
Bass Rock ...103 NT 6087
Basta ...143 HU 5294
Basta Voe ...143 HU 5296
Baston ...62 TF 1114
Bastwick ...65 TG 4217
Batcombe (Dorset.) ...25 ST 6104
Batcombe (Somer.) ...33 ST 6838
Bate Heath ...69 SJ 6879
Bath ...33 ST 7464
Bathampton ...33 ST 7766
Bathealton ...24 ST 0724
Bathford ...33 ST 7866
Bathgate ...102 NS 9768
Bathley ...72 SK 7759
Bathpool ...20 SX 2874
Batley ...79 SE 2424
Batsford ...47 SP 1834
Battersby ...85 NZ 5908
Battersea ...37 TQ 2876
Battery Point ...33 ST 4677
Battisford ...54 TM 0554
Battisford Tye ...54 TM 0254
Battle (E Susx.) ...29 TQ 7416
Battle (Powys) ...41 SO 0031
Battlefield ...59 SJ 5117
Battlesbridge ...38 TQ 7794
Battlesden ...52 SP 9628
Battleton ...23 SS 9127

Boot Brobury

Boot 82 NY 1700
Boothby Graffoe 72 SK 9859
Boothby Pagnell 62 SK 9730
Boothstown 69 SD 7200
Booth Wood Resr. 70 SE 0215
Bootle (Cumbr.) 76 SD 1088
Bootle (Mers.) 68 SJ 3394
Bootle Fell 76 SD 1488
Bootle Station 82 SD 0989
Boquhan 101 NS 5387
Boraston 49 SO 6170
Borden 30 TQ 8863
Bordley 78 SD 9465
Bordon Camp 27 SU 7935
Boreham (Essex) 38 TL 7509
Boreham (Wilts.) 33 ST 8944
Boreham Street 29 TQ 6611
Borehamwood 37 TQ 1996
Boreland (Central) 107 NN 5534
Boreland (Dumf. and Galwy.) 89 NY 1790
Boreland Hill 88 NX 9460
Boreray (North Uist) 124 NF 8581
Boreray (St. Kilda or Hirta) 124 NA 1505
Bore Stane 102 NT 1459
Bore, The 138 HY 4956
Borgie 133 NC 6759
Borgie Forest 133 NC 6655
Borgue (Dumf. and Galwy.) 87 NX 6248
Borgue (Highld.) 135 ND 1325
Borle Brook 49 SO 7087
Borley 54 TL 8442
Bornesketaig 122 NG 3771
Borness 87 NX 6145
Borness Point 87 NX 6144
Boroughbridge 79 SE 3966
Borough Green 29 TQ 6057
Borras Head 58 SJ 3653
Borreraig 122 NG 1853
Borrobol Forest 134 NC 7726
Borrobol Lodge 134 NC 8626
Borrodale Burn 111 NM 7086
Borrowash 60 SK 4134
Borrow Beck 83 NY 5205
Borrowby 85 SE 4289
Borrowdale (Cumbr.) 82 NY 2416
Borrowdale (Cumbr.) 82 NY 2514
Borrowdale (Cumbr.) 83 NY 5703
Borrowdale Fells 82 NY 2512
Borrowfield 119 NO 8293
Borth 56 SN 6089
Borthwickbrae 89 NT 4113
Borthwickshiels 89 NT 4315
Borthwick Water 89 NT 4112
Borve (Barra) 112 NF 6501
Borve (Berneray, North Uist) 124 NF 9181
Borve (Harris, W Isles) 124 NG 0294
Borve (Island of Skye) 123 NG 4448
Borve Point 112 NF 6402
Borve River 131 NB 4254
Borwick 77 SD 5273
Bosavern 18 SW 3730
Bosbury 49 SO 6943
Boscastle 20 SX 0990
Boscobel House (ant.) 59 SJ 8308
Boscombe (Dorset) 26 SZ 1191
Boscombe (Wilts.) 34 SU 2038
Boscoppa 19 SX 0353
Bosham 27 SU 8004
Bosherston 42 SR 9694
Boskednan 18 SW 4434
Bosley 69 SJ 9165
Bossall 80 SE 7160
Bossiney 20 SX 0688
Bossingham 31 TR 1549
Bostock Green 69 SJ 6769
Boston 63 TF 3244
Boston Aerodrome 63 TF 2943
Boston Deeps (chan.) 63 TF 4947
Boston Spa 79 SE 4245
Boswinger 19 SW 9941
Botallack 18 SW 3632
Botany Bay 37 TQ 2999
Botcheston 61 SK 4804
Botesdale 54 TM 0475
Bothal 91 NZ 2386
Bothamsall 71 SK 6773
Bothel 82 NY 1838
Bothenhampton 25 SY 4791
Bothwell 101 NS 7058
Bothwell Water 103 NT 6666
Botley (Bucks.) 36 SP 9802
Botley (Hants.) 27 SU 5112
Botley (Oxon.) 47 SP 4806
Botolphs 28 TQ 1909
Bottacks 128 NH 4860
Bottesford (Humbs.) 74 SE 9107
Bottesford (Leic.) 61 SK 8038
Bottisham 53 TL 5460
Bottle Island 126 NB 9502
Bottomcraig 109 NO 3724
Bottoms 78 SD 9321
Botton Head 77 SD 6661
Botusfleming 20 SX 4061
Botwnnog 66 SH 2631
Boughrood 44 SO 1239
Boughspring 45 ST 5597
Boughton (Norf.) 64 TF 7002
Boughton (Northants.) 51 SP 7565
Boughton (Notts.) 71 SK 6768
Boughton Aluph 31 TR 0348
Boughton Green 29 TQ 7651
Boughton House (ant.) 52 SP 9081
Boughton Lees 31 TR 0247
Boughton Malherbe 30 TQ 8849
Boughton Street 31 TR 0559
Boulby 85 NZ 7519
Bouldon 48 SO 5485
Boulmer 91 NU 2614
Boulmer Haven 91 NU 2613
Boulston 42 SM 9812
Boulsworth Hill 78 SD 9335
Boultenstone 118 NJ 4110
Boultham 72 SK 9568
Bourn 53 TL 3256
Bourne 62 TF 0920
Bourne End (Beds.) 52 SP 9644
Bourne End (Bucks.) 36 SU 8987
Bourne End (Herts.) 36 TL 0206
Bournemouth 26 SZ 0991
Bournemouth (Hurn) Airport 26 SZ 1198
Bournes Green 46 SO 9104
Bournheath 49 SO 9474
Bournmoor 84 NZ 3051
Bournville 50 SP 0480
Bourton (Avon) 32 ST 3864
Bourton (Dorset) 25 ST 7630
Bourton (Oxon.) 34 SU 2387
Bourton (Shrops.) 59 SO 5996
Bourton on Dunsmore 50 SP 4370
Bourton-on-the-Hill 47 SP 1732
Bourton-on-the-Water 47 SP 1620
Bousd 110 NM 2563
Boveney 36 SU 9377
Boverton 41 SS 9868
Bovey Tracey 21 SX 8178
Bovingdon 36 TL 0103
Bovington Camp 25 SY 8389
Bow 37 TQ 3783
Bow (Devon) 23 SS 7201
Bow (Flotta, Orkney) 136 ND 3693
Bowbank 84 NY 9423
Bow Brickhill 52 SP 9034
Bowburn 84 NZ 3038
Bowcombe 27 SZ 4786
Bowd 24 SY 1190
Bowden (Borders) 96 NT 5530
Bowden (Devon) 21 SX 8448
Bowden Hill 34 ST 9367
Bowdon 69 SJ 7586
Bower 90 NY 7583
Bowerchalke 26 SU 0122
Bowermadden 135 ND 2364
Bowers Gifford 38 TQ 7588
Bowershall 102 NT 0991
Bowertower 135 ND 2362
Bowes 84 NY 9913
Bowes Moor 84 NY 9311
Bow Fell 82 NY 2406
Bow Head 138 HY 4553
Bowhill 96 NT 4227
Bowland 96 NT 4540
Bowland Bridge 83 SD 4189
Bowley 45 SO 5352
Bowlhead Green 28 SU 9138
Bowling 101 NS 4473
Bowling Bank 58 SJ 3948
Bowling Green 49 SO 8151
Bowmanstead 82 SD 3096
Bowmont Forest 96 NT 7328
Bowmont Water 97 NT 8125
Bowmore 98 NR 3159
Bowness-on-Solway 89 NY 2262
Bowness-on-Windermere 83 SD 4097
Bow of Fife 103 NO 3112
Bowood House 34 ST 9769
Bowsden 97 NT 9941
Bowside Lodge 134 NC 8261
Bow Street 57 SN 6284
Bowthorpe 65 TG 1709
Box (Glos.) 46 SO 8600
Box (Wilts.) 33 ST 8268
Boxbush 46 SO 7412
Boxford (Berks.) 34 SU 4271
Boxford (Suff.) 54 TL 9640
Boxgrove 27 SU 9007
Boxley 30 TQ 7759
Boxted (Essex) 54 TM 0033
Boxted (Suff.) 54 TL 8250
Boxworth 53 TL 3464
Boylestone 60 SK 1835
Boyndie 121 NJ 6463
Boyndie Bay 121 NJ 6765
Boyndlie 121 NJ 9162
Boyne Bay 121 NJ 6166
Boynton 81 TA 1368
Boysack 109 NO 6249
Boyton (Corn.) 20 SX 3192
Boyton (Suff.) 55 TM 3747
Boyton (Wilts.) 34 ST 9539
Bozeat 52 SP 9059
Braaid 76 SC 3176
Braal Castle 135 ND 1360
Brabling Green 55 TM 2964
Brabourne 31 TR 1041
Brabourne Lees 31 TR 0840
Brabster 135 ND 3269
Bracadale 122 NG 3538
Braceborough 62 TF 0713
Bracebridge Heath 72 SK 9767
Braceby 62 TF 0135
Bracewell 78 SD 8648
Brackenfield 71 SK 3759
Brackenthwaite 82 NY 1522
Bracklesham Bay 36 SU 8095
Brackletter 115 NN 1882
Brackley (Northants.) 51 SP 5837
Brackley (Strath.) 92 NR 7941
Bracknell 36 SU 8769
Brack, The 100 NN 2403
Braco 101 NN 8309
Bracobrae 121 NJ 5053
Braco Castle (ant.) 101 NN 8211
Bracon Ash 65 TM 1899
Bracorina 111 NM 7192
Bracorina 111 NM 7292
Bradbourne 60 SK 2052
Bradbury 84 NZ 3128
Bradda 76 SC 1970
Bradda Head 76 SC 1870
Bradden 51 SP 6448
Braddock 19 SX 1662
Bradenham 36 SU 8297
Bradenham 64 TF 9208
Bradenstoke 34 SU 0079
Bradfield (Berks.) 35 SU 6072
Bradfield (Essex) 55 TM 1430
Bradfield (Norf.) 65 TG 2633
Bradfield Combust 54 TL 8957
Bradfield Green 69 SJ 6859
Bradfield Moors 71 SK 2292
Bradfield St. Clare 54 TL 9057
Bradfield St. George 54 TL 9059
Bradford (Devon) 22 SS 4207
Bradford (Northum.) 97 NU 1532
Bradford (W Yorks.) 78 SE 1633
Bradford Abbas 25 ST 5814
Bradford Leigh 33 ST 8362
Bradford-on-Avon 33 ST 8260
Bradford-on-Tone 24 ST 1722
Bradford Peverell 25 SY 6592
Brading 27 SZ 6087
Bradley (Derby.) 60 SK 2145
Bradley (Hants.) 35 SU 6341
Bradley (Here. and Worc.) 50 SO 9860
Bradley (Humbs.) 75 TA 2406
Bradley (Staffs.) 59 SJ 8717
Bradley Green 50 SO 9861
Bradley in the Moors 60 SK 0541
Bradmore 61 SK 5831
Bradninch 23 SS 9903
Bradnop 60 SK 0155
Bradpole 25 SY 4794
Bradshaw 69 SD 7312
Bradstone 20 SX 3880
Bradwall Green 69 SJ 7563
Bradwell (Bucks.) 52 SP 8339
Bradwell (Derby.) 70 SK 1781
Bradwell (Essex) 38 TL 8023
Bradwell (Norf.) 65 TG 5003
Bradwell Green 69 SJ 7563
Bradwell Grove 47 SP 2308
Bradwell-on-Sea 39 TM 0006
Bradwell Waterside 39 TL 9907
Bradworthy 22 SS 3213
Brae (Highld.) 128 NC 4300
Brae (Highld.) 126 NG 8185
Brae (Highld.) 128 NH 6663
Brae (Shetld.) 141 HU 3567
Braeantra 128 NH 5678
Braedownie 117 NO 2875
Braefield 116 NH 4130
Braegrum 108 NO 0024
Braehead (Orkney) 136 HY 5101
Braehead (Strath.) 95 NS 8134
Braehead (Strath.) 95 NS 9550
Braehead (Tays.) 109 NO 6852
Braehead (Westray) 138 HY 4447
Braehead (Wigtown.) 87 NX 4252
Braehoulland 142 HU 2479
Braelangwell Lodge 128 NH 5192
Braemar (Grampn.) 117 NO 1591
Braemar (Grampn.) (dist.) 117 NO 1493
Braemore 135 ND 0630
Braemore Forest 127 NH 2076
Brae of Achnahaird 132 NC 0013
Brae of Glenbervie 119 NO 7684
Brae of Moan 138 HY 3733
Braeriach (Braigh Riabhach) 117 NN 9599
Braeroy Forest 115 NN 3791
Brae Roy Lodge 115 NN 3391
Braeside 100 NS 2375
Braes of Abernethy 117 NJ 0715
Braes of Balquhidder 107 NN 4921
Braes of Doune 101 NN 7005
Braes of Glenlivet 117 NJ 2522
Braes of Lorn 105 NM 8717
Braes of Ogilvie 102 NN 8907
Braes of the Carse 108 NO 2530
Braes o' Lochaber 115 NN 3280
Braes, The 123 NG 5234
Braeswick 139 HY 6037
Brae Wick 142 HU 2477
Brafferton (Durham) 84 NZ 2921
Brafferton (N Yorks.) 79 SE 4370
Brafield-on-the-Green 52 SP 8158
Braga Ness 140 HU 1948
Bragar 131 NB 2947
Bragbury End 37 TL 2621
Bragleenmore 106 NM 9020
Braich Anelog 56 SH 1427
Braich y Pwll 56 SH 1325
Braides 77 SD 4350
Braid Fell 86 NX 1166
Braid Hills 103 NT 2569
Braidley 78 SE 0380
Braidon Bay 119 NO 8777
Braidwood 95 NS 8448
Bràigh Mòr 130 NA 9916
Bràigh-nam-bàgh 125 NG 0889
Braigh Riabhach 117 NN 9599
Braigh Srón Ghorm 117 NN 9078
Braigo 98 NR 2369
Brailes 50 SP 3139
Brailsford 60 SK 2541
Braintree 38 TL 7622
Braiseworth 55 TM 1371
Braishfield 26 SU 3725
Braithwaite 82 NY 2323
Braithwell 71 SK 5394
Bramber 28 TQ 1810
Bramcote 61 SK 5037
Bramdean 27 SU 6127
Bramerton 65 TG 2904
Bramfield (Herts.) 37 TL 2915
Bramfield (Suff.) 55 TM 4073
Bramford 55 TM 1246
Bramhall 69 SJ 8984
Bramham 79 SE 4242
Bramhope 79 SE 2443
Bramley (Hants.) 36 SU 6358
Bramley (Surrey) 28 TQ 0044
Bramley (S Yorks.) 71 SK 4892
Brampford Speke 21 SX 9298
Brampton (Cambs.) 52 TL 2170
Brampton (Cumbr.) 90 NY 5361
Brampton (Cumbr.) 83 NY 6723
Brampton (Lincs.) 72 SK 8479
Brampton (Norf.) 65 TG 2224
Brampton (Suff.) 55 TM 4381
Brampton (S Yorks.) 71 SE 4101
Brampton Abbotts 45 SO 6026
Brampton Ash 51 SP 7887
Brampton Bryan 48 SO 3672
Brampton Station 55 TM 4183
Bramshall 60 SK 0633
Bramshaw 26 SU 2615
Bramshill 36 SU 7461
Bramshill Plantation 36 SU 7562
Bramshott 27 SU 8432
Brancaster 64 TF 7743
Brancaster Bay 64 TF 7546
Brancaster Roads 64 TF 8049
Brancepeth 84 NZ 2238
Branchill 129 NJ 0852
Branderburgh 120 NJ 2371
Brandesburton 75 TA 1147
Brandeston 55 TM 2460
Brandiston 65 TG 1321
Brandon (Durham) 84 NZ 2439
Brandon (Lincs.) 62 SK 9048
Brandon (Northum.) 91 NU 0417
Brandon (Suff.) 54 TL 7886
Brandon (Warw.) 50 SP 4076
Brandon Bank 54 TL 6289
Brandon Creek 54 TL 6091
Brandon Park 54 TL 7784
Brandon Parva 64 TG 0708
Brandsby 79 SE 5872
Brands Hatch 37 TQ 5764
Brand Side 70 SK 0468
Brane 18 SW 4028
Bran End 54 TL 6525
Branksome Park 26 SZ 0490
Brannie Burn 106 NN 1616
Branscombe 24 SY 1988
Bransdale 85 SE 6296
Bransford 49 SO 7952
Bransgore 26 SZ 1897
Bransly Hill 103 NT 6770
Branston (Leic.) 61 SK 8029
Branston (Lincs.) 72 TF 0167
Branston (Staffs.) 60 SK 2221
Branstone 27 SZ 5583
Brant Broughton 62 SK 9154
Brant Fell 83 SD 6595
Brantham 55 TM 1034
Branthwaite 82 NY 0525
Brantingham 74 SE 9429
Branton 91 NU 0416
Branton 71 SE 6501
Branxholme 89 NT 4611
Branxholm Park 89 NT 4612
Branxton 97 NT 8937
Brassington 60 SK 2354
Brasted 29 TQ 4755
Brasted Chart 29 TQ 4653
Brat Bheinn 98 NR 4966
Brathens 119 NO 6798
Bratoft 73 TF 4765
Brattleby 72 SK 9480
Bratton 33 ST 9152
Bratton Castle (ant.) 33 ST 9051
Bratton Clovelly 20 SX 4691
Bratton Fleming 23 SS 6437
Bratton Seymour 25 ST 6729
Braughing 53 TL 3925
Braunston (Leic.) 62 SK 8306
Braunston (Northants.) 51 SP 5366
Braunstone 61 SK 5502
Braunton 22 SS 4836
Braunton Burrows 22 SS 4535
Brawby 80 SE 7378
Brawl 134 NC 8066
Brawlbin 135 ND 0757
Bray 36 SU 9079
Braybrooke 51 SP 7684
Brayford 23 SS 6834
Bray Shop 20 SX 3374
Braystones 82 NY 0006
Brayton 79 SE 6030
Brazacott 20 SX 2691
Breabag (mt.) 132 NC 2917
Breachacha Castle 110 NM 1553
Breachwood Green 37 TL 1522
Breackerie Water 92 NR 6413
Breaclete 131 NB 1536
Breadalbane (dist.) 107 NN 4735
Breadsall 60 SK 3639
Breadstone 46 SO 7000
Breagach Hill 118 NJ 3313
Breage 18 SW 6128
Breakachy 128 NH 4644
Breakish 123 NG 6723
Breaksea Point 41 ST 0265
Bream 45 SO 6005
Breamore 26 SU 1517
Brean 32 ST 2955
Brean Down 32 ST 2858
Brearton 79 SE 3260
Breasclete 131 NB 2135
Breaston 61 SK 4533
Breast Sand 63 TF 5427
Brechfa 43 SN 5230
Brechin 109 NO 5960
Breckles 64 TL 9594
Breck Ness 136 HY 2209
Breckrey 123 NG 5162
Breck, The 142 HU 3292
Brecon 41 SO 0428
Brecon and Abergavenny Canal 41 SO 1122
Brecon Beacons (mt.) 41 SO 0121
Bredbury 69 SJ 9292
Brede 30 TQ 8218
Bredenbury 45 SO 6056
Bredfield 55 TM 2653
Bredgar 30 TQ 8860
Bredhurst 30 TQ 7962
Bredon 49 SO 9236
Bredon Hill 50 SO 9640
Bredon's Norton 49 SO 9339
Bredwardine 45 SO 3344
Breedon on the Hill 60 SK 4022
Breich 102 NS 9560
Breighton 74 SE 7033
Breinton 45 SO 4739
Breiti Stack 139 HZ 2072
Brei Wick 141 HU 4740
Bremenium (ant.) 90 NY 8398
Bremhill 34 ST 9873
Bremia (ant.) 43 SN 6456
Brenchley 29 TQ 6741
Brendon 23 SS 7648
Brendon Common 23 SS 7645
Brendon Hills 24 ST 0135
Brenfield Bay 99 NR 8582
Brenig Resr. 67 SH 9857
Brenish 130 NA 9926
Brenish Point 124 NF 9089
Brent Eleigh 54 TL 9447
Brentford 37 TQ 1778
Brent Knoll 32 ST 3350
Brent Pelham 53 TL 4330
Brentwood 38 TQ 5993
Brenzett 31 TR 0027
Brereton 60 SK 0516
Brereton Green 69 SJ 7764
Brereton Heath 69 SJ 8064
Bressay 141 HU 5040
Bressay Sound 141 HU 4841
Bressingham 54 TM 0780
Brest Rocks 93 NS 1904
Brest Twrch 41 SN 8120
Bretby 60 SK 2923
Bretford 50 SP 4277
Bretforton 50 SP 0943
Bretherdale Head 83 NY 5705
Bretherton 69 SD 4720
Brettabister 141 HU 4857
Brettenham (Norf.) 54 TL 9383
Brettenham (Suff.) 54 TL 9653
Bretton 68 SJ 3563
Brevig 112 NL 6998
Brewham 25 ST 7136
Brewlands Bridge 108 NO 1961
Brewood 59 SJ 8808
Breydon Water 65 TG 4907
Briantspuddle 25 SY 8193
Brickendon 37 TL 3208
Bricket Wood 37 TL 1301
Bricklehampton 50 SO 9842
Bride 76 NX 4501
Bridekirk 82 NY 1133
Bridell 42 SN 1742
Bride's Ness 139 HY 7752
Bridestowe 20 SX 5189
Bridestowe and Sourton Common 21 SX 5688
Brideswell 121 NJ 5739
Bridford 21 SX 8186
Bridge 31 TR 1854
Bridge End (Lincs.) 62 TF 1436
Bridgefoot 82 NY 0529
Bridge Green 53 TL 4636
Bridgemary 27 SU 5702
Bridgend (Cumbr.) 83 NY 3914
Bridgend (Dumf. and Galwy.) 89 NT 0708
Bridgend (Fife) 103 NO 3911
Bridgend (Grampn.) 121 NJ 3731
Bridgend (Grampn.) 121 NJ 5135
Bridgend (Islay) 98 NR 3362
Bridgend (Lothian) 102 NT 0475
Bridgend (Mid Glam.) 41 SS 9079
Bridgend (Strath.) 99 NR 8592
Bridgend (Strath.) 101 NS 6970
Bridgend (Tays.) 108 NO 1224
Bridgend (Tays.) 109 NO 5368
Bridgend of Lintrathen 108 NO 2854
Bridge of Alford 119 NJ 5617
Bridge of Allan 101 NS 7897
Bridge of Avon 117 NJ 1835
Bridge of Balgie 107 NN 5746
Bridge of Brown 117 NJ 1220
Bridge of Buchat 118 NJ 3915
Bridge of Cally 108 NO 1351
Bridge of Canny 119 NO 6597
Bridge of Craigisla 108 NO 2553
Bridge of Dee 88 NX 7360
Bridge of Don 119 NJ 9409
Bridge of Dun 109 NO 6658
Bridge of Dye 119 NO 6585
Bridge of Earn 108 NO 1318
Bridge of Ericht 107 NN 5258
Bridge of Feugh 119 NO 7094
Bridge of Forss 135 ND 0368
Bridge of Gairn 118 NO 3597
Bridge of Gaur 107 NN 5056
Bridge of Muchalls 119 NO 8991
Bridge of Orchy 106 NN 2939
Bridge of Tilt 108 NN 8765
Bridge of Waithe 136 HY 2811
Bridge of Walls 140 HU 2651
Bridge of Weir 101 NS 3865
Bridgerule 22 SS 2803
Bridges 58 SO 3996
Bridge Sollers 45 SO 4142
Bridge Street 54 TL 8749
Bridgetown 23 SS 9233
Bridge Trafford 68 SJ 4471
Bridgewater Canal 69 SJ 7186
Bridgeyate 33 ST 6873
Bridgham 54 TL 9686
Bridgnorth 59 SO 7193
Bridgtown 60 SJ 9808
Bridgwater 24 ST 3037
Bridgwater Bay 32 ST 1852
Bridlington 81 TA 1766
Bridlington Bay 81 TA 1964
Bridport 25 SY 4692
Bridstow 45 SO 5824
Brierfield 78 SD 8436
Brierley (Glos.) 45 SO 6215
Brierley (Here. and Worc.) 45 SO 4956
Brierley (S Yorks.) 71 SE 4011
Brierley Hill 49 SO 9187
Briga Head 135 ND 1875
Brigg 74 TA 0007
Brigham (Cumbr.) 82 NY 0830
Brigham (Humbs.) 81 TA 0753
Brighouse 78 SE 1423
Brighstone 26 SZ 4282
Brighstone Bay 26 SZ 4180
Brighstone Forest 26 SZ 4285
Brightgate 71 SK 2659
Brighthampton 47 SP 3803
Brightling 29 TQ 6821
Brightlingsea 39 TM 0816
Brighton (Corn.) 19 SW 9054
Brighton (E Susx) 29 TQ 3105
Brighton, Hove & Worthing Municipal Airport 28 TQ 2005
Brightons 102 NS 9277
Brightwalton 34 SU 4278
Brightwell 55 TM 2543
Brightwell Baldwin 36 SU 6594
Brightwell-cum-Sotwell 35 SU 5790
Brignall 84 NZ 0712
Brig o'Turk 101 NN 5306
Brigsley 75 TA 2501
Brigsteer 83 SD 4889
Brigstock 52 SP 9485
Brill 36 SP 6513
Brilley 45 SO 2549
Brimfield 48 SO 5267
Brimington 71 SK 4073
Brimmond Hill 119 NJ 8509
Brimpsfield 46 SO 9312
Brimpton 35 SU 5564
Brims 136 ND 2888
Brims Ness (Highld.) 135 ND 0471
Brims Ness (Hoy, Orkney) 136 ND 2988
Brind 74 SE 7430
Brindister (Shetld.) 140 HU 2757
Brindister (Shetld.) 141 HU 4337
Brindle 77 SD 5924
Brindley Ford 59 SJ 8754
Brindley Heath 60 SJ 9914
Brineton 59 SJ 8013
Bring Deeps (chan.) 136 HY 2902
Bringewood Chase 48 SO 4573
Bring Head (Hoy, Shetld.) 136 HY 2702
Bring Head (Rousay) 138 HY 3733
Bringhurst 52 SP 8492
Brington 52 TL 0875
Briningham 64 TG 0334
Brinkburn Priory (ant.) 91 NZ 1198
Brinkhill 73 TF 3773
Brinkley 54 TL 6254
Brinklow 50 SP 4379
Brinkworth 34 SU 0184
Brinscall 77 SD 6321
Brinsley 61 SK 4548
Brinsop 45 SO 4344
Brinsworth 71 SK 4190
Brinton 64 TG 0335
Brinyan 136 HY 4327
Brisley 64 TF 9421
Brislington 33 ST 6170
Brisons, The 18 SW 3331
Bristol 33 ST 5872
Bristol Airport 33 ST 5064
Bristol Channel 40 SS 4267
Briston 64 TG 0632
Britannia 78 SD 8821
Britford 26 SU 1528
Briton Ferry 40 SS 7394
Britwell Salome 36 SU 6792
Brixham 21 SX 9255
Brixton 21 SX 5452
Brixton 37 TQ 3175
Brixton Deverill 33 ST 8638
Brixworth 51 SP 7470
Brize Norton 47 SP 2907
Broad Bay or Loch a Tuath 131 NB 5037
Broad Bench (pt.) 25 SY 8978
Broad Blunsdon 34 SU 1490
Broadbottom 70 SJ 9993
Broadbridge 27 SU 8105
Broadbridge Heath 28 TQ 1431
Broadbury (dist.) 20 SX 4596
Broad Cairn 117 NO 2481
Broad Campden 50 SP 1537
Broad Chalke 26 SU 0325
Broadclyst 21 SX 9897
Broad Clyst Station 21 SX 9995
Broad Down 24 SY 1793
Broadford 123 NG 6423
Broadford Aerodrome 123 NG 6925
Broadford Bay 123 NG 6524
Broad Green 49 SO 7656
Broadhaugh 89 NT 4509
Broad Haven 42 SM 8613
Broad Head 89 NY 3394
Broadheath (Gtr Mches.) 69 SJ 7689
Broadheath (Here. and Worc.) 49 SO 6665
Broadheath (Here. and Worc.) 49 SO 8156
Broadhembury 24 ST 1004
Broadhempston 21 SX 8066
Broad Hill (Cambs.) 54 TL 5976
Broadhill (Strath.) 95 NT 0029
Broad Hinton 34 SU 1076
Broadlands House 26 SU 3520
Broad Law 95 NT 1423
Broad Laying 34 SU 4362
Broadley (Grampn.) 121 NJ 4161
Broadley (Gtr Mches.) 69 SD 8716
Broadley Common 37 TL 4207
Broad Marston 50 SP 1346
Broadmayne 25 SY 7286
Broadmeadows 96 NT 4130
Broadmere 35 SU 6247
Broad Oak (Cumbr.) 82 SD 1194
Broadoak (Dorset) 25 SY 4496
Broad Oak (E Susx) 29 TQ 6022
Broad Oak (Here. and Worc.) 45 SO 4721
Broadoak (Kent) 31 TR 1661
Broadrashes 121 NJ 4354
Broadsea Bay 86 NW 9659
Broad Sound (Dyfed) 42 SM 7307
Broad Sound (Is. of Sc.) 18 SV 8309
Broadstairs 31 TR 3967
Broadstone (Dorset) 26 SZ 0095
Broadstone (Shrops.) 48 SO 5389
Broad Street 30 TQ 8356
Broad Taing 136 HY 4217
Broad Town 34 SU 0977
Broadwas 49 SO 7555
Broadwater 28 TQ 1504
Broadway (Here. and Worc.) 50 SP 0937
Broadway (Somer.) 24 ST 3215
Broadway Hill 50 SP 1136
Broadwell (Glos.) 47 SP 2027
Broadwell (Oxon.) 47 SP 2503
Broadwell (Warw.) 51 SP 4565
Broadwell House 84 NY 9153
Broadwell Lane End 45 SO 5811
Broadwey 25 SY 6683
Broadwindsor 25 ST 4302
Broadwood-Kelly 23 SS 6105
Broadwoodwidger 20 SX 4089
Brobury 45 SO 3444

Brochel....123 NG 5846
Brockbridge....27 SU 6018
Brockdam....97 NU 1624
Brockdish....55 TM 2179
Brockenhurst....26 SU 2902
Brocketsbrae....95 NS 8239
Brockford Street....55 TM 1166
Brockhall....51 SP 6362
Brockham....28 TQ 2049
Brockhampton....45 SO 5932
Brockholes....70 SE 1411
Brocklesby....73 TA 1311
Brockley....33 ST 4666
Brockley Green....54 TL 8254
Brockloch Hill (Dumf. and Galwy.)....87 NX 5173
Brockloch Hill (Dumf. and Galwy.)....88 NX 8179
Brockloch Rig....88 NS 5801
Brockton (Shrops.)....58 SJ 3104
Brockton (Shrops.)....57 SJ 7103
Brockton (Shrops.)....48 SO 3285
Brockton (Shrops.)....48 SO 5793
Brockweir....45 SO 5301
Brockwood Park....27 SU 6226
Brockworth....46 SO 8916
Brocolitia (ant.)....90 NY 8570
Brocton....60 SJ 9619
Brodick....92 NS 0136
Brodick Bay....92 NS 0237
Brodie Castle....129 NH 9757
Brodsworth....71 SE 5007
Brogborough....52 SP 9638
Brokenborough....33 ST 9189
Broken Cross (Ches.)....69 SJ 6872
Broken Cross (Ches.)....69 SJ 8973
Broken Cross Muir (mt.)....95 NS 8436
Brolass (dist.)....105 NM 4923
Bromborough....68 SJ 3582
Brome....55 TM 1376
Brome Street....55 TM 1576
Bromeswell....55 TM 3050
Bromfield (Cumbr.)....82 NY 1746
Bromfield (Salop)....48 SO 4876
Bromham (Beds.)....52 TL 0051
Bromham (Wilts.)....34 ST 9665
Bromley (Gtr London)....37 TQ 4069
Bromley Common....37 TQ 7668
Brompton (Kent)....30 TQ 7668
Brompton (N Yorks.)....85 SE 3796
Brompton (N Yorks.)....81 SE 9482
Brompton-on-Swale....84 SE 2199
Brompton Ralph....24 ST 0832
Brompton Regis....23 SS 9531
Bromsash....46 SO 6424
Bromsgrove....50 SO 9570
Rromyard....49 SO 6554
Bromyard Downs....49 SO 6555
Bronaber....67 SH 7131
Bronant....57 SN 6467
Bronington....59 SJ 4839
Bronllys....41 SO 1435
Bronygarth....58 SJ 2636
Brook (Hants.)....26 SU 2713
Brook (Hants.)....26 SU 3428
Brook (I. of W.)....26 SZ 3983
Brook (Kent)....31 TR 0644
Brook (Surrey)....28 SU 9338
Brooke (Leic.)....62 SK 8405
Brooke (Norf.)....65 TM 2999
Brookfield....101 NS 4164
Brookhouse....77 SD 5464
Brookhouse Green....69 SJ 8061
Brookland....31 TQ 9825
Brookmans Park....37 TL 2404
Brooks....58 SO 1499
Brook Street....37 TQ 5792
Brookthorpe....46 SO 8312
Brookwood....28 SU 9557
Broom (Beds.)....52 TL 1743
Broom (Warw.)....50 SP 0953
Broome (Here. and Worc.)....49 SO 9078
Broome (Norf.)....55 TM 3591
Broome (Shrops.)....48 SO 3981
Broome Park....91 NU 1112
Broomer's Corners....28 TQ 1221
Broomfield (Essex.)....38 TL 7009
Broomfield (Grampn.)....121 NJ 9532
Broomfield (Kent)....30 TQ 8452
Broomfield (Kent)....31 TR 2066
Broomfield (Somer.)....24 ST 2231
Broomfleet....74 SE 8727
Broom Hall Airfield....66 SH 4137
Broomhead Resr....71 SK 2695
Broom Hill (Dorset)....26 SU 0302
Broomhill (Northum.)....91 NU 2400
Broomlee Lough....90 NY 7969
Broomy Law....96 NT 4131
Broomy Lodge....26 SU 2111
Brora....129 NC 9003
Brosdale Island....98 NR 4962
Broseley....59 SJ 6701
Brothers Water....83 NY 4012
Brothertoft....63 TF 2746
Brotherton....79 SE 4825
Brotton....85 NZ 6819
Broubster....135 ND 0360
Brough (Bressay)....141 HU 5141
Brough (Cumbr.)....83 NY 7914
Brough (Derby.)....70 SK 1882
Brough (Highld.)....135 ND 2273
Brough (Humbs.)....74 SE 9326
Brough (Notts.)....72 SK 8358
Brough (Shetld.)....143 HU 4377
Brough (Whalsay)....141 HU 5564
Brough (Yell)....143 HU 5179
Broughall....59 SJ 5641
Brough Head (Highld.)....135 ND 3663
Brough Head (Orkney)....136 HY 2328
Brough Lodge....143 HU 5892
Brough Ness....136 ND 4482
Brough of Deerness (pt.)....137 HY 5908
Brough Sowerby....83 NY 7912
Brough Taing....143 HP 6304
Brough, The....142 HU 2982
Broughton (Borders)....95 NT 1136
Broughton (Bucks.)....52 SP 8940
Broughton (Cambs.)....53 TL 2878
Broughton (Clwyd)....68 SJ 3363
Broughton (Cumbr.)....82 NY 0731
Broughton (Gtr Mches.)....69 SD 8201
Broughton (Hants.)....26 SU 3132
Broughton (Humbs.)....74 SE 9508
Broughton (Lancs.)....77 SD 5234
Broughton (Mid Glam.)....41 SS 9271
Broughton (Northants.)....52 SP 8375
Broughton (N Yorks.)....78 SD 9451
Broughton (N Yorks.)....80 SE 7673
Broughton (Oxon.)....50 SP 4238
Broughton (Westray)....138 HY 4448
Broughton Astley....51 SP 5292
Broughton Beck....77 SD 2882
Broughton Gifford....33 ST 8763
Broughton Hackett....49 SO 9254
Broughton Heights....95 NT 1241
Broughton in Furness....76 SD 2087
Broughton Mills....82 SD 2290
Broughton Moor....82 NY 0533
Broughton Poggs....47 SP 2303
Broughtown....139 HY 6540
Broughty Ferry....109 NO 4630

Browland....140 HU 2750
Brown Bank Head (mt.)....78 SE 1057
Brown Candover....35 SU 5839
Brown Carrick Hill....93 NS 2815
Brown Caterthun (mt.)....109 NO 5566
Brown Clee Hill....49 SO 5985
Brown Cow Hill....117 NJ 2204
Brown Edge....59 SJ 9053
Brown Head....59 NR 8925
Brownhill (Grampn.)....121 NJ 8640
Brownhills (W Mids)....60 SK 0405
Brownlow Heath....69 SJ 8360
Brownmoor Hill....88 NX 9991
Brownmuir....119 NO 7477
Brown Ridge....78 SE 1077
Brownsea Island....26 SZ 0187
Brownston....21 SX 6952
Brown Willy (mt.)....19 SX 1579
Browsholme Hall (ant.)....77 SD 6845
Broxbourne....37 TL 3707
Broxburn (Lothian)....102 NT 0872
Broxburn (Lothian)....96 NT 6977
Broxted....53 TL 5727
Broxwood....45 SO 3654
Bruach, The (mt.)....117 NJ 1105
Bruan....117 ND 3039
Bruar Lodge....117 NN 8376
Bruar Water (Tays.)....107 NN 8269
Bruar Water (Tays.)....117 NN 8375
Bruchag Point....93 NS 1157
Bruddans, The....142 HU 2077
Brue....68 NB 3349
Bruera....68 SJ 4360
Bruern Abbey....47 SP 2620
Bruernish....112 NF 7102
Bruernish Point....112 NF 7300
Bruichladdich....98 NR 2661
Bruisyard....55 TM 3266
Bruisyard Street....55 TM 3365
Brumby....74 SE 8809
Brund....70 SK 1061
Brundall....65 TG 3208
Brundish....55 TM 2669
Brundish Street....55 TM 2671
Brunerican Bay....92 NR 6874
Brunt Hill....96 NT 6874
Bruntingthorpe....51 SP 6090
Brunton (Fife)....108 NO 3220
Brunton (Northum.)....97 NU 2024
Bruntshiel Hill....89 NY 4182
Bruray....143 HU 6972
Brushford....23 SS 9225
Brushford Barton....23 SS 6707
Bruton....25 ST 6834
Bruton Forest....33 ST 7438
Bruxie Hill....119 NO 8280
Bryanston....25 ST 8706
Brydekirk....89 NY 1870
Bryher (is.)....18 SV 8714
Brymbo....58 SJ 2953
Brympton....38 SD 5701
Bryn (Gtr Mches.)....69 SD 5701
Bryn (Powys)....44 SN 9055
Bryn (Shrops.)....48 SO 2985
Bryn (W Glam.)....41 SS 8192
Brynamlwg....57 SN 9297
Brynamman....40 SN 7114
Brynberian....42 SN 1035
Bryn Brawd....44 SN 6951
Bryncae....41 SS 9983
Bryn-celli-ddu (ant.)....66 SH 5070
Bryncethin....41 SS 9184
Bryncir....66 SH 4641
Bryn-côch....41 SS 7499
Bryncroes....66 SH 2231
Bryncrug....56 SH 6003
Bryn Crwn....44 SN 8258
Bryn du (Clwyd)....58 SJ 1435
Bryn-du (Powys)....44 SN 9342
Bryneglwys....58 SJ 1447
Brynford....68 SJ 1774
Bryn Garw (Dyfed)....57 SN 8077
Bryn Garw (Powys)....44 SN 8361
Bryn Gates....69 SD 5901
Brynglas Station....57 SH 6203
Bryngwran....66 SH 3477
Bryngwyn (Gwent)....45 SO 3909
Bryngwyn (Powys)....45 SO 1849
Bryn-henllan....42 SN 0139
Brynhoffnant....43 SN 3351
Brynmawr....41 SO 1911
Brynmenyn....41 SS 9084
Brynna....41 SS 9883
Bryn Nicol....44 SN 8243
Brynrefail....66 SH 4786
Brynsadler....41 ST 0380
Brynsiencyn....66 SH 4867
Brynteg....66 SH 4982
Bryn, The....45 SO 3309
Bryntrillyn....57 SN 9375
Bryn y Castell....57 SH 9704
Bryn-y-maen (Clwyd)....67 SH 8376
Bryn-y-maen (Powys)....45 SO 1657
Buachaille Etive Beag....106 NN 1854
Buachaille Etive Mòr....106 NN 2146
Buail' a' Ghoill....112 NF 8130
Bualintur....123 NG 4020
Bubbenhall....50 SP 3672
Bubwith....74 SE 7136
Buccleuch....89 NT 3214
Buchan (dist.)....121 NJ 9749
Buchan Smithy....101 NS 4689
Buchan Burn....86 NX 4181
Buchan Ness....87 NX 4281
Buchan Ness....121 NK 1342
Buchanty....108 NN 9328
Buchlyvie....101 NS 5793
Buckabank....83 NY 3749
Buckden (Cambs.)....52 TL 1967
Buckden (N Yorks.)....78 SD 9477
Buckden Pike....78 SD 9678
Buckenham....65 TG 3505
Buckenham....24 ST 1200
Buckfast....21 SX 7367
Buckfastleigh....21 SX 7466
Buckhaven....103 NT 3598
Buckholm....96 NT 4838
Buckhorn Weston....25 ST 7524
Buckhurst Hill....37 TQ 4193
Buckie....121 NJ 4265
Buckies....135 ND 1063
Buckingham....51 SP 6933
Buckland (Bucks.)....36 SP 8812
Buckland (Devon)....21 SX 6743
Buckland (Glos.)....50 SP 0836
Buckland (Herts.)....53 TL 3533
Buckland (Kent)....31 TR 2942
Buckland (Oxon.)....47 SU 3497
Buckland (Surrey)....28 TQ 2250
Buckland Abbey (ant.)....20 SX 4866
Buckland Brewer....22 SS 4120
Buckland Common....36 SP 9306
Buckland Dinham....33 ST 7550
Buckland Filleigh....22 SS 4609
Buckland in the Moor....21 SX 7273
Buckland Monachorum....20 SX 4868
Buckland Newton....25 ST 6905
Buckland St. Mary....24 ST 2713
Buckland-Tout-Saints....21 SX 7645
Bucklebury....35 SU 5570
Bucklerheads....109 NO 4636
Bucklers Hard....26 SZ 4099

Bucklesham....55 TM 2442
Buckley....68 SJ 2764
Buckminster....62 SK 8722
Bucknall (Lincs.)....73 TF 1668
Bucknall (Staffs.)....59 SJ 9147
Bucknell (Oxon.)....47 SP 5525
Bucknell (Shrops.)....48 SO 3574
Buckpool....119 NJ 8909
Buck's Cross....22 SS 3422
Bucks Green....28 TQ 0732
Bucks Hill....36 TL 0500
Bucks Horn Oak....35 SU 8142
Buck's Mills....22 SS 3523
Buck, The (mt.)....121 NJ 4123
Buckton (Here. and Worc.)....48 SO 3873
Buckton (Northum.)....97 NU 0838
Buckworth....52 TL 1476
Budbrooke....50 SP 2565
Budby....62 SK 6169
Buddo Ness....109 NO 5515
Buddon Ness....109 NO 5530
Bude....22 SS 2006
Bude Bay....22 SS 1706
Bude Haven....22 SS 2006
Budle....97 NU 1534
Budle Bay....97 NU 1535
Budleigh Salterton....24 SY 0682
Budock Water....19 SW 7832
Buerton....59 SJ 6843
Bugbrooke....51 SP 6757
Bugeilyn....57 SN 8292
Bught Fell....89 NX 2062
Bugle....19 SX 0158
Bugthorpe....80 SE 7757
Buidhe Bheinn....114 NG 9508
Builg Burn....119 NO 6687
Builth Road....44 SO 0253
Builth Wells....44 SO 0351
Bulbarrow Hill....25 ST 7705
Bulby....62 TF 0526
Buldoo....134 NC 9967
Bulford....34 SU 1643
Bulford Camp....34 SU 5476
Bulgham Bay....76 SC 4685
Bulkeley....59 SJ 5254
Bulkington (Warw.)....50 SP 3986
Bulkington (Wilts.)....34 ST 9458
Bulkworthy....22 SS 3914
Bull (lightship)....75 TA 3809
Bull Bay (Gwyn.)....66 SH 4294
Bull Bay (Gwyn.)....66 SH 4394
Bulldog Sand....64 TF 6027
Bulley....46 SO 7519
Bullie Burn....101 NN 7809
Bull Point....22 SS 4646
Bullpot Farm....77 SD 6681
Bullwood....100 NS 1674
Dulmer (Essex)....54 TL 8440
Bulmer (N Yorks.)....80 SE 6967
Bulmer Tye....38 TL 8438
Bulphan....38 TQ 6385
Bulverhythe....30 TQ 7809
Bulwark....121 NJ 9345
Bulwell....61 SK 5345
Bulwick....62 SP 9694
Bumble's Green....37 TL 4005
Bunacaimb....111 NM 6588
Bun Allt na Criche....106 NM 9256
Bun an Leoib (chan.)....105 NM 4023
Bunarkaig....115 NN 1887
Bunavoneadar....125 NB 1304
Bunbury....69 SJ 5658
Bunchrew....130 NH 6145
Buncton....28 TQ 1413
Bundalloch....114 NG 8927
Bu Ness (Fair Isle)....139 HZ 2272
Buness (Unst)....143 HP 6209
Bunessan....104 NM 3821
Bungay....55 TM 3389
Bunloinn Forest....115 NH 1608
Bunnahabhainn....98 NR 4173
Bunny....61 SK 5829
Buntait....115 NH 3930
Buntingford....53 TL 3629
Bunwell....65 TM 1293
Burach....115 NH 3814
Burbage (Derby.)....70 SK 0472
Burbage (Leic.)....51 SP 4492
Burbage (Wilts.)....34 SU 2261
Burcombe (Somer.) (dist.)....23 SS 7538
Burcombe (Wilts.)....26 SU 0630
Burcot....47 SU 5595
Burdale....81 SE 8762
Bures....54 TL 9034
Burfa Camp (ant.)....48 SO 2861
Burford....47 SP 2512
Burg....104 NM 3745
Burg Water....136 HY 3427
Burgar....140 HU 2354
Burgess Hill....29 TQ 3118
Burgh (Island of Mull)....105 NM 4226
Burgh (Suff.)....55 TM 2251
Burgh by Sands....89 NY 3259
Burgh Castle....65 TG 4805
Burghclere....35 SU 4660
Burghead....129 NJ 1168
Burghead Bay....129 NJ 0767
Burghfield....36 SU 6668
Burghfield Common....36 SU 6466
Burghfield Hill....36 SU 6567
Burgh Head....137 HY 6923
Burgh Heath....37 TQ 2458
Burghill....45 SO 4744
Burgh Island....20 SX 6443
Burgh Le Marsh....73 TF 5065
Burghley House (ant.)....62 TF 0406
Burgh Muir....121 NJ 7622
Burgh next Aylsham....65 TG 2125
Burgh on Bain....73 TF 2186
Burgh St. Margaret....65 TG 4413
Burgh St. Peter....65 TM 4693
Burghwallis....71 SE 5312
Burgi Geus....143 HP 4703
Burham....30 TQ 7262
Burifa Hill....135 ND 2075
Buriton....27 SU 7319
Burland....59 SJ 6153
Burlawn....19 SW 9970
Burlescombe....24 ST 0716
Burleston....25 SY 7794
Burley (Hants.)....26 SU 2103
Burley (Leic.)....62 SK 8810
Burley Gate....45 SO 6042
Burley in Wharfedale....78 SE 1646
Burley Lodge....26 SU 2305
Burley Street....26 SU 2004
Burlingjobb....45 SO 2558
Burlton....58 SJ 4526
Burmarsh....31 TR 1032
Burmington....50 SP 2637
Burn....79 SE 5928
Burnage....69 SJ 8692
Burnaston....60 SK 2832
Burnby....74 SE 8346
Burncrooks Resr....101 NS 4879
Burneside....83 SD 5095
Burness....139 HY 7644
Burneston....79 SE 3084
Burnett....33 ST 6665
Burn Farm, The....109 NO 6072

Burnfoot (Borders)....89 NT 4113
Burnfoot (Borders)....90 NT 5116
Burnfoot (Tays.)....102 NN 9804
Burnfoot Resr....93 NS 4544
Burnham (Berks. - Bucks.)....36 SU 9382
Burnham (Humbs.)....74 TA 0517
Burnham Beeches....36 SU 9585
Burnham Deepdale....64 TF 8044
Burnham Green....37 TL 2616
Burnham Market....64 TF 8342
Burnham Norton....64 TF 8243
Burnham-on-Crouch....39 TQ 9496
Burnham-on-Sea....32 ST 3049
Burnham Overy Staithe....64 TF 8444
Burnham Overy Town....64 TF 8442
Burnham Thorpe....64 TF 8541
Burnhaven....121 NK 1244
Burnhead....88 NX 8595
Burnhervie....119 NJ 7319
Burnhill Green....59 SJ 7800
Burnhope....84 NZ 1948
Burnhope Reservoir....83 NY 8328
Burnhope Seat (mt.)....83 NY 7837
Burnhouse....93 NS 3850
Burn Howe Rigg (mt.)....81 SE 9099
Burniston....81 TA 0193
Burnley....78 SD 8332
Burn Moor....77 SD 7064
Burn Moor Fell....77 SD 7064
Burnmoor Tarn....82 NY 1804
Burnmouth....97 NT 9560
Burnock Water....93 NS 5017
Burn of Acharole....135 ND 2351
Burn of Agie....115 NN 3691
Burn of Arisdale....143 HU 4783
Burn of Aultmore....121 NJ 4556
Burn of Boyne....118 NJ 5858
Burn of Branny....109 NO 4494
Burn of Calletar....109 NO 4769
Burn of Cambus....101 NN 7003
Burn of Cattie....109 NO 5795
Burn of Corrichie....119 NJ 7002
Burn of Dale....140 HU 2053
Burn of Hillside....136 HY 3023
Burn of Houstry....135 ND 1436
Burn of Laxdale....143 HU 4131
Burn of Lochy....117 NJ 1221
Burn of Loin....117 NJ 1409
Burn of Lyth....135 ND 2961
Burn of Ore....136 ND 2893
Burn of Rothes....121 NJ 2248
Burn of Sandvoe....143 HU 3590
Burn of Sandwater....141 HU 4153
Burn of Sheeoch....119 NO 7389
Burn of Tennet....118 NO 5082
Burn of Tulchan....117 NJ 0838
Burn of Turret....119 NO 5480
Burngfield....84 NZ 1756
Burnsall....78 SE 0361
Burns Cottage....93 NS 3318
Burnside (Fife)....102 NO 1607
Burnside (Lothian)....102 NT 0971
Burnside (Shetld.)....142 HU 2778
Burnside (Strath.)....88 NS 5811
Burnside (Tays.)....109 NO 4259
Burnside (Tays.)....109 NO 5050
Burnside of Duntrune....109 NO 4434
Burnswark....89 NY 1878
Burnt Fen....53 TL 6085
Burn, The....109 NO 5971
Burnt Hill....100 NS 3058
Burntisland....103 NT 2385
Burntwood....60 SK 0609
Burnt Yates....78 SE 2461
Burpham (Surrey)....28 TQ 0151
Burpham (W Susx)....28 TQ 0408
Burrach Mòr....116 NH 5808
Burradon (Northum.)....91 NT 9806
Burradon (Tyne and Wear)....91 NZ 2772
Burrafirth (Unst.)....143 HP 6113
Burra Firth (Unst)....143 HP 6116
Burraland (Shetld.)....140 HU 2249
Burraland (Shetld.)....142 HU 3475
Burra Ness (Yell)....143 HU 5595
Burras....18 SW 6835
Burra Sound....136 HY 2234
Burrator Resr....20 SX 5568
Burravoe (Shetld.)....141 HU 3667
Burra Voe (Shetld.)....143 HU 3689
Burra Voe (Yell)....143 HU 5279
Burravoe (Yell)....143 HU 5280
Burray....143 HU 4796
Burray Haas....143 HU 4998
Burray Ness....108 NO 5096
Burrelton....108 NO 1936
Burreldales....121 NJ 7144
Burrells....83 NY 6619
Burridge....27 SU 5110
Burrill....79 SE 2387
Burringham....74 SE 8309
Burrington (Avon)....33 ST 4759
Burrington (Devon)....23 SS 6316
Burrington (Here. and Worc.)....48 SO 4472
Burrough Green....54 TL 6355
Burrow on the Hill....61 SK 7510
Burrow Bridge....33 ST 3530
Burrow Head....87 NX 4534
Burrowhill....36 SU 9763
Burrows Hole....97 NU 1340
Burry Holms....40 SS 3992
Burry Port....40 SN 4400
Burscough....68 SD 4310
Burscough Bridge....68 SD 4411
Bursea....74 SE 8033
Burshill....75 TA 0948
Bursledon....27 SU 4809
Burslem....59 SJ 8749
Burstall....55 TM 0944
Burstock....24 ST 4202
Burston (Norf.)....55 TM 1383
Burston (Staffs.)....59 SJ 9330
Burstow....29 TQ 3141
Burstwick....75 TA 2228
Burtersett....84 SD 8989
Burtle....32 ST 3943
Burton (Ches.)....68 SJ 3174
Burton (Ches.)....59 SJ 5063
Burton (Dorset)....26 SZ 1794
Burton (Dyfed)....42 SM 9805
Burton (Lincs.)....72 SK 9574
Burton (Northum.)....97 NU 1732
Burton (Somer.)....32 ST 1944
Burton (Wilts.)....33 ST 8179
Burton Agnes....81 TA 1063
Burton Bradstock....25 SY 4889
Burton Constable....75 TA 1836
Burton Fleming....81 TA 0872
Burton Green (Clwyd)....68 SJ 3458
Burton Green (Warw.)....50 SP 2675
Burton Hastings....51 SP 4189
Burton-in-Kendal....77 SD 5376
Burton in Lonsdale....78 SD 6572
Burton Joyce....61 SK 6443
Burton Latimer....52 SP 9074
Burton Lazars....61 SK 7716
Burton-Le-Coggles....62 SK 9725
Burton Leonard....79 SE 3363
Burton on the Wolds....61 SK 5821
Burton Overy....51 SP 6798
Burton Pedwardine....73 TF 1142
Burton Pidsea....75 TA 2431
Burton Salmon....79 SE 4927

Burton upon Stather....74 SE 8617
Burton upon Trent....60 SK 2423
Burtonwood....69 SJ 5692
Burwardsley....59 SJ 5156
Burwarton....49 SO 6185
Burwash....29 TQ 6724
Burwash Common....29 TQ 6423
Burwell (Cambs.)....53 TL 5866
Burwell (Lincs.)....73 TF 3579
Bur Wick (Shetld.)....141 HU 3840
Burwick (Shetld.)....141 HU 3940
Burwick (S. Ronaldsay)....136 ND 4384
Bury (Cambs.)....53 TL 2883
Bury (Gtr Mches.)....69 SD 8010
Bury (Somer.)....23 SS 9427
Bury (W Susx)....28 TQ 0113
Bury Ditches (ant.)....48 SO 3283
Bury Green....37 TL 4521
Bury Hill....34 SU 3443
Bury St. Edmunds....54 TL 8564
Burythorpe....80 SE 7964
Bury Walls (ant.)....59 SJ 5727
Busbie Muir Resr....93 NS 2446
Busbridge....28 SU 9842
Busby (Strath.)....94 NS 5856
Busby (Tays.)....108 NO 0327
Buscot....47 SU 2297
Bushbury....59 SJ 9202
Bush Crathie....117 NO 2596
Bushey....37 TQ 1395
Bushey Heath....37 TQ 1594
Bush Green....55 TM 2187
Bushley....46 SO 8734
Bushton....34 SU 0677
Bushy Park....37 TQ 1569
Buss Craig....97 NT 9464
Busta....141 HU 3466
Busta Voe....141 HU 3566
Butcher's Pasture....38 TL 6024
Butcombe....33 ST 5161
Butleigh....25 ST 5233
Butleigh Wootton....25 ST 5034
Butlers Marston....50 SP 3150
Butley....55 TM 3651
Butser Hill....27 SU 7120
Butsfield....84 NZ 1044
Butterburn....90 NY 6774
Buttercrambe....80 SE 7358
Butterknowle....84 NZ 1025
Butterleigh....23 SS 9708
Butterley Reservoir....70 SE 0514
Buttermere (Cumbr.)....82 NY 1717
Buttermere (Cumbr.)....82 NY 1815
Buttermere (Wilts.)....34 SU 3361
Buttershaw....78 SE 1329
Butterstone....108 NO 0646
Butterton....60 SK 0756
Butterwick (Humbs.)....74 SE 8305
Butterwick (Lincs.)....63 TF 3845
Butterwick (N Yorks.)....80 SE 7377
Butterwick (N Yorks.)....81 SF 9971
Butterwick Low (sbk.)....63 TF 4243
Butt Green....59 SJ 6651
Buttington....58 SJ 2408
Buttock Point....100 NS 0074
Butt of Lewis....131 NB 5166
Button Hills....143 HU 3968
Buttonoak....49 SO 7578
Buxey Sand....39 TM 1103
Buxhall....54 TM 0057
Buxted....29 TQ 4923
Buxton (Derby.)....70 SK 0673
Buxton (Norf.)....65 TG 2222
Buxton Heath....65 TG 1821
Bwlch....45 SO 1422
Bwlchgwyn....58 SJ 2653
Bwlchllan....43 SN 5758
Bwlch Mawr (mt.)....66 SH 4247
Bwlchtocyn....56 SH 3126
Bwlch-y-cibau....58 SJ 1717
Bwlch-y-ffridd....57 SO 0695
Bwlch-y-groes (Dyfed)....43 SN 2436
Bwlch-y-groes (Gwyn.)....57 SH 9023
Bwlch-y-sarnau....57 SO 0274
Byerhope Resr....83 NY 8546
Byers Green....84 NZ 2234
Byfield....51 SP 5153
Byfleet....36 TQ 0461
Byford....45 SO 3943
Bygrave....53 TL 2636
Byker....79 NZ 2763
Byland Abbey (ant.)....79 SE 5478
Bylchau....67 SH 9762
Bylchau Rhos-faen....56 SH 7416
Byley....59 SJ 7269
Bynack Burn....117 NN 9784
Bynack More....117 NJ 0406
Byne Hill....86 NX 1794
Byrehope Mount....95 NT 1054
Bythorn....52 TL 0575
Byton....48 SO 3664
Byworth....28 SU 9921

C

Caaf Resr....93 NS 2450
Caar Bheinn....114 NM 9986
Cabaan Forest....127 NH 3650
Caban Coch Resr....44 SN 9163
Cabourne....75 TA 1301
Cabrach (Grampn.)....121 NJ 3826
Cabrach (Jura)....98 NR 4964
Cabus....39 SN 9105
Cadbury....23 SS 9105
Cadbury Barton....23 SS 6917
Cadbury Camp....33 ST 4572
Cadbury Castle....25 ST 6225
Cadder....101 NS 6172
Caddington....36 TL 0619
Caddonfoot....96 NT 4534
Caddon Water....96 NT 4041
Cadeby (Leic.)....51 SK 4202
Cadeby (S Yorks.)....71 SE 5100
Cadeleigh....23 SS 9107
Cademuir Hill....95 NT 2437
Cader Fawr....57 SN 9712
Cader Idris....57 SH 7013
Cade Street....29 TQ 6021
Cadgwith....18 SW 7214
Cadham....103 NO 2701
Cadha na Gaoidhsich (pt.)....128 NG 4399
Cadishead....69 SJ 7091
Cadle....40 SS 6297
Cadley....34 SU 2066
Cadmore End....36 SU 7892
Cadnam....26 SU 2913
Cadney....74 TA 0103
Cadole....68 SJ 2062
Cadzow Resr....94 NS 6951
Cae Afon....57 SH 8114
Caeathro....66 SH 5061
Caehopkin....41 SN 8212
Caenlochan Forest....117 NO 1875
Caeo....43 SN 6739
Caerau (Mid Glam.)....41 SS 8594
Caerau (S Glam.)....41 ST 1375
Caer Caradoc (ant.)....48 SO 3075
Caer Caradoc (mt.)....59 SO 4795
Caerdeon....57 SH 6418
Caergeiliog....66 SH 3178
Caergwrle....68 SJ 3057

Caergybi (ant.)

Castle Heaton

Caergybi (ant.) 66 SH 2682
Caerlaverock Castle (ant.) 88 NY 0265
Caerleon 32 ST 3390
Caer Llan 45 SO 4908
Caernarfon 66 SH 4862
Caernarfon Bay 66 SH 3055
Caerphilly 41 ST 1587
Caersws 57 SO 0392
Caerwent 33 ST 4790
Caerwys 68 SJ 1272
Caesar's Camp (Berks.) (ant.) 36 SU 8665
Caesar's Camp (Hants.) (ant.) 35 SU 8350
Caethle 56 SN 6099
Cagar Feosaig 129 NC 8404
Cailiness Point 86 NX 1535
Cailleach Head 126 NG 9898
Cailleach Uragaig 98 NR 3898
Cairidh nan Ob 122 NG 3570
Cairnacay 117 NJ 2032
Cairn Avel (ant.) 88 NX 5692
Cairnbaan 99 NR 8390
Cairn Baddoch 108 NO 2770
Cairn Bannoch 117 NO 2282
Cairnbanno House 121 NJ 8444
Cairnborrow 121 NJ 4640
Cairnbrallan 121 NJ 3324
Cairnbrogie 121 NJ 8527
Cairnbulg Castle 121 NK 0164
Cairnbulg Point 121 NK 0365
Cairn Cattoch 120 NJ 2247
Cairncross 118 NO 4979
Cairncross 97 NT 8963
Cairndow 100 NN 1810
Cairn Edward Forest 88 NX 6171
Cairness 121 NK 0360
Cairneyhill 102 NT 0486
Cairnfield House 121 NJ 4162
Cairngaan 86 NX 1232
Cairn Galtar 112 NL 6491
Cairngarroch (Dumf. and Galwy.) 86 NX 0649
Cairngarroch (Dumf. and Galwy.) 87 NX 4977
Cairngarroch Bay 86 NX 0449
Cairn Geldie 117 NN 9988
Cairn Gibbs 108 NO 1859
Cairn Gorm 117 NJ 0004
Cairngorm Mountains 117 NJ 0103
Cairngorms Nature Reserve 117 NN 9598
Cairnharrow 87 NX 5356
Cairn Head 87 NX 4838
Cairnhill (Dumf. and Galwy.) 88 NS 8506
Cairnhill (Grampn.) 121 NJ 6732
Cairn Hill (Strath.) 86 NX 3090
Cairn Holy (ant.) 87 NX 5154
Cairnie 121 NJ 4945
Cairn Inks 108 NO 3072
Cairnkinna Hill 88 NS 7901
Cairn Kinny 94 NS 7821
Cairn Leuchan 118 NO 3791
Cairn Mona Gowan 118 NJ 3305
Cairn-mon-earn 119 NO 7891
Cairn Muldonich 117 NJ 2326
Cairn na Burgh Beg 104 NM 3044
Cairnoch Hill 101 NS 6985
Cairn of Barns 108 NO 3171
Cairn o' Mount 119 NO 6480
Cairnorrie 121 NJ 8640
Cairnpapple (ant.) 102 NS 9871
Cairn Pat 86 NX 0456
Cairn Point 86 NX 0668
Cairnryan 86 NX 0668
Cairnscarrow 86 NX 1364
Cairnsmore of Corsphairn 88 NX 5997
Cairnsmore of Fleet 87 NX 5066
Cairns of Coll (is.) 110 NM 2866
Cairntable (Strath.) 93 NS 4313
Cairn Table (Strath.) 94 NS 7224
Cairn Toul (Carn ant-Sabhail) 117 NN 9697
Cairn Uish 129 NJ 1750
Cairn Water 88 NX 8681
Cairnwell, The (mt.) 117 NO 1377
Cairn William 119 NJ 6516
Cairnywellan Head 86 NX 0940
Caisteal Abhail 92 NR 9644
Caister-on-Sea 65 TG 5212
Caistor 75 TA 1101
Caistor St.Edmund 65 TG 2303
Caistron 91 NT 9901
Caiteshal (mt.) 125 NB 2404
Calair Burn 107 NN 5317
Calback Ness 143 HU 3977
Calbha Beag (is.) 132 NC 1536
Calbha Mór (is.) 132 NC 1636
Calbost 131 NB 4117
Calbourne 26 SZ 4286
Calcot 36 SU 6672
Caldback 143 HP 6006
Caldbeck 82 NY 3239
Caldbergh 78 SE 0984
Caldecote (Cambs.) 52 TL 1488
Caldecote (Cambs.) 53 TL 3456
Caldecote (Herts.) 53 TL 2338
Caldecott (Leic.) 62 SP 8693
Caldecott (Northants.) 52 SP 9968
Calderbank 101 NS 7662
Calder Bridge 82 NY 0405
Calderbrook 69 SD 9418
Calder Burn 115 NN 3399
Caldercruix 101 NS 8167
Calder Dam 100 NS 2965
Calder Fell 77 SD 5648
Calder Mains 135 ND 0959
Caldermill 94 NS 6641
Calder Vale 77 SD 5345
Calder Water 94 NS 6041
Caldey Island 42 SS 1496
Caldey Sound 42 SS 1297
Caldhame 109 NO 4748
Caldicot 33 ST 4888
Caldicot Level 33 ST 4285
Caldon Canal (Staffs.) 59 SJ 9453
Caldon Canal (Staffs.) 60 SJ 9949
Caldwell 84 NZ 1613
Caldwell (Derby.) 60 SK 2517
Caldy 68 SJ 2285
Caledonian Canal (Highld.) 127 NH 1380
Caledonian Canal (Highld.) 115 NH 3405
Caledonian Canal (Highld.) 116 NH 6240
Caledrhydiau 43 SN 4753
Calf of Eday 138 HY 5839
Calf of Flotta 136 ND 3896
Calf of Man 76 SC 1565
Calfsound (Eday) 138 HY 5738
Calf Sound (Eday) 138 HY 5739
Calf, The (mt.) 83 SD 6696
Calf Top 77 SD 6585
Calgary 110 NM 3751
Calgary Bay 110 NM 3550
Calgary Point 110 NM 1052
Caliach Point 110 NM 3454
Califer 129 NJ 0857
California (Central) 102 NS 9076
California (Norf.) 65 TG 5114
Calke 60 SK 3722
Calkin Rig 89 NY 2987
Callaly 91 NU 0509
Callander 101 NN 6208
Callanish 131 NB 2133
Callater Burn 117 NO 1687
Callestick 18 SW 7750
Calligarry 111 NG 6202
Callington 20 SX 3669
Callop River 114 NM 9180
Callow 45 SO 4934
Callow End 49 SO 8349
Callow Hill (Here. and Worc.) 49 SO 7473
Callow Hill (Wilts.) 34 SU 0385
Callows Grave 49 SO 5966
Calmore 26 SU 3314
Calmsden 46 SP 0408
Calne 34 ST 9971
Calow 71 SK 4071
Calpa Mór 116 NH 6710
Calshot 27 SU 4701
Calshot Castle (ant.) 27 SU 4802
Calshot Spit (lightship) 27 SU 4901
Calstock 20 SX 4368
Calstone Wellington 34 SU 0268
Calthorpe 65 TG 1831
Calthwaite 83 NY 4640
Caltinish 124 NF 8341
Calton (N Yorks.) 78 SD 9059
Calton (Staffs.) 60 SK 1050
Calvay (South Uist) 112 NF 7728
Calvay (South Uist) 112 NF 8218
Calve Island 111 NM 5254
Calveley 69 SJ 5958
Calver 71 SK 2374
Calverhall 59 SJ 6037
Calver Hill 45 SO 3748
Calverleigh 23 SS 9214
Calverley 78 SE 2036
Calvert 36 SP 6824
Calverton (Bucks.) 51 SP 7938
Calverton (Notts.) 61 SK 6149
Calvine 107 NN 8066
Cam 46 ST 7599
Cama Choire 116 NN 6879
Camas Airigh Shamhraidh 105 NM 8448
Camas Allt nam Bearnach 125 NB 3608
Camas a' Mhoil 130 NA 9825
Camas Baravaig 123 NG 6909
Camas chil Mhalieu 106 NM 9055
Camas Coille 132 NC 0016
Camas Eilean Ghlais 132 NB 9615
Camas Geodhachan an Duilisg 130 NB 0438
Camas Ghaoideil 111 NM 6683
Camas Gorm 105 NM 7742
Camas-luinie 114 NG 9128
Camas Mór (Highld.) 127 NC 1000
Camas Mór (Highld.) 126 NG 7592
Camas Mór (Island of Skye) 122 NG 3770
Camas na Ceardaich 100 NR 9162
Camas Nathais 105 NM 8737
Camas Pliasgaig 111 NG 4002
Camastianavaig 123 NG 5039
Camas Uig 130 NB 0233
Camasunary 123 NG 5118
Camault Muir 116 NH 5040
Camb 143 HU 5192
Cambeak (pt.) 20 SX 1296
Cam Beck 78 SD 7978
Camber 31 TQ 9619
Camber Castle (ant.) 30 TQ 9218
Camberley 36 SU 8760
Camberwell 37 TQ 3376
Camblesforth 79 SE 6425
Cambo 91 NZ 0285
Camboglanna (ant.) 90 NY 6166
Cambois 91 NZ 3083
Cambo Ness 103 NO 6011
Camborne 18 SW 6440
Cambrian Mountains 57 SH 8809
Cambridge 53 TL 4658
Cambridge Airport 53 TL 4858
Cambus 102 NS 8593
Cambusavie 129 NH 7796
Cambusbarron 101 NS 7792
Cambuscurrie Bay 129 NH 7285
Cambuskenneth 101 NS 8094
Cambuslang 101 NS 6459
Cambusmore Lodge 129 NH 7697
Cam Chreag 107 NN 5349
Camddwr 44 SN 7755
Camden Town 37 TQ 2784
Camelford 20 SX 1083
Camelon 102 NS 8680
Cameron Burn 103 NO 4912
Cameron Resr. 103 NO 4711
Camerory 117 NJ 0231
Camerton (Avon) 33 ST 6857
Camerton (Cumbr.) 82 NY 0330
Camesdale 27 SU 8932
Cam Fell 78 SD 8080
Camghouran 107 NN 5556
Cam Loch (Highld.) 132 NC 2113
Càm Loch (Strath.) 99 NR 8187
Camlo Hill 57 SO 0370
Cammachmore 119 NO 9295
Cammachmore Bay 119 NO 9295
Cammeringham 72 SK 9482
Cammoch Hill 108 NN 8959
Campay 131 NB 1442
Campbells Hill 93 NS 5201
Campbelton 93 NS 1950
Campbeltown 92 NR 7120
Campbeltown Loch 92 NR 7420
Camperdown House 109 NO 3532
Camphill Resr. 93 NS 2655
Campmuir 108 NO 2137
Campsall 71 SE 5313
Campsey Ash 55 TM 3356
Campsie Fells 101 NS 6082
Camps Resr. 95 NT 0022
Camps Water 95 NS 9622
Camp, The 46 SO 9109
Campton 52 TL 1238
Camrose 42 SM 9220
Camserney 107 NN 8149
Camster 135 ND 2641
Camster Burn 135 ND 2348
Camulodunum (ant.) 54 TM 0025
Camus Geodhachan an Duilisg 130 NB 0438
Camus-luinie 114 NG 9428
Camusnagaul (Highld.) 127 NH 0689
Camusnagaul (Highld.) 115 NN 0975
Camusrory 111 NM 8595
Camusteel 123 NG 7042
Camusterrach 123 NG 7141
Camusvrachan 107 NN 6248
Camy (pt.) 137 HY 5401
Canada 26 SU 2817
Canal Foot 77 SD 3177
Canaston Bridge 42 SN 0515
Candacraig House 118 NJ 3411
Candlesby 73 TF 4567
Candy Mill 95 NT 0741
Cane End 36 SU 6779
Canewdon 38 TQ 8994
Canford Bottom 26 SU 0300
Canford Cliffs 26 SZ 0689
Canford Heath 26 SZ 0294
Canisbay 135 ND 3472
Canis Dale 143 HU 5082
Canisp (mt.) 132 NC 2018
Cann 25 ST 8620
Canna (is.) 110 NG 2405
Canna Harbour 110 NG 2804
Cann Common 25 ST 8920
Cannich 115 NH 3331
Cannington 32 ST 2539
Cannock 60 SJ 9710
Cannock Chase 60 SJ 9816
Cannock Wood 60 SK 0412
Cannon Street Station 37 TQ 3280
Canonbie 89 NY 3976
Canon Bridge 45 SO 4341
Canon Frome 49 SO 6543
Canon Pyon 45 SO 4549
Canons Ashby 51 SP 5750
Canonstown 18 SW 5335
Canterbury 31 TR 1557
Cantick Head 136 ND 3489
Cantley (Norf.) 65 TG 3704
Cantley (S Yorks.) 71 SE 6202
Cantlop 59 SJ 5205
Canton 41 ST 1577
Cantraydoune 129 NH 7946
Cantraywood 129 NH 7847
Cantref Resr. 41 SN 9915
Cantsfield 77 SD 6172
Canvey Island 38 TQ 7783
Canwell Hall 60 SK 1400
Canwick 72 SK 9869
Canworthy Water 20 SX 2291
Caol 115 NN 1175
Caolard Rubha 99 NR 8783
Caolas a' Mhòrain 124 NF 8480
Caolas an Eilein 130 NA 9821
Caolas an Scarp 130 NA 9913
Caolas Bàn 110 NM 1151
Caolas Beag 126 NG 7478
Caolas Mór (Highld.) 123 NG 7135
Caolas Mór (Strath.) 98 NR 3586
Caolas Scalpay 123 NG 6127
Caoles 104 NM 0848
Caol Ghleann 100 NS 0693
Caolis 112 NL 6397
Caol Lairig 115 NN 2783
Caol Mór 123 NG 5733
Caol Raineach (chan.) 133 NC 6364
Caol Rona 123 NG 6153
Cape Cornwall 18 SW 3431
Capel 28 TQ 1740
Cape Law 89 NT 1314
Capel Bangor 57 SN 6580
Capel Betws Lleucu 43 SN 6058
Capel Carmel 56 SH 1628
Capel Coch 66 SH 4582
Capel Curig 67 SH 7258
Capel Cynon 43 SN 3849
Capel Dewi 43 SN 4542
Capel Fell 89 NT 1607
Capel Garmon 67 SH 8155
Capel Gwyn (Dyfed) 433 SN 4622
Capel Gwyn (Gwyn.) 66 SH 3575
Capel Gwynfe 40 SN 7222
Capel Hendre 43 SN 5911
Capel Isaac 43 SN 5927
Capel Iwan 43 SN 2836
Capel-le-Ferne 31 TR 2439
Capel Llanilterne 41 ST 0979
Capel Parc 66 SH 4486
Capel St. Mary 55 TM 0838
Capel-y-ffin 45 SO 2531
Capenhurst 68 SJ 3673
Capernwray 77 SD 5372
Cape Wrath 132 NC 2574
Capheaton 91 NZ 0380
Capler Camp (ant.) 45 SO 5932
Caplestone Fell 90 NY 5888
Cappercleuch 95 NT 2423
Capstone 30 TQ 7865
Capton 21 SX 8353
Caputh 108 NO 0940
Caradon Hill 20 SX 2770
Cara Island 92 NR 6444
Carbh-Bheinn 123 NG 5323
Carbis Bay 18 SW 5339
Carbost (Island of Skye) 122 NG 3731
Carbost (Island of Skye) 123 NG 4248
Carbrooke 64 TF 9402
Carburton 71 SK 6173
Carcary 109 NO 6455
Carclew 19 SW 7838
Car Colston 61 SK 7142
Carcroft 71 SE 5409
Cardenden 103 NT 2195
Carden Hall (ant.) 58 SJ 4553
Cardeston 58 SJ 3912
Cardiff 41 ST 1877
Cardiff-Wales Airport 41 ST 0667
Cardigan 43 SN 1846
Cardigan Bay 44 SN 4080
Cardigan Island 42 SN 1651
Cardington (Beds.) 52 TL 0847
Cardington (Shrops.) 59 SO 5095
Cardinham 19 SX 1268
Cardney House 108 NO 0545
Cardno 121 NJ 9663
Cardoness Castle (ant.) 87 NX 5955
Cardow 120 NJ 1942
Cardrona 96 NT 3038
Cardrona Forest 96 NT 3036
Cardross (Central) (ant.) 101 NS 6097
Cardross (Strath.) 100 NS 3477
Cardurnock 89 NY 1758
Car Dyke (Cambs.) (ant.) 53 TL 4769
Car Dyke (Lincs.) (ant.) 62 TF 1437
Car Dyke (Northants.) (ant.) 62 TF 1508
Careby 62 TF 0216
Careston 109 NO 5260
Carew 42 SN 0403
Carew Cheriton 42 SN 0402
Carew Newton 42 SN 0404
Carey 45 SO 5631
Carfrae 103 NT 5769
Cargen 88 NX 9672
Cargenbridge 88 NX 9474
Cargill 108 NO 1536
Cargo 89 NY 3659
Cargreen 20 SX 4262
Carham 97 NT 7938
Carhampton 23 ST 0042
Carharrack 18 SW 7241
Carie (Tays.) 107 NN 6157
Carie (Tays.) 107 NN 6437
Carines 19 SW 7959
Carinish 124 NF 8159
Carisbrooke 27 SZ 4888
Cark 77 SD 3676
Carland Cross 19 SW 8554
Carlby 62 TF 0414
Carleatheran 101 NS 6892
Carlecotes 70 SE 1703
Carleton (Cumbr.) 83 NY 4253
Carleton (Lancs.) 77 SD 3339
Carleton (N Yorks.) 78 SD 9749
Carleton Forehoe 65 TG 0805
Carleton Rode 55 TM 1192
Carlingcott 33 ST 6958
Carlingwark Loch 88 NX 7661
Carlin Tooth 90 NT 6302
Carlisle 83 NY 3955
Carlisle Airport 89 NY 4860
Carlock Hill 86 NX 0877
Carlops 95 NT 1656
Carloway 131 NB 2042
Carlton (Beds.) 52 SP 9555
Carlton (Cambs.) 54 TL 6453
Carlton (Cleve.) 85 NZ 3921
Carlton (Leic.) 60 SK 3905
Carlton (Notts.) 61 SK 6141
Carlton (N Yorks.) 78 SE 0684
Carlton (N Yorks.) 79 SE 6086
Carlton (N Yorks.) 79 SE 6423
Carlton (Suff.) 55 TM 3864
Carlton (S Yorks.) 71 SE 3610
Carlton (W Yorks.) 79 SE 3327
Carlton Colville 55 TM 5190
Carlton Curlieu 61 SP 6997
Carlton Husthwaite 79 SE 4976
Carlton in Cleveland 85 NZ 5004
Carlton in Lindrick 71 SK 5984
Carlton-le-Moorland 72 SK 9058
Carlton Miniott 79 SE 3980
Carlton Moor 78 SE 0383
Carlton-on-Trent 72 SK 7963
Carlton Scroop 62 SK 9445
Carluke 95 NS 8450
Carl Wark (ant.) 71 SK 2681
Carmacoup 94 NS 7927
Carmarthen 43 SN 4120
Carmarthen Bay 40 SN 2400
Carmel (Clwyd) 68 SJ 1676
Carmel (Dyfed) 43 SN 5816
Carmel (Gwyn.) 66 SH 3882
Carmel (Gwyn.) 66 SH 4954
Carmel Head 66 SH 2992
Carminish 124 NG 0284
Carminish Islands 124 NG 0185
Carmont 119 NO 8084
Carmunnock 94 NS 5957
Carmyle 101 NS 6461
Carmyllie 109 NO 5542
Carna 111 NM 6259
Carn a' Bhiorain 127 NH 1483
Carn a Bhodaich 116 NH 5637
Carnaby 81 TA 1465
Carnach (Harris) 125 NG 2297
Carnach (Highld.) 114 NH 0228
Carn a' Chaochain 115 NH 2317
Carn a' Choin Deirg 127 NH 3992
Carn a' Choire Mhòir 117 NH 8428
Carn a' Chrasgie 129 NH 8642
Carn a' Chuilinn 116 NH 4103
Carn a' Ghaill 110 NG 2606
Carn a' Gheòidh 117 NO 1076
Carn a' Ghlinne 127 NH 0660
Carn a' Mhaim 117 NN 9995
Carnan (mt.) 112 NL 5582
Carn an Daimh 106 NN 1371
Carnan Eoin 98 NR 4098
Carn an Fhidhleir or Carn Ealar 117 NN 9084
Carn an Fhreiceadain 116 NH 7207
Carnan Mòr 104 NL 9640
Carn an Righ 117 NO 0277
Carn an t-Sabhail 117 NN 9697
Carn an t-Sean liathanaich 117 NH 8632
Carn an t-Suidhe 117 NJ 2726
Carn an Tuire 117 NO 1780
Carn Bàn (Highld.) 127 NH 3341
Carn Bàn (Highld.) 127 NH 3387
Carn Bàn (Highld.) 116 NH 6303
Carn Ban (Island of Mull) 105 NM 7229
Carn Bàn Mòr 117 NN 8896
Carn Beag 127 NH 1055
Carnbee 103 NO 5306
Carn Bhac 117 NO 0482
Carn Bheadhair 117 NJ 0511
Carn Bhrain 128 NH 5287
Carnbo 102 NO 0503
Carn Brea 18 SW 6741
Carn Breac 127 NH 0452
Carn Breac Beag 127 NH 1879
Carn Breugach 105 NM 8127
Carn Cas nan Gabhar 128 NH 5280
Carn Chòis 107 NN 7927
Carn Chuinneag 128 NH 4883
Carn Coire na Creiche 116 NH 6208
Carn Coire na h-Easgainn 116 NH 7313
Carn Daimh 117 NJ 1824
Càrn Dearg 116 NN 5076
Carn Dearg (Highld.) 116 NH 6202
Carn Dearg (Highld.) 115 NN 3488
Carn Dearg (Highld.) 115 NN 3596
Carn Dearg (Highld.-Tays.) 107 NN 4166
Carn Dearg (Strath.) 106 NM 8918
Carn Dearg Mòr 117 NN 8291
Carn Dubh'Ic an Deòir 116 NH 7719
Carn Duchara 100 NM 8910
Carnduncan 98 NR 2467
Carne 19 SW 9138
Carn Ealar or Carn an Fhidhleir 117 NN 9084
Carn Ealasaid 117 NJ 2211
Carn Eàs 117 NO 1298
Carn Easgann Bana 116 NH 4806
Carneddau (mt.) 44 SO 0654
Carnedd Dafydd 67 SH 6663
Carnedd Iago 67 SH 7840
Carnedd Llewelyn 67 SH 6864
Carnedd Moel-siabod 67 SH 7054
Carn Eige 115 NH 1226
Carn Eiric 117 NH 9305
Carnell 93 NS 4632
Car Ness 136 HY 4614
Carn fadrun (ant.) 66 SH 2835
Carnferg 119 NO 5293
Carnforth 77 SD 4970
Carn Garbh 127 NH 2858
Carn Geuradainn 114 NG 9839
Carn Ghriogair 116 NH 6520
Carn Glas-choire 117 NH 8929
Carn Gorm (Highld.) 127 NH 1349
Carn Gorm (Highld.) 115 NH 3235
Carn Gorm (Highld.) 128 NH 4362
Carn Gorm (Highld.) 128 NH 4570
Carn Gorm (Tays.) 107 NN 6350
Carnhell Green 18 SW 6137
Carnie 119 NJ 8105
Carn Kitty 129 NJ 0942
Carn Lea 115 NN 4097
Carn Leac Saighdeir 117 NJ 2706
Carn Liath (Grampn.) 117 NJ 1827
Carn Liath (Grampn.) 117 NJ 2515
Carn Liath (Grampn.) 117 NO 0386
Carn Liath (Highld.) 116 NN 4790
Carn Liath (Tays.) 108 NN 9369
Carn Mairg 107 NN 6851
Carn Meadhonach 117 NJ 1317
Carn Mhartuin 127 NH 1754
Carn Mór (Grampn.) 117 NJ 2618
Carn Mór (Highld.) 127 NH 2487
Carn Mór (Highld.) 128 NH 4271
Carn Mór (Highld.) 116 NH 4334
Carn Mór (Highld.) 114 NM 9090
Carn Mór (Island of Mull) 105 NM 3948
Carn na Cailliche 129 NJ 1847
Carn na Caim 116 NN 6782
Carn na Cloiche Móire 127 NH 3753
Carn na Còinnich 127 NH 3251
Carn na Drochaide 117 NO 1293
Carn na Dubh Choille 127 NH 3867
Carn na Farraidh 117 NJ 1114
Carn na Feannaige 117 NJ 0908
Carn na h-Easgainn 116 NH 7432
Carn na Làraiche Maoile 116 NH 5811
Carn na Lòine 117 NJ 0636
Carn nam Bad 115 NH 4033
Carn nam Bain-tighearna 117 NH 8425
Carn nam Buailtean 126 NH 0087
Carn nan Con Ruadha 128 NH 4174
Carn nan Iomairean 114 NG 9135
Carn nan Sgeir (is.) 126 NC 0101
Carn nan Tri-tighearnan 117 NH 8239
Carn na Saobhaidh 116 NH 6724
Carn na Saobhaidhe 116 NH 5914
Carn na Sean-lùibe 114 NH 0235
Carno 57 SN 9696
Carnock 102 NT 0489
Carn Odhar 116 NH 6317
Carnon Downs 19 SW 7940
Carnousie 121 NJ 6650
Carnoustie 109 NO 5634
Càrn Phris Mhóir 116 NH 8021
Carn Ruigh Chorrach 117 NH 9834
Carn Sgùlain 116 NH 6909
Carn Sgùmain 117 NH 8740
Carn Sleamhuinn 117 NH 8516
Carn Towan 18 SW 3626
Carnwath 95 NS 9746
Carnyorth 18 SW 3733
Carperby 84 SE 0089
Carracks, The 18 SW 4640
Carradale 92 NR 8138
Carradale Bay 92 NR 8137
Carradale Point 92 NR 8136
Carradale Water 92 NR 7843
Carragreich 125 NG 1998
Carraig Bhàn 98 NR 2572
Carraig Dhubh 98 NR 3062
Carraig Fhada 98 NR 3444
Carraig Mhór 98 NR 4656
Carrbridge 117 NH 9022
Carr Brigs (pt.) 103 NO 6411
Carreg Ddu 66 SH 2742
Carreg-gwylan-fach 42 SM 7730
Carreglefn 66 SH 3889
Carreg-lem 41 SN 8017
Carreg-lwyd 41 SN 8615
Carreg Ti-pw 56 SN 5370
Carregwastad Point 42 SM 9340
Carreg yr Imbill 66 SH 3834
Carr End (pt.) 97 NU 2232
Carrick (Fife) 109 NO 4422
Carrick (Strath.) 100 NR 9087
Carrick (Strath.) 100 NS 1994
Carrick (Strath.) (dist.) 86 NX 3394
Carrick Forest 86 NX 4093
Carrick House 138 HY 5638
Carrick Roads 19 SW 8335
Carriden 102 NT 0181
Carrine 92 NR 6709
Carrington (Gtr Mches.) 69 SJ 7492
Carrington (Lincs.) 63 TF 3155
Carrington (Lothian) 103 NT 3160
Carrington Moss 69 SJ 7491
Carrog 67 SJ 1043
Carron (Central) 102 NS 8882
Carron (Grampn.) 120 NJ 2241
Carron Bridge (Central) 101 NS 7483
Carronbridge (Dumf. and Galwy.) 88 NX 8697
Carronshore 102 NS 8983
Carron Valley Forest 101 NS 6982
Carron Valley Resr. 101 NS 6983
Carrot Hill 109 NO 4540
Carr Shield 83 NY 8047
Carrs, The 81 SE 9678
Carrutherstown 89 NY 1071
Carruth House 100 NS 3566
Carr Vale 71 SK 4669
Carrville 84 NZ 3043
Carrycoats Hall 90 NY 9279
Carsaig 105 NM 5421
Carsaig Bay 105 NM 5320
Carscreugh 86 NX 2260
Carsegowan 87 NX 4258
Carse Gray 109 NO 4653
Carse House 99 NR 7461
Carse of Gowrie (dist.) 108 NO 2726
Carseriggan 86 NX 3167
Carsethorn 88 NX 9959
Carsgailoch Hill 93 NS 5414
Carshalton 37 TQ 2764
Carsington 60 SK 2553
Carsington Reservoir 60 SK 2652
Carskiey 92 NR 6508
Carsluith 87 NX 4854
Carsphairn 88 NX 5693
Carsphairn Forest 88 NS 5701
Caarstairs 95 NS 9345
Carstairs Junction 95 NS 9545
Carswell Marsh 47 SU 3198
Carter Bar 90 NT 6906
Carter's Clay 26 SU 3024
Carterton 47 SP 2706
Carterway Heads 84 NZ 0451
Carthagena Bank (sbk.) 108 NO 2722
Carthew 19 SX 0055
Carthorpe 79 SE 3083
Cartington 91 NU 0304
Cartland 95 NS 8646
Cartmel 77 SD 3778
Cartmel Fell 77 SD 4188
Cartmel Sands 77 SD 3375
Cartmel Wharf (sbk.) 77 SD 3668
Carway 43 SN 4606
Cas 99 NR 7364
Casfad Loch 88 NX 6086
Cashel Dhu 133 NC 4450
Cashlie 107 NN 4942
Cashmoor 26 ST 9813
Cashtel yn Ard (ant.) 76 SC 4689
Cassington 47 SP 4510
Cassiobury Park 36 TQ 0897
Casswell's Bridge 62 TF 1627
Castallack 18 SW 4525
Castellau 41 ST 0586
Castell Dinas (ant.) 41 SO 1730
Castell Howell 43 SN 4448
Castell Odo (ant.) 56 SH 1828
Castell y Bere (ant.) 57 SH 6708
Castell-y-bŵch 32 ST 2792
Castell-y-geifr 41 SN 8216
Casterley Camp (ant.) 34 SU 1153
Casterton 77 SD 6279
Castle 136 HY 2113
Castle Acre 64 TF 8115
Castle-an-Dinas (ant.) 19 SW 9462
Castle Ashby 52 SP 8659
Castlebay 112 NL 6698
Castle Bolton 84 SE 0391
Castle Bromwich 50 SP 1489
Castle Bytham 62 SK 9818
Castlebythe 42 SN 0229
Castle Caereinion 58 SJ 1605
Castle Campbell (ant.) 102 NS 9699
Castle Camps 54 TL 6343
Castle Carrock 83 NY 5455
Castle Cary (Somer.) 25 ST 6332
Castlecary (Strath.) 101 NS 7878
Castle Combe 33 ST 8477
Castlecraig (Borders) 95 NT 1344
Castlecraig (Highld.) 129 NH 8169
Castle Ditches (Hants.) (ant.) 26 SU 1219
Castle Ditches (S Glam.) (ant.) 41 ST 0570
Castle Ditches (W Glam.) (ant.) 41 SS 9667
Castle Donington 61 SK 4427
Castle Douglas 88 NX 7662
Castle Eaton 47 SU 1495
Castle Eden 85 NZ 4338
Castle Forbes 119 NJ 6219
Castleford 79 SE 4225
Castle Fraser 119 NJ 7212
Castle Frome 49 SO 6645
Castle Gresley 60 SK 2718
Castle Haven 119 NO 8884
Castle Heaton 97 NT 9041

Castle Hedingham	54	TL	7835
Castlehill (Highld.)	135	ND	1968
Castle Hill (Highld.)	117	NH	9505
Castlehill (Strath.)	95	NS	8452
Castle Hill (Suff.)	55	TM	1646
Castlehill Point	87	NX	8552
Castle Howard	80	SE	7170
Castle Huntly	108	NO	3029
Castle Kennedy	86	NX	1059
Castle Lachlan	100	NS	0195
Castle Leod	128	NH	4858
Castle Loch (Dumf. and Galwy.)	86	NX	2853
Castle Loch (Dumf. and Galwy.)	89	NY	0881
Castlemaddy	87	NX	5589
Castlemartin	42	SR	9198
Castlemilk	89	NY	1577
Castle Morris	42	SM	9031
Castlemorton	49	SO	7937
Castle O'er	89	NY	2492
Castle O'er Forest	89	NY	2493
Castle of Mey	135	ND	2973
Castle of Old Wick (ant.)	135	ND	3648
Castle of Park (ant.)	86	NX	2057
Castle Point	97	NU	1441
Castle Ring (ant.)	60	SK	0412
Castle Rising	64	TF	6624
Castleshaw Moor	71	SE	0111
Castleside	84	NZ	0748
Castle Stuart	129	NH	7449
Castle Sween	99	NR	7178
Castle, The (pt.)	143	HU	3787
Castlethorpe	51	SP	7944
Castleton (Derby.)	70	SK	1582
Castleton (Gwent)	32	ST	2583
Castleton (N Yorks.)	80	NZ	6808
Castleton (Strath.)	100	NR	8884
Castle Toward	100	NS	1168
Castletown (Highld.)	135	ND	1967
Castletown (I. of M.)	76	SC	2667
Castletown (Tyne and Wear)	91	NZ	3558
Caston	64	TL	9598
Castor	62	TL	1298
Catacol	92	NR	9149
Catacol Bay	92	NR	9049
Cat and Fiddle	70	SK	0071
Cata Sand	139	HY	7040
Catbrain	33	ST	5580
Catcleugh Resr.	90	NT	7303
Catcliffe	71	SK	4288
Catcott	32	ST	3939
Cateran Hill	97	NU	1023
Caterham	29	TQ	3455
Cater's Beam	21	SX	6369
Catesby	51	SP	5159
Catfield	65	TG	3821
Catfirth (Shetld.)	141	HU	4354
Cat Firth (Shetld.)	141	HU	4552
Catford	37	TQ	3872
Catforth	77	SD	4735
Cath.	42	SM	7525
Cathcart	101	NS	5960
Cathedine	41	SO	1425
Catherington	27	SU	6914
Catherton	49	SO	6578
Cati Geo	138	HY	4342
Cat Law (mt.)	108	NO	3160
Catlodge	116	NN	6392
Catlowdy	89	NY	4676
Catlow Fell	77	SD	7060
Catmore	35	SU	4579
Caton	77	SD	5364
Caton Moor	77	SD	5763
Cator Court	21	SX	6877
Catrine	93	NS	5225
Cat's Ash	32	ST	3790
Catsfield	29	TQ	7213
Catshill	50	SO	9674
Cattal	79	SE	4454
Cattawade	55	TM	1033
Catterall	77	SD	4942
Catterick	84	SE	2397
Catterick Bridge	84	SE	2299
Catterick Garrison	84	SE	1897
Catterlen	83	NY	4833
Catterline	119	NO	8678
Catterton	79	SE	5045
Catthorpe	51	SP	5578
Cattistock	25	SY	5999
Catton (Norf.)	65	TG	2312
Catton (Northum.)	83	NY	8257
Catton (N Yorks.)	79	SE	3778
Catton Hall	60	SK	2015
Catwick	75	TA	1245
Catworth	52	TL	0873
Caulcott	47	SP	5024
Cauldcleuch Head	89	NT	4600
Cauldcots	109	NO	6547
Cauldhame	101	NS	6494
Cauldon	60	SK	0749
Cauldron Snout	83	NY	8228
Cauldrus (pt.)	136	HY	2116
Cauldshiels Hill	96	NT	5131
Caulkerbush	88	NX	9257
Caulside	89	NY	4480
Caunsall	49	SO	8481
Caunton	72	SK	7460
Causamul (is.)	124	NF	6670
Caus Castle (ant.)	58	SJ	3308
Causeway Grain Head	89	NY	3598
Causewayhead	101	NS	8195
Causeyend	119	NJ	9419
Causey Park	91	NZ	1794
Causey Pike	82	NY	2120
Cautley	83	SD	6994
Cava (is.)	136	ND	3299
Cavendish	54	TL	8046
Cavenham	54	TL	7669
Caversfield	47	SP	5824
Caversham	36	SU	7274
Caver's Hill	96	NT	3921
Caversta	131	NB	3619
Caverswall	60	SJ	9442
Caw (mt.)	82	SD	2294
Cawdor	129	NH	8449
Caw Fell	82	NY	1210
Cawood	79	SE	5737
Cawsand	20	SX	4350
Cawsand Hill	21	SX	6391
Cawston	65	TG	1324
Cawthorne	71	SE	2807
Cawton	79	SE	6476
Caxton	53	TL	3058
Caynham	48	SO	5473
Caynham Camp (ant.)	48	SO	5473
Caythorpe (Lincs.)	62	SK	9348
Caythorpe (Notts.)	61	SK	6845
Cayton	81	TA	0583
Cayton Bay	81	TA	0784
Ceannacroc Forest	127	NH	1613
Ceanna Mòr	111	NM	8551
Ceann Creag-arighe	110	NG	2205
Ceann Ear (is.)	124	NF	6461
Ceann Leathad nam Bò (pt.)	135	NO	1323
Ceann na Beinne	123	NG	4217
Ceann-na-Cleithe	125	NG	1794
Ceann Riobha	98	NR	3585
Ceathramh Garbh (dist.)	132	NC	2252
Cedig	57	SH	9922
Cefn-brith	67	SH	9350
Cefn Bryn	40	SS	5089
Cefn Carnedd (ant.)	57	SO	0189
Cefn Carn-Fadog	41	SN	7617
Cefncennarth	57	SN	9776
Cefn Coch (Clwyd-Gwyn.)	67	SJ	0035
Cefn Coch (Powys)	57	SJ	1026
Cefn-coch (Powys)	44	SN	8254
Cefn-coed-y-cymmer	41	SO	0307
Cefn Cribwr	41	SS	8582
Cefn-crin	57	SO	0272
Cefn Cross	41	SS	8682
Cefn-ddwysarn	67	SH	9638
Cefndeuddwr	57	SH	7226
Cefn Drum	43	SN	6205
Cefn Du	67	SJ	9303
Cefn-Einion	48	SO	2886
Cefn Fannog	44	SN	8251
Cefn Grug	41	SN	8802
Cefn Gwrhyd	40	SN	7208
Cefn Hirgoed	41	SS	9383
Cefni Resr.	66	SH	4477
Cefn Llwydlo	44	SN	8642
Cefn-mawr (Clwyd)	58	SJ	2842
Cefn Mawr (Powys)	44	SN	7915
Cefn Merthyr	41	ST	0899
Cefn Morfudd	41	SS	7997
Cefn Onneu	40	SN	4800
Cefn Padrig	40	SO	1716
Cefn Pyllau-duon	41	SO	1111
Cefn Rhyswg	45	ST	2395
Cefn Sidan Sands	40	SN	3702
Cefn-y-bedd	58	SJ	3156
Cefn-y-coed	58	SO	2093
Cefn-y-pant	43	SN	1925
Cefn yr Arail	41	SO	1905
Cefnyresgair	57	SN	7489
Ceidio	66	SH	4085
Ceidio Fawr	66	SH	2838
Ceint	66	SH	4874
Cellan	43	SN	6149
Cellar Head (Isle of Lewis)	131	NB	5656
Cellarhead (Staffs.)	60	SJ	9547
Celtic or Deil's Dike (ant.)	88	NS	7011
Cemaes	66	SH	3693
Cemaes Bay	66	SH	3694
Cemaes Head	42	SN	1350
Cemlyn Bay	66	SH	3393
Cemmaes	57	SH	8306
Cemmaes Road	57	SH	8204
Cenarth	43	SN	2641
Cennin	66	SH	4645
Ceol na mara	111	NM	7561
Ceres	103	NO	4011
Cerne Abbas	25	ST	6601
Cerney Wick	46	SU	0796
Cerrigceinwen	66	SH	4273
Cerrigydrudion	67	SH	9548
Cessford	96	NT	7323
Cessnock Water	93	NS	5028
Chaceley	46	SO	8530
Chacewater	18	SW	7444
Chackmoro	51	SP	6835
Chacombe	51	SP	4943
Chadderton	69	SD	9005
Chaddesden	60	SK	3737
Chaddesley Corbett	49	SO	8973
Chaddleworth	34	SU	4177
Chadlington	47	SP	3221
Chadshunt	50	SP	3453
Chad Valley	50	SP	0385
Chadwell St. Mary	38	TQ	6478
Chadwick End	50	SP	2073
Chaffcombe	24	ST	3510
Chagford	21	SX	7087
Chailey	29	TQ	3919
Chainhurst	29	TQ	7347
Chaipaval (is.)	124	NF	9792
Chalbury Common	26	SU	0106
Chaldon	29	TQ	3155
Chaldon Down	25	SY	7881
Chaldon Herring or East Chaldon	25	SY	7983
Chale	27	SZ	4877
Chale Bay	27	SZ	4777
Chale Green	27	SZ	4879
Chalfont and Latimer Station	36	SU	9997
Chalfont Common	36	SU	9892
Chalfont St. Giles	36	SU	9993
Chalfont St. Peter	36	SU	9990
Chalford	46	SO	8902
Chalgrove	36	SU	6396
Chalk	30	TQ	6772
Challacombe	23	SS	6941
Challister Ness	141	HU	5766
Challoch	86	NX	3867
Challoch Hill	86	NX	1658
Challock	31	TR	0050
Chalton (Beds.)	52	TL	0326
Chalton (Hants.)	27	SU	7316
Chalvington	29	TQ	5109
Champany	102	NT	0278
Chancellor, The (mt.)	106	NN	1957
Chandler's Cross	36	TQ	0698
Chandler's Ford	26	SU	4320
Changue Plantation	86	NX	3193
Channelkirk	96	NT	4753
Channerwick	141	HU	4023
Channony Point	129	NH	7555
Chantry (Somer.)	33	ST	7146
Chantry (Suff.)	55	TM	1443
Chapel	103	NT	2593
Chapel Allerton (Somer.)	32	SM	9400
Chapel Allerton (W Yorks.)	79	SE	2936
Chapel Amble	19	SW	9975
Chapel Brampton	51	SP	7266
Chapel Chorlton	59	SJ	8037
Chapeldonald Way	54	TL	7039
Chapel-en-le-Frith	70	SK	0580
Chapelfell Top	84	NY	8734
Chapel Finian (ant.)	86	NX	2849
Chapelgate	63	TF	4124
Chapel Haddlesey	79	SE	5826
Chapelhall	101	NS	7862
Chapel Hill (Gramp.)	121	NK	0635
Chapel Hill (Gwent)	45	SO	5200
Chapelhill (Highld.)	129	NH	8273
Chapel Hill (Lincs.)	62	TF	2054
Chapelhill (Tays.)	108	NO	0030
Chapel Hill (Tays.)	108	NO	2021
Chapelknowe	89	NY	3173
Chapel Lawn	48	SO	3176
Chapel Le Dale	77	SD	7377
Chapel Ness	103	NT	4799
Chapel of Garioch	121	NJ	7124
Chapel Point (Corn.)	19	SX	0243
Chapel Point (Dyfed)	42	SS	1495
Chapel Rossan Bay	86	NX	1145
Chapel Row	35	SU	5669
Chapel Stile	82	NY	3205
Chapel St. Leonards	73	TF	5572
Chapelton (Devon)	23	SS	5826
Chapelton (Strath.)	94	NS	6848
Chapelton (Tays.)	109	NO	6247
Chapeltown (Gramp.)	117	NJ	2421
Chapeltown (Lancs.)	69	SD	7315
Chapeltown (S Yorks.)	71	SK	3596
Chapman Sands	38	TQ	8383
Chapmanslade	33	ST	8348
Chappel	54	TL	8928
Chard	24	ST	3208
Chardstock	24	ST	3004
Charfield	33	ST	7292
Charing	30	TQ	9549
Charing Cross Station	37	TQ	3080
Charing Heath	30	TQ	9148
Charingworth	50	SP	1939
Charlbury	47	SP	3519
Charlcombe	33	ST	7467
Charlecote	50	SP	2656
Charlecote Park (ant.)	50	SP	2656
Charles	23	SS	6832
Charleston	109	NO	3845
Charlestown (Corn.)	19	SX	0351
Charlestown (Dorset)	25	SY	6579
Charlestown (Fife.)	102	NT	0683
Charlestown (Gramp.)	121	NJ	9300
Charlestown (Highld.)	123	NG	8175
Charlestown (Highld.)	128	NH	6448
Charlestown of Aberlour	120	NJ	2642
Charles Tye	54	TM	0252
Charlesworth	71	SK	0092
Charleton House	103	NO	4603
Charlton (Gtr London)	37	TQ	4278
Charlton (Here. and Worc.)	50	SP	0045
Charlton (Northants.)	51	SP	5236
Charlton (Wilts.)	25	ST	9021
Charlton (Wilts.)	34	SU	9689
Charlton (Wilts.)	34	SU	1155
Charlton (Wilts.)	25	SU	1723
Charlton (W Susx.)	27	SU	8812
Charlton Abbots	46	SP	0324
Charlton Adam	25	ST	5328
Charlton Down	25	ST	8700
Charlton Horethorne	25	ST	6623
Charlton Kings	46	SO	9620
Charlton Mackrell	25	ST	5228
Charlton Marshall	25	ST	8903
Charlton Musgrove	25	ST	7229
Charlton-on-Otmoor	47	SP	5615
Charlwood	28	TQ	2441
Charlynch	24	ST	2337
Charminster	25	SY	6792
Charmouth	24	SY	3693
Charndon	36	SP	6724
Charney Bassett	34	SU	3894
Charnock Richard	69	SD	5415
Charnwood Forest	61	SK	4914
Charsfield	55	TM	2556
Charter Alley	35	SU	5957
Charterhouse	33	ST	4955
Charterville Allotments	47	SP	3110
Chartham	31	TR	1054
Chartham Hatch	31	TR	1056
Chartridge	36	SP	9303
Chart Sutton	30	TQ	8049
Charwelton	51	SP	5355
Chase Terrace	60	SK	0409
Chasetown	60	SK	0408
Chasewater	60	SK	0307
Chastleton	47	SP	2429
Chatburn	78	SD	7644
Chatcull	59	SJ	7934
Chatham	30	TQ	7567
Chathill	97	NU	1826
Chat Moss	69	SJ	7095
Chatsworth House (ant.)	71	SK	2670
Chattenden	30	TQ	7672
Chatteris	53	TL	3986
Chatteris Fen	53	TL	3979
Chattisham	55	TM	0942
Chatto	90	NT	7717
Chatton	97	NU	0528
Chawleigh	23	SS	7112
Chawston	52	TL	1556
Chawton	27	SU	7037
Cheadle (Gtr Mches.)	69	SJ	8788
Cheadle (Staffs.)	60	SK	0043
Cheadle Hulme	69	SJ	8686
Cheam	37	TQ	2463
Chearsley	36	SP	7110
Chebsey	59	SJ	8528
Checkendon	36	SU	6682
Checkley (Ches.)	59	SJ	7245
Checkley (Staffs.)	60	SK	0237
Chedburgh	54	TL	7957
Cheddar	33	ST	4553
Cheddar Gorge	33	ST	4653
Cheddar Reservoir	33	ST	4453
Cheddington	36	SP	9217
Cheddleton	60	SJ	9651
Cheddon Fitzpaine	24	ST	2427
Chedgrave	65	TM	3699
Chedington	25	ST	4805
Chediston	55	TM	3577
Chedworth	46	SP	0511
Chedzoy	24	ST	3337
Cheeseman's Green	31	TR	0338
Cheetham Hill	69	SD	8401
Cheldon	23	SS	7313
Chelford	78	SJ	8174
Chelker Resr.	60	SK	3830
Chellaston	60	SK	3830
Chellington	52	SP	9656
Chelmarsh	49	SO	7187
Chelmark Resr.	49	SO	7187
Chelmondiston	55	TM	2037
Chelmorton	70	SK	1169
Chelmsford	38	TL	7006
Chelsea	37	TQ	2778
Chelsfield	37	TQ	4864
Chelsworth	54	TL	9748
Cheltenham	46	SO	9422
Chelveston	52	SP	9969
Chelvey	33	ST	4668
Chelwood	33	ST	6361
Chelwood Gate	29	TQ	4130
Cheney Longville	48	SO	4184
Chenies	36	TQ	0198
Chepstow	45	ST	5393
Chepstow Park Wood	45	SO	4897
Cherhill	34	SU	0370
Cherington (Glos.)	46	ST	9098
Cherington (Warw.)	50	SP	2936
Cheriton (Devon)	23	SS	7346
Cheriton (Devon)	24	ST	1001
Cheriton (Hants.)	27	SU	5828
Cheriton (Somer.)	25	ST	6825
Cheriton (W Glam.)	40	SS	4593
Cheriton Bishop	21	SX	7793
Cheriton Fitzpaine	23	SS	8606
Cherrington	59	SJ	6619
Cherry Burton	74	SE	9842
Cherry Cobb Sands	75	TA	2121
Cherry Hinton	53	TL	4857
Cherry Willingham	72	TF	0173
Chertsey	36	TQ	0466
Cheselbourne	25	SY	7699
Chesham	36	SP	9601
Chesham Bois	36	SU	9698
Cheshunt	37	TL	3502
Chesil Beach	25	SY	5882
Cheslyn Hay	60	SJ	9707
Chessington	37	TQ	1863
Chester	68	SJ	4066
Chesterblade	33	ST	6641
Chesterfield (Derby.)	71	SK	3871
Chesterfield (Staffs.)	60	SK	1005
Chesterfield Canal (Notts.)	71	SK	6582
Chesterfield Canal (Notts.)	72	SK	7284
Chester-le-Street	84	NZ	2751
Chesters (Borders)	96	NT	6022
Chesters (Borders)	90	NT	6210
Chesterton (Cambs.)	62	TL	1295
Chesterton (Cambs.)	53	TL	4560
Chesterton (Oxon.)	47	SP	5621
Chesterton (Staffs.)	59	SJ	8249
Chesterton Green	50	SP	3558
Chesterwood	90	NY	8364
Chestfield	31	TR	1365
Cheswardine	59	SJ	7129
Cheswick	97	NU	0346
Cheswick Black Rocks	97	NU	0347
Cheswick Green	50	SP	1275
Chetney Marshes	30	TQ	8871
Chetnole	25	ST	6008
Chettiscombe	23	SS	9614
Chettisham	53	TL	5483
Chettle	25	ST	9513
Chetton	49	SO	6690
Chetwode	51	SP	6429
Chetwynd Aston	59	SJ	7517
Cheveley	54	TL	6760
Chevening	37	TQ	4857
Chevington	54	TL	7859
Chevington Drift	91	NZ	2699
Cheviot Hills, The	90	NT	8211
Cheviot, The (mt.)	90	NT	9020
Chevithorne	23	SS	9715
Chew Magna	33	ST	5763
Chew Reservoir	70	SE	0301
Chew Stoke	33	ST	5561
Chewton Mendip	33	ST	5952
Chew Valley Lake	33	ST	5659
Cheyries (is.)	141	HU	3438
Chicheley	52	SP	9046
Chichester	27	SU	8605
Chichester (Goodwood) Airfield	27	SU	8707
Chichester Harbour	27	SU	7703
Chicken Head	131	NB	5029
Chicken Rock	76	SC	1464
Chickerell	25	SY	6480
Chicklade	25	ST	9134
Chicksands	52	TL	1239
Chidden	27	SU	6517
Chiddingfold	28	SU	9635
Chiddingly	29	TQ	5414
Chiddingstone	29	TQ	5045
Chiddingstone Causeway	29	TQ	5147
Chideock	24	SY	4292
Chidham	27	SU	7803
Chieveley	35	SU	4773
Chignall Smealy	38	TL	6611
Chignall St. James	38	TL	6709
Chigwell	37	TQ	4493
Chigwell Row	37	TQ	4693
Chilbolton	34	SU	3939
Chilcomb (Hants.)	27	SU	5028
Chilcombe (Dorset)	25	SY	5291
Chilcompton	33	ST	6452
Chilcote	60	SK	2811
Childer Thornton	68	SJ	3677
Child Okeford	25	ST	8312
Childrey	34	SU	3687
Child's Ercall	59	SJ	6625
Childswickham	50	SP	0738
Childwall	68	SJ	4089
Chilfrome	25	SY	5898
Chilgrove	27	SU	8314
Chilham	31	TR	0753
Chillaton	20	SX	4381
Chillenden	31	TR	2753
Chillerton	27	SZ	4883
Chillesford	55	TM	3852
Chillingham	97	NU	0625
Chillington (Devon)	21	SX	7942
Chillington (Somer.)	24	ST	3811
Chillington Hall	59	SJ	8606
Chilmark	26	ST	9632
Chilson	47	SP	3119
Chilsworthy (Corn.)	20	SX	4172
Chilsworthy (Devon)	22	SS	3206
Chiltern Hills	36	SU	7799
Chiltern Hundreds (dist.)	36	SU	9390
Chilthorne Domer	25	ST	5219
Chilton (Bucks.)	36	SP	6811
Chilton (Durham)	84	NZ	2929
Chilton (Oxon.)	35	SU	4885
Chilton Cantelo	25	ST	5621
Chilton Chine	26	SZ	4181
Chilton Foliat	34	SU	3170
Chilton Lane	84	NZ	3031
Chilton Polden	32	ST	3739
Chilton Street	54	TL	7547
Chilton Trinity	32	ST	2939
Chilworth	26	SU	4018
Chimney	47	SP	3500
Chineham	35	SU	6554
Chingford	37	TQ	3893
Chinley	70	SK	0382
Chinley Head	70	SK	0484
Chinnor	36	SP	7500
Chipchase Castle	90	NY	8875
Chipnall	59	SJ	7231
Chippenham (Cambs.)	54	TL	6669
Chippenham (Wilts.)	33	SU	9173
Chipperfield	36	TL	0401
Chipping (Herts.)	53	TL	3532
Chipping (Lancs.)	77	SD	6243
Chipping Campden	50	SP	1539
Chipping Hill	38	TL	8215
Chipping Norton	47	SP	3127
Chipping Ongar	37	TL	5502
Chipping Sodbury	33	ST	7282
Chipping Warden	51	SP	4948
Chipstable	24	ST	0427
Chipstead (Kent)	29	TQ	5056
Chipstead (Surrey)	28	TQ	2756
Chirbury	58	SO	2698
Chirdon Burn	90	NY	7481
Chirk	58	SJ	2937
Chirk Castle	58	SJ	2638
Chirmorie	86	NX	2076
Chirnside	97	NT	8756
Chirnsidebridge	97	NT	8556
Chirton	34	SU	0757
Chisbury	34	SU	2766
Chiselborough	25	ST	4614
Chiselbury (ant.)	26	SU	0127
Chiselhampton	47	SU	5999
Chisledon	34	SU	1879
Chislehurst	37	TQ	4470
Chislet	31	TR	2264
Chiswell Green	52	TL	1303
Chiswick	37	TQ	2077
Chisworth	70	SJ	9991
Chithurst	27	SU	8423
Chittering	53	TL	4970
Chitterne	33	ST	9843
Chittlehamholt	23	SS	6520
Chittlehampton	23	SS	6325
Chittoe	34	ST	9666
Chivelstone	21	SX	7838
Chno Dearg	115	NN	3774
Chobham	36	SU	9761
Chobham Common	36	SU	9665
Chobham Ridges	36	SU	9159
Cholderton	34	SU	2242
Cholesbury	36	SP	9307
Chollerton	90	NY	9372
Cholmondeley Castle	59	SJ	5351
Cholsey	35	SU	5886
Cholstrey	45	SO	4659
Chon (mt.)	91	NZ	2583
Chopwell	91	NZ	1158
Chorley (Ches.)	59	SJ	5650
Chorley (Lancs.)	77	SD	5817
Chorley (Shrops.)	49	SO	6983
Chorley (Staffs.)	60	SK	0711
Chorleywood	36	TQ	0396
Chorlton	59	SJ	7250
Chorlton-cum-Hardy	69	SJ	8093
Chorlton Lane	58	SJ	4547
Chowley	59	SJ	4756
Chrishall	53	TL	4439
Christchurch (Cambs.)	63	TL	4996
Christchurch (Dorset)	26	SZ	1593
Christchurch (Glos.)	45	SO	5713
Christchurch Bay	26	SZ	2291
Christian Malford	34	ST	9678
Christleton	68	SJ	4365
Christmas Common	36	SU	7193
Christon	32	ST	3956
Christon Bank	97	NU	2122
Christow	21	SX	8385
Christ's Hospital	28	TQ	1428
Chudleigh	21	SX	8679
Chudleigh Knighton	21	SX	8477
Chulmleigh	23	SS	6814
Chunal	70	SK	0391
Church	77	SD	7428
Churcham	46	SO	7618
Church Aston	59	SJ	7317
Church Bay	66	SH	2989
Church Brampton	51	SP	7165
Church Broughton	60	SK	2033
Church Cove	18	SW	7112
Church Crookham	35	SU	8152
Churchdown	46	SO	8819
Church Eaton	59	SJ	8417
Church End (Beds.)	36	SP	9921
Church End (Beds.)	52	TL	1937
Church End (Cambs.)	63	TF	3909
Church End (Cambs.)	53	TL	4857
Church End (Essex)	53	TL	5841
Church End (Essex)	38	TL	6323
Churchend (Essex)	39	TR	0092
Church End (Hants.)	35	SU	6756
Church End (Warw.)	50	SP	2892
Church End (Wilts.)	34	SU	0278
Church Fenton	79	SE	5136
Church Gresley	60	SK	2918
Church Handborough	47	SP	4212
Church Houses	85	SE	6697
Churchill (Avon)	33	ST	4359
Churchill (Here. and Worc.)	50	SO	8779
Churchill (Oxon.)	47	SP	2824
Churchingford	24	ST	2112
Church Knowle	25	SY	9481
Church Langton	61	SP	7293
Church Lawford	51	SP	4476
Church Lawton	59	SJ	8255
Church Leigh	60	SK	0235
Church Lench	50	SP	0251
Church Minshull	59	SJ	6660
Church Norton	27	SZ	8695
Churchover	51	SP	5080
Church Preen	59	SO	5398
Church Pulverbatch	58	SJ	4303
Churclistanton	24	ST	1914
Church Stoke	58	SO	2694
Churchstow (Devon)	21	SX	7145
Church Stowe (Northants.)	51	SP	6357
Church Street	30	TQ	7174
Church Stretton	58	SO	4593
Churchtown (I. of M.)	76	SC	4294
Churchtown (Lancs.)	77	SD	4842
Churchtown (Mers.)	68	SD	3618
Church Village	41	ST	0886
Church Warsop	71	SK	5668
Churn Clough Resr.	90	NY	6677
Churnsike Lodge	90	NY	6777
Churt	35	SU	8538
Churton	68	SJ	4156
Churwell	79	SE	2729
Chute Causeway (ant.)	34	SU	2856
Chwefru	44	SN	9854
Chwilog	66	SH	4338
Chyandour	18	SW	4731
Ciaran Water	106	NN	2861
Cilan Uchaf	56	SH	2923
Cilcain	67	SJ	1765
Cilcennin	43	SN	5160
Cilfaesty Hill	50	SO	1384
Cilfor	67	SH	6237
Cilfrew	41	ST	0892
Cilfynydd	41	ST	0892
Cilgerran	43	SN	1943
Cilgwyn	41	SN	7430
Ciliau-Aeron	43	SN	5058
Cilieni	41	SN	9035
Cilmery	44	SO	0051
Cilrhedyn	43	SN	2734
Cilsan	43	SN	5821
Citalgarth	67	SH	8840
Cilurnum (ant.)	90	NY	9170
Cilwendeg	43	SN	2238
Cilybebyll	41	SN	7404
Cilycwm	44	SN	7540
Cinderford	46	SO	6513
Cioch Mhòr	128	NH	5063
Cirean Geardail	132	NC	0134
Cirencester	46	SP	0201
Cir Mhòr	92	NR	9743
Cissbury Ring (ant.)	28	TQ	1408
Ciste Dhubh	115	NH	0616
City Dulas	66	SH	4687
City of London	37	TQ	3281
City, The	100	NS	1181
Clabhach	92	NM	6940
Clachaig Water	92	NR	9360
Clachan (Island of Raasay)	123	NG	5436
Clachan (Lismore Island)	105	NM	8543
Clachan (Strath.)	105	NM	7819
Clachan (Strath.)	99	NR	7656
Clachan (Strath.)	100	NM	8065
Clachan (Tays.)	107	NN	8065
Clachan-a-Luib	124	NF	8163
Clachan Burn	133	NC	7261
Clachan Mòr	104	NL	9847
Clachan of Campsie	101	NS	6179
Clachan of Glendaruel	100	NR	9984
Clachan-Seil	105	NM	7718
Clachan Yell (mt.)	110	NO	4491
Clach Bheinn	100	NS	2195
Clachbreck	99	NR	7675
Clach Leathad	106	NN	2449
Clachtoll	132	NC	0427
Clackmannan	101	NS	9191
Clacton-on-Sea	39	TM	1715
Cladach an Eilein	131	NB	5365
Cladach Cuiashader	131	NB	5653
Cladach Dibadale	131	NB	5554
Claddach Kirkibost	124	NF	7865
Cladich	106	NN	0921
Cladich River	106	NN	0921
Claerwen Resr.	44	SN	8565
Claggain Bay	98	NR	4553
Claggan River	111	NM	7504
Clagh Ouyr	76	SC	4189
Claife Heights	82	SD	3798
Claigan	122	NG	2353
Claig Castle	99	NR	4762
Claines	49	SO	8559
Clandown	33	ST	6855
Clanfield (Hants.)	27	SU	6916
Clanfield (Oxon.)	47	SP	2801
Clannaborough Barton	23	SS	7402
Clanville	34	SU	3148
Clanyard	86	NX	1037

Clanyard Bay Corney

Clanyard Bay 86 NX 0938
Claonaig 92 NR 8656
Claonaig Bay 92 NR 8755
Claonel 128 NC 5604
Clapgate 26 SU 0102
Clapham (Beds.) 52 TL 0252
Clapham (Gtr London) 37 TQ 2875
Clapham (N Yorks.) 77 SD 7469
Clapham (W Susx) 28 TQ 0906
Clappers 97 NT 9455
Clappersgate 82 NY 3603
Clapton (Somer.) 24 ST 4106
Clapton-in-Gordano 33 ST 4774
Clapton-on-the-Hill 47 SP 1617
Clapworthy 23 SS 6724
Clarbeston 42 SN 0421
Clarbeston Road 42 SN 0121
Clarborough 72 SK 7383
Clardon 135 ND 1468
Clardon Head 135 ND 1570
Clare 54 TL 7645
Clarebrand 88 NX 7666
Claremont Park 37 TQ 1363
Clarencefield 89 NY 0968
Clarkston 94 NS 5757
Clashindarroch 121 NJ 4831
Clashindarroch Forest 121 NJ 4633
Clashmach Hill 121 NJ 4938
Clashmore 132 NC 0331
Clashmore Wood 129 NH 7390
Clashnessie 132 NC 0530
Clashnessie Bay 132 NC 0631
Clashnoir 117 NJ 2222
Clathy 108 NN 9919
Clatt 121 NJ 5426
Clatter 57 SN 9994
Clattering Brig 119 NO 6678
Clatteringshaws Loch 87 NX 5477
Clatto Hill 103 NO 3506
Clatto Resr. 103 NO 3607
Clatworthy 24 ST 0530
Clatworthy Reservoir 24 ST 0431
Clauchlands Point 92 NS 0533
Claughton (Lancs.) 77 SD 5242
Claughton (Lancs.) 77 SD 5666
Clava Cairns (ant.) 129 NH 7544
Claverdon 50 SP 1964
Claverham 33 ST 4566
Clavering 53 TL 4832
Claverley 59 SO 7993
Claverton 33 ST 7864
Clawdd-du-bach 57 SN 8770
Clawdd-newydd 67 SJ 0852
Clawton 20 SX 3599
Claxby (Lincs.) 73 TF 1194
Claxby (Lincs.) 73 TF 4571
Claxton (Norf.) 65 TG 3303
Claxton (N Yorks.) 80 SE 6960
Clay 108 NO 1463
Claybokie 117 NO 0989
Claybrooke Magna 51 SP 4988
Clay Common 55 TM 4781
Clay Coton 51 SP 5977
Clay Cross 71 SK 3963
Claydon (Oxon.) 51 SP 4550
Claydon (Suff.) 55 TM 1350
Claygate 37 TQ 1563
Claygate Cross 29 TQ 6155
Clayhanger (Devon) 24 ST 0222
Clayhanger (W Mids) 60 SK 0404
Clay Head 76 SC 4480
Clayhidon 24 ST 1615
Clayock 135 ND 1659
Clay of Allan 129 NH 8276
Claypole 62 SK 8449
Clayton (Staffs.) 59 SJ 8443
Clayton (S Yorks.) 71 SE 4507
Clayton (W Susx) 29 TQ 3014
Clayton (W Yorks.) 78 SE 1131
Clayton-le-Moors 77 SD 7431
Clayton-le-Woods 77 SD 5722
Clayton West 71 SE 2511
Clayworth 72 SK 7288
Cleadale 111 NM 4788
Cleadon 91 NZ 3862
Cleann Tanagaidh 127 NH 0868
Clearbury Ring (ant.) 26 SU 1524
Clearwell 45 SO 5708
Cleasby 84 NZ 2713
Cleasby Hill 84 NY 9707
Cleat (Barra) 112 NF 6604
Cleat (S. Ronaldsay) 136 ND 4584
Cleatlam 84 NZ 1118
Cleator 82 NY 0113
Cleator Moor 82 NY 0214
Cleckheaton 78 SE 1825
Cledan 44 SN 8644
Cleedownton 48 SO 5880
Cleehill 49 SO 5975
Clee St. Margaret 48 SO 5684
Cleethorpes 75 TA 3008
Cleeton St. Mary 49 SO 6178
Cleeve 33 ST 4566
Cleeve Hill 46 SO 9827
Cleeve Prior 50 SP 0849
Clehonger 45 SO 4637
Cleigh 105 NM 8725
Cleish 102 NT 0998
Cleish Hills 102 NT 0796
Cleite Leathann (mt.) 130 NB 0428
Cleland 101 NS 7958
Clench Common 34 SU 1765
Clenchwarton 63 TF 5820
Clent 49 SO 9179
Clent Hills 49 SO 9380
Cleobury Mortimer 49 SO 6775
Cleobury North 49 SO 6187
Cleongart 92 NR 6734
Clephanton 129 NH 8150
Clerklands 96 NT 5024
Clestrain 136 HY 3006
Clestrain Sound 136 HY 2806
Clett 135 ND 1071
Clett Ard 125 NB 1808
Clett Nisabost 124 NG 0495
Clettraval 124 NF 7471
Cleughbrae 89 NY 0673
Clevancy 34 SU 0475
Clevedon 32 ST 4071
Clevedon Court 33 ST 4271
Cleveland 85 NZ 6213
Cleveland Hills 85 SE 5899
Cleveleys 77 SD 3142
Cleverton 34 ST 9785
Clewer 33 ST 4350
Cley Hill 33 ST 8344
Cley next the Sea 64 TG 0444
Cliad Bay 110 NM 1960
Cliasmol 125 NB 0706
Cliburn 83 NY 5824
Cliddesden 35 SU 6349
Cliffe (Kent) 30 TQ 7376
Cliffe (N Yorks.) 79 SE 6631
Cliffe Hill 29 TQ 4310
Cliff End 30 TQ 8813
Cliffe Woods 30 TQ 7373
Clifford (Here. and Worc.) 45 SO 2445
Clifford (W Yorks.) 79 SE 4244
Clifford Chambers 50 SP 1952
Clifford's Mesne 46 SO 7023
Cliffs End 31 TR 3464
Clift Hills 141 HU 3931
Clifton (Avon) 33 ST 5673
Clifton (Beds.) 52 TL 1739
Clifton (Central) 106 NN 3230
Clifton (Cumbr.) 82 NY 0429
Clifton (Cumbr.) 83 NY 5326
Clifton (Derby.) 60 SK 1644
Clifton (Here. and Worc.) 49 SO 8446
Clifton (Lancs.) 77 SD 4630
Clifton (Northum.) 91 NZ 2082
Clifton (Notts.) 61 SK 5434
Clifton (Oxon.) 47 SP 4831
Clifton Campville 60 SK 2510
Clifton Hampden 47 SU 5495
Clifton Reynes 52 SP 9051
Clifton upon Dunsmore 51 SP 5276
Clifton upon Teme 49 SO 7161
Clift Sound 141 HU 3933
Clifts, The 142 HU 3281
Climping 28 TQ 0002
Clint 79 SE 2559
Clintburn 90 NY 7279
Clinterty 119 NJ 8311
Clint Green 64 TG 0210
Clintmains 96 NT 6132
Clints Dod 103 NT 6268
Clints of Dromore (mt.) 87 NX 5464
Clippesby 65 TG 4214
Clipsham 62 SK 9616
Clipston (Northants.) 51 SP 7181
Clipston (Notts.) 61 SK 6333
Clisham (mt.) 125 NB 1507
Clitheroe 77 SD 7441
Clive 59 SJ 5124
Clivocast 143 HP 6000
Clocaenog 67 SJ 0854
Clocaenog Forest 67 SJ 0152
Clochan 121 NJ 4060
Cloch Point 100 NS 2075
Clock Face 69 SJ 5291
Cloddymoss 129 NH 9859
Clodock 45 SO 3227
Clola 121 NK 0043
Clophill 52 TL 0838
Clopton 52 TL 0680
Clopton Green 54 TL 7654
Closeburn 88 NX 8992
Close Clark 76 SC 2775
Clothall 53 TL 2732
Clothan 143 HU 4581
Clotton 69 SJ 5263
Clougha Pike 77 SD 5559
Clough Foot 78 SD 9123
Cloughton 81 TA 0094
Cloughton Newlands 81 TA 0096
Cloughton Wyke (pt.) 81 TA 0295
Clousta 141 HU 3157
Clova (Grampn.) 121 NJ 4522
Clova (Tays.) 118 NO 3273
Clovelly 22 SS 3124
Clovelly Dykes (ant.) 22 SS 3123
Clove Lodge 84 NY 9317
Clovenfords 96 NT 4436
Clovenstone 119 NJ 7717
Clovullin 106 NN 0063
Clowbridge Resr. 78 SD 8328
Clowne 71 SK 4975
Clows Top 49 SO 7171
Cluanie Forest 115 NH 0409
Cluanie Lodge 115 NH 0910
Cluas Deas 132 NC 0032
Cluer 125 NG 1490
Clumber Park 71 SK 6274
Clun 48 SO 3081
Clunas 129 NH 8846
Clunas Reservoir 129 NH 8545
Clunbury 48 SO 3780
Clunes 115 NN 2088
Clunes Forest 115 NN 2290
Clun Forest 48 SO 2286
Clungunford 48 SO 3978
Clunie (Grampn.) 121 NJ 6350
Clunie (Tays.) 108 NO 1043
Clunie Water 117 NO 1486
Clunton 48 SO 3381
Cluny 103 NT 2495
Cluny Castle (Grampn.) 119 NJ 6812
Cluny Castle (Highld.) 116 NN 6494
Cluster 143 HU 5890
Clutton (Avon) 33 ST 6159
Clutton (Ches.) 58 SJ 4654
Clwt-y-bont 66 SH 5763
Clwydian Range 68 SJ 1464
Clydach (Gwent) 41 SO 2213
Clydach (W Glam.) 40 SN 6801
Clydach Vale 41 SS 9793
Clydebank 101 NS 5069
Clyde Law 88 NT 0217
Clydesdale (dist.) 95 NS 8347
Clydey 43 SN 2535
Clyffe Pypard 34 SU 0776
Clynder 100 NS 2484
Clynderwen 42 SN 1219
Clynelish 129 NC 8905
Clynnog-fawr 66 SH 4149
Clyro 45 SO 2143
Clyro Hill 45 SO 2046
Clyst Honiton 21 SX 9893
Clyst Hydon 24 ST 0301
Clyst St. George 21 SX 9888
Clyst St. Lawrence 24 ST 0200
Clyst St. Mary 21 SX 9890
Clyth 135 ND 2937
Cnap Chaochan Aitinn 117 NJ 1409
Cnap na Feola (mt.) 127 NH 2253
Cnicht 67 SH 6446
Cnoc a'Bhaile-shios 99 NR 8662
Cnoc a'Chapuill 92 NR 9730
Cnoc a'Choire 128 NC 5004
Cnoc a' Ghiubhais (Highld.) 132 NC 2670
Cnoc a' Ghiubhais (Highld.) 133 NC 5423
Cnoc a' Ghriama 132 NC 4026
Cnoc a'Mhadaidh 100 NS 1684
Cnoc an Alaskie 133 NC 4827
Cnocan Conachreag 135 ND 1136
Cnoc an dà Chinn 105 NM 4444
Cnoc an Earrannaiche 135 ND 2441
Cnoc an Eireannaich 134 NC 9527
Cnoc an Fhuarain Bhàin 134 NC 9553
Cnoc an Ime 98 NR 5880
Cnoc an Liath-bhaid Mhòir 134 NC 7529
Cnoc an t-Sabhail 128 NH 6978
Cnoc Badaireach na Gaoithe 134 NC 8452
Cnoc Bad Mhairtein 134 NC 9354
Cnoc Breac 126 NG 7884
Cnoc Buidhe 92 NR 6930
Cnoc Ceann nam Bad 128 NC 5500
Cnoc Céislein 128 NH 5870
Cnoc Coinnich 100 NN 2300
Cnoc Coire na Feàrna 134 NC 9329
Cnoc Corr Guinie 128 NH 6775
Cnoc Craggie 133 NC 6052
Cnoc Creagach 92 NR 8455
Cnoc Donn 92 NR 7452
Cnoc Dubh 98 NR 2262
Cnoc Eille Mòr 128 NH 4547
Cnoc Fraing 116 NH 8014
Cnoc Leamhnachd 134 NC 7511
Cnoc Loch Mhadadh 134 NC 9932
Cnoc Meadhonach 134 NC 8417
Cnoc Mòr 92 NR 6809
Cnoc Mòr na Claigin 98 NR 4553
Cnoc Moy 92 NR 6115
Cnoc Muigh-bhlàraidh 128 NH 6382
Cnoc na Breun-choille 134 NC 7824
Cnoc na Carraige 100 NR 9768
Cnoc na Glas Choille 127 NC 2708
Cnoc na h'Airighe 100 NS 2290
Cnoc na Maoile 135 ND 0021
Cnoc na Meine 100 NR 9060
Cnoc nan Craobh 92 NR 7345
Cnoc nan Cuilean 133 NC 5946
Cnoc nan Gabhar 92 NR 8039
Cnoc nan Tri-chlach 134 NC 7943
Cnoc Odhar 92 NR 6613
Cnoc Preas a'Mhadaidh 134 NC 9848
Cnoc Reamhar (Island of Arran) 92 NR 9224
Cnoc Reamhar (Strath.) 99 NR 7690
Cnoc Stighseir 99 NR 7176
Cnwch Coch 57 SN 6775
Coad's Green 20 SX 2976
Coal Aston 71 SK 3679
Coalbrookdale 59 SJ 6604
Coalburn 95 NS 8034
Coalcleugh 83 NY 8045
Coaley 46 SO 7701
Coall Head 141 HU 4433
Coalpit Heath 33 ST 6780
Coalport 59 SJ 6902
Coalsnaughton 102 NS 9195
Coaltown of Balgonie 103 NT 2999
Coaltown of Wemyss 103 NT 3295
Coalville 60 SK 4214
Coast 126 NG 9290
Coatbridge 101 NS 7265
Coatdyke 101 NS 7464
Coate 34 SU 0361
Coates (Cambs.) 63 TL 3097
Coates (Glos.) 46 SO 9700
Coatham 85 NZ 5925
Coatham Mundeville 84 NZ 2919
Coatsgate 89 NT 0605
Cobbaton 23 SS 6127
Cobbin's Brook 37 TL 4001
Cobbinshaw Resr. 95 NT 0157
Cobbler, The (mt.) 100 NN 2505
Coberley 46 SO 9615
Cobham (Kent) 30 TQ 6768
Cobham (Surrey) 37 TQ 1060
Cobnash 45 SO 4560
Cochno Loch 101 NS 4976
Cochrage Muir 108 NO 1349
Cockayne 85 SE 6298
Cockayne Hatley 53 TL 2549
Cockayne Ridge 85 NZ 6000
Cock Beck 79 SE 4738
Cock Bridge 117 NJ 2509
Cockburnspath 96 NT 7770
Cock Cairn 118 NO 4688
Cock Clarks 38 TL 8102
Cockenzie and Port Seton 103 NT 4075
Cockerham 77 SD 4651
Cockerington 73 TF 3789
Cockermouth 82 NY 1230
Cockernhoe 37 TL 1223
Cockfield (Durham) 84 NZ 1224
Cockfield (Suff.) 54 TL 9054
Cockfosters 37 TQ 2896
Cock Hill 119 NO 5387
Cocking 27 SU 8717
Cockington 21 SX 8964
Cocklake 33 ST 4349
Cock Law 90 NT 8616
Cocklaw Hill 96 NT 7271
Cockley Beck 82 NY 2401
Cockley Cley 64 TF 7904
Cock of Arran 92 NR 9552
Cockpole Green 36 SU 7981
Cocks Hill 21 SX 5679
Cockshutt 58 SJ 4329
Cockthorpe 64 TF 9842
Cockwood 21 SX 9780
Cod Beck 79 SE 4277
Codda 19 SX 1878
Coddenham 55 TM 1354
Coddington (Ches.) 58 SJ 4455
Coddington (Here. and Worc.) 49 SO 7142
Coddington (Notts.) 62 SK 8354
Codford St. Mary 34 ST 9739
Codford St. Peter 34 ST 9640
Codicote 37 TL 2118
Codnor 60 SK 4149
Codrington 33 ST 7278
Codsall 59 SJ 8603
Codsall Wood 59 SJ 8405
Coedely 41 ST 0285
Coedkernew 32 ST 2783
Coedpoeth 58 SJ 2850
Coed-y-gaer 57 SO 0084
Coed-y-paen 45 ST 3398
Coelbren 41 SN 8411
Coffinswell 21 SX 8868
Cofton Hackett 50 SP 0075
Cogan 41 ST 1772
Cogenhoe 52 SP 8360
Coggeshall 38 TL 8522
Cogra Moss 82 NY 0919
Coigach (dist.) 127 NC 1103
Coignafearn Forest 116 NH 6412
Coignafearn Lodge 116 NH 6815
Coilacriech 118 NO 3287
Coilantogle 101 NN 5906
Coillaig 106 NN 0120
Coille Mhorgil 115 NH 1001
Coillore 122 NG 3537
Coirc Bheinn 105 NM 4832
Coire a' Chonachair 127 NC 3302
Coire Bhachdaidh Lodge 107 NN 5471
Coirefrois Burn 133 NC 7015
Coire na Beinne 135 ND 1440
Coire Odhar (Highld.) 116 NH 5006
Coire Odhar (Tays.) 107 NN 8213
Coire Thomag 99 NR 7974
Coity 41 SS 9281
Coity Mountain 45 SO 2308
Coker 25 ST 5312
Colaboll 133 NC 5610
Coladoir River 105 NM 5529
Colan 19 SW 8661
Colaton Raleigh 24 SY 0787
Col-bheinn 134 NC 8810
Colbost 122 NG 2148
Colbost Point 122 NG 3039
Colby (Cumbr.) 83 NY 6620
Colby (I. of M.) 76 SC 2370
Colby (Norf.) 65 TG 2131
Colchester 54 TM 0025
Cold Ash 35 SU 5169
Cold Ashby 51 SP 6576
Cold Ashton 33 ST 7472
Cold Aston 47 SP 1219
Coldbackie 133 NC 6160
Coldblow 37 TQ 5173
Cold Brayfield 52 SP 9252
Coldean 29 TQ 3408
Coldeast 21 SX 8274
Colden (mt.) 76 SC 3484
Colden Common 27 SU 4822
Coldfair Green 55 TM 4361
Cold Fell 83 NY 6055
Cold Hanworth 72 TF 0383
Coldharbour 28 TQ 1443
Cold Hesledon 85 NZ 4147
Cold Higham 51 SP 6653
Coldingham 97 NT 9065
Coldingham Bay 97 NT 9266
Coldingham Moor 97 NT 8666
Cold Kirby 79 SE 5384
Cold Law 97 NT 9523
Cold Newton 61 SK 7106
Cold Norton 38 TL 8500
Cold Overton 62 SK 8110
Coldrain 102 NO 0700
Coldred 31 TR 2747
Coldridge 23 SS 6907
Coldsmouth Hill 97 NT 8528
Coldstream 97 NT 8439
Coldwaltham 28 TQ 0216
Coldwells 121 NK 1039
Coldwells Croft 121 NJ 5722
Cole 25 ST 6633
Colebatch 48 SO 3187
Colebrook 23 ST 0006
Colebrooke 21 SX 7799
Coleburn 84 SE 2098
Coleby (Humbs.) 74 SE 8919
Coleby (Lincs.) 72 SK 9760
Coleford (Devon) 23 SS 7701
Coleford (Glos.) 45 SO 5710
Coleford (Somer.) 33 ST 6848
Colehill 26 SU 0300
Coleman's Hatch 29 TQ 4533
Colemere 58 SJ 4232
Colenden 108 NO 1029
Coleorton 60 SK 3917
Colerne 33 ST 8171
Colesbourne 46 SO 9913
Colesden 52 TL 1255
Coleshill (Bucks.) 36 SU 9495
Coleshill (Oxon.) 47 SU 2393
Coleshill (Warw.) 50 SP 1989
Colgate 28 TQ 2332
Colgrain 100 NS 3280
Colgrave Sound 143 HU 5789
Colinsburgh 103 NO 4703
Colinton 103 NT 2169
Colintraive 100 NS 0374
Colkirk 64 TF 9126
Coll (Isle of Lewis) 131 NB 4739
Coll (Strath.) (is.) 110 NM 1957
Collace 108 NO 2032
Coll Aerodrome 110 NM 1756
Collafirth (Shetld.) 142 HU 3583
Colla Firth (Shetld.) 142 HU 3683
Collafirth (Shetld.) 143 HU 4368
Colla Firth (Shetld.) 143 HU 4469
Collaton St. Mary 21 SX 8660
College Burn 97 NT 8824
Collessie 103 NO 2813
Collie Law 96 NT 4850
Collier Law 84 NZ 0141
Collier Row 37 TQ 4991
Colliers End 37 TL 3720
Collier Street 29 TQ 7145
Colliery Row 85 NZ 3449
Collieston 121 NK 0328
Colliford Reservoir 19 SX 1772
Collin 88 NY 0276
Collingbourne Ducis 34 SU 2453
Collingbourne Kingston 34 SU 2355
Collingham (Notts.) 72 SK 8261
Collingham (W Yorks.) 79 SE 3845
Collington 49 SO 6460
Collingtree 51 SP 7555
Colliston 109 NO 6045
Coll Sands 131 NB 4638
Collynie 121 NJ 8436
Collyweston 62 SK 9903
Colmonell 86 NX 1586
Colmworth 52 TL 1058
Colnabaichin 117 NJ 2908
Colnbrook 36 TQ 0277
Colne (Cambs.) 53 TL 3776
Colne (Lancs.) 78 SD 8839
Colne Engaine 54 TL 8530
Colne Point 39 TM 1012
Colne Valley 54 TL 8529
Colney 65 TG 1808
Colney Heath 37 TL 2005
Colney Street 37 TL 1502
Con Rogers 46 SP 0809
Coln St. Aldwyns 47 SP 1405
Coln St. Dennis 46 SP 0810
Colonel's Bed, The (mt.) 117 NO 1086
Colonsay (is.) 98 NR 3794
Colp 121 NJ 7448
Colpy 121 NJ 6432
Colsay 141 HU 3618
Colsterdale 78 SE 1280
Colsterdale Moor 78 SE 1181
Colsterworth 62 SK 9224
Colston Bassett 61 SK 7033
Colt Crag Resr. 90 NY 9378
Coltfield 129 NJ 1163
Colt Hill 88 NX 6998
Coltishall 65 TG 2619
Colton (Cumbr.) 77 SD 3186
Colton (Norf.) 65 TG 1009
Colton (N Yorks.) 79 SE 5444
Colton (Staffs.) 60 SK 0520
Colvend 87 NX 8654
Colvister 143 HU 5197
Colwall Green 49 SO 7541
Colwall Stone 49 SO 7542
Colwell 90 NY 9575
Colwell Bay 26 SZ 3288
Colwich 60 SK 0121
Colwinston 41 SS 9475
Colworth 28 SU 9102
Colwyn Bay 67 SH 8478
Colyford 24 SY 2492
Colyton 24 SY 2493
Combe (Berks.) 34 SU 3760
Combe (Here. and Worc.) 48 SO 3463
Combe (Oxon.) 47 SP 4115
Combe Florey 24 ST 1531
Combe Hay 33 ST 7359
Combeinteignhead 21 SX 9071
Combe Martin 23 SS 5846
Combe Martin Bay 23 SS 5748
Combe Moor 48 SO 3663
Combe Raleigh 24 ST 1502
Comberbach 69 SJ 6477
Comberton 53 TL 3856
Combe St. Nicholas 24 ST 3011
Comb Fell 90 NT 9118
Comb Hill 89 NT 3900
Comb Law 88 NS 9407
Combrook 50 SP 3051
Combs (Derby.) 70 SK 0478
Combs (Suff.) 54 TM 0456
Combs Ford 54 TM 0457
Combs Reservoir 70 SK 0379
Combwich 32 ST 2542
Comers 119 NJ 6707
Comlongon Castle (ant.) 89 NY 0868
Commins Coch 57 SH 8403
Commondale 85 NZ 6610
Common Edge 77 SD 3232
Commonedge Hill 102 NN 9701
Common Hill 95 NS 8222
Common Law 95 NT 0732
Common Moor 19 SX 2369
Common of Dunning 102 NO 0109
Common Side 71 SK 3375
Common, The 26 SU 2432
Compstall 70 SJ 9690
Compton (Berks.) 35 SU 5279
Compton (Devon) 21 SX 8664
Compton (Hants.) 27 SU 4625
Compton (Surrey) 28 SU 9547
Compton (Wilts.) 34 SU 1352
Compton (W Susx) 27 SU 7714
Compton Abbas 25 ST 8718
Compton Abbas Airfield 25 ST 8918
Compton Abdale 46 SP 0516
Compton Bassett 34 SU 0372
Compton Bay 26 SZ 3684
Compton Beauchamp 34 SU 2887
Compton Bishop 32 ST 3955
Compton Chamberlayne 26 SU 0229
Compton Dando 33 ST 6464
Compton Down 34 SU 1050
Compton Dundon 25 ST 4933
Compton Martin 33 ST 5456
Compton Pauncefoot 25 ST 6425
Compton Valence 25 SY 5993
Compton Wynyates (ant.) 50 SP 3342
Comrie 107 NN 7722
Conachcraig 117 NO 2786
Cona Glen 106 NM 9471
Conaglen House 106 NN 0268
Conan House 128 NH 5353
Cona River 106 NM 9372
Conchra 100 NS 0288
Concraigie 108 NO 1044
Conderton 50 SO 9637
Condicote 47 SP 1528
Condorrat 101 NS 7373
Condover 59 SJ 4906
Coneyhurst 28 TQ 1024
Coneysthorpe 80 SE 7171
Coney Weston 54 TL 9578
Congerstone 60 SK 3605
Congham 64 TF 7123
Conglass Water 117 NJ 1818
Congleton 69 SJ 8562
Congresbury 33 ST 4363
Conicavel 129 NH 9953
Conic Hill 101 NS 4392
Conie Glen 92 NR 6912
Conieglen Water 92 NR 6914
Coningsby 73 TF 2258
Conington (Cambs.) 52 TL 1785
Conington (Cambs.) 53 TL 3266
Conisbrough 71 SK 5098
Conisby 98 NR 2661
Conisholme 73 TF 3995
Coniston (Cumbr.) 82 SD 3097
Coniston (Humbs.) 75 TA 1535
Coniston Cold 78 SD 9054
Conistone 78 SD 9867
Conistone Moor 78 SE 0270
Coniston Water 82 SD 3094
Connah's Quay 68 SJ 2869
Connel 106 NM 9134
Connel Airfield 106 NM 9035
Connel Park 88 NS 6012
Connor Downs 18 SW 5939
Conon Bridge 128 NH 5455
Cononley 78 SD 9846
Conrig Hill 88 NS 8112
Consall 60 SJ 9748
Consett 84 NZ 1150
Constable Burton 84 SE 1690
Constantine 18 SW 7229
Constantine Bay 19 SW 8574
Contin 128 NH 4555
Contlaw 119 NJ 8402
Contrary Head 76 SC 2282
Conwy 67 SH 7777
Conwy Bay 67 SH 7180
Conwy Falls 67 SH 8053
Conwy Sands 67 SH 7679
Conyer 31 TQ 9664
Cookbury 22 SS 4005
Cookham 36 SU 8985
Cookham Dean 36 SU 8785
Cookham Rise 36 SU 8884
Cookhill 50 SP 0558
Cookley (Here. and Worc.) 49 SO 8480
Cookley (Suff.) 55 TM 3475
Cookley Green 36 SU 6990
Cookney 119 NO 8793
Cooksbridge 29 TQ 4013
Cooksmill Green 38 TL 6306
Coolham 28 TQ 1222
Cooling 30 TQ 7575
Coombe (Corn.) 22 SS 2011
Coombe (Corn.) 19 SW 9551
Coombe Abbey (ant.) 50 SP 4080
Coombe Bissett 26 SU 1026
Coombe Hill 46 SO 8827
Coombe Keynes 25 SY 8484
Coombes 28 TQ 1908
Coopersale Common 37 TL 4702
Cooran Lane 87 NX 4782
Copdock 55 TM 1141
Copeland Forest 82 NY 1507
Copford Green 38 TL 9222
Copinsay 137 HY 6101
Copister 143 HU 4878
Cople 52 TL 1048
Copley 84 NZ 0825
Coplow Dale 70 SK 1679
Copmanthorpe 79 SE 5646
Coppathorne 20 SS 2000
Coppay 124 NF 9393
Coppenhall 59 SJ 9019
Coppingford 52 TL 1680
Copplestone 23 SS 7702
Coppull 69 SD 5613
Copsale 28 TQ 1724
Copster Green 77 SD 6734
Copt Heath 50 SP 1778
Copt Hewick 79 SE 3371
Copthorne 29 TQ 3139
Copt Oak 61 SK 4812
Copythorne 26 SU 3014
Coquetdale 90 NZ 0999
Coquet Island 91 NU 2904
Coracharabic Forest 127 NH 3246
Corb Law 102 NO 0009
Corbridge 91 NY 9964
Corby 52 SP 8988
Corby Glen 62 SK 9925
Corby Loch 119 NJ 9214
Corby Pike 90 NT 8401
Core Hill (Grampn.) 121 NJ 7632
Core Hill (Tays.) 102 NN 8804
Coreley 49 SO 6173
Corfe 24 ST 2319
Corfe Castle 26 SY 9681
Corfe Mullen 26 SY 9798
Corfton 48 SO 4985
Corgarff 117 NJ 2708
Corhampton 27 SU 6120
Corinium (ant.) 46 SP 0201
Corkickle Station 82 NX 9717
Corlan-fraith 57 SH 6300
Corlarach Forest 100 NS 1573
Corley 50 SP 3085
Corley Ash 50 SP 2886
Corley Moor 50 SP 2884
Cornabus 98 NR 3346
Cornal Burn 89 NT 1104
Corndon Hill 58 SO 3096
Cornelly 41 SS 8281
Corney 82 SD 1191

Cornforth Cruach an Lochain

Cornforth 84 NZ 3034
Corngafallt 57 SN 9464
Cornhill 121 NJ 5858
Cornhill-on-Tweed 97 NT 8639
Corn Holm (Copinsay) 137 HY 5901
Cornholme (W Yorks.) 78 SD 9025
Cornish Hall End 54 TL 6836
Cornquoy 137 ND 5299
Cornriggs 83 NY 8441
Cornsay 84 NZ 1443
Corntown 128 NH 5555
Cornwell 47 SP 2727
Cornwood 21 SX 6059
Cornworthy 21 SX 8255
Corpach 115 NN 0976
Corpach Bay 98 NR 5691
Corpusty 65 TG 1129
Corra-bheinn 105 NM 5732
Corran (Highld.) 123 NG 8509
Corran (Highld.) 106 NN 0163
Corran Narrows 106 NN 0163
Corran River 98 NR 5373
Corrany 76 SC 4589
Correen Hills 121 NJ 5222
Corrennie Forest 119 NJ 6410
Corrennie Moor 119 NJ 6110
Corrie 92 NS 0243
Corrie Common 89 NY 2085
Corriehallie Forest 127 NH 3748
Corriekinloch 132 NC 3625
Corriemoillie 127 NH 3563
Corriemoillie Forest 127 NH 3566
Corriemulzie River 127 NH 3194
Corrievorrie 116 NH 7724
Corrieyairack Forest 116 NN 4497
Corrieyairack Hill 116 NN 4299
Corrieyairack Pass 116 NN 4298
Corrimony 115 NH 3830
Corringham (Essex) 38 TQ 7183
Corringham (Lincs.) 72 SK 8691
Corris Uchaf 57 SH 7408
Corrour Forest 107 NN 4167
Corrour Shooting Lodge 107 NN 4169
Corrour Station 106 NN 3566
Corrow 100 NN 1800
Corry 123 NG 6424
Corryhabbie Hill 117 NJ 2829
Corrymuckloch 108 NN 8934
Corrynachenchy 105 NM 6441
Corry of Ardnagrask 128 NH 5048
Corscombe 25 ST 5105
Corse 121 NJ 6040
Corse Hill (Dumf. and Galwy.) 88 NS 6803
Corse Hill (Strath.) 94 NS 5946
Corse House 119 NJ 5407
Corsehouse Resr. 93 NS 4850
Corse of Kinnoir 121 NJ 5443
Corserine (mt.) 87 NX 4987
Corsewall Point 86 NW 9072
Cors-goch Glan Teifi 57 SN 6863
Corsham 33 ST 8669
Corsindae 119 NJ 6808
Corsley 33 ST 8246
Corsley Heath 33 ST 8245
Corsock 88 NX 7576
Corston (Avon) 33 ST 6965
Corston (Wilts.) 33 ST 9284
Corstopitum (ant.) 91 NY 9864
Corstorphine 103 NT 1972
Cortachy 109 NO 3959
Cortes House 121 NJ 9959
Corton (Suff.) 65 TM 5497
Corton (Wilts.) 34 ST 9340
Corton Denham 25 ST 6322
Coruanan Lodge 106 NN 0668
Corve Dale 48 SO 5488
Corwar House 86 NX 2780
Corwen 67 SJ 0743
Coryton (Devon) 20 SX 4583
Coryton (Essex) 38 TQ 7482
Cosby 61 SP 5495
Coseley 59 SO 9494
Cosford Station 59 SJ 7905
Cosgrove 51 SP 7942
Cosham 27 SU 6605
Cosheston 42 SN 0003
Cossall 61 SK 4842
Cosses 86 NX 1182
Cossington (Leic.) 61 SK 6013
Cossington (Somer.) 32 ST 3540
Costa 136 HY 3328
Costa Beck 80 SE 7682
Costa Head 138 HY 3130
Costessey 65 TG 1712
Costock 61 SK 5726
Coston 62 SK 8422
Cotebrook 69 SJ 5765
Cotehele House (ant.) 20 SX 4268
Cotehill 83 NY 4750
Cotes (Cumbr.) 77 SD 4886
Cotes (Leic.) 61 SK 5520
Cotes (Staffs.) 59 SJ 8434
Cotesbach 51 SP 5382
Cotgrave 61 SK 6435
Cothall 119 NJ 8716
Cotham 61 SK 7947
Cothelstone 24 ST 1831
Cotherstone 84 NZ 0119
Cotherstone Moor 84 NY 9316
Cothill 47 SU 4699
Cotleigh 24 ST 2002
Coton (Cambs.) 53 TL 4158
Coton (Northants.) 51 SP 6771
Coton (Staffs.) 60 SJ 9832
Coton Clanford 59 SJ 8723
Coton in the Elms 60 SK 2415
Cotswold Hills 46 SO 9302
Cott 21 SX 7861
Cottam (Lancs.) 77 SD 4932
Cottam (Notts.) 72 SK 8179
Cottartown 117 NJ 0331
Cottenham 53 TL 4567
Cotterdale 83 SD 8393
Cottered 53 TL 3129
Cotterstock 52 TL 0490
Cottesbrooke 51 SP 7073
Cottesmore 62 SK 9013
Cottingham (Humbs.) 74 TA 0532
Cottingham (Northants.) 52 SP 8490
Cottisford 47 SP 5831
Cotton 54 TM 0667
Cotton End 52 TL 0845
Cot-town (Grampn.) 121 NJ 5026
Cottown (Grampn.) 119 NJ 7715
Cot-town (Grampn.) 121 NJ 8140
Cotwalton 59 SJ 9234
Coughton 50 SP 0760
Coul 98 NR 2064
Coulags 126 NG 9645
Coulin Forest 126 NG 9954
Coulin Lodge 126 NH 0056
Coull 118 NJ 5102
Coul Point 98 NR 1864
Coulport 100 NS 2087
Coulsdon 37 TQ 3059
Coulter 95 NT 0233
Coulton 79 SE 6374
Cound 59 SJ 5504
Cound Brook 59 SJ 5206
Coundon 84 NZ 2329
Coundon Grange 84 NZ 2327
Countam (Dumf. and Galwy.) (mt.) 88 NX 7698
Countam (Dumf. and Galwy.) (mt.) 88 NS 7101
Countersett 78 SD 9287
Countess Wear 21 SX 9489
Countesthorpe 61 SP 5895
Countisbury 23 SS 7449
Coupar Angus 108 NO 2139
Coupland 97 NT 9331
Cour 92 NR 8248
Cour Bay 92 NR 8248
Courteachan 111 NM 6897
Courteenhall 51 SP 7653
Cour, The 115 NN 2276
Court Henry 43 SN 5522
Courtsend 39 TR 0293
Courtway 24 ST 2033
Cousland 103 NT 3768
Cousley Wood 29 TQ 6533
Cove (Devon) 23 SS 9519
Cove (Hants.) 35 SU 8555
Cove (Highld.) 126 NG 8090
Cove (Strath.) 100 NS 2281
Cove Bay (Grampn.) 119 NJ 9500
Cove Bay (Strath.) 100 NS 2182
Covehithe 55 TM 5281
Coven 59 SJ 9006
Coveney 53 TL 4882
Covenham Resr. 73 TF 3496
Covenham St. Bartholomew 73 TF 3395
Covenham St. Mary 73 TF 3394
Coventry 50 SP 3379
Coventry Airport 50 SP 3574
Coventry Canal (Warw.) 60 SP 3196
Coventry Canal (Warw.) 50 SP 3786
Cove Point 92 NR 7107
Coverack 19 SW 7818
Coverdale 78 SE 0682
Coverham 78 SE 1086
Cover Head Bents 78 SD 9978
Covesea Skerries 120 NJ 1971
Covington 52 TL 0570
Cowan Bridge 77 SD 6476
Cowbeech 29 TQ 6114
Cowbit 63 TF 2618
Cowbridge 41 SS 9974
Cowden 29 TQ 4640
Cowdenbeath 102 NT 1691
Cowdenburn 95 NT 2052
Cowden Station 29 TQ 4741
Cowes 27 SZ 4995
Cowesby 85 SE 4689
Cowes Roads 27 SZ 4997
Cowfold 28 TQ 2122
Cowgask Burn 108 NN 9419
Cow Green Resr. 83 NY 7930
Cowick 79 SE 6521
Cowie 101 NS 8389
Cowie Water 119 NO 7687
Cowley (Devon) 21 SX 9095
Cowley (Glos.) 46 SO 9614
Cowley (Gtr London) 36 TQ 0582
Cowley (Oxon.) 47 SP 5404
Cowling (N Yorks.) 78 SD 9743
Cowling (N Yorks.) 79 SE 2387
Cowlinge 54 TL 7154
Cowm Resr. 69 SD 8819
Cowpen Bewley 85 NZ 4824
Cowplain 27 SU 7011
Cow Ridge 85 SE 5496
Cowshill 83 NY 8540
Cowstrandburn 102 NT 0390
Cowbank 59 SJ 6541
Coxbench 60 SK 3743
Cox Common 55 TM 4082
Coxheath 30 TQ 7451
Coxhoe 84 NZ 3235
Coxley 33 ST 5343
Coxwold 79 SE 5377
Coychurch 41 SS 9379
Coyles of Muick, The (mt.) 118 NO 3291
Coylton 93 NS 4119
Coylumbridge 117 NH 9110
Coynach 118 NJ 4405
Coynachie 121 NJ 4934
Craach Mhòr 100 NN 0514
Crabadon 21 SX 7555
Crabbs Cross 50 SP 0464
Crab Rocks 81 TA 1974
Crabtree 28 TQ 2225
Crabtree Green 58 SJ 3344
Crackenthorpe 83 NY 6622
Crackington Haven 20 SX 1496
Crackleybank 59 SJ 7611
Crackpot 84 SD 9796
Cracoe 78 SD 9760
Cradley 49 SO 7347
Crafthole 20 SX 3654
Cragabus 98 NR 3345
Cragdale Moor 78 SD 9282
Cragg 78 SE 0023
Craggan (Grampn.) 117 NJ 0226
Craggan (Strath.) 100 NS 2699
Craggie 126 NC 8719
Craggie Water 134 NC 8819
Craghead 84 NZ 2150
Crag Hill 77 SD 7083
Crag Lough 90 NY 7667
Crai 41 SN 8924
Craibstone (Grampn.) 121 NJ 4959
Craibstone (Grampn.) 119 NJ 8611
Craichie 109 NO 5047
Craig (Dumf. and Galwy.) 88 NX 6875
Craig (Highld.) 126 NH 0349
Craigairie Fell 86 NX 2373
Craiganour Forest 107 NN 6064
Craiganour Lodge 107 NN 6159
Craig Castle 121 NJ 4724
Craigcefnparc 40 SN 6703
Craigdallie 108 NO 2428
Craigdam 121 NJ 8430
Craigdarroch 88 NS 6306
Craig Ddrwg 67 SH 6537
Craigearn 119 NJ 7214
Craigellachie (Grampn.) 120 NJ 2844
Craigellachie (Highld.) 117 NH 8811
Craigend 108 NO 1120
Craigendoran 100 NS 3181
Craigendunton Resr. 93 NS 5245
Craigenlee Fell 86 NX 0157
Craigens 98 NR 2967
Craig Fell 86 NX 1761
Craiggiecat 119 NO 8592
Craig Goch Resr. 57 SN 8969
Craig Gyfynys 67 SH 6838
Craighall 108 NO 1748
Craighat 101 NS 4984
Craig Hill 107 NN 8045
Craighoar Hill 88 NT 0002
Craighouse 98 NR 5267
Craigie (Grampn.) 119 NJ 9119
Craigie (Strath.) 93 NS 4232
Craigie (Tays.) 108 NO 1143
Craigievar Castle (ant.) 119 NJ 5609
Craiglee 87 NX 4796
Craigleith (is.) 103 NT 5588
Craiglich 119 NJ 5305
Craiglockhart 103 NT 2270
Craig Lodge 100 NS 0077
Craiglowrie 87 NX 5467
Craigluscar Hill 102 NT 0690
Craigmahandle 118 NO 4891
Craigmaid 89 NT 0717
Craigmaud 121 NJ 8858
Craigmillar 103 NT 2871
Craig nan Caisean 107 NN 7760
Craignane 88 NS 5804
Craignant 58 SJ 2535
Craignarget Hill 86 NX 2652
Craignelder 87 NX 5070
Craigneuk (Strath.) 94 NS 7656
Craigneuk (Strath.) 101 NS 7764
Craignish Castle 99 NM 7701
Craignish Point 99 NR 7599
Craignure 105 NM 7236
Craignure Bay 105 NM 7137
Craigo 109 NO 6864
Craig of Bunzeach 118 NJ 3609
Craig of Dalfro 119 NO 6789
Craigow 102 NO 0806
Craig Rhiwarth 57 SJ 0527
Craig River 123 NG 7864
Craig Rossie 102 NN 9812
Craig Rostan 100 NN 3404
Craigrothie 103 NO 3710
Craigruie 107 NN 5020
Craigston Castle 121 NJ 7655
Craigton (Grampn.) 119 NJ 8301
Craigton (Highld.) 128 NH 6296
Craigton (Tays.) 108 NO 3250
Craigton (Tays.) 109 NO 5138
Craigtown 134 NC 8856
Craig Twrch 43 SN 6649
Craig Veann 117 NJ 1811
Craigvinean Forest 108 NN 9745
Craig-y-cae 57 SH 7022
Craig y Llyn 41 SN 9103
Craig-y-nos 41 SN 8315
Craig yr Hyrddod 67 SH 8237
Craik 89 NT 3408
Craik Cross Hill 89 NT 3004
Craik Forest 89 NT 3309
Craik Moor 90 NT 8118
Crail 103 NO 6107
Crailing 96 NT 6824
Crailinghall 96 NT 6921
Crailzie Hill 95 NT 1945
Crakehall 84 SE 2490
Cramalt 95 NT 1922
Crambe 80 SE 7364
Cramlington 91 NZ 2776
Crammag Head 86 NX 0834
Cramond 102 NT 1876
Cramond Bridge 102 NT 1775
Cramond Island 103 NT 1978
Cranage 69 SJ 7568
Cranberry 59 SJ 8236
Cranborne 26 SU 0513
Cranborne Chase 26 ST 9417
Cranbourne 36 SU 9272
Cranbrook 30 TQ 7735
Cranbrook Common 30 TQ 7938
Crane Islands 18 SW 6344
Cranfield 52 SP 9542
Cranfield Airfield 52 SP 9543
Cranford 37 TQ 1077
Cranford St. Andrew 52 SP 9277
Cranford St. John 52 SP 9276
Cranham (Essex) 37 TQ 5787
Cranham (Glos.) 46 SO 8912
Crank 69 SJ 5099
Cranleigh 28 TQ 0638
Cranmore (I. of W.) 26 SZ 3990
Cranmore (Somer.) 33 ST 6843
Cranna 121 NJ 6352
Crannach 121 NJ 4954
Cranoe 61 SP 7695
Cransford 55 TM 3164
Cranshaws 96 NT 6961
Cranshaws Hill 103 NT 6761
Cranstackie (mt.) 132 NC 3555
Cranstal 76 NX 4602
Crantock 19 SW 7860
Cranwell 62 TF 0349
Cranwich 64 TL 7795
Cranworth 64 TF 9804
Crapstone 20 SX 5067
Crarae 100 NR 9897
Craro Island 92 NR 6247
Crask Inn 133 NC 5224
Craskins 118 NJ 5105
Crask of Aigas 128 NH 4642
Craster 91 NU 2519
Cratfield 55 TM 3175
Crathes 119 NO 7596
Crathes Castle (ant.) 119 NO 7396
Crathie (Grampn.) 117 NO 2695
Crathie (Highld.) 116 NN 5893
Crathorne 85 NZ 4407
Craufurdland Castle (ant.) 93 NS 4540
Craven Arms 48 SO 4382
Crawcrook 91 NZ 1363
Crawford 88 NS 9520
Crawfordjohn 95 NS 8823
Crawick 88 NS 7710
Crawick Water 88 NS 8014
Crawley (Hants.) 26 SU 4234
Crawley (Oxon.) 47 SP 3312
Crawley (W Susx) 28 TQ 2636
Crawley Down 29 TQ 3237
Crawleyside 84 NY 9940
Crawshawbooth 78 SD 8125
Crawton 119 NO 8779
Crawton Bay 119 NO 8779
Cray (N Yorks.) 78 SD 9479
Crayford 37 TQ 5175
Crayke 79 SE 5670
Crays Hill 38 TQ 7192
Cray's Pond 36 SU 6380
Creachan Mòr 100 NS 1891
Creach Beinn (Island of Mull) 105 NM 6427
Creach Bheinn (Highld.) 111 NM 8757
Creach Bheinn (Island of Mull) 105 NM 4228
Creach Bheinn (Strath.) 106 NN 0242
Creach Bheinn Lodge 105 NM 6425
Creacombe 23 SS 8119
Creag a' Chaorainn 126 NH 0043
Creag a Chlachain 116 NH 6533
Creag a'Lain 123 NG 4658
Creagan 106 NM 9744
Creagan a' Chaise 117 NJ 1024
Creagan an Eich 100 NN 1003
Creag an Doil Bheag 117 NO 1598
Creag an Eunan 118 NJ 3819
Creagan Glas 128 NC 6701
Creag an Lòin 116 NH 6901
Creagan Mòr 116 NN 6180
Creagantairbh Mòr 99 NM 8401
Creag an t-Sithein 108 NO 0365
Creag a'Phuill 100 NN 1005
Creag Beinn nan Eun 101 NN 7213
Creag Bhalg 117 NO 0991
Creag Bhàn (Highld.) 111 NM 7884
Creag Bhàn (Strath.) 92 NR 6450
Creag Dhubh (Highld.) 115 NN 3282
Creag Dhubh (Highld.) 116 NN 6897
Creag Dhubh (Tays.) 108 NO 0261
Creag Fhraoch 131 NB 5142
Creag Gharbh 107 NN 6332
Creag Island 105 NM 8337
Creag Leacach 117 NO 1574
Creag Liath (Highld.) 129 NH 7295
Creag Liath (Highld.) 117 NJ 0031
Creag Loch nan Dearcag 127 NH 3356
Creag Loisgte 127 NH 3695
Creag Meagaidh 116 NN 4187
Creag Mholach 100 NS 0993
Creag Mhòr (Central) 107 NN 5134
Creag Mhòr (Highld.) 133 NC 6924
Creag Mhòr (Highld.) 116 NN 4997
Creag Mhòr (Isle of Lewis) 131 NB 1741
Creag Mhòr (Strath.) 105 NM 8202
Creag Mhòr (Strath.) 100 NR 9273
Creag Mhòr (Tays.) 107 NN 3936
Creag na h-Iolaire (Highld.) 133 NC 6728
Creag na h-Iolaire (Highld.) 127 NH 1398
Creag na h-Iolaire (Highld.) 127 NH 1749
Creag nam Bodach 116 NN 7596
Creag nam Fiadh 134 NC 8323
Creag nam Mial 108 NO 0554
Creag-nan-Eun Forest 116 NH 4519
Creag nan Gabhar 117 NO 1584
Creag nan Gall 117 NO 2691
Creagorry 124 NF 7948
Creag Riabhach 132 NC 2763
Creag Riabhach na Greighe 133 NC 6120
Creag Scalabsdale 134 NC 9624
Creaguaineach Lodge 106 NN 3069
Creag Uchdag 107 NN 7032
Creaton 51 SP 7071
Creca 89 NY 2270
Credenhill 45 SO 4543
Crediton 21 SS 8300
Creech St. Michael 24 ST 2725
Creed 19 SW 9347
Creedy Park 23 SS 8301
Creekmouth 37 TQ 4581
Creeting St. Mary 55 TM 0956
Creeton 62 TF 0120
Creetown 87 NX 4758
Creggans 100 NN 0802
Cregneish 76 SC 1967
Cregrina 44 SO 1252
Creich (Fife.) 108 NO 3221
Creich (Island of Mull) 104 NM 3124
Creigh Hill 108 NO 2759
Creigiau 41 ST 0881
Cressage 59 SJ 5904
Cresselly 42 SN 0606
Cressing 38 TL 7920
Cresswell (Dyfed) 42 SN 0506
Cresswell (Northum.) 91 NZ 2993
Cresswell (Staffs.) 60 SJ 9739
Creswell 71 SK 5274
Cretingham 55 TM 2260
Cretshengan 99 NR 7167
Creuch Hill 100 NS 2668
Crewe (Ches.) 58 SJ 4253
Crewe (Ches.) 59 SJ 7055
Crewe Hall 59 SJ 7353
Crew Green 58 SJ 3215
Crewkerne 25 ST 4409
Crews Hill 37 TL 3000
Crianlarich 107 NN 3825
Cribba Head 18 SW 4022
Cribbie (pt.) 140 HU 1562
Cribin Fawr 57 SH 8014
Crib Law 103 NT 5259
Cribyn 43 SN 5251
Criccieth 66 SH 4938
Crich 60 SK 3554
Crichie 121 NJ 9544
Crichton 103 NT 3862
Crick (Gwent) 33 ST 4890
Crick (Northants.) 51 SP 5872
Crickadarn 44 SO 0942
Cricket St. Thomas 24 ST 3708
Crickheath 58 SJ 2923
Crickhowell 41 SO 2118
Cricklade 46 SU 0993
Cridling Stubbs 79 SE 5221
Crieff 108 NN 8621
Criffel 88 NX 9561
Crigdon Hill 90 NT 8604
Criggion 58 SJ 2915
Crigglestone 71 SE 3116
Crimond 121 NK 0556
Crimonmogate 121 NK 0458
Crimplesham 64 TF 6503
Crim Rocks 18 SV 8009
Crinaglack 116 NH 4240
Crinan 99 NR 7894
Crinan Canal 99 NR 8391
Cringate Law 101 NS 6888
Cringleford 65 TG 1905
Crinow 42 SN 1214
Crionaig (mt.) 125 NB 2906
Cripplesease 18 SW 5036
Cripp's Corner 30 TQ 7821
Croachy 116 NH 6527
Croasdale Fell 77 SD 6857
Crockenhill 37 TQ 5067
Crockernwell 21 SX 7592
Crockerton 33 ST 8642
Crocketford or Ninemile Bar 88 NX 8272
Crockey Hill 79 SE 6246
Crockham Hill 29 TQ 4450
Crockleford Heath 54 TM 0426
Crockness 136 ND 3192
Croeserw 41 SS 8695
Croesgoch 42 SM 8330
Croesor 67 SH 6344
Croesyceiliog (Gwent) 45 ST 3196
Croesyceiliog 43 SN 4016
Croes-y-mwyalch 32 ST 3092
Croft (Ches.) 69 SJ 6393
Croft (Leic.) 61 SP 5195
Croft (Lincs.) 73 TF 5162
Croft Ambrey (ant.) 48 SO 4466
Croftamie 101 NS 4786
Croftgarbh 107 NN 7246
Croft Head 89 NT 1505
Croft Marsh 73 TF 5460
Crofton 71 SE 3717
Croft-on-Tees 84 NZ 2909
Crofts of Benachielt 135 ND 1838
Crofts of Blackburn 121 NJ 5334
Crofts of Haddo 121 NJ 8337
Crofts of Inverthernie 121 NJ 7343
Crofts of Meikle Ardo 121 NJ 8541
Crofts of Savoch 121 NK 0459
Crofts of Shanquhar 121 NJ 5435
Crofty 40 SS 5295
Crogary Mòr (mt.) 124 NF 8673
Crogary na Hoe 124 NF 9772
Crogen 67 SJ 0036
Croggan 105 NM 7027
Croglin 83 NY 5747
Croglin Water 83 NY 5646
Croic-bheinn 123 NG 7652
Croick 128 NH 4591
Croir 131 NB 1539
Crom Bheinn 111 NM 8177
Cròm Allt 116 NH 5404
Crom Allt (Highld.) 127 NC 2506
Cromalt Hills 127 NC 2205
Cromar (dist.) 118 NJ 4703
Cromarty 129 NH 7867
Cromarty Bay 129 NH 7466
Cromarty Firth 128 NH 6667
Cromblet 121 NJ 7734
Cromdale 117 NJ 0728
Cromer (Herts.) 53 TL 2928
Cromer (Norf.) 65 TG 2142
Cromer Point 81 TA 0392
Cromford 60 SK 2956
Cromhall 33 ST 6990
Cromhall Common 33 ST 6989
Cromlet (mt.) 101 NN 7811
Crom Loch 127 NH 3982
Cromore 131 NB 4021
Cromra 116 NN 5489
Cromwell 72 SK 7961
Cronberry 94 NS 6022
Crondall 35 SU 7948
Cronkley Fell 83 NY 8427
Cronk Sumark (ant.) 76 SC 3893
Cronk, The 76 SC 3495
Cronk-y-Voddy 76 SC 3086
Cronton 69 SJ 4988
Crook (Cumbr.) 83 SD 4694
Crook (Durham) 84 NZ 1635
Crookedshaws Hill 97 NT 8024
Crookfoot Resr. 85 NZ 4331
Crookham (Berks.) 35 SU 5364
Crookham (Northum.) 97 NT 9138
Crookham Village 35 SU 7952
Crookhouse 96 NT 7626
Crook Inn 95 NT 1026
Crooklands 77 SD 5383
Crook of Devon 102 NO 0301
Croome Court 49 SO 8844
Cropredy 51 SP 4646
Cropston 61 SK 5511
Cropston Resr. 61 SK 5410
Cropthorne 50 SO 9944
Cropton 80 SE 7589
Cropwell Bishop 61 SK 6835
Cropwell Butler 61 SK 6837
Crosbie 93 NS 2150
Crosby (Cumbr.) 82 NY 0738
Crosby (I. of M.) 76 SC 3279
Crosby (Lincs.) 74 SE 8711
Crosby (Mers.) 68 SJ 3099
Crosby Channel 68 SJ 2799
Crosby Court 85 SE 3992
Crosby Garrett 83 NY 7309
Crosby Ravensworth 83 NY 6214
Crosby Ravensworth Fell 83 NY 6010
Croscombe 33 ST 5844
Cross (Isle of Lewis) 131 NB 5061
Cross (Somerset) 32 ST 4154
Crossaig 92 NR 8351
Crossaig Glen 92 NR 8152
Crossapol 104 NL 9943
Crossapol Bay 110 NM 1352
Cross Ash 45 SO 4019
Crossbost 131 NB 3924
Crosscanonby 82 NY 0739
Crossdale Street 65 TG 2239
Crossdougal 112 NF 7520
Cross Drain 62 TF 1514
Crossens 68 SD 3719
Cross Fell 83 NY 6834
Crossford (Fife) 102 NT 0686
Crossford (Strath.) 95 NS 8246
Crossgates (Fife) 102 NT 1488
Crossgates (Powys) 57 SO 0865
Crossgill 77 SD 5562
Cross Green (Devon) 20 SX 3888
Cross Green (Suff.) 54 TL 9952
Cross Hands 43 SN 5612
Cross Hill (Borders) 89 NT 2507
Crosshill (Fife) 102 NT 1796
Crosshill (Strath.) 93 NS 3206
Crosshouse (Strath.) 93 NS 3938
Cross Houses (Shrops.) 59 SJ 5307
Crossings 90 NY 5177
Cross in Hand 29 TQ 5621
Cross Inn (Dyfed) 43 SN 3957
Cross Inn (Dyfed) 56 SN 5464
Cross Inn (Mid Glam.) 41 ST 0582
Crosskeys (Gwent) 41 ST 2292
Crosskeys (Strath.) 100 NS 3365
Crosskirk 135 ND 0370
Cross Lanes (Clwyd) 58 SJ 3746
Crosslanes (N Yorks.) 79 SE 5264
Crosslanes (Shrops.) 58 SJ 3218
Cross Law 97 NT 8767
Crosslee 89 NT 3018
Crossmichael 88 NX 7267
Crossmoor 77 SD 4438
Cross of Jackston 121 NJ 7432
Crossraguel Abbey (ant.) 93 NS 2708
Crossroads 119 NO 7594
Cross Sands 131 NB 4962
Cross Water of Luce 86 NX 1867
Crossway 45 SO 4419
Crossway Green 49 SO 8368
Crosswell 42 SN 1236
Crosswood Resr. 95 NT 0557
Crosthwaite 83 SD 4491
Croston 69 SD 4818
Crostwick 65 TG 2515
Crostwight 65 TG 3329
Crouch Hill 25 ST 7010
Croughton 47 SP 5433
Crovie 121 NJ 8065
Crowan 18 SW 6434
Crowborough 29 TQ 5130
Crowcombe 24 ST 1336
Crowdecote 70 SK 1065
Crowdundle Beck 83 NY 6631
Crowdy Reservoir 20 SX 1483
Crowfield (Northants.) 51 SP 6141
Crowfield (Suff.) 55 TM 1557
Crow Hill 45 SO 6326
Crowhurst (E Susx) 29 TQ 7512
Crowhurst (Surrey) 29 TQ 3947
Crowland 63 TF 2310
Crowlas 18 SW 5133
Crowle (Here. and Worc.) 49 SO 9256
Crowle (Humbs.) 74 SE 7713
Crowlin Islands 123 NG 6934
Crowlista 130 NB 0433
Crowmarsh Gifford 36 SU 6189
Crownhill 20 SX 4857
Crownthorpe 65 TG 0803
Crow Rock 42 SR 8894
Crow Sound 18 SV 9312
Crowthorne 36 SU 8464
Crowthorn School 69 SD 7418
Crowton 69 SJ 5774
Croxall 60 SK 1913
Croxdale 84 NZ 2636
Croxden 60 SK 0639
Croxley Green 36 TQ 0795
Croxton (Cambs.) 53 TL 2459
Croxton (Humbs.) 75 TA 0912
Croxton (Norf.) 54 TL 8786
Croxton (Staffs.) 59 SJ 7832
Croxton Kerrial 62 SK 8329
Croxton Park 62 SK 8227
Croy (Highld.) 129 NH 7949
Croy (Strath.) 101 NS 7275
Croyde 22 SS 4439
Croyde Bay 22 SS 4239
Croydon (Cambs.) 53 TL 3149
Croydon (Gtr London) 37 TQ 3365
Croydon Hill 23 SS 9739
Cruach a'Bhuie 100 NS 1693
Cruachan 100 NN 3507
Cruachan Beinn a'Chearcaill 122 NG 3546
Cruachan Druim na Croise 111 NM 4549
Cruach an Eachlaich 105 NM 8606
Cruach an Locha 99 NR 7865
Cruach an Lochain 100 NS 0493

Eastchurch....31 TQ 9871
East Clandon....28 TQ 0651
East Claydon....51 SP 7325
Eastcombe (Glos.)....46 SO 8804
East Combe (Somer.)....24 ST 1631
Eastcote (Gtr London)....37 TQ 1188
Eastcote (W Mids)....50 SP 1979
Eastcott (Corn.)....22 SS 2515
Eastcott (Wilts.)....34 SU 0255
East Cottingwith....74 SE 7042
East Coulston....34 ST 9454
Eastcourt....34 ST 9792
East Cowes....27 SZ 5095
East Cowton....84 NZ 3103
East Cramlinton....91 NZ 2876
East Creech....25 SY 9282
East Croftmore....117 NH 9519
East Dart River....21 SX 6676
East Dean (E Susx)....29 TV 5598
East Dean (Hants.)....26 SU 2726
East Dean (W Susx)....27 SU 9013
East Dereham....64 TF 9913
East Down....23 SS 5941
East Drayton....72 SK 7775
East End (Avon)....33 ST 4770
East End (Dorset)....26 SY 9998
East End (Hants.)....34 SU 4161
East End (Hants.)....26 SZ 3697
East End (Herts.)....53 TL 4527
East End (Kent)....30 TQ 8335
East End (Oxon.)....47 SP 3914
Easter Ardross....128 NH 6373
Easter Balloch....118 NO 3480
Easter Balmoral....117 NO 2693
Easter Boleskine....116 NH 5122
Easter Compton....33 ST 5782
Easter Davoch....118 NJ 4607
Easter Fearn....128 NH 6486
Easter Fearn Burn....128 NH 6384
Easter Galcantray....129 NH 8148
Eastergate....28 SU 9405
Easter Kinkell....128 NH 5755
Easter Lednathie....108 NO 3363
Easter Moniack....128 NH 5543
Easter Muckovie....129 NH 7044
Eastern Green....50 SP 2780
Eastern Isles....22 SV 9514
Easter Ord....119 NJ 8304
Easter Ross (dist.)....128 NH 5878
Easter Rova Head....141 HU 4745
Easter Skeld....141 HU 3044
Easterton....34 SU 0154
Eastertown....32 ST 3454
Easter Whyntie....121 NJ 6264
East Farleigh....29 TQ 7353
East Farndon....51 SP 7185
East Fen....64 TF 4255
East Fenton....97 NT 9733
East Ferry....74 SK 8199
Eastfield (N Yorks.)....81 TA 0484
Eastfield (Strath.)....101 NS 7574
Eastfield (Strath.)....102 NS 8964
Eastfield Hall....91 NU 2206
East Garston....34 SU 3676
Eastgate (Durham)....84 NY 9538
Eastgate (Norf.)....65 TG 1423
East Ginge....35 SU 4486
East Glenquoich Forest....115 NH 1003
East Glen River....62 TF 0426
East Goscote....61 SK 6413
East Grafton....34 SU 2560
East Grimstead....26 SU 2227
East Grinstead....29 TQ 3938
East Guldeford....30 TQ 9321
East Haddon....51 SP 6668
East Hagbourne....35 SU 5388
East Halton....75 TA 1419
East Halton Skitter....75 TA 1423
East Ham (Essex)....37 TQ 4283
Eastham (Mers.)....68 SJ 3580
Easthampstead....36 SU 8667
Eastham Sands....68 SJ 3980
East Hanney....34 SU 4192
East Hanningfield....38 TL 7601
East Hardwick....71 SE 4618
East Harling....54 TL 9986
East Harlsey....85 SE 4299
East Harptree....33 ST 5655
East Hartford....91 NZ 2679
East Harting....27 SU 7919
East Hatley....53 TL 2850
East Hauxwell....84 SE 1693
East Haven....109 NO 5836
East Heckingham....62 TF 1944
East Hedleyhope....84 NZ 1540
East Hendred....35 SU 4588
East Heslerton....81 SE 9276
East Hoathly....29 TQ 5216
Easthope....59 SO 5695
Easthorpe....38 TL 9121
East Horrington....33 ST 5846
East Horsley....28 TQ 0952
East Hoyle Bank (sbk.)....68 SJ 2090
East Huntspill....32 ST 3444
East Hyde....37 TL 1317
East Ilsley....35 SU 4981
Eastington (Glos.)....46 SO 7705
Eastington (Glos.)....47 SP 1213
East Kame (mt.)....141 HU 4257
East Kennett....34 SU 1167
East Keswick....79 SE 3544
East Kilbride....94 NS 6354
East Kirkby....73 TF 3362
East Knighton....25 SY 8185
East Knoyle....25 ST 8830
East Lambrook....25 ST 4319
East Lamington....129 NH 7577
East Langdon....31 TR 3346
East Langton....51 SP 7292
East Langwell....129 NC 7206
East Lavington....28 SU 9416
East Layton....84 NZ 1609
Eastleach Martin....47 SP 2005
Eastleach Turville....47 SP 1905
East Leake....61 SK 5526
East Leigh (Devon)....23 SS 6905
Eastleigh (Hants.)....27 SU 4518
East Lexham....64 TF 8617
East Lilburn....97 NU 0423
Eastling....31 TQ 9656
East Linga (is.)....141 HU 6162
East Linton....103 NT 5977
East Liss....27 SU 7827
East Loch Roag....131 NB 1837
East Loch Tarbert (Isle of Lewis)....125 NG 1896
East Loch Tarbert (Strath.)....99 NR 8769
East Lochussie....128 NH 5056
East Lound....74 SK 7899
East Lulworth....25 SY 8581
East Mains....119 NO 6797
East Malling....30 TQ 7057
East March....109 NO 4436
East Marden....27 SU 8014
East Markham....72 SK 7472
East Marsh....43 SK 3586
East Marton....78 SD 9050
East Meon....27 SU 6822
East Mersea....39 TM 0414
East Midlands Airport....61 SK 4525
East Molesey....37 TQ 1568
East Monar Forest....127 NH 1842

East Moor....71 SK 2870
East Morden....25 SY 9194
East Morton....78 SE 1042
Eastney....27 SZ 6698
Eastnor....49 SO 7337
East Norton....61 SK 7800
East Oakley....35 SU 5749
Eastoft....74 SE 8016
East Ogwell....21 SX 8370
Easton (Cambs.)....52 TL 1371
Easton (Cumbr.)....89 NY 4372
Easton (Devon)....21 SX 7288
Easton (Dorset)....25 SY 6871
Easton (Hants.)....27 SU 5132
Easton (I.of W.)....26 SZ 3485
Easton (Lincs.)....62 SK 9226
Easton (Norf.)....65 TG 1311
Easton (Somer.)....33 ST 5147
Easton (Suff.)....55 TM 2858
Easton Grey....33 ST 8787
Easton Hill....34 SU 2059
Easton-in-Gordano....33 ST 5175
Easton Maudit....52 SP 8858
Easton on the Hill....62 TF 0004
Easton Royal....34 SU 2060
East Ord....97 NT 9851
East Panson....20 SX 3692
East Peckham....29 TQ 6649
East Pennard....25 ST 5937
East Portlemouth....21 SX 7438
East Prawle....21 SX 7736
East Preston....28 TQ 0702
East Putford....22 SS 3616
East Quantoxhead....32 ST 1343
East Rainton....84 NZ 3347
East Ravendale....75 TF 2399
East Raynham....64 TF 8825
Eastrea....63 TL 2997
East Retford....72 SK 7080
East Rhidorroch Lodge....127 NH 2393
Eastriggs....89 NY 2465
Eastrington....74 SE 7929
East Road....31 TR 1123
East Rudham....64 TF 8228
East Runton....65 TG 1942
East Ruston....65 TG 3427
Eastry....31 TR 3155
East Saltoun....103 NT 4767
East Sleekburn....91 NZ 2785
East Stoke (Dorset)....25 SY 8787
East Stoke (Notts.)....61 SK 7549
East Stour....25 ST 8022
East Stourmouth....31 TR 2662
East Stour River....31 TR 0837
East Stratton....35 SU 5440
East Studdal....31 TR 3149
East Taphouse....19 SX 1863
East Tarbert Bay....92 NR 6552
East Thirston....91 NZ 1999
East Tilbury....38 TQ 6878
East Tisted....27 SU 7032
East Torrington....73 TF 1483
East Tuddenham....65 TG 0811
East Tytherley....26 SU 2929
East Tytherton....33 ST 9074
East Village....23 SS 8405
Eastville....73 TF 4057
East Voe of Quarff....141 HU 4335
East Wall....59 SO 5293
East Walton....64 TF 7416
East Wear Bay....31 TR 2537
Eastwell....61 SK 7728
East Wellow....26 SU 3020
Eastwell Park....31 TR 0147
East Wemyss....103 NT 3396
East Whitburn....102 NS 9665
Eastwick....37 TL 4311
East Wickham....37 TQ 4576
East Williamston....42 SN 0905
East Winch....64 TF 6916
East Wittering....27 SZ 7996
East Witton....78 SE 1486
Eastwood (Essex)....38 TQ 8588
Eastwood (Notts.)....61 SK 4646
Eastwood (W Yorks.)....78 SD 9625
East Woodhay....34 SU 4061
East Worldham....35 SU 7538
East Wretham....54 TL 9190
East Yell....143 HU 5284
Eathorpe....50 SP 3969
Eaton (Ches.)....69 SJ 5763
Eaton (Ches.)....69 SJ 8765
Eaton (Leic.)....61 SK 7929
Eaton (Norf.)....65 TG 2006
Eaton (Notts.)....72 SK 7077
Eaton (Oxon.)....47 SP 4403
Eaton (Shrops.)....48 SO 3789
Eaton (Shrops.)....48 SO 4989
Eaton Bishop....45 SO 4439
Eaton Bray....36 SP 9720
Eaton Constantine....59 SJ 5906
Eaton Hall....68 SJ 4160
Eaton Socon....52 TL 1658
Eaton upon Tern....59 SJ 6523
Eaval (mt.)....124 NF 8960
Ebberston....81 SE 8983
Ebbesborne Wake....26 ST 9824
Ebbw River....32 ST 2489
Ebbw Vale (Gwent)....41 SO 1609
Ebbw Vale (Gwent)....41 ST 2094
Ebchester....84 NZ 1055
Ebford....21 SX 9887
Ebrington....50 SP 1840
Eburacum (ant.)....79 SE 6052
Ecchinswell....35 SU 5060
Ecclaw....96 NT 7568
Ecclefechan....89 NY 1974
Eccles (Borders)....96 NT 7641
Eccles (Gtr Mches.)....69 SJ 7798
Eccles (Kent)....30 TQ 7260
Ecclesfield....71 SK 3393
Ecclesgreig....109 NO 7365
Eccleshall....59 SJ 8329
Eccleshill....78 SE 1736
Ecclesmachan....102 NT 0573
Eccles Road....54 TM 0190
Eccleston (Ches.)....68 SJ 4162
Eccleston (Lancs.)....69 SD 5216
Eccleston (Mers.)....68 SJ 4895
Eccup....79 SE 2842
Eccup Reservoir....79 SE 2941
Echnaloch Bay....136 ND 4797
Echt....119 NJ 7305
Eckford....96 NT 7125
Eckington (Derby.)....71 SK 4379
Eckington (Here. and Worc.)....49 SO 9241
Ecton....52 SP 8263
Edale....70 SK 1285
Edale Cross (mt.)....70 SK 0886
Eday....138 HY 5634
Eday Sound....138 HY 5833
Edburton....29 TQ 2311
Edderton....129 NH 7184
Eddisbury Hill....69 SJ 5669
Eddleston....95 NT 2447
Eddleston Water....95 NT 2346
Eddrachillis Bay....132 NC 1336
Eddystone Rocks....20 SX 3833
Edenbridge....29 TQ 4446
Edendon Water....116 NN 7176
Edenfield....69 SD 8019
Edenhall....83 NY 5632
Edenham....62 TF 0621

Edenhope Hill....48 SO 2688
Eden Mouth....109 NO 5021
Eden Park....37 TQ 3868
Edensor....71 SK 2469
Edentaggart....100 NS 3394
Edenthorpe....71 SE 6206
Eden Water....96 NT 6345
Edgarhope Wood....96 NT 5549
Edgbaston....50 SP 0684
Edgcott....36 SP 6722
Edge....58 SJ 3908
Edgebolton....59 SJ 5721
Edge End....45 SO 5913
Edgefield....65 TG 0934
Edgefield Street....65 TG 0933
Edge Hill....50 SP 3747
Edgelaw Resr....103 NT 3058
Edgeworth....46 SO 9406
Edgmond....59 SJ 7119
Edgmond Marsh....59 SJ 7120
Edgton....48 SO 3885
Edgware....37 TQ 2091
Edgworth....69 SD 7416
Edinample....107 NN 6022
Edinbane....122 NG 3451
Edinburgh....103 NT 2674
Edinburgh Airport....102 NT 1573
Edingale....60 SK 2112
Edingight House....121 NJ 5155
Edingley....61 SK 6655
Edingthorpe....65 TG 3132
Edington (Somer.)....32 ST 3939
Edington (Wilts.)....33 ST 9252
Edithmead....32 ST 3249
Edith Weston....62 SK 9205
Edlesborough....36 SP 9719
Edlingham....91 NU 1108
Edlington....73 TF 2371
Edmondsham....26 SU 0611
Edmondsley....84 NZ 2348
Edmondthorpe....62 SK 8517
Edmonstone....137 HY 5220
Edmonton....37 TQ 3493
Edmundbyers....84 NZ 0150
Ednam....96 NT 7337
Edradour House....108 NN 9558
Edradynate....108 NN 8852
Edrom....97 NT 8255
Edstaston....59 SJ 5131
Edstone....50 SP 1761
Edvin Loach....49 SO 6658
Edwalton....61 SK 5935
Edwardstone....54 TL 9442
Edwinsford....43 SN 6334
Edwinstowe....71 SK 6266
Edworth....53 TL 2241
Edwyn Ralph....49 SO 6457
Edzell....109 NO 5968
Eela Water....142 HU 3378
Efail Isaf....41 ST 0884
Efailnewydd....66 SH 3536
Efenechtyd....58 SJ 1155
Effingham....28 TQ 1253
Effingham Junction Station....28 TQ 1055
Efford....141 HU 3152
Egerton (Gtr Mches.)....69 SD 7014
Egerton (Kent)....30 TQ 9047
Egerton Forstal....30 TQ 8946
Egga Field (mt.)....142 HU 3617
Eggardon Hill....25 SY 5494
Eggerness Point....87 NX 4946
Eggesford Station....23 SS 6811
Eggington....52 SP 9525
Egginton....60 SK 2628
Egglescliffe....85 NZ 4213
Eggleston....84 NZ 0023
Eggleston Common....84 NZ 0615
Egglestone Abbey (ant.)....84 NZ 0615
Egham....36 TQ 0170
Egilsay (Orkney) (is.)....136 HY 4729
Egilsay (Shetld.) (is.)....142 HU 3169
Egleton....62 SK 8707
Eglingham....91 NU 1019
Egloshayle....19 SX 0071
Egloskerry....20 SX 2786
Eglwysbach....67 SH 8070
Eglwys-Brewis....41 ST 0168
Eglwyseg Mountain....58 SJ 2347
Eglwys Nunydd Resr....42 SS 7985
Eglwyswrw....42 SN 1438
Egmanton....72 SK 7368
Egremont....82 NY 0110
Egton....80 NZ 8006
Egton Bridge....80 NZ 8005
Egton High Moor....80 NZ 7701
Eididh nan Clach Geala (mt.)....127 NH 2584
Eigg (is.)....111 NM 4786
Eigg, The (pt.)....143 HU 4495
Eight Ash Green....54 TL 9425
Eignaig....111 NM 7944
Eigneig Bheag (pt.)....124 NF 9260
Eigneig Mhòr (pt.)....124 NF 9361
Eil....117 NH 8217
Eilanreach....123 NG 8017
Eildon Hills....96 NT 5432
Eileach an Naoimh....105 NM 6409
Eilean a' Bhreitheimh....132 NC 1339
Eilean a'Chalmain....104 NM 3017
Eilean a'Chladaich....98 NR 3392
Eileanach Lodge....128 NH 5468
Eilean a'Chùirn....98 NR 4749
Eilean a' Ghaill....111 NM 6282
Eilean Annraidh....104 NM 2926
Eilean an Ròin Mòr....132 NC 1758
Eilean an Tighe....125 NG 4297
Eilean an t-Snidhe....125 NG 6381
Eilean Aoidhe....100 NR 9367
Eilean Balnagowan....106 NM 9554
Eilean Beag (Highld.)....123 NG 6836
Eilean Beag (Islay)....98 NR 2774
Eilean Bhride....98 NR 4547
Eilean Chaluim Chille....131 NB 3821
Eilean Chathastail....111 NM 4883
Eilean Choraidh....133 NC 4258
Eilean Chrona....132 NC 0633
Eilean Clùimhrig....133 NC 4666
Eilean Craobhach....98 NR 4649
Eilean Creagach....122 NG 0965
Eilean Dallaig....112 NG 6908
Eilean Dioghlum....104 NM 3242
Eilean Dubh (Highld.)....105 NB 9703
Eilean Dubh (Highld.)....105 NM 8338
Eilean Dubh (Strath.)....105 NM 8742
Eilean Dubh (Strath.)....99 NR 7187
Eilean Dubh Cruinn....105 NM 4433
Eilean Dubh Mòr....105 NM 6910
Eilean Duin....105 NM 7821
Eilean Fladday....123 NG 5851
Eilean Flodigarry....123 NG 4771
Eilean Furadh Mòr....126 NG 7993
Eilean Garbh (Gigha Island)....98 NR 6554
Eilean Garbh (Island of Rona)....123 NG 6056
Eilean Ghaoideamal....98 NR 3687
Eilean Glas (Isle of Lewis)....125 NG 2494
Eilean Grianain....92 NR 8142
Eilean Heast....123 NG 6415
Eilean Hoan....133 NC 4467
Eilean Horrisdale....123 NG 7874

Eilean Ighe....111 NM 6388
Eilean Imersay....98 NR 4346
Eilean Iosal....122 NG 2865
Eilean Iubhard....131 NB 3809
Eilean Kearstay....131 NB 1933
Eilean Leathan....98 NB 3290
Eilean Loain....99 NR 7585
Eilean Loch Oscair....105 NM 8645
Eilean Mhic Chrion....105 NM 8003
Eilean Mhuire....125 NG 4398
Eilean Mòr (Coll. Strath.)....110 NM 2765
Eilean Mòr (Highld.)....132 NC 0517
Eilean Mòr (Highld.)....123 NG 6934
Eilean Mòr (Island of Skye)....122 NG 3557
Eilean Mòr (Strath.)....99 NR 6675
Eilean Mòr (Strath.) (is.)....106 NM 8834
Eilean Mòr a' Bhàigh....125 NB 2600
Eilean Mullagrach....132 NB 9511
Eilean Musdile....105 NM 7835
Eilean na Bà....123 NG 6938
Eilean na Creiche....104 NM 3837
Eilean na h-Airde....123 NG 5211
Eilean na h-Aon Chaorach....104 NM 2520
Eilean nam Muc....104 NM 2819
Eilean nan Caorach....106 NM 9046
Eilean nan Coinean....99 NR 7186
Eilean nan Each....111 NM 3981
Eilean nan Gamhna....105 NM 8130
Eilean nan Gobhar....111 NM 6979
Eilean nan Ròn (Colonsay)....98 NR 3386
Eilean nan Ròn (Highld.)....133 NC 6365
Eilean Ona....105 NM 7602
Eilean Orasaidh....131 NB 4121
Eilean Ornsay....110 NM 2255
Eilean Ràrsaidh....123 NG 8111
Eilean Righ....99 NM 8001
Eilean Ruairidh Mòr....126 NG 8973
Eilean Shona....111 NM 6474
Eilean Sùbhainn....126 NG 9272
Eilean Thòraidh....131 NB 4220
Eilean Thuilm....104 NM 4891
Eilean Tigh....123 NG 6053
Eilean Treadhrach....98 NR 3788
Eilean Trodday....125 NG 4478
Eishken....131 NB 3211
Eitshal (mt.)....131 NB 3030
Elan Village....57 SN 9365
Elberton (Avon)....33 ST 6088
Elburton (Devon)....21 SX 5353
Elchies Forest....120 NJ 2246
Elcho....108 NO 1620
Elcombe....34 SU 1280
Eldernell....63 TL 3298
Eldersfield....46 SO 7931
Elderslie....101 NS 4462
Eldrable Hill....134 NC 9816
Eldrick Hill....86 NX 3693
Eldrig Fell....86 NX 2568
Eldroth....78 SD 7665
Eldwick....78 SE 1240
Elford (Northum.)....97 NU 1830
Elford (Staffs.)....60 SK 1810
Elgin....120 NJ 2162
Elgol....123 NG 5214
Elham....31 TR 1744
Elibank and Traquair Forest....96 NT 3635
Elie....103 NO 4900
Elim....131 NB 3584
Elishader....123 NG 5065
Elishaw....90 NY 8694
Elkesley....72 SK 6875
Elkstone....46 SO 9612
Elland....78 SE 1020
Ellary....99 NR 7476
Ellastone....60 SK 1143
Ellemford....96 NT 7360
Ellenhall....59 SJ 8426
Ellen's Green....28 TQ 1035
Ellen's Isle....101 NN 4808
Eller Beck (N Yorks.)....85 SD 9854
Ellerbeck (N Yorks.)....85 SE 4396
Ellerby (N Yorks.)....85 NZ 7914
Ellerdine Heath....59 SJ 6121
Elleric....106 NN 0348
Ellerker....74 SE 7039
Ellerton (Humbs.)....74 SE 7039
Ellerton (Shrops.)....59 SJ 7125
Ellesborough....36 SP 8306
Ellesmere....58 SJ 3934
Ellesmere Port....68 SJ 4077
Ellingham (Norf.)....55 TM 3592
Ellingham (Northum.)....97 NU 1725
Ellingstring....78 SE 1783
Ellington (Cambs.)....52 TL 1671
Ellington (Northum.)....91 NZ 2792
Elliot Water....109 NO 5841
Ellis Crag....90 NT 7401
Ellisfield....35 SU 6345
Ellister....98 NR 1852
Ellistown....60 SK 4311
Ellon....121 NJ 9530
Ellough....55 TM 4486
Elloughton....74 SE 9428
Ellwood....45 SO 5808
Elm....63 TF 4607
Elmbridge....49 SO 8967
Elmdon (Essex)....53 TL 4639
Elmdon (W Mids)....50 SP 1783
Elmdon Heath....50 SP 1580
Elmesthorpe....61 SP 4696
Elmhurst....60 SK 1112
Elmley Castle....50 SO 9841
Elmley Island....30 TQ 9468
Elmley Lovett....49 SO 8669
Elmore....46 SO 7715
Elmore Back....46 SO 7716
Elm Park....37 TQ 5385
Elmscott....22 SS 2321
Elmsett....54 TM 0546
Elmstead Market....39 TM 0624
Elmsted Court....31 TR 1145
Elmstone....31 TR 2660
Elmstone Hardwicke....46 SO 9125
Elmswell....54 TL 9964
Elmton....71 SK 5073
Elphin....132 NC 2111
Elphinstone....103 NT 3970
Elrick....119 NJ 8206
Elrick Burn....116 NH 6811
Elrig....86 NX 3247
Elsdon....90 NY 9393
Elsecar....71 SE 3800
Elsenham....53 TL 5425
Elsfield....47 SP 5409
Elsham....74 TA 0312
Elsing....64 TG 0516
Elslack....78 SD 9349
Els Ness....137 HY 6738
Elsrickle....95 NT 0643
Elstead (Surrey)....28 SU 9043
Elsted (W Susx)....27 SU 8119
Elston....61 SK 7548
Elstone....23 SS 6716
Elstow....52 TL 0547
Elstree....37 TQ 1895
Elstree Aerodrome....37 TL 1596
Elstronwick....75 TA 2232
Elswick....77 SD 4138
Elsworth....53 TL 3163
Elterwater....82 NY 3204

Eltham....37 TQ 4274
Eltisley....53 TL 2759
Elton (Cambs.)....62 TL 0893
Elton (Ches.)....68 SJ 4575
Elton (Cleve.)....85 NZ 4017
Elton (Derby.)....71 SK 2261
Elton (Glos.)....46 SO 6914
Elton (Here. and Worc.)....48 SO 4571
Elton (Notts.)....61 SK 7638
Elvanfoot....88 NS 9517
Elvan Water....88 NS 9216
Elvaston....61 SK 4132
Elveden....54 TL 8279
Elvingston....103 NT 4674
Elvington (Kent)....31 TR 2750
Elvington (N Yorks.)....74 SE 6947
Elwick (Cleve.)....85 NZ 4532
Elwick (Northum.)....97 NU 1136
Elworth....69 SJ 7361
Elworthy....24 ST 0835
Ely (Cambs.)....53 TL 5380
Ely (S Glam.)....41 ST 1476
Ely River....41 ST 0185
Ely Valley....41 ST 0579
Emberton....52 SP 8849
Emblehope Moor....90 NY 7395
Embleton (Cumbr.)....82 NY 1630
Embleton (Northum.)....97 NU 2322
Embleton Bay....97 NU 2423
Embo....129 NH 8192
Emborough....33 ST 6151
Embsay....78 SE 0053
Embsay Moor....78 SE 0056
Embsay Resr....78 SE 0054
Emery Down....26 SU 2808
Emley....71 SE 2413
Emmer Green....35 SU 7177
Emmington....36 SP 7402
Emneth....63 TF 4807
Emneth Hungate....63 TF 5107
Empingham....62 SK 9408
Empshott....27 SU 7531
Emsworth....27 SU 7405
Emsworth Channel....27 SU 7403
Enaclete....131 NB 1228
Enard Bay....132 NC 0416
Enborne....34 SU 4365
Enchmarsh....59 SO 4996
Enderby....51 SP 5399
End Moor....77 SD 5584
Endon....59 SJ 9253
Endrick Water....101 NS 6087
Enfield....37 TQ 3296
Enfield Chase....37 TQ 2998
Enford....34 SU 1351
Enford Down....34 SU 1049
Engine Common....33 ST 6984
Englefield....36 SU 6272
Englefield Green....36 SU 9870
English Bicknor....45 SO 5815
Englishcombe....33 ST 7162
English Frankton....58 SJ 4529
English Stones (pt.)....33 ST 5285
Enham-Alamein....34 SU 3648
Enmore....24 ST 2335
Ennerdale Bridge....82 NY 0615
Ennerdale Fell....82 NY 1313
Ennerdale Water....82 NY 1015
Enoch....88 NS 8801
Enochdhu....108 NO 0662
Enoch Hill....88 NS 5606
Ensay (Harris)....124 NF 9786
Ensay (Island of Mull)....110 NM 3648
Ensbury....26 SZ 0896
Ensdon....58 SJ 4016
Ensis....23 SS 5626
Enstone....47 SP 3724
Enterkinfoot....88 NS 8504
Entwistle Station....69 SD 7217
Enville....49 SO 8286
Enyas Hill....136 HY 4020
Eochar....124 NF 7846
Eolaigarry....124 NF 7007
Eorabus....104 NM 3823
Eoropie....131 NB 5165
Eorsa (is.)....105 NM 4837
Epperstone....61 SK 6548
Epping....37 TL 4602
Epping Forest....37 TQ 4197
Epping Green (Essex)....37 TL 4305
Epping Green (Herts.)....37 TL 2906
Epping Upland....37 TL 4404
Eppleby....84 NZ 1713
Epsom....37 TQ 2160
Epsom Downs Station....37 TQ 2258
Epwell....50 SP 3540
Epworth....74 SE 7803
Erbistock....58 SJ 3541
Erbusaig....123 NG 7629
Erchless Castle....115 NH 4040
Erchless Forest....128 NH 4145
Erdington....50 SP 1291
Eredine....100 NM 9609
Eredine Forest (Strath.)....100 NM 9507
Eredine Forest (Strath.)....100 NN 0012
Eriboll....133 NC 4356
Ericstane....89 NT 0710
Eridge Green....29 TQ 5535
Eridge Station....29 TQ 5434
Erines....99 NR 8575
Eriskaig....109 NM 3832
Eriska (dist.)....106 NM 8943
Eriskay....112 NF 7910
Eriswell....54 TL 7278
Erith....37 TQ 5177
Erlestoke....34 ST 9653
Ermine Street (Cambs.) (ant.)....62 TL 1593
Ermine Street (Herts.) (ant.)....53 TL 2667
Ermine Street (Herts.) (ant.)....37 TL 3720
Ermine Street (Lincs.) (ant.)....72 SK 9685
Ermington....21 SX 6353
Ermin Way (ant.)....46 SO 9611
Ernan Water....117 NJ 2712
Erne Stack....141 HU 3067
Erpingham....65 TG 1931
Errid (is.)....104 NM 2919
Errochty Water....107 NN 7663
Errogie....116 NH 5622
Errol....108 NO 2522
Errwood Resr....70 SK 0175
Erskine....101 NS 4670
Erskine Bridge....101 NS 4672
Ervie....86 NX 0067
Erwarton....39 TM 2234
Erwood....44 SO 0943
Eryholme....84 NZ 3208
Eryrys....68 SJ 2057
Esclusham Mountain....58 SJ 2550
Escrick....79 SE 6243
Esgair Ambor....57 SN 7559
Esgair Berfa....56 SH 6309
Esgair Cerrig....57 SN 7556
Esgair Cwmowen....57 SJ 0100
Esgair Ddu....57 SN 7057
Esgair Fraith....44 SN 8364
Esgair Garthen....57 SH 7605
Esgair Hir....57 SN 7254
Esgair Llyn-du....57 SN 7661
Esgairmaesnant....48 SN 1762
Esgair Priciau....57 SH 9304
Esgair Ychion....57 SN 8480

Esgair y Maesnant Ford (Mers.)

Esgair y Maesnant 57 SN 8386
Esh 84 NZ 1944
Esha Ness 142 HU 2279
Esher 37 TQ 1464
Eshott 91 NZ 2097
Eshton 78 SD 9356
Esh Winning 84 NZ 1942
Eskadale 116 NH 4539
Eskbank 103 NT 3266
Eskdale (Cumbr.) 82 NY 1800
Eskdale (Dumf. and Galwy.) 89 NY 3489
Esk Dale (N Yorks.) 80 NZ 7407
Eskdale Green 82 NY 1400
Eskdalemuir 89 NY 2597
Eskdalemuir Forest 89 NT 2503
Eskielawn (mt.) 108 NO 2766
Esknish 98 NR 3664
Espley Hall 91 NZ 1790
Esprick 77 SD 4035
Essendine 62 TF 0412
Essendon 37 TL 2708
Essich 116 NH 6539
Essington 60 SJ 9603
Esslemont 121 NJ 9329
Esthwaite Water 82 SD 3596
Eston 85 NZ 5518
Etal 97 NT 9339
Etchilhampton 34 SU 0460
Etchingham 29 TQ 7126
Etchinghill (Kent) 31 TR 1639
Etchinghill (Staffs.) 60 SK 0218
Ethie Castle 109 NO 6846
Eton 36 SU 9678
Etteridge 116 NN 6892
Ettington 50 SP 2649
Etton (Humbs.) 74 SE 9743
Etton (Northants.) 62 TF 1306
Ettrick 89 NT 2714
Ettrick Bay 100 NS 0365
Ettrickbridge 96 NT 3824
Ettrick Forest 96 NT 3724
Ettrick Pen 89 NT 1907
Ettrick Water 89 NT 3118
Etwall 60 SK 2732
Euchan Water 88 NS 7206
Euston 54 TL 8978
Euston Station 37 TQ 2982
Euximoor Fen 63 TL 4799
Euxton 77 SD 5518
Evanton 128 NH 6066
Evedon 62 TF 0947
Evelix 129 NH 7691
Evenjobb 48 SO 2662
Evenley 47 SP 5834
Evenlode 47 SP 2229
Eventide Home 119 NJ 9618
Evenwood 84 NZ 1524
Everbay 137 HY 6724
Evercreech 33 ST 6438
Everdon 51 SP 5957
Everingham 74 SE 8042
Everleigh 34 SU 1953
Everley 81 SE 9789
Eversholt 52 SP 9933
Evershot 25 ST 5704
Eversley 36 SU 7762
Eversley Cross 36 SU 7961
Everton (Beds.) 52 TL 2051
Everton (Hants.) 26 SZ 2993
Everton (Notts.) 72 SK 6891
Evertown 89 NY 3576
Evesbatch 49 SO 6848
Evesham 50 SP 0344
Evington 61 SK 6203
Ewden Village 71 SK 2796
Ewe Hill 95 NT 0540
Ewelairs Hill 89 NT 1602
Ewell 37 TQ 2262
Ewell Minnis 31 TR 2643
Ewelme 36 SU 6491
Ewen 46 SU 0097
Ewenny 41 SS 9077
Ewerby 62 TF 1247
Ewes 89 NY 3690
Eweslees Knowe 89 NT 3201
Ewesley 91 NZ 0592
Ewes Water 89 NY 3791
Ewhurst (Surrey) 28 TQ 0940
Ewhurst Green 30 TQ 7924
Ewloe 68 SJ 3066
Eworthy 20 SX 4494
Ewshot 35 SU 8149
Ewyas Harold 45 SO 3828
Exbourne 23 SS 6002
Exbury 26 SU 4200
Exebridge 23 SS 9324
Exelby 79 SE 2986
Exeter 21 SX 9292
Exeter Airport 21 SX 9993
Exe Valley 23 SS 9415
Exford 23 SS 8538
Exhall 50 SP 1055
Exminster 21 SX 9487
Exmoor Forest 23 SS 7642
Exmouth 21 SY 0080
Exnaboe 141 HU 3912
Exning 54 TL 6265
Exton (Devon) 21 SX 9886
Exton (Hants.) 27 SU 6121
Exton (Leic.) 62 SK 9211
Exton (Somer.) 23 SS 9233
Eyam 70 SK 2176
Ey Burn 117 NO 0886
Eydon 51 SP 5450
Eye (Here. and Worc.) 48 SO 4963
Eye (Northants.) 63 TF 2202
Eye (Suffolk) 55 TM 1473
Eye Brook 61 SK 7602
Eyebrook Resr. 62 SP 8595
Eyebroughy (pt.) 103 NT 4986
Eyemouth 97 NT 9464
Eye Peninsula 131 NB 5332
Eye Water 97 NT 8263
Eyeworth 53 TL 2545
Eyhorne Street 30 TQ 8354
Eyke 55 TM 3151
Eynesbury 52 TL 1859
Eynhallow (is.) 136 HY 3529
Eynhallow Sound 136 HY 3827
Eynort 122 NG 3826
Eynort River 122 NG 3727
Eynsford 37 TQ 5365
Eynsham 47 SP 4309
Eype 25 SY 4491
Eyre 123 NG 4152
Eyre Point 123 NG 5834
Eythorne 31 TR 2849
Eyton (Here. and Worc.) 48 SO 4761
Eyton (Salop) 48 SO 3687
Eyton upon the Weald Moors 59 SJ 6414

F

Faan Hill 142 HU 3480
Faccombe 34 SU 3857
Faceby 85 NZ 4903
Faddiley 59 SJ 5752
Fadmoor 85 SE 6789
Faifley 101 NS 5073
Failand 33 ST 5272
Failford 93 NS 4526
Failsworth 69 SD 9002
Fairbourne 56 SH 6113
Fairburn 79 SE 4727
Fairfield 49 SO 9475
Fairford 47 SP 1501
Fairham Brook 61 SK 5531
Fair Isle 139 HZ 2172
Fairlie 93 NS 2155
Fairlie Roads 93 NS 1753
Fairlight 30 TQ 8612
Fairmile 24 SY 0997
Fairmilehead 103 NT 2567
Fairnington House 96 NT 6427
Fair Oak (Hants.) 27 SU 4918
Fairoak (Staffs.) 59 SJ 7632
Fairoaks Airport 36 TQ 0062
Fairseat 30 TQ 6261
Fair Snape Fell 77 SD 5947
Fairstead (Essex) 38 TL 7616
Fairwarp 29 TQ 4626
Fairy Cross 22 SS 4024
Fairy Glen 67 SH 8054
Faither, The (pt.) 142 HU 2585
Fakenham 64 TF 9229
Fala 103 NT 4361
Fala Dam 103 NT 4261
Falahill 96 NT 3956
Fala Moor 103 NT 4258
Faldingworth 72 TF 0684
Falfield 46 ST 6893
Falkenham 55 TM 2939
Falkirk 102 NS 8880
Falkland 103 NO 2507
Falla 90 NT 7013
Fallin 101 NS 8391
Fall of Glomach 114 NH 0325
Fall of Warness (chan.) 137 HY 5427
Fallowlees Burn 91 NY 9992
Falls of Acharn 107 NN 7543
Falls of Bruar The 107 NN 8267
Falls of Cruachan 106 NN 0727
Falls of Falloch 106 NN 3420
Falls of Garbh Allt 117 NO 2089
Falls of Keltie 108 NN 8625
Falls of Lochay 107 NN 5434
Falls of Lora 106 NM 9134
Falls of Moness 108 NN 8547
Falls of Rogie 128 NH 4458
Falls of Tummel 108 NN 9159
Falmer 29 TQ 3508
Falmouth 19 SW 8032
Falmouth Bay 19 SW 8130
Falstone 90 NY 7287
Fambridge Station 38 TQ 8597
Fanagmore 132 NC 1750
Fan Fawr 41 SN 9619
Fangdale Beck 85 SE 5694
Fangfoss 80 SE 7653
Fan-Gihirych 41 SN 8819
Fan Hill 57 SN 9388
Fan Hir (mt.) 41 SN 8220
Fan Llia 41 SN 9318
Fanmore 105 NM 4244
Fanna Hill 90 NT 5603
Fannich Forest 127 NH 1968
Fannich Lodge 127 NH 2166
Fannyside Lochs 101 NS 8073
Fans 96 NT 6140
Fara (is.) 136 ND 3295
Faraclett Head 138 HY 4433
Faraid Head 132 NC 3971
Faray 138 HY 5336
Farcet 62 TL 2094
Farcet Fen 53 TL 2392
Far Cotton 51 SP 7458
Farden 48 SO 5776
Fareham 27 SU 5806
Farewell 60 SK 0811
Farigaig Forest 116 NH 5221
Faringdon 47 SU 2895
Farington 77 SD 5425
Farlam 90 NY 5558
Farland Head 93 NS 1748
Farlary 129 NC 7606
Farleigh 37 TQ 3660
Farleigh Hungerford 33 ST 8057
Farleigh Wallop 35 SU 6246
Farlesthorpe 73 TF 4774
Farleton 77 SD 5380
Farley (Salop.) 58 SJ 3808
Farley (Staffs.) 60 SK 0644
Farley (Wilts.) 26 SU 2229
Farley Green 28 TQ 0645
Farley Hill 36 SU 7564
Farley Mount 26 SU 3928
Farleys End 46 SO 7615
Farlington 79 SE 6167
Farlow 49 SO 6380
Farmborough 33 ST 6560
Farmcote 46 SP 0629
Farmers 43 SN 6444
Farmington 47 SP 1315
Farmoor 47 SP 4407
Farmoor Resr. 47 SP 4406
Farmtown 121 NJ 5051
Farnborough (Berks.) 34 SU 4381
Farnborough (Gtr London) 37 TQ 4464
Farnborough (Hants.) 35 SU 8753
Farnborough (Warw.) 50 SP 4349
Farncombe 28 SU 9755
Farndale 80 SE 6895
Farndale Moor 85 NZ 6500
Farndish 52 SP 9263
Farndon (Ches.) 58 SJ 4154
Farndon (Notts.) 61 SK 7651
Farne Islands 97 NU 2337
Farnell 109 NO 6255
Farnham (Dorset) 26 ST 9514
Farnham (Essex) 37 TL 4724
Farnham (N Yorks.) 79 SE 3460
Farnham (Suff.) 55 TM 3660
Farnham (Surrey) 35 SU 8446
Farnham Common 36 SU 9584
Farnham Green 53 TL 4625
Farnham Royal 36 SU 9682
Farningham 37 TQ 5566
Farnley 78 SE 2147
Farnley Tyas 70 SE 1612
Farnsfield 61 SK 6456
Farnworth (Ches.) 69 SJ 5187
Farnworth (Gtr Mches.) 69 SD 7305
Farquhar's Point 111 NM 6272
Farr (Highld.) 134 NC 7163
Farr (Highld.) 116 NH 6833
Farr (Highld.) 117 NH 8203
Farragon Hill 107 NN 8455
Farr Bay 133 NC 7063
Farr House 116 NH 6831
Farringdon 24 SY 0191
Farrington Gurney 33 ST 6255
Farrmheall (mt.) 132 NC 3058
Farr Point 134 NC 7164
Farsley 78 SE 2135
Farthinghoe 51 SP 5339
Farthingstone 51 SP 6155
Farway 24 SY 1895
Fascadale 111 NM 5070
Faseny Water 103 NT 6162
Fasheilach 118 NO 3485
Fashven (mt.) 132 NC 3167
Faslane Bay 100 NS 2489
Fasnacloich 106 NN 0247
Fasnakyle 115 NH 3128
Fasnakyle Forest 115 NH 2630
Fasque 119 NO 6475
Fassfern 114 NN 0278
Fast Castle (ant.) 97 NT 8671
Fastheugh Hill 96 NT 3927
Fatfield 84 NZ 3053
Fathan Glinne 107 NN 4917
Fattahead 121 NJ 6657
Faugh 83 NY 5155
Fauldhouse 102 NS 9260
Faulkbourne 38 TL 7917
Faulkland 33 ST 7354
Fauls 59 SJ 5933
Faversham 31 TR 0161
Favillar 117 NJ 2734
Fawfieldhead 70 SK 0763
Fawkham Green 37 TQ 5865
Fawler 47 SP 3717
Fawley (Berks.) 34 SU 3981
Fawley (Bucks.) 36 SU 7586
Fawley (Hants.) 27 SU 4503
Fawley Chapel 45 SO 5829
Faw Side (mt.) 89 NY 3596
Faxfleet 74 SE 8624
Faygate 28 TQ 2134
Fazeley 60 SK 2001
Feadda Ness 141 HU 5438
Feall Bay 110 NM 1354
Fearby 78 SE 1981
Feardar Burn 117 NO 1995
Fearnan 107 NN 7244
Fearnbeg 123 NG 7359
Fearnhead 69 SJ 6290
Fearn Lodge 128 NH 6387
Fearnmore 123 NG 7260
Fearnoch Forest 106 NM 9631
Fearn Station 129 NH 8178
Featherbed Top 70 SK 0892
Featherstone (Staffs.) 59 SJ 9305
Featherstone (W Yorks.) 79 SE 4222
Featherstone Castle 90 NY 6761
Feckenham 50 SP 0061
Fedderate 121 NJ 8949
Feering 38 TL 8720
Feetham 84 SD 9898
Feinne-bheinn Mhòr 133 NC 4346
Fèith a'Chaoruinn 133 NC 5522
Fèith Gaineimh Mhòr 134 NC 9332
Fèith Talagain 116 NN 5497
Feizor 78 SD 7968
Felbridge 29 TQ 3739
Felbrigg 65 TG 2039
Felcourt 29 TQ 3841
Felden 36 TL 0404
Felindre (Dyfed) 40 SN 7027
Felindre (Powys) 48 SO 1681
Felindre (W Glam.) 40 SN 6302
Felinfach 41 SO 0933
Felinfoel 40 SN 5202
Felingwm Uchaf 43 SN 5024
Felixkirk 79 SE 4684
Felixstowe 55 TM 3034
Felkington 97 NT 9444
Felling 91 NZ 2762
Fell of Barhullion 86 NX 3742
Fell of Carleton 86 NX 4037
Fell of Fleet 88 NX 5670
Fell Side 82 NY 3037
Fell Top 77 SD 5751
Felmersham 52 SP 9957
Felmingham 65 TG 2529
Felpham 28 SZ 9599
Felsham 54 TL 9457
Felsted 38 TL 6720
Feltham 36 TQ 1072
Felthorpe 65 TG 1618
Felton (Avon) 33 ST 5165
Felton (Here. and Worc.) 45 SO 5748
Felton (Northum.) 91 NU 1800
Felton Butler 58 SJ 3917
Feltwell 54 TL 7190
Feltwell Anchor 54 TL 6789
Fence 78 SD 8237
Fencote 84 SE 2893
Fender Burn 108 NN 9169
Fendike Corner 73 TF 4560
Fen Ditton 53 TL 4860
Fen Drayton 53 TL 3468
Fen End 50 SP 2274
Feniscowles 77 SD 6425
Feniton 24 SY 1199
Fenn's Moss 59 SJ 4937
Fenny Bentley 60 SK 1750
Fenny Bridges 24 SY 1198
Fenny Compton 50 SP 4152
Fenny Drayton 60 SP 3597
Fenny Stratford 52 SP 8834
Fen Road (ant.) 63 TL 4698
Fenrother 91 NZ 1792
Fenstanton 53 TL 3168
Fenton (Cambs.) 53 TL 3279
Fenton (Lincs.) 72 SK 8476
Fenton (Lincs.) 62 SK 8750
Fenton (Staffs.) 59 SJ 8944
Fenwick (Northum.) 91 NU 0639
Fenwick (Northum.) 91 NZ 0572
Fenwick (Strath.) 93 NS 4643
Fenwick (S Yorks.) 71 SE 5916
Fenwick Water 93 NS 4541
Feochaig 92 NR 7613
Feochan Bheag 106 NM 8824
Feock 19 SW 8238
Feolin Ferry 98 NR 4469
Ferinquarrie 122 NG 1750
Fern 109 NO 4861
Ferndale 41 SS 9997
Ferndown 26 SU 0700
Ferness 129 NH 9645
Fernham 34 SU 2991
Fernhill Heath 49 SO 8659
Fernhurst 27 SU 9028
Fernie 108 NO 3115
Ferniehirst Castle (ant.) 90 NT 6517
Fernilea 122 NG 3634
Fernilee 70 SK 0178
Fernilee Resr. 70 SK 0176
Fernworthy Reservoir 21 SX 6684
Ferrensby 79 SE 3660
Ferring 28 TQ 0902
Ferrybridge 79 SE 4824
Ferryden 109 NO 7156
Ferryhill 84 NZ 2832
Ferryside 43 SN 3610
Fersfield 54 TM 0682
Fersit 115 NN 3577
Fers Ness 138 HY 5334
Fersness Bay 138 HY 5434
Fersness Hill 138 HY 5332
Feshiebridge 117 NH 8504
Fetcham 28 TQ 1555
Fethaland 143 HU 3793
Fetlar (is.) 143 HU 6291
Fetterangus 121 NJ 9850
Fettercairn 119 NO 6573
Fetteresso Forest 119 NO 7786
Fewston 78 SE 1954
Fewston Resr. 78 SE 1754
Ffairfach 43 SN 6220
Ffestiniog 67 SH 7042
Fforest 43 SN 5804
Fforest Fach (Powys) 41 SN 9027
Fforest-fach (Powys) 48 SO 1867
Fforest-fach (W Glam.) 40 SS 6396
Fforest Fawr 41 SN 9018
Ffostrasol 43 SN 3747
Ffridd 57 SH 9603
Ffridd Faldwyn (ant.) 58 SO 2196
Ffridd Fawr 67 SJ 0560
Ffridd-uchaf 66 SH 5751
Ffrith 58 SJ 2855
Ffrwdgrech 41 SO 0227
Ffynnonddrain 43 SN 4021
Ffynnongroew 68 SJ 1382
Ffynnon Llugwy Reservoir 67 SH 6962
Fiag Lodge (ruin) 133 NC 4528
Fiarach (mt.) 106 NN 3425
Fiaray 112 NF 7010
Fiavig Bàgh 130 NB 0335
Fidden 104 NM 3021
Fiddes 119 NO 8181
Fiddington (Glos.) 46 SO 9231
Fiddington (Somer.) 32 ST 2140
Fiddlers Hamlet 37 TL 4701
Fidra (is.) 103 NT 5186
Field 60 SK 0233
Field Broughton 77 SD 3881
Field Dalling 64 TG 0039
Field Head 61 SK 4909
Fifehead Magdalen 25 ST 7721
Fifehead Neville 25 ST 7610
Fife Ness 103 NO 6309
Fifield (Berks.) 36 SU 9076
Fifield (Oxon.) 47 SP 2318
Figheldean 34 SU 1547
Figsbury Ring (ant.) 26 SU 1833
Filby 65 TG 4613
Filey 81 TA 1180
Filey Bay 81 TA 1378
Filgrave 52 SP 8748
Filkins 47 SP 2304
Filla (is.) 143 HU 6668
Filleigh (Devon) 23 SS 6628
Filleigh (Devon) 23 SS 7410
Fill Geo 143 HP 5708
Fillingham 72 SK 9485
Fillongley 50 SP 2787
Filton 33 ST 6079
Filton Airfield 33 ST 5880
Fimber 81 SE 8960
Finalty Hill 117 NO 2074
Finavon 109 NO 4957
Finavon Castle 109 NO 4956
Finbracks (mt.) 109 NO 4070
Finchale Priory (ant.) 84 NZ 2947
Fincham 64 TF 6806
Finchampstead 36 SU 7963
Fincharn 100 NM 9003
Finchdean 27 SU 7312
Finchingfield 54 TL 6832
Finchley 37 TQ 2890
Findern 60 SK 3030
Findhorn 129 NJ 0464
Findhorn Bay 129 NJ 0462
Findhorn Bridge 116 NH 8027
Findhu Glen 107 NN 7115
Findochty 121 NJ 4667
Findo Gask 108 NO 0020
Findon (Grampn.) 119 NO 9397
Findon (W Susx) 28 TQ 1208
Findon Forest 128 NH 6458
Findon Mains 128 NH 6060
Findon Ness 119 NO 9497
Findrack House 119 NJ 6004
Finedon 52 SP 9272
Fingal's Cave 104 NM 3234
Fingal Street 55 TM 2169
Fingask 121 NJ 7827
Fingask Castle 108 NO 2227
Fingest 36 SU 7791
Finghall 84 SE 1889
Fingland 88 NS 7517
Fingland Fell 89 NY 1495
Finglen Burn 107 NN 6734
Finglen Rig 95 NT 1332
Fingringhoe 39 TM 0220
Finiskaig 111 NM 8694
Finlarig 107 NN 5733
Finlas Water 100 NS 3389
Finlaystone House 101 NS 3673
Finmere 51 SP 6333
Finnart 107 NN 5157
Finnarts Bay 86 NX 0472
Finningham 54 TM 0669
Finningly 71 SK 6699
Finnygaud 121 NJ 6054
Finsbay 125 NG 0786
Finsbury 37 TQ 3282
Finsthwaite 77 SD 3687
Finstock 47 SP 3516
Finstown 136 HY 3513
Fintry (Central) 101 NS 6186
Fintry (Grampn.) 121 NJ 7554
Fionn Bheinn 127 NH 1462
Fionn Bheinn Mhòr 127 NC 3704
Fionn Lighe 114 NM 9682
Fionn Loch (Highld.) 132 NC 1317
Fionn Loch (Highld.) 126 NG 9578
Fionn Loch Mòr 132 NC 3323
Fionnphort (Island of Mull) 104 NM 2923
Fionn Phort (Strath.) 100 NR 9065
Firbank 83 SD 6294
Firbeck 71 SK 5688
Fire Beacon Point 20 SX 1092
Firgrove 69 SD 9113
Firle Beacon 29 TQ 4806
Firsby 73 TF 4563
Firth 143 HU 4473
Firth of Clyde 93 NS 1354
Firth of Forth 103 NT 3786
Firth of Lorn 105 NM 7221
Firth of Tay 109 NO 3727
Firths Voe 143 HU 4474
Firth, The 141 HU 3450
Fir Tree 84 NZ 1334
Fishbourne (I. of W.) 27 SZ 5592
Fishbourne (W Susx) 27 SU 8304
Fishburn 85 NZ 3632
Fishcross 102 NS 8995
Fisherfield Forest 126 NH 0080
Fisherford 121 NJ 6635
Fisher's Pond 27 SU 4820
Fisherstreet 28 SU 9531
Fisher Tarn Reservoir 83 SD 5592
Fisherton (Highld.) 129 NH 7451
Fisherton (Strath.) 93 NS 2717
Fishguard 42 SM 9637
Fishguard Bay 42 SM 9839
Fish Holm 143 HU 4774
Fishlake 71 SE 6513
Fishnish Bay 105 NM 6442
Fishpool 69 SD 8009
Fishtoft 63 TF 3642
Fishtoft Drove 63 TF 3148
Fishtown of Usan 109 NO 7254
Fishwick 97 NT 9151
Fiskavaig 122 NG 3234
Fiskerton (Lincs.) 72 TF 0472
Fiskerton (Notts.) 61 SK 7351
Fistral Bay 19 SW 7862
Fitful Head 141 HU 3413
Fittleton 34 SU 1449
Fittleworth 28 TQ 0119
Fitton End 63 TF 4312
Fitty Hill 138 HY 4244
Fitz 58 SJ 4417
Fitzhead 24 ST 1228
Fitzwilliam 71 SE 4115
Fiunary 105 NM 6246
Fiunary Forest 105 NM 6447
Five Ashes 29 TQ 5525
Fivehead 24 ST 3522
Five Oak Green 29 TQ 6445
Five Oaks 28 TQ 0928
Five Penny Borve 131 NB 4056
Five Penny Ness 131 NB 5364
Five Roads 43 SN 4905
Five Sisters 114 NG 9617
Flackwell Heath 36 SU 8890
Fladbury 50 SO 9946
Fladda (is.) 104 NM 2943
Fladdabister 141 HU 4332
Fladda-chùain (is.) 125 NG 3681
Flag Fen 63 TL 2894
Flagg 70 SK 1368
Flamborough 81 TA 2270
Flamborough Head 81 TA 2570
Flamstead 36 TL 0814
Flanders Moss (Central) 101 NS 5595
Flanders Moss (Central) 101 NS 6398
Flannan Isles 130 NA 7146
Flansham 28 SU 9601
Flasby 78 SD 9456
Flash 70 SK 0267
Flashader 122 NG 3553
Flashes, The (pt.) 85 NZ 6125
Flat Holm (is.) 41 ST 2265
Flatt, The 90 NY 5678
Flaunden 36 TL 0100
Flawborough 61 SK 7842
Flawith 79 SE 4865
Flax Bourton 33 ST 5069
Flaxby 79 SE 3957
Flaxley 46 SO 6915
Flaxpool 24 ST 1435
Flaxton 79 SE 6762
Fleam Dyke (ant.) 53 TL 5553
Fleckney 61 SP 6493
Flecknoe 51 SP 5163
Fleet (Hants.) 35 SU 8054
Fleet (Lincs.) 63 TF 3823
Fleet Bay 87 NX 5651
Fleet Hargate 63 TF 3925
Fleetwood 77 SD 3247
Flemingston 41 ST 0170
Flemington 101 NS 6559
Flempton 54 TL 8169
Fleshwick Bay 76 SC 2071
Fletching 29 TQ 4323
Flexford 28 SU 9350
Flimby 82 NY 0233
Flimwell 29 TQ 7131
Flint 68 SJ 2472
Flintham 61 SK 7446
Flint Mountain 68 SJ 2369
Flinton 75 TA 2136
Flitcham 64 TF 7226
Flitton 52 TL 0536
Flitwick 52 TL 0335
Flixborough 74 SE 8715
Flixton (Gtr Mches.) 69 SJ 7494
Flixton (N Yorks.) 81 TA 0479
Flixton (Suff.) 55 TM 3186
Float Bay 86 NX 0647
Flockton 71 SE 2314
Flodabay 125 NG 0988
Floday (Isle of Lewis) 131 NB 1033
Floday (Isle of Lewis) 131 NB 1241
Flodda (is.) 124 NF 8455
Flodday (Barra) 112 NF 7502
Flodday (W Isles) 112 NL 6192
Floddaybeg 124 NF 9158
Floddaymore 124 NF 9157
Flodden 97 NT 9235
Flodigarry 123 NG 4671
Flookburgh 77 SD 3675
Floors Castle 96 NT 7134
Flordon 65 TM 1897
Flore 51 SP 6460
Flossnan 122 NG 2337
Flotta (Orkney) (is.) 136 ND 3593
Flotta (Shetld.) (is.) 141 HU 3746
Flotterton 91 NT 9902
Flowerdale Forest 126 NG 8867
Flowton 55 TM 0847
Flushing (Corn.) 19 SW 8034
Flushing (Grampn.) 121 NK 0546
Flyford Flavell 50 SO 9754
Fobbing 38 TQ 7183
Fochabers 121 NJ 3458
Fochno 57 SN 6493
Fochriw 41 SO 1005
Fockerby 74 SE 8419
Fodder Fen 53 TL 5287
Fodderletter 117 NJ 1421
Fodderty 128 NH 5159
Foel 57 SH 9911
Foel-cwmcerwyn 42 SN 0931
Foel-drych 42 SN 1630
Foeleryr 42 SN 0632
Foel Fenlli (ant.) 68 SJ 1660
Foel Figenau 57 SH 9128
Foel Fraith 41 SN 7517
Foel-Fras 67 SH 6968
Foel Fynyddau 41 SS 7893
Foel Goch 67 SH 9542
Foel Gurig 57 SN 9279
Foel Rhiwlas 58 SJ 2032
Foel Rhudd 57 SH 8924
Foel Wen 67 SJ 0933
Foel-y-ffridd 57 SH 8312
Foel y Geifr 57 SH 9327
Foffarty 109 NO 4145
Foggathorpe 74 SE 7537
Fogla Skerry 140 HU 1461
Fogo 96 NT 7749
Foinaven (mt.) 132 NC 3149
Foindle 132 NC 1948
Folda 108 NO 1964
Fole 60 SK 0437
Foleshill 50 SP 3582
Folke 25 ST 6513
Folkestone 31 TR 2336
Folkingham 62 TF 0733
Folkington 29 TQ 5604
Folksworth 52 TL 1490
Folkton 81 TA 0579
Folla Rule 121 NJ 7333
Follifoot 79 SE 3452
Folly Gate 21 SX 5797
Fontburn Resr 91 NZ 0493
Fonthill Bishop 26 ST 9332
Fonthill Gifford 25 ST 9231
Fontmell Magna 25 ST 8616
Fontwell 28 SU 9407
Foolow 70 SK 1976
Foots Cray 37 TQ 4770
Foot, The 137 HY 5316
Fora Ness (Shetld.) 141 HU 3517
Fora Ness (Shetld.) 143 HU 4571
Forcett 84 NZ 1712
Ford (Bucks.) 36 SP 7709
Ford (Devon) 21 SX 7840
Ford (Glos.) 46 SP 0829
Ford (Mers.) 68 SJ 3598

Ford (Northum.) Gisborough Moor

Ford (Northum.) 97 NT 9437
Ford (Shrops.) 58 SJ 4113
Ford (Staffs.) 60 SK 0654
Ford (Strath.) 105 NM 8603
Ford (Wilts.) 33 ST 8475
Ford (W Susx) 28 TQ 0003
Fordcombe 29 TQ 5240
Forde Abbey (ant.) 24 ST 3505
Fordell 102 NT 1588
Fordell Castle (ant.) 102 NT 1485
Forden 58 SJ 2201
Ford End 38 TL 6716
Forder Green 21 SX 7867
Fordham (Cambs.) 54 TL 6370
Fordham (Essex) 54 TL 9228
Fordham (Norf.) 64 TL 6199
Fordham Abbey 54 TL 6369
Fordingbridge 26 SU 1413
Fordon 81 TA 0475
Fordoun 119 NO 7475
Fordstreet (Essex) 54 TL 9227
Ford Street (Somer.) 24 ST 1518
Fordwells 47 SP 3013
Fordwich 31 TR 1859
Fordyce 121 NJ 5563
Fore Holm 141 HU 3544
Foreland (pt.) 27 SZ 6687
Foreland House 98 NR 2664
Foreland Point 23 SS 7551
Foreland, The, or Handfast Point 26 SZ 0582
Foremark 60 SK 3326
Foremark Resr 60 SK 3324
Foreness Point 31 TR 3871
Forest 84 NY 8629
Forestburn Gate 91 NZ 0696
Forestfield 102 NS 8566
Forest Gate 37 TQ 4085
Forest Green 28 TQ 1241
Forest Hall 83 NY 5401
Forest Head 83 NY 5857
Forest Hill 47 SP 5807
Forest Lodge (Highld.) 117 NJ 0216
Forest Lodge (Strath.) 106 NN 2742
Forest Lodge (Tays.) 117 NN 9274
Forest Mill 102 NS 9594
Forest Moor 79 SE 2256
Forest of Ae 88 NX 9991
Forest of Alyth 108 NO 1755
Forest of Atholl 116 NN 7973
Forest of Bere 27 SU 6711
Forest of Birse 119 NO 5291
Forest of Bowland 77 SD 6455
Forest of Clunie 108 NO 0850
Forest of Dean 45 SO 6310
Forest of Deer 121 NJ 9750
Forest of Glenartney 107 NN 6818
Forest of Glenavon 117 NJ 1005
Forest of Glen Tanar 118 NO 4995
Forest of Harris 130 NB 0609
Forest of Mamlorn 107 NN 4034
Forest of Mar 117 NO 0292
Forest of Pendle, The 78 SD 8239
Forest of Rossendale 78 SD 8424
Forest of Trawden, The 78 SD 9437
Forest Row 29 TQ 4235
Forestside 27 SU 7512
Forest Town 71 SK 5662
Forfar 109 NO 4550
Forgandenny 108 NO 0818
Forgie 121 NJ 3954
Forglen House 121 NJ 6952
Formartine (dist.) 121 NJ 8729
Formby 68 SD 2907
Formby Hills 68 SD 2708
Forncett End 65 TM 1493
Forncett St. Mary 65 TM 1694
Forncett St. Peter 65 TM 1693
Forneth 108 NO 0945
Fornham All Saints 54 TL 8367
Fornham St. Martin 54 TL 8566
Forres 129 NJ 0358
Forrestburn Resr. 102 NS 8765
Forrest Lodge 87 NX 5586
Forret Hill 109 NO 3920
Forsbrook 60 SJ 9641
Forse 135 ND 2234
Forse House 135 ND 2135
Forsie 135 ND 0463
Forsinain 134 NC 9149
Forsinain Burn 134 NC 9247
Forsinard 134 NC 8842
Forsnaval (mt.) 130 NB 0635
Forss House 135 ND 0369
Forss Water 135 ND 0360
Forston 25 SY 6695
Fort Augustus 115 NH 3709
Forter 108 NO 1864
Forteviot 108 NO 0517
Fort George 129 NH 7656
Forth 95 NS 9453
Forthampton 46 SO 8532
Forth and Clyde Canal 101 NS 6674
Forth Bridge 102 NT 1379
Forth Road Bridge 102 NT 1279
Fortingall 107 NN 7447
Forton (Lancs.) 77 SD 4851
Forton (Shrops.) 58 SJ 4216
Forton (Somer.) 24 ST 3306
Forton (Staffs.) 59 SJ 7521
Fortree 121 NJ 9640
Fortrie 121 NJ 6645
Fortrose 129 NH 7256
Fortuneswell 25 SY 6873
Fort William 115 NN 1074
Forty Foot or Vermuden's Drain 53 TL 3888
Forty Hill 37 TQ 3398
Forvie Ness or Hackley Head 121 NK 0226
Forward Green 55 TM 1059
Fosbury 34 SU 3157
Fosdyke 63 TF 3133
Foss 107 NN 7958
Fossdyke Navigation 72 SK 9274
Fossebridge 46 SP 0811
Foss Way (Devon - Somer.) (ant.) 24 ST 3102
Foss Way (Glos. - Wilts.) (ant.) 46 ST 9394
Foss Way (Lincs.) (ant.) 72 SK 9064
Foss Way (Somer.) (ant.) 25 ST 4920
Foss Way (Somer.) (ant.) 33 ST 6345
Foss Way (Warw.) (ant.) 50 SP 3358
Foss Way (Wilts.) (ant.) 33 ST 8277
Foss-y-ffin 43 SN 4460
Foster Street 37 TL 4909
Foston (Derby.) 60 SK 1831
Foston (Lincs.) 62 SK 8542
Foston (N Yorks.) 80 SE 6965
Foston Beck 62 SK 8739
Foston on the Wolds 81 TA 1055
Fotherby 73 TF 3191
Fotheringhay 62 TL 0593
Fothringham Hill 109 NO 4645
Foubister 136 HY 5104
Foula (is.) 140 HT 9638
Foulden (Borders) 97 NT 9355
Foulden (Norf.) 64 TL 7699
Foulholme Sands 75 TA 1920
Foulis Castle 128 NH 5864
Foul Mile 29 TQ 6215
Foulmire Heights 90 NY 5794
Foulnaze (sbk) 77 SD 3124
Foulness 65 TG 2441
Foulness Island 33 TR 0192
Foulness Point 33 TR 0495
Foulness Sands 33 TR 0997
Foulney Island 76 SD 2463
Foulridge 78 SD 8942
Foulsham 64 TG 0324
Fountainhall 96 NT 4349
Fountains Abbey (ant.) 79 SE 2768
Fountains Fell 78 SD 8671
Four Ashes 54 TM 0070
Four Crosses (Powys) 57 SJ 0508
Four Crosses (Powys) 58 SJ 2718
Four Crosses (Staffs.) 60 SJ 9509
Four Elms 29 TQ 4648
Four Forks 24 ST 2336
Four Gotes 63 TF 4516
Four Lanes 18 SW 6838
Fourlanes End 69 SJ 8059
Fourman Hill 121 NJ 5745
Four Marks 27 SU 6634
Four Mile Bridge 66 SH 2778
Four Oaks (E Susx) 30 TQ 8624
Four Oaks (W Mids) 60 SP 1198
Four Oaks (W Mids) 50 SP 2480
Fourpenny 129 NH 8094
Fourstones 90 NY 8967
Four Throws 30 TQ 7729
Fovant 26 SU 0028
Foveran 121 NJ 9824
Foveran Burn 121 NJ 9323
Fowberry Tower 97 NU 0429
Fowey 19 SX 1251
Fowlis 108 NO 3133
Fowlis Wester 108 NN 9223
Fowlmere 53 TL 4245
Fownhope 45 SO 5734
Foxcote Reservoir 51 SP 7136
Foxdale 76 SC 2878
Foxearth 54 TL 8344
Foxfield 76 SD 2085
Foxham 34 ST 9777
Foxhole (Corn.) 19 SW 9654
Foxholes (N Yorks.) 81 TA 0173
Fox Lane 35 SU 8557
Foxley (Norf.) 64 TG 0321
Foxley (Wilts.) 33 ST 8985
Foxt 60 SK 0348
Foxton (Cambs.) 53 TL 4148
Foxton (Leic.) 51 SP 7090
Foxup 78 SD 8676
Foxwist Green 69 SJ 6168
Foy 45 SO 5928
Foyers 116 NH 4921
Fraddon 19 SW 9158
Fradley 60 SK 1513
Fradswell 60 SJ 9831
Fraisthorpe 81 TA 1561
Framfield 29 TQ 4920
Framingham Earl 65 TG 2702
Framingham Pigot 65 TG 2703
Framlingham 55 TM 2863
Frampton (Dorset) 25 SY 6294
Frampton (Lincs.) 63 TF 3239
Frampton Cotterell 33 ST 6582
Frampton Mansell 46 SO 9202
Frampton on Severn 46 SO 7407
Frampton West End 63 TF 3040
Framsden 55 TM 1959
Framwellgate Moor 84 NZ 2644
Franche 49 SO 8178
Frankby 68 SJ 2486
Frankley 50 SO 9980
Frank Lockwood's Island 105 NM 6219
Frankton 50 SP 4270
Frant 29 TQ 5835
Fraochaidh 106 NN 0251
Fraserburgh 121 NJ 9966
Fraserburgh Bay 121 NK 0165
Frating Green 39 TM 0923
Fratton 27 SU 6600
Freathy 20 SX 3952
Freckenham 54 TL 6672
Freckleton 77 SD 4228
Fredden Hill 97 NT 9526
Freeby 61 SK 8020
Freeland 47 SP 4112
Freester 141 HU 4553
Freethorpe 65 TG 4105
Freethorpe Common 65 TG 4004
Freevater Forest 127 NH 3588
Freiston 63 TF 3743
Fremington 22 SS 5132
Frenchay 33 ST 6377
Frenchbeer 21 SX 6785
Freni-fawr 43 SN 2035
Frensham 35 SU 8441
Fresgoe 134 NC 9566
Freshfield 68 SD 2807
Freshford 33 ST 7860
Freshwater 26 SZ 3487
Freshwater Bay 26 SZ 3485
Freshwater West 42 SR 8899
Fressingfield 55 TM 2677
Freston 55 TM 1739
Freswick 135 ND 3667
Freswick Bay 135 ND 3867
Fretherne 46 SO 7309
Frettenham 65 TG 2417
Freuchie 103 NO 2806
Friar's Gate 29 TQ 4933
Friday Bridge 63 TF 4605
Fridaythorpe 81 SE 8759
Friern Barnet 37 TQ 2892
Friesland 110 NM 1853
Friesthorpe 72 TF 0683
Frieth 36 SU 7990
Frilford 47 SU 4497
Frilsham 35 SU 5373
Frimley 36 SU 8758
Frindsbury 30 TQ 7369
Fring 64 TF 7334
Fringford 47 SP 6028
Frinsted 30 TQ 8957
Frinton-on-Sea 39 TM 2319
Friockheim 109 NO 5949
Frisby on the Wreake 61 SK 6917
Friskney 63 TF 4555
Friskney Flats (sbk.) 63 TF 4851
Friston (E Susx) 29 TV 5498
Friston (Suff.) 55 TM 4160
Fritchley 60 SK 3553
Fritham 26 SU 2413
Frith Bank 63 TF 3147
Frith Common 49 SO 6969
Frithelstock 22 SS 4619
Frithville 63 TF 3250
Frittenden 30 TQ 8141
Fritton (Norf.) 65 TG 4700
Fritton (Norf.) 65 TM 2293
Fritwell 47 SP 5229
Frizington 82 NY 0316
Frocester 46 SO 7803
Frodesley 59 SJ 5101
Frodsham 69 SJ 5177
Froggatt 71 SK 2476
Froghall 60 SK 0247
Frogmore 36 SU 8360
Frogmore House 36 SU 9775
Frolesworth 51 SP 5090
Frome 33 ST 7747
Fromes Hill 49 SO 6846
Frome St. Quintin 25 ST 5902
Fron (Gwyn.) 66 SH 3539
Fron (Powys) 58 SJ 2203
Fron (Powys) 57 SO 0865
Fron Cysyllte 58 SJ 2741
Fron-goch 67 SH 9039
Frosterley 84 NZ 0237
Frosty Hill 118 NJ 4510
Froxfield 34 SU 2967
Froxfield Green 27 SU 7025
Fruid Reservoir 93 NS 1019
Fryerning 38 TL 6400
Fryton 80 SE 6875
Fuar Bheinn 111 NM 8556
Fuar Larach (mt.) 92 NR 8154
Fuday 112 NF 7308
Fugla Ness (Shetld.) 142 HU 3091
Fugla Ness (Shetld.) 142 HU 3674
Fugla Ness (West Burra) 141 HU 3635
Fugla Stack 141 HU 3529
Fugla Water 143 HU 5172
Fuiay 112 NF 7402
Fulbeck 62 SK 9450
Fulbourn 53 TL 5256
Fulbrook 47 SP 2513
Fulford (N Yorks.) 79 SE 6149
Fulford (Somer.) 24 ST 2129
Fulford (Staffs.) 59 SJ 9438
Fulham 37 TQ 2576
Fulking 28 TQ 2411
Fuller's Moor 59 SJ 4953
Fuller Street 38 TL 7415
Fullerton 34 SU 3739
Fulletby 73 TF 2973
Full Sutton 80 SE 7455
Fullwood 93 NS 4450
Fulmer 36 SU 9985
Fulmodeston 64 TF 9931
Fulnetby 73 TF 0979
Fulstow 73 TF 3297
Fulwell 91 NZ 3959
Fulwood (Lancs.) 77 SD 5331
Fulwood (S Yorks.) 71 SK 3085
Funlack Burn 116 NH 7833
Funtington 27 SU 7908
Funtley 27 SU 5607
Funzie 143 HU 6690
Funzie Bay 143 HU 6689
Furnace 100 NN 0200
Furness Abbey (ant.) 76 SD 2271
Furness Fells 82 NY 2900
Furneux Pelham 53 TL 4327
Furzehill 23 SS 7245
Fyfett 24 ST 2314
Fyfield (Essex) 37 TL 5707
Fyfield (Glos.) 47 SP 2003
Fyfield (Hants.) 34 SU 2946
Fyfield (Oxon.) 47 SU 4298
Fyfield (Wilts.) 34 SU 1468
Fylingdales Moor 81 SE 9199
Fylingthorpe 81 NZ 9405
Fyvie 121 NJ 7637

G

Gablon 129 NH 7191
Gabroc Hill 93 NS 4551
Gaddesby 61 SK 6813
Gadie Burn 121 NJ 6424
Gaer 41 SO 1721
Gaer-fawr 45 ST 4498
Gaerllwyd 45 ST 4496
Gaerwen 66 SH 4871
Gagingwell 47 SP 4025
Gaick Forest 116 NN 7584
Gaick Lodge 116 NN 7584
Gailey 59 SJ 9110
Gainford 84 NZ 1716
Gainsborough 72 SK 8189
Gainsford End 54 TL 7235
Gairbeinn 116 NN 4698
Gairich (mt.) 114 NN 0299
Gairletter Point 100 NS 1984
Gairloch 123 NG 8076
Gairlochy 115 NN 1784
Gairney Bank 102 NT 1299
Gairnshiel Lodge 117 NJ 2900
Gairsay 136 HY 4422
Gairsay Sound 136 HY 4424
Gairy Craig 87 NX 5490
Gairy Hill 136 ND 4685
Gaitnip Hill 136 HY 4505
Gaitsgill 83 NY 3946
Gala Lane 87 NX 4792
Galashiels 96 NT 4936
Gala Water 96 NT 4152
Galby 61 SK 6901
Galgate 77 SD 4855
Galhampton 25 ST 6329
Gallanach (Coll, Strath.) 110 NM 2160
Gallanach (Strath.) 105 NM 8226
Gallan Head 130 NB 0539
Gallatown 103 NT 2994
Galley Common 50 SP 3192
Galleyend 38 TL 7103
Galloway (dist.) 87 NX 4867
Gallowfauld 109 NO 4342
Gallow Hill (Dumf. and Galwy.) 89 NT 0806
Gallow Hill (Tays.) 109 NO 3841
Gallrope Bank (sbk.) 129 NH 7885
Galltair 123 NG 8120
Galmisdale 111 NM 4883
Galmpton (Devon) 21 SX 6940
Galmpton (Devon) 21 SX 8856
Galphay 79 SE 2572
Galson 131 NB 4358
Galston 93 NS 5036
Galtachean (is.) 125 NG 3998
Galtrigill 122 NG 1854
Galt, The (pt.) 136 HY 4821
Gamallt (Dyfed) 44 SN 7756
Gamallt (Powys) 57 SN 9570
Gamblesby 83 NY 6039
Gamhna Gigha 92 NR 6854
Gamlingay 53 TL 2452
Gamrie 121 NJ 7962
Gamrie Bay 121 NJ 7965
Gamriw 57 SN 9461
Gamston (Notts.) 61 SK 6037
Gamston (Notts.) 72 SK 7076
Gana Hill 88 NS 9500
Ganarew 45 SO 5216
Ganavan 105 NM 8632
Ganllwyd 57 SH 7224
Gannochy 109 NO 5970
Ganstead 75 TA 1434
Ganthorpe 80 SE 6870
Ganton 81 SE 9877
Ganu Mór 132 NC 3150
Gaodhail 105 NM 6038
Gaor Bheinn or Gulvain 114 NM 9987
Garadhban Forest 101 NS 4790
Garbat 128 NH 4167
Garbat Forest 128 NH 4368
Garbh-allt (Highld.) 134 NC 7738
Garbhallt (Strath.) 100 NS 0295
Garbh Bheinn (Highld.) 106 NM 9062
Garbh Bheinn (Highld.) 106 NN 1659
Garbh-bheinn (Island of Skye) 123 NG 5323
Garbh Eileach 105 NM 6612
Garbh Eilean (Island of Rona) 123 NG 6153
Garbh Eilean (Shiant Islands) 125 NG 4198
Garbh Ghaoir 107 NN 4356
Garbh-mheall Mór 116 NN 7292
Garbh Phort 104 NM 3325
Garbh Rèisa 99 NR 7597
Garbh Shlios 105 NM 7542
Garbh Thorr 92 NR 9335
Garboldisham 54 TM 0081
Gardenstown 121 NJ 7964
Garderhouse 141 HU 3347
Gardie House 141 HU 4842
Gareg Lâs 41 SN 7720
Gare Hill 33 ST 7840
Gare Loch 100 NS 2486
Garelochhead 100 NS 2491
Garenin 131 NB 1944
Garford 47 SU 4296
Garforth 79 SE 4033
Garf Water 95 NS 9032
Gargrave 78 SD 9354
Gargunnock 101 NS 7094
Gargunnock Hills 101 NS 6891
Garioch (dist.) 121 NJ 7024
Garleffin Fell 86 NX 3598
Garleton Hills 103 NT 5076
Garlick Hill 87 NX 4372
Garlies Castle (ant.) 87 NX 4269
Garlieston 87 NX 4746
Garlogie 119 NJ 7805
Garmond 121 NJ 8052
Garmony 105 NM 6740
Garmouth 121 NJ 3364
Garmsley Camp (ant.) 49 SO 6162
Garmus Taing 142 HU 3594
Garn 66 SH 2734
Garnant 40 SN 6813
Garn Boduan (ant.) 66 SH 3139
Garn Caws 41 SO 1317
Garn Ddu 41 SO 0212
Garn-Dolbenmaen 66 SH 4944
Garnedd-goch 66 SH 5149
Garnett Bridge 83 SD 5299
Garnkirk 101 NS 6768
Garn Prys 67 SH 8848
Garpol Water 88 NT 0103
Garrabost 131 NB 5133
Garragie Lodge 116 NH 5211
Garraron 105 NM 8008
Garras 18 SW 7023
Garreg 66 SH 6141
Garreg Bank 58 SJ 2811
Garreg-ddu Resr. 57 SN 9165
Garrick 101 NN 8412
Garrigill 83 NY 7441
Garrisdale Point 110 NG 2005
Garrison, The 18 SV 8910
Garroch 88 NX 5981
Garroch Head 93 NS 0951
Garron Point 119 NO 8987
Garros 123 NG 4963
Garrow 107 NN 8240
Garrow Tor 19 SX 1478
Garrynamonie 112 NF 7416
Garsdale 83 SD 7389
Garsdale Head 83 SD 7992
Garsdon 34 ST 9687
Garshall Green 60 SJ 9633
Garsington 47 SP 5802
Garso Wick 139 HY 7755
Garstang 77 SD 4945
Garston 68 SJ 4083
Garswood 69 SJ 5599
Gartbreck 98 NR 2858
Gartcosh 101 NS 6968
Garth (Clwyd) 58 SJ 2542
Garth (I. of M.) 76 SC 3177
Garth (Mid Glam.) 41 SS 8690
Garth (Powys) 44 SN 9549
Garth (Shetld.) 140 HU 2157
Garthbrengy 41 SO 0433
Gartheli 43 SN 5956
Garth Head 136 ND 3188
Garthmyl 58 SO 1999
Garthorpe (Humbs.) 74 SE 8419
Garthorpe (Leic.) 62 SK 8320
Garths Ness 141 HU 3611
Garths, The 143 HP 6615
Garths Voe 143 HU 4073
Gartmore 101 NS 5297
Gartmore House 101 NS 5297
Gartnagrenach 99 NR 7959
Gartness (Central) 101 NS 5086
Gartness (Strath.) 101 NS 7864
Gartocharn 101 NS 4286
Garton 75 TA 2635
Garton-on-the-Wolds 81 SE 9859
Gartymore 135 ND 0114
Garvald 103 NT 5870
Garvard 98 NR 3691
Garvary Burn 134 NC 7222
Garve 127 NH 3961
Garvellachs (is.) 105 NM 6511
Garveston 64 TG 0207
Garvock 100 NS 2571
Garwall Hill 86 NX 3483
Garway 45 SO 4522
Garynahine 131 NB 2331
Gasay 124 NF 8443
Gaskan 111 NM 8072
Gasker (is.) 130 NA 8711
Gastard 33 ST 8868
Gasthorpe 54 TL 9780
Gatcombe 27 SZ 4885
Gatebeck 77 SD 5485
Gate Burton 72 SK 8382
Gateforth 79 SE 5528
Gatehead 93 NS 3936
Gate Helmsley 80 SE 6955
Gateholm Island 42 SM 7707
Gatehouse 90 NY 7988
Gatehouse of Fleet 87 NX 5956
Gatelawbridge 88 NX 9096
Gateley 64 TF 9624
Gatenby 79 SE 3287
Gatescarth Pass 83 NY 4709
Gateshead 91 NZ 2562
Gatesheath 69 SJ 4760
Gateside (Fife) 102 NO 1809
Gateside (Strath.) 93 NS 3653
Gateside (Tays.) 109 NO 3749
Gateside (Tays.) 109 NO 4344
Gathurst 69 SD 5307
Gatley 69 SJ 8387
Gat Sand 63 TF 4738
Gattonside 96 NT 5435
Gatwick Airport - London 28 TQ 2740
Gauldry 109 NO 3723
Gauls 108 NO 0734
Gaunt's Common 26 SU 0205
Gautby 73 TF 1772
Gavinton 96 NT 7652
Gawber 71 SE 3207
Gawcott 51 SP 6831
Gawdy Hall (ant.) 55 TM 2485
Gawsworth 69 SJ 8869
Gawthorpe Hall (ant.) 78 SD 8033
Gawthrop 77 SD 6987
Gawthwaite 77 SD 2784
Gaydon 50 SP 3654
Gayhurst 52 SP 8446
Gayle Moor 78 SD 8082
Gayles 84 NZ 1207
Gay Street 28 TQ 0820
Gayton (Mers.) 68 SJ 2680
Gayton (Norf.) 64 TF 7219
Gayton (Northants.) 51 SP 7054
Gayton (Staffs.) 60 SJ 9728
Gayton le Marsh 73 TF 4284
Gayton Sands 68 SJ 2478
Gayton Thorpe 64 TF 7418
Gaywood 64 TF 6320
Gazeley 54 TL 7264
Geal Charn (Grampn.) 117 NJ 2810
Geal Charn (Highld.) 117 NJ 0812
Geal Charn (Highld.) 115 NN 1594
Geal Charn (Highld.) 116 NN 5081
Geal Charn (Highld.) 116 NN 5698
Geal Charn (Highld.) 116 NN 5978
Geal-charn Mór 117 NH 8312
Geallaig Hill 117 NO 2998
Gealldruig Mhór (is.) 130 HW 8131
Geanies House 129 NH 8979
Gearr Garry 115 NH 0801
Geary 122 NG 2661
Geddes House 129 NH 8852
Gedding 54 TL 9457
Geddington 52 SP 8983
Gedintailor 123 NG 5235
Gedney 63 TF 4024
Gedney Broadgate 63 TF 4022
Gedney Drove End 63 TF 4629
Gedney Dyke 63 TF 4126
Gedney Hill 63 TF 3311
Gedney Marsh 63 TF 4329
Gee Cross 70 SJ 9593
Geifas (mt.) 57 SN 8172
Geilston 100 NS 3477
Geise 135 ND 1064
Geldeston 55 TM 3891
Geldie Burn 117 NN 9687
Gell 67 SH 8569
Gelligaer 41 ST 1397
Gelli-gaer Common 41 ST 1298
Gelli Gynan 58 SJ 1854
Gellilydan 67 SH 6839
Gellioedd 67 SH 9344
Gelly 42 SN 0819
Gellyburn 108 NO 0939
Gellywen 43 SN 2723
Gelston 88 NX 7758
Geltsdale Middle 83 NY 6052
Genie Fea (mt.) 136 ND 2494
Genoch Mains 86 NX 1356
Gentlemens' Cave 138 HY 3948
Gentleshaw 60 SK 0511
Geocrab 125 NG 1190
Geodh'a' Bhrideoin 133 NC 4867
Geodha Daraich 122 NG 3719
Geodha Mór (Highld.) 127 NC 0802
Geodha Mór (Island of Skye) 122 NG 2039
Geodha na Crich 131 NB 1538
Geodha nan Calman 131 NB 1339
Geodha nan Each 122 NG 1554
Geodha Nasavig 130 NB 0336
Geodha Ruadh 132 NC 2368
Geodha Ruadh na Fola 132 NC 2471
Geo Dubh 125 NB 2200
Geo Luon 137 HY 5429
Geo of Hellia 136 HY 1904
Geo of Markamouth 143 HP 4701
Geo of Odderaber 138 HY 4954
Geo of the Uin 141 HU 4118
Geo of Vigon 143 HP 4704
Geordie's Hill 89 NY 4396
Georgeham 22 SS 4639
Georgemas Junction Station 135 ND 1559
George Nympton 23 SS 7023
Georgetown 101 NS 4567
Georgia 18 SW 4836
Georth 136 HY 3625
Germansweek 20 SX 4394
Germoe 18 SW 5829
Gerrans 19 SW 8735
Gerrans Bay 19 SW 8937
Gerrards Cross 36 TQ 0088
Geshader 131 NB 1131
Gestingthorpe 54 TL 8138
Geuffordd 58 SJ 2114
Geufron 57 SN 8885
Geur Rubha 111 NG 5501
Ghlas-bheinn 132 NC 3161
Giant's Leg (pt.) 141 HU 5135
Giant, The (ant.) 25 ST 6601
Gibbet Hill 27 SU 9035
Gibbon Hill 84 SE 0096
Gibraltar 73 TF 5558
Gidea Park 37 TQ 5390
Gidleigh 21 SX 6788
Gifford 103 NT 5368
Gigalum Island 92 NR 6445
Giggleswick 78 SD 8163
Gigha Island 92 NR 6449
Gighay 112 NF 7604
Gilberdyke 74 SE 8329
Gilchriston 103 NT 4865
Gilcrux 82 NY 1138
Gilderdale Forest 83 NY 6644
Gildersome 79 SE 2429
Gildingwells 71 SK 5585
Gileston 41 ST 0167
Gilfach Goch 41 SS 9890
Gilfachrheda 43 SN 4058
Gilgarran 82 NY 0323
Gilkicker Point 27 SZ 6097
Gillamoor 80 SE 6890
Gillaval Glas (mt.) 125 NB 1402
Gill Burn 135 ND 3368
Gillies Hill 101 NS 7791
Gilling East 79 SE 6176
Gillingham (Dorset) 25 ST 8026
Gillingham (Kent) 30 TQ 7768
Gillingham (Norf.) 55 TM 4191
Gilling West 84 NZ 1805
Gill of Garth 136 HY 4707
Gillow Heath 69 SJ 8858
Gills 135 ND 3172
Gills Bay 135 ND 3373
Gilmanscleuch 96 NT 3321
Gilmerton (Lothian) 103 NT 2968
Gilmerton (Tays.) 108 NN 8823
Gilmorton 51 SP 5787
Gilsay 124 NG 0279
Gilsland 90 NY 6366
Gilsland Spa 90 NY 6367
Gilston 96 NT 4456
Giltar Point 42 SS 1298
Giltarump (is.) 140 HU 2742
Gilwern 45 SO 2414
Gilwern Hill 44 SO 0958
Gimingham 65 TG 2836
Ginst Point 43 SN 3207
Gipping 54 TM 0763
Gipsey Bridge 63 TF 2850
Girdle Fell 90 NT 7001
Girdle Ness 119 NJ 9705
Girlsta 141 HU 4250
Girnock Burn 118 NO 3191
Girsby 85 NZ 3508
Girthon 87 NX 6053
Girtley Hill 100 NS 2361
Girton (Cambs.) 53 TL 4262
Girton (Notts.) 72 SK 8266
Girvan 86 NX 1897
Gisborough Moor 85 NZ 6213

Gisburn 78 SD 8248
Gisla River 131 NB 1126
Gisleham 55 TM 5188
Gislingham 54 TM 0771
Gissing 55 TM 1485
Gittisham 24 SY 1398
Giùr-bheinn 98 NR 3772
Glackossian 116 NH 5938
Gladestry 45 SO 2355
Gladhouse Reservoir 96 NT 2953
Gladsmuir 103 NT 4573
Glais 40 SN 7000
Glais Bheinn 105 NM 7143
Glaisdale (N Yorks.) 80 NZ 7603
Glaisdale (N Yorks.) 80 NZ 7705
Glaisdale Moor 80 NZ 7101
Glaisdale Rigg 80 NZ 7404
Glamaig (mt.) 123 NG 5129
Glam Burn 123 NG 5542
Glame 123 NG 5542
Glamis 109 NO 3846
Glamis Castle (ant.) 109 NO 3848
Glanaber Terrace 67 SH 7547
Glanaman 40 SN 6713
Glan-Conwy 67 SH 8352
Glandford 64 TG 0441
Glandwr (Dyfed) 43 SN 1928
Glandŵr (Gwent) 41 SO 2101
Glangrwyne 45 SO 2316
Glan-Mule 48 SO 1690
Glanrhyd 42 SN 1442
Glanton 91 NU 0714
Glanton Pyke 91 NU 0514
Glanvilles Wootton 25 ST 6708
Glan-y-don 68 SJ 1679
Glan-yr-afon (Clwyd-Gwyn.) 67 SJ 0242
Glan-yr-afon (Gwyn.) 67 SH 9141
Glapthorn 52 TL 0290
Glapwell 71 SK 4766
Glaramara 82 NY 2410
Glas-allt Shiel 117 NO 2782
Glas Bheinn (Highld.) 132 NC 2526
Glas Bheinn (Highld.) 123 NG 9043
Glas Bheinn (Highld.) 115 NN 1397
Glas Bheinn (Highld.) 106 NN 2564
Glas Bheinn (Islay) 98 NR 4259
Glas Bheinn (Jura) 98 NR 5069
Glas Bheinn Mhòr 123 NG 5525
Glasbury 45 SO 1739
Glas-charn 111 NM 8483
Glascoed 45 SO 3301
Glascorrie 118 NO 3997
Glascote 60 SK 2203
Glascwm 44 SO 1553
Glascwm Hill 44 SO 1552
Glasdrum 106 NM 0046
Glas Eilean (Highld.) 111 NG 7000
Glas Eilean (Highld.) 123 NG 8425
Glas Eilean (Jura) 98 NR 4465
Glas-eileanan 124 NF 8641
Glasfryn 67 SH 9150
Glasfynydd Forest 41 SN 8524
Glasgow 101 NS 5865
Glasgow Airport 101 NS 4766
Glasha Burn 127 NH 3792
Glasinfryn 66 SH 5868
Glaslaw 119 NO 8584
Glas-leac Beag (is.) 126 NB 9205
Glas-leac Mòr (is.) 132 NB 9509
Glas-loch Mòr 133 NC 6619
Glaslyn 57 SN 8294
Glas Maol (mt.) 117 NO 1676
Glas Mheall Mòr 116 NN 6876
Glasnakille 123 NG 5313
Glaspwll 57 SN 7397
Glassburn 115 NH 3634
Glasserton 87 NX 4238
Glassford 94 NS 7247
Glasshouse Hill 46 SO 7020
Glasshouses 78 SE 1764
Glasslaw 121 NJ 8659
Glasslie 103 NO 2305
Glasson (Cumbr.) 89 NY 2560
Glasson (Lancs.) 76 SD 4455
Glassonby 83 NY 5738
Glasterlaw 109 NO 6051
Glaston 62 SK 8900
Glastonbury 33 ST 4938
Glas Tulaichean 117 NO 0576
Glatton 52 TL 1586
Glazebury 69 SJ 6796
Glazeley 49 SO 7088
Gleadless Townend 71 SK 3883
Gleadsmoss 69 SJ 8469
Gleann a'Chilleine 107 NN 7336
Gleann a'Choilich 115 NH 0926
Gleann Airigh 100 NR 9195
Gleann an Dubh-Lochain 111 NG 8100
Gleann an Fhiodh 106 NN 0855
Gleann Aoistail 98 NR 6085
Gleann Astaile 98 NR 4871
Gleann Beag 127 NH 3383
Gleann Bhruthadail 131 NB 3443
Gleann Camghararaidh 114 NM 9988
Gleann Casaig 101 NN 5410
Gleann Cia-aig 115 NN 1891
Gleann Còsaidh 114 NG 9402
Gleann Da-Eig 107 NN 6045
Gleann Da-ghob 107 NN 6945
Gleann Diridh 117 NN 8775
Gleann Dubh (Highld.) 132 NC 2402
Gleann Dubh (Highld.) 132 NC 3033
Gleann Dubh (Highld.) 111 NM 7353
Gleann Dubh Lighe 114 NM 9582
Gleann Duibhe 107 NN 4655
Gleann Feàrnach 108 NO 0368
Gleann Fhiodhaig 127 NH 1448
Gleann Fionnlighe 114 NM 9782
Gleann Geal 111 NM 7250
Gleann Goibhnaidh 115 NH 0519
Gleann Goibhre 128 NH 4247
Gleann Leireag 132 NC 1730
Gleann Leòra 98 NR 4254
Gleann Màma 111 NH 7485
Gleann Meadhonach 111 NG 5904
Gleann Mèinich 127 NH 2553
Gleann Mòr (Highld.) 127 NH 4085
Gleann Mòr (South Uist) 112 NF 8125
Gleann Mòr (Tays.) 117 NO 0276
Gleann nam Barvas 131 NB 3845
Gleann na Guiserein 111 NG 7803
Gleann nam Fiadh 115 NH 1726
Gleann Oraid 122 NG 3330
Gleann Salach 106 NM 9738
Gleann Seilisdeir 105 NM 4730
Gleann Sithidh 115 NH 0727
Gleann Tanagaidh 127 NH 0866
Gleann Udalain 114 NG 8831
Gleann Ullibh 98 NR 4666
Gleaston 76 SD 2570
Glemanuilt Hill 92 NR 6408
Glemsford 54 TL 8247
Glen 87 NX 5457
Glenacardoch Point 92 NR 6637
Glen Achall 127 NH 2294
Glen Affric 115 NH 1922
Glen Affric Forest 115 NH 1020
Glen Aldie 129 NH 7779
Glenalla Field 86 NS 3500
Glen Almond (Tays.) 108 NN 9128

Glenalmond (Tays.) 108 NN 9627
Glen Ample 107 NN 5918
Glenan Bay 100 NR 9170
Glenancross 111 NM 6691
Glen App 86 NX 0774
Glenapp Castle 86 NX 0980
Glen Aray 86 NN 0913
Glen Arnisdale 123 NG 8709
Glenaros House 105 NM 5544
Glen Arroch 123 NG 7321
Glen Artney 98 NN 7218
Glenastle 98 NR 3044
Glen Auldyn 76 SC 4393
Glen Avon 117 NJ 1106
Glen Banchor 116 NN 6798
Glenbarr 92 NR 6736
Glen Barrisdale 114 NG 9003
Glen Barry 121 NJ 5554
Glen Batrick 98 NR 5178
Glen Beasdale 111 NM 7385
Glen Beg (Grampn.) 117 NJ 0028
Glen Beg (Highld.) 111 NM 5862
Glen Bernisdale 123 NG 4048
Glenbervie 119 NO 7680
Glenboig 101 NS 7268
Glenborrodale 111 NM 6060
Glen Bragar 131 NB 3041
Glenbranter 100 NS 1097
Glenbranter Forest 100 NS 1097
Glen Breackerie 92 NR 6511
Glenbreck 95 NT 0521
Glen Brein 116 NH 4809
Glenbrein Lodge 116 NH 4211
Glen Brerachan 108 NO 0063
Glen Brittle 123 NG 4123
Glen Brittle Forest 123 NG 4026
Glenbrittle House 123 NG 4121
Glen Bruar 117 NN 8274
Glenbuchat Lodge 118 NJ 3318
Glenbuck 94 NS 7429
Glenburn 101 NS 4761
Glencaird Hill 86 NX 3580
Glen Callater 117 NO 1883
Glencalvie Forest 128 NH 4387
Glencalvie Lodge 128 NH 4689
Glencanisp Forest 132 NC 1619
Glencanisp Lodge 132 NC 1122
Glen Cannel 105 NM 5935
Glen Cannich 123 NH 1930
Glencannich Forest 115 NH 2433
Glencaple 88 NX 9968
Glen Carron 127 NH 0852
Glencarron and Glenuig Forest 127 NH 1249
Glencarron Lodge 127 NH 0651
Glencarse 101 NO 1922
Glen Cassley 132 NC 4112
Glencassley Castle 132 NC 4407
Glenceitlein 106 NN 1447
Glen Clachaig 105 NM 5735
Glen Clova 109 NO 3570
Glencloy 92 NS 0036
Glen Cochill 106 NN 9042
Glencoe (Highld.) 106 NN 1058
Glen Coe (Highld.) 106 NN 1557
Glen Convinth 116 NH 5137
Glen Coralde 112 NF 8331
Glencorse Resr 103 NT 2163
Glen Coul 132 NC 2829
Glencraig 102 NT 1795
Glen Creran 106 NN 0448
Glencripesdale Burn 111 NM 6658
Glen Croe 131 NB 5160
Glen Cross 122 NG 1847
Glen Dale 108 NO 2567
Glen Damff 117 NO 2397
Glendaruel 119 NR 9985
Glendaruel Forest 100 NS 0288
Glendavan House 118 NJ 4301
Glendebadel Bay 99 NR 6295
Glen Dee 114 NN 9894
Glen Dessarry 114 NM 9593
Glen Devon (Tays.) 102 NN 9504
Glendevon (Tays.) 102 NN 9804
Glendevon Forest 102 NN 0006
Glendevon Reservoirs 102 NN 9204
Glendhu Forest 132 NC 2834
Glendhu Hill 90 NY 5686
Glen Diebidale 128 NH 4482
Glen Dochart 107 NN 4828
Glen Docherty 127 NH 0559
Glenduckie 108 NO 2818
Glendue Fell 83 NY 6454
Glen Duror 106 NN 0153
Glen Dye 119 NO 6384
Glendye Lodge 119 NO 6486
Glen Eagles 102 NN 9306
Gleneagles 102 NN 9308
Gleneagles Station 102 NN 9210
Glen Effock 118 NO 4478
Glenegedale 98 NR 3351
Glenegedale River 98 NR 3352
Glen Einig 127 NH 3698
Glen Elchaig 114 NG 9627
Glenelg 123 NG 8119
Glenelg Bay 123 NG 8019
Glen Ernan 118 NJ 3112
Glen Errochty 107 NN 7663
Glen Esk 119 NO 5377
Glen Etive 106 NN 1751
Glen Euchar 105 NM 8319
Glen Ey 117 NO 0985
Glen Falloch 107 NN 3622
Glenfarg (Tays.) 102 NO 1310
Glen Farg (Tays.) 102 NO 1413
Glenfarg Resr 102 NO 1011
Glenfarquhar Lodge 119 NO 7281
Glen Fenzie 118 NJ 3202
Glen Feochan 106 NM 8924
Glenferness House 129 NH 9342
Glen Feshie 117 NN 8594
Glenfeshie Forest 117 NN 8790
Glenfeshie Lodge 117 NN 8493
Glen Fiag 133 NC 4524
Glen Fiddich 121 NJ 3234
Glen Fiddich 121 NJ 3130
Glenfiddich Lodge 121 NJ 3132
Glenfield 61 SK 5306
Glen Finart 100 NS 1790
Glenfinart Forest 100 NS 1887
Glenfinart House 100 NS 1888
Glen Finglas 101 NN 5010
Glen Finglas Resr 101 NN 5209
Glen Finlet 108 NO 2267
Glenfinnan (Highld.) 114 NM 9080
Glen Finnan (Highld.) 114 NM 9083
Glenfoot 108 NO 1715
Glen Fruin 100 NS 2888
Glen Fyne (Strath.) 106 NN 2115
Glen Fyne (Strath.) 106 NS 1173
Glenfyne Lodge 106 NN 2215
Glen Gairn 118 NO 3399

Glengap Forest 88 NX 6460
Glengarnock 93 NS 3252
Glengarrisdale Bay 99 NR 6497
Glen Garry (Highld.) 115 NH 1300
Glen Garry (Tays.) 107 NN 7568
Glengarry Forest 115 NN 2396
Glen Garvan 114 NM 9675
Glengavel Reservoir 94 NS 6634
Glengavel Water 94 NS 6535
Glen Gelder 117 NO 2689
Glen Girnaig 108 NN 9366
Glen Glass 128 NH 5668
Glen Gloy 116 NN 2790
Glen Golly 133 NC 4243
Glen Golly River 132 NC 4144
Glengorm Castle 111 NM 4357
Glen Gour 106 NM 9463
Glengrasco 123 NG 4444
Glen Grudie 123 NG 9665
Glenhead Fm 108 NO 2562
Glenhoul 88 NX 6087
Glen Hurich 92 NR 7932
Glen House 96 NT 2932
Glen Iorsa 92 NR 9239
Gleniron Fell 86 NX 1962
Glenkens, The (dist.) 88 NX 5887
Glenkerry 89 NT 2710
Glen Kin 100 NS 1279
Glenkindie 114 NJ 4313
Glen Kingie 114 NN 0397
Glen Kinglass (Strath.) 116 NN 2109
Glen Kinglass (Strath.) 106 NN 1435
Glen Kyllachy 116 NH 7225
Glenlatterach 120 NJ 1954
Glenlatterach Resr 120 NJ 1953
Glen Lean 100 NS 0982
Glen Lednock 107 NN 7327
Glenlee (Dumf. and Galwy.) 88 NX 6080
Glen Lee (Tays.) 118 NO 3781
Glenlichorn 107 NN 7912
Glen Liver 106 NN 0835
Glenlivet 117 NJ 1929
Glenlivet 117 NJ 2126
Glen Loch 108 NN 9872
Glen Lochay 107 NN 4936
Glen Lochy 106 NN 2428
Glen Logie 108 NO 3168
Glen Lonan 106 NN 9427
Glenlood Hill 95 NT 0828
Glen Loth 134 NC 9312
Glen Loy 115 NN 1084
Glen Loyne 115 NH 1404
Glenluce 86 NX 1957
Glen Lui 108 NO 0492
Glen Luss 100 NS 3394
Glen Lussa 92 NR 7426
Glenlussa Water 92 NR 7226
Glen Lyon 107 NN 5646
Glenlyon House 107 NN 7347
Glenmaid Moor 88 NX 9689
Glen Mallie 115 NN 0887
Glen Mark 118 NO 3684
Glen Markie (Highld.) 116 NH 5708
Glen Markie (Highld.) 116 NN 5898
Glen Massan 100 NS 1286
Glenmavis 101 NS 7467
Glenmaye 76 SC 2380
Glen Mazeran 116 NH 7121
Glen More (Highld.) 116 NG 8818
Glen More (Highld.) 117 NH 9809
Glen More (Island of Mull) 105 NM 6029
Glenmore (Island of Skye) 123 NG 4340
Glen More (Strath.) 105 NM 8412
Glenmore Loch 117 NJ 0833
Glenmore Lodge 117 NH 9709
Glenmore River 123 NG 8519
Glen Moriston 115 NH 2411
Glen Mòr or Glen Albyn 116 NH 4211
Glenmorven Cottage 111 NM 5651
Glenmoy 109 NO 4064
Glenmuck Height 95 NT 0724
Glen Muick 118 NO 3187
Glenmuir 94 NS 6321
Glenmuirshaw 88 NS 6920
Glenmuir Water 88 NS 6719
Glen Nant 106 NN 0128
Glen Nevis 106 NN 1468
Glen Nevis House 106 NN 1272
Glen Noe 106 NN 0633
Glen of Artloch Croft 121 NJ 4839
Glen of Coachford 121 NJ 4646
Glen of Rothes 120 NJ 2454
Glen Ogle 107 NN 5726
Glen Orchy 106 NN 2635
Glen Orrin 128 NH 3449
Glen Oykel 132 NC 3111
Glen Parva 61 SP 5798
Glen Pean 114 NM 9490
Glen Prosen 108 NO 2967
Glenprosen Village 108 NO 3265
Glen Quaich 108 NN 8638
Glenquiech 109 NO 4211
Glen Quoich 114 NH 0206
Glenquoich Forest 114 NH 0304
Glenridding 83 NY 3817
Glenrigh Forest 106 NN 0663
Glen Rinnes 117 NJ 2834
Glenrisdell 99 NR 8658
Glen Rosa 92 NR 9838
Glen Rossal 128 NC 4604
Glenrothes 103 NO 2600
Glen Roy 116 NN 3088
Glensanda 105 NM 8246
Glen Sannox 92 NR 9844
Glensaugh 119 NO 6778
Glen Scaddle 106 NM 9667
Glen Shee (Tays.) 108 NN 9735
Glenshee (Tays.) 108 NN 9834
Glen Shee (Tays.) 108 NO 1362
Glenshero Lodge 116 NN 5493
Glen Shiel 114 NG 9614
Glenshieldaig Forest 123 NG 8349
Glenshiel Forest 114 NG 9413
Glen Shira 100 NN 1314
Glenshirra Forest 116 NN 4793
Glenside 131 NB 3615
Glen Sletdale 134 NC 9112
Glen Sligachan 123 NG 4927
Glensluain 100 NS 0999
Glens of Foudland 121 NJ 5934
Glen Spean 116 NN 3479
Glenstockadale 86 NX 0061
Glen Strae 106 NN 1531
Glen Strathfarrar 115 NH 3339
Glen Strathfarrar Forest 115 NH 2339
Glenstriven 100 NS 0878
Glen Tanar 118 NO 4594
Glen Tanar House 118 NO 4795
Glen Tarbert 115 NM 8960
Glen Tarff 115 NH 3902
Glen Tarken 107 NN 6626
Glen Tarsan 100 NS 0785
Glentenmont Height 89 NY 2986
Glentham 72 TF 0090
Glen Tig 86 NX 1382
Glen Tilt 108 NN 9172
Glen Tolsta 131 NB 5244
Glentoo Loch 88 NX 7062
Glen Torridon 126 NG 9456

Glentress 95 NT 2839
Glentress Forest 95 NT 2841
Glen Tromie 116 NN 7694
Glentromie Lodge 116 NN 7796
Glen Trool 86 NX 4080
Glen Trool Forest 86 NX 4180
Glentrool Forest 86 NX 3581
Glentrool Village 86 NX 3578
Glentrosdale Bay 98 NM 6700
Glen Truim 116 NN 6789
Glentruim House 116 NN 6895
Glen Turret 107 NN 8226
Glentworth 72 SK 9488
Glenuig Bay 111 NM 6778
Glen Urquhart 106 NN 0647
Glenurquhart Forest 116 NH 4430
Glen Village 116 NH 4428
Glen Varragill 123 NG 4837
Glen Vine 102 NS 8878
Glen Water 94 NS 5739
Glenwhappen Rig 95 NT 0625
Glenwhilly 86 NX 1772
Gleouraich (mt.) 115 NH 0405
Glespin 95 NS 8028
Gletness 141 HU 4651
Glevum (ant.) 46 SO 8318
Glewstone 45 SO 5522
Glimps Holm 136 ND 4799
Glinton 62 TF 1506
Glog Hill 45 SO 2169
Glooston 61 SP 7596
Glossop 79 SK 0393
Gloster Hill 91 NU 2504
Gloucester 46 SO 8318
Gloucester and Sharpness Canal 46 SO 7305
Gloucester & Cheltenham (Staverton) Airport 46 SO 8821
Gloup 143 HP 5004
Gloup Holm 143 HP 5004
Gloup Ness 143 HP 5005
Glusburn 78 SE 0344
Gluss 142 HU 3477
Gluss Isle 142 HU 3778
Gluss Voe 142 HU 3678
Gluss Water 142 HU 2581
Glutt Lodge 134 NC 9936
Glutt Water 134 NC 9935
Glyder Fawr (mt.) 67 SH 6457
Glympton 47 SP 4221
Glynarthen 43 SN 3148
Glyn Ceiriog 58 SJ 2038
Glyncorrwg 41 SS 8799
Glyn-Cywarch 41 SH 6034
Glynde 29 TQ 4509
Glyndebourne 29 TQ 4510
Glyn Dyfrdwy 58 SJ 1542
Glyn-Neath 41 SN 8806
Glynogwr 41 SS 9587
Glyntaff 41 ST 0889
Glyn Tarell 41 SN 9823
Glynteg 43 SN 3637
Glyntrefnant 57 SN 9192
Gnosall 59 SJ 8220
Gnosall Heath 59 SJ 8220
Goadby 61 SP 7598
Goadby Marwood 61 SK 7826
Goatacre 34 SU 0176
Goat Fell 92 NR 9941
Goathill 32 ST 6717
Goathland 80 NZ 8301
Goathland Moor 80 SE 8597
Goathurst 32 ST 2534
Gob a' Chuaille 126 NG 8496
Gob an Tolmachain 125 NB 0904
Gob Dubh 58 NR 6385
Gobernuisgach Lodge 133 NC 4341
Goblin's Cave 101 NN 4807
Gob na h-Airde Moire 130 NB 0117
Gob na h-Oa 122 NG 3134
Gob na Hoe 122 NG 1954
Gob na Milaid 131 NB 4211
Gobowen 58 SJ 3033
Gob Rubh' Uisenis 125 NB 3503
Gob Shilldinish 131 NB 4631
Gob y Deigan 76 SC 2887
Gödag (is.) 111 NM 4181
Godalming 28 SU 9743
Godington 31 SP 6327
Godmanchester 53 TL 2470
Godmanstone 17 SY 6697
Godmersham 31 TR 0650
Godney 33 ST 4842
Godolphin Cross 4 SW 6031
Godre'r-graig 41 SN 7507
Godrevy Island 18 SW 5743
Godshill (Hants.) 26 SU 1714
Godshill (I. of W.) 27 SZ 5281
Godstone 29 TQ 3551
Godstone Station 29 TQ 3648
Goetre 45 SO 3205
Goff's Oak 37 TL 3202
Gogar 102 NT 1672
Goginan 57 SN 6981
Gog Magog Hills 53 TL 4954
Golan 66 SH 5242
Golant 19 SX 1254
Golberdon 4 SX 3271
Golborne 69 SJ 6097
Golcar 78 SE 0915
Goldcliff 32 ST 3683
Golden Cross 29 TQ 5312
Golden Green 29 TQ 6348
Golden Grove 43 SN 5919
Goldenhill 59 SJ 8553
Golden Pot 35 SU 7143
Golden Valley (Glos.) 46 SO 9022
Golden Valley (Here. and Worc.) 45 SO 3537
Golders Green 37 TQ 2488
Goldhanger 38 TL 9009
Golding 59 SJ 5403
Goldsborough (N Yorks.) 85 NZ 8314
Goldsborough (N Yorks.) 79 SE 3856
Goldsithney 18 SW 5430
Goldthorpe 71 SE 4604
Gollanfield 129 NH 8053
Golspie 129 NH 8399
Golspie Burn 129 NC 8103
Golval 134 NC 8962
Gomersal 78 SE 2026
Gometra (is.) 104 NM 3640
Gomshall 37 TQ 0847
Gonachan 94 NS 6187
Gonalston 71 SK 6847
Gon Firth (Shetld.) 141 HU 3662
Gonfirth (Shetld.) 141 HU 3761
Goodber Common 77 SD 6263
Good Easter 38 TL 6212
Gooderstone 63 TF 7602
Goodleigh 23 SS 5934
Goodmanham 74 SE 8842
Goodnestone (Kent) 31 TR 0461
Goodnestone (Kent) 31 TR 2554
Goodrich 45 SO 5719
Goodrington 19 SX 8958
Goodwick 42 SM 9438
Goodwin Sands 31 TR 4455
Goodwood House 28 SU 8808
Goodworth Clatford 34 SU 3642
Goodyers End 50 SP 3385
Goole 74 SE 7423

Goole Fields 74 SE 7519
Goonbell 18 SW 7249
Goonhavern 19 SW 7953
Goonhilly Downs 18 SW 7120
Gooseham 22 SS 2316
Goosetrey 69 SJ 7769
Goosey 34 SU 3591
Gop Hill 67 SJ 0880
Gordon 96 NT 6443
Gordonbush 134 NC 8409
Gordonstoun 129 NJ 1868
Gordonstown (Grampn.) 121 NJ 5656
Gordonstown (Grampn.) 121 NJ 7138
Gorebridge 103 NT 3461
Gorefield 63 TF 4112
Gore Sand 32 ST 2851
Goring 35 SU 6080
Goring-by-Sea 28 TQ 1102
Gorleston on Sea 65 TG 5203
Gorley 26 SU 1511
Gorllwyn 44 SN 9159
Gorm Loch 132 NC 2144
Gorm-loch Beag 133 NC 7027
Gorm-loch (Highld.) 132 NC 3124
Gorm-loch Mòr (Highld.) 134 NC 7123
Gorple Resrs 78 SD 9123
Gorpley Resr 78 SD 9123
Gorrachie 121 NJ 7358
Gorran Haven 19 SX 0141
Gors 57 SN 6277
Gorsedd 68 SJ 1476
Gorsedd Brân 67 SH 9760
Gorseinon 40 SS 5998
Gorseness 136 HY 4119
Gors-goch 57 SN 9393
Gorslas 45 SN 5713
Gorsley 46 SO 6826
Gorstan 127 NH 3862
Gorsty Common 45 SO 4537
Gortantaoid 98 NR 3373
Gortantaoid Point 98 NR 3374
Gorton 55 SJ 8996
Gosbeck 55 TM 1555
Gosberton 63 TF 2331
Goseland Hill 95 NT 0735
Gosfield 54 TL 7829
Gosford Bay 103 NT 4478
Gosford House 103 NT 4578
Gosforth (Cumbr.) 82 NY 0603
Gosforth (Tyne and Wear) 91 NZ 2467
Gosmore 52 TL 1927
Gosport 27 SZ 6199
Gossabrough 141 HU 5383
Gossa Water (Shetld.) 141 HU 3045
Gossa Water (Shetld.) 141 HU 4360
Gossa Water (Yell) 143 HU 4899
Goswick 97 NU 0545
Gote o' Tram (pt.) 135 ND 3648
Gotham 61 SK 5330
Gotherington 46 SO 9629
Gott 141 HU 4345
Gott Bay 104 NM 0546
Goudhurst 29 TQ 7337
Goulceby 73 TF 2579
Gourdas 121 NJ 7741
Gourdon 109 NO 8270
Gourock 100 NS 2477
Gouthwaite Reservoir 79 SE 1368
Govan 101 NS 5464
Goveton 21 SX 7546
Govig 130 NB 0109
Gowanhill 121 NK 0363
Gowanwell 56 SE 6122
Gower (Highld.) 128 NH 5057
Gower (W Glam.) 40 SS 5290
Gowerton 40 SS 5896
Gowkhall 102 NT 0589
Goxhill (Humbs.) 75 TA 1021
Goxhill (Humbs.) 75 TA 1844
Goyle Hill 119 NO 6881
Goyt's Moss 70 SK 0072
Graddon Moor 22 SS 4602
Graemsay 136 HY 2505
Graffham (W Susx) 28 SU 9216
Graffham (Cambs.) 52 TL 1669
Grafham Water 52 TL 1468
Grafton (Here. and Worc.) 45 SO 4937
Grafton (Here. and Worc.) 45 SO 5761
Grafton (N Yorks.) 79 SE 4163
Grafton (Oxon.) 47 SP 2600
Grafton Flyford 50 SO 9655
Grafton Regis 51 SP 7546
Grafton Underwood 52 SP 9280
Grafty Green 30 TQ 8748
Graianrhyd 58 SJ 2156
Graig (Clwyd.) 67 SJ 0872
Graig (Gwyn.) 67 SH 8071
Graig Fawr 56 SN 6207
Graig-fechan 58 SJ 1454
Graig Goch 67 SH 7108
Graig Penllyn 41 SS 9777
Graig Wen 67 SH 7339
Grain 30 TQ 8876
Grainsby 73 TF 2799
Grainthorpe 73 TF 3896
Graizelound 71 SK 7798
Grampian Mountains (Central - Tays.) 107 NN 4151
Grampian Mountains (Grampn.) 117 NJ 9200
Grampound 19 SW 9348
Grampound Road 19 SW 9150
Gramsdale 124 NF 8255
Granborough 51 SP 7625
Granby 62 SK 7536
Grandborough 50 SP 4866
Grandtully 108 NN 9152
Grandtully Castle 108 NN 8951
Grandtully Hill 108 NN 9147
Grand Union Canal (Bucks.) 36 SP 8742
Grand Union Canal (Warw.) 50 SP 2466
Grange (Cumbr.) 82 NY 2517
Grange (Mers.) 68 SJ 2286
Grange (N Yorks.) 85 SE 5796
Grange (Tays.) 108 NO 2725
Grange Crossroads 121 NJ 4754
Grange Hall 129 NJ 0660
Grange Heath 25 SY 9083
Grange Hill 37 TQ 4492
Grange Moor 78 SE 2216
Grangemouth 102 NS 9281
Grange of Lindores 108 NO 2516
Grange-over-Sands 77 SD 4077
Grangepans 102 NT 0282
Grange, The 18 SU 5636
Grangetown 84 NZ 5420
Grange Villa 84 NZ 2352
Granish 117 NH 8914
Gransmoor 81 TA 1259
Granston 42 SM 8934
Grantchester 53 TL 4355
Grantham 62 SK 9135
Grantham Canal 61 SK 7431
Grantley 79 SE 2369
Grantlodge 121 NJ 7017
Granton (Dumf. and Galwy.) 89 NT 0709
Granton (Lothian) 103 NT 2277
Grantown-on-Spey 117 NJ 0327
Grantshouse 97 NT 8065

Grappenhall ... 69 SJ 6385
Grasby ... 74 TA 0804
Grasmere (Cumbr.) ... 82 NY 3307
Grasmere (Cumbr.) ... 82 NY 3406
Grasscroft ... 70 SD 9804
Grassendale ... 68 SJ 3985
Grassholme ... 84 NY 9221
Grassholme Resr ... 84 NY 9422
Grassington ... 78 SE 0064
Grassmoor ... 71 SK 4067
Grass Point ... 105 NM 7430
Grassthorpe ... 72 SK 7967
Grassy Cletts ... 136 ND 2887
Grateley ... 34 SU 2741
Gratwich ... 60 SK 0231
Graveley (Cambs.) ... 53 TL 2564
Graveley (Herts.) ... 53 TL 2328
Gravelly Hill ... 50 SP 1090
Gravels ... 58 SJ 3300
Graveney ... 31 TR 0562
Gravesend ... 30 TQ 6473
Gravir ... 131 NB 3815
Grayingham ... 72 SK 9395
Grayrigg ... 83 SD 5797
Grays ... 30 TQ 6177
Grayshott ... 27 SU 8735
Grayswood ... 28 SU 9234
Graythorp ... 85 NZ 5227
Grazeley ... 36 SU 6966
Gréabhal (mt.) ... 124 NG 0089
Grean ... 112 NF 6703
Greanamul (Barra) ... 112 NF 7305
Greanamul (W Isles) ... 112 NL 6289
Greanamul Deas ... 124 NF 8848
Greasbrough ... 71 SK 4195
Greasby ... 68 SJ 2587
Great Abington ... 53 TL 5348
Great Addington ... 52 SP 9575
Great Altar ... 50 SP 1159
Great Altcar ... 68 SD 3206
Great Amwell ... 37 TL 3712
Great Asby ... 83 NY 6813
Great Ashfield ... 54 TM 0068
Great Ayton ... 85 NZ 5510
Great Baddow ... 38 TL 7204
Great Bardfield ... 54 TL 6730
Great Barford ... 52 TL 1352
Great Barr ... 60 SP 0495
Great Barrington ... 47 SP 2013
Great Barrow ... 68 SJ 4668
Great Barton ... 54 TL 8967
Great Barugh ... 80 SE 7478
Great Bavington ... 91 NY 9880
Great Bedwyn ... 34 SU 2764
Great Bentley ... 39 TM 1121
Great Bernera (is.) ... 131 NB 1635
Great Billing ... 52 SP 8162
Great Bircham ... 64 TF 7632
Great Blakenham ... 55 TM 1150
Great Bolas ... 59 SJ 6421
Great Bookham ... 28 TQ 1454
Great Borne (mt.) ... 82 NY 1216
Great Bosullow ... SW 4133
Great Bourton ... 52 SP 4545
Great Bowden ... 51 SP 7488
Great Bradley ... 54 TL 6753
Great Braxted ... 38 TL 8614
Great Bricett ... 54 TM 0350
Great Brickhill ... 52 SP 9030
Great Bridgeford ... 59 SJ 8827
Great Brington ... 51 SP 6665
Great Bromley ... 55 TM 0826
Great Broughton ... 85 NZ 5406
Great Budworth ... 69 SJ 6677
Great Burbo Bank (sbk.) ... 68 SJ 2597
Great Burdon ... 84 NZ 3116
Great Burstead ... 38 TQ 6892
Great Busby ... 85 NZ 5105
Great Calva ... 82 NY 2831
Great Canfield ... 38 TL 5917
Great Carlton ... 73 TF 4185
Great Casterton ... 62 TF 0009
Great Chart ... 31 TQ 9842
Great Chatwell ... 59 SJ 7914
Great Chesterford ... 53 TL 5042
Great Cheverell ... 34 ST 9858
Great Chishill ... 53 TL 4238
Great Clacton ... 39 TM 1716
Great Coates ... 75 TA 2310
Great Comberton ... 50 SO 9542
Great Corby ... 83 NY 4754
Great Cornard ... 54 TL 8840
Great Coxwell ... 47 SU 2693
Great Cransley ... 52 SP 8376
Great Cressingham ... 64 TF 8501
Great Crosby ... 68 SJ 3199
Great Cubley ... 60 SK 1637
Great Cumbrae Island ... 93 NS 1656
Great Dalby ... 61 SK 7414
Great Dodd (mt.) ... 82 NY 3420
Great Doddington ... 52 SP 8864
Great Driffield ... 81 TA 0257
Great Dunham ... 64 TF 8714
Great Dunmow ... 38 TL 6221
Great Durnford ... 34 SU 1338
Great Easton (Essex) ... 54 TL 6125
Great Easton (Leic.) ... 62 SP 8493
Great Eau ... 73 TF 4485
Great Eccleston ... 77 SD 4240
Great Edstone ... 80 SE 7084
Great Ellingham ... 64 TM 0196
Great Elm ... 33 ST 7449
Great End (mt.) ... 82 NY 2208
Great Eversden ... 53 TL 3653
Great Fen ... 54 TL 5978
Great Finborough ... 54 TM 0157
Greatford ... 62 TF 0811
Great Fransham ... 64 TF 8913
Great Gable ... 82 NY 2110
Great Gaddesden ... 36 TL 0211
Great Gidding ... 52 TL 1183
Great Givendale ... 80 SE 8153
Great Glemham ... 55 TM 3361
Great Glen ... 61 SP 6597
Great Gonerby ... 62 SK 8938
Great Gransden ... 53 TL 2756
Great Green (Norf.) ... 55 TM 2789
Great Green (Suff.) ... 54 TL 9155
Great Habton ... 80 SE 7576
Great Hallingbury ... 37 TL 5119
Greatham (Cleve.) ... 85 NZ 4927
Greatham (Hants.) ... 27 SU 7730
Greatham (W Susx) ... 28 TQ 0415
Great Hampden ... 36 SP 8402
Great Harrowden ... 52 SP 8871
Great Harwood ... 77 SD 7332
Great Haseley ... 36 SP 6401
Great Hatfield ... 75 TA 1842
Great Haw (mt.) ... 78 SE 0779
Great Haywood ... 60 SJ 9922
Great Heck ... 71 SE 5920
Great Henny ... 54 TL 8738
Great Hill ... 88 NX 9492
Great Hinton ... 33 ST 9058
Great Hockham ... 54 TL 9592
Great Holland ... 39 TM 2119
Great Horkesley ... 54 TL 9731
Great Hormead ... 53 TL 4030
Great Horwood ... 51 SP 7731
Great Houghton (Northants.) ... 51 SP 7958
Great Houghton (S Yorks.) ... 71 SE 4206
Great Hucklow ... 70 SK 1777

Great Kelk ... 81 TA 1058
Great Kingshill ... 36 SU 8798
Great Lake (Notts.) ... 71 SK 5773
Great Lake (N Yorks) ... 80 SE 7170
Great Langton ... 84 SE 2996
Great Law ... 96 NT 4041
Great Leighs ... 38 TL 7317
Great Limber ... 75 TA 1308
Great Linford ... 52 SP 8542
Great Livermere ... 54 TL 8871
Great Longstone ... 70 SK 1971
Great Lumley ... 84 NZ 2949
Great Lyth ... 58 SJ 4507
Great Malvern ... 49 SO 7845
Great Maplestead ... 54 TL 8034
Great Marton ... 77 SD 3335
Great Massingham ... 64 TF 7922
Great Mew Stone (is.) ... 20 SX 5047
Great Milton ... 36 SP 6302
Great Missenden ... 36 SP 8901
Great Mis Tor ... 21 SX 5676
Great Mitton ... 77 SD 7138
Great Mongeham ... 31 TR 3451
Greatmoor Hill ... 89 NT 4800
Great Moulton ... 55 TM 1690
Great Musgrave ... 83 NY 7613
Great Ness ... 58 SJ 3918
Great Oakley (Essex) ... 55 TM 1927
Great Oakley (Northants.) ... 52 SP 8686
Great Offley ... 52 TL 1427
Great Ormes Head ... 67 SH 7584
Great Ormside ... 83 NY 7017
Great Orton ... 82 NY 3254
Great Oxendon ... 51 SP 7383
Great Palgrave ... 64 TF 8312
Great Pardon ... 37 TL 4308
Great Paxton ... 52 TL 2164
Great Pinseat (mt.) ... 84 NY 9702
Great Plumstead ... 65 TG 2910
Great Ponton ... 62 SK 9230
Great Postland ... 63 TF 2612
Great Preston ... 78 SE 4029
Great Raveley ... 53 TL 2581
Great Ridge ... 25 ST 9236
Great Rissington ... 47 SP 1917
Great Rollright ... 47 SP 3231
Great Ryburgh ... 64 TF 9627
Great Ryle ... 91 NU 0212
Great Saling ... 38 TL 7025
Great Salkeld ... 83 NY 5536
Great Sampford ... 54 TL 6435
Great Sankey ... 69 SJ 5688
Great Saxham ... 54 TL 7862
Great Shefford ... 34 SU 3875
Great Shelford ... 53 TL 4652
Great Shunner Fell ... 83 SD 8497
Great Shutter Rock ... SS 1343
Great Smeaton ... 85 NZ 3404
Great Snoring ... 64 TF 9434
Great Somerford ... 34 ST 9682
Great Stainton ... 85 NZ 3322
Great Stambridge ... 38 TQ 8991
Great Staughton ... 73 TF 4364
Great Steeping ... 73 TF 4364
Great Stonar ... 31 TR 3359
Greatstone-on-Sea ... 31 TR 0822
Great Stour ... 31 TR 0651
Great Strickland ... 83 NY 5522
Great Stukeley ... 53 TL 2275
Great Sturton ... 73 TF 2176
Great Swinburne ... 90 NY 9375
Great Tew ... 47 SP 3929
Great Tey ... 54 TL 8925
Great Torrington ... 22 SS 4919
Great Tosson ... 91 NU 0300
Great Totham (Essex) ... 38 TL 8511
Great Totham (Essex) ... 38 TL 8613
Great Wakering ... 38 TQ 9487
Great Waldingfield ... 54 TL 9143
Great Walsingham ... 64 TF 9437
Great Waltham ... 38 TL 6913
Great Warley ... 37 TQ 5890
Great Washbourne ... 46 SO 9834
Great Welnetham ... 54 TL 8759
Great Wenham ... 54 TM 0738
Great Whernside (mt.) ... 78 SE 0074
Great Whittington ... 91 NZ 0070
Great Wigborough ... 39 TL 9615
Great Wilbraham ... 53 TL 5557
Great Wishford ... 26 SU 0835
Great Witcombe ... 46 SO 9014
Great Witley ... 49 SO 7566
Great Wolford ... 47 SP 2434
Greatworth ... 51 SP 5542
Great Wratting ... 54 TL 6848
Great Wyrley ... 60 SJ 9907
Great Wytheford ... 59 SJ 5719
Great Yarmouth ... 65 TG 5207
Great Yeldham ... 54 TL 7638
Greave ... 104 NM 2420
Greeb Point ... 19 SW 8733
Greenbooth Resr ... 69 SD 8915
Greenburn ... 102 NS 9360
Greendikes ... 91 NU 0628
Greenfield (Beds.) ... 52 TL 0534
Greenfield (Clwyd) ... 68 SJ 1977
Greenfield (Gtr Mches.) ... 70 SD 9904
Greenfield (Highld.) ... 115 NH 2000
Greenfield (Oxon.) ... 36 SU 7191
Greenford ... 37 TQ 1382
Greengairs ... 101 NS 7870
Greenham ... 34 SU 4865
Green Hammerton ... 79 SE 4656
Greenhaugh ... 91 NY 7987
Green Head (Hoy, Orkney) ... 136 ND 3099
Greenhead (Northum.) ... 90 NY 6665
Greenhill (Central) ... 101 NS 8278
Greenhill (Gtr London) ... 37 TQ 1688
Green Hill (Northum.) ... 84 NY 8647
Greenhill (S Yorks) ... 71 SK 3481
Green Hill (Wilts.) ... 34 SU 0686
Greenhithe ... 30 TQ 5974
Greenholm ... 94 NS 5637
Greenholme ... 83 NY 5905
Greenhouse ... 96 NT 5523
Greenhow Hill ... 78 SE 1164
Greenigoe ... 136 HY 4107
Greenland ... 135 ND 2367
Green Law (Borders) ... 97 NT 6304
Greenlaw (Borders) ... 96 NT 7145
Greenlee Lough ... 90 NY 7669
Greenli Ness ... 137 HY 6221
Greenloaning ... 101 NN 8307
Green Lowther ... 88 NS 8911
Green Mount ... 69 SD 7714
Greenock ... 100 NS 2776
Greenodd ... 82 SD 3182
Green Ore ... 33 ST 5749
Green Road Station ... 76 SD 1984
Green Scar ... 42 SM 7922
Greenside ... 91 NZ 1362
Greensidehill ... 91 NT 9716
Greenside Reservoir ... 101 NS 4775
Greensides (mt.) ... 86 NX 2889
Greenskairs ... 121 NJ 7863
Greens Norton ... 51 SP 6649
Greenstead Green ... 54 TL 8227
Greensted ... 37 TL 5302
Greenstone Point ... 126 NG 8598
Green Street ... 37 TQ 1998
Green Street Green ... 37 TQ 4663
Green, The (Cumbr.) ... 76 SD 1784

Green, The (Wilts.) ... 25 ST 8731
Greenwich ... 37 TQ 4077
Greet ... 46 SP 0230
Greeta River or River Creed ... 131 NB 3632
Greete ... 48 SO 5770
Greetham (Leic.) ... 62 SK 9214
Greetham (Lincs.) ... 73 TF 3070
Greetland ... 78 SE 0821
Greg Ness ... 119 NJ 9704
Gregson Lane ... 77 SD 5926
Greian Head ... 112 NF 6404
Greinton ... 24 ST 4136
Gremista ... 141 HU 4643
Grendon (Northants.) ... 52 SP 8760
Grendon (Warw.) ... 60 SP 2799
Grendon Common ... 60 SP 2799
Grendon Green ... 45 SO 5957
Grendon Underwood ... 36 SP 6720
Grenitote ... 124 NF 8275
Grenoside ... 71 SK 3394
Gresford ... 58 SJ 3454
Gresham ... 65 TG 1738
Greshornish ... 122 NG 3454
Greshornish Point ... 122 NG 3456
Gress ... 131 NB 4942
Gressenhall ... 64 TF 9615
Gressenhall Green ... 64 TF 9616
Gressingham ... 77 SD 5769
Gress River ... 131 NB 4545
Greta Bridge ... 84 NZ 0813
Gretna ... 89 NY 3167
Gretna Green ... 89 NY 3268
Gretton (Glos.) ... 46 SP 0030
Gretton (Northants.) ... 52 SP 8994
Gretton (Shrops.) ... 59 SO 5195
Grewelthorpe ... 78 SE 2276
Grey Cairns (ant.) ... 135 ND 2544
Greygarth ... 78 SE 1872
Grey Head ... 138 HY 5740
Grey Hill ... 86 NX 1692
Grey Mare's Tail (mt.) ... 89 NT 1814
Greysouthen ... 82 NY 0729
Greystoke ... 83 NY 4330
Greystone ... 109 NO 5343
Greywell ... 35 SU 7151
Gribbin Head ... 19 SX 0949
Griff ... 50 SP 3588
Griffithstown ... 45 ST 2999
Grif Skerry ... 141 HU 6362
Grigghall ... 83 SD 4691
Grike (mt.) ... 82 NY 0814
Grimeford Village ... 69 SD 6112
Grime's Graves (ant.) ... 54 TL 8189
Grimes Hill ... 77 SD 6286
Grimethorpe ... 71 SE 4109
Griminish ... 124 NF 7851
Griminish Point ... 124 NF 7276
Grimister ... 143 HU 4693
Grimley ... 49 SO 8360
Grimness (S. Ronaldsay) ... 136 ND 4793
Grim Ness (S.Ronaldsay) ... 136 ND 4992
Grimoldby ... 73 TF 3988
Grimsargh ... 77 SD 5834
Grimsay ... 124 NF 8656
Grimsby ... 75 TA 2810
Grimscote ... 51 SP 6553
Grimscott ... 23 SS 2606
Grimshader ... 131 NB 4025
Grimspound (ant.) ... 21 SX 7080
Grimsthorpe ... 62 TF 0423
Grimston (Leic.) ... 61 SK 6821
Grimston (Norf.) ... 64 TF 7221
Grimstone ... 25 SY 6393
Grimwith Resr. ... 78 SE 0664
Grindale ... 81 TA 1371
Grindle ... 59 SJ 7403
Grindleford ... 71 SK 2477
Grindleton ... 78 SD 7545
Grindlow ... 70 SK 1877
Grind of the Navir (pt.) ... 142 HU 2180
Grindon (Northum.) ... 97 NT 9144
Grindon (Staffs.) ... 60 SK 0854
Gringley on the Hill ... 72 SK 7390
Grinsdale ... 82 NY 3758
Grinshill ... 59 SJ 5223
Grinton ... 84 SE 0498
Griomaval (mt.) ... 130 NB 0122
Grisedale ... 83 NY 3715
Grisedale Pike ... 82 NY 1922
Grisedale Tarn ... 82 NY 3512
Grishipoll ... 110 NM 1959
Griskerry ... 141 HU 3622
Gristhorpe ... 81 TA 0882
Griston ... 64 TL 9499
Gritley ... 137 HY 5605
Grittenham ... 34 SU 0382
Grittleton ... 33 ST 8579
Grizebeck ... 76 SD 2384
Grizedale ... 82 SD 3394
Grizedale Forest ... 82 SD 3394
Groatay ... 124 NF 9773
Groay ... 124 NG 0079
Groban (mt.) ... 127 NH 0970
Grob Bàgh ... 92 NR 6346
Grobister ... 137 HY 6524
Groby ... 61 SK 5207
Groemeshall Burn ... 136 HY 4704
Groes (Clwyd) ... 67 SJ 0064
Groes (W Glam.) ... 41 SS 7986
Groes-faen ... 41 ST 0780
Groesffordd Marli ... 67 SJ 0073
Groeslon ... 66 SH 4755
Grogport ... 92 NR 8044
Gronant ... 67 SJ 0883
Groombridge ... 29 TQ 5337
Grosebay ... 125 NG 1592
Grosmont (Gwent) ... 45 SO 4024
Grosmont (N Yorks.) ... 80 NZ 8205
Groton ... 54 TL 9641
Grove (Dorset) ... 25 SY 6972
Grove (Kent) ... 31 TR 2362
Grove (Notts.) ... 72 SK 7379
Grove (Oxon.) ... 34 SU 4090
Grovely Wood ... 26 SU 0534
Grove Park ... 37 TQ 4172
Grovesend ... 40 SN 5900
Grudie Burn ... 128 NC 5305
Grudie River ... 132 NC 3161
Gruids ... 128 NC 5604
Gruinard Bay ... 126 NG 9293
Gruinard House ... 126 NG 9692
Gruinard Island ... 126 NG 9494
Gruinard River ... 126 NG 9789
Gruinart ... 98 NR 2866
Grula ... 122 NG 3826
Gruline ... 105 NM 5440
Gruline House ... 105 NM 5539
Grumbla ... 18 SW 4029
Grumby Rock ... 133 NC 7010
Gruna (is.) ... 142 HU 2859
Grunasound ... 141 HU 3733
Gruna Stack ... 142 HU 2886
Grunay ... 143 HU 6971
Grundisburgh ... 55 TM 2251
Gruney (is.) ... 143 HU 3896
Grunka Hellier ... 143 HP 5815
Gruting ... 140 HU 2849
Gruting Voe ... 140 HU 2647
Grutness ... 141 HU 4009

Grut Wick ... 141 HU 5138
Grwyne Fechan ... 45 SO 2324
Gryfe Reservoirs ... 100 NS 2871
Gualachulain ... 106 NN 1145
Gualann (mt.) ... 101 NS 4594
Gualann Mhòr ... 119 NR 9062
Guardbridge ... 109 NO 4519
Guarlford ... 49 SO 8145
Guay ... 108 NO 0049
Guens, The (is.) ... 143 HU 6568
Guestling Green ... 30 TQ 8513
Guestwick ... 64 TG 0627
Gugh ... 18 SV 8908
Guide Post ... 91 NZ 2585
Guilden Morden ... 53 TL 2744
Guilden Sutton ... 68 SJ 4468
Guildford ... 28 TQ 0049
Guildtown ... 108 NO 1331
Guillamon Island ... 123 NG 6327
Guilsborough ... 51 SP 6773
Guilsfield ... 58 SJ 2111
Guiraсdeal ... 105 NM 6907
Guirdil Bay ... 110 NG 3101
Guisachan Forest ... 115 NH 2520
Guisborough ... 85 NZ 6115
Guiseley ... 78 SE 1941
Guist ... 64 TF 9925
Guiting Power ... 46 SP 0924
Gulber Wick ... 141 HU 4438
Gulf of Corryvreckan ... 99 NM 6901
Gulland Rock ... 19 SW 8778
Gullane ... 103 NT 4882
Gullane Bay ... 103 NT 4783
Gull Point ... 93 NS 1450
Gulval ... 18 SW 4831
Gulvain or Gaor Bheinn ... 114 NM 9987
Gumfreston ... 42 SN 1101
Gumley ... 51 SP 6890
Gunby (Humbs.) ... 74 SE 7135
Gunby (Lincs.) ... 62 SK 9021
Gundleton ... 27 SU 6133
Gunfleet Sand ... 39 TM 2611
Gunn ... 138 SS 6333
Gunna (is.) ... 110 NM 0951
Gunnerside ... 84 SD 9598
Gunnerton ... 90 NY 9074
Gunness ... 74 SE 8411
Gunnislake ... 20 SX 4371
Gunnista ... 141 HU 5043
Gunthorpe (Norf.) ... 64 TG 0135
Gunthorpe (Notts.) ... 61 SK 6744
Gunton Hall ... 65 TG 2234
Gunton Sta ... 65 TG 2535
Gunver Head ... 19 SW 8977
Gunwalloe Fishing Cove ... 18 SW 6522
Gurnard ... 27 SZ 4795
Gurnard Bay ... 27 SZ 4795
Gurnard's Head ... 18 SW 4338
Gurn Ddu ... 66 SH 4046
Gurney Slade ... 33 ST 6249
Gurnos ... 41 SN 7709
Gussage All Saints ... 26 SU 0010
Gussage St. Michael ... 26 ST 9811
Guston ... 31 TR 3244
Gutcher ... 143 HU 5498
Guthrie ... 109 NO 5650
Gutter Sound ... 136 ND 3197
Guyhirn ... 63 TF 3903
Guy's Head ... 63 TF 4825
Guy's Marsh ... 25 ST 8420
Guyzance ... 91 NU 2103
Gwaelod-y-garth ... 41 ST 1183
Gwaenysgor ... 67 SJ 0780
Gwalchmai ... 66 SH 3975
Gwastad ... 42 SO 2305
Gwastedyn Hill ... 57 SN 9866
Gwaun-Cae-Gurwen ... 40 SN 7011
Gwaunceste Hill ... 44 SO 1555
Gwaun Nant-ddu ... 45 SO 0017
Gwaynynog ... 67 SJ 0365
Gwbert-on-Sea ... 55 SN 1650
Gweek ... 18 SW 7026
Gwehelog ... 45 SO 3804
Gwenddwr ... 44 SO 0643
Gwendraeth (sbk.) ... 43 SN 3606
Gwendraeth Fàch ... 43 SN 4714
Gwendraeth Fawr ... 43 SN 5011
Gwennap ... 18 SW 7340
Gwennap Head ... 18 SW 3621
Gwenter ... 18 SW 7418
Gwernaffield ... 68 SJ 2064
Gwernesney ... 45 SO 4101
Gwernogle ... 43 SN 5234
Gwernymynydd ... 68 SJ 2162
Gwespyr ... 68 SJ 1183
Gwinear ... 18 SW 5937
Gwithian ... 18 SW 5841
Gwrhyd ... 44 SN 9339
Gwrych Castle ... 67 SH 9277
Gwyddelwern ... 67 SJ 0746
Gwyddgrug ... 43 SN 4635
Gwytherin ... 67 SH 8761
Gylchedd ... 67 SH 8644
Gypsey Race ... 81 TA 0970

H

Haaf Gruney (is.) ... 143 HU 6398
Haa, The (pt.) ... 141 HU 5560
Habberley (Here. and Worc.) ... 49 SO 8077
Habberley (Shrops.) ... 58 SJ 3903
Habitancum (ant.) ... 90 NY 8986
Habost (Isle of Lewis) ... 131 NB 3219
Habost (Isle of Lewis) ... 131 NB 5262
Habrough ... 75 TA 1514
Haccombe ... 21 SX 8970
Haceby ... 62 TF 0236
Hacheston ... 55 TM 3059
Hackenthorpe ... 71 SK 4183
Hackford ... 64 TG 0502
Hackforth ... 84 SE 2493
Hackland ... 136 HY 3920
Hacklete ... 131 NB 1534
Hackleton ... 51 SP 8055
Hackley Head or Forvie Ness ... 121 NK 0226
Hackness (N Yorks...) ... 81 SE 9690
Hackness (South Walls) ... 136 ND 3391
Hacko's Ness ... 137 HY 5215
Hackpen Hill (Devon) ... 24 ST 1112
Hackpen Hill (Wilts.) ... 34 SU 1274
Hacks Ness ... 139 HY 6134
Hackthorn ... 72 SK 9882
Hackthorpe ... 83 NY 5423
Haconby ... 62 TF 1025
Hadden ... 97 NT 7836
Haddenham (Bucks.) ... 36 SP 7408
Haddenham (Cambs.) ... 53 TL 4675
Haddington ... 103 NT 5174
Haddiscoe ... 65 TM 4497
Haddock Sands (chan.) ... 140 HU 3443
Haddon House ... 121 NJ 8634
Haddon ... 71 TM 1392
Haddon Hall (ant.) ... 71 SK 2366
Haddon Hill ... 24 SS 9628
Hademore ... 60 SK 1708
Hadfield ... 70 SK 0296
Hadham Cross ... 37 TL 4218

Hadham Ford ... 37 TL 4321
Hadleigh (Essex) ... 38 TQ 8087
Hadleigh (Suff.) ... 54 TM 0242
Hadley ... 59 SJ 6712
Hadley End ... 60 SK 1320
Hadlow ... 29 TQ 6349
Hadlow Down ... 29 TQ 5324
Hadnall ... 59 SJ 5120
Hadrian's Wall (Cumbr.) (ant.) ... 89 NY 2661
Hadrian's Wall (Cumbr.) (ant.) ... 83 NY 3757
Hadrian's Wall (Cumbr.) (ant.) ... 89 NY 4561
Hadrian's Wall (Northum.) (ant.) ... 90 NY 7167
Hadrian's Wall (Northum.) (ant.) ... 90 NY 8069
Hadrian's Wall (Northum.) (ant.) ... 91 NZ 0568
Hadstock ... 53 TL 5645
Hadston Carrs (pt.) ... 91 NU 2800
Hadyard Hill ... 86 NX 2799
Hadzor ... 49 SO 9162
Haffenden Quarter ... 30 TQ 8841
Hafod-Dinbych ... 67 SH 8953
Haggbeck ... 89 NY 4774
Haggerston Castle ... 97 NU 0443
Hagley (Here. and Worc.) ... 51 SO 5641
Hagley (Here. and Worc.) ... 49 SO 9181
Hagshaw Hill ... 94 NS 7831
Hagworthingham ... 73 TF 3469
Haigh ... 69 SD 6108
Haighton Green ... 77 SD 5634
Haile ... 82 NY 0308
Hailes ... 46 SP 0530
Hailes Castle (ant.) ... 103 NT 5775
Hailey (Herts.) ... 37 TL 3710
Hailey (Oxon.) ... 47 SP 3512
Hailsham ... 29 TQ 5909
Hail Weston ... 52 TL 1662
Hainault ... 37 TQ 4691
Hainford ... 65 TG 2218
Hainton ... 73 TF 1784
Haisborough (lightship) ... 65 TG 4049
Haisthorpe ... 81 TA 1264
Halam ... 61 SK 6754
Halberry Head ... 135 ND 3037
Halberton ... 23 ST 0012
Halcro ... 135 ND 2260
Halcro Head ... 136 ND 4785
Hale (Ches.) ... 68 SJ 4682
Hale (Gtr Mches.) ... 69 SJ 7786
Hale (Hants.) ... 26 SU 1919
Hale (Lincs.) ... 62 TF 1443
Hale Bank ... 68 SJ 4784
Halebarns ... 69 SJ 7985
Hales (Norf.) ... 65 TM 3897
Hales (Staffs.) ... 59 SJ 7134
Halesowen ... 50 SO 9683
Hales Place ... 31 TR 1459
Hale Street ... 29 TQ 6749
Halesworth ... 55 TM 3877
Halewood ... 68 SJ 4585
Halford (Shrops.) ... 48 SO 4383
Halford (Warw.) ... 50 SP 2545
Halfpenny Green ... 60 SO 8292
Halfpenny Green Airport ... 49 SO 8291
Halfway (Berks.) ... 34 SU 4068
Halfway (Dyfed) ... 43 SN 6430
Halfway (Dyfed) ... 41 SN 8232
Halfway House ... 58 SJ 3411
Halfway Houses ... 30 TQ 9373
Halidon Hill ... 97 NT 9655
Halifax ... 78 SE 0825
Halistra ... 122 NG 2459
Halket ... 93 NS 4252
Halkirk ... 135 ND 1359
Halkyn ... 68 SJ 2071
Halkyn Mountain ... 68 SJ 1971
Halladale River ... 134 NC 8855
Halland ... 29 TQ 5016
Hallaton ... 61 SP 7896
Hallatrow ... 33 ST 6356
Hallbankgate ... 90 NY 5859
Hall Dunnerdale ... 82 SD 2193
Hallen ... 33 ST 5479
Hall Green ... 50 SP 1181
Hallhills Loch ... 89 NY 1688
Halliburton ... 96 NT 6748
Halliman Skerries ... 120 NJ 2172
Hallin ... 122 NG 2558
Hallington ... 91 NY 9875
Hallington Resr ... 91 NY 9776
Hallival (mt) ... 111 NM 3996
Hall of Clestrain ... 136 HY 2907
Hall of Tankerness ... 137 HY 5208
Hall of the Forest ... 48 SO 2083
Halloughton ... 61 SK 6851
Hallow ... 49 SO 8258
Hall Road Station ... 68 SD 3000
Hallrule ... 90 NT 5914
Halls ... 103 NT 6572
Hallsands ... 21 SX 8138
Hall's Green ... 53 TL 2728
Hall, The ... 143 HU 6098
Hallthwaites ... 76 SD 1884
Hallworthy ... 20 SX 1787
Hallyburton Forest ... 108 NO 2333
Hallyne ... 95 NT 1940
Halmer End ... 59 SJ 7949
Halmore ... 46 SO 6902
Halmyre Mains ... 95 NT 1749
Halnaker ... 28 SU 9108
Halsall ... 68 SD 3710
Halse (Northants.) ... 51 SP 5640
Halse (Somer.) ... 24 ST 1327
Halsetown ... 18 SW 5038
Halsham ... 75 TA 2627
Halsinger ... 22 SS 5138
Halstead (Essex) ... 54 TL 8130
Halstead (Kent) ... 37 TQ 4960
Halstead (Leic.) ... 61 SK 7505
Halstock ... 25 ST 5308
Halstow Marshes ... 30 TQ 7877
Haltham ... 73 TF 2463
Haltoft End ... 63 TF 3645
Halton (Bucks.) ... 36 SP 8710
Halton (Ches.) ... 68 SJ 5381
Halton (Clwyd) ... 58 SJ 3039
Halton (Lancs.) ... 77 SD 5065
Halton East ... 78 SE 0454
Halton Gill ... 83 SD 8876
Halton Holegate ... 73 TF 4165
Halton Lea Gate ... 90 NY 6558
Halton West ... 78 SD 8454
Haltwhistle ... 90 NY 7064
Halvergate ... 65 TG 4206

Halwell ... 21 SX 7753
Halwill ... 20 SS 4299
Halwill Junction ... 20 SS 4400
Ham (Foula) ... 140 HT 9739
Ham (Glos.) ... 46 ST 6898
Ham (Gtr London) ... 37 TQ 1672
Ham (Highld.) ... 135 ND 2373
Ham (Kent) ... 31 TR 3254
Ham (Wilts.) ... 34 SU 3262
Hamar (pt.) ... 141 HU 5136
Hamara River ... 122 NG 1947
Hamars Ness ... 143 HU 5894
Hamble ... 27 SU 4806

Hamble Airfield Heskin Green

Hamble Airfield	27	SU 4707
Hambleden (Bucks.)	36	SU 7886
Hambledon (Hants.)	27	SU 6414
Hambledon (Surrey)	28	SU 9638
Hambledon Hill (ant.)	25	ST 8412
Hambleton (Lancs.)	77	SD 3742
Hambleton (N Yorks.)	79	SE 5430
Hambleton Hill	78	SE 1573
Hambleton Hills, The	79	SE 5286
Hambridge	24	ST 3921
Hambrook (Avon)	33	ST 6378
Hambrook (W Susx)	27	SU 7806
Hameldon Hill	78	SD 7928
Hameldown Tor	21	SX 7080
Hamera Head	141	HU 4862
Hameringham	73	TF 3167
Hamerton	52	TL 1379
Hametoun	140	HT 9637
Hamford Water	55	TM 2325
Ham Green (Avon)	33	ST 5575
Ham Green (Here. and Worc.)	50	SP 0063
Ham Hill (ant.)	25	ST 4816
Hamilton	94	NS 7255
Hamly Hill	136	HY 4904
Hammersmith	37	TQ 2279
Hammerwich	60	SK 0707
Hammond Beck	62	TF 2038
Hammond Street	37	TL 3304
Hammoon	25	ST 8114
Hamna Voe (Papa Stour)	140	HU 1659
Hamna Voe (Shetld.)	142	HU 2380
Hamnavoe (Shetld.)	142	HU 2381
Hamnavoe (Shetld.)	143	HU 4971
Hamnavoe (West Burra)	141	HU 3735
Hamna Voe (Yell)	143	HU 4879
Hamnavoe (Yell)	143	HU 4980
Ham of Muness	143	HP 6301
Hampden Park	29	TQ 6002
Hampnett	46	SP 0915
Hampole	71	SE 5010
Hampreston	26	SZ 0598
Hampstead	37	TQ 2485
Hampstead Norreys	35	SU 5276
Hampsthwaite	79	SE 2558
Hampton	50	SP 0243
Hampton (Gtr London)	37	TQ 1369
Hampton (Shrops.)	49	SO 7486
Hampton Bishop	45	SO 5538
Hampton Court (ant.)	37	TQ 1568
Hampton Heath	59	SJ 4949
Hampton in Arden	50	SP 2081
Hampton Lovett	49	SO 8865
Hampton Lucy	50	SP 2557
Hampton on the Hill	50	SP 2564
Hampton Poyle	47	SP 5015
Hamsey	29	TQ 4112
Hamstall Ridware	60	SK 1019
Hamstead (I. of W.)	26	SZ 3991
Hamstead (W Mids)	60	SP 0593
Hamstead Marshall	34	SU 4165
Hamsterley (Durham)	84	NZ 1131
Hamsterley (Durham)	84	NZ 1156
Hamsterley Forest	84	NZ 0328
Hamstreet (Kent)	31	TR 0034
Ham Street (Somer.)	25	ST 5534
Hamworthy	26	SY 9990
Hanbury (Here and Worc.)	50	SO 9663
Hanbury (Staffs.)	60	SK 1727
Hanchurch	59	SJ 8441
Handa Island	132	NC 1348
Handbridge	68	SJ 4164
Handcross	28	TQ 2630
Handfast Point or The Foreland	26	SZ 0582
Handforth	69	SJ 8883
Handley	68	SJ 4657
Handsacre	60	SK 0916
Handsworth (S Yorks.)	71	SK 4086
Handsworth (W Mids)	50	SP 0490
Hanford	59	SJ 8642
Hanging Langford	26	SU 0237
Hanham	33	ST 6372
Hankelow	59	SJ 6645
Hankerton	34	ST 9690
Hankham	29	TQ 6105
Hanley	59	SJ 8847
Hanley Castle	49	SO 8342
Hanley Childe	49	SO 6565
Hanley Swan	49	SO 8143
Hanley William	49	SO 6765
Hanlith	78	SD 9061
Hanmer	58	SJ 4540
Hanningfield Resr.	38	TQ 7398
Hannington (Hants.)	35	SU 5355
Hannington (Northants.)	52	SP 8171
Hannington (Wilts.)	47	SU 1793
Hannington Wick	47	SU 1795
Hanslope	51	SP 8046
Hanthorpe	62	TF 0824
Hanwell	50	SP 4343
Hanwood	58	SJ 4309
Hanworth (Gtr London)	37	TQ 1271
Hanworth (Norf.)	65	TG 1935
Happendon	95	NS 8533
Happisburgh	65	TG 3731
Happisburgh Common	65	TG 3729
Happyland Hall	84	NZ 0932
Hapsford	69	SJ 4774
Hapton (Lancs.)	78	SD 7931
Hapton (Norf.)	65	TM 1796
Harberton	21	SX 7758
Harbertonford	21	SX 7856
Harbledown	31	TR 1358
Harborne	50	SP 0384
Harborough Magna	51	SP 4779
Harbottle	90	NT 9304
Harbury	50	SP 3759
Harby (Leic.)	61	SK 7431
Harby (Notts.)	72	SK 8770
Harcombe	24	SY 1590
Harden	78	SE 0838
Hardgate	119	NJ 7801
Hardham	28	TQ 0317
Hardhorn	77	SD 3538
Hardingham	64	TG 0403
Hardingstone	51	SP 7657
Hardings Wood	59	SJ 8054
Hardington	33	ST 7452
Hardington Mandeville	25	ST 5111
Hardington Marsh	25	ST 5009
Hard Knott Pass	82	NY 2301
Hardley	26	SU 4205
Hardley Street	65	TG 3801
Hardmead	52	SP 9347
Hardrow	84	SD 8691
Hardstoft	71	SK 4463
Hardway (Hants.)	27	SU 6101
Hardway (Somer.)	25	ST 7134
Hardwick (Bucks.)	36	SP 8019
Hardwick (Cambs.)	53	TL 3758
Hardwick (Norf.)	55	TM 2290
Hardwick (Northants.)	52	SP 8569
Hardwick (Oxon.)	47	SP 3706
Hardwick (Oxon.)	47	SP 5729
Hardwicke (Glos.)	46	SO 7912
Hardwicke (Glos.)	46	SO 9127
Hardwick Hall (ant.)	71	SK 4663
Hareby	73	TF 3365
Hareden	77	SD 6350
Hare Faulds (ant.)	96	NT 5750
Harefield	36	TQ 0590
Hare Hatch	36	SU 8077
Hare Hill (Strath.)	88	NS 6509
Hare Hill (Strath.)	95	NS 9153
Harehope	91	NU 0920
Harelaw Dam	93	NS 4753
Hare Ness	119	NO 9599
Harescombe	46	SO 8410
Haresfield	46	SO 8110
Hareshaw Hill	94	NS 7629
Hare Street	53	TL 3929
Harewood	79	SE 3245
Harewood Forest	34	SU 3943
Harford	21	SX 6359
Hargrave (Ches.)	69	SJ 4862
Hargrave (Northants.)	52	TL 0370
Hargrave (Suff.)	54	TL 7759
Harker	89	NY 3960
Harkstead	55	TM 1935
Harland Hill	78	SE 0284
Harlaston	60	SK 2111
Harlaw House	121	NJ 7424
Harlaw Resr.	102	NT 1865
Harlaxton	62	SK 8832
Harlech	66	SH 5831
Harlesden	37	TQ 2383
Harleston (Devon)	21	SX 7945
Harleston (Norf.)	55	TM 2483
Harleston (Suff.)	54	TM 0160
Harlestone	51	SP 7064
Harle Syke	78	SD 8634
Harley	59	SJ 5901
Harling Road Station	54	TL 9788
Harlington	52	TL 0330
Harlosh	122	NG 2841
Harlosh Island	122	NG 2739
Harlosh Point	122	NG 2840
Harlow	37	TL 4711
Harlow Hill	91	NZ 0768
Harlthorpe	74	SE 7337
Harlton	53	TL 3852
Harman's Cross	26	SY 9880
Harmby	84	SE 1289
Harmer Green	37	TL 2516
Harmer Hill	59	SJ 4822
Harmston	72	SK 9762
Harnham	26	SU 1229
Harnhill	46	SP 0600
Harold Hill	37	TQ 5391
Haroldston West	42	SM 8615
Haroldswick (Unst)	143	HP 6312
Harold's Wick (Unst)	143	HP 6411
Harold Wood	37	TQ 5590
Harome	79	SE 6482
Harpenden	37	TL 1314
Harperleas Resr.	103	NO 2105
Harperrig Reservoir	102	NT 0961
Harper's Brook	52	SP 9286
Harpford	24	SY 0890
Harpham	81	TA 0961
Harpley (Here. and Worc.)	49	SO 6861
Harpley (Norf.)	64	TF 7826
Harpole	51	SP 6961
Harpsdale	135	ND 1256
Harpsden	36	SU 7680
Harpswell	72	SK 9389
Harpurhey	69	SD 8701
Harpur Hill	70	SK 0671
Harrabrough Head	136	ND 4190
Harrapool	123	NG 6522
Harrier	140	HT 9540
Harrietfield	108	NN 9829
Harrietsham	30	TQ 8753
Harrington (Cumbr.)	82	NX 9926
Harrington (Lincs.)	73	TF 3671
Harrington (Northants.)	51	SP 7780
Harringworth	62	SP 9197
Harris (Rhum)	110	NM 3395
Harris (W Isles) (dist.)	125	NG 1198
Harriseahead	59	SJ 8656
Harrogate	79	SE 3055
Harrold	52	SP 9456
Harrow	37	TQ 1388
Harrowbarrow	20	SX 3969
Harrowden	52	TL 0646
Harrow Hill	28	TQ 0810
Harrow on the Hill	37	TQ 1586
Harsgeir	131	NB 1040
Harston (Cambs.)	53	TL 4251
Harston (Leic.)	62	SK 8331
Hart	85	NZ 4735
Harta Corrie	123	NG 4723
Hartamul	112	NF 8311
Hartburn	91	NZ 0886
Harter Fell (Cumbr.)	83	NY 4609
Harter Fell (Cumbr.)	82	SD 2199
Hartest	54	TL 8352
Hart Fell (Dumf. and Galwy.)	89	NT 1113
Hart Fell (Dumf. and Galwy.)	89	NY 2289
Hartfield	29	TQ 4735
Hartford (Cambs.)	53	TL 2572
Hartford (Ches.)	69	SJ 6372
Hartfordbridge	35	SU 7757
Hartford End	38	TL 6817
Harthill (Ches.)	59	SJ 4955
Harthill (Lothian)	102	NS 9064
Harthill (S Yorks.)	71	SK 4980
Harthope Burn	97	NT 9623
Hartington	70	SK 1360
Hartland	22	SS 2624
Hartland Point	22	SS 2227
Hartland Quay	22	SS 2224
Hartlebury	49	SO 8470
Hartlepool	85	NZ 5032
Hartlepool Bay	85	NZ 5232
Hartley (Cumbr.)	83	NY 7808
Hartley (Kent)	30	TQ 6166
Hartley (Kent)	29	TQ 7634
Hartley (Northum.)	91	NZ 3475
Hartley Wespall	36	SU 6958
Hartley Wintney	35	SU 7756
Hartlip	30	TQ 8364
Harton (N Yorks.)	80	SE 7061
Harton (Shrops.)	48	SO 4888
Harton (Tyne and Wear)	91	NZ 3864
Hartpury	46	SO 7924
Hartshill	60	SP 3293
Hartshorne	60	SK 3221
Hartshorn Pike	90	NT 6201
Hartsop	83	NY 4013
Hartwell	51	SP 7850
Hartwood	101	NS 8459
Harvel	30	TQ 6563
Harvington	50	SP 0548
Harvington Cross	50	SP 0549
Harwell	35	SU 4989
Harwich	55	TM 2431
Harwich Harbour	55	TM 2632
Harwood (Durham)	83	NY 8133
Harwood (Gtr Mches.)	69	SD 7411
Harwood Beck	83	NY 8321
Harwood Dale	81	SE 9595
Harwood Forest	91	NY 9994
Harworth	71	SK 6291
Hascombe	28	TQ 0039
Hascosay	143	HU 5592
Hascosay Sound	143	HU 5492
Haselbech	51	SP 7177
Haselbury Plucknett	25	ST 4711
Haseley	50	SP 2368
Haselor	50	SP 1257
Hasfield	46	SO 8227
Hasguard	42	SM 8509
Haskayne	68	SD 3507
Haskeir Eagach (is.)	124	NF 5980
Haskeir Island	124	NF 6182
Hasketon	55	TM 2550
Hasland	71	SK 3969
Haslemere	27	SU 9032
Haslingden	78	SD 7823
Haslingden Grane	78	SD 7523
Haslingfield	53	TL 4052
Haslington	59	SJ 7355
Hassall	69	SJ 7657
Hassall Green	69	SJ 7758
Hassell Street	31	TR 0946
Hassendean	90	NT 5420
Hassingham	65	TG 3605
Hassocks	29	TQ 3015
Hassop	71	SK 2272
Hastigrow	135	ND 2661
Hastingleigh	31	TR 0945
Hastings	30	TQ 8009
Hastingwood	37	TL 4807
Hastoe	36	SP 9209
Haswell	85	NZ 3743
Hatch (Beds.)	52	TL 1547
Hatch (Hants.)	35	SU 6752
Hatch (Wilts.)	25	ST 9228
Hatch Beauchamp	24	ST 3020
Hatch End	37	TQ 1391
Hatching Green	37	TL 1313
Hatchmere	69	SJ 5571
Hatcliffe	75	TA 2100
Hatfield (Here. and Worc.)	45	SO 5859
Hatfield (Herts.)	37	TL 2309
Hatfield (S Yorks.)	71	SE 6609
Hatfield Aerodrome	37	TL 2009
Hatfield Broad Oak	37	TL 5516
Hatfield Chase	74	SE 7109
Hatfield Heath	37	TL 5215
Hatfield House (ant.)	37	TL 2308
Hatfield Moors	74	SE 7006
Hatfield Peverel	38	TL 7911
Hatfield Woodhouse	71	SE 6708
Hatford	47	SU 3394
Hatherden	34	SU 3450
Hatherleigh	23	SS 5404
Hathern	61	SK 5022
Hatherop	47	SP 1505
Hathersage	71	SK 2381
Hatherton (Ches.)	59	SJ 6847
Hatherton (Staffs.)	60	SJ 9610
Hatley St. George	53	TL 2851
Hatt	20	SX 3962
Hatterrall Hill	45	SO 3025
Hattingley	27	SU 6437
Hatton (Ches.)	69	SJ 5982
Hatton (Derby.)	60	SK 2130
Hatton (Grampn.)	121	NK 0537
Hatton (Gtr London)	37	TQ 1075
Hatton (Lincs.)	73	TF 1776
Hatton (Shrops.)	48	SO 4690
Hatton (Warw.)	50	SP 2367
Hatton Castle (ant.)	121	NJ 7546
Hattoncrook	121	NJ 8424
Hatton Heath	68	SJ 4561
Hatton of Fintray	119	NJ 8316
Hattons Lodge	34	SU 0688
Haugham	73	TF 3381
Haugh Head	97	NU 0026
Haughley	54	TM 0262
Haughley Green	54	TM 0364
Haugh of Glass	121	NJ 3239
Haugh of Urr	88	NX 8066
Haughs of Cromdale	117	NJ 0927
Haughton (Notts.)	71	SK 6772
Haughton (Shrops.)	58	SJ 3727
Haughton (Shrops.)	59	SJ 5516
Haughton (Shrops.)	59	SO 6795
Haughton (Staffs.)	59	SJ 8620
Haughton Common	90	NY 8172
Haughton Green	69	SJ 9393
Haughton Moss	59	SJ 5756
Haunn	104	NM 3347
Haunton	60	SK 2411
Hauxley	91	NU 2703
Hauxley Haven	91	NU 2902
Hauxton	53	TL 4351
Havant	27	SU 7106
Haven	45	SO 4054
Havengore Island	39	TQ 9788
Havenhouse Station	73	TF 5259
Havenstreet	27	SZ 5690
Haven, The	63	TF 3540
Haverfordwest	42	SM 9515
Haverhill	54	TL 6745
Haverigg	76	SD 1578
Havering-atte-Bower	37	TQ 5193
Haversham	52	SP 8343
Haverthwaite	77	SD 3483
Hawarden	68	SJ 3165
Hawarden Airport	68	SJ 3565
Hawes	84	SD 8789
Haweswater Resr.	83	NY 4814
Hawford	49	SO 8460
Hawick (Borders)	89	NT 5014
Ha Wick (Hoy, Orkney)	136	ND 2589
Hawkchurch	24	ST 3400
Hawkedon	54	TL 7952
Hawkeridge	33	ST 8653
Hawkerland	24	SY 0588
Hawkesbury	33	ST 7687
Hawkesbury Upton	33	ST 7786
Hawkes End	50	SP 2983
Hawkhill	91	NU 2212
Hawkhope	90	NY 7188
Hawkhurst	29	TQ 7630
Hawkinge	31	TR 2139
Hawkley	27	SU 7429
Hawkridge	23	SS 8630
Hawkridge Reservoir	24	ST 2036
Hawkshead	82	SD 3598
Hawksland	95	NS 8439
Hawks Ness	141	HU 4648
Hawkswick	78	SD 9570
Hawksworth (Notts.)	61	SK 7543
Hawksworth (W Yorks.)	78	SE 1641
Hawkwell	38	TQ 8691
Hawkwood Hill	94	NS 6838
Hawley (Hants.)	36	SU 8558
Hawley (Kent)	37	TQ 5571
Hawling	46	SP 0623
Hawnby	85	SE 5389
Haworth	78	SE 0337
Haworth Moor	78	SD 9935
Hawsker	81	NZ 9207
Hawstead	54	TL 8559
Hawthorn	85	NZ 4145
Hawthorn Hill	36	SU 8873
Hawthornthwaite Fell	77	SD 5752
Hawton	61	SK 7851
Haxby	79	SE 6057
Haxey	74	SK 7699
Haxton Down	34	SU 2049
Hay Bluff	45	SO 2436
Haycock	82	NY 1410
Haydock	69	SJ 5696
Haydon	25	ST 6615
Haydon Bridge	90	NY 8464
Haydon Dean	97	NT 9743
Haydon Wick	34	SU 1388
Haydown Hill	34	SU 3155
Haye	20	SX 3570
Hayes (Gtr London)	36	TQ 0980
Hayes (Gtr London)	37	TQ 4165
Hayfield	70	SK 0386
Hayhillock	109	NO 5242
Hayle	18	SW 5537
Hayling Bay	27	SZ 7198
Hayling Island	27	SU 7201
Haylot Fell	77	SD 5861
Haynes	52	TL 1042
Haynes Church End	52	TL 0841
Hay-on-Wye	45	SO 2342
Hayscastle	42	SM 8925
Hayscastle Cross	42	SM 9125
Hay Stacks	82	NY 2013
Hayton (Cumbr.)	82	NY 1041
Hayton (Cumbr.)	83	NY 5057
Hayton (Humbs.)	74	SE 8145
Hayton (Notts.)	72	SK 7284
Hayton's Bent	48	SO 5280
Haytor Vale	21	SX 7677
Haywards Heath	29	TQ 3324
Haywood Oaks	61	SK 6055
Hazelbank	95	NS 8344
Hazelbury Bryan	25	ST 7408
Hazeley	36	SU 7459
Hazel Grove	69	SJ 9287
Hazelrigg	97	NU 0533
Hazelslade	60	SK 0212
Hazelton Walls	108	NO 3321
Hazelwood	60	SK 3245
Hazlemere	36	SU 8895
Hazlerigg	91	NZ 2472
Hazleton	46	SP 0718
Heacham	64	TF 6737
Headbourne Worthy	27	SU 4831
Headcorn	30	TQ 8344
Headington	47	SP 5407
Headlam	84	NZ 1818
Headless Cross	50	SP 0365
Headley (Hants.)	35	SU 5162
Headley (Hants.)	27	SU 8236
Headley (Surrey)	28	TQ 2054
Head o' da Taing	140	HT 9739
Head of Bratta	143	HU 4799
Head of Brough	143	HU 4484
Head of Garness	121	NJ 7464
Head of Holland	136	HY 4812
Head of Hosta	143	HU 6791
Head of Lambhoga	143	HU 6287
Head of Moclett	138	HY 4949
Head of Muir	101	NS 8080
Head of Stanshi	142	HU 2180
Headon	72	SK 7476
Heads Nook	83	NY 4955
Heads of Ayr	93	NS 2818
Heage	60	SK 3650
Healabhal Bheag (mt.)	122	NG 2242
Healabhal Mhór (mt.)	122	NG 2244
Healaugh (N Yorks.)	84	SE 0198
Healaugh (N Yorks.)	79	SE 4947
Healaval (mt.)	122	NG 2464
Heald Green	69	SJ 8385
Heald Moor	78	SD 8726
Heale	23	SS 6446
Healey (Lancs.)	69	SD 8817
Healey (Northum.)	91	NZ 0158
Healey (N Yorks.)	78	SE 1780
Healeyfield	84	NZ 0648
Healing	75	TA 2110
Heamoor	18	SW 4631
Heanish	104	NM 0343
Heanor	60	SK 4346
Heanton Punchardon	22	SS 5035
Heapham	72	SK 8788
Hearnish (pt.)	124	NF 6263
Hearthstane	95	NT 1125
Heart Law	96	NT 7166
Heast	123	NG 6417
Heath (Derby.)	71	SK 4466
Heath (S Glam.)	41	ST 1779
Heath and Reach	52	SP 9228
Heathcote	70	SK 1460
Heath End (Hants.)	35	SU 5762
Heath End (Hants.)	35	SU 8550
Heather	60	SK 3910
Heathfield (Devon)	21	SX 8376
Heathfield (E Susx)	29	TQ 5821
Heathfield (Somer.)	24	ST 1526
Heathfield (Strath.)	100	NS 3262
Heathfield Moor	78	SE 1067
Heath Hayes	60	SK 0110
Heath Hill	59	SJ 7614
Heath House	32	ST 4146
Heathrow Airport - London	36	TQ 0875
Heath, The	54	TL 9043
Heathton	49	SO 8192
Heatley	69	SJ 6988
Heaton (Lancs.)	77	SD 4460
Heaton (Staffs.)	69	SJ 9462
Heaton (Tyne and Wear)	91	NZ 2665
Heaton Moor	69	SJ 8691
Heaval (mt.)	112	NL 6799
Heaverham	37	TQ 5758
Heaviley	69	SJ 9088
Hebburn	91	NZ 3265
Hebden	78	SE 0263
Hebden Bridge	78	SD 9927
Hebden Green	69	SJ 6365
Hebden Moor	78	SE 0465
Hebden Water	78	SD 9631
Hebrides or Western Isles	112	NG 0239
Hebron	91	NZ 1989
Heckfield	36	SU 7260
Heckington	62	TF 1444
Heckmondwike	78	SE 2123
Hecla (mt.)	112	NF 8234
Heddington	34	ST 9966
Heddle	136	HY 3512
Heddon-on-the-Wall	91	NZ 1366
Heddon's Mouth	23	SS 6549
Hedenham	65	TM 3193
Hedge End	27	SU 4812
Hedgehope Hill	90	NT 9419
Hedgerley	36	SU 9787
Hedging	24	ST 3029
Hedley on the Hill	91	NZ 0759
Hednesford	60	SK 0012
Hedon	75	TA 1828
Hedsor	36	SU 9086
Hegdon Hill	45	SO 5854
Heglibister	141	HU 3851
Heighington (Durham)	84	NZ 2522
Heighington (Lincs.)	72	TF 0269
Heights of Brae	128	NH 5161
Heights of Kinlochewe	127	NH 0764
Heilam	133	NC 4659
Heillia	142	HU 2684
Heishival Mór (mt.)	112	NL 6296
Heisker or Monach Islands	124	NF 6262
Heiskers (is.)	112	NL 5786
Heiton	96	NT 7130
Heldale Water	136	ND 2592
Heldon Hill	129	NJ 1257
Hele (Devon)	23	SS 5347
Hele (Devon)	23	SS 9902
Helensburgh	100	NS 2982
Helford	18	SW 7526
Helford River	18	SW 7626
Helhoughton	64	TF 8626
Helions Bumpstead	54	TL 6541
Hellabrick's Wick	140	HT 9536
Helland	19	SX 0770
Hellesdon	65	TG 1810
Helliar Holm	136	HY 4815
Hellidon	51	SP 5158
Hellifield	78	SD 8556
Helli Ness	141	HU 4628
Hellingly	29	TQ 5812
Hellington	65	TG 3103
Hellir (pt.)	143	HU 3892
Hellisay	112	NF 7504
Hellister	141	HU 3949
Hellmoor Loch	89	NT 3816
Hell's Glen	100	NN 1806
Hell's Mouth or Porth Neigwl	56	SH 2626
Helman Head	135	ND 3646
Helmdon	51	SP 5843
Helmingham	55	TM 1857
Helmsdale	135	ND 0215
Helmshore	78	SD 7821
Helmsley	79	SE 6183
Helmsley Moor	85	SE 5991
Helperby	79	SE 4369
Helperthorpe	81	SE 9570
Helpringham	62	TF 1340
Helpston	62	TF 1205
Helsby	69	SJ 4875
Helston	18	SW 6527
Helstone	20	SX 0881
Helton	83	NY 5122
Helvellyn (mt.)	82	NY 3315
Helwick (lightship)	40	SS 3281
Helwith Bridge	78	SD 8169
Hemblington	65	TG 3411
Hembury (ant.)	24	ST 1103
Hemel Hempstead	36	TL 0506
Hemingbrough	79	SE 6730
Hemingby	73	TF 2374
Hemingford Abbots	53	TL 2870
Hemingford Grey	53	TL 2970
Hemingstone	55	TM 1453
Hemington (Northants.)	52	TL 0985
Hemington (Somer.)	33	ST 7253
Hemley	55	TM 2842
Hempholme	81	TA 0850
Hempnall	65	TM 2494
Hempnall Green	65	TM 2593
Hempriggs	129	NJ 1064
Hempriggs House	135	ND 3547
Hempstead (Essex)	54	TL 6338
Hempstead (Norf.)	65	TG 4028
Hempsted (Glos.)	46	SO 8117
Hempsted (Norf.)	65	TG 1037
Hempton (Norf.)	64	TF 9129
Hempton (Oxon.)	47	SP 4431
Hemsby	65	TG 4917
Hemsby Hole	65	TG 5118
Hemswell	72	SK 9290
Hemsworth	71	SE 4213
Hemyock	24	ST 1313
Henbury (Avon)	33	ST 5478
Henbury (Ches.)	69	SJ 8873
Hendersyde Park	96	NT 7435
Hendon (Gtr London)	37	TQ 2389
Hendon (Tyne and Wear)	85	NZ 4055
Hendreys Course	102	NS 9758
Hendy	43	SN 5804
Heneglwys	66	SH 4276
Henfield	28	TQ 2116
Hen Gerrig	57	SH 9518
Hengistbury Head	26	SZ 1790
Hengoed (Mid Glam.)	41	ST 1495
Hengoed (Powys)	45	SO 2253
Hengoed (Shrops.)	58	SJ 2833
Hengrave	54	TL 8268
Hengynwydd-fawr	57	SN 9882
Henham	53	TL 5428
Heniarth	58	SJ 1108
Henley (Shrops.)	48	SO 5476
Henley (Somer.)	25	ST 4232
Henley (Suff.)	55	TM 1551
Henley (W Susx)	27	SU 8926
Henley-in-Arden	50	SP 1465
Henley-on-Thames	36	SU 7682
Henley Park	28	SU 9352
Henllan (Clwyd)	67	SJ 0268
Henllan (Dyfed)	43	SN 3540
Henllan Amgoed	43	SN 1820
Henllys	45	ST 2693
Henlow	52	TL 1738
Hennock	21	SX 8380
Henryd	67	SH 7674
Henry's Moat (Castell Hendre)	42	SN 0428
Hensall	79	SE 5923
Hensbarrow Downs	19	SW 9957
Henshaw	90	NY 7664
Henstead	55	TM 4986
Henstridge	25	ST 7219
Henstridge Marsh	25	ST 7420
Henton (Oxon.)	36	SP 7602
Henton (Somer.)	33	ST 4845
Henwick	49	SO 8354
Henwood	20	SX 2673
Heogan	141	HU 4743
Heoga Ness	143	HU 5379
Heol Senni	41	SN 9223
Heol-y-Cyw	41	SS 9484
Hepburn	97	NU 0724
Hepple	91	NT 9800
Hepscott	91	NZ 2284
Heptonstall	78	SD 9827
Heptonstall Moor	78	SD 9330
Hepworth (Suff.)	54	TL 9874
Hepworth (W Yorks.)	70	SE 1606
Herbrandston	42	SM 8707
Hereford	45	SO 5040
Hergest	45	SO 2655
Hergest Ridge	45	SO 2556
Heriot	96	NT 3952
Herma Ness	143	HP 6018
Hermaness Hill	143	HP 6017
Herman Law	89	NT 2115
Hermetray	124	NF 9874
Hermitage (Berks.)	35	SU 5072
Hermitage (Borders)	89	NY 5095
Hermitage (Dorset.)	25	ST 6306
Hermitage (Hants.)	27	SU 7505
Hermitage, The	28	TQ 2253
Hermon (Dyfed)	43	SN 2032
Hermon (Dyfed)	43	SN 3630
Hermon (Gwyn.)	66	SH 3868
Herne	31	TR 1866
Herne Bay	31	TR 1768
Herner	23	SS 5926
Herne, The	53	TL 2590
Hernhill	31	TR 0660
Herodsfoot	19	SX 2160
Herongate	38	TQ 6391
Heronsgate	36	TQ 0294
Herra, The	143	HU 4693
Herriard	35	SU 6645
Herringfleet	65	TM 4797
Herringswell	54	TL 7170
Herrington	85	NZ 3553
Herscha Hill	119	NO 7380
Hersden	31	TR 1961
Hersham	37	TQ 1164
Herstmonceux	29	TQ 6312
Herston	136	ND 4291
Herston Head	136	ND 4191
Hertford	37	TL 3212
Hertford Heath	37	TL 3511
Hertingfordbury	37	TL 3112
Hesketh Bank	77	SD 4323
Hesketh Lane	77	SD 6141
Hesket Newmarket	82	NY 3438
Heskin Green	69	SD 5315

Kelynack ....18 SW 3729
Kemback ....109 NO 4115
Kemberton ....59 SJ 7204
Kemble ....46 ST 9897
Kemerton ....49 SO 9437
Kemeys Commander ....45 SO 3405
Kemnay ....119 NJ 7315
Kemnay Forest ....119 NJ 7418
Kempley ....46 SO 6729
Kempock Point ....100 NS 2478
Kempsey ....49 SO 8549
Kempsford ....47 SU 1596
Kempston ....52 TL 0347
Kempston Hardwick ....52 TL 0244
Kempton ....48 SO 3582
Kemp Town ....29 TQ 3303
Kemsing ....37 TQ 5558
Kenardington ....31 TQ 9732
Kencot ....47 SP 2504
Kendal ....83 SD 5192
Kenderchurch ....45 SO 4028
Kendoon Loch ....88 NX 6090
Kenfig ....41 SS 8081
Kenfig Burrows ....41 SS 7981
Kenfig Hill ....41 SS 8483
Kengharair Farm ....105 NM 4348
Kenilworth ....50 SP 2872
Kenknock ....107 NN 4636
Kenley (Gtr. London) ....37 TQ 3259
Kenley (Shrops.) ....59 SJ 5600
Kenmore (Highld.) ....123 NG 7557
Kenmore (Tays.) ....107 NN 7745
Kenmure Castle (ant.) ....88 NX 6376
Kenn (Avon) ....32 ST 4168
Kenn (Devon) ....21 SX 9285
Kennacraig ....99 NR 8262
Kenna Craig ....99 NR 8267
Kennedy's Pass ....86 NX 1493
Kennerleigh ....23 SS 8107
Kennet ....102 NS 9291
Kennet and Avon Canal (Wilts.) ....33 ST 8761
Kennet and Avon Canal (Wilts.) ....34 SU 2363
Kennethmont ....121 NJ 5328
Kennett ....54 TL 6968
Kennford ....21 SX 9186
Kennick Resr. ....21 SX 8084
Kenninghall ....54 TM 0386
Kennington (Kent) ....31 TR 0245
Kennington (Oxon.) ....47 SP 5202
Kennoway ....103 NO 3402
Kenny Hill ....54 TL 6680
Kennythorpe ....80 SE 7865
Kenovay ....104 NL 9946
Kensaleyre ....123 NG 4251
Kensington ....37 TQ 2579
Kensworth ....36 TL 0318
Kensworth Common ....36 TL 0317
Kentallen ....106 NN 0057
Kentchurch ....45 SO 4125
Kentchurch Court (ant.) ....45 SO 4225
Kentford ....54 TL 7056
Kentisbeare ....23 ST 0608
Kentisbury ....23 SS 6144
Kentmere ....83 NY 4504
Kentmere Reservoir ....83 NY 4408
Kent Oil Refinery ....30 TQ 8674
Kenton (Devon) ....21 SX 9583
Kenton (Suff.) ....55 TM 1965
Kentra ....111 NM 6568
Kentra Bay ....111 NM 6468
Kents Bank ....77 SD 3975
Kent's Green ....46 SO 7423
Kent's Oak ....26 SU 3224
Kentwell Hall (ant.) ....54 TL 8647
Kenwick ....58 SJ 4230
Kenwyn ....19 SW 8145
Kenyon ....69 SJ 6295
Keoldale ....132 NC 3866
Keose ....131 NB 3521
Keppanach ....106 NN 0262
Keppoch ....114 NG 9621
Keprigny ....85 SE 4690
Keresley ....50 SP 3182
Kerloch (mt.) ....119 NO 6987
Kerne Bridge ....45 SO 5819
Kerran Hill ....92 NR 7313
Kerrera (is.) ....105 NM 8128
Kerridge ....69 SJ 9376
Kerris ....18 SW 4427
Kerry ....48 SO 1490
Kerrycroy ....100 NS 1061
Kerry Hill ....48 SO 1386
Kerrysdale ....123 NG 8273
Kerry's Gate ....45 SO 3933
Kersall ....72 SK 7162
Kersey ....54 TM 0044
Kershader ....131 NB 3420
Kershope Burn ....89 NY 5083
Kershopefoot ....89 NY 4782
Kershope Forest ....90 NY 5181
Kersoe ....49 SO 9939
Kerswell ....24 ST 0806
Kerswell Green ....49 SO 8646
Kesgrave ....55 TM 2245
Kessingland ....55 TM 5286
Kestle Mill ....19 SW 8459
Keston ....37 TQ 4164
Keswick (Cumbr.) ....82 NY 2723
Keswick (Norf.) ....65 TG 2004
Keswick (Norf.) ....65 TG 3533
Ketligill Head ....142 HU 2784
Kettering ....52 SP 8778
Ketteringham ....65 TG 1503
Kettins ....108 NO 2338
Kettla Ness ....141 HU 3428
Kettlebaston ....54 TL 9650
Kettlebridge ....103 NO 3007
Kettlebrook ....60 SK 2103
Kettleburgh ....55 TM 2660
Kettleness ....85 NZ 8315
Kettleshulme ....70 SJ 9879
Kettlesing ....79 SE 2257
Kettlesing Bottom ....79 SE 2257
Kettlestone ....64 TF 9631
Kettlethorpe ....72 SK 8475
Kettletoft ....139 HY 6538
Kettletoft Bay ....139 HY 6638
Kettlewell ....78 SD 9772
Ketton ....62 SK 9704
Kew ....37 TQ 1877
Kewstoke ....32 ST 3363
Kex Beck ....78 SE 0953
Kexbrough ....71 SE 3009
Kexby (Lincs.) ....72 SK 8785
Kexby (N Yorks.) ....80 SE 7050
Key Green ....69 SJ 8963
Keyham ....61 SK 6606
Keyhaven ....26 SZ 3091
Keyingham ....75 TA 2425
Keymer ....29 TQ 3115
Keynsham ....33 ST 6568
Keysley Down ....25 ST 8634
Keysoe ....52 TL 0763
Keysoe Row ....52 TL 0861
Keyston ....52 TL 0475
Keyworth ....61 SK 6130
Kibblesworth ....84 NZ 2456
Kibworth Beauchamp ....61 SP 6893
Kibworth Harcourt ....61 SP 6894
Kidbrooke ....37 TQ 4076
Kiddemore Green ....59 SJ 8509
Kidderminster ....49 SO 8376

Kiddington ....47 SP 4122
Kidlington ....47 SP 4913
Kidmore End ....36 SU 6979
Kidsgrove ....59 SJ 8354
Kidstones ....78 SD 9781
Kidwelly ....43 SN 4106
Kielder ....90 NY 6293
Kielder Castle ....90 NY 6494
Kielder Burn ....90 NY 6393
Kielder Forest ....90 NY 6591
Kielderhead Moor ....90 NT 6600
Kielder Reservoir ....90 NY 6689
Kiells ....98 NR 4168
Kierfea Hill ....138 HY 4132
Kierfield House ....136 HY 2518
Kiessimul Castle (ant.) ....112 NL 6697
Kilbarchan ....101 NS 4063
Kilbeg ....111 NG 6506
Kilberry ....99 NR 7164
Kilberry Head ....99 NR 7064
Kilbirnie ....93 NS 3154
Kilbirnie Loch ....93 NS 3354
Kilblaan Burn ....100 NN 1413
Kilbrannan Sound ....92 NR 8441
Kilbraur Hill ....129 NC 8208
Kilbride (Island of Skye) ....122 NG 5820
Kilbride (South Uist) ....112 NF 7614
Kilbride (Strath.) ....105 NM 8525
Kilbride Bay ....100 NR 9666
Kilbride Point ....122 NG 3766
Kilbryde Castle (ant.) ....101 NN 7503
Kilburn (Derby.) ....60 SK 3845
Kilburn (N Yorks.) ....79 SE 5179
Kilby ....61 SP 6295
Kilcadzow ....95 NS 8848
Kilchamaig ....99 NR 8061
Kilchattan (Bute) ....93 NS 1054
Kilchattan (Colonsay) ....98 NR 3795
Kilchattan Bay ....93 NS 1055
Kilchenzie ....92 NR 6725
Kilcheran ....105 NM 8238
Kilchiaran ....98 NR 2060
Kilchiaran Bay ....98 NR 1960
Kilchoan ....111 NM 4963
Kilchoan Bay ....111 NM 4762
Kilchoman ....98 NR 2163
Kilchrenan ....106 NN 0322
Kilchurn Castle (ant.) ....106 NN 1327
Kilconquhar ....103 NO 4802
Kilconquhar Loch ....103 NO 4801
Kilcot ....46 SO 6925
Kilcoy ....128 NH 5751
Kilcoy Forest ....128 NH 6355
Kilcreggan ....100 NS 2380
Kildale ....85 NZ 6009
Kildalloig ....92 NR 7518
Kildalton Castle ....98 NR 4347
Kildalton Cross (ant.) ....98 NR 4650
Kildary ....129 NH 7775
Kildavanan ....100 NS 0266
Kildermorie Forest ....128 NH 4678
Kildermorie Lodge ....128 NH 5177
Kildonan (Island of Arran) ....92 NS 0321
Kildonan Burn ....134 NC 9122
Kildonan Lodge ....134 NC 9022
Kildonnan ....111 NM 4885
Kildrummy ....118 NJ 4617
Kildwick ....78 SE 0145
Kilfinan ....100 NR 9378
Kilfinan Bay ....100 NR 9278
Kilfinichen Bay ....105 NM 4827
Kilgetty ....42 SN 1207
Kilgwrrwg Common ....45 ST 4797
Kilham (Humbs.) ....81 TA 0564
Kilham (Northum.) ....97 NT 8832
Kili Holm ....138 HY 4732
Kilkenneth ....104 NL 9444
Kilkerran ....93 NS 3003
Kilkhampton ....22 SS 2511
Killamarsh ....71 SK 4680
Killay ....40 SS 6092
Killichianaig ....98 NR 6486
Killean ....92 NR 6944
Killearn ....101 NS 5286
Killegray ....124 NF 9783
Killen ....128 NH 6758
Killerby ....84 NZ 1919
Killichonan ....107 NN 5458
Killichonan Burn ....107 NN 5660
Killichronan ....105 NM 5441
Killiechonate ....115 NN 2481
Killiechonate Forest ....115 NN 2074
Killiecrankie ....108 NN 9162
Killiemor ....105 NM 4939
Killilan ....114 NG 9430
Killilan Forest ....114 NH 0333
Killimster ....135 ND 3156
Killin ....107 NN 5732
Killinallan ....98 NR 3171
Killinghall ....79 SE 2858
Killingholme ....75 TA 1416
Killington ....77 SD 6188
Killington Resr. ....83 SD 5991
Killin Lodge ....116 NH 5209
Killochan (ant.) ....86 NS 2200
Killochyett ....96 NT 4545
Killocraw ....92 NR 6630
Killundine ....111 NM 5849
Kilmacolm ....100 NS 3569
Kilmahumaig ....99 NR 7893
Kilmalieu ....106 NM 8955
Kilmaluag ....123 NG 4374
Kilmaluag Bay ....123 NG 4475
Kilmannan Resr. ....101 NS 4978
Kilmany ....109 NO 3821
Kilmarie ....123 NG 5417
Kilmarnock ....93 NS 4237
Kilmaron Castle ....109 NO 3516
Kilmartin ....99 NR 8398
Kilmar Tor ....20 SX 2574
Kilmaurs ....93 NS 4141
Kilmelford ....105 NM 8413
Kilmeny ....98 NR 3965
Kilmersdon ....33 ST 6952
Kilmeston ....27 SU 5825
Kilmichael Forest ....100 NR 9095
Kilmichael Glassary ....99 NR 8593
Kilmichael of Inverlussa ....99 NR 7785
Kilmington (Devon) ....24 SY 2798
Kilmington (Wilts.) ....25 ST 7736
Kilmorack ....128 NH 4944
Kilmore (Island of Skye) ....111 NG 6507
Kilmore (Strath.) ....106 NM 8824
Kilmory (Highld.) ....111 NM 5270
Kilmory (Island of Arran) ....92 NR 9621
Kilmory (Rhum) ....110 NG 3503
Kilmory (Strath.) ....99 NR 7075
Kilmory Bay ....99 NR 6974
Kilmory Castle ....99 NR 8686
Kilmory Glen ....110 NG 3602
Kilmory Lodge ....98 NM 7105
Kilmory Water ....92 NR 9622
Kilmuir (Highld.) ....128 NH 6749
Kilmuir (Highld.) ....129 NH 7573
Kilmuir (Island of Skye) ....122 NG 2547
Kilmun ....100 NS 1781
Kilndown ....29 TQ 7035
Kilnhurst ....71 SK 4697

Kilninian ....105 NM 3945
Kilninver ....105 NM 8221
Kiln Pit Hill ....84 NZ 0454
Kilnsea ....75 TA 4015
Kilnsey ....78 SD 9767
Kilnwick ....81 SE 9949
Kiloran ....98 NR 3996
Kiloran Bay ....98 NR 3999
Kilpatrick ....98 NR 9027
Kilpatrick Hills ....101 NS 4776
Kilpeck ....45 SO 4430
Kilphedar ....112 NF 7419
Kilphedir ....134 NC 9818
Kilpin ....74 SE 7726
Kilrenny ....103 NO 5705
Kilsby ....51 SP 5671
Kilspindie ....108 NO 2225
Kilstay Bay ....86 NX 1338
Kilsyth ....101 NS 7178
Kilsyth Hills ....101 NS 6980
Kiltarlity ....128 NH 5041
Kilton ....32 ST 1644
Kilt Rock ....123 NG 5066
Kilvaxter ....122 NG 3869
Kilve ....32 ST 1443
Kilvington ....61 SK 7942
Kilwinning ....93 NS 3043
Kimberley (Norf.) ....64 TG 0704
Kimberley (Notts.) ....61 SK 4944
Kimberley House ....65 TG 0904
Kimble ....36 SP 8206
Kimblesworth ....84 NZ 2547
Kimble Wick ....36 SP 8007
Kimbolton (Cambs.) ....52 TL 0967
Kimbolton (Here. and Worc.) ....48 SO 5261
Kimcote ....51 SP 5886
Kimmeridge ....25 SY 9179
Kimmerston ....97 NT 9535
Kimpton (Hants.) ....34 SU 2746
Kimpton (Herts.) ....37 TL 1718
Kinbrace ....134 NC 8631
Kinbrace Burn ....134 NC 8828
Kinbuck ....101 NN 7905
Kincaple ....109 NO 4518
Kincardine (Fife) ....102 NS 9387
Kincardine (Highld.) ....128 NH 6089
Kincardine Castle (Tays.) ....102 NN 9411
Kincardine O'Neil ....119 NO 5999
Kinclaven ....108 NO 1538
Kincorth ....119 NJ 9303
Kincorth House ....129 NJ 0161
Kincraig ....117 NH 8305
Kincraigie ....108 NN 9849
Kindallachan ....108 NN 9950
Kinder Reservoir ....70 SK 0588
Kinder Scout (mt.) ....70 SK 0888
Kineton (Glos.) ....46 SP 0926
Kineton (Warw.) ....50 SP 3351
Kinfauns ....108 NO 1622
Kinfauns Forest ....108 NO 1923
Kingairloch (dist.) ....111 NM 8553
Kingairloch House ....111 NM 8353
Kingarth ....93 NS 0956
Kingcoed ....45 SO 4205
Kingham ....47 SP 2523
Kingholm Quay ....88 NX 9773
Kinghorn ....103 NT 2686
Kinglassie ....103 NT 2298
Kingoodie ....108 NO 3329
King Orry's Grave (ant.) ....76 SC 4485
Kingsand ....20 SX 4350
Kingsbarns ....103 NO 5912
Kingsbridge (Devon) ....21 SX 7344
Kingsbridge (Somer.) ....23 SS 9837
King's Bromley ....60 SK 1216
Kingsburgh ....123 NG 3955
Kingsbury (Gtr London) ....37 TQ 1989
Kingsbury (Warw.) ....60 SP 2196
Kingsbury Episcopi ....25 ST 4320
Kings Caple ....45 SO 5628
King's Cave ....129 NH 8371
Kingsclere ....35 SU 5258
King's Cliffe ....62 TL 0097
Kingscote ....46 ST 8196
Kingscott ....23 SS 5318
King's Coughton ....50 SP 0858
Kingscross ....92 NS 0428
Kingscross Point ....92 NS 0528
King's Cross Station ....37 TQ 3083
King's Delph ....63 TL 2595
Kingsdon ....25 ST 5126
Kingsdown ....31 TR 3748
Kingseat ....102 NT 1290
Kingsey ....36 SP 7406
Kingsfold ....28 TQ 1636
Kingsford ....49 SO 8281
King's Forest of Geltsdale ....83 NY 5853
Kingsforth ....74 TA 0219
Kingshall Street ....54 TL 9161
King's Heath ....50 SP 0781
Kingshouse ....107 NN 5620
Kingskerswell ....21 SX 8767
Kingskettle ....103 NO 3008
Kingsland ....48 SO 4461
Kingsley (Ches.) ....69 SJ 5474
Kingsley (Hants.) ....35 SU 7838
Kingsley (Staffs.) ....60 SK 0047
Kingsley Green ....28 SU 8930
King's Lynn ....64 TF 6220
Kings Meaburn ....83 NY 6221
Kings Muir (Borders) ....96 NT 2539
Kingsmuir (Fife) ....103 NO 5409
Kingsmuir (Tays.) ....109 NO 4849
Kingsnorth (Kent) ....31 TR 0039
Kingsnorth (Kent) ....30 TQ 8072
King's Norton (Leic.) ....61 SK 6800
King's Norton (W Mids) ....50 SP 0579
King's Nympton ....23 SS 6819
King's Pyon ....45 SO 4350
Kings Ripton ....52 TL 2576
King's Seat (mt.) ....108 NO 2333
King's Seat Hill ....102 NS 9399
King's Sedge Moor ....25 ST 4433
King's Somborne ....26 SU 3631
King's Stag ....25 ST 7210
King's Stanley ....46 SO 8103
Kings Sutton ....51 SP 4936
Kingstanding ....60 SP 0794
Kingsteignton ....21 SX 8773
King Sterndale ....70 SK 0972
Kingsthorne ....45 SO 4932
Kingsthorpe ....51 SP 7563
Kingston (Cambs.) ....53 TL 3455
Kingston (Devon) ....21 SX 6347
Kingston (Dorset) ....25 SY 7509
Kingston (Dorset) ....25 SY 9579
Kingston (Grampn.) ....121 NJ 3365
Kingston (Hants.) ....25 SU 1401
Kingston (I. of W.) ....27 SZ 4781
Kingston (Kent) ....31 TR 1951
Kingston (Lothian) ....103 NT 5482
Kingston Bagpuize ....47 SU 4098
Kingston Blount ....36 SU 7399
Kingston by Sea ....28 TQ 2205
Kingston Deverill ....25 ST 8436
Kingstone (Here. and Worc.) ....45 SO 4235
Kingstone (Somer.) ....24 ST 3713
Kingstone (Staffs.) ....60 SK 0629
Kingston Lisle ....34 SU 3287
Kingston near Lewes ....29 TQ 3908

Kingston on Soar ....61 SK 5027
Kingston Russell ....25 SY 5891
Kingston Seymour ....32 ST 3966
Kingston St. Mary ....24 ST 2229
Kingston upon Hull ....75 TA 0929
Kingston upon Thames ....37 TQ 1869
Kingstown ....89 NY 3959
King Street (Ches.) (ant.) ....69 SJ 6969
King Street (Northants.) (ant.) ....62 TF 1108
King's Walden ....37 TL 1623
Kingswear ....21 SX 8851
Kingswells ....119 NJ 8606
Kingswinford ....49 SO 8888
Kings Wood ....30 TQ 8351
Kingswood (Avon) ....33 ST 6473
Kingswood (Bucks.) ....36 SP 6819
Kingswood (Glos.) ....33 ST 7491
Kingswood (Powys) ....58 SJ 2402
Kingswood (Surrey) ....28 TQ 2455
Kingswood (Warw.) ....50 SP 1871
Kingswood Common ....45 SO 2854
Kings Worthy ....27 SU 4932
Kington (Here. and Worc.) ....45 SO 2956
Kington (Here. and Worc.) ....50 SO 9955
Kington Langley ....33 ST 9276
Kington Magna ....25 ST 7622
Kington St. Michael ....33 ST 9077
Kingussie ....116 NH 7500
King Water ....90 NY 5365
Kingweston ....25 ST 5230
Kinharrachie ....121 NJ 9231
Kinnivie House ....121 NJ 3144
Kinkell Bridge ....108 NN 9316
Kinkell Church (ant.) ....119 NJ 7819
Kinkell Ness ....109 NO 5315
Kinknockie ....121 NK 0041
Kinlet ....49 SO 7280
Kinloch (Fife) ....103 NO 2812
Kinloch (Highld.) ....132 NC 3434
Kinloch (Island of Skye) ....123 NG 6917
Kinloch (Tays.) ....108 NO 1444
Kinloch (Tays.) ....108 NO 2644
Kinlochard ....101 NN 4502
Kinlochbervie ....132 NC 2156
Kinloch Castle ....111 NM 4099
Kinlochcheil ....114 NM 9779
Kinlochewe ....126 NH 0261
Kinlochewe Forest ....127 NH 0766
Kinloch Glen ....110 NG 3600
Kinloch Hourn ....114 NG 9407
Kinloch Laggan ....116 NN 5999
Kinloch Lodge ....133 NC 5552
Kinlochluichart Forest ....127 NH 2769
Kinlochmore ....106 NN 1962
Kinloch Rannoch ....107 NN 6658
Kinloch River ....133 NC 5450
Kinlochspelve ....105 NM 6525
Kinloss ....129 NJ 0661
Kinmel Bay ....67 SH 9881
Kinmount House ....89 NY 1368
Kinmuck ....119 NJ 8119
Kinmundy ....119 NJ 8817
Kinnadie ....121 NJ 9643
Kinnaird ....108 NO 2428
Kinnaird Castle ....109 NO 6357
Kinnaird Head ....121 NJ 9967
Kinneff ....119 NO 8574
Kinneil House (ant.) ....102 NS 9880
Kinnelhead ....88 NT 0201
Kinnell ....109 NO 6050
Kinnersley (Here. and Worc.) ....45 SO 3449
Kinnersley (Here. and Worc.) ....49 SO 8743
Kinnerton (Ches.) ....68 SJ 3361
Kinnerton (Powys) ....48 SO 2463
Kinnesswood ....102 NO 1702
Kinninvie ....84 NZ 0521
Kinnordy ....109 NO 3654
Kinnoull Hill ....108 NO 1322
Kinoulton ....61 SK 6730
Kinpurney Hill ....108 NO 3241
Kinrive Hill ....128 NH 6875
Kinross ....102 NO 1102
Kinrossie ....108 NO 1832
Kinsham ....48 SO 3664
Kinsley ....71 SE 4114
Kinson ....26 SZ 0696
Kintail Forest ....114 NG 9917
Kintarvie ....131 NB 2317
Kintbury ....34 SU 3866
Kintessack ....129 NJ 0060
Kintillo ....108 NO 1317
Kintocher ....118 NJ 5709
Kintore ....119 NJ 7916
Kintour ....98 NR 4551
Kintra ....98 NR 3248
Kintra River ....98 NR 3249
Kintyre (dist.) ....100 NR 7540
Kinuachdrach ....99 NR 7098
Kinuachdrach Harbour ....99 NR 7098
Kinveachy ....117 NH 9118
Kinver ....49 SO 8483
Kippax ....79 SE 4030
Kippax Park ....79 SE 4228
Kippen ....101 NS 6594
Kipperross House ....101 NN 7800
Kippford or Scaur ....88 NX 8355
Kirbister (Orkney) ....136 HY 3607
Kirbister (Stronsay) ....137 HY 6823
Kirby Bedon ....65 TG 2705
Kirby Bellars ....61 SK 7117
Kirby Cane ....65 TM 3794
Kirby Cross ....55 TM 2120
Kirby Grindalythe ....81 SE 9067
Kirby Hill (ant.) ....62 SP 9293
Kirby Hill (N Yorks.) ....84 NZ 1306
Kirby Hill (N Yorks.) ....79 SE 3868
Kirby Knowle ....79 SE 4687
Kirby-le-Soken ....55 TM 2222
Kirby Mills ....80 SE 7185
Kirby Misperton ....80 SE 7779
Kirby Muxloe ....61 SK 5104
Kirby Row ....55 TM 3792
Kirby Sigston ....85 SE 4194
Kirby Underdale ....80 SE 8158
Kirby Wiske ....79 SE 3784
Kirdford ....28 TQ 0226
Kirivick ....131 NB 2041
Kirk ....135 ND 2859
Kirkabister ....141 HU 4938
Kirkaig Point ....132 NC 0521
Kirkandrews on Eden ....89 NY 3558
Kirkbampton ....89 NY 3056
Kirkbean ....88 NX 9859
Kirk Bramwith ....71 SE 6111
Kirkbride ....89 NY 2356
Kirkbuddo ....109 NO 5043
Kirk Burn (Highld.) ....135 ND 3164
Kirkburn (Humbs.) ....81 SE 9856
Kirkburton ....71 SE 1912
Kirkby (Lincs.) ....72 TF 0692
Kirkby (Mers.) ....68 SJ 4098
Kirkby (N Yorks.) ....85 NZ 5306
Kirkby Fell ....78 SD 8664
Kirkby Fleetham ....84 SE 2894
Kirkby Green ....72 TF 0857
Kirkby in Ashfield ....61 SK 4956
Kirkby Industrial Estate ....68 SJ 4398
Kirkby-in-Furness ....76 SD 2282

Kirkby la Thorpe ....62 TF 0946
Kirkby Lonsdale ....77 SD 6178
Kirkby Malham ....78 SD 8960
Kirkby Mallory ....61 SK 4500
Kirkby Malzeard ....79 SE 2374
Kirkbymoorside ....80 SE 6986
Kirkby on Bain ....73 TF 2362
Kirkby Overblow ....79 SE 3249
Kirkby Stephen ....83 NY 7708
Kirkby Thore ....83 NY 6325
Kirkby Underwood ....62 TF 0727
Kirkcaldy ....103 NT 2791
Kirkcambeck ....90 NY 5368
Kirkcarswell ....87 NX 7549
Kirkcolm ....86 NX 0268
Kirk Connel (Dumf. and Galwy.) ....88 NS 7312
Kirk Connel (Dumf. and Galwy.) (ant.) ....89 NY 2575
Kirkconnell (Dumf. and Galwy.) ....88 NX 9767
Kirkcowan ....86 NX 3260
Kirkcudbright ....87 NX 6851
Kirkcudbright Bay ....87 NX 6644
Kirk Deighton ....79 SE 3950
Kirk Ella ....74 TA 0129
Kirk Fell ....82 NY 1910
Kirkfieldbank ....95 NS 8643
Kirkgunzeon ....88 NX 8666
Kirk Hallam ....61 SK 4540
Kirkham (Lancs.) ....76 SD 4231
Kirkham (N Yorks.) ....80 SE 7365
Kirkhamgate ....79 SE 2922
Kirk Hammerton ....79 SE 4655
Kirkharle ....91 NZ 0182
Kirkheaton (Northum.) ....91 NZ 0177
Kirkheaton (W Yorks.) ....70 SE 1817
Kirkhill (Highld.) ....128 NH 5545
Kirkhill (Tays.) ....109 NO 6860
Kirkhope (Borders) ....96 NT 3823
Kirk Hope (South Walls) ....136 ND 3490
Kirkhouse ....96 NT 3233
Kirkhouse Point ....136 ND 4790
Kirkibost (Island of Skye) ....123 NG 5518
Kirkibost (Isle of Lewis) ....131 NB 1834
Kirkibost Island ....124 NF 7564
Kirkinch ....108 NO 3144
Kirkinner ....87 NX 4251
Kirkintilloch ....101 NS 6573
Kirk Ireton ....60 SK 2650
Kirkland (Cumbr.) ....82 NY 0718
Kirkland (Cumbr.) ....83 NY 6432
Kirkland (Dumf. and Galwy.) ....88 NS 7214
Kirkland (Dumf. and Galwy.) ....88 NX 8090
Kirkland Hill ....60 SK 7215
Kirk Langley ....60 SK 2838
Kirkleatham ....85 NZ 5921
Kirklevington ....85 NZ 4309
Kirkley ....55 TM 5491
Kirklington (Notts.) ....71 SK 6757
Kirklington (N Yorks.) ....79 SE 3181
Kirklinton ....89 NY 4366
Kirkliston ....102 NT 1274
Kirkmaiden ....86 NX 1236
Kirk Merrington ....84 NZ 2631
Kirk Michael (I. of M.) ....76 SC 3190
Kirkmichael (Strath.) ....86 NS 3408
Kirkmichael (Tays.) ....108 NO 0860
Kirkmond le Mire ....73 TF 1892
Kirkmuirhill ....94 NS 7943
Kirknewton (Lothian) ....102 NT 1166
Kirknewton (Northum.) ....97 NT 9130
Kirkney Water ....121 NJ 4830
Kirk of Shotts ....101 NS 8462
Kirkoswald (Cumbr.) ....83 NY 5541
Kirkoswald (Strath.) ....93 NS 2407
Kirkpatrick Durham ....88 NX 7870
Kirkpatrick-Fleming ....89 NY 2770
Kirk Sandall ....71 SE 6007
Kirksanton ....76 SD 1380
Kirk Smeaton ....71 SE 5116
Kirkstall ....79 SE 2635
Kirkstile (Grampn.) ....121 NJ 5235
Kirkstone Pass ....83 NY 4008
Kirk Taing ....138 HY 5633
Kirkton (Borders) ....90 NT 5413
Kirkton (Dumf. and Galwy.) ....89 NX 9781
Kirkton (Fife) ....109 NO 3625
Kirkton (Grampn.) ....119 NJ 6112
Kirkton (Grampn.) ....121 NJ 6425
Kirkton (Grampn.) ....121 NJ 6950
Kirkton (Grampn.) ....119 NJ 8243
Kirkton (Highld.) ....114 NH 1050
Kirkton (Highld.) ....126 NG 9141
Kirkton (Highld.) ....117 NH 7998
Kirkton (Strath.) ....88 NS 9320
Kirkton (Tays.) ....109 NO 9618
Kirkton (Tays.) ....109 NO 4246
Kirkton Head ....121 NK 1250
Kirkton Manor ....95 NT 2137
Kirkton of Airlie ....108 NO 3151
Kirkton of Auchterhouse ....108 NO 3338
Kirkton of Barevan ....128 NH 8347
Kirkton of Collace ....108 NO 1931
Kirkton of Craig ....109 NO 7055
Kirkton of Culsalmond ....121 NJ 6432
Kirkton of Durris ....119 NO 7796
Kirkton of Glenbuchat ....118 NJ 3715
Kirkton of Glenisla ....108 NO 2160
Kirkton of Kingoldrum ....108 NO 3354
Kirkton of Largo ....103 NO 4203
Kirkton of Lethendy ....108 NO 1441
Kirkton of Logie Buchan ....121 NJ 9829
Kirkton of Maryculter ....119 NO 8599
Kirkton of Menmuir ....109 NO 5364
Kirkton of Monikie ....109 NO 5138
Kirkton of Rayne ....121 NJ 6930
Kirkton of Skene ....119 NJ 8007
Kirkton of Strathmartine ....109 NO 3735
Kirkton of Tealing ....109 NO 4037
Kirktown ....121 NK 0952
Kirktown of Alvah ....121 NJ 6760
Kirktown of Auchterless ....121 NJ 7141
Kirktown of Bourtie ....121 NJ 8024
Kirktown of Deskford ....121 NJ 5061
Kirktown of Fetteresso ....119 NO 8585
Kirkwall ....136 HY 4410
Kirkwall Airport ....136 HY 4808
Kirkwhelpington ....91 NY 9984
Kirk Yetholm ....97 NT 8227
Kirn ....100 NS 1878
Kirriemuir ....109 NO 3854
Kirriereoch Hill ....87 NX 4287
Kirroughtree Forest ....87 NX 4473
Kirstead Green ....65 TM 2997
Kirtivary ....79 NY 2372
Kirtle Water ....89 NY 2577
Kirtling ....54 TL 6857
Kirtling Green ....54 TL 6855
Kirtlington ....47 SP 4919
Kirtomy ....134 NC 7463
Kirtomy Point ....134 NC 7566
Kirton (Highld.) ....123 NG 8227
Kirton (Lincs.) ....73 TF 3038
Kirton (Notts.) ....72 SK 6869
Kirton (Suff.) ....55 TM 2739
Kirton End ....73 TF 2840
Kirton Holme ....63 TF 2642
Kirton in Lindsey ....74 SK 9398
Kishorn Island ....123 NG 8037
Kislingbury ....51 SP 6959
Kites Hardwick ....51 SP 4668
Kit Hill ....20 SX 3771

Kithurst Hill ... 28 TQ 0712
Kit's Coty House (ant.) ... 30 TQ 7461
Kittybrewster ... 119 NJ 9208
Kitwood ... 27 SU 6633
Kiveton Park ... 71 SK 4982
Klibreck ... 133 NC 5834
Klibreck Burn ... 133 NC 5832
Knaith ... 72 SK 8284
Knap Corner ... 25 ST 8023
Knapdale (dist.) ... 99 NR 8176
Knapdale Forest ... 99 NR 7890
Knaphill ... 36 SU 9658
Knap of Howar (ant.) ... 138 HY 4851
Knap of Trowieglen ... 136 ND 2398
Knapp (Somer.) ... 24 ST 3025
Knapp (Tays.) ... 108 NO 2831
Knaps Longpeak (Pt.) ... 22 SS 2018
Knapton (Norf.) ... 65 TG 3034
Knapton (N Yorks.) ... 79 SE 5652
Knapton (N Yorks.) ... 81 SE 8775
Knapwell ... 53 TL 3362
Knaresborough ... 79 SE 3557
Knarsdale ... 83 NY 6753
Knaven ... 121 NJ 8943
Knayton ... 79 SE 4188
Knayton ... 79 SE 4387
Knebworth ... 37 TL 2520
Kneesall ... 72 SK 7064
Kneesworth ... 53 TL 3444
Kneeton ... 61 SK 7146
Knelston ... 40 SS 4689
Knightacott ... 23 SS 6439
Knightcote ... 50 SP 3954
Knighton (Devon) ... 21 SX 5249
Knighton (Leic.) ... 61 SK 6001
Knighton (Powys) ... 48 SO 2872
Knighton (Staffs.) ... 59 SJ 7240
Knighton (Staffs.) ... 59 SJ 7427
Knighton Down ... 25 SU 1245
Knightwick ... 49 SO 7355
Knill ... 45 SO 2960
Knipe, The (mt.) ... 88 NS 6410
Knipton ... 62 SK 8231
Knipton Reservoir ... 62 SK 8130
Knitsley ... 84 NZ 1148
Kniveton ... 60 SK 2050
Knock (Cumbr.) ... 83 NY 6826
Knock (Grampn.) ... 121 NJ 5452
Knock (Grampn.) ... 105 NM 5438
Knock (Isle of Lewis) ... 131 NB 4931
Knockally ... 135 ND 1428
Knockan ... 132 NC 2110
Knockandhu ... 117 NJ 2123
Knockando ... 121 NJ 1941
Knockando House ... 120 NJ 2042
Knockandy Hill ... 121 NJ 5431
Knockangle Point ... 98 NR 3151
Knockbain ... 117 NH 8255
Knock Bay ... 111 NG 6708
Knockbrex ... 87 NX 5849
Knock Castle ... 100 NS 1963
Knockcoid ... 86 NX 0168
Knockdaw Hill ... 86 NX 1688
Knockdee ... 135 ND 1761
Knockdhu ... 86 NX 1483
Knockdolian ... 86 NX 1184
Knockdolian Castle ... 86 NX 1285
Knockdow ... 100 NS 1070
Knockendon Resr. ... 93 NS 2452
Knockenkelly ... 92 NS 0426
Knockentiber ... 83 NS 3939
Knockespock House ... 121 NJ 5424
Knockfin Heights ... 121 NJ 9134
Knock Head ... 121 NT 6565
Knock Hill (Fife) ... 102 NT 0593
Knock Hill (Grampn.) ... 121 NJ 5355
Knockholt ... 37 TQ 4658
Knockholt Pound ... 37 TQ 4859
Knockie Lodge ... 116 NH 4413
Knockin ... 58 SJ 3322
Knockinlochie ... 86 NX 2889
Knockintorran ... 124 NF 7367
Knock Moss ... 86 NX 2057
Knocknaha ... 86 NR 6817
Knocknain ... 86 NW 9764
Knocknevis ... 86 NX 5474
Knock of Balmyle ... 108 NO 1156
Knock of Braemoray ... 129 NJ 0141
Knockrome ... 98 NR 5571
Knocksharry ... 76 SC 2785
Knock, The ... 89 NY 7291
Knodishall ... 55 TM 4261
Knole (ant.) ... 28 TQ 5354
Knolls Green ... 69 SJ 8079
Knolton ... 58 SJ 3738
Knook ... 34 ST 9341
Knossington ... 61 SK 8008
Knott ... 82 NY 2932
Knott End-on-Sea ... 77 SD 3548
Knotting ... 52 TL 0063
Knottingley ... 71 SE 5023
Knotty Green ... 36 SU 9392
Knowbury ... 48 SO 5774
Knowe ... 86 NX 3171
Knowehead ... 86 NX 6090
Knowesgate ... 91 NY 9885
Knowes Hill ... 96 NT 4338
Knoweside ... 93 NS 2512
Knowetownhead ... 90 NT 5418
Knowle (Avon) ... 33 ST 6170
Knowle (Devon) ... 22 SS 4938
Knowle (Devon) ... 23 SS 7801
Knowle (W Mids) ... 50 SP 1876
Knowl Green ... 77 SD 6337
Knowl Hill ... 36 SU 8279
Knowlton ... 31 TR 2853
Knowsley ... 68 SJ 4396
Knowsley Hall ... 68 SJ 4494
Knowstone ... 23 SS 8223
Knox Hill ... 109 NO 8171
Knox Knowe ... 90 NT 6502
Kneydart (dist.) ... 111 NG 8301
Knucklas ... 48 SO 2574
Knutsford ... 69 SJ 7578
Knypersley ... 59 SJ 8856
Kokoarrah (pt.) ... 82 SD 0496
Kuggar ... 18 SW 7216
Kyle (dist.) ... 93 NS 5022
Kyleakin (Highld.) ... 123 NG 7526
Kyle Akin (Highld.) ... 123 NG 7527
Kylechorky Lodge ... 115 NH 4029
Kyle Forest ... 93 NS 4911
Kyle of Durness ... 132 NC 3765
Kyle of Lochalsh ... 123 NG 7527
Kyle of Sutherland ... 128 NH 5795
Kyle of Tongue ... 133 NC 5757
Kylerhea (Highld.) ... 123 NG 7820
Kyle Rhea (Highld.) ... 123 NG 7922
Kyles Lodge ... 124 NF 9987
Kylesmorar ... 111 NM 8093
Kyles of Bute (Strath.) ... 100 NR 9969
Kyles of Bute (Strath.) ... 100 NS 0473
Kyles Stockinish ... 125 NG 1391
Kylestrome ... 132 NC 2234
Kyllachy House ... 117 NH 7825
Kyloe ... 97 NU 0540
Kyloe Hills ... 97 NU 0439
Kynance Cove ... 18 SW 6813
Kynnersley ... 59 SJ 6716
Kype Muir ... 94 NS 7138
Kype Water ... 94 NS 7439
Kyre Park ... 49 SO 6263

L

Labost ... 131 NB 2749
Lacasital ... 131 NB 4240
Laceby ... 75 TA 2106
Lacey Green ... 36 SP 8200
Lach Dennis ... 69 SJ 7071
Lachlan Bay ... 100 NS 0095
Lackalee ... 125 NG 1292
Lackford ... 54 TL 7970
Lacock ... 33 ST 9168
Ladbroke ... 50 SP 4158
Ladder Burn ... 118 NJ 4185
Ladder Hills ... 117 NJ 2718
Laddingford ... 29 TQ 6948
Laddus Fens ... 63 TF 4701
Lade Bank ... 63 TF 3954
Ladhar Bheinn ... 111 NG 8204
Ladock ... 19 SW 8950
Ladybank (Fife) ... 103 NO 3009
Ladybank (Strath.) ... 93 NS 2102
Ladybower Resr. ... 70 SK 1888
Lady Isle ... 93 NS 2729
Ladykirk ... 97 NT 8847
Ladyland Moor ... 100 NS 3059
Ladylea Hill ... 118 NJ 3416
Ladysford ... 121 NJ 9060
Lady's Holm ... 141 HU 3709
Ladyside Height ... 96 NT 3647
Lael Forest ... 127 NH 1982
Lagavulin ... 98 NR 4045
Lagg (Island of Arran) ... 92 NR 9521
Lagg (Jura) ... 98 NR 5978
Laggan (Highld.) ... 115 NN 2997
Laggan (Highld.) ... 116 NN 6194
Laggan (Islay) ... 98 NR 2855
Laggan (Islay) ... 86 NX 2582
Laggan Bay (Island of Mull) ... 105 NM 4440
Laggan Bay (Islay) ... 98 NR 2951
Laggan Deer Forest ... 105 NM 6221
Laggan Lodge ... 105 NM 6223
Laggan Point ... 98 NR 2755
Laggantalluch Head ... 86 NX 0836
Lagganulva ... 105 NM 4541
Laid ... 132 NC 4159
Laide ... 126 NG 8991
Laiken Forest ... 129 NH 9052
Laindon ... 38 TQ 6889
Lair ... 126 NH 0148
Lairg ... 128 NC 5806
Lairg Lodge ... 128 NC 5707
Lairg Station ... 128 NC 5803
Lairig a'Mhuic ... 107 NN 5749
Lairig Breisleich ... 107 NN 5641
Lairig Ghru ... 117 NH 9603
Lairig Leacach ... 115 NN 2972
Lair of Aldararie (mt.) ... 118 NO 3177
Laival a Tuath (mt.) ... 131 NB 0224
Lake ... 34 SU 1239
Lake Cottage ... 86 NX 0968
Lakenham ... 65 TG 2307
Lakenheath ... 54 TL 7182
Lakenheath Station ... 54 TL 7286
Lakenheath Warren ... 54 TL 7581
Lake of Menteith ... 101 NS 5699
Lakesend ... 63 TL 5196
Lakeside ... 77 SD 3787
Lake Vyrnwy ... 57 SH 9821
Laleham ... 36 TQ 0568
Laleston ... 41 SS 8779
Lamachan Hill ... 87 NX 4376
Lamaload Resr. ... 70 SJ 9775
Lamarsh ... 54 TL 8935
Lamas ... 65 TG 2423
Lamba (is.) ... 143 HU 3881
Lamba Ness ... 143 HP 6715
Lamba Taing ... 141 HU 4326
Lamba Water ... 141 HU 3836
Lamberhurst ... 29 TQ 6735
Lamberton ... 97 NT 9654
Lamberton Beach ... 97 NT 9758
Lambeth ... 37 TQ 3078
Lambfell Moar ... 76 SC 2984
Lambgarth Head ... 141 HU 4550
Lamb Head ... 137 HY 6921
Lamb Hoga ... 143 HU 6088
Lambhoga Head ... 141 HU 4013
Lamb Holm ... 137 HY 4800
Lamb Hill ... 90 NT 9071
Lambley (Northum.) ... 90 NY 6758
Lambley (Notts.) ... 61 SK 6245
Lambourn ... 35 SU 3278
Lambourn Downs ... 34 SU 3481
Lambourne End ... 37 TQ 4894
Lambrigg Fell ... 83 SD 5893
Lambs Green ... 28 TQ 2136
Lambston ... 42 SM 9016
Lamerton ... 21 SX 4476
Lamesley ... 84 NZ 2557
Lamford Hill ... 87 NX 5398
Lamb Dearg ... 108 NO 1163
Lamington (Highld.) ... 129 NH 7577
Lamington (Strath.) ... 95 NS 9730
Lamlash ... 92 NS 0231
Lamlash Bay ... 92 NS 0330
Lammer Law ... 102 NT 5261
Lammermuir (dist.) ... 96 NT 6170
Lammermuir Hills ... 103 NT 5863
Lamonby ... 83 NY 4135
Lamorna ... 18 SW 4524
Lamorran ... 19 SW 8741
Lampeter ... 43 SN 5748
Lampeter Velfrey ... 42 SN 1514
Lamphey ... 42 SN 0100
Lamplugh ... 82 NY 0820
Lamport ... 51 SP 7574
Lamyatt ... 25 ST 6535
Lana ... 20 SX 3496
Lanark ... 95 NS 8843
Lancaster ... 77 SD 4761
Lancaster Canal ... 77 SD 5041
Lanchester ... 84 NZ 1647
Landbeach ... 53 TL 4765
Landcross ... 22 SS 4524
Landerberry ... 119 NJ 7404
Landford ... 26 SU 2519
Landford Manor ... 26 SU 2620
Landimore ... 40 SS 4693
Landkey ... 23 SS 5931
Landore ... 40 SS 6595
Landrake ... 20 SX 3760
Landscove ... 21 SX 7766
Land's End (pt.) ... 18 SW 3425
Land's End (St. Just) Aerodrome ... 18 SW 3728
Landshipping ... 42 SN 0211
Landulph ... 20 SX 4261
Landwade ... 54 TL 6268
Landywood ... 60 SJ 9806
Laneast ... 20 SX 2283
Lane End ... 36 SU 8091
Lane Green ... 59 SJ 8802
Laneham ... 72 SK 8076
Lanercost Priory (ant.) ... 90 NY 5563
Laneshaw Bridge ... 78 SD 9240
Laneshaw Resr. ... 78 SD 9441
Langa (is.) ... 141 HU 3739
Langar ... 61 SK 7234
Langatoon Point ... 135 ND 3579

Langay ... 124 NG 0181
Langbank ... 101 NS 3873
Langbar ... 78 SE 0951
Langcliffe ... 78 SD 8264
Lang Clodie Wick ... 142 HU 3088
Lang Craig ... 109 NO 7048
Langdale End ... 81 SE 9391
Langdale Fell ... 83 NY 6400
Langdale Pikes (mt.) ... 82 NY 2707
Langdon Beck ... 83 NY 8521
Langdon Common ... 83 NY 8532
Langdon Hills ... 38 TQ 6786
Langdyke ... 103 NO 3304
Langenhoe ... 39 TM 0018
Langford (Beds.) ... 52 TL 1841
Langford (Devon) ... 51 ST 0203
Langford (Essex) ... 38 TL 8408
Langford (Notts.) ... 72 SK 8258
Langford (Oxon.) ... 47 SP 2402
Langford Budville ... 24 ST 1122
Langford End ... 52 TL 1654
Langford Grounds ... 32 ST 3568
Langham (Essex) ... 54 TM 0233
Langham (Leic.) ... 62 SK 8411
Langham (Norf.) ... 64 TG 0041
Langham (Suff.) ... 54 TL 9769
Lang Head ... 142 HU 3070
Langho ... 77 SD 7034
Langholm ... 89 NY 3684
Langlee Crags ... 97 NT 9721
Langleeford ... 97 NT 9521
Langley (Ches.) ... 36 TQ 0078
Langley (Ches.) ... 69 SJ 9471
Langley (Essex) ... 53 TL 4435
Langley (Hants.) ... 26 SU 4400
Langley (Herts.) ... 37 TL 2122
Langley (Kent) ... 30 TQ 8051
Langley (Warw.) ... 50 SP 1962
Langley (W Susx) ... 27 SU 8029
Langley Burrell ... 33 ST 9275
Langley Hill ... 46 SP 0028
Langley Marsh ... 24 ST 0729
Langley Park ... 84 NZ 2144
Langley Street ... 65 TG 3601
Langness ... 76 SC 2966
Langney ... 29 TQ 6302
Langney Point ... 29 TQ 6401
Langold ... 71 SK 5887
Langore ... 20 SX 3086
Langport ... 25 ST 4226
Langrick ... 63 TF 2648
Langridge ... 33 ST 7369
Langrish ... 27 SU 7023
Langsett ... 70 SE 2100
Langsett Reservoir ... 70 SE 2000
Langshaw ... 96 NT 5139
Langskaill ... 138 HY 4342
Langstone Harbour ... 27 SU 7104
Langstone ... 27 SU 6901
Langstrothdale Chase (dist.) ... 78 SD 8879
Langthorne ... 84 SE 2491
Langthorpe ... 79 SE 3867
Langthwaite ... 84 NZ 0002
Langtoft (Humbs.) ... 81 TA 0166
Langtoft (Lincs.) ... 62 TF 1212
Langton (Durham) ... 84 NZ 1719
Langton (Lincs.) ... 73 TF 2368
Langton (Lincs.) ... 73 TF 3970
Langton (N Yorks.) ... 80 SE 7967
Langton by Wragby ... 73 TF 1476
Langton Green ... 29 TQ 5439
Langton Herring ... 25 SY 6182
Langton Matravers ... 26 SY 9978
Langtree ... 22 SS 4415
Langwathby ... 83 NY 5733
Langwell Forest ... 135 ND 0325
Langwell House ... 135 ND 1122
Langwell Lodge ... 127 NC 1702
Langwell Water ... 135 ND 0324
Langwood Fen ... 53 TL 4385
Langworth ... 72 TF 0676
Lanherne or Vale of Mawgan ... 19 SW 8964
Lanhydrock House ... 19 SX 0863
Lanivet ... 19 SX 0364
Lank Rigg ... 82 NY 0912
Lanlivery ... 19 SX 0759
Lanllwest ... 48 SN 1756
Lanner ... 18 SW 7139
Lanreath ... 19 SX 1756
Lanrick Castle ... 101 NN 6803
Lansallos ... 19 SX 1751
Lanton (Borders) ... 96 NT 6221
Lanton (Northum.) ... 97 NT 9231
Lanyar Taing ... 143 HU 3893
Lapford ... 23 SS 7308
Laphroaig ... 98 NR 3845
Lapley ... 59 SJ 8713
Lapworth ... 50 SP 1671
Larachbeg ... 105 NM 6948
Larbert ... 102 NS 8582
Larg Hill ... 86 NX 4175
Largie ... 121 NJ 6131
Largie Castle ... 92 NR 7046
Largiemore ... 100 NR 9486
Largo Bay ... 103 NO 4201
Largo Law ... 103 NO 4204
Largoward ... 103 NO 4607
Largs ... 100 NS 2058
Largs Bay ... 100 NS 1959
Largybeg ... 92 NS 0423
Largybeg Point ... 92 NS 0523
Largymore ... 92 NS 0424
Larig Hill ... 117 NJ 0840
Larkfield ... 100 NS 2376
Larkhall ... 94 NS 7651
Larkhill ... 34 SU 1243
Larling ... 54 TL 9889
Larriston ... 90 NY 5494
Larriston Fells ... 90 NY 5792
Lartington ... 84 NZ 0117
Lary ... 118 NJ 3300
Lasham ... 35 SU 6742
Lashy Sound ... 137 HY 5938
Lassodie ... 102 NT 1292
Lastingham ... 80 SE 7290
Latchingdon ... 38 TL 8800
Latchley ... 20 SX 4173
Lately Common ... 69 SJ 6797
Lathbury ... 52 SP 8745
Latheron ... 135 ND 1933
Latheronwheel ... 135 ND 1832
Latheronwheel House ... 135 ND 1832
Lathones ... 103 NO 4708
Latimer ... 36 TQ 0099
Latrigg ... 82 NY 2724
Latteridge ... 33 ST 6684
Lattiford ... 25 ST 6926
Latton ... 46 SU 0995
Lauchintilly ... 119 NJ 7412
Laudale House ... 111 NM 7459
Lauder ... 96 NT 5347
Lauder Common ... 96 NT 5046
Lauderdale ... 96 NT 5746
Laugharne ... 43 SN 3011
Laugharne Sands ... 43 SN 3006
Laughterton ... 72 SK 8375
Laughton (E Susx) ... 29 TQ 4913
Laughton (Leic.) ... 51 SP 6589
Laughton (Lincs.) ... 73 SK 8497
Laughton (Lincs.) ... 72 SK 5188
Laughton en le Morthen ... 71 SK 5188
Launcells ... 22 SS 2405

Launceston ... 20 SX 3384
Launde Abbey ... 61 SK 7904
Launton ... 47 SP 6022
Laurencekirk ... 109 NO 7171
Laurieston ... 88 NX 6864
Laurieston Forest ... 88 NX 6564
Lauriston Castle ... 109 NO 7666
Lavan Sands ... 66 SH 6375
Lavant ... 27 SU 8608
Lavendon ... 52 SP 9153
Lavenham ... 54 TL 9149
Lavernhay ... 89 NY 1498
Lavernock Point ... 41 ST 1868
Laverstock ... 26 SU 1530
Laverstoke ... 35 SU 4948
Laverton (Glos.) ... 46 SP 0735
Laverton (N Yorks.) ... 79 SE 2273
Laverton (Somer.) ... 33 ST 7753
Law ... 95 NS 8252
Lawers (Tays.) ... 107 NN 6739
Lawers (Tays.) ... 107 NN 7923
Lawers Burn ... 107 NN 6742
Lawford ... 55 TM 0830
Lawhitton ... 20 SX 3582
Lawkland ... 78 SD 7766
Law Kneis ... 89 NT 2912
Lawley ... 59 SJ 6608
Lawnhead ... 59 SJ 8224
Lawrenny ... 42 SN 0107
Lawshall ... 54 TL 8654
Lawton ... 45 SO 4459
Laxa Burn ... 143 HU 4988
Laxadale Lochs ... 125 NB 1801
Laxay ... 131 NB 3321
Laxdale ... 131 NB 4234
Laxey ... 76 SC 4384
Laxey Bay ... 76 SC 4483
Laxey Head ... 76 SC 4483
Laxfield ... 55 TM 2972
Laxfirth (Shetld.) ... 141 HU 4346
Lax Firth (Shetld.) ... 141 HU 4447
Laxford Bridge ... 132 NC 2347
Laxo ... 141 HU 4463
Laxobigging ... 143 HU 4173
Laxton (Humbs.) ... 74 SE 7825
Laxton (Northants.) ... 62 SP 9496
Laxton (Notts.) ... 72 SK 7266
Layavad ... 131 NF 7723
Laycock ... 78 SE 0340
Layer Breton ... 38 TL 9417
Layer de la Haye ... 39 TL 9620
Layham ... 54 TM 0340
Laytham ... 74 SE 7439
Lazenby ... 85 NZ 5719
Lazonby ... 83 NY 5439
Lea (Derby.) ... 71 SK 3357
Lea (Here. and Worc.) ... 46 SO 6521
Lea (Lincs.) ... 72 SK 8286
Lea (Shrops.) ... 58 SJ 4108
Lea (Shrops.) ... 48 SO 3589
Lea (Wilts.) ... 34 ST 9586
Leacann Doire Bainneir (mt.) ... 115 NN 2994
Leac Dhonn ... 126 NH 0199
Leac Eskadale ... 125 NG 2399
Leachie Hill ... 102 NO 7385
Leachkin ... 128 NH 6344
Leac nam Faoileann ... 123 NG 4214
Leac Shoilleir ... 111 NM 6165
Leac Tressirnish ... 123 NG 5257
Leadburn ... 95 NT 2355
Leadenham ... 62 SK 9452
Leaden Roding ... 38 TL 5913
Leader Water ... 97 NT 5151
Leadgate (Cumbr.) ... 83 NY 7043
Leadgate (Durham) ... 84 NZ 1251
Leadhills ... 88 NS 8814
Leafield ... 47 SP 3115
Lea Green ... 69 SJ 6561
Leake Common Side ... 63 TF 3952
Leake Hurn's End ... 63 TF 4248
Lealholm ... 80 NZ 7607
Lealholm Moor ... 80 NZ 7509
Lealt (Island of Skye) ... 123 NG 5060
Lealt (Jura) ... 99 NR 6690
Lea Marston ... 60 SP 2093
Leamington Hastings ... 51 SP 4467
Leanachan Forest ... 115 NN 1977
Leanoch Burn ... 129 NJ 1851
Leap Hill (Borders) ... 89 NT 5001
Leap Hill (Northum.) ... 90 NT 7207
Leap Moor ... 100 NS 2269
Leargybreck ... 98 NR 5371
Learin ... 98 NR 3548
Learmouth ... 97 NT 8537
Leasgill ... 77 SD 4984
Leasingham ... 62 TF 0548
Leask ... 121 NK 0232
Lea Taing (pt.) ... 137 HY 5410
Leatherhead ... 28 TQ 1656
Leathley ... 78 SE 2346
Leaton ... 58 SJ 4618
Lea Town ... 77 SD 4930
Leavening ... 80 SE 7863
Leavesden Airport ... 36 TL 0900
Leaves Green ... 37 TQ 4162
Lea Yeat ... 83 SD 7587
Lebberston ... 81 TA 0882
Lechlade ... 46 SU 2199
Lecht Road ... 117 NJ 2413
Leck Beck ... 77 SD 6376
Leck Fell ... 77 SD 6678
Leckford ... 26 SU 3737
Leckfurin ... 133 NC 7059
Leckgruinart ... 98 NR 2769
Leckhampstead (Berks.) ... 34 SU 4375
Leckhampstead (Bucks.) ... 51 SP 7237
Leckhampton ... 46 SO 9419
Leckie ... 101 NS 6894
Leckmelm ... 127 NH 1690
Leckwith ... 41 ST 1574
Leconfield ... 74 TA 0143
Leconfield Aerodrome ... 74 TA 0343
Ledaig ... 106 NM 9037
Ledaig Point ... 106 NM 9034
Ledbeg River ... 132 NC 2413
Ledburn ... 36 SP 9022
Ledbury ... 49 SO 7037
Ledcharrie ... 107 NN 5027
Ledgemoor ... 45 SO 4150
Ledgowan Forest ... 127 NH 1256
Ledicot ... 45 SO 4162
Ledmore ... 132 NC 2412
Ledsham (Ches.) ... 68 SJ 3574
Ledsham (W Yorks.) ... 79 SE 4529
Ledston ... 79 SE 4328
Ledwell ... 47 SP 4128
Lee (Devon) ... 22 SS 4846
Lee (Hants.) ... 26 SU 3617
Lee (Island of Mull) ... 105 NM 4022
Lee (Lancs.) ... 77 SD 5655
Lee (Shrops.) ... 58 SJ 4032
Leebotten ... 141 HU 4324
Leebotwood ... 59 SJ 4798
Lee Brockhurst ... 59 SJ 5426
Leece ... 76 SD 2469
Lee Clump ... 36 SP 9004
Leeds (Kent) ... 30 TQ 8253
Leeds (W Yorks.) ... 79 SE 3034
Leeds and Bradford Airport ... 79 SE 2241

Leeds and Liverpool Canal ... 78 SE 1338
Leedstown ... 18 SW 6034
Lee Fell ... 77 SD 5657
Leek ... 60 SJ 9856
Leek Wootton ... 50 SP 2868
Leeming ... 84 SE 2989
Leeming Bar ... 84 SE 2889
Lee Mill ... 21 SX 5955
Lee Moor ... 21 SX 5862
Lee-on-the-Solent ... 27 SU 5600
Lees (Derby.) ... 60 SK 2637
Lees (Gtr Mches) ... 70 SD 9504
Leeswood ... 68 SJ 2759
Lee, The ... 36 SP 8904
Leet Water ... 97 NT 8043
Leez Lodge Lakes ... 38 TL 7118
Legbourne ... 73 TF 3684
Legerwood ... 96 NT 5843
Legsby ... 73 TF 1385
Leicester ... 61 SK 5904
Leicester East Aerodrome ... 61 SK 6602
Leicester Forest East ... 61 SK 5203
Leigh (Dorset) ... 25 ST 6108
Leigh (Gtr Mches) ... 69 SJ 6699
Leigh (Here. and Worc.) ... 49 SO 7853
Leigh (Kent) ... 29 TQ 5546
Leigh (Shrops.) ... 58 SJ 3303
Leigh (Surrey) ... 28 TQ 2246
Leigh (Wilts.) ... 34 SU 0692
Leigh Beck ... 38 TQ 8182
Leigh Common ... 25 ST 7329
Leigh Delamere ... 33 ST 8879
Leigh Green ... 30 TQ 8933
Leigh-on-Sea ... 38 TQ 8385
Leigh Sinton ... 49 SO 7750
Leighterton ... 33 ST 8290
Leighton, The ... 46 SO 8725
Leighton (Powys) ... 58 SJ 2405
Leighton (Shrops.) ... 59 SJ 6105
Leighton (Somer.) ... 33 ST 7043
Leighton Bromswold ... 52 TL 1175
Leighton Buzzard ... 52 SP 9225
Leighton Resr. ... 78 SE 1578
Leigh upon Mendip ... 33 ST 6847
Leigh Woods ... 33 ST 5572
Leinthall Earls ... 48 SO 4467
Leinthall Starkes ... 48 SO 4369
Leintwardine ... 48 SO 4074
Leire ... 51 SP 5290
Leirinmore ... 133 NC 4267
Leishmore ... 115 NH 3940
Leiston ... 55 TM 4462
Leiston Abbey (ant.) ... 55 TM 4464
Leitfie ... 108 NO 2545
Leith ... 103 NT 2676
Leithen Water ... 96 NT 3043
Leith Hall ... 121 NJ 5429
Leith Hill ... 28 TQ 1342
Leitholm ... 97 NT 7944
Leithope Forest ... 90 NT 7408
Lelant ... 18 SW 5437
Lelley ... 75 TA 2032
Lem Hill ... 49 SO 7274
Lemington Hall ... 55 NU 1211
Lempitlaw ... 97 NT 7832
Lemreway ... 131 NB 3811
Lendalfoot ... 86 NX 1390
Lendrick ... 101 NN 5506
Lendrick Hill ... 102 NO 0103
Lenham ... 30 TQ 8952
Lenham Heath ... 30 TQ 9249
Lenie ... 116 NH 5127
Lennel ... 97 NT 8540
Lennoxtown ... 101 NS 6277
Lenton ... 62 TF 0230
Lentran House ... 128 NH 5745
Lenwade ... 65 TG 0918
Leny House ... 101 NN 6108
Lenzie ... 101 NS 6571
Leoch ... 109 NO 3636
Leochel Cushnie ... 119 NJ 5210
Leominster ... 45 SO 4959
Leonach Burn ... 117 NH 9236
Leonard Stanley ... 46 SO 8003
Leosaval (mt.) ... 130 NB 0039
Lephin ... 122 NG 1749
Lephinmore ... 100 NR 9892
Leppington ... 80 SE 7661
Lepton ... 70 SE 2015
Lerryn ... 19 SX 1356
Lerwick (Shetld.) ... 141 HU 4741
Ler Wick (Yell) ... 143 HU 4492
Lesbury ... 91 NU 2311
Leslie (Fife) ... 103 NO 2401
Leslie (Grampn.) ... 121 NJ 5924
Lesmahagow ... 95 NS 8139
Lessendrum ... 121 NJ 5741
Lessingham ... 65 TG 3928
Lessonhall ... 82 NY 2250
Leswalt ... 86 NX 0263
Letchmore Heath ... 37 TQ 1597
Letchworth ... 52 TL 2132
Letcombe Bassett ... 34 SU 3785
Letcombe Regis ... 34 SU 3786
Letham (Fife) ... 103 NO 3014
Letham (Tays.) ... 109 NO 5248
Letham Grange ... 109 NO 6245
Lethenty ... 121 NJ 8041
Letheringham ... 55 TM 2757
Letheringsett ... 64 TG 0638
Letocetum (ant.) ... 21 SK 0906
Lettaford ... 21 SX 7084
Letterewe ... 126 NG 9571
Letterewe Forest ... 126 NG 9772
Letterfearn ... 114 NG 8823
Lettermore ... 105 NM 4948
Letters ... 127 NH 1687
Letterston ... 42 SM 9429
Lettoch (Grampn.) ... 117 NJ 0932
Lettoch (Highld.) ... 117 NJ 0219
Letton (Here. and Worc.) ... 45 SO 3346
Letton (Here. and Worc.) ... 45 SO 3770
Letton Hall ... 64 TF 9705
Letty Green ... 37 TL 2810
Letwell ... 71 SK 5687
Leuchar Burn ... 119 NJ 7804
Leuchars ... 109 NO 4521
Leuchars Airport ... 109 NO 4620
Leuchars Junction Station ... 109 NO 4420
Leum Uilleim ... 106 NN 3364
Leurbost ... 131 NB 3725
Levedale ... 59 SJ 8916
Leven (Fife) ... 103 NO 3700
Leven (Humbs.) ... 75 TA 1045
Levenish (is.) ... 124 NF 1396
Levens ... 77 SD 4886
Levenshulme ... 69 SJ 8794
Levenwick ... 141 HU 4021
Levenwick Ness ... 141 HU 4121
Leverburgh ... 124 NG 0186
Leverington ... 63 TF 4411
Levers Water ... 82 SD 2799
Leverton ... 63 TF 3947
Levington ... 55 TM 2339

Levisham....80 SE 8390
Levishie Forest....115 NH 3919
Lew....47 SP 3206
Lewannick....20 SX 2780
Lewdown....20 SX 4486
Lewes....29 TQ 4110
Leweston....42 SM 9422
Lewisham....37 TQ 3674
Lewiston....116 NH 5029
Lewknor....36 SU 7197
Leworthy....23 SS 6638
Lews Castle....131 NB 4133
Lewtrenchard....20 SX 4586
Ley (Corn.)....19 SX 1766
Ley (Grampn.)....119 NJ 5312
Leybourne....30 TQ 6858
Leyburn....84 SE 1190
Leycett....59 SJ 7846
Leyland....77 SD 5421
Leylodge....119 NJ 7713
Leys (Grampn.)....121 NK 0052
Leys (Tays.)....108 NO 2537
Leys Castle....128 NH 6841
Leysdown on Sea....31 TR 0370
Leysmill....109 NO 6047
Leys of Cossans....109 NO 3749
Leysters....48 SO 5563
Leyton....37 TQ 3886
Lezant....20 SX 3378
Lhanbryde....120 NJ 2761
Lhen, The....76 NX 3801
Liathach (mt.)....126 NG 9257
Liath Eilean....100 NR 8883
Libbers Hill....58 HP 5813
Liberton....95 NS 9943
Liberton....103 NT 2769
Lichfield....60 SK 1209
Lickey....50 SO 9975
Lickey End....50 SO 9772
Lickfold....28 SU 9225
Licklyhead Castle....121 NJ 6223
Liddel....136 ND 4683
Liddel Water....89 NY 4478
Liddesdale (Dumf. and Galwy.)....89 NY 4787
Liddesdale (Highld.)....111 NM 7859
Liddington....34 SU 2081
Liddington Castle (ant.)....34 SU 2079
Lidgate....54 TL 7258
Lidlington....52 SP 9939
Lidstone....47 SP 3524
Liernish (dist.)....124 NF 8758
Lieurary (dist.)....135 ND 0762
Liff....108 NO 3332
Lifton....20 SX 3885
Ligger or Perran Bay....18 SW 7256
Lighthazles....70 SE 0220
Lighthorne....50 SP 3355
Lightwater....36 SU 9262
Lightwood....59 SJ 9041
Lightwood Green....58 SJ 3840
Liksto....125 NG 1292
Lilbourne....51 SP 5677
Lilburn Tower....97 NU 0224
Lilford Hall (ant.)....52 TL 0284
Lilleshall....59 SJ 7315
Lilley....52 TL 1226
Lilliesleaf....96 NT 5325
Lillingstone Dayrell....51 SP 7039
Lillingstone Lovell....51 SP 7140
Lillington....25 ST 6212
Lilly Loch....101 NS 8267
Lilstock....32 ST 1644
Limbrick....69 SD 6016
Limefield....69 SD 8012
Limekilns....95 NS 7050
Limekilns....102 NT 0783
Limerigg....102 NS 8570
Limington....25 ST 5422
Limmerhaugh....94 NS 6126
Limpenhoe....65 TG 3903
Limpley Stoke....33 ST 7760
Limpsfield....29 TQ 4152
Linacre Resrs....71 SK 3372
Linby....61 SK 5350
Linchmere....27 SU 8630
Lincluden College (ant.)....88 NX 9678
Lincoln....72 SK 9771
Lincomb....49 SO 8268
Lincombe....21 SX 7458
Lindale....77 SD 4180
Lindal in Furness....76 SD 2575
Lindean....96 NT 4931
Lindfield....29 TQ 3425
Lindford....27 SU 8136
Lindisfarne (ant.)....97 NU 1343
Lindley Wood Resr....78 SE 2149
Lindores....108 NO 2616
Lindores Loch....108 NO 2616
Lindridge....49 SO 6769
Lindsell....54 TL 6427
Lindsey....54 TL 9744
Linfern Lock....86 NX 3697
Linford (Essex)....38 TQ 6779
Linford (Hants.)....26 SU 1707
Linga (Hildasay) (is.)....141 HU 3639
Linga (Shetld.) (is.)....141 HU 3563
Linga (Shetld.) (is.)....143 HU 4673
Linga (Yell) (is.)....143 HU 5598
Lingague....76 SC 2172
Linga Holm....137 HY 6127
Lingarabay Island....125 NG 0684
Linga Sound (Stronsay)....137 HY 6228
Linga Sound (Whalsay)....141 HU 5464
Lingay (Harris, W Isles)....124 NG 0178
Lingay (North Uist)....124 NF 8778
Lingay (South Uist)....112 NF 7511
Lingay (W Isles)....112 NL 6089
Lingdale....85 NZ 6716
Lingen....48 SO 3667
Lingfield....29 TQ 3943
Linglie Hill....96 NT 4530
Lingmell....82 NY 2007
Ling Ness....141 HU 4954
Lingwood....65 TG 3609
Linhope Water....102 NT 0662
Liniclate....124 NF 7949
Linicro....123 NG 3967
Linkenholt....34 SU 3657
Linkinhorne....20 SX 3173
Linklater....136 ND 4587
Linklet Bay....139 HY 7754
Linksness (Hoy, Shetld.)....136 HY 2403
Linksness (Orkney)....137 HY 5210
Links Ness (Stronsay)....137 HY 6129
Linktown....103 NT 2790
Linley....58 SO 3593
Linley Green....49 SO 6953
Linley Hill....58 SO 3594
Linlithgow....102 NS 9977
Linlithgow Bridge....102 NS 9877
Linney....42 SR 8996
Linney Head....42 SR 8896
Linn of Dee....117 NO 0589
Linshader (Isle of Lewis)....131 NB 2032
Linshiels....90 NT 8906
Linsidemore....134 NH 5499
Linslade....52 SP 9125
Linstead Parva....55 TM 3377
Linstock....89 NY 4258
Linthwaite....70 SE 0913
Lintlaw....97 NT 8258
Lintmill....121 NJ 5165

Linton (Borders)....96 NT 7726
Linton (Cambs.)....53 TL 5646
Linton (Derby.)....60 SK 2716
Linton (Here. and Worc.)....46 SO 6625
Linton (Kent)....29 TQ 7549
Linton (N Yorks.)....78 SD 9962
Linton Hill....97 NT 7827
Linton-on-Ouse....79 SE 4960
Linwood (Hants.)....26 SU 1809
Linwood (Lincs.)....73 TF 1186
Linwood (Strath.)....101 NS 4464
Lionel....131 NB 5363
Liphook....27 SU 8431
Liscombe....23 SS 8732
Lisgear Mhòr....130 HW 8133
Liskeard....19 SX 2564
Lismore....105 NM 8441
Liss....27 SU 7727
Lisset....81 TA 1458
Liss Forest....27 SU 7929
Lissington....73 TF 1083
Lisvane....41 ST 1983
Litcham....64 TF 8817
Litchborough....51 SP 6354
Litchfield....35 SU 4553
Litherland....68 SJ 3397
Litlington (Cambs.)....53 TL 3142
Litlington (E Susx)....29 TQ 5201
Little Abington....53 TL 5349
Little Addington....52 SP 9573
Little Alne....50 SP 1361
Little Aston....60 SK 0900
Little Atherfield....27 SZ 4680
Little Ayre (Hoy, Orkney)....136 ND 3091
Little-ayre (Muckle Roe)....141 HU 3262
Little Ayton....85 NZ 5710
Little Baddow....38 TL 7807
Little Badminton....33 ST 8084
Little Ballinluig....108 NN 9152
Little Bardfield....54 TL 6530
Little Barford....52 TL 1857
Little Barningham....65 TG 1333
Little Barrington....47 SP 2012
Little Barugh....80 SE 7579
Little Bedwyn....34 SU 2966
Little Bentley....55 TM 1125
Little Berkhamsted....37 TL 2907
Little Bernera (is.)....131 NB 1441
Little Billing....51 SP 8061
Little Birch....45 SO 5031
Little Blakenham....55 TM 1048
Littleborough (Gtr Mches)....69 SD 9316
Littleborough (Notts.)....72 SK 8282
Littlebourne....31 TR 2057
Little Bowden....51 SP 7487
Little Bradley....54 TL 6852
Little Brampton....48 SO 3681
Little Brechin....109 NO 5862
Littlebredy....25 SY 5888
Little Brickhill....52 SP 9032
Little Brington....51 SP 6663
Little Bromley....55 TM 0928
Little Budworth....69 SJ 5965
Little Burstead....38 TQ 6691
Littlebury....53 TL 5139
Littlebury Green....53 TL 4938
Little Bytham....62 TF 0118
Little Carlton....73 TF 3985
Little Casterton....62 TF 0109
Little Cawthorpe....73 TF 3583
Little Chalfont....36 SU 9997
Little Chart....30 TQ 9245
Little Chesterford....53 TL 5141
Little Cheverell....34 ST 9853
Little Chishill....53 TL 4237
Little Clacton....39 TM 1618
Little Colonsay (is.)....104 NM 3736
Little Comberton....50 SO 9643
Little Common....29 TQ 7107
Little Compton....47 SP 2530
Littlecote (ant.)....34 SU 3070
Little Cowarne....45 SO 6051
Little Coxwell....47 SU 2893
Little Cressingham....64 TF 8600
Little Cumbrae Island....93 NS 1451
Little Dalby....61 SK 7714
Littledale....77 SD 5761
Little Dart River....23 SS 7814
Littledean....46 SO 6713
Little Dens....121 NK 0744
Little Dewchurch....45 SO 5231
Little Don or The Porter River....71 SE 2399
Little Downham....53 TL 5284
Little Dunham....64 TF 8613
Little Dunkeld....108 NO 0242
Little Dunmow....38 TL 6521
Little Easton....38 TL 6023
Little Eaton....60 SK 3641
Little Ellingham....64 TM 0099
Little End....37 TL 5400
Little Eversden....53 TL 3752
Little Fakenham....54 TL 9076
Little Faringdon....47 SP 2201
Little Fen....53 TL 5868
Little Fenton....79 SE 5135
Littleferry....129 NH 8095
Little Fransham....64 TF 9011
Little Gaddesden....36 SP 9913
Little Garway....45 SO 4424
Little Gidding....52 TL 1382
Little Glemham....55 TM 3458
Little Gransden....53 TL 2755
Little Gruinard....126 NG 9489
Little Gruinard River....126 NG 9486
Little Hadham....37 TL 4422
Little Haldon (dist.)....21 SX 9176
Little Hallingbury....37 TL 5017
Littleham (Devon)....22 SS 4323
Littleham (Devon)....24 SY 0281
Little Hampden....36 SP 8603
Littlehampton....28 TQ 0202
Little Harrowden....52 SP 8771
Little Hartmidden (mt.)....94 NS 6032
Little Haseley....36 SP 6400
Little Hautbois....65 TG 2521
Little Haven....42 SM 8513
Little Hay....60 SK 1202
Little Haywood....60 SK 0021
Littlehempston....21 SX 8162
Little Hereford....48 SO 5568
Little Hill....40 SO 1267
Little Holm....143 HU 4086
Little Horkesley....54 TL 9631
Little Horsted....29 TQ 4718
Little Horwood....51 SP 7930
Little Houghton (Northants.)....51 SP 8059
Littlehoughton (Northum.)....91 NU 2316
Little Hucklow....71 SK 1678
Little Hulton....69 SD 7103
Little John's Haven....119 NO 8574
Little Kingshill....36 SU 8999
Little Langdale....82 NY 3103
Little Langford....26 SU 0436
Little Laver....37 TL 5409
Little Leigh....69 SJ 6175
Little Leighs....38 TL 7116
Little Lever....69 SD 7507
Little Loch Broom....126 NH 0292
Little Loch Roag....131 NB 1327
Little London (E Susx)....29 TQ 5420
Little London (Hants.)....34 SU 3749
Little London (Hants.)....36 SU 6259

Little London (Lincs.)....63 TF 2321
Little Longstone....70 SK 1871
Little Linturk....119 NJ 5712
Little Malvern....49 SO 7741
Little Maplestead....54 TL 8233
Little Marcle....49 SO 6736
Little Marlow....36 SU 8788
Little Massingham....64 TF 7924
Little Melton....65 TG 1506
Little Mill (Gwent)....45 SO 3102
Littlemill (Highld.)....129 NH 9150
Littlemill (Strath.)....93 NS 4515
Little Milton....36 SP 6100
Little Minch, The....125 NG 0560
Little Minch, The (chan.)....122 NG 0661
Little Missenden....36 SU 9298
Littlemore....47 SP 5302
Little Ness (I. of M.)....76 SC 3673
Little Ness (Shrops.)....58 SJ 4019
Little Newcastle....42 SM 9829
Little Newsham....84 NZ 1217
Little Oakley (Essex)....55 TM 2229
Little Oakley (Northants.)....52 SP 8985
Little Ormes Head....67 SH 8182
Little Orton....82 NY 3555
Little Ouse River....54 TL 8387
Littleover....60 SK 3234
Little Paxton....52 TL 1862
Little Petherick....19 SW 9172
Little Pitlurg....121 NJ 4245
Little Plumstead....65 TG 3112
Littleport....53 TL 5686
Little Rack Wick....136 ND 2392
Little Rahane....100 NS 2386
Little Raveley....53 TL 2579
Little Ribston....79 SE 3853
Little Rissington....47 SP 1819
Little River....135 ND 1548
Little Roe (is.)....143 HU 4079
Little Ross....87 NX 6543
Little Ryburgh....64 TF 9628
Little Ryle....91 NU 0211
Little Salkeld....83 NY 5636
Little Sampford....54 TL 6533
Little Saxham....54 TL 7963
Little Scatwell....127 NH 3756
Little Shelford....53 TL 4551
Little Shillay....124 NF 8790
Little Skerry....143 HU 6371
Little Smeaton....71 SE 5219
Little Snoring....64 TF 9532
Little Somerford....34 ST 9684
Little Stainton....85 NZ 3420
Little Stanney....68 SJ 4173
Little Staughton....52 TL 1062
Little Steeping....73 TF 4362
Littlestone-on-Sea....31 TR 0824
Little Stonham....55 TM 1160
Little Stretton (Leic.)....61 SK 6600
Little Stretton (Shrops.)....48 SO 4491
Little Strickland....83 NY 5619
Little Stukeley....52 TL 2075
Little Tew....47 SP 3828
Little Thetford....53 TL 5376
Littlethorpe....79 SE 3269
Little Thurrock....30 TQ 6477
Littleton (Ches.)....68 SJ 4366
Littleton (Hants.)....27 SU 4532
Littleton (Somer.)....25 ST 4830
Littleton (Surrey)....36 TQ 0768
Littleton (Tays.)....108 NO 2633
Littleton Down....34 SU 9751
Littleton Drew....33 ST 8280
Littleton-on-Severn....33 ST 5990
Littleton Pannell....34 ST 9954
Little Torrington....22 SS 4816
Little Totham....38 TL 8812
Little Town (Cumbr.)....82 NY 2319
Littletown (Durham)....84 NZ 3343
Little Wakering....39 TQ 9388
Little Walden....53 TL 5441
Little Waldingfield....54 TL 9245
Little Walsingham....64 TF 9336
Little Waltham....38 TL 7012
Little Warley....38 TQ 6090
Little Water....121 NJ 8441
Little Weighton....74 SE 9833
Little Welnetham....54 TL 8859
Little Wenlock....59 SJ 6406
Little Whernside....78 SE 0277
Little Whittingham Green....55 TM 2877
Littlewick Green....36 SU 8379
Little Wilbraham....53 TL 5458
Little Witley....49 SO 7863
Little Wittenham....47 SU 5693
Little Wolford....47 SP 2635
Littleworth (Here. and Worc.)....49 SO 8850
Littleworth (Oxon.)....47 SU 3197
Littleworth (Staffs.)....60 SK 0111
Little Wyrley....60 SK 0105
Little Wyvis (mt.)....128 NH 4364
Little Yeldham....54 TL 7739
Litton (Derby.)....70 SK 1674
Litton (N Yorks.)....78 SD 9074
Litton (Somer.)....33 ST 5954
Litton Cheney....25 SY 5490
Littondale....78 SD 9011
Liundale....98 NR 5478
Liuthaid (mt.)....131 NB 1713
Liverpool....68 SJ 3591
Liverpool Airport....68 SJ 4183
Liverpool Bay....68 SJ 1599
Liverpool Street Station....37 TQ 3381
Liversedge....78 SE 2024
Liverton....102 NZ 7115
Livingston....102 NT 0568
Livingston Village....102 NT 0366
Lixwm....68 SJ 1671
Lizard....18 SW 6912
Lizard Point....18 SW 6911
Llanaber....56 SH 6018
Llanaelhaearn....66 SH 3844
Llanafan....57 SN 6872
Llanafan-fechan....44 SN 9650
Llanallgo....66 SH 5085
Llanarmon....66 SH 4239
Llanarmon Dyffryn Ceiriog....58 SJ 1532
Llanarmon-yn-Ial....58 SJ 1856
Llanarth (Dyfed)....43 SN 4257
Llanarth (Gwent)....45 SO 3711
Llanarthney....43 SN 5320
Llanasa....67 SJ 1081
Llanbabo....66 SH 3786
Llanbadarn Fawr....57 SN 6080
Llanbadarn Fynydd....44 SO 0977
Llanbadarn-y-garreg....44 SO 1148
Llanbadoc....66 SH 3794
Llanbeder....32 ST 3890
Llanbedr (Gwyn.)....56 SH 5826
Llanbedr (Powys)....44 SO 1346
Llanbedr (Powys)....45 SO 2320
Llanbedr-Dyffryn-Clwyd....68 SJ 1459
Llanbedrgoch....66 SH 5180
Llanbedrog....66 SH 3231
Llanbedr-y-cennin....66 SH 7569
Llanberis....66 SH 5760
Llanbister....45 SO 1073
Llanbister Road Station....45 SO 1771
Llanblethian....41 SS 9873
Llanboidy....43 SN 2123
Llanbradach....41 ST 1490

Llanbrynmair....57 SH 9002
Llancarfan....41 ST 0570
Llancynfelyn....57 SN 6492
Llandaff....41 ST 1578
Llandanwg....56 SH 5728
Llandawke....43 SN 2811
Llanddanael Fab....66 SH 4970
Llanddarog....43 SN 5016
Llanddeiniol....56 SN 5672
Llanddeiniolen....66 SH 5465
Llandderfel....67 SH 9837
Llanddeusant (Dyfed)....41 SN 7724
Llanddeusant (Gwyn.)....66 SH 3485
Llanddew....41 SO 0530
Llanddewi....40 SS 4689
Llanddewi Brefi....43 SN 6655
Llanddewi'r Cwm....44 SO 0348
Llanddewi Rhydderch....45 SO 3412
Llanddewi Velfrey....42 SN 1417
Llanddewi Ystradenni....57 SO 1068
Llanddoged....67 SH 8063
Llanddona....66 SH 5779
Llanddowror....43 SN 2514
Llanddulas....67 SH 9078
Llanddwyn Island....66 SH 3862
Llanddyfnan....66 SH 5078
Llandefaelog....43 SN 4111
Llandefaelog Fach....41 SO 0332
Llandefaelog-tre'r-graig....41 SO 1230
Llandefalle....41 SO 1135
Llandefalle Hill....44 SO 0637
Llandegai....66 SH 5970
Llandegfan....66 SH 5674
Llandegfedd Resr....45 ST 3299
Llandegla....58 SJ 1952
Llandegley....48 SO 1363
Llandegley Rhos....44 SO 1360
Llandegveth....45 ST 3395
Llandeilo....43 SN 6322
Llandeilo Graban....44 SO 0944
Llandeilo Hill....44 SO 0946
Llandeilo'r Fan....44 SN 8934
Llandeloy....42 SM 8526
Llandenny....45 SO 4104
Llandevenny....32 ST 4186
Llandinabo....45 SO 5128
Llandinam....57 SO 0288
Llandissilio....42 SN 1221
Llandogo....45 SO 5204
Llandough (S Glam)....41 SS 9972
Llandough (S Glam)....41 ST 1673
Llandovery....41 SN 7634
Llandow....41 SS 9473
Llandre (Dyfed)....57 SN 6286
Llandre (Dyfed)....43 SN 6641
Llandrillo....67 SJ 0337
Llandrillo-yn-Rhos....67 SH 8380
Llandrindod Wells....57 SO 0561
Llandrinio....58 SJ 2917
Llandudno....67 SH 7782
Llandudno Junction....67 SH 7977
Llandwrog....66 SH 4556
Llandybie....43 SN 6215
Llandyfan....43 SN 6417
Llandyfriog....43 SN 3241
Llandyfrydog....66 SH 4485
Llandygwydd....43 SN 2443
Llandyrnog....67 SJ 1064
Llandyssil....58 SO 1995
Llandysul....43 SN 4140
Llanegryn....56 SH 5905
Llanegwad....43 SN 5121
Llanelian-yn-Rhos....67 SH 8376
Llanelidan....67 SJ 1050
Llanelieu....45 SO 1834
Llanellen....45 SO 3010
Llanelli (Dyfed)....40 SN 5000
Llanelltyd....57 SH 7119
Llanelly (Gwent)....45 SO 2314
Llanelwedd....44 SO 0451
Llanenddwyn....56 SH 5823
Llanengan....56 SH 2927
Llanerchymedd....66 SH 4183
Llanerfyl....57 SJ 0309
Llanfachraeth....66 SH 3182
Llanfachreth....57 SH 7522
Llanfaelog....66 SH 3373
Llanfaes....66 SH 6077
Llanfaethlu....66 SH 3186
Llanfaglan....66 SH 4760
Llanfair....56 SH 5729
Llanfair Caereinion....57 SJ 1006
Llanfair Clydogau....43 SN 6251
Llanfair Dyffryn Clwyd....58 SJ 1355
Llanfairfechan....67 SH 6874
Llanfair-green....45 SO 3919
Llanfair-Nant-Gwyn....42 SN 1637
Llanfairpwllgwyngyll....66 SH 5371
Llanfair Talhaiarn....67 SH 9269
Llanfair Waterdine....48 SO 2476
Llanfairynghornwy....66 SH 3290
Llanfair-yn-Neubwll....66 SH 3077
Llanfallteg....42 SN 1520
Llanfallteg West....42 SN 1519
Llanfaredd....44 SO 0651
Llanfechain....58 SJ 1820
Llanfechell....66 SH 3691
Llanfendigaid....56 SH 5605
Llanferres....68 SJ 1860
Llanfflewyn....66 SH 3689
Llanfihangel ar-Arth....43 SN 4539
Llanfihangel Crucorney....45 SO 3220
Llanfihangel Glyn Myfyr....67 SH 9849
Llanfihangel Nant Bran....41 SN 9434
Llanfihangel-nant-Melan....45 SO 1758
Llanfihangel Rhydithon....48 SO 1466
Llanfihangel Rogiet....33 ST 4487
Llanfihangel-Tal-y-llyn....45 SO 1128
Llanfihangel uwch-Gwili....43 SN 4822
Llanfihangel-y-Creuddyn....57 SN 6676
Llanfihangel-yng-Ngwynfa....58 SJ 0817
Llanfihangel-y-pennant (Gwyn.)....66 SH 5245
Llanfihangel-y-Pennant (Gwyn.)....57 SH 6708
Llanfihangel Ystern Llywern....45 SO 4313
Llanfihangel-y-traethau....66 SH 5935
Llanfilo....44 SO 1133
Llanfoist....45 SO 2813
Llanfor....67 SH 9336
Llanfrechfa....45 SO 3193
Llanfrothen....67 SH 6241
Llanfrynach....44 SO 0726
Llanfwrog (Clwyd)....68 SJ 1157
Llanfwrog (Gwyn.)....66 SH 3083
Llanfyllin....58 SJ 1419
Llanfynydd (Clwyd)....58 SJ 2756
Llanfynydd (Dyfed)....43 SN 5527
Llanfyrnach....43 SN 2231
Llangadog....57 SJ 0010
Llangadwaladr (Clwyd)....58 SJ 1730
Llangadwaladr (Gwyn.)....66 SH 3869
Llangaffo....66 SH 4468
Llangain....43 SN 3815
Llangammarch Wells....44 SN 9347
Llangan....45 SS 9577
Llangarron....45 SO 5221
Llangasty-Talyllyn....44 SO 1426
Llangathen....43 SN 5822
Llangattock....41 SO 2117

Llangattock Lingoed....45 SO 3620
Llangattock-Vibon-Avel....45 SO 4515
Llangedwyn....58 SJ 1824
Llangefni....66 SH 4575
Llangeinor....41 SS 9187
Llangeitho....43 SN 6159
Llangeler....43 SN 3739
Llangelynin....56 SH 5707
Llangendeirne....40 SN 4514
Llangennech....40 SN 5601
Llangennith....40 SS 4291
Llangenny....45 SO 2418
Llangernyw....67 SH 8767
Llangian....56 SH 2928
Llangiwg....40 SN 7205
Llanglydwen....43 SN 1826
Llangoed....66 SH 6079
Llangoed Castle (ant.)....44 SO 1140
Llangoedmor....43 SN 2045
Llangollen....58 SJ 2141
Llangollen Canal (Ches.)....59 SJ 5847
Llangollen Canal (Clwyd)....58 SJ 2342
Llangolman....43 SN 1127
Llangorse....41 SO 1327
Llangorse Lake....41 SO 1326
Llangorwen....56 SN 6084
Llangovan....45 SO 4505
Llangower....67 SH 9032
Llangranog....43 SN 3154
Llangristiolus....66 SH 4373
Llangrove....45 SO 5219
Llangunllo....48 SO 2171
Llangunnor....43 SN 4219
Llangurig....57 SN 9080
Llangwm (Clwyd)....67 SH 9644
Llangwm (Dyfed)....42 SM 9909
Llangwm (Gwent)....45 SO 4200
Llangwnnadl....66 SH 2033
Llangwyfan....68 SJ 1266
Llangwyllog....66 SH 4379
Llangwyryfon....56 SN 5970
Llangybi (Dyfed)....43 SN 6053
Llangybi (Gwent)....45 ST 3796
Llangybi (Gwyn.)....56 SH 4240
Llangyfelach....40 SS 6499
Llangynhafal....68 SJ 1263
Llangynidr....41 SO 1519
Llangynin....43 SN 2519
Llangynog (Dyfed)....43 SN 3316
Llangynog (Powys)....57 SJ 0526
Llanhamlach....41 SO 0926
Llanharan....41 ST 0083
Llanharry....41 ST 0080
Llanhennock....32 ST 3592
Llanhilleth....45 SO 2101
Llanidloes....57 SN 9584
Llanieston....66 SH 2633
Llanigon....52 SO 2139
Llanilid....57 SN 6275
Llanishen (Gwent)....45 SO 4703
Llanishen (S Glam.)....41 ST 1781
Llanllawddog....43 SN 8977
Llanllechid....67 SH 6268
Llanllowell....44 SO 9350
Llanllugan....58 SJ 0402
Llanllwch....43 SN 3818
Llanllwchaiarn....48 SO 1192
Llanllyfni....66 SH 4651
Llanmadoc....40 SS 4493
Llanmaes....41 SS 9869
Llanmartin....32 ST 3989
Llanmerewig....58 SO 1593
Llanmihangel....45 SS 9771
Llanmorlais....40 SS 5294
Llannefydd....67 SH 9770
Llannerch Hall....67 SJ 0572
Llannon....59 SN 5408
Llannor....66 SH 3537
Llanon....43 SN 5167
Llanpumsaint....43 SN 4129
Llanreithan....42 SM 8628
Llanrhaeadr....67 SJ 0763
Llanrhaeadr-ym-Mochnant....58 SJ 1226
Llanrhain....42 SM 8131
Llanrhidian....40 SS 4992
Llanrhidian Sands....40 SS 4895
Llanrhos....67 SH 7880
Llanrhyddlad....66 SH 3389
Llanrhystud....56 SN 5369
Llanrothal....45 SO 4618
Llanrug....66 SH 5363
Llanrwst....67 SH 7961
Llansadwrnen....43 SN 2810
Llansadwrn (Dyfed)....40 SN 6931
Llansadwrn (Gwyn.)....66 SH 5575
Llansaint....43 SN 3808
Llansamlet....40 SS 6997
Llansanffraid....67 SH 9365
Llansannor....41 SS 9977
Llansantffraed....44 SO 1223
Llansantffraed-Cwmdeuddwr....57 SN 9667
Llansantffraed-in-Elvel....44 SO 0954
Llansantffraid....56 SN 5167
Llansantffraid Glan Conwy....67 SH 8075
Llansantffraid-ym-Mechain....58 SJ 2220
Llansawel....43 SN 6136
Llansilin....58 SJ 2028
Llansoy....45 SO 4402
Llanspyddid....41 SO 0328
Llanstadwell....42 SM 9505
Llanstephan (Dyfed)....43 SN 3511
Llanstephan (Powys)....44 SO 1142
Llanthony....45 SO 2827
Llantilio-Crossenny....45 SO 3914
Llantilio Pertholey....45 SO 3116
Llantrisant (Gwent)....45 ST 3996
Llantrisant (Mid Glam.)....41 ST 0483
Llantrithyd....41 ST 0472
Llantwit Fardre....41 ST 0785
Llantwit Major....41 SS 9768
Llantysilio Hall....58 SJ 1943
Llantysilio Mountain....58 SJ 1545
Llanuwchllyn....67 SH 8730
Llanvaches....33 ST 4391
Llanvair-Discoed....33 ST 4492
Llanvapley....45 SO 3614
Llanvetherine....45 SO 3617
Llanveynoe....45 SO 3031
Llanvihangel Gobion....45 SO 3409
Llanwarne....45 SO 5028
Llan-wen Hill....48 SO 3069
Llanwenog....43 SN 4945
Llanwern....32 ST 3688
Llanwinio....43 SN 2626
Llanwnda (Dyfed)....42 SM 9339
Llanwnda (Gwyn.)....66 SH 4758
Llanwnnen....43 SN 5347
Llanwnog....57 SO 0293
Llanwrda....57 SN 7131
Llanwrin....57 SH 7803
Llanwrthwl....57 SN 9763
Llanwrtyd....44 SN 8647
Llanwrtyd Wells....44 SN 8746
Llanwyddelan....57 SJ 0801
Llanyblodwel....58 SJ 2322
Llanybri....43 SN 3312
Llanybyther....43 SN 5244
Llanycefn....42 SN 0923

Name	Page	Grid
Llanychaer	42	SM 9835
Llancrwys	43	SN 6445
Llanmawddwy	57	SH 9019
Llanmynech	58	SJ 2620
Llanynghenedl	66	SH 3181
Llanynys	67	SJ 1062
Llanyre	57	SO 0462
Llanystumdwy	66	SH 4738
Llanywern	41	SO 1028
Llawhaden	42	SN 0717
Llawlech (mt.)	57	SH 6321
Llawnt	58	SJ 2430
Llawr-y-dre	56	SH 2728
Llawryglyn	57	SN 9291
Llay	57	SJ 3255
Llechcynfarwy	66	SH 3881
Llechfaen	41	SO 0828
Llechryd (Dyfed)	43	SN 2243
Llechryd (Mid Glam.)	41	SO 1009
Llechrydau	58	SJ 2234
Lledrod (Clwyd)	58	SJ 2229
Lledrod (Dyfed)	57	SN 6470
Lleyn Peninsula	66	SH 3237
Llidiadnenog	43	SN 5437
Llidiardau	66	SH 1929
Llithfaen	66	SH 3543
Lliw Resrs.	43	SN 6505
Llong	68	SJ 2562
Llowes	41	SO 1941
Llwydcoed	41	SN 9905
Llwydiarth	57	SJ 0315
Llwyn	58	SO 2880
Llwyncelyn	43	SN 4459
Llwyndafydd	43	SN 3755
Llwynderw	58	SJ 2004
Llwyndyrys	66	SH 3741
Llwyngwril	56	SH 5909
Llwynhendy	40	SS 5599
Llwynmawr	58	SJ 2236
Llwyn-on Resr.	41	SO 0011
Llwynypia	41	SS 9993
Llyn Alaw	66	SH 3986
Llyn Aled	67	SH 9157
Llyn Alwen	67	SH 8956
Llyn Arennig-Fawr	44	SH 8437
Llyn Berwyn	44	SN 7456
Llyn Bodlyn	67	SH 6423
Llyn Brân	67	SH 9659
Llyn Brianne	44	SN 8050
Llyn Celyn	67	SH 8640
Llynclys	58	SJ 2924
Llyn Clywedog	57	SN 8989
Llyn Coch-hwyad	57	SH 9211
Llyn Conwy	67	SH 7746
Llyn Coron	66	SH 3770
Llyn Cowlyd Resr.	67	SH 7262
Llyn Crafnant Resr.	67	SH 7461
Llyn Cwellyn	66	SH 5554
Llyn Cwmystradllyn	66	SH 5644
Llyn Dinas	66	SH 6149
Llyn Dulyn Resr.	57	SH 7066
Llyn-dŵr Hill.	57	SO 0583
Llyn Eigiau Resr.	67	SH 7065
Llyn Elsi Resr.	67	SH 7855
Llynfaes	66	SH 4178
Llyn Frogwy	66	SH 4477
Llyn Gwyddior	57	SH 9307
Llyn Gwynant	67	SH 6452
Llyn Helyg	68	SJ 1177
Llyn Hywel	67	SH 6626
Llyn Llydaw	67	SH 6254
Llyn Llywenan	66	SH 3481
Llyn Mawr	57	SO 0097
Llyn Nantle Uchaf	66	SH 5153
Llyn Ogwen	67	SH 6560
Llyn Padarn	66	SH 5761
Llyn Peris	66	SH 5959
Llyn Syfydrin	57	SN 7284
Llyn Tegid or Bala Lake	67	SH 9033
Llyn Teifi	57	SN 7867
Llyn-y Fan Fawr	41	SN 8321
Llynytarw	57	SO 0297
Llysfaen	67	SH 8977
Llyswen	44	SO 1337
Llysworney	41	SS 9674
Llys-y-frân	42	SN 0424
Llys-y-frân Resr.	42	SN 0425
Llywel	41	SN 8630
Loadpot Hill	83	NY 4518
Loan	102	NS 9575
Loanend	97	NT 9450
Loanhead	103	NT 2765
Loans	93	NS 3431
Lòba Sgeir	130	HW 8031
Lochaber (dist.)	115	NN 1492
Lochaber Loch	88	NX 9270
Loch a' Bhaid-luachraich	126	NG 8986
Loch a'Bhealaich (Highld.)	133	NC 6026
Loch a'Bhealaich (Highld.)	123	NG 8664
Loch a'Bhealaich (Highld.)	114	NH 0221
Loch a'Bhealaich Bheithe	107	NN 5171
Loch a'Bhràige	123	NG 6261
Loch a'Bhraoin	127	NH 1374
Loch a'Bhùrra	99	NR 6696
Loch a'Chàirn Bhàin	132	NC 1934
Loch Achall	127	NH 1795
Loch Achanalt	127	NH 2761
Loch a'Chaorainn	128	NH 4678
Loch a'Chaoruinn	99	NR 7866
Loch Achilty	128	NH 4356
Loch Achnamoine	134	NC 8132
Loch a'Chnuic Bhric	98	NR 4473
Loch a' Choire	111	NM 8452
Loch a' Choire Mhòir	127	NH 3088
Loch Achonachie	128	NH 4354
Loch a'Chraeaich	123	NG 7657
Loch a'Chràthaich	115	NH 3621
Loch Achray	101	NN 5106
Loch a' Chròisg	127	NH 1258
Loch Affric	115	NH 1522
Loch a' Gharbh-bhaid Mòr	132	NC 2748
Loch a'Gheòidh	99	NR 6695
Loch a' Ghlinne	130	NB 0212
Loch a'Ghorm-choire	133	NC 4433
Loch a'Ghriama	132	NC 3926
Loch Ailort (Highld.)	111	NM 7379
Lochailort (Highld.)	111	NM 7682
Loch Ailsh	132	NC 3110
Loch Ainort	123	NG 5528
Loch Airdeglais	105	NM 6228
Loch Airigh na Beinne	132	NC 3266
Loch Airigh na h-Airde	131	NB 2123
Loch Akran	134	NC 9260
Loch a' Laip	124	NF 8647
Lochaline (Highld.)	105	NM 6744
Loch Aline (Highld.)	105	NM 6845
Loch Alsh	123	NG 8125
Loch Alvie	117	NH 8609
Loch a' Mhuilinn	135	NO 0142
Loch a' Mhuillidh	115	NH 2738
Lochan a' Chairn	128	NH 5184
Loch an Aircill	98	NR 5076
Loch an Alltan Fhearna	134	NC 7533
Lochan Breaclaich	107	NN 6231
Lochan Burn	88	NT 0000
Loch an Daimh (Highld.)	127	NH 2794
Loch an Daimh (Tays.)	107	NN 4846
Loch an Dherue	133	NC 5448
Loch an Doire Dhuibh	132	NC 1310
Loch an Draing	126	NG 7790
Lochan Dubh nan Geodh	135	NO 0248
Loch an Dùin	116	NN 7279
Loch an Easain Uaine	132	NC 3246
Loch an Eircill	132	NC 3027
Loch an Eoin	132	NG 9251
Lochan Fada	126	NH 0271
Lochan Gaineamhach	106	NN 3053
Loch an Iasaich	114	NG 9535
Loch an Laoigh	126	NH 0241
Loch an Leathaid Bhuain	132	NC 2736
Loch an Leothaid	132	NC 1729
Lochan na Bì	106	NN 3031
Lochan na h-Achlaise	106	NN 3147
Lochan na h-Earba	106	NN 4883
Lochan na Làirige	107	NN 5940
Loch an Ruathair	134	NC 8636
Lochans	86	NX 0656
Lochan Shira	106	NN 1720
Lochan Sron Mòr	106	NN 1619
Loch an Tachdaidh	115	NH 0937
Lochan Thulachan	135	ND 1041
Loch an t-Seilich	116	NN 7586
Loch a'Phuill	104	NL 9542
Loch Arail	99	NR 8179
Locharbriggs	88	NX 9980
Loch Ard	101	NN 4601
Loch Ard Forest	101	NS 4898
Loch Arichlinie	134	NC 8435
Loch Arienas	111	NM 6851
Loch Arkaig	115	NN 0891
Loch Arklet Reservoir	101	NN 3708
Lochar Moss	89	NY 0371
Loch Arnish	123	NG 5848
Loch Arthur	88	NX 9069
Lochar Water	88	NY 0178
Loch Ascaig	134	NC 8425
Loch a' Sguirr	123	NG 5952
Loch Ashie	116	NH 6334
Loch Assapol	105	NM 4020
Loch Assynt	132	NC 2024
Lochassynt Lodge	132	NC 1726
Loch a Tuath or Broad Bay	131	NB 5037
Loch Aulasay	124	NF 9474
Loch Avich (Strath.)	100	NM 9314
Loch Avon	117	NJ 0102
Loch Awe (Highld.)	132	NC 2415
Loch Awe (Strath.)	100	NM 9610
Lochawe (Strath.)	106	NN 1227
Loch Bà (Island of Mull)	105	NM 5637
Loch Bà (Strath.)	106	NN 3259
Loch Bad a' Chreamh	126	NG 8180
Loch Bad a' Ghaill	132	NC 0710
Loch Badanloch	134	NC 7734
Loch Bad an Sgalaig	123	NG 8571
Loch Baligill	98	NC 8562
Loch Ballygrant	98	NR 4066
Loch Bay	122	NG 2655
Loch Beanie	106	NO 1668
Loch Beannach (Highld.)	132	NC 1326
Loch Bconnach (Highld)	133	NC 6012
Loch Beannacharain	127	NH 2351
Loch Beannacharan	115	NH 3039
Loch Bee	124	NF 7743
Loch Beinn a' Mheadhoin	115	NH 2224
Loch Beinn Uraraidh	98	NR 4053
Loch Benachally	108	NO 0750
Loch Benisval	131	NB 0819
Loch Beoraid	111	NM 8285
Loch Bhac	107	NN 8262
Loch Bharcasaig	122	NG 2542
Loch Bhrodainn	116	NN 7483
Loch Bhrollum	125	NB 3103
Loch Blàir	115	NN 0594
Loch Bodavat	130	NB 0619
Lochboisdale (South Uist)	112	NF 7919
Loch Boisdale (South Uist)	112	NF 8018
Loch Boltachan	107	NN 6926
Loch Borralan	132	NC 2810
Loch Borralie	132	NC 3867
Loch Bracadale	122	NG 2837
Loch Bradan Reservoir	87	NX 4297
Loch Braigh an Achaidh	123	NG 8443
Loch Brandy	118	NO 3375
Loch Breac	135	ND 0745
Loch Breachacha	110	NM 1653
Loch Breivat	131	NB 3345
Loch Brittle	123	NG 4019
Loch Broom (Highld.)	127	NH 1392
Loch Broom (Tays.)	107	NO 0158
Loch Brora	129	NC 8508
Loch Bruicheach	128	NH 4536
Loch Buidhe	128	NH 6698
Loch Buidhe Mòr	127	NC 7758
Loch Buie (Strath.)	105	NM 5922
Lochbuie (Strath.)	105	NM 6125
Loch Builg	117	NJ 1803
Loch Calavie	115	NH 0538
Loch Calder	135	ND 0760
Loch Callater	117	NO 1883
Loch Calum	135	ND 0251
Loch Cam	98	NM 8646
Loch Caoldair	116	NN 6189
Loch Caolisport	99	NR 7374
Loch Caravat	124	NF 8461
Loch Carloway	131	NB 1842
Lochcarnan	124	NF 8043
Loch Càrnan	124	NF 8043
Loch Caroy	122	NG 2941
Loch Carron (Highld.)	123	NG 8735
Lochcarron (Highld.)	114	NG 8939
Loch Ceann Dibrig	125	NG 1597
Loch Chaolartan	130	NB 0624
Loch Chaorunn Reservoir	99	NR 8371
Loch Choire	133	NC 6228
Loch Choire Forest	133	NC 6229
Loch Choire Lodge	133	NC 6530
Loch Chon	101	NN 4205
Loch Ciaran	92	NR 7754
Loch Ciardh	125	NB 2702
Loch Clàir (Highld.)	123	NG 7771
Loch Clair (Highld.)	126	NH 0057
Loch Clash	132	NC 2156
Loch Cliad	110	NM 2058
Loch Cliff	115	NH 1409
Loch Coire na Saighe Duibhe	133	NC 4436
Loch Coirigerod	131	NB 1721
Loch Con	107	NN 6867
Loch Connan	122	NG 3843
Loch Connell	86	NX 0168
Loch Coruisk	123	NG 4820
Lochcote Resr.	102	NS 9874
Loch Coulin	126	NH 0155
Loch Coulside	133	NC 5843
Loch Coulter Reservoir	101	NS 7686
Loch Cracail Mòr	128	NC 6202
Loch Craggie (Highld.)	127	NC 3205
Loch Craggie (Highld.)	133	NC 6152
Loch Craggie (Highld.)	128	NC 6207
Lochcraig Head	89	NT 1617
Lochcraignish	99	NM 7800
Lochcraig Reservoir	93	NS 5351
Loch Cravadale	130	NB 0114
Loch Creran	106	NM 9442
Loch Crinan	99	NR 7795
Loch Cròcach (Highld)	132	NC 1027
Loch Cròcach (Highld.)	132	NC 1939
Loch Crocach (Highld.)	133	NC 4249
Loch Cròcach (Highld.)	134	NC 8043
Loch Crò Criosdaig	131	NB 0820
Loch Crunachdan	116	NN 5492
Loch Cruoshie	115	NH 0536
Loch Cuaich	116	NN 6987
Loch Culag	132	NC 0921
Loch Dallas	129	NJ 0947
Loch Damh	123	NG 8650
Loch Davan	118	NJ 4400
Loch Dee	87	NX 4678
Loch Derculich	108	NN 8655
Loch Derry	86	NX 2573
Lochdhu Hotel	135	ND 0144
Loch Diabaigas Airde	126	NG 8159
Loch Dionard	132	NC 3549
Loch Dochard	106	NN 2141
Loch Dochart	107	NN 4025
Lochdochart House	107	NN 4327
Loch Doilet	111	NM 8067
Loch Doine	105	NN 4719
Loch Don	105	NM 7332
Lochdon	87	NM 7333
Loch Doon	87	NX 4997
Loch Doon Hill	86	NX 1068
Loch Dornal	86	NX 2976
Loch Droma	127	NH 2675
Loch Druidibeg	112	NF 7937
Loch Druim a'Chliabhain	134	NC 8041
Loch Drunkie	101	NN 5404
Loch Duagrich	123	NG 3939
Loch Dubh	123	ND 0536
Loch Dubh a' Chuail	132	NC 3428
Loch Dùghaill (Highld.)	132	NC 1852
Loch Dùghaill (Highld.)	126	NH 0047
Loch Duich	114	NG 9121
Loch Dungeon	87	NX 5284
Loch Duntelchaig	116	NH 6231
Loch Dunvegan	122	NG 2153
Lochead	99	NR 7778
Loch Earn	107	NN 6423
Lochearnhead	107	NN 5823
Loch Eatharna	100	NM 2256
Loch Eck	105	NS 1391
Loch Eck Forest	100	NS 1494
Loch Eigheach	107	NN 4557
Loch Eil	114	NN 0277
Loch Eilde Beag	106	NN 2565
Loch Eilde Mòr	106	NN 2364
Loch Eileanach (Highld.)	133	NC 5940
Loch Eileanach (Highld.)	127	ND 0747
Locheil Forest	115	NN 0788
Locheilside Station	111	NM 9978
Loch Eilt	111	NM 8182
Loch Einich	123	NG 9198
Loch Eishort	123	NG 6114
Lochend (Highld.)	128	ND 2668
Lochend (Highld.)	116	NH 5937
Loch Enoch	87	NX 4485
Locheport (North Uist)	124	NF 8563
Loch Eport (North Uist)	124	NF 8863
Locherben	88	NX 9597
Loch Eriboll	133	NC 4360
Loch Ericht	107	NN 5371
Loch Ericht Forest	116	NN 5981
Loch Erisort	131	NB 3420
Loch Errochty	107	NN 6965
Locher Water	101	NS 3663
Loch Esk	118	NO 2379
Loch Etchachan	117	NJ 0000
Loch Etive	106	NN 0434
Loch Ewe	126	NG 8387
Loch Eye	128	NH 8379
Loch Eynort (Island of Skye)	122	NG 3624
Loch Eynort (South Uist)	112	NF 8026
Loch Fad	100	NS 0661
Loch Fada (Colonsay)	98	NR 3895
Loch Fada (Highld.)	126	NG 9186
Loch Fada (Island of Skye)	123	NG 4949
Loch Fada (North Uist)	124	NF 8770
Loch Fannich	127	NH 2165
Loch Faskally	108	NN 9258
Loch Feith an Leòthaid	132	NC 1822
Loch Fell	89	NT 1704
Loch Feochan	105	NM 8423
Loch Fiag	132	NC 4429
Loch Fiart	105	NM 8037
Loch Finlaggan	98	NR 3867
Loch Finlas	87	NX 4598
Loch Finsbay	131	NG 0886
Loch Fitty	102	NT 1291
Loch Fleet	128	NH 7896
Loch Flodabay	125	NG 1087
Lochfoot	88	NX 8973
Loch Freuchie	105	NN 8637
Loch Frisa	105	NM 4848
Loch Fuaroil	131	NB 1224
Loch Fuaron	105	NM 5826
Loch Fyne	100	NN 9591
Loch Gaineamhach (Highld.)	133	NC 5824
Loch Gaineamhach (Highld.)	123	NG 7553
Loch Gaineamhach (Strath.)	100	NN 9100
Lochgair	100	NR 9290
Loch Gairloch	123	NG 7676
Loch Garasdale	92	NR 7651
Loch Garbhaig	126	NH 0070
Loch Garry (Highld.)	115	NH 2302
Loch Garry (Tays.)	107	NN 6270
Loch Garten	117	NH 9718
Lochgarthside	116	NH 5219
Loch Garve	128	NH 4159
Lochgelly	102	NT 1893
Loch Gelly	102	NT 2092
Loch Ghuilbinn	116	NN 4174
Loch Gilp	99	NR 8584
Lochgilphead	99	NR 8687
Loch Glascarnoch	127	NH 3172
Loch Glashan	100	NR 9193
Loch Glass	128	NH 5172
Loch Glencoul	132	NC 2531
Loch Glendhu	132	NC 2633
Loch Glow	102	NT 0895
Loch Goil	100	NS 1996
Lochgoilhead	100	NN 1901
Lochgoin Reservoir	93	NS 5447
Loch Gorm	98	NR 2365
Loch Gowan	127	NH 1409
Loch Grannoch	87	NX 5469
Loch Greshornish	122	NG 3454
Loch Grosebay	125	NG 1691
Loch Grogarry	124	NF 8870
Loch Grunavat	131	NB 0827
Loch Haluim	133	NC 5545
Loch Harport	123	NG 3734
Loch Harrow	87	NX 5286
Loch Heilen	135	ND 2568
Loch Hempriggs	135	ND 3447
Loch Heurabhagh	124	NB 4250
Loch Heron	86	NX 2764
Lochhill	120	NJ 2964
Loch Hoil	108	NN 8643
Loch Hope	133	NC 4654
Loch Hourn	123	NG 8309
Loch Humphrey	101	NS 4576
Loch Huna	124	NF 8166
Loch Hunish	123	NG 4076
Loch Inchard	132	NC 2454
Lochinch Castle	86	NX 1061
Loch Indaal	98	NR 2758
Lochindorb	117	NH 9736
Lochindorb Lodge	117	NH 9635
Loch Insh	117	NH 8304
Loch Inshore	133	NC 3389
Lochinvar	87	NX 6585
Loch Inver (Highld.)	132	NC 0721
Lochinver (Highld.)	132	NC 0922
Loch Iubhair	107	NN 4226
Loch Kanaird	127	NH 1099
Loch Katrine	101	NN 4409
Loch Keisgaig	132	NC 2668
Loch Ken	88	NX 6474
Loch Kennard	108	NN 9046
Loch Kernsary	126	NG 8880
Loch Kildonan	112	NF 7327
Loch Killin	116	NH 5210
Loch Kinardochy	107	NN 7755
Loch Kindar	88	NX 9664
Loch Kinnabus	98	NR 3042
Loch Kinord	118	NO 4499
Loch Kirkaig	132	NC 0719
Loch Kishorn	123	NG 8138
Loch Knockie	116	NH 4513
Loch Laggan	116	NN 4886
Loch Laidon	107	NN 3854
Lochlane	107	NN 8320
Loch Langass (Harris, W Isles)	124	NF 8464
Loch Langavat (Harris, W Isles)	124	NG 0489
Loch Langavat (Isle of Lewis)	131	NB 1718
Loch Langavat (Isle of Lewis)	131	NB 5254
Loch Laro	128	NH 6099
Loch Laxavat Ard	131	NB 2438
Loch Laxford	132	NC 2049
Loch Leacann	100	NM 9903
Loch Leathan	123	NG 5051
Loch Leathaun an Sgorra	98	NR 4052
Loch Lednock Reservoir	107	NN 7129
Loch Lee	118	NO 4279
Loch Lesgamaill	98	NR 5777
Loch Leven (Highld.)	106	NN 1260
Loch Leven (Tays.)	102	NO 1401
Loch Linnhe	105	NN 9354
Loch Loch	116	NN 9874
Loch Lochy	115	NN 2390
Loch Lomond	100	NS 3598
Loch Long (Highld.)	114	NG 9029
Loch Long (Strath.)	100	NS 2292
Loch Losait	122	NG 2759
Loch Loyal	133	NC 6247
Loch Loyal Lodge	133	NC 6146
Loch Loyne	115	NH 1705
Loch Lubnaig	101	NN 5713
Lochluichart	127	NH 3262
Loch Luichart	127	NH 3661
Loch Lundie	123	NG 8049
Loch Lurgainn	127	NC 1208
Loch Lyon	107	NN 3839
Lochmaben	89	NY 0882
Lochmaben Stone	89	NY 3166
Loch Maberry	86	NX 2874
Loch Macaterick	87	NX 4491
Lochmaddy (North Uist)	124	NF 9168
Loch Maddy (North Uist)	124	NF 9368
Loch Mahaick	101	NN 7006
Loch Mannoch	88	NX 6660
Loch Maree	126	NG 9570
Loch ma Stac	115	NH 3421
Loch Meadaidh	133	NC 3964
Loch Meadie (Highld.)	133	NC 5041
Loch Meadie (Highld.)	132	NC 7560
Loch Meadie (Highld.)	135	ND 0948
Loch Meala	134	NC 7856
Loch Meallbrodden	108	NN 9125
Loch Mealt	123	NG 5065
Loch Meig	127	NH 3655
Loch Meiklie	116	NH 4330
Loch Melfort	105	NM 8012
Loch Merkland	132	NC 3831
Loch Mhairc	117	NN 8879
Loch Mhaoicheil	116	NH 5419
Loch Migdale	128	NH 6390
Loch Moan	86	NX 3485
Loch Moidart	111	NM 6472
Loch Monar	127	NH 1440
Loch Moraig	108	NN 9066
Loch Mòr an Stàirr	123	NB 3938
Loch Morar	111	NM 7790
Loch More (Highld.)	132	NC 3237
Loch More (Highld.)	135	ND 0745
Lochmore Cottage	135	ND 0846
Lochmore Lodge	132	NC 2938
Loch Morie	128	NH 5376
Loch Morlich	117	NH 9609
Loch Mòr na Caorach	134	NC 7654
Loch Mòr Sandavat	131	NB 4882
Loch Morsgail	131	NB 1322
Loch Moy	116	NH 7734
Loch Muck	135	NS 5100
Loch Mudle	111	NM 5466
Loch Muick	117	NO 2882
Loch Mullardoch	127	NH 1931
Loch na Beinne Baine	115	NH 2819
Loch na Caoidhe	128	NH 2246
Loch na Cille	99	NR 6878
Loch na Claise Càrnaich	132	NC 2852
Loch na Claise Mòire	127	NC 3805
Loch na Conaire	99	NR 6796
Loch na Craige	108	NN 8845
Loch na Creige Duibhe	123	NC 2836
Loch na Crèitheach	123	NG 5120
Loch na Dal	123	NG 7114
Loch na Fuaralaich	128	NC 4806
Loch na Gainmh (Highld.)	127	NC 1718
Loch na Gainmich (Highld.)	132	NC 2061
Lochnagar (mt.)	117	NO 2485
Loch na h-Oidhche	126	NG 8965
Loch na Keal	105	NM 5038
Loch na Lairach	104	NM 3623
Loch na Leitreach	114	NH 0227
Loch nam Bonnach	128	NH 4848
Loch nam Brac	132	NC 1848
Loch nam Breac	98	NC 8247
Loch nam Breac Dearga	116	NH 4522
Loch nam Falcag	98	NB 2927
Loch na Mile	111	NR 5470
Loch nan Ceall	111	NM 6486
Loch nan Clach (Highld.)	134	NC 7752
Loch nan Clach (Highld.)	132	NM 7846
Loch nan Clàr	134	NC 7535
Loch nan Eilean	131	NB 3617
Loch nan Eun	131	NO 0678
Loch nan Eun (Highld.)	123	NG 7048
Loch nan Eun (Highld.)	115	NH 1519
Loch nan Geireann	124	NF 8973
Loch nan Stearnag	106	NB 3236
Loch Nant	106	NN 0024
Loch nan Torran	99	NR 7568
Loch nan Uamh	111	NM 6982
Loch na Saobhaidhe	98	NB 8047
Loch na Scaravat	131	NB 3540
Loch na Sealga	126	NH 0383
Loch na Seilg	133	NC 4951
Loch na Seilge	127	NC 9258
Loch na Sgeire	133	NC 6136
Lochnaw Castle	86	NW 9962
Loch Nedd	132	NC 7132
Loch Neldricken	87	NX 4482
Loch Nell	105	NM 8927
Lochnell House	106	NM 8838
Loch Ness	111	NH 5023
Loch Nevis	111	NM 7695
Loch Niarsco	123	NG 3947
Loch Obisary	124	NF 8961
Loch Ochiltree	86	NX 3174
Loch Odhairn	131	NB 4114
Loch of Boardhouse	136	HY 2626
Loch of Cliff	143	HP 6011
Loch of Girlsta	141	HU 4352
Loch of Harray	136	HY 2915
Loch of Hundland	136	HY 2926
Loch of Kirbister	136	HY 3608
Loch of Lintrathen	108	NO 2754
Loch of Lowes	108	NO 0544
Loch of Mey	135	ND 2773
Loch of Skaill	136	HY 2418
Loch of Skellister	141	HU 4656
Loch of Skene	119	NJ 7807
Loch of Spiggie	141	HU 3716
Loch of Stenness	136	HY 2813
Loch of Strathbeg	121	NK 0758
Loch of Strom	141	HU 4048
Loch of St. Tredwell	138	HY 4950
Loch of Swannay	136	HY 3128
Loch of the Lowes	89	NT 2319
Loch of Tingwall	141	HU 4142
Loch of Toftingall	135	ND 1852
Loch of Vaara	141	HU 3256
Loch of Vatsetter	143	HU 5389
Loch of Voxterby	140	HU 2653
Loch of Watlee	143	HP 5905
Loch of Wester	135	ND 3259
Loch of Yarrows	135	ND 3201
Loch Oich	115	NH 3201
Loch Olginey	135	ND 0857
Loch Ollay	112	NF 7531
Loch Orasay	131	NB 3928
Loch Ordie	108	NO 0350
Loch Ore	102	NT 1695
Lochore	102	NT 1796
Loch Osgaig	132	NC 0412
Loch Ossian	107	NN 3967
Loch Pattack	116	NN 5479
Loch Poit na h-I	104	NM 3122
Loch Poll	132	NC 1030
Loch Pooltiel	122	NG 1650
Loch Quien	100	NS 0659
Loch Quoich	114	NH 0102
Loch Rangag	135	ND 1741
Loch Rannoch	107	NN 5857
Loch Ranza (Island of Arran)	92	NR 9251
Lochranza (Island of Arran)	92	NR 9350
Loch Resort	130	NB 0617
Loch Riddon	100	NS 0076
Loch Riecawr	87	NX 4393
Loch Righ Mòr	98	NR 5185
Loch Rimsdale	134	NC 7335
Loch Roag	131	NB 1233
Loch Ronald	86	NX 2664
Lochrosque Forest	127	NH 2162
Loch Ruard	135	ND 1443
Loch Rumsdale	134	NC 9641
Loch Rusky	101	NN 6103
Loch Ruthven	116	NH 6127
Lochrutton Loch	88	NX 8972
Loch Ryan	86	NX 0565
Loch Sand	132	NC 9540
Loch Scadavay (North Uist)	124	NF 8568
Loch Scadavay (North Uist)	124	NF 8766
Loch Scammadale	106	NM 8820
Loch Scarmclate	135	ND 1859
Loch Scaslavat	130	NB 0231
Loch Scavaig	123	NG 5015
Loch Scoly	108	NN 9147
Loch Scresort	111	NM 4199
Loch Scridain	105	NM 4625
Loch Skye	135	ND 0055
Loch Seaforth	125	NB 2106
Loch Sealg or Loch Shell	131	NB 3410
Loch Sgamhain	127	NH 1052
Loch Sgeireach Mòr	131	NB 4945
Loch Sgibacleit	131	NB 3116
Loch Sguabain	105	NM 6230
Loch Sguod	126	NB 8187
Loch Shanndabhat	131	NB 3413
Loch Shell or Loch Sealg	131	NB 3410
Loch Shiel	111	NM 8072
Loch Shieldaig	123	NG 8055
Loch Shin	133	NC 4816
Loch Shira	106	NN 1009
Loch Shurrery	135	ND 0455
Lochside (Gramp.)	109	NO 7464
Lochside (Highld.)	133	NC 4758
Lochside (Highld.)	134	NC 8735
Loch Sionascaig	132	NC 1113
Loch Skealtar	124	NF 8968
Loch Skeen	89	NT 1716
Loch Skerrow	88	NX 6068
Lochskipport (South Uist)	112	NF 8238
Loch Skipport (South Uist)	112	NF 8438
Loch Slapin	123	NG 5718
Loch Sletill	134	NC 9547
Loch Sligachan	123	NG 5132
Loch Sloy	100	NN 2811
Loch Smigeadail	98	NR 3875
Loch Smuaisaval	131	NB 2030
Loch Snigisclett	112	NF 8025
Loch Snizort	122	NG 3261
Loch Snizort Beag	123	NG 3954
Lochs of Beosetter	141	HU 4943
Lochs of Lumbister	143	HU 4896
Loch Spallander Resr.	93	NS 3908
Loch Spelve	105	NM 6927
Loch Spey	116	NN 4293
Loch Spynie	121	NJ 2366
Loch Stack	132	NC 3042
Lochstack Lodge	132	NC 2643
Loch Staosnaig	98	NR 3993
Loch Steisevat	124	NG 0187
Loch Stornoway	99	NR 7260
Loch Strandavat	131	NB 2519
Loch Strathy	134	NC 7747
Loch Striven	100	NS 0776
Loch Stulaval	112	NF 7922
Loch Suainaval	131	NB 0629
Loch Sunart	111	NM 7262
Loch Sween	99	NR 7382
Loch Syre	133	NC 6644
Loch Tamanavay	130	NB 0220
Loch Tanna	92	NR 9242
Loch Tarbert	98	NR 5481
Loch Tarff	116	NH 4210
Loch Tay	107	NN 6838
Loch Teacuis	111	NM 6355
Loch Tealasavay	130	NB 0218
Loch Tearnait	105	NM 7446
Loch Thom	100	NS 2572
Loch Thota Bridein	131	NB 3327
Loch Tollaidh	126	NG 8478
Lochton	109	NO 7592
Loch Torridon	123	NG 7560
Loch Tralaig	105	NM 8716
Loch Trealaval	131	NB 2723
Loch Treig	107	NN 3372
Loch Trollamarig	125	NB 2201
Loch Tromlee	100	NN 0425
Loch Trool	86	NX 4179
Loch Truderscaig	134	NC 7132
Loch Tuath	105	NM 3943
Loch Tuim Ghlais	134	NN 9852
Loch Tulla	106	NN 2942
Loch Tummel	107	NN 8259
Loch Tungavat	131	NB 1628
Loch Turret Reservoir	107	NN 8028
Loch Urgisg	116	NH 6325
Lochuisge (Highld.)	111	NM 7955
Loch Uisge (Highld.)	111	NM 8054
Loch Uiskevagh	124	NF 8551
Loch Uraval	131	NB 3032

Loch Urigill ... 132 NC 2409
Loch Urr ... 88 NX 7584
Loch Urrahag ... 131 NB 3247
Loch Ussie ... 128 NH 5057
Loch Vaich ... 127 NH 3477
Loch Valigan ... 108 NN 9769
Loch Valley ... 87 NX 4481
Loch Venachar ... 101 NN 5705
Loch Veyatie ... 132 NC 1813
Loch Voil ... 107 NN 5019
Loch Vrotachan ... 117 NO 1278
Loch Walton ... 101 NS 6686
Loch Watten ... 135 ND 2256
Loch Whinyeon ... 88 NX 6260
Lochwinnoch ... 100 NS 3558
Lochwood (Dumf. and Galwy.) ... 89 NY 0896
Lochwood (Strath.) ... 101 NS 6966
Lock Awe (Argyll.) ... 100 NM 9610
Lockengate ... 19 SX 0361
Lockerbie ... 89 NY 1381
Lockeridge ... 34 SU 1467
Lockerley ... 26 SU 2925
Lockerley Hall ... 26 SU 2928
Locking ... 32 ST 3659
Lockington (Humbs.) ... 74 SE 9947
Lockington (Leic.) ... 61 SK 4628
Lockleywood ... 59 SJ 6828
Lockmaddy ... 124 NF 9168
Locks Heath ... 27 SU 5207
Lockton ... 80 SE 8489
Lockwood Beck Resr. ... 85 NZ 6713
Loddington (Leic.) ... 61 SK 7802
Loddington (Northants.) ... 52 SP 8178
Loddiswell ... 21 SX 7148
Loddon ... 65 TM 3698
Lode ... 53 TL 5362
Loder Head ... 141 HU 5243
Loders ... 25 SY 4994
Lodsworth ... 28 SU 9223
Loe, The ... 18 SW 6425
Loft Hill ... 90 NT 8513
Lofthouse (N Yorks.) ... 78 SE 1073
Lofthouse (W Yorks.) ... 79 SE 3325
Loftus ... 85 NZ 7118
Logan ... 88 NS 5820
Loganlea Resr. ... 103 NT 1962
Logan Mains ... 86 NX 0942
Logan Rock ... 18 SW 3523
Logan Water ... 94 NS 7537
Loggerheads ... 59 SJ 7336
Loggie ... 127 NH 1490
Logie (Fife) ... 109 NO 4020
Logie (Grampn.) ... 121 NK 0356
Logie (Tays.) ... 109 NO 6963
Logiealmond (dist.) ... 108 NN 9731
Logiealmond Lodge ... 108 NN 9531
Logie Coldstone ... 118 NJ 4304
Logie Head ... 121 NJ 5267
Logie Hill ... 129 NH 7776
Logie Newton ... 121 NJ 6638
Logie Pert ... 109 NO 6664
Logierait ... 108 NN 9752
Login ... 42 SN 1623
Lolworth ... 53 TL 3664
Lomond Hills ... 103 NO 2106
Lonbain ... 123 NG 6852
Londesborough ... 74 SE 8645
Londinium (ant.) ... 37 TQ 3079
London ... 37 TQ 3079
London Airport (Gatwick.) ... 138 HY 5634
London Airport (Gatwick.) ... 28 TQ 2740
London Airport (Heathrow) ... 36 TQ 0875
London Colney ... 37 TL 1603
Londonderry ... 79 SE 3087
Londonthorpe ... 62 SK 9537
Londubh ... 126 NG 8680
Lonemore ... 129 NH 7688
Longa Island ... 126 NG 7377
Longannet Point ... 102 NS 9485
Long Ashton ... 33 ST 5470
Longay ... 123 NG 6531
Long Bennington ... 62 SK 8344
Longbenton ... 91 NZ 2668
Longborough ... 47 SP 1729
Long Bredy ... 25 SY 5690
Longbridge (Warw.) ... 50 SP 2662
Longbridge (W Mids.) ... 50 SP 0178
Longbridge Deverill ... 33 ST 8640
Long Buckby ... 51 SP 6267
Longburton ... 25 ST 6412
Long Clawson ... 61 SK 7227
Longcliffe ... 60 SK 2255
Long Common ... 27 SU 5014
Long Compton (Staffs.) ... 59 SJ 8522
Long Compton (Warw.) ... 47 SP 2832
Longcot ... 34 SU 2790
Long Crag ... 91 NU 0606
Long Craig ... 109 NO 7254
Long Crendon ... 36 SP 6908
Long Crichel ... 26 ST 9710
Longcroft ... 101 NS 7979
Longden ... 58 SJ 4306
Longdendale ... 70 SK 0397
Long Ditton ... 37 TQ 1666
Longdon (Here. and Worc.) ... 49 SO 8336
Longdon (Staffs.) ... 60 SK 0714
Longdon on Tern ... 59 SJ 6215
Longdown ... 21 SX 8691
Longdowns ... 18 SW 7434
Long Drax ... 79 SE 6528
Long Duckmanton ... 71 SK 4371
Long Eaton ... 61 SK 4933
Long Fell ... 88 NX 9064
Longfield ... 30 TQ 6068
Longford (Derby.) ... 60 SK 2137
Longford (Glos.) ... 46 SO 8320
Longford (Gtr London) ... 36 TQ 0576
Longford (Shrops.) ... 59 SJ 6433
Longford (Shrops.) ... 59 SJ 7218
Longford (W Mids.) ... 50 SP 3583
Longford Castle (ant.) ... 26 SU 1626
Longforgan ... 108 NO 3129
Longformacus ... 96 NT 6957
Longframlington ... 91 NU 1201
Long Geo ... 136 HY 4404
Long Gill ... 78 SD 7858
Longham (Dorset) ... 26 SZ 0697
Longham (Norf.) ... 64 TF 9415
Long Hanborough ... 47 SP 4114
Long Haven ... 121 NK 1240
Long Hermiston ... 102 NT 1770
Longhirst ... 91 NZ 2289
Long Holcombe ... 23 SS 7636
Longhope (Glos.) ... 46 SO 6819
Longhope (Hoy, Orkney) (chan.) ... 136 ND 3191
Longhorsley ... 91 NZ 1494
Longhoughton ... 91 NU 2414
Long Itchington ... 50 SP 4165
Long Lawford ... 51 SP 4775
Longleat House (ant.) ... 33 ST 8042
Longley Green ... 49 SO 7350
Long Load ... 25 ST 4623
Long Loch (Strath.) ... 93 NS 4752
Long Loch (Tays.) ... 108 NO 2938
Longmanhill ... 121 NJ 7462
Longman Point ... 128 NH 6747
Long Man, The (ant.) ... 29 TQ 5403
Long Marston (Herts.) ... 36 SP 8915
Long Marston (N Yorks.) ... 79 SE 4951
Long Marston (Warw.) ... 50 SP 1548

Long Marton ... 83 NY 6624
Long Melford ... 54 TL 8646
Longmoor Camp ... 27 SU 7930
Long Mountain ... 58 SJ 2808
Long Mynd, The (mt.) ... 58 SO 4093
Long Newton (Glos.) ... 33 ST 9092
Longnewton (Borders) ... 96 NT 5827
Longnewton (Cleve.) ... 85 NZ 3816
Longnewton Forest ... 96 NT 6227
Longney ... 46 SO 7612
Longniddry ... 103 NT 4476
Longnor (Shrops.) ... 59 SJ 4800
Longnor (Staffs.) ... 70 SK 0864
Long Nose Spit ... 31 TR 3771
Longparish ... 34 SU 4344
Long Preston ... 78 SD 8357
Longridge (Lancs.) ... 77 SD 6037
Longridge (Lothian) ... 102 NS 9462
Longridge Fell ... 77 SD 6540
Longridge Towers ... 97 NT 9549
Longriggend ... 101 NS 8270
Long Riston ... 75 TA 1242
Longsdon ... 60 SJ 9554
Longships ... 18 SW 3225
Longside ... 121 NK 0347
Longsleddale ... 83 NY 4902
Longslow ... 59 SJ 6535
Longstanton ... 53 TL 3966
Longstock ... 26 SU 3536
Longstone Wells ... 23 SS 7633
Long Stowe ... 53 TL 3054
Long Stratton ... 55 TM 1992
Long Street ... 51 SP 7947
Long Sutton (Hants.) ... 35 SU 7347
Long Sutton (Lincs.) ... 63 TF 4322
Long Sutton (Somer.) ... 25 ST 4625
Long Taing ... 143 HU 3785
Longthorpe ... 62 TL 1698
Longton (Lancs.) ... 77 SD 4725
Longton (Staffs.) ... 59 SJ 9043
Longtown (Cumbr.) ... 89 NY 3768
Longtown (Here. and Worc.) ... 45 SO 3228
Long Valley ... 35 SU 8351
Longville in the Dale ... 59 SO 5393
Long Whatton ... 61 SK 4723
Longwick ... 36 SP 7805
Long Wittenham ... 47 SU 5493
Longwitton ... 91 NZ 0788
Longwood House ... 27 SU 5324
Longwood Warren ... 27 SU 5226
Longworth ... 47 SU 3899
Longyester ... 103 NT 5465
Lón Liath ... 111 NM 6590
Lonmore ... 122 NG 2646
Looe ... 19 SX 2553
Looe Bay ... 20 SX 2753
Looe or St. George's Island ... 19 SX 2551
Loose ... 29 TQ 7552
Loosley Row ... 36 SP 8100
Lootcherbrae ... 121 NJ 6054
Lopcombe Corner ... 26 SU 2435
Lopen ... 25 ST 4214
Lop Ness ... 139 HY 7643
Loppington ... 58 SJ 4629
Lorbottle ... 91 NU 0306
Lorbottle Hall ... 91 NU 0407
Lord Arthur's Cairn ... 118* NJ 5019
Lord's Seat (mt.) ... 71 SP 2026
Lorn (dist.) ... 106 NN 0735
Lornty ... 108 NO 1746
Lornty Burn ... 108 NO 1048
Lorton ... 82 NY 1625
Lorton Vale ... 82 NY 1526
Loscoe ... 60 SK 4247
Lossie Forest ... 120 NJ 2767
Lossiemouth ... 120 NJ 2370
Lossit ... 98 NR 1856
Lossit Bay ... 98 NR 1755
Lossit Point ... 98 NR 1756
Lostock Gralam ... 69 SJ 6874
Lostock Junction ... 69 SD 6708
Lostwithiel ... 19 SX 1059
Lothbeg ... 134 NC 9410
Lothbeg Point ... 134 NC 9609
Lothersdale ... 78 SD 9545
Lothmore ... 134 NC 9611
Lotus Hill ... 88 NX 9067
Loudoun Hill ... 94 NS 6037
Loudwater ... 36 SU 8990
Loughborough ... 61 SK 5319
Loughor ... 40 SS 5898
Loughton (Bucks.) ... 52 SP 8337
Loughton (Essex) ... 38 TQ 4296
Loughton (Shrops.) ... 49 SO 6183
Lound (Lincs.) ... 62 TF 0618
Lound (Notts.) ... 72 SK 6986
Lound (Suff.) ... 65 TM 5099
Lount ... 60 SK 3819
Louth ... 73 TF 3287
Love Clough ... 78 SD 8126
Lover ... 26 SU 2120
Loversall ... 71 SK 5798
Loves Green ... 38 TL 6404
Loveston ... 42 SN 0808
Lovington ... 25 ST 5931
Low Bentham ... 77 SD 6469
Low Bradfield ... 71 SK 2691
Low Bradley ... 78 SE 0048
Low Braithwaite ... 83 NY 4242
Lowbridge House ... 83 NY 5301
Low Brunton ... 90 NY 9269
Low Burnham ... 74 SE 7702
Lowca ... 82 NX 9821
Low Catton ... 80 SE 7053
Low Coniscliffe ... 84 NZ 2514
Low Crosby ... 89 NY 4459
Lowdham ... 61 SK 6646
Low Dinsdale ... 85 NZ 3411
Low Eggborough ... 79 SE 5522
Lower Aisholt ... 24 ST 2035
Lower Assendon ... 36 SU 7484
Lower Basildon ... 35 SU 6078
Lower Beeding ... 28 TQ 2227
Lower Benefield ... 52 SP 9888
Lower Boddington ... 51 SP 4752
Lower Bullingham ... 45 SO 5038
Lower Cam ... 46 SO 7401
Lower Chapel ... 41 SO 0235
Lower Chute ... 34 SU 3153
Lower Cwmtwrch ... 41 SN 7710
Lower Darwen ... 77 SD 6824
Lower Diabaig ... 123 NG 7960
Lower Down ... 48 SO 3384
Lower Dunsforth ... 79 SE 4464
Lower Farringdon ... 27 SU 7035
Lower Frankton ... 58 SJ 3732
Lower Froyle ... 35 SU 7544
Lower Gledfield ... 128 NH 5990
Lower Green ... 64 TF 9837
Lower Halstow ... 30 TQ 8567
Lower Hardres ... 31 TR 1453
Lower Heryford ... 47 SP 4824
Lower Higham ... 30 TQ 7172
Lower Hope, The (chan.) ... 30 TQ 7077
Lower Hordley ... 58 SJ 3929
Lower Icknield Way (ant.) ... 36 SP 8912
Lower Killeyan ... 98 NR 2743
Lower Langford ... 33 ST 4660
Lower Largo ... 103 NO 4102
Lower Lemington ... 47 SP 2134

Lower Lye ... 48 SO 4067
Lower Machen ... 41 ST 2288
Lower Maes-coed ... 45 SO 3431
Lower Moor ... 50 SO 9847
Lower Nazeing ... 37 TL 3906
Lower Penarth ... 41 ST 1869
Lower Penn ... 59 SO 8696
Lower Pennington ... 26 SZ 3193
Lower Peover ... 69 SJ 7474
Lower Quinton ... 50 SP 1847
Lower Sharpnose Point ... 22 SS 1912
Lower Shelton ... 52 SP 9942
Lower Shiplake ... 36 SU 7779
Lower Shuckburgh ... 51 SP 4862
Lower Slaughter ... 47 SP 1622
Lower Stanton St. Quintin ... 33 ST 9180
Lower Sundon ... 52 TL 0526
Lower Swanwick ... 27 SU 4909
Lower Swell ... 47 SP 1725
Lower Tamar Lake ... 22 SS 2910
Lower Thurlton ... 65 TM 4299
Lower Tysoe ... 50 SP 3445
Lower Upham ... 27 SU 5219
Lower Vexford ... 24 ST 1135
Lower Weare ... *32 ST 4053
Lower Wield ... 35 SU 6340
Lower Winchendon or Nether
  Winchendon ... 36 SP 7312
Lower Woodend ... 36 SU 8088
Lower Woodford ... 26 SU 1235
Lowesby ... 61 SK 7207
Lowestoft ... 65 TM 5493
Lowestoft End ... 65 TM 5394
Loweswater ... 82 NY 1421
Loweswater Fell ... 82 NY 1319
Low Gate ... 90 NY 9064
Lowgill (Cumbr.) ... 83 SD 6297
Lowgill (Lancs.) ... 77 SD 6564
Low Ham ... 25 ST 4329
Low Hartsop ... 83 NY 4013
Low Hesket ... 83 NY 4646
Low Hesleyhurst ... 91 NZ 0997
Lowick (Cumbr.) ... 83 SD 2985
Lowick (Northants.) ... 52 SP 9781
Lowick (Northum.) ... 97 NU 0139
Lowlandman's Bay ... 98 NR 5672
Low Mill ... 85 SE 6795
Low Moor ... 77 SD 7241
Lownie Moor ... 109 NO 4848
Lowood ... 96 NT 5235
Low Redford ... 84 NZ 0731
Low Row (Cumbr.) ... 90 NY 5863
Low Row (N Yorks.) ... 84 SD 9897
Lowsonford ... 50 SP 1867
Lowther Castle ... 83 NY 5223
Lowther College ... 67 SH 9975
Lowther Hill ... 88 NS 8810
Lowther Hills ... 88 NS 8910
Lowthorpe ... 81 TA 0860
Lowton ... 69 SJ 6197
Lowton Common ... 69 SJ 6397
Low Torry ... 102 NT 0086
Low Waters ... 94 NS 7353
Low Worsall ... 85 NZ 3909
Loxbeare ... 23 SS 9116
Loxhill ... 28 TQ 0037
Loxhore ... 23 SS 6138
Loxley ... 50 SP 2553
Loxton ... 32 ST 3755
Loxwood ... 28 TQ 0431
Lubcroy ... 127 NC 3501
Lubenham ... 51 SP 7087
Lub Score ... 122 NG 3973
Luccombe ... 24 SS 9144
Luccombe Chine ... 27 SZ 5879
Luccombe Village ... 27 SZ 5880
Luce Bay ... 86 NX 2244
Luce Sands ... 86 NX 1453
Lucker ... 97 NU 1530
Luckett ... 20 SX 3873
Luckington ... 33 ST 8383
Lucklawhill ... 109 NO 4222
Luckwell Bridge ... 23 SS 9038
Lucton ... 48 SO 4364
Ludag ... 124 NF 7714
Ludborough ... 73 TF 2995
Ludchurch ... 42 SN 1411
Luddenden ... 78 SE 0425
Luddenham Court ... 31 TQ 9963
Luddesdown ... 30 TQ 6766
Luddington ... 50 SE 8216
Lude House ... 108 NN 8865
Ludford (Lincs.) ... 73 TF 1989
Ludford (Shrops.) ... 48 SO 5173
Ludgershall (Bucks.) ... 36 SP 6617
Ludgershall (Wilts.) ... 34 SU 2650
Ludgvan ... 18 SW 5033
Ludham ... 65 TG 3818
Ludlow ... 48 SO 5175
Ludwell ... 26 ST 9122
Ludworth ... 85 NZ 3641
Luffincott ... 22 SX 3394
Lugar ... 94 NS 5821
Lugar Water ... 94 NS 5022
Lugate Water ... 96 NT 4145
Luggate Burn ... 103 NT 6074
Luggiebank ... 101 NS 7672
Lugton ... 93 NS 4152
Lugton Water ... 93 NS 3848
Lugwardine ... 45 SO 5441
Luib ... 123 NG 5627
Luing (is.) ... 105 NM 7410
Luinga Bheag (is.) ... 111 NM 6181
Luinga Mhór (is.) ... 111 NM 6086
Luinne Bheinn ... 111 NG 8600
Luirsay Dubh ... 124 NF 8640
Luithaid ... 111 NB 1713
Lui Water ... 117 NO 0592
Lulham ... 45 SO 4041
Lullingstone Castle ... 37 TQ 5364
Lullington (Derby.) ... 60 SK 2513
Lullington (Somer.) ... 33 ST 7851
Lulsgate Bottom ... 33 ST 5065
Lulsley ... 49 SO 7455
Lulworth Cove ... 25 SY 8279
Lumb ... 78 SE 0221
Lumby ... 79 SE 4830
Lumley Moor Resr. ... 78 SE 2270
Lumloch ... 101 NS 6369
Lumphanan ... 119 NJ 5804
Lumphinnans ... 102 NT 1692
Lumsdaine ... 97 NT 8769
Lumsden ... 121 NJ 4722
Lunan ... 109 NO 6851
Lunan Bay ... 109 NO 7051
Lunanhead ... 109 NO 4752
Lunan Water ... 109 NO 6149
Luncarty ... 108 NO 0929
Lund (Humbs.) ... 81 SE 9648
Lund (N Yorks.) ... 80 SE 6532
Lund (Notts.) ... 143 HP 1453
Lunda Wick ... 143 HP 5604
Lundenston Bay ... 100 NS 1873
Lundie (Highld.) ... 115 NH 1410
Lundie (Tays.) ... 108 NO 2836
Lundin Links ... 103 NO 4002
Lundy ... 22 SS 1443
Lune Forest ... 83 NY 8323
Lune Moor ... 84 NY 9023
Lunga (Island of Mull) (is.) ... 104 NM 2741

Lunga (Strath.) (is.) ... 105 NM 7008
Lunga Hotel ... 105 NM 7906
Lunna ... 143 HU 4869
Lunna Holm ... 143 HU 5274
Lunnasting (dist.) ... 141 HU 4865
Lunning ... 141 HU 5066
Lunning Sound ... 141 HU 5165
Lunsford's Cross ... 29 TQ 7210
Lunt ... 68 SD 3401
Luntley ... 45 SO 3955
Luppitt ... 24 ST 1606
Lupton ... 77 SD 5581
Lupton Beck ... 77 SD 5580
Lurgashall ... 28 SU 9326
Lurg Hill ... 121 NJ 5057
Lurg Mhòr (mt.) ... 115 NH 0640
Lurgmore ... 116 NH 5937
Lusby ... 73 TF 3367
Luskentyre ... 125 NG 0699
Lusragan Burn ... 106 NM 9031
Luss ... 100 NS 3592
Lussa Loch ... 92 NR 7130
Lussa Point ... 99 NR 6486
Lussa River (Island of Mull) ... 105 NM 6531
Lussa River (Jura) ... 99 NR 6292
Lusta ... 122 NG 2756
Lustleigh ... 21 SX 7881
Luston ... 48 SO 4863
Luthermuir ... 109 NO 6568
Luther Water ... 109 NO 6870
Luthrie ... 108 NO 3219
Luton (Beds.) ... 36 TL 0821
Luton (Devon) ... 21 SX 9076
Luton (Kent) ... 30 TQ 7766
Luton Airport ... 37 TL 1221
Lutterworth ... 51 SP 5484
Lutton (Devon) ... 21 SX 5959
Lutton (Lincs.) ... 63 TF 4325
Lutton (Northants.) ... 52 TL 1187
Luxborough ... 23 SS 9738
Luxley ... 46 SO 6921
Luxulyan ... 19 SX 0458
Lybster ... 135 ND 2435
Lydbury North ... 48 SO 3486
Lydcott ... 23 SS 6936
Lydd ... 31 TR 0421
Lydd Airport ... 31 TR 0621
Lydden ... 31 TR 2645
Lyddington ... 62 SP 8797
Lydd-on-Sea ... 31 TR 0819
Lydeard St. Lawrence ... 24 ST 1232
Lydford (Devon) ... 20 SX 5084
Lydford (Somer.) ... 25 ST 5731
Lydgate ... 78 SD 9225
Lydham ... 48 SO 3391
Lydiard Millicent ... 34 SU 0886
Lydiate ... 68 SD 3604
Lydlinch ... 25 ST 7413
Lydney ... 45 SO 6203
Lydney Sand ... 45 SE 6399
Lydstep ... 42 SS 0898
Lye ... 49 SO 9284
Lye Green ... 36 SP 9703
Lyford ... 47 SU 3994
Lymbridge Green ... 31 TR 1243
Lyme Park (ant.) ... 70 SJ 9682
Lyme Regis ... 24 SY 3492
Lyminge ... 31 TR 1641
Lyminge Forest ... 31 TR 1545
Lymington ... 26 SZ 3295
Lymington River ... 26 SU 3102
Lyminster ... 28 TQ 0204
Lymm ... 69 SJ 6786
Lymore ... 26 SZ 2992
Lympne ... 31 TR 1235
Lympsham ... 32 ST 3454
Lympstone ... 21 SX 9984
Lynaberack ... 116 NN 7694
Lynchat ... 116 NH 7801
Lyn Cwmdulyn Reservoir ... 66 SH 4949
Lyndale House ... 122 NG 3654
Lyndale Point ... 122 NG 3654
Lyndhurst ... 26 SU 2907
Lyndhurst Road Station ... 26 SU 3309
Lyndon ... 62 SK 9004
Lyne ... 36 TQ 0166
Lyneal ... 58 SJ 4433
Lyneham (Oxon.) ... 47 SP 2720
Lyneham (Wilts.) ... 34 SU 0179
Lyne House ... 28 TQ 1938
Lynemouth ... 91 NZ 2991
Lyne of Gorthleck ... 116 NH 5420
Lyne of Skene ... 119 NJ 7610
Lyness ... 136 ND 3094
Lyne Water ... 95 NT 1645
Lyng (Norf.) ... 64 TG 0617
Lyng (Somer.) ... 24 ST 3328
Lynmouth ... 23 SS 7249
Lynn Deeps (chan.) ... 63 TF 5846
Lynn of Lorn ... 105 NM 8639
Lynsted ... 30 TQ 9461
Lyniton ... 23 SS 7149
Lyon's Gate ... 25 ST 6605
Lyonshall ... 45 SO 3356
Lype Hill ... 23 SS 9537
Lyrawa Burn ... 136 ND 2699
Lyrie Geo ... 136 ND 2096
Lytchett Matravers ... 26 SY 9495
Lytchett Minster ... 26 SY 9593
Lyth ... 135 ND 2763
Lytham ... 76 SD 3727
Lytham St. Anne's ... 77 SD 3427
Lythe ... 85 NZ 8413
Lythes ... 136 ND 4589

M

Maaey Riabhach ... 124 NF 8850
Maaruig ... 125 NB 1906
Maa Water ... 141 HU 3755
Mabe Burnthouse ... 18 SW 7634
Mabie ... 88 NX 9570
Mablethorpe ... 73 TF 5085
Macaterick ... 87 NX 4390
Macclesfield ... 69 SJ 9173
Macclesfield Canal (Ches.) ... 69 SJ 9166
Macclesfield Canal (Ches.) ... 69 SJ 9482
Macclesfield Forest ... 70 SJ 9772
Macduff ... 121 NJ 7064
Macduff's Castle (ant.) ... 103 NT 3497
Machany Water ... 107 NN 8415
Macharioch ... 92 NR 7309
Machars, The (dist.) ... 86 NX 3753
Machen ... 41 ST 2189
Machir Bay ... 98 NR 1962
Machrie Bay ... 92 NR 8834
Machrie Water ... 92 NR 9334
Machrihanish ... 92 NR 6220
Machrihanish Airfield ... 92 NR 6622
Machrihanish Bay ... 92 NR 6423
Machrihanish Water ... 92 NR 6520
Machynlleth ... 57 SH 7401
Mackworth ... 60 SK 3137
Maclean's Nose ... 111 NM 5361
Macleod's Maidens (is.) ... 122 NG 2436
Macleod's Tables (mt.) ... 122 NG 2243
Macmerry ... 103 NT 4372
Madadh Gruamach (is.) ... 124 NF 9566
Madderty ... 108 NN 9522
Maddiston ... 102 NS 9476

Madehurst ... 28 SU 9810
Madeley (Shrops.) ... 59 SJ 6904
Madeley (Staffs.) ... 59 SJ 7744
Madingley ... 53 TL 3960
Madley ... 45 SO 4138
Madresfield ... 49 SO 8047
Madron ... 18 SW 4532
Mad Wharf (sbk.) ... 68 SD 2607
Maelienydd ... 48 SO 1271
Maenclochog ... 42 SN 0827
Maendy ... 41 ST 0176
Mae Ness ... 138 HY 4831
Maentwrog ... 67 SH 6640
Maer ... 59 SJ 7938
Maerdy (Clwyd) ... 67 SJ 0144
Maerdy (Mid Glam.) ... 41 SS 9798
Maesbrook ... 58 SJ 3121
Maesbury Marsh ... 58 SJ 3125
Maes-glas ... 32 ST 2985
Maesgwynne ... 42 SN 2024
Maeshafn ... 68 SJ 2061
Maes Howe (ant.) ... 136 HY 3112
Maesllyn ... 43 SN 3644
Maesmynis ... 44 SO 0148
Maesteg ... 41 SS 8592
Maesybont ... 43 SN 5616
Maesycwmmer ... 41 ST 1594
Maesyrchen Mountain ... 58 SJ 1846
Magdalen Laver ... 38 TL 5108
Maggieknockater ... 121 NJ 3145
Magham Down ... 29 TQ 6111
Maghannan ... 21 NB 0821
Maghull ... 68 SD 3702
Magor ... 33 ST 4287
Maiden Bradley ... 33 ST 8038
Maiden Castle (ant.) ... 25 SY 6688
Maidencombe ... 21 SX 9268
Maidenhead ... 36 SU 8881
Maidenhead Bay ... 86 NS 2008
Maiden Island ... 105 NM 8432
Maiden Law ... 84 NZ 1749
Maiden Newton ... 25 SY 5997
Maidenpap (Dumf. and Galwy.) (mt.) ... 88 NX 8961
Maiden Pap (Highld.) (mt.) ... 135 ND 0429
Maiden Paps (Borders) (mt.) ... 89 NT 5002
Maidens ... 93 NS 2107
Maiden Stone (ant.) ... 121 NJ 7024
Maiden Way (Cumbr.) (ant.) ... 83 NY 6535
Maiden Way (Northum.) (ant.) ... 83 NY 6756
Maidenwell ... 73 TF 2479
Maidford ... 51 SP 6052
Maids Moreton ... 51 SP 7035
Maidstone ... 29 TQ 7656
Maidwell ... 51 SP 7477
Mail ... 141 HU 4228
Mainland (Orkney) ... 136 HY 3711
Mainland (Shetld.) ... 141 HU 4051
Mains ... 116 NH 4239
Mains of Ardestie ... 109 NO 5034
Mains of Balhall ... 109 NO 5163
Mains of Ballindarg ... 109 NO 4051
Mains of Dalvey ... 117 NJ 1132
Mains of Dillavaird ... 119 NO 7481
Mains of Drum ... 119 NO 8099
Mains of Melgund ... 109 NO 5456
Mains of Thornton ... 109 NO 6071
Mainstone ... 48 SO 2687
Main Water of Luce ... 86 NX 1468
Maisemore ... 46 SO 8121
Maisgeir (is.) ... 104* NM 3539
Malacleit ... 124 NF 7573
Malaggair (mt.) ... 121 NB 3017
Malborough ... 21 SX 7039
Malcolm's Head ... 139 HZ 1970
Malcolm's Point ... 105 NM 4918
Maldon ... 38 TL 8506
Malham ... 78 SD 9062
Malham Tarn ... 78 SD 8966
Mallaig ... 111 NM 6796
Mallart River ... 133 NC 6737
Mallerstang Common ... 83 SD 7798
Mallowdale Fell ... 77 SD 6159
Malltraeth Bay ... 66 SH 3764
Malltraeth Marsh ... 66 SH 4471
Malltraeth Sands ... 66 SH 4066
Mallwyd ... 57 SH 8612
Malmesbury ... 34 ST 9387
Malpas (Ches.) ... 59 SJ 4847
Malpas (Cornwall) ... 18 SW 8442
Malpas (S Glam.) ... 32 ST 3091
Maltby (Cleve.) ... 85 NZ 4613
Maltby (S Yorks.) ... 71 SK 5392
Maltby le Marsh ... 73 TF 4681
Maltman's Hill ... 30 TQ 9043
Malton ... 80 SE 7871
Malvern Hills ... 49 SO 7641
Malvern Link ... 49 SO 7848
Malvern Wells ... 49 SO 7742
Màm an Staing ... 123 NG 7813
Mamble ... 49 SO 6871
Mam na Gualainn ... 106 NN 1162
Mamore Forest ... 106 NN 1765
Màm Sodhail ... 115 NH 1225
Màm Suim ... 117 NJ 0109
Mam Tor (ant.) ... 70 SK 1283
Manaccan ... 19 SW 7625
Manacle Point ... 19 SW 8121
Manacles, The (pt.) ... 19 SW 8120
Manafon ... 58 SJ 1102
Man and his man or Bawden Rocks ... 18 SW 6953
Manar House ... 119 NJ 7319
Manaton ... 21 SX 7481
Manby ... 73 TF 3986
Mancetter ... 50 SP 3196
Manchester ... 69 SJ 8397
Manchester Airport ... 69 SJ 8184
Manchester Ship Canal ... 69 SJ 6989
Mancot ... 59 SJ 3267
Mandally ... 115 NH 2900
Manea ... 53 TL 4789
Manfield ... 84 NZ 2213
Mangaster ... 142 HU 3270
Mangersta ... 130 NB 0131
Mangotsfield ... 33 ST 6676
Manish (Harris, W Isles) ... 125 NG 1089
Manish (Scarp) ... 130 NA 9513
Manish Point (Island of Raasay) ... 123 NG 5648
Manish Point (North Uist) ... 124 NF 7173
Mankinholes ... 78 SD 9523
Manley ... 69 SJ 5071
Manmoel ... 41 SO 1703
Mannal ... 104 NL 9840
Manningford Bohune ... 34 SU 1357
Manningford Bruce ... 34 SU 1359
Manning's Heath ... 28 TQ 2028
Mannington ... 26 SU 0605
Manningtree ... 55 TM 1031
Mannofield ... 119 NJ 9104
Manorbier ... 42 SS 0698
Manorhill ... 96 NT 6632
Manorowen ... 42 SM 9336
Manor Water ... 95 NT 2031
Man o' Scord (mt.) ... 142 HU 3283
Manquhill Hill ... 88 NX 6694
Mansell Gamage ... 45 SO 3944
Mansell Lacy ... 45 SO 4245
Mansergh ... 77 SD 6082
Mansfield (Notts.) ... 71 SK 5361
Mansfield (Strath.) ... 88 NS 6214
Mansfield Woodhouse ... 71 SK 5363

Mansie's Berg (pt.) ...141 HU 5341
Mansriggs ...77 SD 2880
Manston ...25 ST 8115
Manston Aerodrome ...31 TR 3366
Manthorpe ...62 TF 0616
Manton (Humbs.) ...74 SE 9302
Manton (Leic.) ...62 SK 8704
Manton (Wilts.) ...34 SU 1768
Mantyn Dyke (ant.) ...48 SO 2090
Manuden ...53 TL 4926
Maole Lumdaidh (mt.) ...127 NM 1345
Maol Breac ...106 NN 2515
Maol Buidhe ...98 NR 2945
Maol Chean-dearg ...126 NG 9249
Maol Chinn-dearg ...115 NH 0407
Maol nan Damh ...99 NR 6288
Maovally (mt.) ...132 NC 3721
Maplebeck ...72 SK 7160
Maple Cross ...36 TQ 0392
Mapledurham ...36 SU 6776
Mapledurwell ...35 SU 6851
Maplehurst ...28 TQ 1924
Mapleton ...60 SK 1648
Maplin Sands ...39 TR 0388
Mapperley ...60 SK 4343
Mapperton ...9 SY 5099
Mappleborough Green ...50 SP 0866
Mappleton ...75 TA 2244
Mappowder ...9 ST 7105
Maragay Mór ...124 NB 8952
Marazion ...18 SW 5130
Marbury ...59 SJ 5545
March ...63 TL 4197
Marcham ...47 SU 4596
Marchamley ...59 SJ 5929
Marchbankwood ...89 NY 0899
Marchington ...60 SK 1330
Marchington Woodlands ...60 SK 1128
Marchnant ...57 SN 7470
Marchwiel ...58 SJ 3547
Marchwood ...26 SU 3809
Marcross ...41 SS 9269
Mardale Common ...83 NY 4811
Marden (Here. and Worc.) ...45 SO 5247
Marden (Kent) ...29 TQ 7444
Marden (Wilts.) ...34 SU 0857
Mardy ...45 SO 3016
Mare Fen ...53 TL 5488
Marefield ...61 SK 7408
Mareham le Fen ...73 TF 2761
Mareham on the Hill ...73 TF 2867
Maresfield ...29 TQ 4624
Mare Tail (sbk.) ...63 TF 4437
Marfleet ...75 TA 1329
Margam ...41 SS 7887
Margam Burrows ...41 SS 7785
Margaret Marsh ...25 ST 8218
Margaret Roding ...30 TL 5912
Margaretting ...38 TL 6601
Margate ...31 TR 3670
Marg na Craige ...116 NN 6297
Margnaheglish ...92 NS 0331
Marham ...64 TF 7110
Marhamchurch ...22 SS 2203
Marholm ...62 TF 1402
Marian-glas ...66 SH 5084
Mariansleigh ...23 SS 7422
Marishader ...123 NG 4963
Maristow ...20 SX 4764
Mark ...32 ST 3747
Marka Ber ...137 HY 5907
Markbeech ...29 TQ 4842
Markby ...73 TF 4878
Mark Causeway ...32 ST 3547
Mark Cross ...29 TQ 5831
Market Bosworth ...60 SK 4003
Market Deeping ...62 TF 1310
Market Drayton ...59 SJ 6734
Market Harborough ...51 SP 7387
Markethill ...108 NO 2239
Market Lavington ...34 SU 0154
Market Overton ...62 SK 8816
Market Rasen ...73 TF 1089
Market Stainton ...73 TF 2279
Market Weighton ...74 SE 8741
Market Weston ...54 TL 9877
Markfield ...61 SK 4810
Markham ...41 SO 1600
Markinch ...103 NO 2901
Markington ...79 SE 2864
Marksbury ...33 ST 6662
Marks Tey ...38 TL 9123
Markwell ...20 SX 3658
Markyate ...36 TL 0616
Marlborough ...34 SU 1869
Marlborough Downs ...34 SU 1574
Marlcliff ...50 SP 0950
Marldon ...21 SX 8663
Marlesford ...55 TM 3258
Marley Green ...59 SJ 5745
Marlingford ...65 TG 1208
Marloes ...42 SM 7908
Marlow ...36 SU 8587
Marlpit Hill ...29 TQ 4447
Marnhull ...25 ST 7718
Marnoch (Grampn.) ...121 NJ 5950
Marnoch (Strath.) ...101 NS 7168
Marple ...70 SJ 9588
Marr ...71 SE 5105
Marrick ...84 SE 0798
Marrister ...141 HU 5464
Marrival (mt.) ...124 NF 8070
Marros ...43 SN 2008
Marscalloch Hill ...88 NX 6192
Marsco (mt.) ...123 NG 5025
Marsden ...70 SE 0411
Marsden Bay ...91 NZ 4065
Marsett ...78 SD 9086
Marsh ...24 ST 2410
Marshalls Heath ...37 TL 1515
Marsham ...65 TG 1924
Marshaw ...77 SD 5853
Marsh Baldon ...47 SU 5699
Marshborough ...31 TR 2958
Marshbrook ...48 SO 4389
Marshchapel ...75 TA 3598
Marshfield (Avon) ...33 ST 7773
Marshfield (Gwent) ...32 ST 2582
Marshgate ...20 SX 1592
Marsh Gibbon ...36 SP 6423
Marsh Green (Devon) ...24 SY 0493
Marsh Green (Kent) ...29 TQ 4344
Marsh Green (Shrops.) ...59 SJ 6014
Marshland (Humbs.) ...74 SE 7820
Marshland (Norf.) ...63 TF 5412
Marshland Fen ...63 TF 5407
Marshland St. James ...63 TF 5108
Marshside ...68 SD 3419
Marsh, The ...58 SO 3197
Marshwood ...24 SY 3899
Marshwood Vale ...24 SY 4097
Marske ...84 NZ 1000
Marske-by-the-Sea ...85 NZ 6322
Marston (Ches.) ...69 SJ 6474
Marston (Here. and Worc.) ...45 SO 3657
Marston (Lincs.) ...62 SK 8943
Marston (Oxon.) ...47 SP 5208
Marston (Staffs.) ...59 SJ 8314
Marston (Staffs.) ...59 SJ 9227
Marston (Warw.) ...60 SP 2095

Marston (Wilts.) ...34 ST 9656
Marston Green ...50 SP 1685
Marston Magna ...25 ST 5922
Marston Meysey ...47 SU 1297
Marston Montgomery ...60 SK 1338
Marston Moor ...79 SE 4853
Marston Moretaine ...52 SP 9941
Marston on Dove ...60 SK 2329
Marston Stannett ...45 SO 5655
Marston St. Lawrence ...51 SP 5342
Marston Trussell ...51 SP 6986
Marstow ...45 SO 5519
Marsworth ...36 SP 9214
Marten ...34 SU 2860
Marthall ...69 SJ 8076
Martham ...65 TG 4518
Martin (Hants.) ...26 SU 0719
Martin (Lincs.) ...73 TF 1259
Martindale ...83 NY 4218
Martindale Common ...83 NY 4417
Martin Dales ...73 TF 1761
Martin Drove End ...26 SU 0420
Martinhoe ...23 SS 6648
Martin Hussingtree ...49 SO 8860
Martinscroft ...69 SJ 6589
Martinstown ...9 SY 6488
Martlesham ...55 TM 2547
Martlesham Heath ...55 TM 2545
Martletwy ...42 SN 0310
Martley ...49 SO 7559
Martnaham Loch ...93 NS 3917
Martock ...25 ST 4619
Marton (Ches.) ...69 SJ 8468
Marton (Cleve.) ...85 NZ 5115
Marton (Lincs.) ...72 SK 8381
Marton (N Yorks.) ...79 SE 4162
Marton (N Yorks.) ...80 SE 7383
Marton (Shrops.) ...58 SJ 2802
Marton (Warw.) ...50 SP 4069
Marton Abbey ...79 SE 5869
Marvig ...131 NB 4119
Mar Wick (Orkney) ...136 HY 2224
Marwick (Orkney) ...136 HY 2325
Marwick Head ...136 HY 2225
Marwood ...23 SS 5437
Marybank ...128 NH 4753
Maryburgh ...128 NH 5456
Marygold ...97 NT 8160
Maryhill ...121 NJ 8245
Marykirk ...109 NO 6865
Marylebone ...69 SD 5807
Marylebone ...37 TQ 2881
Marypark ...117 NJ 1938
Maryport (Cumbr.) ...82 NY 0336
Maryport (Dumf. and Galwy.) ...86 NX 1429
Maryport (Strath.) ...86 NX 1434
Marystow ...20 SX 4382
Mary Tavy ...20 SX 5079
Maryton ...109 NO 6856
Marywell (Grampn.) ...119 NO 5896
Marywell (Tays.) ...109 NO 6544
Masham ...79 SE 2280
Masham Moor ...78 SE 1079
Mashbury ...38 TL 6511
Mason ...91 NZ 2073
Massacamber (pt.) ...124 NF 9382
Massingham Heath ...64 TF 7620
Mastrick ...119 NJ 9007
Matching ...37 TL 5212
Matching Green ...37 TL 5311
Matching Tye ...37 TL 5111
Matfen ...91 NZ 0371
Matfield ...29 TQ 6541
Mathern ...33 ST 5291
Mathon ...49 SO 7345
Mathry ...42 SM 8832
Matlaske ...65 TG 1534
Matlock ...71 SK 3060
Matlock Bath ...71 SK 2958
Matson ...46 SO 8316
Matterdale End ...83 NY 3923
Mattersey ...71 SK 6889
Mathew's Port ...93 NS 1903
Mattingley ...35 SU 7357
Mattishall ...64 TG 0510
Mattishall Burgh ...64 TG 0511
Mauchline ...93 NS 4927
Maud ...121 NJ 9247
Maugersbury ...47 SP 1925
Maughold ...76 SC 4991
Maughold Head ...76 SC 4991
Maulden ...52 TL 0538
Maulds Meaburn ...83 NY 6216
Maunby ...79 SE 3486
Maund Bryan ...45 SO 5550
Mautby ...65 TG 4712
Mavesyn Ridware ...60 SK 0817
Mavis Enderby ...73 TF 3666
Mavis Grind ...142 HU 3469
Mawbray ...82 NY 0846
Mawdesley ...69 SD 4914
Mawgan ...18 SW 7024
Mawgan Porth ...19 SW 8467
Maw Green ...60 SW 0197
Mawla ...18 SW 6945
Mawnan ...19 SW 7827
Mawnan Smith ...18 SW 7728
Maxey ...62 TF 1208
Maxstoke ...50 SP 2386
Maxton ...96 NT 6129
Maxwellheugh ...96 NT 7333
Maxwellston ...86 NS 2600
Mayar (mt.) ...117 NO 2373
Maybole ...93 NS 3009
Mayfield ...103 NT 3465
Mayfield (E Susx) ...29 TQ 5827
Mayfield (Staffs.) ...60 SK 1545
Mayford ...28 SU 9956
May Hill ...46 SO 6921
Mayland ...38 TL 9101
Maypole ...43 SO 4716
Maypole Green ...66 TM 4195
Maywick ...141 HU 3724
McArthur's Head ...98 NR 4659
McFarlane's Rock ...122 NG 3031
McFarquhar's Cave ...129 NH 7965
Meadie Burn ...133 NC 5038
Meadle ...36 SP 8005
Meadowtown ...58 SJ 3101
Mealasta ...130 NA 9721
Mealasta Island ...130 NB 0122
Meal Bank ...83 SD 5495
Mealdarroch Point ...100 NR 8868
Mealfuarvonie ...116 NH 4522
Mealisval (mt.) ...130 NB 0227
Meall a' Bhata ...133 NC 6326
Meall a' Bhreacraibh ...116 NH 7935
Meall a' Bhuachaille ...117 NH 9811
Meall a' Chàise ...105 NM 7517
Meall a' Chaorainn ...116 NH 1364
Meall a' Choire Bhuidhe ...108 NO 0671
Meall a' Chrasgaidh ...115 NH 1873
Meall a' Chràthaich ...115 NH 3622
Meall a' Churain ...106 NN 4632
Meall a' Ghrianain ...127 NH 3677
Meall a' Mhadaidh ...107 NN 5925
Meall a' Mhuic ...107 NN 5750
Meall an Aonaich ...132 NC 3316
Meall an Arbhair ...98 NN 3990
Meallan Buidhe (Highld.) ...115 NH 1337
Meallan Buidhe (Highld.) ...127 NH 3344

Meall an Damhain ...111 NM 7259
Meall an Doirein ...123 NG 8675
Meall an Fhuarain (Highld.) ...127 NC 2802
Meall an Fhuarain (Highld.) ...133 NC 5130
Meall an Fhuarain (Island of Skye) ...123 NG 4535
Meall an Inbhire ...111 NM 4656
Meallan Liath ...133 NC 5150
Meallan Liath Beag ...132 NC 8815
Meallan Liath Coire Mhic Dhughaill ...132 NC 3539
Meallan Liath Mór ...133 NC 6517
Meall an t-Seallaidh ...107 NN 5423
Meall an t-Sithe ...128 NH 1376
Meall an Tuirc ...128 NH 5471
Meall a' Phiobaire ...133 NC 6915
Meall a' Phubuill ...114 NN 0385
Meall Bhenneit ...128 NH 5483
Meall Blàir ...115 NN 0795
Meall Buidhe ...98 NN 8095
Meall Buidhe (Highld.) ...111 NM 8498
Meall Buidhe (Strath.) ...92 NR 7332
Meall Buidhe (Tays.) ...107 NN 4245
Meall Buidhe (Tays.) ...107 NN 4949
Meall Cala ...101 NN 5012
Meall Cruaidh ...116 NN 5780
Meall Cruinn ...107 NN 4547
Meall Dearg ...108 NN 8841
Meall Dheirgidh ...128 NH 4794
Meall Dubh (Argyll.) ...100 NS 0789
Meall Dubh (Highld.) ...128 NH 2089
Meall Dubh (Highld.) ...115 NH 2407
Meall Fuar-mhonaidh ...116 NH 4522
Meall Gainmheich ...101 NN 5109
Meall Garbh (Strath.) ...106 NN 1636
Meall Garbh (Tays.) ...107 NN 6443
Meall Geal ...131 NB 5660
Meall Ghaordaidh ...107 NN 5139
Meall Gorm (Grampn.) ...117 NO 1894
Meall Gorm (Highld.) ...123 NG 7840
Meall Gorm (Highld.) ...127 NH 2269
Meall Leacachain ...127 NH 2477
Meall Liath Choire ...127 NH 2296
Meall Loch Airigh Alasdair ...123 NG 7436
Meall Luaidhe ...107 NN 5843
Meall Luidh Mór ...116 NN 4179
Meall Meadhonach ...132 NC 4162
Meall Mhic Iomhair ...128 NH 3167
Meall Mór (Highld.) ...128 NH 5174
Meall Mór (Highld.) ...116 NH 7335
Meall Mór (Highld.) ...106 NN 1056
Meall Mór (Highld.) (is.) ...132 NC 1237
Meall Moraig ...128 NH 6694
Meall na Caorach ...135 NO 0927
Meall na Drochaide ...128 NH 5069
Meall na h-Aisre ...116 NH 5100
Meall na h-Eilde ...116 NN 5332
Meall na h-Uamha ...123 NG 7765
Meall na Leitreach ...107 NN 6470
Meall nam Bràdhan ...127 NH 2690
Meall na Mèine ...106 NN 9081
Meall nam Fuaran ...107 NN 8236
Meall na Caorach ...116 NH 4735
Meall na Caorach (Tayside) ...108 NN 9234
Meall na Con (Highld.) ...133 NC 5830
Meall na Con (Highld.) ...111 NM 5068
Meall na Creag Leac ...111 NM 8674
Meall na Each ...111 NM 6364
Meall na Ruadhag ...106 NN 2957
Meall na Tarmachan ...107 NN 5838
Meall na Tighearn ...106 NN 2323
Meall na Speireig ...128 NH 4966
Meall na Suiramach ...123 NG 4469
Meall Odhar (Strath.) ...106 NN 9416
Meall Odhar (Tays.) ...101 NN 6414
Meall Odhar (Tays.) ...107 NN 6639
Meall Reamhar (Strath.) ...99 NR 8370
Meall Reamhar (Tays.) ...107 NN 6721
Meall Reamhar (Tays.) ...108 NN 8924
Meall Reamhar (Tays.) ...108 NN 8732
Meall Reamhar (Tays.) ...100 NO 0356
Meall Tairneachan ...107 NN 8054
Meall Tarsuinn ...108 NN 8729
Meall Tarvie ...107 NN 4838
Meall Uaine ...108 NO 1167
Mealna Letter or Duchray Hill ...108 NO 1667
Meal nan Damh ...92 NN 9342
Mealsgate ...82 NY 2141
Mearbeck ...78 SD 8160
Meare ...32 ST 4541
Meare Green ...24 ST 3326
Mears Ashby ...52 SP 8366
Measham ...60 SK 3312
Meathop ...77 SD 4380
Meaul (mt.) ...87 NX 5091
Meaux ...75 TA 0939
Meavag ...125 NG 1596
Meavaig ...125 NB 0905
Meavaig River ...125 NB 0908
Meavy ...21 SX 5467
Medbourne ...61 SP 7993
Medburn ...91 NZ 1270
Meddon ...22 SS 2717
Meden Vale ...71 SK 5869
Medmenham ...36 SU 8084
Medstead ...27 SU 6537
Meerbrook ...70 SJ 9860
Meer End ...50 SP 2474
Meesden ...53 TL 4432
Meeth ...23 SS 5408
Meggat Water ...89 NY 2996
Meggernie Castle ...107 NN 5546
Meggethead ...95 NT 1621
Megget Reservoir (under constn.) ...95 NT 1922
Meg's Craig ...109 NO 6844
Meidrim ...43 SN 2820
Meifod ...58 SJ 1513
Meigle ...108 NO 2844
Meikle Hill ...96 NT 4636
Meikle Black Law ...97 NT 8268
Meikle Carewe Hill ...119 NO 8291
Meikle Conval ...117 NJ 2937
Meikle Craigs ...93 NS 3228
Meikle Earnock ...94 NS 7253
Meikle Float ...86 NX 0748
Meikle Hard Hill ...88 NX 9363
Meikle Hill ...129 NJ 1450
Meikleour ...108 NO 1539
Meikle Says Law ...103 NT 5861
Meikle Strath ...109 NO 6471
Meikle Tarty ...121 NJ 9928
Meikle Wartle ...121 NJ 7230
Meinciau ...43 SN 4610
Meir ...59 SJ 9342
Meith Bheinn ...111 NM 8287
Melbecks Moor ...84 NY 9400
Melbost ...131 NB 4632
Melbost Sands ...131 NB 4535
Melbourn (Cambs.) ...53 TL 3844
Melbourne (Derby.) ...60 SK 3825
Melbourne (Humbs.) ...74 SE 7543
Melbury ...22 SS 3719
Melbury Bubb ...25 ST 5906
Melbury Osmond ...25 ST 5707
Melbury Sampford ...25 ST 5705
Melby House ...140 HU 1857
Melchbourne ...52 TL 0265
Melcombe Bingham ...25 ST 7602
Meldon (Devon) ...23 SX 5592
Meldon (Northum.) ...91 NZ 1284

Meldon Reservoir ...21 SX 5691
Meldreth ...53 TL 3746
Meldrum House ...121 NJ 8129
Melfort ...105 NM 8314
Melgarve ...116 NN 4695
Meliden ...67 SJ 0580
Melincourt ...41 SN 8201
Melin-y-coed ...67 SH 8160
Melin-y-ddol ...57 SJ 0807
Melin-y-grug ...57 SJ 0507
Melin-y-wig ...67 SJ 0448
Melkinthorpe ...83 NY 5525
Melkridge ...90 NY 7363
Melksham ...33 ST 9063
Melldalloch ...100 NR 9375
Mellerstain Ho. ...96 NT 6439
Mell Head ...135 ND 3476
Melling (Lancs.) ...77 SD 5970
Melling (Mers.) ...68 SD 3800
Mellis ...55 TM 0974
Mellon Charles ...126 NG 8491
Mellon Udrigle ...126 NG 8895
Mellor (Gtr Mches.) ...70 SJ 9888
Mellor (Lancs.) ...77 SD 6530
Mellor Brook ...77 SD 6331
Mells ...33 ST 7249
Melmerby (Cumbr.) ...83 NY 6137
Melmerby (N Yorks.) ...78 SE 0785
Melmerby (N Yorks.) ...79 SE 3376
Melmerby Fell ...83 NY 6538
Melowther Hill ...93 NS 5548
Melplash ...25 SY 4797
Melrose ...96 NT 5433
Melsetter ...136 ND 2689
Melsonby ...84 NZ 1908
Meltham ...70 SE 0910
Melton ...55 TM 2850
Meltonby ...80 SE 7952
Melton Constable ...64 TG 0433
Melton Mowbray ...61 SK 7518
Melton Ross ...74 TA 0610
Meluncart (mt.) ...119 NO 6382
Melvaig ...126 NG 7486
Melverley ...58 SJ 3316
Melvich ...134 NC 8864
Melvich Bay ...134 NC 8865
Membury ...24 ST 2703
Memsie ...121 NJ 9762
Memus ...109 NO 4258
Menabilly ...19 SX 0951
Menai Bridge ...66 SH 5572
Menai Strait ...66 SH 5471
Mendham ...55 TM 2783
Mendick Hill ...95 NT 1250
Mendip Forest ...33 ST 4954
Mendip Hills ...33 ST 5255
Mendlesham ...55 TM 1065
Mendlesham Green ...55 TM 0963
Menheniot ...20 SX 2862
Mennock ...88 NS 8008
Men of Mey (pt.) ...135 NU 3175
Menston ...78 SE 1743
Menstrie ...102 NS 8596
Menteith Hills ...101 NN 5502
Mentmore ...36 SP 9019
Meoir Langwell ...128 NH 4298
Meole Brace ...58 SJ 4811
Meon Hill ...50 SP 1745
Meonstoke ...27 SU 6119
Meon Valley ...27 SU 5915
Meopham ...30 TQ 6466
Meopham Station ...30 TQ 6467
Mepal ...53 TL 4481
Meppershall ...52 TL 1336
Merbach ...45 SO 3045
Mere (Ches.) ...69 SJ 7281
Mere (Wilts.) ...25 ST 8132
Mere Brow ...68 SD 4118
Mereclough ...77 SD 8730
Mere Green ...60 SP 1298
Mere, The ...58 SJ 4133
Mereworth ...29 TQ 6553
Mereworth Castle ...29 TQ 6653
Mergie ...119 NO 7988
Meriden ...50 SP 2482
Merkadale ...122 NG 3831
Merkland ...86 NX 2491
Merkland Lodge ...132 NC 4029
Merkland Point ...92 NS 0339
Merlin's Bridge ...42 SM 9414
Merrick ...87 NX 4285
Merrington ...59 SJ 4621
Merriott ...25 ST 4412
Merrivale ...20 SX 5475
Merrymeet ...20 SX 2766
Merse (dist.) ...97 NT 8247
Mersea Flats (sbk.) ...39 TM 0513
Mersea Island ...39 TM 0314
Mersehead Sands ...88 NX 9153
Mersham ...31 TR 0539
Merstham ...37 TQ 2953
Merston ...27 SU 8903
Merstone ...27 SZ 5285
Merther ...19 SW 8644
Merthyr ...43 SN 3520
Merthyr Cynog ...44 SN 9837
Merthyr Dyfan ...41 ST 1169
Merthyr Mawr ...41 SS 8877
Merthyr Tydfil ...41 SO 0406
Merthyr Vale ...41 ST 0899
Merton (Devon) ...23 SS 5212
Merton (Gtr London) ...37 TQ 2569
Merton (Norf.) ...64 TL 9098
Merton (Oxon.) ...47 SP 5717
Mervinslaw ...90 NT 6713
Meshaw ...23 SS 7519
Messing ...38 TL 8918
Messingham ...74 SE 8904
Metfield ...55 TM 2980
Metheringham ...72 TF 0661
Methil ...103 NT 3699
Methley ...79 SE 3826
Methlick ...121 NJ 8537
Methven ...108 NO 0225
Methwold ...64 TL 7394
Methwold Fens ...64 TL 6593
Methwold Hythe ...64 TL 7195
Mettingham ...55 TM 3689
Mevagissey ...19 SX 0144
Mevagissey Bay ...19 SX 0246
Mew Stone ...21 SX 4449
Mexborough ...71 SK 4799
Mey ...135 ND 2872
Meysey Hampton ...46 SU 1199
Miavaig ...131 NB 0834
Michaelchurch ...45 SO 5125
Michaelchurch Escley ...45 SO 3134
Michaelchurch-on-Arrow ...45 SO 2450
Michaelston-le-Pit ...41 ST 1573
Michaelston-y-Fedw ...32 ST 2484
Michaelstow ...19 SX 0778
Micheldever ...35 SU 5138
Micheldever Forest ...35 SU 5741
Micheldever Station ...35 SU 5142
Micheldever Wood ...35 SU 5337
Michelmersh ...26 SU 3426
Mickfield ...55 TM 1361
Mickleby ...85 NZ 8013
Mickle Fell ...79 NY 8024
Micklefield ...79 SE 4443
Mickleham ...37 TQ 1753
Mickleover ...60 SK 3034

Mickleton (Durham) ...84 NY 9623
Mickleton (Glos.) ...50 SP 1543
Mickle Trafford ...68 SJ 4469
Mickley ...79 SE 2576
Mickley Square ...91 NZ 0761
Mid Ardlaw ...121 NJ 9464
Mid Barrow (lightship) ...39 TR 1992
Midbea ...138 HY 4444
Mid Beltie ...119 NJ 6200
Midberg (pt.) ...143 HU 5988
Middle Assendon ...36 SU 7385
Middle Aston ...47 SP 4726
Middle Barton ...47 SP 4326
Middlebere Heath ...26 SY 9484
Middlebie ...89 NY 2176
Middle Claydon ...51 SP 7125
Middle Drums ...109 NO 5957
Middle Fell ...83 NY 7444
Middle Fen ...53 TL 5679
Middlefield Law ...96 NS 6730
Middle Grounds (sbk.) ...32 ST 3577
Middleham ...78 SE 1287
Middle Hambleton ...62 SK 9007
Middlehope ...48 SO 4988
Middlehope Moor ...84 NY 8842
Middle Level Main Drain ...62 TF 5506
Middle Littleton ...50 SP 0747
Middle Maes-coed ...45 SO 3334
Middlemarsh ...25 ST 6707
Middle Mill ...42 SM 8025
Middle Moor (Cambs.) ...53 TL 2589
Middle Moor (Northum.) ...97 NU 1423
Middle Mouse (is.) ...66 SH 3895
Middle Muir ...95 NS 8425
Middlemuir Farm ...121 NJ 9420
Middle Rasen ...72 TF 0889
Middle Rigg ...107 NO 0608
Middlesbrough ...85 NZ 4920
Middle Shield Park ...90 NY 6070
Middlesmoor ...78 SE 0974
Middlestone Moor ...84 NZ 2532
Middlestown ...71 SE 2617
Middleton (Cumbr.) ...77 SD 6286
Middleton (Derby.) ...71 SK 1963
Middleton (Derby.) ...60 SK 2755
Middleton (Essex) ...54 TL 8639
Middleton (Grampn.) ...119 NJ 8419
Middleton (Gtr Mches.) ...70 SD 8606
Middleton (Hants.) ...34 SU 4243
Middleton (Here. and Worc.) ...48 SO 5469
Middleton (Lancs.) ...77 SD 4258
Middleton (Lothian) ...96 NT 3657
Middleton (Norf.) ...64 TF 6616
Middleton (Northants.) ...52 SP 8489
Middleton (Northum.) ...90 NU 0024
Middleton (Northum.) ...97 NU 1035
Middleton (N Yorks.) ...80 SE 7885
Middleton (N Yorks. W Yorks.) ...78 SE 1249
Middleton (Shrops.) ...58 SJ 3128
Middleton (Shrops.) ...50 SO 2999
Middleton (Shrops.) ...48 SO 5377
Middleton (Suff.) ...55 TM 4267
Middleton (Tays.) ...102 NO 1206
Middleton (Tays.) ...108 NO 1447
Middleton (Tiree) ...104 NL 9443
Middleton (Warw.) ...50 SP 1798
Middleton (W Yorks.) ...79 SE 3027
Middleton Cheney ...51 SP 4941
Middleton Common ...26 NY 9630
Middleton Green ...60 SJ 9935
Middle Tongue (mt.) ...78 SD 9181
Middleton Hall ...97 NT 9825
Middleton in Teesdale ...84 NY 9425
Middleton-on-Sea ...28 SU 9800
Middleton on the Hill ...48 SO 5464
Middleton-on-the-Wolds ...81 SE 9449
Middleton Priors ...49 SO 6290
Middleton Scriven ...49 SO 6787
Middleton St. George ...85 NZ 3412
Middleton Stoney ...47 SP 5323
Middleton Tyas ...84 NZ 2205
Middletown ...58 SJ 3012
Middle Tysoe ...50 SP 3344
Middle Wallop ...26 SU 2937
Middlewich ...69 SJ 7066
Middle Winterslow ...26 SU 2432
Middle Witchyburn ...121 NJ 6356
Middle Woodford ...26 SU 1136
Middlewood Green ...55 TM 0961
Middlewood Station ...59 SJ 9484
Middleyard ...93 NS 5132
Middlezoy ...24 ST 3733
Middridge ...84 NZ 2526
Midfield ...133 NC 5864
Midge Hall ...77 SD 5123
Midgeholme ...90 NY 6458
Midgham ...35 SU 5567
Midgley ...78 SE 0226
Mid Hill (Dumf. and Galwy.) ...88 NS 6907
Mid Hill (Orkney) ...136 HY 3324
Midhope Moors ...70 SK 2098
Midhopestones ...70 SK 2399
Midhurst ...27 SU 8821
Mid Kame (mt.) ...141 HU 4158
Midland Ness ...136 HY 3203
Midlem ...96 NT 5227
Midmar Forest ...119 NJ 7104
Mid Moile (mt.) ...133 NX 0972
Mid Sannox ...100 NS 0145
Midsomer Norton ...33 ST 6654
Mid Thundergay ...100 NR 8846
Midtown ...126 NG 8285
Midtown of Buchromb ...121 NJ 4144
Mid Urchany ...129 NH 8849
Midville ...73 TF 3857
Mid Yell ...143 HU 5190
Mid Yell Voe ...143 HU 5191
Miefield ...88 NX 6559
Migneint ...57 NH 7642
Migvie ...118 NJ 4306
Milborne Port ...25 ST 6718
Milborne St. Andrew ...25 SY 7997
Milborne Wick ...25 ST 6620
Milbourne ...91 NZ 1175
Milburn (Cumbr.) ...76 NY 6529
Milburn Forest ...83 NY 7332
Milburn Geo ...141 HU 4012
Milbury Heath ...33 ST 6690
Milcombe ...47 SP 4134
Milden ...54 TL 9546
Mildenhall (Suff.) ...54 TL 7074
Mildenhall (Wilts.) ...34 SU 2069
Mildenhall Fen ...54 TL 6578
Milebrook ...48 SO 3172
Milebush ...29 TQ 7546
Mile End ...34 SJ 9968
Mile Oak ...29 TQ 5822
Mileham ...64 TF 9119
Mile Hill ...80 NO 3157
Milesmark ...102 NT 0688
Milfield ...97 NT 9333
Milford (Derby.) ...60 SK 3445
Milford (Staffs.) ...60 SJ 9721
Milford (Surrey) ...28 SU 9442
Milford Haven (Dyfed) ...42 SM 9006
Milford Haven (Dyfed) (chan.) ...42 SM 8804
Milford on Sea ...26 SZ 2891
Milk Hill ...34 SU 1064
Milkieston Rings ...95 NT 2545
Milkwall ...45 SO 5809
Milland ...27 SU 8228

North Charlton ... 97 NU 1622
North Cheek or Ness Point ... 81 NZ 9506
Northchurch ... 36 SP 9708
North Cliffe ... 74 SE 8737
North Clifton ... 72 SK 8272
Northcote Manor ... 23 SS 6218
North Cotes ... 75 TA 3400
Northcott ... 20 SX 3392
North Cove ... 55 TM 4689
North Cowton ... 84 NZ 2803
North Crawley ... 36 SP 9244
North Cray ... 37 TQ 4972
North Creake ... 64 TF 8538
North Curry ... 24 ST 3125
North Dalton ... 81 SE 9352
North Dawn ... 136 HY 4803
North Deep ... 108 NO 2219
North Deighton ... 79 SE 3851
North Downs (Hants.) ... 27 SU 8207
North Downs (Kent) ... 30 TQ 6763
North Drove Drain ... 62 TF 1817
North Duffield ... 74 SE 6837
Northdyke ... 136 HY 2320
North Elkington ... 73 TF 2890
North Elmham ... 64 TF 9820
North End (Avon) ... 32 ST 4167
Northend (Avon) ... 33 ST 7867
North End (Berks.) ... 34 SU 4063
North End (Bucks.) ... 36 SU 7392
North End (Hants.) ... 27 SU 6502
Northend (Warw.) ... 51 SP 3852
North End (W Susx) ... 28 TQ 1209
North Erradale ... 126 NG 7481
North Esk Resr. ... 102 NT 1558
Northey Island ... 38 TL 8706
North Fearns ... 123 NG 5935
North Fen (Cambs.) ... 63 TF 2909
North Fen (Cambs.) ... 53 TL 5169
North Ferriby ... 74 SE 9826
Northfield (Borders) ... 97 NT 9167
Northfield (Grampn.) ... 119 NJ 9008
Northfield (W Mids.) ... 50 SP 0179
Northfleet ... 30 TQ 6274
North Foreland ... 31 TR 4069
North Frodingham ... 81 TA 1053
North Glen Sannox ... 92 NR 9746
North Green ... 55 TM 2288
North Greetwell ... 72 TF 0173
North Grimston ... 80 SE 8467
North Harris (dist.) ... 125 NB 1207
North Haven (Fair Isle) ... 139 HZ 2272
North Haven (Grampn.) ... 121 NK 1138
North Havra (is.) ... 141 HU 3642
North Hayling ... 27 SU 7203
North Head (Highld.) ... 135 ND 3851
North Head (Swona) ... 136 ND 3985
North Heasley ... 23 SS 7333
North Heath ... 28 TQ 0621
North Hill (Corn.) ... 20 SX 2776
North Hill (Papa Westray) ... 138 HY 4954
North Hill (Somer.) ... 23 SS 9347
North Hill (Westray) ... 138 HY 4048
North Hinksey Village ... 47 SP 4806
North Holms ... 143 HP 5611
North Holmwood ... 28 TQ 1646
North Huish ... 21 SX 7156
North Hykeham ... 72 SK 9465
Northiam ... 30 TQ 8324
Northill (Beds.) ... 52 TL 1446
Northington ... 27 SU 5637
North Kelsey ... 74 TA 0401
North Kelsey Beck ... 74 TA 0102
North Kessock ... 128 NH 6548
North Kilvington ... 79 SE 4285
North Kilworth ... 51 SP 6183
North Kingennie ... 109 NO 4736
North Kyme ... 62 TF 1452
North Lancing ... 28 TQ 1805
Northlands ... 63 TF 3453
Northleach ... 46 SP 1114
North Lee (Bucks.) ... 36 SP 8309
North Lee (North Uist) (mt.) ... 124 NF 9366
Northleigh (Devon) ... 24 SY 1995
North Leigh (Oxon.) ... 47 SP 3813
North Leverton with Habblesthorpe ... 72 SK 7882
Northlew ... 20 SX 5099
North Littleton ... 50 SP 0847
North Loch ... 139 HY 7545
North Lopham ... 54 TM 0383
North Luffenham ... 62 SK 9303
North Marden ... 27 SU 8015
North Marston ... 36 SP 7722
North Medwin ... 95 NT 0149
North Middleton ... 103 NT 3559
North Molton ... 23 SS 7329
Northmoor ... 47 SP 4202
Northmoor Green or Moorland ... 24 ST 3332
North Morar (dist.) ... 111 NM 7892
North Moreton ... 35 SU 5689
Northmuir ... 109 NO 3855
North Muskham ... 72 SK 7958
North Neaps ... 143 HP 4805
North Ness ... 140 HU 1861
North Nesting (dist.) ... 141 HU 4559
North Nevi (pt.) ... 137 HY 6101
North Newbald ... 74 SE 9136
North Newington ... 47 SP 4139
North Newnton ... 34 SU 1257
North Newton ... 24 ST 2931
North Nibley ... 46 ST 7396
North Oakley ... 35 SU 5354
North Ockendon ... 38 TQ 5984
Northolt ... 37 TQ 1285
Northop ... 68 SJ 2468
Northop Hall ... 68 SJ 2767
North Ormsby ... 73 TF 2893
Northorpe (Lincs.) ... 72 SK 8996
Northorpe (Lincs.) ... 62 TF 0917
North Otterington ... 85 SE 3589
Northover ... 25 ST 5223
North Owersby ... 72 TF 0594
Northowram ... 78 SE 1127
North Perrott ... 25 ST 4709
North Petherton ... 24 ST 2832
North Petherwin ... 20 SX 2889
North Pickenham ... 64 TF 8606
North Piddle ... 50 SO 9654
North Poorton ... 25 SY 5197
Northpunds ... 141 HU 4022
North Queensferry ... 102 NT 1380
Northrepps ... 65 TG 2439
North Rigton ... 79 SE 2749
North Rode ... 69 SJ 8866
North Roe ... 142 HU 3689
North Roe (dist.) ... 142 HU 3487
North Ronaldsay ... 139 HY 7654
North Ronaldsay Aerodrome ... 139 HY 7653
North Ronaldsay Firth ... 139 HY 7549
North Runcton ... 64 TF 6416
North Sandwick ... 143 HU 5496
North Scale ... 76 SD 1769
North Scarle ... 72 SK 8466
North Seaton ... 91 NZ 2986
North Shian ... 106 NM 9143
North Shields ... 91 NZ 3468
North Shoebury ... 38 TQ 9286
North Shore ... 77 SD 3037
North Side ... 63 TL 2799
North Somercotes ... 73 TF 4296
North Sound, The ... 138 HY 5845
North Stack (pt.) ... 66 SH 2183

North Stainley ... 79 SE 2876
North Stainmore ... 83 NY 8215
North Stane ... 143 HP 6613
North Stifford ... 38 TQ 6080
North Stoke (Avon) ... 33 ST 7068
North Stoke (Oxon.) ... 36 SU 6186
North Stoke (W Susx) ... 28 TQ 0211
North Street ... 27 SU 6433
North Sunderland ... 97 NU 2131
North Sutor (pt.) ... 129 NH 8168
North Taing (Auskerry) ... 137 HY 6716
North Taing (Stronsay) ... 137 HY 6225
North Tamerton ... 20 SX 3197
North Tawton ... 23 SS 6601
North Third Resr. ... 101 NS 7588
North Thoresby ... 75 TF 2998
North Tidworth ... 34 SU 2248
North Tolsta ... 131 NB 5347
Northton ... 124 NF 9989
Northtown ... 136 ND 4797
North Tuddenham ... 64 TG 0413
North Uist (is.) ... 124 NF 8370
Northwaa ... 139 HY 7544
North Walsham ... 65 TG 2730
North Waltham ... 35 SU 5546
North Warnborough ... 35 SU 7351
North Water Bridge ... 109 NO 6566
North Watten ... 135 ND 2458
Northway ... 46 SO 9234
North Weald Basset ... 37 TL 4904
North West Passage ... 14 SV 8411
North West Point ... 22 SS 1347
North Wharf (sbk.) ... 77 SD 3149
North Whilborough ... 21 SX 8766
Northwich ... 69 SJ 6573
Northwick (Avon) ... 33 ST 5586
North Wick (Avon) ... 33 ST 5865
North Widcombe ... 33 ST 5758
North Willingham ... 73 TF 1688
North Wingfield ... 71 SK 4064
North Witham ... 62 SK 9221
Northwold ... 64 TL 7596
Northwood (Gtr London) ... 37 TQ 1090
Northwood (I. of W.) ... 27 SZ 4992
Northwood (Shrops.) ... 58 SJ 4633
Northwood Green ... 46 SO 7216
North Wootton (Dorset) ... 25 ST 6614
North Wootton (Norf.) ... 64 TF 6424
North Wootton (Somer.) ... 33 ST 5641
North Wraxall ... 33 ST 8174
North Yardhope ... 90 NT 9201
North York Moors ... 80 SE 7398
North Yorkshire Moors Railway ... 80 SE 8495
Norton (Ches.) ... 69 SJ 5581
Norton (Cleve.) ... 85 NZ 4421
Norton (Glos.) ... 46 SO 8624
Norton (Here. and Worc.) ... 49 SO 8750
Norton (Here. and Worc.) ... 50 SP 0447
Norton (Herts.) ... 53 TL 2234
Norton (I. of W.) ... 26 SZ 3489
Norton (Northants.) ... 51 SP 6063
Norton (Notts.) ... 71 SK 5772
Norton (N Yorks.) ... 80 SE 7971
Norton (N Yorks.) ... 71 SK 3581
Norton (Powys) ... 48 SO 3067
Norton (Shrops.) ... 59 SJ 5609
Norton (Shrops.) ... 59 SJ 7200
Norton (Shrops.) ... 48 SO 4581
Norton (Suff.) ... 54 TL 9565
Norton (S Yorks.) ... 71 SE 5415
Norton (Wilts.) ... 33 ST 8884
Norton (W Susx) ... 28 SU 9306
Norton Bavant ... 33 ST 9043
Norton Bridge ... 59 SJ 8730
Norton Canes ... 60 SK 0108
Norton Canon ... 45 SO 3847
Norton Disney ... 72 SK 8859
Norton Ferris ... 25 ST 7936
Norton Fitzwarren ... 24 ST 1925
Norton Green ... 26 SZ 3388
Norton Hawkfield ... 33 ST 5964
Norton Heath ... 38 TL 6004
Norton in Hales ... 59 SJ 7038
Norton-in-the-Moors ... 59 SJ 8951
Norton-Juxta-Twycross ... 60 SK 3207
Norton-le-Clay ... 79 SE 4071
Norton Lindsey ... 50 SP 2263
Norton Malreward ... 33 ST 6064
Norton Mandeville ... 37 TL 5804
Norton Marshes ... 65 TG 4200
Norton St. Philip ... 33 ST 7755
Norton Subcourse ... 65 TM 4098
Norton sub Hamdon ... 25 ST 4615
Norwell ... 72 SK 7661
Norwell Woodhouse ... 72 SK 7462
Norwich ... 65 TG 2308
Norwich Airport ... 65 TG 2213
Norwick (Unst) ... 143 HP 6514
Nor Wick (Unst) ... 143 HP 6614
Norwood Green ... 37 TQ 1378
Norwood Hill ... 28 TQ 2443
Noseley ... 61 SP 7398
Noss Head ... 135 ND 3854
Noss Mayo ... 21 SX 5447
Nosterfield ... 79 SE 2780
Nostie ... 123 NG 8527
Notgrove ... 46 SP 1020
Nottage ... 41 SS 8278
Nottingham ... 61 SK 5741
Nottingham Airport ... 61 SK 6236
Notton (Wilts.) ... 33 ST 9169
Notton (W Yorks.) ... 71 SE 3413
Nounsley ... 38 TL 7910
Noup Head ... 138 HY 3950
Noup of Noss ... 141 HU 5539
Noup, The (pt.) ... 143 HP 6318
Noutard's Green ... 49 SO 7966
Novar House ... 128 NH 6167
Nox ... 58 SJ 4010
Nuffield ... 36 SU 6687
Nunburnholme ... 80 SE 8548
Nuneaton ... 50 SP 3592
Nuneham Courtenay ... 47 SU 5599
Nun Monkton ... 79 SE 5057
Nunney ... 33 ST 7345
Nunnington ... 79 SE 6679
Nunnykirk ... 91 NZ 0892
Nunthorpe ... 85 NZ 5313
Nunton (Benbecula) ... 124 NF 7653
Nunton (Wilts.) ... 26 SU 1525
Nunwick ... 90 NY 8774
Nursling ... 26 SU 3615
Nursted ... 27 SU 7621
Nutbourne Hill ... 94 NS 7433
Nutbourne ... 28 TQ 0718
Nutfield ... 29 TQ 3150
Nuthall ... 61 SK 5144
Nuthampstead ... 53 TL 4134
Nutley ... 29 TQ 4427
Nutwell ... 71 SE 6303
Nybster ... 135 ND 3663
Nyetimber ... 27 SZ 8998
Nyewood ... 27 SU 8021
Nyland Hill ... 33 ST 4550
Nymet Rowland ... 23 SS 7108
Nymet Tracey ... 21 SS 7200
Nympsfield ... 46 SO 8000
Nynehead ... 24 ST 1422
Nyton ... 28 SU 9305

O

Oadby ... 61 SK 6200
Oad Street ... 30 TQ 8762
Oakamoor ... 60 SK 0544
Oakbank ... 102 NT 0866
Oakdale ... 41 ST 1898
Oake ... 24 ST 1525
Oaken ... 59 SJ 8502
Oakenclough ... 77 SD 5447
Oakengates ... 59 SJ 7010
Oakenshaw (Durham) ... 84 NZ 2036
Oakenshaw (W Yorks.) ... 78 SE 1727
Oakford (Devon) ... 23 SS 9021
Oakford (Dyfed) ... 69 SJ 9169
Oakgrove ... 62 SK 8509
Oakhanger ... 27 SU 7635
Oakhill ... 33 ST 6347
Oakington ... 53 TL 4164
Oaklands ... 67 SH 8158
Oakle Street ... 46 SO 7517
Oakley (Beds.) ... 52 TL 0153
Oakley (Bucks.) ... 36 SP 6412
Oakley (Fife) ... 102 NT 0289
Oakley (Hants.) ... 35 SU 5650
Oakley (Suff.) ... 55 TM 1678
Oakley Green ... 36 SU 9376
Oakley Park ... 57 SN 9886
Oakridge ... 46 SO 9103
Oaks ... 58 SJ 4204
Oaksey ... 33 ST 9893
Oakthorpe ... 60 SK 3213
Oakwoodhill ... 28 TQ 1337
Oakworth ... 78 SE 0238
Oare (Kent) ... 31 TR 0062
Oare (Somer.) ... 23 SS 8047
Oare (Wilts.) ... 34 SU 1563
Oasby ... 62 TF 0039
Oa, The (dist.) ... 98 NR 3144
Oathlaw ... 109 NO 4756
Oban ... 105 NM 8630
Oban Bay ... 105 NM 8530
Obney ... 108 NO 0336
Obney Hills ... 108 NO 0238
Oborne ... 25 ST 6518
Occlestone Green ... 69 SJ 6962
Occold ... 55 TM 1570
Ochertyre ... 107 NO 0509
Ochiltree ... 93 NS 5121
Ochtermuthill ... 107 NN 8216
Ockbrook ... 60 SK 4235
Ockham ... 28 TQ 0756
Ockle ... 111 NM 5570
Ockle Point ... 111 NM 5471
Ockley ... 28 TQ 1640
Ockran Head ... 142 HU 2484
Ocle Pychard ... 45 SO 5946
Odcombe ... 25 ST 5015
Oddendale ... 83 NY 5913
Odda's Chapel (ant.) ... 46 SO 8629
Oddingley ... 49 SO 9159
Oddington (Glos.) ... 47 SP 2225
Oddington (Oxon.) ... 47 SP 5514
Odell ... 52 SP 9658
Odie ... 137 HY 6229
Odiham ... 35 SU 7350
Odin Bay ... 137 HY 6824
Odness ... 137 HY 6926
Odstock ... 26 SU 1426
Odstock Down ... 26 SU 1324
Odstone ... 60 SK 3907
Offa's Dyke (Clwyd) (ant.) ... 67 SJ 1079
Offa's Dyke (Clwyd) (ant.) ... 58 SJ 2948
Offa's Dyke (Here. and Worc.) (ant.) ... 45 SO 2959
Offa's Dyke (Salop) (ant.) ... 48 SO 2578
Offchurch ... 50 SP 3565
Offenham ... 50 SP 0546
Offham (E Susx) ... 29 TQ 4012
Offham (Kent) ... 29 TQ 6557
Offord Cluny ... 52 TL 2267
Offord D'Arcy ... 53 TL 2266
Offton ... 54 TM 0649
Offwell ... 24 SY 1999
Ogbourne Maizey ... 34 SU 1871
Ogbourne St. Andrew ... 34 SU 1872
Ogbourne St. George ... 34 SU 2074
Ogbury (ant.) ... 34 SU 1438
Ogden Reservoir (Lancs.) ... 78 SD 7622
Ogden Reservoir (Lancs.) ... 78 SD 8140
Ogil ... 109 NO 4561
Ogle ... 91 NZ 1378
Ogmore ... 41 SS 8877
Ogmore-by-Sea ... 41 SS 8674
Ogmore Forest ... 41 SS 9489
Ogmore Vale ... 41 SS 9490
Ogston Reservoir ... 71 SK 3760
Oh Me Edge ... 90 NY 7099
Oigh-sgeir ... 110 NM 1596
Oisgill Bay ... 122 NG 1349
Oitir Fhiadhaich ... 124 NF 7465
Oitir Mhór (Barra) ... 112 NF 7306
Oitir Mhór (Benbecula) ... 124 NF 8157
Okeford Fitzpaine ... 25 ST 8010
Okehampton ... 21 SX 5895
Okehampton Camp ... 21 SX 5893
Okement Hill ... 21 SX 6087
Okraquoy ... 141 HU 4331
Olantigh ... 31 TR 0648
Old ... 51 SP 7873
Old Aberdeen ... 119 NJ 9408
Old Alresford ... 27 SU 5834
Oldany Island ... 132 NC 0834
Old Bedford River ... 53 TL 4888
Oldberrow ... 50 SP 1165
Old Bewick ... 97 NU 0621
Old Bolingbroke ... 73 TF 3564
Oldborough ... 23 SS 7706
Old Brampton ... 71 SK 3371
Old Bridge of Urr ... 88 NX 7767
Old Buckenham ... 54 TM 0691
Old Burghclere ... 35 SU 4657
Oldbury (Shrops.) ... 59 SO 7092
Oldbury (Warw.) ... 60 SP 3194
Oldbury (W Mids.) ... 50 SO 9889
Oldbury Castle (ant.) ... 34 SU 0469
Oldbury-on-Severn ... 33 ST 6092
Oldbury on the Hill ... 33 ST 8089
Oldbury Sands ... 45 ST 5793
Old Byland ... 79 SE 5486
Oldcastle ... 50 SO 3224
Old Castle Head ... 42 SS 0796
Old Cleeve ... 32 ST 0342
Old Clipstone ... 71 SK 6064
Oldcoates ... 71 SK 5888
Old Colwyn ... 67 SH 8678
Old Croft River ... 63 TL 4996
Old Dailly ... 86 NX 2299
Old Dalby ... 61 SK 6723
Old Deer ... 121 NJ 9747
Old Denaby ... 71 SK 4899
Old Ellerby ... 75 TA 1637
Old Felixstowe ... 55 TM 3135
Oldfield ... 49 SO 8464
Old Fletton ... 62 TL 1997
Oldford ... 33 ST 7849
Old Hall, The (Humbs.) ... 75 TA 2717
Oldham ... 69 SD 9305

Oldhamstocks ... 96 NT 7470
Old Head ... 136 ND 4683
Old Heath ... 39 TM 0122
Old Howe ... 81 TA 1156
Oldhurst ... 53 TL 3077
Old Hutton ... 77 SD 5688
Old Kea ... 19 SW 8441
Old Kilpatrick ... 101 NS 4673
Old Knebworth ... 37 TL 2320
Oldland ... 33 ST 6771
Old Leake ... 63 TF 4050
Old Lynn Channel ... 63 TF 5234
Old Malton ... 80 SE 7972
Old Man of Coniston, The ... 82 SD 2797
Old Man of Hoy (mt.) ... 136 HY 1700
Old Man of Storr (mt.) ... 123 NG 5054
Oldmeldrum ... 121 NJ 8027
Old Milverton ... 50 SP 2967
Old Monkland ... 101 NS 7163
Old Montsale ... 39 TR 0097
Old Newton ... 54 TM 0662
Old Oswestry (ant.) ... 58 SJ 2931
Oldpark ... 59 SJ 6909
Old Peak or South Cheek ... 81 NZ 9802
Old Philpstoun ... 102 NT 0577
Old Radnor ... 45 SO 2559
Old Rayne ... 121 NJ 6728
Old River Ancholme ... 74 SE 9615
Old River Don ... 74 SE 7613
Old Romney ... 31 TR 0325
Old Sarum (ant.) ... 26 SU 1332
Old Scone ... 108 NO 1226
Oldshoremore ... 132 NC 2059
Old Soar Manor (ant.) ... 29 TQ 6254
Old Sodbury ... 33 ST 7581
Old Somerby ... 62 SK 9633
Old South (sbk.) ... 63 TF 4735
Oldstead ... 79 SE 5280
Old Town (Cumbr.) ... 77 SD 6082
Old Town (Northum.) ... 90 NY 8891
Oldtown of Ord ... 121 NJ 6259
Old Warden ... 52 TL 1343
Oldways End ... 23 SS 8624
Old Weston ... 52 TL 0977
Old West River or River Great Ouse ... 53 TL 4671
Oldwhat ... 121 NJ 8551
Old Windsor ... 36 SU 6420
Old Winchester Hill (ant.) ... 27 SU 6420
Old Windsor ... 36 SU 9874
Old Wives Lees ... 31 TR 0755
Olgrinmore ... 135 ND 0955
Oliver ... 95 NT 0924
Oliver's Battery ... 27 SU 4527
Ollaberry ... 142 HU 3680
Ollach ... 123 NG 5136
Ollerton (Ches.) ... 69 SJ 7776
Ollerton (Notts.) ... 71 SK 6567
Ollerton (Shrops.) ... 59 SJ 6425
Ollisgarth (pt.) ... 141 HU 4430
Ollisdal Geo ... 122 NG 2138
Olna Firth ... 141 HU 3864
Olney ... 52 SP 8851
Olrig House ... 135 ND 1866
Olton ... 50 SP 1282
Olveston ... 33 ST 6087
Ombersley ... 49 SO 8463
Ompton ... 72 SK 6865
Onchan ... 76 SC 4078
Onchan Head ... 76 SC 4077
Onecote ... 60 SK 0555
Ongar Hill ... 63 TF 5724
Ongar Street ... 48 SO 3967
Onibury ... 48 SO 4579
Onich ... 106 NN 0261
Onllwyn ... 41 SN 8310
Onneley ... 59 SJ 7542
Onslow Village ... 28 SU 9849
Opinan (Highld.) ... 123 NG 7472
Opinan (Highld.) ... 126 NG 8796
Opsay ... 124 NF 9876
Orbost ... 122 NG 2543
Orby ... 73 TF 4967
Orby Marsh ... 73 TF 5266
Orchard ... 25 ST 8216
Orchardleigh House ... 33 ST 7750
Orchard Portman ... 24 ST 2421
Orcheston ... 34 SU 0545
Orcheston Down ... 34 SU 0747
Orcop ... 45 SO 4726
Orcop Hill ... 45 SO 4628
Ord ... 123 NG 6113
Ordhead ... 119 NJ 6610
Ordie Burn ... 108 NO 0534
Ordiquish ... 121 NJ 3357
Ord River ... 123 NG 6212
Ords, The ... 141 HU 3413
Ord, The (pt.) ... 141 HU 4936
Ore ... 30 TQ 8311
Ore Bay ... 136 ND 3094
Oreham Common ... 28 TQ 2214
Oreton ... 49 SO 6580
Oreval (mt.) ... 131 NB 0809
Orfasay ... 143 HU 4977
Orford (Ches.) ... 69 SJ 6090
Orford (Suff.) ... 55 TM 4250
Orford Ness ... 55 TM 4549
Orgreave ... 60 SK 1415
Orinsay ... 131 NB 3612
Orka Voe ... 143 HU 4077
Orknagable (pt.) ... 143 HP 5713
Orkney Islands ... 136 HY 4821
Orlestone ... 31 TR 0034
Orleton (Here. and Worc.) ... 48 SO 4967
Orleton (Here. and Worc.) ... 49 SO 6967
Orlingbury ... 52 SP 8572
Ormesby ... 85 NZ 5317
Ormesby St. Margaret ... 65 TG 4915
Ormesby St. Michael ... 65 TG 4814
Ormiclate Castle ... 112 NF 7331
Ormiscaig ... 126 NG 8590
Ormiston ... 103 NT 4169
Ormsaigmore ... 111 NM 4763
Ormsary House ... 99 NR 7372
Ormskirk ... 68 SD 4107
Ornish Island ... 112 NF 8538
Ornsay ... 123 NG 7112
Oronsay (Colonsay) (is.) ... 98 NR 3588
Oronsay (Highld.) ... 111 NM 5959
Oronsay (Island of Skye) ... 122 NG 3136
Oronsay (North Uist) ... 124 NF 8475
Orosay (Barra) ... 112 NF 7106
Orosay (South Uist) ... 112 NF 7217
Orphir ... 136 HY 3404
Orpington ... 37 TQ 4665
Orrell ... 69 SD 5203
Orrin Falls ... 128 NH 4751
Orrin Reservoir ... 127 NH 3850
Orrisdale Head ... 76 SC 3192
Orroland ... 87 NX 7746
Orsay ... 98 NR 1651
Orsett ... 38 TQ 6481
Orslow ... 59 SJ 8015
Orston ... 61 SK 7741
Orton (Cumbr.) ... 83 NY 6208
Orton (Northants.) ... 51 SP 8079
Orton Longueville ... 62 TL 1696
Orton-on-the-Hill ... 60 SK 3004
Orton Waterville ... 62 TL 1596
Orval (mt.) ... 110 NM 3399
Orwell ... 53 TL 3650
Osbaldeston ... 77 SD 6431
Osbaston ... 60 SK 4204

Osborne Bay ... 27 SZ 5395
Osborne House ... 27 SZ 5194
Osbournby ... 62 TF 0638
Oscroft ... 69 SJ 5066
Ose ... 122 NG 3141
Osea Island ... 38 TL 9106
Osgathorpe ... 60 SK 4219
Osgodby (Lincs.) ... 72 TF 0792
Osgodby (N Yorks.) ... 79 SE 6433
Osgodby (N Yorks.) ... 81 TA 0585
Oskaig ... 123 NG 5438
Oskamull ... 105 NM 4540
Osmaston ... 60 SK 1944
Osmington ... 25 SY 7282
Osmington Mills ... 25 SY 7381
Osmotherley ... 85 SE 4597
Osnaburgh or Dairsie ... 109 NO 4117
Ospisdale ... 129 NH 7189
Ospringe ... 31 TQ 9960
Ossett ... 71 SE 2720
Ossington ... 72 SK 7564
Ostend ... 38 TQ 9397
Osterley Park ... 37 TQ 1577
Oswaldkirk ... 79 SE 6279
Oswaldtwistle ... 77 SD 7327
Oswestry ... 58 SJ 2829
Otford ... 37 TQ 5359
Otham ... 30 TQ 7954
Othery ... 24 ST 3831
Othona (ant.) ... 39 TM 0308
Otley (Suff.) ... 55 TM 2055
Otley (W Yorks.) ... 78 SE 2045
Ot Moor ... 47 SP 5614
Otterbourne ... 27 SU 4522
Otterburn (Northum.) ... 90 NY 8893
Otterburn (N Yorks.) ... 78 SD 8857
Otterburn Camp ... 90 NY 8995
Otterden Place ... 30 TQ 9454
Otter Ferry ... 100 NR 9384
Otterham ... 20 SX 1690
Ottershaw ... 36 TQ 0264
Otters Wick (Sanday, Orkney) ... 139 HY 6944
Otterswick (Yell) ... 143 HU 5185
Otters Wick (Yell) ... 143 HU 5285
Otterton ... 24 SY 0785
Ottery St. Mary ... 24 SY 0995
Ottringham ... 75 TA 2624
Oughterard ... 78 SD 8781
Oughtibridge ... 71 SK 3093
Oulston ... 79 SE 5474
Oulton (Cumbr.) ... 82 NY 2551
Oulton (Norf.) ... 65 TG 1328
Oulton (Staffs.) ... 59 SJ 9035
Oulton (Suff.) ... 65 TM 5194
Oulton (W Yorks.) ... 65 TM 3627
Oulton Broad ... 55 TM 5292
Oulton Street ... 65 TG 1527
Oundle ... 52 TL 0488
Ousby ... 83 NY 6134
Ousdale ... 135 ND 0620
Ousden ... 54 TL 7359
Ouseburn ... 79 SE 4461
Ousefleet ... 74 SE 8223
Ouse Ness ... 79 HY 4549
Ouston ... 84 NZ 2554
Outer Hebrides ... 130 NG 0085
Outertown ... 136 HY 2310
Out Gate ... 77 SD 3599
Outhgill ... 83 NY 7801
Outlane ... 78 SE 0817
Out Newton ... 75 TA 3822
Out Rawcliffe ... 77 SD 4041
Outshore Point ... 136 HY 2222
Out Skerries ... 143 HU 6771
Out Stack ... 143 HP 6120
Outward Bound Mountain School (Cumbr.) ... 82 NY 1400
Outward Bound Mountain School (Cumbr.) ... 83 NY 4021
Outwell ... 63 TF 5104
Outwood (Surrey) ... 29 TQ 3246
Outwood (W Yorks.) ... 79 SE 3223
Oval, The ... 33 ST 7363
Ovenden ... 78 SE 0727
Over (Avon) ... 33 ST 5882
Over (Cambs.) ... 53 TL 3770
Overbister ... 139 HY 6840
Overbury ... 50 SO 9537
Overcombe ... 25 SY 6982
Over Haddon ... 70 SK 2066
Over Kellet ... 77 SD 5169
Over Kiddington ... 47 SP 4122
Over Norton ... 47 SP 3128
Overseal ... 60 SK 2915
Over Silton ... 85 SE 4593
Overstone ... 51 SP 8066
Overstrand ... 65 TG 2440
Overton (Clwyd) ... 58 SJ 3741
Overton (Dumf. and Galwy.) ... 88 NX 9864
Overton (Grampn.) ... 119 NJ 8714
Overton (Hants.) ... 35 SU 5149
Overton (Lancs.) ... 77 SD 4357
Overton (Shrops.) ... 48 SO 4972
Overton Green ... 57 SJ 7960
Overtown ... 95 NS 8052
Over Wallop ... 34 SU 2838
Over Water ... 82 NY 2535
Over Whitacre ... 50 SP 2591
Oving (Bucks.) ... 36 SP 7821
Oving (W Susx) ... 28 SU 9005
Ovingdean ... 29 TQ 3503
Ovingham ... 91 NZ 0863
Ovington (Durham) ... 84 NZ 1314
Ovington (Essex) ... 54 TL 7742
Ovington (Hants.) ... 27 SU 5631
Ovington (Norf.) ... 64 TF 9202
Ovington (Northum.) ... 91 NZ 0663
Ower ... 26 SU 3216
Owermoigne ... 25 SY 7685
Owlswick ... 36 SP 7906
Owmby-by-Spittal ... 72 TF 0087
Owslebury ... 27 SU 5123
Owston ... 61 SK 7708
Owston Ferry ... 74 SE 8000
Owstwick ... 75 TA 2732
Owthorpe ... 61 SK 6733
Oxborough ... 64 TF 7401
Oxcars ... 103 NT 2081
Oxenford Castle ... 103 NT 3865
Oxenhall ... 46 SO 6926
Oxenhope ... 78 SE 0334
Oxen Park ... 77 SD 3187
Oxenton ... 46 SO 9531
Oxenwood ... 34 SU 3059
Oxford ... 47 SP 5106
Oxford Airport ... 47 SP 4615
Oxford Canal ... 51 SP 4837
Ox Hill (Dumf. and Galwy.) ... 94 NS 7200
Oxhill (Warw.) ... 50 SP 3145
Oxley ... 59 SJ 9002
Oxley's Green ... 30 TQ 6921
Oxna (is.) ... 141 HU 3537
Oxnam ... 90 NT 7018
Oxnam Water ... 90 NT 7017
Oxspring ... 71 SE 2601
Oxted ... 29 TQ 3852
Oxton (Borders) ... 96 NT 4953
Oxton (Notts.) ... 61 SK 6351
Oxwich ... 40 SS 4986
Oxwich Bay ... 40 SS 5386
Oxwick ... 64 TF 9125

Place	Page	Grid
Oykel Bridge	127	NC 3800
Oyne	121	NJ 6725

P

Place	Page	Grid
Pabay (Highld.)	123	NG 6727
Pabay Mòr	131	NB 1037
Pabbay (North Uist)	124	NF 8887
Pabbay (W Isles)	112	NL 6087
Packington	60	SK 3614
Padanaram	109	NO 4251
Padbury	51	SP 7130
Paddaburn Moor	90	NY 6378
Paddington	37	TQ 2482
Paddington Station	37	TQ 2681
Paddlesworth	31	TR 1939
Paddockhaugh	120	NJ 2058
Paddock Wood	29	TQ 6645
Paddolgreen	59	SJ 5032
Padeswood	68	SJ 2761
Padiham	78	SD 7933
Padon Hill	90	NY 8292
Padstow	19	SW 9175
Padstow Bay	19	SW 9179
Pagham	27	SZ 8897
Page Hill	95	NS 8528
Paglesham Churchend	38	TQ 9292
Paglesham Eastend	38	TQ 9492
Paible (North Uist)	124	NF 7367
Paible (Taransay)	124	NG 0299
Paignton	21	SX 8960
Pailton	51	SP 4781
Painscastle	45	SO 1646
Painshawfield	91	NZ 0660
Painswick	46	SO 8609
Pairc or Park (dist.)	131	NB 3112
Paisley	101	NS 4864
Pakefield	55	TM 5390
Pakenham	54	TL 9267
Pale	67	SH 9836
Palestine	34	SU 2640
Paley Street	36	SU 8776
Palgowan	86	NX 3783
Palgrave	55	TM 1178
Pallinsburn House	97	NT 8939
Palmerstown	41	ST 1369
Palnackie	87	NX 8257
Palnure	87	NX 4563
Palnure Burn	87	NX 4668
Palterton	71	SK 4768
Pamber End	36	SU 6158
Pamber Green	35	SU 6059
Pamber Heath	36	SU 6262
Pamphill	26	ST 9900
Pampisford	53	TL 4948
Pan	136	ND 3794
Panbride	109	NO 5635
Pancrasweek	22	SS 2905
Pandy (Clwyd)	58	SJ 1935
Pandy (Gwent)	45	SO 3322
Pandy (Powys)	57	SN 9004
Pandy Tudur	67	SH 8564
Panfield	54	TL 7325
Pangbourne	36	SU 6376
Pan Hope	136	ND 3794
Pannal	79	SE 3051
Pannanich Hill	118	NO 3994
Panorama Walk	57	SH 6216
Panshanger Aerodrome	37	TL 2712
Pant	58	SJ 2722
Pant-glas (Gwyn.)	66	SH 4747
Pant Glas (Powys)	57	SN 7798
Pantglas Hall	43	SN 5425
Pantgwyn	43	SN 2446
Pant Mawr	57	SN 8482
Panton	73	TF 1778
Pant-pastynog	67	SJ 0461
Pantperthog	57	SH 7504
Pant Sychbant	44	SN 9809
Pant-y-dŵr	57	SN 9875
Pant-y-ffridd	58	SJ 1502
Pantyffynnon	43	SN 6210
Panxworth	65	TG 3413
Papa (is.)	141	HU 3637
Papa Little (is.)	141	HU 3361
Papa Sound	138	HY 4752
Papa Stour (is.)	140	HU 1660
Papa Stronsay	137	HY 6629
Papa Westray (is.)	138	HY 4952
Papa Westray Aerodrome	138	HY 4852
Papcastle	82	NY 1131
Papil Ness	143	HP 5404
Papley	136	ND 4691
Pap of Glencoe (mt.)	106	NN 1259
Papple	103	NT 5972
Papplewick	61	SK 5451
Paps of Jura (mt.)	98	NR 4974
Papworth Everard	53	TL 2862
Papworth St. Agnes	53	TL 2664
Par	19	SX 0653
Parbold	69	SD 4911
Parbrook	25	ST 5736
Parcllyn	43	SN 2451
Pardshaw	82	NY 0924
Parham	55	TM 3060
Parham House (ant.)	28	TQ 0514
Park (Grampn.)	119	NO 7798
Park (Strath.)	106	NM 9340
Park Corner	36	SU 6988
Parkend (Glos.)	45	SO 6108
Park End (Northum.)	90	NY 8775
Parkeston	55	TM 2332
Parkgate (Ches.)	68	SJ 2778
Parkgate (Ches.)	69	SJ 7874
Parkgate (Dumf. and Galwy.)	88	NY 0288
Park Gate (Hants.)	27	SU 5108
Parkgate (Surrey)	28	TQ 2043
Parkham	22	SS 3821
Parkham Ash	22	SS 3620
Park Head	19	SW 8370
Parkhill House	119	NJ 8914
Parkhouse	45	SO 5002
Parkhurst	27	SZ 4991
Parkhurst Forest	27	SZ 4790
Parkneuk	119	NO 7976
Park or Pairc (Isle of Lewis) (dist.)	131	NB 3112
Parkstone	26	SZ 0491
Parley Common	26	SZ 0999
Parley Cross	26	SZ 0898
Parracombe	23	SS 6744
Parrog	42	SN 0439
Parson Drove	63	TF 3708
Partick	101	NS 5567
Partington	69	SJ 7191
Partney	73	TF 4168
Parton (Cumbr.)	82	NX 9720
Parton (Dumf. and Galwy.)	88	NX 6970
Partridge Green	28	TQ 1919
Parwich	60	SK 1854
Parys Mountain	66	SH 4390
Passenham	51	SP 7839
Pass of Aberglaslyn	66	SH 5946
Pass of Brander	106	NN 0627
Pass of Drumochter	116	NN 6376
Pass of Killiecrankie	108	NN 9162
Pass of Leny	101	NN 5908
Pass of Llanberis	67	SH 6355
Pass of Melfort	105	NM 8315
Paston	65	TG 3235

Place	Page	Grid
Patcham	29	TQ 3009
Patching	28	TQ 0806
Patchole	23	SS 6142
Patchway	33	ST 6082
Pateley Bridge	78	SE 1565
Pateley Moor	78	SE 1967
Pathhead (Fife)	103	NT 2892
Pathhead (Gramp.)	109	NO 7363
Pathhead (Lothian)	103	NT 3964
Pathhead (Strath.)	88	NS 6114
Path of Condie	102	NO 0711
Patmore Heath	53	TL 4526
Patna	93	NS 4110
Patney	34	SU 0758
Patrick	76	SC 2482
Patrick Brompton	84	SE 2290
Patrington	75	TA 3122
Patrixbourne	31	TR 1855
Patshull Hall	59	SJ 8001
Patterdale	83	NY 3915
Patterton Station	93	NS 5357
Pattingham	59	SO 8299
Pattishall	51	SP 6654
Patton Bridge	83	SD 5597
Paul	18	SW 4627
Paulerspury	51	SP 7145
Paull	75	TA 1626
Paull Holme Sands	75	TA 1823
Paulton	33	ST 6456
Pauperhaugh	91	NZ 1099
Pavenham	52	SP 9955
Pawlaw Pike	84	NZ 0032
Pawlett	32	ST 2942
Pawston	97	NT 8532
Paxford	50	SP 1837
Paxton	97	NT 9352
Payhembury	24	ST 0801
Paythorne	78	SD 8251
Peacehaven	29	TQ 4101
Peachley	49	SO 8057
Peak Dale	70	SK 0976
Peak Forest	70	SK 1179
Peakirk	62	TF 1606
Peanmeanach	111	NM 7180
Pearsie	109	NO 3659
Peasedown St. John	33	ST 7057
Peasemore	35	SU 4576
Peasenhall	55	TM 3569
Peaslake	28	TQ 0844
Peasmarsh	30	TQ 8822
Peaston	103	NT 4265
Peaston Bank	103	NT 4466
Peathill (Grampn.)	121	NJ 9365
Peat Hill (Tays.)	109	NO 5067
Peat Inn	103	NO 4509
Peatling Magna	51	SP 5992
Peatling Parva	51	SP 5889
Peaton	48	SO 5385
Pebmarsh	54	TL 8533
Pebworth	50	SP 1347
Pecket Well	78	SD 9929
Peckforton	59	SJ 5356
Peckleton	61	SK 4701
Peddars Way (ant.)	64	TF 8312
Pedmore	49	SO 9182
Pedwell	25	ST 4236
Peebles	95	NT 2540
Peel	76	SC 2484
Peel Fell	90	NY 6299
Peffer Burn	103	NT 5778
Pegal Burn	136	ND 2798
Pegswood	91	NZ 2287
Pegwell Bay	31	TR 3563
Peinchorran	123	NG 5233
Peinlich	123	NG 4158
Pelaw	91	NZ 2962
Peldon	39	TL 9816
Pelsall	60	SK 0103
Pelton	84	NZ 2553
Pelutho	82	NY 1249
Pelynt	19	SX 2055
Pembrey	40	SN 4201
Pembridge	45	SO 3858
Pembroke	42	SM 9901
Pembroke Dock	42	SM 9603
Pembury	29	TQ 6240
Penallt	45	SO 5210
Pen Allt-mawr	44	SO 2024
Penally	42	SS 1199
Penant	56	SN 5163
Penare	19	SW 9940
Penarth	41	ST 1871
Pen-bont Rhydybeddau	57	SN 6783
Pen Brush	42	SM 8839
Penbryn	43	SN 2952
Penbwchdy	42	SM 8737
Pencader	43	SN 4436
Pen Caer	42	SM 9140
Pencaitland	103	NT 4468
Pencarreg	43	SN 5345
Pencarreg-gopa	57	SN 7294
Pencarrow Head	19	SX 1450
Pencelli	44	SO 0925
Pen Cerrig-calch	44	SO 2122
Penclawdd	40	SS 5495
Penclegyr (Dyfed)	42	SM 7629
Penclegyr (Dyfed)	42	SM 8032
Pen Coed (Mid Glam.)	43	SS 9581
Pen Coed (Powys)	57	SH 9808
Pencombe	45	SO 5952
Pencoyd	45	SO 5126
Pencraig (Here. and Worc.)	45	SO 5621
Pencraig (Powys)	57	SJ 0427
Pendeen	18	SW 3834
Pendeen Watch (pt.)	18	SW 3736
Pendennis Point	19	SW 8231
Penderry Hill	41	NX 0675
Penderyn	44	SN 9408
Penderyn Resr.	41	SN 9407
Pen Dinas (ant.)	56	SN 5880
Pendine	43	SN 2308
Pendine Sands	43	SN 2706
Pendlebury	69	SD 7802
Pendle Hill	78	SD 7941
Pendleton	78	SD 7539
Pendock	46	SO 7832
Pendoggett	19	SX 0279
Pendoylan	41	ST 0576
Penegoes	57	SH 7701
Pen-ffordd	42	SN 0722
Penge	37	TQ 3570
Pengorffwysfa	66	SH 4692
Pengwern	67	SJ 0176
Pen Gwyllt-meirch	45	SO 2524
Penhale Point	18	SW 7559
Penhale Sands	18	SW 7656
Penhalvean	18	SW 7037
Penhill	33	ST 0486
Penhow	33	ST 4290
Penhurst	29	TQ 6916
Peniarth	56	SH 6105
Penicuik	103	NT 2359
Peniel Heugh	96	NT 6526
Penifiler	123	NG 4841
Peninver	92	NR 7524
Pen-isa'r-cwm	45	SO 0018
Penisa'r Waun	66	SH 5564
Penistone	71	SE 2402
Penjerrick	18	SW 7730
Penketh	69	SJ 5687
Penkill	86	NX 2398

Place	Page	Grid
Penkill Burn	87	NX 4369
Penkridge	59	SJ 9214
Penlee Point	20	SX 4448
Penley	58	SJ 4039
Penllechwen	42	SM 7429
Penllergaer	40	SS 6199
Pen Lithrig-y-wrâch	67	SH 7162
Pen-llyn (Gwyn.)	66	SH 3482
Penllyn (S Glam.)	41	SS 9776
Penmachno	67	SH 7950
Penmaen	40	SS 5288
Penmaenmawr	67	SH 7176
Penmaenpool	57	SH 6918
Penmaen Swatch	67	SH 6577
Penmark	41	ST 0568
Pen Milan	41	SN 9923
Penmon	67	SH 6381
Penmorfa	66	SH 5440
Penmynydd	66	SH 5174
Penn	36	SU 9193
Pennal	57	SH 6900
Pennan	121	NJ 8465
Pennan Head	121	NJ 8565
Pennant	57	SN 8897
Pennant-Melangell	57	SJ 0226
Pennard	40	SS 5688
Pennerley	58	SO 3599
Pennies, The	78	SE 0077
Penninghame Forest	86	NX 3568
Pennington	76	SD 2577
Penn Street	36	SU 9296
Pennycross	105	NM 5025
Pennygown	105	NM 6042
Pennymoor	23	SS 8611
Penparc	43	SN 2148
Penparcau	56	SN 5980
Penperlleni	45	SO 3204
Penpillick	19	SX 0756
Penpol	19	SW 8139
Penpont (Dumf. and Galwy.)	88	NX 8494
Penpont (Powys)	41	SN 9728
Pen Pumlumon-Arwystli	57	SN 8187
Penrherber	43	SN 2839
Penrhiwceiber	41	ST 0597
Penrhiwllan	43	SN 3742
Penrhiwpal	43	SN 3445
Pen-rhos (Gwent)	45	SO 4111
Penrhos (Gwyn.)	66	SH 2781
Penrhos (Gwyn.)	66	SH 3433
Penrhos (Powys)	41	SN 8011
Penrhyn Bay	66	SH 8281
Penrhyn Castle (ant.)	66	SH 6071
Penrhyncoch	57	SN 6484
Penrhyndeudraeth	66	SH 6139
Penrhyn Mawr (Gwyn.)	66	SH 1632
Penrhyn Mawr (Gwyn.)	66	SH 2080
Penrhyn-side	67	SH 8181
Penrice	40	SS 4988
Penrith	83	NY 5130
Penrose	19	SW 8770
Penruddock	83	NY 4227
Pensarn (Clwyd)	67	SH 9478
Pen-Sarn (Gwyn.)	66	SH 4344
Pen-Sarn (Gwyn.)	56	SH 5728
Pensax	49	SO 7269
Pensby	68	SJ 2683
Penselwood	25	ST 7531
Pensford	33	ST 6163
Penshaw	84	NZ 3253
Penshurst	29	TQ 5243
Penshurst Place (ant.)	29	TQ 5243
Penshurst Station	29	TQ 5246
Pensilva	20	SX 2969
Pentewan	19	SX 0147
Pentir	66	SH 5767
Pentire	19	SW 7961
Pentre Point	19	SW 9280
Pentland Firth	136	NO 3082
Pentland Hills	102	NT 1459
Pentland Skerries	135	ND 4777
Pentney	64	TF 7213
Penton Mewsey	34	SU 3247
Pentraeth	66	SH 5278
Pentre (Clwyd)	67	SJ 0862
Pentre (Clwyd)	58	SJ 1334
Pentre (Clwyd)	58	SJ 2840
Pentre (Powys)	57	SO 0686
Pentre (Powys)	57	SO 2466
Pentre (Shrops.)	58	SJ 3617
Pentrebach (Mid Glam.)	41	SO 0604
Pentre-bâch (Powys)	41	SN 9033
Pentrebeirdd	58	SJ 1913
Pentre Berw	66	SH 4772
Pentre-celyn (Clwyd)	58	SJ 1453
Pentre-celyn (Powys)	57	SH 8806
Pentre-cwrt	43	SN 3938
Pentre-Dolau-Honddu	44	SN 9943
Pentredwr	58	SJ 1946
Pentrefelin	66	SH 5239
Pentrefelin	66	SH 8231
Pentrefoelas	67	SH 8751
Pentregat	43	SN 3551
Pentre-Gwenlais	43	SN 6116
Pentre Halkyn	68	SJ 2072
Pentre'r-felin	41	SN 9130
Pentre-tafarn-y-fedw	67	SH 8161
Pentre ty gwyn	43	SN 8135
Pentrich	60	SK 3852
Pentridge	26	SU 0317
Pentridge Hill	26	SU 0416
Pen Trum-gwr	57	SH 6503
Pen-twyn (Gwent)	45	SO 5209
Pentwyn (S Glam.)	41	ST 2081
Pentwyn Resr.	41	SO 0515
Pentyrch	41	ST 1082
Penuwch	56	SN 5962
Penwhapple Resr.	86	NX 2697
Penwhirn Resr.	86	NX 1269
Penwithick	19	SX 0256
Penybanc	43	SN 6124
Pen-y-bont (Clwyd)	58	SJ 2123
Penybont (Powys)	48	SO 1164
Penybontfawr	57	SJ 0824
Pen-y-bryn	57	SH 6919
Pen-y-bwlch	57	SN 7763
Penycae (Clwyd)	58	SJ 2745
Pen-y-cae (Powys)	44	SN 8413
Pen-y-cae-mawr	45	ST 4195
Pen-y-cefn	68	SJ 1175
Pen-y-chain	66	SH 4335
Pen-y-Cil	66	SH 1524
Pen-y-clawdd	45	SO 4508
Penycloddiau (ant.)	68	SJ 1267
Pen y-coedcae	41	ST 0587
Pen y crug (ant.)	44	SO 0230
Penyffordd	68	SJ 3061
Pen y Ffridd Gownwy	57	SH 9717
Pen-y-garn	43	SN 5731
Pen-y-garnedd	57	SJ 1023
Pen-y-garreg Resr.	57	SN 9067
Pen-y-Ghent (mt.)	78	SD 8373
Pen-y-Gogarth	67	SH 7584
Penygraig	41	SS 9991
Penygroes (Dyfed)	43	SN 5813
Penygroes (Gwyn.)	66	SH 4753
Pen y Gurnos	44	SN 7751

Place	Page	Grid
Pen y Manllwyn	41	SO 2131
Penysarn	66	SH 4690
Penywaun	41	SN 9704
Penzance	18	SW 4730
Peopleton	49	SO 9350
Peover Heath	69	SJ 7973
Peper Harow	28	SU 9344
Peplow	59	SJ 6324
Percie	119	NO 5991
Percyhorner	121	NJ 9565
Perivale	37	TQ 1682
Perranarworthal	18	SW 7738
Perran or Ligger Bay	18	SW 7256
Perranuthnoe	18	SW 5329
Perranzabuloe	18	SW 7752
Perry	52	TL 1466
Perry Barr	50	SP 0791
Perry Green	37	TL 4317
Pershore	49	SO 9446
Pert	109	NO 6565
Pertenhall	52	TL 0865
Perth	108	NO 1123
Perth Aerodrome	108	NO 1528
Perthy	58	SJ 3633
Perton	59	SO 8598
Peter Black Sand	64	TF 6231
Peterborough	62	TL 1999
Peterborough Airport (Conington)	52	TL 1887
Peterburn	126	NG 7483
Peterchurch	45	SO 3438
Peterculter	119	NJ 8400
Peterhead	121	NK 1346
Peterhead Bay	121	NK 1345
Peter Hill	119	NO 5788
Peterlee	85	NZ 4440
Petersfield	27	SU 7423
Peter's Hill	118	NO 3600
Peters Green	37	TL 1419
Peterstone Wentlooge	32	ST 2680
Peterston-super-Ely	41	ST 0876
Peterstow	45	SO 5624
Peter Tavy	20	SX 5177
Petertown	136	HY 3105
Petham	31	TR 1251
Petrockstow	22	SS 5109
Pett	30	TQ 8714
Pettaugh	55	TM 1659
Pettinain	95	NS 9542
Pettistree	55	TM 2954
Petton (Devon)	23	ST 0024
Petton (Shrops.)	58	SJ 4326
Petty	121	NJ 7636
Pettycur	103	NT 2686
Pettymuk	121	NJ 9024
Petworth	28	SU 9721
Petworth House (ant.)	28	SU 9721
Pevensey	29	TQ 6405
Pevensey Bay	29	TQ 6603
Pevensey Levels	29	TQ 6307
Peveril Castle (ant.)	70	SK 1482
Peveril Point	26	SZ 0378
Pewsey Down	34	SU 1656
Philham	22	SS 2522
Philiphaugh	96	NT 4427
Philip Law	90	NT 7210
Phillack	18	SW 5539
Philleigh	19	SW 8639
Philpstoun	102	NT 0577
Phoenix Green	35	SU 7655
Pibble Hill	87	NX 5360
Pica	82	NY 0222
Piccotts End	36	TL 0509
Pickering	80	SE 7983
Picket Piece	34	SU 3947
Picket Post	26	SU 1905
Pickhill	79	SE 3483
Picklescott	58	SO 4399
Pickmere	69	SJ 6876
Pickwell (Devon)	22	SS 4540
Pickwell (Leic.)	61	SK 7811
Pickworth (Leic.)	62	SK 9913
Pickworth (Lincs.)	62	TF 0433
Picton (Ches.)	68	SJ 4371
Picton (N Yorks.)	85	NZ 4107
Piddinghoe	29	TQ 4303
Piddington (Northants.)	51	SP 8054
Piddington (Oxon.)	36	SP 6317
Piddlehinton	25	SY 7197
Piddletrenthide	25	SY 7099
Pidley	53	TL 3377
Pidley Fen	53	TL 3480
Piel Bar (pt.)	76	SD 2361
Piel Island	76	SD 2363
Piercebridge	84	NZ 2115
Pierowall	138	HY 4348
Pigdon	91	NZ 1588
Pike Fell	89	NY 4193
Pikehall	70	SK 1959
Pike Hill	89	NY 3505
Pike Hill Moss	89	NZ 7600
Pikeston Fell	84	NZ 0432
Pike, The	89	NT 4904
Pikey Hill	120	NJ 2151
Pilgrims Hatch	37	TQ 5895
Pilgrims' Way (ant.)	30	TQ 6561
Pilham	72	SK 8693
Pill	33	ST 5275
Pillar (mt.)	82	NY 1712
Pillar Bank (sbk.)	100	NS 3475
Pillaton	20	SX 3664
Pillerton Hersey	50	SP 2948
Pillerton Priors	50	SP 2947
Pilleth	48	SO 2568
Pilley	71	SE 3300
Pilling	77	SD 4048
Pilling Lane	77	SD 3749
Pils Brook	54	TL 7126
Pilsbury	70	SK 1163
Pilsdon	24	SY 4199
Pilsdon Pen	24	ST 4101
Pilsley (Derby.)	71	SK 2471
Pilsley (Derby.)	71	SK 4262
Pilton (Leic.)	62	SK 9102
Pilton (Northants.)	52	TL 0284
Pilton (Somer.)	33	ST 5940
Pimperne	25	ST 9009
Pimperne Down	25	ST 8910
Pinchbeck	63	TF 2425
Pinchbeck West	63	TF 2024
Pinderachy (mt.)	109	NO 4565
Pindonnan Craigs	86	NX 2787
Pinhoe	21	SX 9694
Pinkworthy Pond	23	SS 7242
Pinminnoch Burn	86	NX 0356
Pinmore	86	NX 2092
Pinner	37	TQ 1289
Pinvin	50	SO 9548
Pinwherry	86	NX 1987
Pinwherry Hill	86	NX 1885
Pinxton	61	SK 4555
Pipe and Lyde	45	SO 5044
Pipe Gate	59	SJ 7340
Piperhill	129	NH 8651
Pipewell	52	SP 8385
Pippacott	22	SS 5237
Pirbright	28	SU 9455
Pirnmill	92	NR 8744
Pirton (Here. and Worc.)	49	SO 8847

Place	Page	Grid
Pirton (Herts.)	52	TL 1431
Pishill	36	SU 7289
Pistyll	66	SH 3242
Pitagowan	107	NN 8266
Pitblae	121	NJ 9865
Pitcairlie Hill	108	NO 2115
Pitcairngreen	108	NO 0627
Pitcaple	121	NJ 7225
Pitchcombe	46	SO 8408
Pitchcott	36	SP 7720
Pitchford	59	SJ 5303
Pitch Green	36	SP 7703
Pitch Place	28	SU 9752
Pitcombe	25	ST 6732
Pitcox	103	NT 6475
Pitcur	108	NO 2536
Pitfichie	119	NJ 6716
Pitfichie Forest	119	NJ 6415
Pitforthie	119	NO 8079
Pitfour Castle	108	NO 1921
Pitgrudy	129	NH 7991
Pitkennedy	109	NO 5454
Pitkevy	103	NO 2403
Pitlessie	103	NO 3309
Pitlochry	108	NN 9458
Pitmain	116	NH 7400
Pitmedden	121	NJ 8927
Pitmedden Forest	103	NO 2114
Pitmedden House	121	NJ 8828
Pitminster	24	ST 2119
Pitmuies	109	NO 5649
Pitmunie	119	NJ 6615
Pitney	25	ST 4428
Pitroddie	108	NO 2224
Pitscottie	103	NO 4113
Pitsea	38	TQ 7488
Pitsford	51	SP 7568
Pitsford Reservoir	51	SP 7669
Pitt Down	26	SU 4128
Pittendreich	120	NJ 1961
Pittentrail	129	NC 7202
Pittenweem	103	NO 5402
Pittington	84	NZ 3245
Pittodrie	121	NJ 6924
Pitton	26	SU 2131
Pixey Green	55	TM 2475
Place Newton	81	SE 8872
Pladda (Island of Arran) (is.)	92	NS 0219
Pladda Island	105	NM 8337
Plains	101	NS 7966
Plaish	59	SO 5296
Plaistow	28	TQ 0030
Plaitford	26	SU 2719
Plâs	43	SN 6283
Plas Gogerddan	57	SN 6250
Plas Gwynant	67	SH 6250
Plas Isaf	57	SJ 0442
Plas Llwyd	67	SH 9073
Plas Llwyngwern	57	SH 7504
Plas Llysyn	57	SN 9597
Plas Nantyr	58	SJ 1537
Plastow Green	35	SU 5361
Plas-yn-Cefn	67	SJ 0171
Platt	29	TQ 6257
Plawsworth	84	NZ 2647
Plaxtol	29	TQ 6053
Playden	30	TQ 9121
Playford	55	TM 2148
Play Hatch	36	SU 7376
Playing Place	19	SW 8141
Plealey	58	SJ 4206
Plean	101	NS 8387
Pleasington	77	SD 6425
Pleasley	71	SK 5064
Plemeller	67	SH 7162
Plemmeller Common	90	NY 7361
Pleshey	38	TL 6614
Plock of Kyle (pt.)	123	NG 7527
Plockton	123	NG 8033
Plockton Aerodrome	123	NG 7933
Plocrapool Point	125	NG 1893
Ploughfield	45	SO 3841
Plover Hill	78	SD 8575
Plowden	48	SO 3888
Ploxgreen	58	SJ 3604
Pluckley	30	TQ 9245
Pluckley Station	30	TQ 9243
Plumbland	82	NY 1438
Plumley	69	SJ 7275
Plumpton (E Susx)	29	TQ 3613
Plumpton (Lancs.)	77	SD 3732
Plumpton Green	29	TQ 3616
Plumpton Head	83	NY 5035
Plumpton Wall	83	NY 4937
Plumstead	65	TG 1335
Plungar	61	SK 6133
Pluscarden	129	NJ 1455
Pluscarden Priory	129	NJ 1457
Plush	25	ST 7102
Plwmp	43	SN 3652
Plymouth	20	SX 4755
Plymouth Airport	20	SX 5060
Plymouth Breakwater	20	SX 4750
Plympton	21	SX 5356
Plymstock	20	SX 5152
Plymtree	24	ST 0502
Plynlimon (Pumlumon Fawr) (mt.)	57	SN 7885
Pocan Smoo (pt.)	133	NC 4267
Pockley	79	SE 6385
Pocklington	80	SE 8048
Pocklington Canal	74	SE 7445
Pock Stones Moor	78	SE 1060
Pode Hole	62	TF 2122
Podimore	25	ST 5424
Podington	52	SP 9462
Podmore	59	SJ 7835
Pods Brook	54	TL 7126
Point Clear	39	TM 0915
Point Lynas	66	SH 4793
Point of Ardnamurchan	111	NM 4167
Point of Ayr (Clwyd)	68	SJ 1285
Point of Ayr (I. of M.)	76	NX 4605
Point of Ayre (Orkney)	137	HY 5904
Point of Backaquoy	136	HY 3915
Point of Cairndoon	86	NX 3738
Point of Fethaland	143	HU 3795
Point of Howana Geo	136	HY 2220
Point of Huro	138	HY 4938
Point of Knap	99	NR 6972
Point of Neven	138	HY 2406
Point of Oxan	136	HY 2406
Point of Sinsoss	139	HY 7856
Point of Sleat	111	NM 5699
Point of Stoer	132	NC 0235
Point of the Graand	136	HY 4726
Pointon	62	TF 1131
Pokesdown	26	SZ 1292
Polapit Tamar	20	SX 3389
Polbae	86	NX 2873
Polbain	132	NB 9910
Polbathic	20	SX 3456
Polbeth	102	NT 0364
Polchar	117	NH 8909
Poldhu Point	18	SW 6519
Poldullie (chan)	123	NG 4771
Polebrook	52	TL 0687
Polegate	29	TQ 5805
Pole Hill (Highld.)	133	NC 6441

Pole Hill (Tays.) Reawick

Pole Hill (Tays.) 108 NO 1926
Pole of Itlaw, The 121 NJ 6856
Polesworth 60 SK 2602
Polglass 126 NC 0307
Polgooth 19 SW 9950
Poling 28 TQ 0405
Polkerris 19 SX 0952
Polla 132 NC 3854
Pollachar 112 NF 7414
Pollagach Burn 118 NO 3992
Poll Gainmhich (roadstead) 131 NB 1343
Pollington 71 SE 6119
Polliwilline Bay 92 NR 7409
Poll na h-Ealaidh 122 NG 3759
Polloch 111 NM 7968
Pollokshaws 101 NS 5560
Pollokshields 101 NS 5663
Polmaddie Hill 86 NX 3391
Polmassick 19 SW 9745
Polnessan 93 NS 4111
Polperro 19 SX 2051
Polruan 19 SX 1250
Polsham 33 ST 5142
Polskeoch 88 NS 6802
Polstead 54 TL 9938
Poltalloch 99 NR 8196
Poltimore 21 SX 9696
Polton 103 NT 2964
Polwarth 96 NT 7450
Polyphant 20 SX 2682
Polzeath 19 SW 9378
Pondersbridge 53 TL 2691
Ponders End 37 TQ 3695
Ponsanooth 18 SW 7336
Ponsworthy 21 SX 7073
Pontamman 43 SN 6312
Pontantwn 43 SN 4412
Pontardawe 40 SN 7204
Pontardulais 43 SN 5903
Pontarsais 43 SN 4428
Pont Cwm Pydew 67 SJ 0031
Pont Cyfyng 67 SH 7357
Pontefract 79 SE 4522
Ponteland 91 NZ 1672
Ponterwyd 57 SN 7481
Pontesbury 58 SJ 3905
Pontfadog 58 SJ 2338
Pontfaen (Dyfed) 42 SN 0234
Pont-faen (Powys) 41 SN 9934
Pont-Henri 43 SN 4709
Ponthirwaun 43 SN 2645
Pontllanfraith 41 ST 1895
Pontlliw 40 SN 6101
Pontlottyn 41 SO 1206
Pontlyfni 66 SH 4352
Pont Nêdd Fechan 41 SN 9007
Pont Pentryal 67 SJ 0351
Pont Pen-y-benglog 67 SH 6460
Pontrhydfendigaid 57 SN 7366
Pont Rhyd-y-cyff 41 SS 8788
Pont-rhyd-y-fen 41 SS 7994
Pontrhydygroes 57 SN 7472
Pontrilas 45 SO 3927
Pontrobert 58 SJ 1112
Pont-rug 66 SH 5163
Ponts Green 29 TQ 6717
Pontshaen 43 SN 4346
Pontshill 45 SO 6321
Pontsticill 41 SO 0511
Pontsticill Resr. 41 SO 0513
Pontyates 43 SN 4708
Pontyberem 43 SN 4911
Pontybodkin 68 SJ 2759
Pontyclun 41 ST 0381
Pontycymer 41 SS 9091
Pontymister 32 ST 2490
Pont-y-pant 67 SH 7554
Pontypool 45 SO 2701
Pontypridd 41 ST 0690
Pontywaun 41 ST 2293
Pooksgreen 26 SU 3710
Pool (W Yorks.) 79 SE 2445
Poole (Dorset) 26 SZ 0190
Poole Bay 26 SZ 1089
Poole Harbour 26 SZ 0189
Poole Keynes 46 ST 9995
Poolewe 126 NG 8580
Pooley Bridge 83 NY 4724
Poolhill (Glos.) 46 SO 7329
Pool Hill (Powys) 48 SO 1775
Pool of Virkie 141 HU 3911
Pool o'Muckart 102 NO 0001
Pool Quay 58 SJ 2512
Popham 35 SU 5543
Popham's Eau (ant.) 63 TF 5300
Poplar 37 TQ 3781
Porchfield 27 SZ 4491
Porin 127 NH 3155
Poringland 65 TG 2701
Porkellis 18 SW 6933
Porlock 23 SS 8846
Porlock Bay 23 SS 8848
Port a'Bhata (Colonsay) 98 NR 4195
Port a'Bhata (Ulva) 105 NM 4237
Port a'Bhorrain 92 NR 6635
Port a'Chaisteil An Stuadh 105 NM 8246
Portachoillan 92 NR 7557
Port a' Ghàraidh 123 NG 8017
Port Allen 87 NX 4741
Port Allt a' Mhuilinn 134 NC 8167
Port Alsaig 98 NR 3048
Port a'Mhadaidh 100 NR 9269
Port a' Mhurain 110 NM 1251
Port an Eas 98 NR 2840
Port an Fhearainn 123 NG 6159
Port Ann 100 NR 9086
Port an Obain 98 NR 3994
Port an Righ 129 NH 8573
Port Appin 106 NM 9045
Port Askaig 98 NR 4369
Portavadie 100 NR 9369
Port Bàn 111 NM 5170
Port Bannatyne 100 NS 0867
Port Bharrapol 104 NL 9342
Port Bun a' Ghlinne 131 NB 5244
Portbury 33 ST 4975
Port Cam 123 NG 7731
Port Carlisle 89 NY 2461
Port Castle Bay 86 NX 4136
Port Ceann a'Gharraidh 98 NR 4298
Port Charlotte 98 NR 2558
Portchester 27 SU 6105
Port Cill Maluaig 99 NR 7270
Portclair Forest 115 NH 3815
Port Corbert 92 NR 6528
Port Cornaa 76 SC 4787
Port Dinorwic 66 SH 5267
Port Doir' a'Chrorain 98 NR 5875
Port Driseach 100 NR 9973
Port Ellen 98 NR 3645
Port Elphinstone 119 NJ 7719
Portencross 93 NS 1748
Port Erin 76 SC 1969
Porter or Little Don River, The 71 SK 2399
Port Erradale 126 NG 7381
Portesham 25 SY 6085
Port e Vullen 76 SC 4793
Port-Eynon 40 SS 4685
Port-Eynon Bay 40 SS 4884
Port-Eynon Point 40 SS 4784
Portfield Gate 42 SM 9115
Portgate 20 SX 4185
Portgaverne 19 SX 0080
Port Glasgow 100 NS 3274
Port Gleann na Gaoidh 98 NR 2153
Portgordon 121 NJ 3964
Portgower 135 ND 0013
Port Groudle 76 SC 4278
Porth 41 ST 0291
Porthallow 19 SW 7923
Porthcawl 41 SS 8176
Porth Colmon 66 SH 1934
Porthcothan Bay 19 SW 8572
Porthcurno 18 SW 3822
Porth Dinllaen 66 SH 2741
Port Henderson 123 NG 7573
Porth-gain 42 SM 8132
Porthkerry 41 ST 0866
Porthleven 18 SW 6225
Porthmadog 66 SH 5638
Porth-mawr or Whitesand Bay 42 SM 7227
Porthmeor 18 SW 4337
Porth Navas 18 SW 7428
Porth Neigwl or Hell's Mouth 56 SH 2626
Portholland 19 SW 9541
Porthor 66 SH 1630
Porthoustock 19 SW 8021
Porthpean 19 SX 0350
Porth Resr. 19 SW 8662
Porthtowan 18 SW 6847
Porthyrhyd (Dyfed) 43 SN 5115
Porthyrhyd (Dyfed) 44 SN 7137
Porth Ysglaig 66 SH 2137
Portincaple 100 NS 2393
Portington 74 SE 7830
Portinnisherrich 100 NM 9711
Port Isaac 19 SW 9980
Port Isaac Bay 19 SX 0181
Portishead 33 ST 4676
Port Kemin 86 NX 1231
Portknockie 121 NJ 4868
Portland Grounds (sbk.) 33 ST 4283
Portland Harbour 25 SY 6876
Port Leathan 100 NR 9176
Portlethen 119 NO 9396
Portloe 19 SW 9339
Port Logan 86 NX 0940
Port Logan or Port Nessock Bay 86 NX 0941
Portmahomack 129 NH 9184
Port Mary 87 NX 7545
Port Mean 92 NR 6407
Portmeirion 66 SH 5937
Portmellon 19 SX 0143
Port Mine 110 NM 1254
Port Mooar 76 SC 4890
Port Mór (Gigha Island) 92 NR 6654
Port Mòr (Muck) 111 NM 4279
Port Mór (Strath.) 99 NR 7161
Port Mór (Tiree) 104 NL 9343
Portmore (Hants) 26 SZ 3397
Portmore Loch 95 NT 2650
Port Mór na Carraig 98 NR 2355
Port Mulgrave 85 NZ 7917
Port na Birlinne 98 NR 5265
Port na Croise 105 NM 4326
Portnacroish 106 NM 9247
Port na Cuilce 98 NM 4100
Port na Cullaidh 123 NG 5113
Port na Feannaiche 92 NR 9122
Portnaguran 131 NB 5536
Portnahaven 98 NR 1652
Port na h-Eather 110 NM 2053
Portnalong 122 NG 3434
Port nam Bothaig 131 NB 5446
Port nam Partan 110 NM 3452
Port na Muice Duibhe 105 NM 7023
Portnancon 133 NC 4260
Port nan Crullach 105 NM 7226
Port nan Laogh 99 NR 6792
Portneora 123 NG 7732
Port Nessock or Port Logan Bay 86 NX 0941
Portobello (Dumf. and Galwy.) 86 NW 9666
Portobello (Lothian) 103 NT 3073
Port of Menteith 101 NN 5801
Port of Ness 131 NB 5363
Port of Spittal Bay 86 NX 0152
Porton 26 SU 1836
Portpatrick 86 NX 0054
Portquin 19 SW 9780
Port Quin Bay 19 SW 9480
Port Ramsay 106 NM 8845
Portreath 18 SW 6545
Portree 123 NG 4843
Port Righ 92 NR 8237
Portrye 100 NS 1758
Portscatho 19 SW 8735
Ports Down 27 SU 6406
Portsea 27 SU 6300
Portsea Island 27 SU 6501
Portskerra 134 NC 8765
Portskewett 33 ST 4988
Port Skigersta 131 NB 5562
Portslade 28 TQ 2506
Portslade-by-Sea 28 TQ 2604
Portsmouth 27 SU 6501
Portsmouth Harbour 27 SU 6202
Port Snoig 104 NL 9638
Port Soderick 76 SC 3472
Portsoy 121 NJ 5865
Port St. Mary 76 SC 2067
Port Sunlight 68 SJ 3483
Portswood 26 SU 4314
Port Talbot 41 SS 7690
Portuairk 111 NM 4468
Port Vasgo 133 NC 5865
Portvoller 131 NB 5636
Portvoller Bay 131 NB 5636
Portway (Warw.) 50 SP 0872
Portway, The (Shrops.) (Ant.) 58 SO 4295
Port Wemyss 98 NR 1751
Port William 86 NX 3343
Portwrinkle 20 SX 3553
Portyerrock Bay 87 NX 4839
Poslingford 54 TL 7648
Possingworth Park 29 TQ 5420
Postbridge 21 SX 6579
Postcombe 36 SU 7099
Postling 31 TR 1439
Post Rocks 98 NR 4079
Postwick 65 TG 2907
Potarch 119 NO 6097
Potrail Water 88 NS 9308
Potsgrove 52 SP 9529
Potten End 36 TL 0108
Potterhanworth 72 TF 0566
Potter Heigham 65 TG 4119
Potteries, The 59 SJ 8744
Potterne 34 ST 9958
Potterne Wick 34 ST 9957
Potters Bar 37 TL 2501
Potter's Cross 49 SO 8484
Potterspury 51 SP 7543
Potter Street 37 TL 4608
Potto 85 NZ 4703
Potton 53 TL 2249
Potton Island 38 TQ 9591
Pott Row 64 TF 7021
Pott Shrigley 69 SJ 9479
Poughill (Corn.) 22 SS 2207
Poughill (Devon) 23 SS 8508
Poulshot 34 ST 9659
Poulton 46 SP 1001
Poulton-le-Fylde 77 SD 3439
Pound Bank 49 SO 7373
Pound Hill 29 TQ 2937
Poundon 51 SP 6425
Poundsgate 21 SX 7072
Poundstock 20 SX 2099
Pow Burn (Central) 102 NS 8886
Powburn (Northum.) 91 NU 0616
Powderham 21 SX 9784
Powerstock 25 SY 5196
Powfoot 89 NY 1465
Powick 49 SO 8351
Powis Castle (ant.) 58 SJ 2106
Powmill 102 NT 0197
Pow Water 108 NN 9723
Poxwell 25 SY 7484
Poyle 36 TQ 0376
Poynings 28 TQ 2612
Poyntington 25 ST 6419
Poynton 69 SJ 9283
Poynton Green 59 SJ 5618
Poys Street 55 TM 3570
Poystreet Green 54 TL 9858
Praa Sands 18 SW 5828
Prail Castle 109 NO 6946
Pratt's Bottom 37 TQ 4762
Prawle Point 21 SX 7735
Praze-an-Beeble 18 SW 6336
Precipice Walk (mt.) 57 SH 7321
Predannack Wollas 18 SW 6616
Prees 59 SJ 5533
Preesall 77 SD 3646
Prees Green 59 SJ 5631
Preesgweene 58 SJ 3135
Prees Higher Heath 59 SJ 5636
Prendwick 91 NU 0012
Pren-gwyn 43 SN 4244
Prenteg 66 SH 5841
Prenton 68 SJ 3184
Prescot (Mers.) 68 SJ 4692
Prescott (Shrops.) 58 SJ 4221
Preshaw House 27 SU 5723
Press Castle 97 NT 8765
Pressen 97 NT 8335
Pressendye 118 NJ 4909
Prestatyn 67 SJ 0682
Prestbury (Ches.) 69 SJ 8976
Prestbury (Glos.) 46 SO 9724
Presteigne 48 SO 3164
Presthope 59 SO 5897
Prestleigh 33 ST 6340
Preston (Borders) 97 NT 7957
Preston (Devon) 21 SX 8574
Preston (Dorset) 25 SY 7082
Preston (E Susx) 29 TQ 3107
Preston (Glos.) 46 SO 6734
Preston (Glos.) 46 SP 0400
Preston (Herts.) 37 TL 1724
Preston (Humbs.) 75 TA 1830
Preston (Kent) 31 TR 2561
Preston (Lancs.) 77 SD 5329
Preston (Leic.) 62 SK 8602
Preston (Lothian) 103 NT 5977
Preston (Northum.) 97 NU 1825
Preston (Wilts.) 34 SU 0377
Preston Bagot 50 SP 1766
Preston Bissett 51 SP 6530
Preston Brockhurst 59 SJ 5324
Preston Brook 69 SJ 5680
Preston Candover 35 SU 6041
Preston Capes 51 SP 5754
Preston Gubbals 59 SJ 4819
Preston Hill 97 NT 9223
Preston Law 95 NT 2535
Preston on Stour 50 SP 2049
Preston on Wye 45 SO 3842
Prestonpans 103 NT 3874
Preston St. Mary 54 TL 9450
Preston-under-Scar 84 SE 0791
Preston upon the Weald Moors 59 SJ 6815
Preston Wynne 45 SO 5646
Prestwich 69 SD 8103
Prestwick (Northum.) 91 NZ 1872
Prestwick (Strath.) 93 NS 3525
Prestwick Scotland Airport 93 NS 3626
Prestwood 36 SP 8700
Price Town 41 SS 9392
Prickeny Hill 93 NS 5405
Prickwillow 54 TL 5982
Priddy 33 ST 5250
Priesthope Hill 96 NT 3539
Priest Hutton 77 SD 5273
Priest Island 126 NB 9202
Priestside Bank (sbk.) 89 NY 1164
Priestweston 58 SO 2997
Primethorpe 61 SP 5293
Primrose Green 64 TG 0616
Primrose Hill (Cambs.) 53 TL 3889
Prince Charles's Cave (Island of Skye) 123 NG 5112
Prince Charles's Cave (Island of Skye) 123 NG 5148
Prince Charlie's Cave (Highld.) 107 NN 4968
Prince's Cave 112 NF 8331
Princes Risborough 36 SP 8003
Princethorpe 50 SP 3970
Princetown 21 SX 5873
Prinknash Park (ant.) 46 SO 8713
Prior Muir 103 NO 5213
Prior Park 82 SD 1490
Priors Hardwick 51 SP 4756
Priors Marston 51 SP 4857
Priory, The 27 SZ 6390
Priory Wood 45 SO 2545
Priston 33 ST 6960
Prittlewell 38 TQ 8787
Privett 27 SU 6726
Probus 19 SW 8947
Proncy 129 NH 7792
Prudhoe 91 NZ 0962
Ptarmigan Lodge 100 NN 3500
Puckeridge 37 TL 3823
Puckington 24 ST 3718
Pucklechurch 33 ST 6976
Puckpool Point 27 SZ 6192
Puddington (Ches.) 68 SJ 3273
Puddington (Devon) 23 SS 8310
Puddledock 54 TM 0592
Puddletown 25 SY 7594
Pudleston 45 SO 5659
Pudsey 79 SE 2232
Puffin Island 67 SH 6481
Pulborough 28 TQ 0418
Puldrite Skerry 136 HY 4318
Puleston 59 SJ 7322
Pulford 68 SJ 3758
Pulham 25 ST 7008
Pulham Market 55 TM 1986
Pulham St. Mary 55 TM 2185
Pulloxhill 52 TL 0634
Pulpit Rock 100 NN 3414
Pulverbatch 58 SJ 4202
Pumsaint 43 SN 6540
Puncheston 42 SN 0029
Puncknowle 25 SY 5388
Pund Head 140 HU 1655
Punnett's Town 29 TQ 6220
Purbeck Hills 25 SY 9081
Purbrook 27 SU 6707
Purfleet 37 TQ 5578
Puriton 32 ST 3241
Purleigh 38 TL 8301
Purley (Berks.) 36 SU 6676
Purley (Gtr London) 37 TQ 3161
Purlogue 48 SO 2877
Purls Bridge 53 TL 4787
Purse Caundle 25 ST 6917
Purslow 48 SO 3680
Purston Jaglin 71 SE 4319
Purton (Glos.) 46 SO 6605
Purton (Glos.) 46 SO 6904
Purton (Wilts.) 34 SU 0887
Purton Stoke 34 SU 0890
Purves Hall 96 NT 7644
Pury End 51 SP 7045
Pusey 47 SU 3596
Putley 49 SO 6437
Putney 37 TQ 2274
Puttenham (Herts.) 36 SP 8814
Puttenham (Surrey) 28 SU 9347
Puxton 32 ST 4063
Pwll 40 SN 4801
Pwllcrochan 42 SM 9202
Pwlldefaid 56 SH 1526
Pwlldu Head 40 SS 5786
Pwllheli 66 SH 3735
Pwllmeyric 33 ST 5192
Pwll-y-glaw 41 SS 7993
Pwllygranant 42 SN 1147
Pyecombe 29 TQ 2912
Pye Corner 32 ST 3485
Pykestone Hill 95 NT 1731
Pyle (I. of W.) 27 SZ 4879
Pyle (Mid Glam.) 41 SS 8282
Pylle 33 ST 6038
Pymore 53 TL 4986
Pyrford 36 TQ 0458
Pyrton 36 SU 6895
Pytchley 52 SP 8574
Pyworthy 22 SS 3102

Q

Quabbs 48 SO 2080
Quadring 63 TF 2233
Quainton 36 SP 7419
Quandale 138 HY 3632
Quanter Ness 136 HY 4114
Quantock Forest 24 ST 1736
Quantock Hills 24 ST 1537
Quarff 141 HU 4135
Quarley 34 SU 2743
Quarndon 60 SK 3340
Quarrier's Homes 101 NS 3666
Quarrington 62 TF 0544
Quarrington Hill 84 NZ 3337
Quarrybank (Ches.) 69 SJ 5465
Quarry Bank (W Mids.) 49 SO 9386
Quarry Head 121 NJ 9065
Quarryhill 129 NH 7481
Quarry, The 46 ST 7399
Quarrywood 129 NJ 1864
Quarter 94 NS 7251
Quarter Fell 86 NX 1969
Quatford 49 SO 7390
Quatt 49 SO 7588
Quebec 84 NZ 1743
Quedgeley 46 SO 8114
Queen Adelaide 53 TL 5681
Queenborough 30 TQ 9471
Queen Camel 25 ST 5924
Queen Charlton 33 ST 6366
Queensberry (mt.) 88 NX 9899
Queensbury 78 SE 1030
Queen's Cairn 128 NH 4672
Queensferry (Clwyd) 68 SJ 3168
Queensferry (Lothian) 102 NT 1278
Queen's Forest, The 117 NH 9710
Queen's Ground 64 TL 6793
Queenside Muir 100 NS 2864
Queen's View 108 NN 8560
Queenzieburn 101 NS 6977
Quendale 141 HU 3713
Quendon 53 TL 5130
Queniborough 61 SK 6412
Quenington 47 SP 1404
Quernmore 77 SD 5160
Quethiock 20 SX 3164
Quey Firth 142 HU 3682
Quholm 136 HY 2412
Quidenham 54 TM 0287
Quidhampton (Hants.) 35 SU 5150
Quidhampton (Wilts.) 26 SU 1030
Quien Hill 100 NS 0559
Quies 19 SW 8376
Quilquox 121 NJ 9038
Quilva Taing 140 HU 1757
Quinag (mt.) 132 NC 2028
Quindry 136 ND 4392
Quine's Hill 76 SC 3473
Quinish (Island of Mull) (dist.) 111 NM 4254
Quinish (Pabbay) (is.) 124 NF 8886
Quinish Point 111 NM 4056
Quintin Knowe 88 NS 6508
Quinton 51 SP 7754
Quoditch 20 SX 4097
Quoig 107 NN 8222
Quorndon (Quorn) 61 SK 5616
Quothquan 95 NS 9939
Quoyloo 136 HY 2420
Quoy Ness 139 HY 6236
Quoys 143 HP 6112

R

Raasay House 123 NG 5436
Rabbit Islands 133 NC 6063
Raby 68 SJ 3179
Raby Castle (ant.) 84 NZ 1321
Rachub 67 SH 6268
Rackenford 23 SS 8418
Rackham 28 TQ 0514
Rackheath 65 TG 2814
Racks 89 NY 0374
Rackwick (Hoy, Orkney) 136 ND 1999
Rack Wick (Hoy, Orkney) 136 ND 2098
Rackwick (Westray) 138 HY 4449
Rack Wick (Westray) 138 HY 4450
Rack Wick (Westray) 138 HY 5042
Radcliffe (Gtr Mches) 69 SD 7806
Radcliffe (Northum.) 91 NU 2602
Radcliffe on Trent 61 SK 6439
Radclive 51 SP 6734
Radcot 47 SU 2899
Raddery 129 NH 7159
Radernie 103 NO 4609
Radford Semele 50 SP 3464
Radlett 37 TL 1600
Radley 47 SU 5398
Radnage 36 SU 7897
Radnor Forest 48 SO 1864
Radstock 33 ST 6854
Radstone 51 SP 5840
Radway 50 SP 3648
Radway Green 59 SJ 7754
Radwell 53 TL 2335
Radwinter 54 TL 6037
Radyr 41 ST 1380
Raera 105 NM 8320
Raerinish Point 131 NB 4224
Raes Knowes 89 NY 2882
Rafford 129 NJ 0656
Ragdale 61 SK 6619
Raglan 45 SO 4107
Ragnall 72 SK 8073
Rainberg Mór 98 NR 5687
Rainford 69 SD 4700
Rainham (Gtr London) 37 TQ 5282
Rainham (Kent) 30 TQ 8165
Rainhill 69 SJ 4990
Rainhill Stoops 69 SJ 5090
Rainow 70 SJ 9575
Rainton 79 SE 3775
Rainworth 71 SK 5958
Raisbeck 83 NY 6407
Rait 108 NO 2226
Raithby (Lincs.) 73 TF 3084
Raithby (Lincs.) 73 TF 3767
Raitts Burn 116 NH 7604
Rake 27 SU 8027
Rake Law 88 NS 8717
Ralfland Forest 83 NY 5413
Ramasaig 122 NG 1644
Rame (Corn.) 18 SW 7233
Rame (Corn.) 20 SX 4249
Rame Head 20 SX 4148
Ram Lane 31 TQ 9646
Ramna Stacks 143 HU 3797
Rampisham 25 ST 5502
Rampside 76 SD 2366
Rampton (Cambs.) 53 TL 4268
Rampton (Notts.) 72 SK 7978
Ramsbottom 69 SD 7916
Ramsbury 34 SU 2771
Ramscraigs 135 ND 1427
Ramsdean 27 SU 7021
Ramsdell 35 SU 5957
Ramsden 47 SP 3515
Ramsden Bellhouse 38 TQ 7194
Ramsden Heath 38 TQ 7195
Ramsey (Cambs.) 53 TL 2885
Ramsey (Essex) 55 TM 2130
Ramsey (I. of M.) 76 SC 4594
Ramsey Bay 76 SC 4796
Ramseycleuch 89 NT 2714
Ramsey Forty Foot 53 TL 3187
Ramsey Hollow 53 TL 3186
Ramsey Island (Dyfed) 42 SM 7023
Ramsey Island (Essex) 39 TL 9605
Ramsey Knowe 89 NT 2516
Ramsey Mereside 53 TL 2889
Ramsey Sound 42 SM 7124
Ramsey St. Mary's 53 TL 2588
Ramsgate 31 TR 3865
Ramsgate Municipal Airport 31 TR 3767
Ramsgill 78 SE 1170
Ramshorn 60 SK 0845
Rams Ness 143 HU 6087
Ranachan Hill 92 NR 6825
Ranby 71 SK 6480
Rand 73 TF 1078
Randwick 46 SO 8206
Ranfurly 101 NS 3865
Rangemore 60 SK 1822
Rangeworthy 33 ST 6886
Ranish 131 NB 4024
Rankinston 93 NS 4514
Rannoch Forest 107 NN 4565
Rannoch Moor 107 NN 3852
Rannoch River 105 NM 7046
Rannoch Station 107 NN 4257
Ranskill 71 SK 6587
Ranson Moor 63 TL 3893
Ranton 59 SJ 8524
Ranworth 65 TG 3514
Rapness 138 HY 5141
Rapness Sound 138 HY 5138
Rappach (dist.) 127 NC 2401
Rappach Water 127 NH 3098
Rascarrel 87 NX 7948
Rascarrel Bay 87 NX 8047
Raskelf 79 SE 4971
Rassau 41 SO 1411
Rastrick 78 SE 1321
Ratagan 114 NG 9220
Ratagan Forest 114 NG 8919
Ratby 61 SK 5105
Ratcliffe Culey 60 SP 3299
Ratcliffe on the Wreake 61 SK 6314
Rathen 121 NK 0060
Rathillet 109 NO 3620
Rathmell 78 SD 8059
Ratho 102 NT 1370
Ratho Station 102 NT 1372
Rathven 121 NJ 4465
Rat Island 22 SS 1443
Ratley 50 SP 3847
Ratlinghope 58 SO 4096
Rattar 135 ND 2672
Ratten Row 77 SD 4241
Rattery 21 SX 7361
Rattlesden 54 TL 9758
Rattray 108 NO 1745
Rattray Head 121 NK 1057
Rauceby 62 TF 0146
Rauceby Station 62 TF 0344
Raughton Head 83 NY 3745
Raunds 52 SP 9972
Ravenfield 71 SK 4895
Ravenglass 82 SD 0896
Raveningham 65 TM 3996
Ravenscar 81 NZ 9801
Ravensdale 76 SC 3592
Ravensden 52 TL 0754
Ravenshead 61 SK 5654
Ravens Knowe 90 NT 7806
Ravensmoor 59 SJ 6250
Ravensthorpe (Northants.) 51 SP 6670
Ravensthorpe (W Yorks.) 71 SE 2220
Ravensthorpe Resr. 51 SP 6770
Ravenstone (Bucks.) 52 SP 8450
Ravenstone (Leic.) 60 SK 4013
Ravenstonedale 83 NY 7203
Ravenstonedale Common 83 NY 6900
Ravenstown 77 SD 3574
Ravenstruther 95 NS 9245
Ravensworth 84 NZ 1407
Raw 81 NZ 9305
Rawcliffe (Humbs.) 74 SE 6822
Rawcliffe (N Yorks.) 79 SE 5855
Rawcliffe Bridge 74 SE 6921
Rawmarsh 71 SK 4396
Rawreth 38 TQ 7793
Rawridge 24 ST 2006
Rawtenstall 78 SD 8122
Rayburn Lake 91 NZ 1192
Raydon 54 TM 0438
Raylees 90 NY 9291
Rayleigh 38 TQ 8090
Rayne 38 TL 7222
Ray Sand 39 TM 0500
Rea Brook 49 SO 6586
Reach 53 TL 5666
Read 78 SD 7634
Reading 36 SU 7272
Reading Street 30 TQ 9230
Read's Island 74 SE 9622
Reagill 83 NY 6017
Rearquhar 129 NH 7492
Rearsby 61 SK 6514
Rease Heath 59 SJ 6454
Reaster 135 ND 2565
Reawick 141 HU 3244

Reay ... 134 NC 9664
Reay Forest ... 132 NC 2939
Reculver ... 31 TR 2269
Redberth ... 42 SN 0804
Redbourn ... 34 TL 1012
Redbourne ... 74 SK 9699
Redbrook ... 45 SO 5310
Redbrook Street ... 30 TQ 9336
Redburn (Highld.) ... 128 NH 5767
Redburn (Highld.) ... 129 NH 9447
Redcar ... 85 NZ 6024
Redcastle (Highld.) ... 128 NH 5849
Redcastle (Tays.) ... 109 NO 6850
Redcleuch Edge (mt.) ... 89 NT 3410
Redcliff Bay ... 33 ST 4475
Red Dial ... 82 NY 2545
Redding ... 102 NS 9178
Reddingmuirhead ... 102 NS 9177
Reddish ... 69 SJ 8993
Redditch ... 50 SP 0468
Red Down ... 20 SX 2685
Rede ... 54 TL 8055
Redenhall ... 55 TM 2684
Redesdale ... 90 NY 8396
Redesdale Camp ... 90 NY 8298
Redesdale Forest ... 90 NY 7601
Redesmouth ... 90 NY 8681
Redford ... 109 NO 5644
Redfordgreen ... 89 NT 3615
Redgrave ... 54 TM 0478
Red Head (Eday) ... 138 HY 5640
Red Head (Stroma) ... 135 ND 3477
Red Head (Tays.) ... 109 NO 7047
Redheugh ... 109 NO 4463
Redhill (Avon) ... 33 ST 4962
Redhill (Grampn.) ... 121 NJ 6837
Redhill (Grampn.) ... 119 NJ 7704
Red Hill (Powys) ... 44 SO 1550
Redhill (Surrey) ... 29 TQ 2850
Redhill Aerodrome & Heliport ... 29 TQ 3047
Redhythe Point ... 121 NJ 5767
Redisham ... 55 TM 4084
Redland (Avon) ... 33 ST 5875
Redland (Orkney) ... 136 HY 3724
Redlingfield ... 55 TM 1871
Red Lion Hill ... 57 SO 0577
Redlynch (Somer.) ... 25 ST 6933
Redlynch (Wilts.) ... 26 SU 2020
Redmarley D'Abitot ... 46 SO 7531
Redmarshall ... 85 NZ 3821
Redmile ... 61 SK 7935
Redmire ... 84 SE 0491
Redmire Moor ... 84 SE 0593
Redmires Dam ... 78 SD 9327
Redmires Reservoirs ... 71 SK 2685
Redmoor ... 19 SX 0761
Redmyre Loch ... 108 NO 2733
Rednal ... 58 SJ 3628
Red Nev (pt.) ... 138 HY 4145
Redpath ... 96 NT 5835
Red Pike ... 82 NY 1615
Red Point (Highld.) ... 134 NG 9265
Redpoint (Highld.) ... 123 NG 7369
Red Rock ... 69 SD 5809
Red Roses ... 43 SN 2012
Red Row ... 91 NZ 2599
Redruth ... 18 SW 6941
Redshin Cove ... 97 NU 0150
Red Street ... 59 SJ 8251
Red Wharf Bay (Gwyn.) ... 66 SH 5281
Red Wharf Bay (Gwyn.) ... 66 SH 5480
Redwick (Avon) ... 33 ST 5485
Redwick (Gwent) ... 33 ST 4184
Redworth ... 84 NZ 2423
Reed ... 53 TL 3636
Reedham ... 65 TG 4201
Reedness ... 74 SE 7922
Reed Point ... 96 NT 7772
Reef ... 131 NB 1134
Reeker Pike ... 90 NY 6682
Reepham (Lincs.) ... 72 TF 0373
Reepham (Norf.) ... 65 TG 1023
Reeth ... 84 SE 0499
Regaby ... 76 SC 4397
Regents Park ... 37 TQ 2882
Regoul ... 129 NH 8851
Rèidh Eilean ... 104 NM 2426
Reiff ... 132 NB 9614
Reigate ... 28 TQ 2550
Reighton ... 81 TA 1275
Reighton Sands ... 81 TA 1476
Reisa an t-Sruith ... 99 NR 7399
Reisa Mhic Phaideain ... 99 NM 7400
Reisgill Burn ... 135 ND 2238
Reiss ... 135 ND 3354
Rejerrah ... 19 SW 8055
Relubbus ... 18 SW 5632
Relugas ... 129 NH 9948
Remenham ... 26 SU 7784
Remenham Hill ... 36 SU 7883
Remony ... 107 NN 7644
Rempstone ... 61 SK 5724
Remuil Hill ... 92 NR 6212
Rendcomb ... 46 SP 0109
Rendham ... 55 TM 3564
Rendlesham Forest ... 55 TM 3449
Renfrew ... 101 NS 4967
Renhold ... 52 TL 0953
Renishaw ... 71 SK 4477
Renish Point ... 124 NG 0481
Rennington ... 91 NU 2118
Renton ... 101 NS 3878
Renwick ... 83 NY 5943
Repps ... 65 TG 4116
Repton ... 60 SK 3026
Rerwick Head ... 137 HY 5411
Rescobie ... 109 NO 5152
Resipole ... 111 NM 7264
Resolis ... 128 NH 6765
Resolven ... 41 SN 8202
Rest and be thankful ... 100 NN 2307
Reston ... 97 NT 8861
Reswallie ... 109 NO 5051
Retew ... 19 SW 9256
Rettendon ... 38 TQ 7698
Rettendon Place ... 38 TQ 7796
Revesby ... 73 TF 2961
Rewe ... 21 SX 9499
Reydon ... 55 TM 4977
Reymerston ... 64 TG 0206
Reynalton ... 42 SN 0909
Reynoldston ... 40 SS 4890
Rhaeadr Cynfal ... 67 SH 7041
Rhandirmwyn ... 44 SN 7843
Rhayader ... 57 SN 9668
Rhedyn ... 66 SH 3032
Rheindown ... 128 NH 5147
Rhemore ... 111 NM 5750
Rhenigidale ... 125 NB 2201
Rhes-y-cae ... 68 SJ 1870
Rhewl (Clwyd) ... 67 SJ 1060
Rhewl (Clwyd) ... 58 SJ 1744
Rhian ... 133 NC 5616
Rhicarn ... 132 NC 0825
Rhiconich ... 132 NC 2552
Rhicullen ... 128 NH 6971
Rhidorroch Forest ... 127 NH 2497
Rhidorroch House ... 127 NH 1795
Rhidorroch River ... 127 NH 2294
Rhifail ... 134 NC 7249
Rhigos ... 41 SN 9205
Rhilean Burn ... 117 NH 8937

Rhilochan ... 129 NC 7407
Rhinns of Kells (mt.) ... 87 NX 5083
Rhinog Fawr (mt.) ... 57 SH 6428
Rhins, The (dist.) ... 86 NX 0454
Rhiroy ... 127 NH 1589
Rhiwbryfdir ... 67 SH 6946
Rhiwderin ... 32 ST 2587
Rhiwlas (Clwyd) ... 58 SJ 1931
Rhiwlas (Gwyn.) ... 66 SH 5765
Rhiwlas (Gwyn.) ... 67 SH 9237
Rhobell Fawr ... 57 SH 7825
Rhodesia ... 71 SK 5680
Rhodes Minnis ... 31 TR 1542
Rhôd-mâd ... 56 SN 5974
Rhondda ... 41 SS 9696
Rhondda Fach ... 41 SS 9996
Rhondda Fawr ... 41 SS 9993
Rhonehouse or Kelton Hill ... 88 NX 7459
Rhoose ... 41 ST 0666
Rhôs (Dyfed) ... 43 SN 3835
Rhos (W Glam.) ... 40 SN 7303
Rhoscolyn ... 66 SH 2675
Rhoscrowther ... 42 SM 9002
Rhos Dirion ... 41 SO 2133
Rhosesmor ... 68 SJ 2168
Rhos-fawr ... 66 SH 3838
Rhosgadfan ... 66 SH 5057
Rhosgoch (Gwyn.) ... 66 SH 4189
Rhosgoch (Powys) ... 45 SO 1847
Rhoslan ... 66 SH 4841
Rhoslefain ... 56 SH 5705
Rhosllanerchrugog ... 58 SJ 2946
Rhosmeirch ... 66 SH 4677
Rhosneigr ... 66 SH 3172
Rhosnesni ... 58 SJ 3451
Rhos-on-Sea ... 67 SH 8480
Rhossili ... 40 SS 4188
Rhossili Bay ... 40 SS 3990
Rhosson ... 42 SM 7254
Rhostryfan ... 66 SH 4958
Rhos-y-llan ... 66 SH 2337
Rhos-y-mawn ... 67 SH 8566
Rhu (Kintyre) ... 99 NR 8364
Rhu (Strath.) ... 100 NS 2783
Rhuallt ... 67 SJ 0774
Rhuddlan ... 67 SJ 0277
Rhue ... 127 NH 0997
Rhulen ... 44 SO 1350
Rhum (is.) ... 110 NM 3798
Rhunahaorine ... 92 NR 7048
Rhu Nòa ... 126 NH 0064
Rhyd (Gwyn.) ... 66 SH 6341
Rhyd (Powys) ... 57 SN 9700
Rhydargaeau ... 43 SN 4326
Rhydcymerau ... 43 SN 5738
Rhydd ... 50 SO 8345
Rhyd Ddu ... 66 SH 5652
Rhyddhywel ... 57 SO 0279
Rhydding ... 41 SS 7498
Rhyd Galed ... 44 SN 7142
Rhydlewis ... 43 SN 3447
Rhydlios ... 66 SH 1830
Rhydlydan ... 58 SH 8950
Rhydowen ... 43 SN 4445
Rhydrosser ... 56 SN 5667
Rhydtalog ... 58 SJ 2354
Rhyd-y-clafdy ... 66 SH 3235
Rhydycroesau ... 58 SJ 2330
Rhydyfelin (Dyfed) ... 56 SN 5979
Rhydyfelin (Mid Glam.) ... 41 ST 0988
Rhyd-y-fro ... 41 SN 7105
Rhydymain ... 57 SH 7922
Rhyd-y-meirch ... 45 SO 3107
Rhydymwyn ... 68 SJ 2066
Rhyd-yr-onnen ... 56 SH 6102
Rhyl ... 67 SJ 0181
Rhymney ... 41 SO 1107
Rhymney River ... 41 ST 2283
Rhymney Valley ... 41 ST 1491
Rhyn ... 58 SJ 3136
Rhynd ... 108 NO 1520
Rhynie (Grampn.) ... 121 NJ 4927
Rhynie (Highld.) ... 129 NH 8579
Ribbesford ... 49 SO 7874
Ribblehead ... 78 SD 7879
Ribblesdale ... 78 SD 8059
Ribbleton ... 77 SD 5630
Ribchester ... 77 SD 6435
Ribigill ... 133 NC 5854
Riby ... 74 TA 1807
Riccall ... 79 SE 6237
Riccarton ... 93 NS 4235
Richards Castle ... 48 SO 4969
Richmond ... 84 NZ 1701
Richmond (Surrey) ... 37 TQ 1874
Richmond Park ... 37 TQ 1972
Rickarton ... 119 NO 8188
Rickets Head ... 42 SM 8529
Rickinghall ... 54 TM 0475
Rickling ... 53 TL 4931
Rickmansworth ... 36 TQ 0594
Riddell ... 96 NT 5124
Riddlecombe ... 23 SS 6013
Riddlesden ... 78 SE 0742
Ridge (Dorset) ... 25 SY 9386
Ridge (Herts.) ... 37 TL 2100
Ridge (Wilts.) ... 26 ST 9531
Ridgehill (Avon) ... 33 ST 5362
Ridge Hill (Here. and Worc.) ... 45 SO 5035
Ridge Lane ... 60 SP 2994
Ridge Way (Berks.) (ant.) ... 34 SU 5381
Ridge Way (Oxon.) (ant.) ... 34 SU 3484
Ridge Way (Wilts.) (ant.) ... 34 SU 0151
Ridge Way (Wilts.) (ant.) ... 34 SU 1168
Ridgeway Cross ... 49 SO 7147
Ridgewell ... 54 TL 7340
Ridgewood ... 29 TQ 4719
Ridgmont ... 52 SP 9736
Riding Mill ... 91 NZ 0161
Ridlees Cairn ... 90 NT 8404
Ridlington (Leic.) ... 62 SK 8402
Ridlington (Norf.) ... 65 TG 3430
Ridsdale ... 90 NY 9084
Riechip ... 108 NO 0647
Riemore Lodge ... 108 NO 0449
Riereach Burn ... 129 NH 8445
Rievaulx ... 79 SE 5785
Rigg ... 89 NY 2966
Riggend ... 101 NS 7670
Riggs Moor ... 78 SE 0373
Rigg, The ... 90 NY 6499
Rigmaden Park ... 77 SD 6184
Rig of the Shalloch ... 86 NX 3892
Rigside ... 95 NS 8734
Rileyhill ... 60 SK 1115
Rilla Mill ... 20 SX 2973
Rillington ... 80 SE 8574
Rimington ... 78 SD 8045
Rimpton ... 25 ST 6021
Rimsdale Burn ... 134 NC 7440
Rimswell ... 75 TA 3128
Rinaston ... 42 SM 9825
Ringford ... 87 NX 6857
Ringland ... 65 TG 1313
Ringmer ... 29 TQ 4412
Ringmore ... 21 SX 6545
Ringorm ... 120 NJ 2644
Ring's End ... 63 TF 3902
Ringsfield ... 55 TM 4088

Ringsfield Corner ... 55 TM 4187
Ringshall (Bucks.) ... 36 SP 9814
Ringshall (Suff.) ... 54 TM 0452
Ringshall Stocks ... 54 TM 0551
Ringstead (Norf.) ... 64 TF 7040
Ringstead (Northants.) ... 51 SP 9875
Ringstead Bay ... 25 SY 7579
Ringwood ... 26 SU 1405
Ringwood Forest ... 26 SU 1108
Ringwould ... 31 TR 3648
Rinmore ... 118 NJ 4117
Rinn Druim Tallig ... 131 NB 3150
Rinnigill ... 136 ND 3193
Rinns of Islay ... 98 NR 2056
Rinns Point ... 98 NR 1751
Rinn Thorbhais ... 104 NL 9340
Rinsey ... 18 SW 5927
Ripe ... 29 TQ 5010
Ripley (Derby.) ... 60 SK 3950
Ripley (Hants.) ... 26 SZ 1698
Ripley (N Yorks.) ... 79 SE 2860
Ripley (Surrey) ... 28 TQ 0556
Riplingham ... 74 SE 9631
Ripon ... 79 SE 3171
Rippingale ... 62 TF 0927
Ripple (Here. and Worc.) ... 49 SO 8737
Ripple (Kent) ... 31 TR 3550
Ripponden ... 70 SE 0319
Rippon Tor ... 21 SX 7475
Rireavach ... 126 NH 0295
Risabus ... 98 NR 3143
Risbury ... 50 SO 5455
Risby (Humbs.) ... 74 SE 9214
Risby (Suff.) ... 54 TL 7966
Risca ... 32 ST 2391
Rise ... 75 TA 1541
Risegate ... 62 TF 2029
Rise Hill ... 77 SD 7388
Riseley (Beds.) ... 52 TL 0463
Riseley (Berks.) ... 36 SU 7263
Rishangles ... 55 TM 1568
Rishton ... 77 SD 7229
Rishworth ... 70 SE 0317
Rishworth Moor ... 70 SD 9917
Risley (Ches.) ... 69 SJ 6592
Risley (Staffs.) ... 60 SK 4635
Rispith ... 79 SE 2467
Rispond ... 133 NC 4565
Rivar ... 34 SU 3161
Rivenhall End ... 38 TL 8316
River Add ... 99 NR 8192
River Adur ... 28 TQ 2118
River Affric (Highld.) ... 115 NH 0920
River Affric (Highld.) ... 115 NH 2627
River Aire ... 79 SE 3630
River Alde ... 55 TM 2967
River Allen (Corn.) ... 19 SX 0678
River Allen (Dorset) ... 26 SU 0006
River Allen (Northern.) ... 90 NY 7962
River Almond (Highld.) ... 107 NN 7833
River Almond (Tays.) ... 107 NO 0228
River Aln ... 91 NU 1214
River Alne ... 50 SP 1562
River Alport ... 71 SK 1292
River Alt ... 68 SD 3105
River Alun ... 90 SM 7627
River Alwin ... 90 NT 9110
River Alyn ... 58 SJ 3656
River Amber ... 71 SK 3463
River Anker ... 60 SP 2859
River Annan (Dumf. and Galwy.) ... 89 NT 0901
River Annan (Dumf. and Galwy.) ... 89 NY 1176
River Ant ... 65 TG 3617
River Applecross ... 123 NG 7448
River Ardle ... 108 NO 1054
River Arnol ... 131 NB 3045
River Arrow (Here. and Worc.) ... 45 SO 4058
River Arrow (Warw.) ... 50 SP 0861
River Arun ... 28 TQ 0422
River Ash ... 37 TL 4216
River Ashop ... 71 SK 1389
River Attadale ... 114 NG 9337
River Averon ... 128 NH 6372
River Avon (Avon) ... 33 ST 5476
River Avon (Avon) ... 33 ST 6966
River Avon (Central) ... 102 NS 8773
River Avon (Devon) ... 21 SX 7157
River Avon (Grampn.) ... 117 NJ 1614
River Avon (Warw.) ... 50 SP 2659
River Avon (Wilts.) ... 26 SU 1301
River Awe ... 106 NN 0229
River Axe (Dorset) ... 24 ST 3303
River Axe (Somer.) ... 33 ST 4647
River Ayr ... 94 NS 5826
River Ba ... 106 NN 2648
River Bain ... 73 TF 2473
River Bank ... 53 TL 5368
River Barle ... 23 SS 8829
River Barrisdale ... 114 NG 8803
River Beauly ... 128 NH 4641
River Bellart ... 105 NM 4448
River Beult ... 30 TQ 7747
River Blackwater ... 38 TL 8322
River Bladnoch ... 86 NX 3657
River Bleng ... 82 NY 0804
River Blithe ... 60 SK 0424
River Blyth (Northern.) ... 91 NZ 1877
River Blyth (Suff.) ... 55 TM 4376
River Blythe (Warw.) ... 50 SP 2184
River Bogie ... 121 NJ 5234
River Bollin ... 69 SJ 7785
River Borgie ... 133 NC 6655
River Bourne ... 34 SU 2038
River Bovey ... 21 SX 7583
River Braan ... 108 NN 9438
River Brain ... 38 TL 7918
River Bran ... 127 NH 2160
River Brant ... 62 SK 9356
River Brathay ... 82 NY 3102
River Bray ... 23 SS 6932
River Breamish ... 90 NT 9515
River Brede ... 30 TQ 8217
River Brent ... 54 TM 0145
River Brit ... 24 SY 4795
River Brittle ... 123 NG 4023
River Brock ... 77 SD 5140
River Broom ... 127 NH 1881
River Brora ... 133 NC 6613
River Brue (Somer.) ... 32 ST 4044
River Brue (Somer.) ... 25 ST 6032
River Bure ... 65 TG 2521
River Calder (Cumbr.) ... 82 NY 0609
River Calder (Highld.) ... 116 NN 6698
River Calder (Lancs.) ... 77 SD 7437
River Calder (Lancs.) ... 78 SD 7833
River Calder (Lancs.) ... 100 NS 3162
River Calder (W Yorks.) ... 71 SE 2620
River Cale ... 25 ST 7422
River Cam (Cambs.) ... 53 TL 5268
River Camel ... 19 SW 9440
River Cam or Granta (Essex) ... 53 TL 5231
River Cam or Rhee (Cambs.) ... 53 TL 3648
River Can ... 38 TL 6807
River Cannich ... 115 NH 2833
River Carey ... 20 SX 3687
River Carron (Central) ... 101 NS 7684
River Carron (Central) ... 101 NS 7684
River Carron (Highld.) ... 126 NG 9442
River Carron (Highld.) ... 128 NH 4890

River Cary ... 25 ST 4530
River Cassley ... 132 NC 4012
River Ceiriog ... 58 SJ 2237
River Char ... 24 SY 3996
River Chater ... 62 SK 8303
River Chelmer ... 38 TL 6520
River Chelmer ... 38 TL 7709
River Cherwell (Northants.) ... 51 SP 4947
River Cherwell (Oxon.) ... 47 SP 5212
River Chess ... 36 TQ 0695
River Chet ... 65 TM 3799
River Churn ... 46 SP 0108
River Churnet ... 60 SK 0147
River Claw ... 20 SX 3498
River Clun ... 48 SO 3976
River Clwyd ... 67 SJ 0276
River Clyde (Strath.) ... 94 NS 7753
River Clyde (Strath.) ... 95 NS 9933
River Clydedog ... 57 SN 9998
River Clyst ... 21 SX 9998
River Coille ... 116 NH 4426
River Cole (Oxon.) ... 47 SU 2195
River Cole (W Mids.) ... 50 SP 1587
River Coll ... 131 NB 4540
River Coln ... 47 SP 1305
River Colne ... 54 TL 9327
River Colne ... 54 TL 5051
River Conder ... 77 SD 4958
River Conon (Highld.) ... 128 NH 4255
River Conon (Isle of Skye) ... 123 NG 4163
River Cononish ... 106 NN 3228
River Conwy (Gwyn.) ... 67 SH 7769
River Conwy (Gwyn.) ... 67 SH 8145
River Coquet ... 91 NT 1599
River Corfe ... 26 SY 9685
River Corve ... 48 SO 5286
River Coulin ... 126 NH 0254
River Coupall ... 106 NN 2054
River Cover ... 78 SE 1186
River Cree ... 86 NX 3184
River Creed or Greeta River ... 131 NB 3632
River Crouch ... 38 TQ 8095
River Culm ... 24 ST 0207
River Cur ... 100 NN 1000
River Dalch ... 23 SS 7510
River Dane (Ches.) ... 69 SJ 6868
River Dane (Staffs.) ... 69 SJ 9463
River Dart ... 21 SX 7565
River Darwen ... 77 SD 6129
River Dean ... 69 SJ 8781
River Dearne ... 71 SE 3408
River Dee (Clwyd) ... 58 SJ 3543
River Dee (Cumbr.) ... 77 SD 6788
River Dee (Dumf. and Galwy.) ... 88 NX 7463
River Dee (Grampn.) ... 117 NN 9991
River Dee (Grampn.) ... 118 NO 3396
River Dee (Grampn.) ... 119 NO 8298
River Dee or Black Water of Dee ... 88 NX 5973
River Deer ... 20 SS 3200
River Delph ... 53 TL 5090
River Derwent (Cumbr.) ... 82 NY 2312
River Derwent (Derby.) ... 71 SK 2564
River Derwent (Derby.) ... 60 SK 4333
River Derwent (Durham-Northum.) ... 84 NZ 0350
River Derwent (Humbs. - N Yorks.) ... 74 SE 7035
River Derwent (N Yorks.) ... 80 SE 8578
River Dessarry ... 114 NM 9393
River Deveron (Grampn.) ... 121 NJ 4439
River Deveron (Grampn.) ... 121 NJ 6247
River Devon (Central) ... 102 NS 9497
River Devon (Notts.) ... 61 SK 7847
River Dibb ... 78 SE 0563
River Dionard ... 132 NC 3357
River Divie ... 129 NJ 0344
River Dochart ... 107 NN 5430
River Doe ... 78 NN 1914
River Don (Grampn.) ... 117 NJ 2707
River Don (Grampn.) ... 119 NJ 6519
River Don (S Yorks.) ... 71 SK 4696
River Doon ... 93 NS 4308
River Dorn ... 47 SP 4420
River Douchary ... 127 NH 2490
River Douglas ... 68 SD 4619
River Dove (Derby.) ... 60 SK 1132
River Dove (N Yorks.) ... 85 SE 6793
River Dove (Staffs.) ... 70 SK 1163
River Dove (Suff.) ... 55 TM 1370
River Dovey (Afon Dyfi) ... 56 SN 6395
River Drolsay ... 98 NR 3366
River Druie ... 117 NH 9011
River Drynoch ... 123 NG 4330
River Duddon ... 82 NY 2398
River Dudwell ... 29 TQ 6824
River Dulnain ... 117 NH 8419
River Dyke ... 118 NC 8547
River E ... 116 NH 5413
River Eamont ... 83 NY 4725
River Earn (Tays.) ... 107 NN 7821
River Earn (Tays.) ... 108 NN 9318
River East Allen ... 83 NY 8354
River Eau ... 72 SK 9097
River Ebble ... 26 SU 1126
River Eden (Cumbr.) ... 89 NY 3462
River Eden (Cumbr.) ... 83 NY 5342
River Eden (Cumbr.) ... 83 NY 6241
River Eden (Fife) ... 103 NO 3209
River Eden (Kent) ... 29 TQ 4645
River Ehen ... 82 NY 0213
River Eidart ... 117 NN 9193
River Einig ... 127 NH 3799
River Elchaig ... 114 NG 9628
River Ellen ... 82 NY 1541
River Elwy ... 58 SH 9972
River Enrick ... 116 NH 3526
River Erewash ... 61 SK 4743
River Ericht ... 107 NN 5161
River Erme ... 21 SX 6355
River Erradale ... 123 NG 7669
River Esk (Cumbr.) ... 82 NY 3289
River Esk (Cumbr.) ... 82 SD 1297
River Esk (Lothian) ... 103 NT 3470
River Esk (N Yorks.) ... 85 NZ 7407
River Eskin ... 116 NH 6110
River Esragan ... 106 NM 9835
River Etherow ... 70 SJ 9791
River Evelix ... 129 NH 7293
River Evenlode ... 47 SP 3220
River Ewe ... 126 NG 8679
River Exe (Devon) ... 23 SS 9409
River Exe (Devon) ... 21 SX 9882
River Eye ... 51 SK 8118
River Fal ... 19 SW 9246
River Falloch ... 107 NN 3723
River Farigaig ... 116 NH 5625
River Farrar ... 116 NH 3339
River Feehlin ... 116 NH 5012
River Feshie ... 117 NN 8522
River Fiag ... 133 NC 4524
River Fiddich ... 121 NJ 3232
River Findhorn ... 117 NH 8839
River Finnan ... 114 NM 9182
River Fleet ... 129 NH 7301
River Forsa ... 105 NM 6041
River Forth ... 101 NS 6496
River Fothless ... 109 SE 7839
River Fowey ... 19 SX 0962
River Foyers ... 116 NH 4917
River Freshney ... 75 TA 2308

River Frome (Avon) ... 33 ST 6376
River Frome (Dorset) ... 25 SY 7490
River Frome (Here. and Worc.) ... 49 SO 6544
River Frome (Somer.) ... 33 ST 7643
River Fyne ... 106 NN 2215
River Gairn ... 117 NJ 2501
River Garnock ... 93 NS 3050
River Garry (Highld.) ... 115 NH 1400
River Garry (Tays.) ... 107 NN 7668
River Gaur ... 107 NN 4857
River Gele ... 67 SH 9476
River Gelt ... 83 NY 5654
River Gilpin ... 83 SD 4687
River Gipping ... 55 TM 1152
River Glass (Highld.) ... 115 NH 3734
River Glass (Highld.) ... 128 NH 5666
River Glass (I. of M.) ... 76 SC 3680
River Glaven ... 64 TG 0440
River Glen (Lincs.) ... 62 TF 0711
River Glen (Lincs.) ... 63 TF 2427
River Glen (Northum.) ... 97 NT 9030
River Glenderamackin ... 82 NY 3426
River Gloy ... 115 NN 2588
River Glyme ... 47 SP 4418
River Gour ... 106 NM 9364
River Gowy ... 69 SJ 4864
River Granta ... 53 TL 5051
River Granta or Cam ... 53 TL 5231
River Great Ouse (Bucks.) ... 51 SP 5936
River Great Ouse (Bucks.) ... 52 SP 8646
River Great Ouse or Old West River (Cambs.) ... 53 TL 4671
River Greta (Cumbr.) ... 77 NY 2924
River Greta (Durham) ... 84 NZ 0511
River Greta (Lancs.) ... 77 SD 6271
River Grudie (Highld.) ... 126 NG 9666
River Grudie (Highld.) ... 127 NH 2964
River Gryfe ... 101 NS 3666
River Gwash ... 62 SK 8906
River Hamble ... 27 SU 5214
River Hart ... 36 TL 7659
River Haultin ... 123 NG 4451
River Hayle ... 18 SW 5622
Riverhead ... 29 TQ 5156
River Helmsdale ... 134 NC 8925
River Hepste ... 41 SN 9612
River Hertford ... 85 TA 0281
River Hindburn ... 77 SD 6366
River Hinnisdal ... 123 NG 4158
River Hiz ... 52 TL 1833
River Hodder ... 77 SD 7050
River Hope ... 133 NC 4760
River Hull ... 74 TA 0646
River Humber ... 75 TA 2316
River Hurich ... 111 NM 8267
River Idle ... 72 SK 7497
River Inny ... 20 SX 2383
River Inver ... 132 NC 1123
River Irt ... 82 NY 1000
River Irthing ... 90 NY 6469
River Irvine ... 93 NS 4737
River Irwell ... 69 SD 7913
River Isbourne ... 46 SP 0334
River Isis or Thames (Oxon.) ... 47 SP 4302
River Isis or Thames (Wilts.) ... 47 SU 1596
River Isla (Grampn.) ... 121 NJ 4046
River Isla (Tays.) ... 108 NO 1738
River Isla (Tays.) ... 117 NO 1974
River Isla (Tays.) ... 108 NO 2357
River Isle ... 24 ST 3722
River Itchen (Hants.) ... 27 SU 4616
River Itchen (Warw.) ... 50 SP 4062
River Ithon ... 57 SO 1066
River Ivel ... 52 TL 1938
River Kanaird ... 127 NC 1602
River Keekle ... 82 NY 0118
River Keer ... 77 SD 5472
River Kelvin ... 101 NS 6775
River Kenn (Avon) ... 33 ST 4269
River Kenn (Devon.) ... 21 SX 9385
River Kennet (Berks.) ... 34 SU 3669
River Kennet (Wilts.) ... 34 SU 2369
River Kennett (Cambs.) ... 54 TL 6969
River Kent (Cumbr.) ... 83 NY 4502
River Kent (Cumbr.) ... 77 SD 5086
River Kerry ... 123 NG 8371
River Kiachnish ... 106 NN 0969
River Killin ... 134 NH 5308
River Kingie ... 114 NN 0197
River Kirkaig ... 132 NC 1018
River Knaik ... 101 NN 8012
River Kym ... 52 TL 1066
River Lael ... 127 NH 2284
River Laggan ... 98 NR 3156
River Làir ... 126 NG 9850
River Lambourn ... 34 SU 4370
River Lark ... 54 TL 6476
River Laver ... 78 SE 2072
River Laxay ... 131 NB 3022
River Laxdale ... 131 NB 3935
River Laxford ... 132 NC 2545
River Leach ... 47 SP 1708
River Leadon ... 46 SO 7628
River Lea ... 37 TL 4568
River Lea or Lee (Gtr London) ... 37 TQ 3695
River Lea or Lee (Herts.) ... 37 TL 2609
River Lednock ... 107 NN 7625
River Lee ... 61 SK 5450
River Lee or Lea (Gtr London) ... 37 TQ 3695
River Lee or Lea (Herts.) ... 37 TL 2609
River Len ... 30 TQ 8054
River Leven (Fife) ... 103 NO 2601
River Leven (Highld.) ... 106 NN 2160
River Leven (N Yorks.) ... 85 NZ 4906
River Leven (Strath.) ... 101 NS 5301
River Lew ... 23 SS 5301
River Liever ... 100 NM 8907
River Ling ... 114 NG 9834
River Livet ... 117 NJ 2523
River Liza ... 82 NY 1313
River Loanan ... 132 NC 2418
River Lochay ... 107 NN 5037
River Lochy (Highld.) ... 115 NN 1581
River Lochy (Highld.) ... 106 NN 2629
River Lochy (Strath.) ... 106 NN 2568
River Loddon ... 36 SU 7568
River Lodon ... 46 SO 6152
River Lossie (Grampn.) ... 129 NJ 1045
River Lossie (Grampn.) ... 121 NJ 2564
River Lostock ... 69 SD 5119
River Loughor ... 41 SN 6007
River Lovat or Ouzel ... 52 SP 8831
River Lowther ... 83 NY 5120
River Loxley ... 71 SK 2989
River Loy ... 115 NN 1183
River Loyne ... 115 NH 0706
River Lugg (Here. and Worc.) ... 45 SO 5263
River Lugg (Powys) ... 48 SO 3264
River Luineag ... 117 NH 9209
River Lune (Cumbr.) ... 83 NY 6105
River Lune (Durham) ... 84 NY 8720
River Lune (Lancs.) ... 77 SD 3653
River Lune (Lancs.) ... 84 SD 6075
River Lydden ... 25 ST 7208
River Lyne ... 89 NY 4871
River Lyon ... 107 NN 6147
River Lyvennet ... 83 NY 6122
River Mallie ... 115 NN 0687
River Manifold ... 60 SK 1054
River Mashie ... 116 NN 5787
River Maun ... 71 SK 6166

River Mease

Rubha Sgorr an t-Snidhe

River Mease	60	SK 2711
River Meden	71	SK 5565
River Medina	27	SZ 5094
River Medway	29	TQ 6446
River Meig	127	NH 3655
River Meoble	111	NM 7986
River Meon	27	SU 5407
River Mersey (Gtr Mches.)	69	SJ 8092
River Mersey (Mers.)	68	SJ 3684
River Misbourne	36	SU 9696
River Mite	82	SD 0998
River Moidart	111	NM 7471
River Mole (Devon)	23	SS 7327
River Mole (Surrey)	37	TQ 1263
River Mole (Surrey)	28	TQ 2347
River Monnow (Afon Mynwy)	45	SO 4716
River Moriston	115	NH 3414
River Mudale	133	NC 5135
River Muick	118	NO 3389
River Nadder	26	SU 0130
River Nairn	129	NH 7947
River Nar	64	TF 6812
River Naver	134	NC 7255
River Neath	41	SN 9013
River Neb	76	SC 2883
River Nene (Cambs.)	63	TL 2398
River Nene (Northants.)	51	SP 5959
River Nene (Northants.)	52	TL 0385
River Nene (Old Course) (Cambs.)	53	TL 3291
River Ness	116	NH 6139
River Nethan	94	NS 7835
River Nethy	117	NJ 0214
River Nevis	106	NN 1370
River Nidd	79	SE 3357
River Nith	88	NS 7012
River Noe	70	SK 1485
River North Esk (Lothian)	103	NT 2158
River North Esk (Tays.)	118	NO 5078
River North Tyne	90	NY 6887
River Ock	47	SU 4095
River Oich	115	NH 3405
River Okement	23	SS 5901
River Orchy	106	NN 2534
River Ore (Fife)	103	NT 2796
River Ore (Suff.)	55	TM 3845
River Orrin	128	NH 4250
River Orwell	55	TM 2138
River Ose	122	NG 3442
River Ossian	107	NN 4172
River Otter	24	SY 0996
River Ottery	20	SX 2788
River Oude	105	NM 8415
River Ouse (E Susx)	29	TQ 4208
River Ouse (Norf.)	64	TF 5903
River Ouse (N Yorks.)	79	SE 4959
River Ouzel or Lovat	52	SP 8831
River Oykel	127	NC 3503
River Pang	36	SU 6173
River Pant	54	TL 6631
River Parrett (Somer.)	32	ST 2842
River Parrett (Somer.)	24	ST 3928
River Pattack	116	NN 5483
River Pean	114	NM 9290
River Penk	59	SJ 8905
River Perry	58	SJ 3828
River Petteril	83	NY 4839
River Piddle or Trent	25	SY 8392
River Plym	21	SX 5464
River Polly	132	NC 0812
River Pont	91	NZ 1676
River Poulter	71	SK 6475
River Quaich	107	NN 7939
River Quin	53	TL 3927
River Ray (Oxon.)	47	SP 5917
River Ray (Wilts.)	34	SU 1191
River Rea	49	SO 6673
River Rede	90	NY 7899
River Rha	123	NG 4065
River Rhee or Cam	53	TL 3647
River Rhiw	58	SJ 1102
River Rib	37	TL 3818
River Ribble	77	SD 6434
River Riccal	79	SE 6382
River Roach	38	TQ 9592
River Roch	69	SD 8712
River Roden	59	SJ 5915
River Roding	37	TQ 4294
River Romesdal	123	NG 4354
River Rother (E Susx)	29	TQ 6125
River Rother (Hants.)	27	SU 7625
River Rother (W Susx)	28	SU 9420
River Roy	115	NN 3088
River Rue	100	NS 0188
River Runie	127	NC 1302
River Rye	79	SE 5784
River Ryton	71	SK 6185
River Sand	126	NG 7779
River Sark	89	NY 3273
River Scaddle	106	NM 9567
River Seaton	20	SX 2959
River Sence (Leic.)	60	SK 3503
River Sence (Leic.)	61	SP 5997
River Seph	85	SE 5691
River Seven	80	SE 7380
River Severn (Avon)	33	ST 5992
River Severn (Here. and Worc.)	49	SO 8448
River Severn (Powys)	58	SJ 2612
River Severn (Powys)	57	SO 0890
River Severn (Shrops.)	59	SJ 6901
River Sgitheach	128	NH 5765
River Sheaf	71	SK 3282
River Shiel	114	NG 9813
River Shin	128	NH 5798
River Shira	106	NN 1518
River Skerne	84	NZ 3026
River Skinsdale	134	NC 7518
River Skirfare	78	SD 8875
River Slea	62	TF 1149
River Sligachan	123	NG 4927
River Snizort	123	NG 4244
River Soar (Leic.)	61	SP 5599
River Soar (Notts.)	61	SK 4925
River Solva	42	SM 8527
River Sorn	98	NR 3563
River South Esk (Lothian)	103	NT 3262
River South Esk (Tays.)	109	NO 3471
River South Tyne	83	NY 6854
River Sow	59	SJ 8628
River Sowe	50	SP 3777
River Spean	115	NN 2481
River Spey (Grampn.)	120	NJ 3050
River Spey (Highld.)	117	NH 9315
River Spey (Highld.)	116	NN 5094
River Sprint	83	NY 4903
River Stiffkey	64	TF 9233
River Stinchar	86	NX 2291
River Stort	53	TL 4829
River Stour (Dorset)	25	ST 7619
River Stour (Dorset)	26	SZ 1096
River Stour (Essex)	54	TL 9233
River Stour (Here. and Worc.)	49	SO 8278
River Stour (Kent)	31	TR 2763
River Stour (Warw.)	50	SP 2249
River Strae	106	NN 1833
River Strathy	134	NC 8051
River Swale	84	SE 2796
River Swere	47	SP 4733
River Swift	51	SP 5283
River Taff	41	ST 1578
River Tale	24	ST 0702
River Tamar	20	SX 3682
River Tame (Gtr Mches.)	69	SJ 9092
River Tame (Staffs.)	60	SK 1807
River Tame (Warw.)	50	SP 2091
River Tarbert	106	NM 9259
River Tarff	115	NH 3805
River Tavy	20	SX 4765
River Taw (Devon)	23	SS 6614
River Tawe (W Glam.)	40	SS 6799
River Tay (Tays.)	108	NO 1138
River Tay (Tays.)	108	NO 1221
River Tees (Cumbr. - Durham)	83	NY 7733
River Tees (Durham - N Yorks.)	84	NZ 2711
River Teign	21	SX 7689
River Teith	101	NN 6306
River Teme (Here. and Worc.)	49	SO 7067
River Teme (Shrops.)	48	SO 3073
River Ter	38	TL 7714
River Tern	59	SJ 7037
River Test	26	SU 3637
River Teviot	96	NT 6424
River Thames (Essex - Kent)	37	TQ 5577
River Thames (Oxon.)	35	SU 5985
River Thames or Isis (Oxon.)	47	SP 4302
River Thames or Isis (Wilts.)	47	SU 1596
River Thet	54	TL 9584
River Thrushel	20	SX 4789
River Thurne	65	TG 4017
River Thurso	135	ND 1055
River Tiddy	20	SX 3064
River Til (Beds.)	52	TL 0268
River Till (Lincs.)	72	SK 9077
River Till (Northum.)	97	NT 9533
River Tillingham	30	TQ 8720
River Tilt	117	NN 9575
River Tirry	133	NC 5318
River Tone	24	ST 3227
River Torne	71	SE 6502
River Torridge	23	SS 5509
River Torridon	126	NG 9255
River Toscaig	123	NG 7438
River Tove	51	SP 7746
River Traligill	132	NC 2720
River Trent (Humbs.)	74	SE 8619
River Trent (Notts.)	61	SK 6239
River Trent (Staffs.)	59	SJ 9231
River Trent or Piddle (Dorset)	25	SY 8392
River Tromie	116	NN 7694
River Truim	116	NN 6485
River Tud	65	TG 0812
River Tummel (Tays.)	107	NN 7459
River Tummel (Tays.)	108	NN 9555
River Turret	115	NN 3394
River Tweed (Borders)	95	NT 0722
River Tweed (Borders)	96	NT 4235
River Tweed (Borders)	96	NT 7737
River Tyne (Lothian)	103	NT 5474
River Tyne (Northum.)	91	NZ 0361
River Ugie	121	NK 0849
River Ure (N Yorks.)	78	SE 2085
River Ure (N Yorks.)	79	SE 4662
River Urie	121	NJ 6629
River Usk	45	SO 2515
River Ver	37	TL 1209
River Waldon	22	SS 3610
River Wampool	82	NY 2454
River Wansbeck	91	NZ 1285
River Washburn	78	SE 1458
River Waveney	55	TM 2381
River Waver	82	NY 1850
River Wear	84	NZ 1134
River Weaver	69	SJ 5877
River Welland (Lincs.)	63	TF 2828
River Welland (Northants.)	62	SP 8894
River Wenning	77	SD 7167
River Wensum	64	TG 0518
River Went	71	SE 5917
River West Allen	83	NY 7854
River Wey (Hants.)	35	SU 7742
River Wey (Surrey)	28	TQ 0557
River Wharfe	78	SE 0262
River Wheelock	69	SJ 7063
River Whitelake	33	ST 5340
River Windrush	47	SP 1817
River Winster	77	SD 4185
River Wiske	85	SE 3497
River Wissey	64	TF 8401
River Witham (Lincs.)	62	SK 9328
River Witham (Lincs.)	72	SK 9463
River Witham (Lincs.)	63	TF 2548
River Wolf	20	SX 4290
River Worfe	59	SO 7698
River Worth	78	SE 0137
River Wreake	61	SK 6616
River Wye (Afon Gwy) (Here. and Worc.)	45	SO 3045
River Wye (Derby.)	70	SK 2069
River Wylye	26	SU 0536
River Wyre	77	SD 4341
River Wyre	77	SD 5553
River Yar	27	SZ 6186
River Yare	65	TG 1108
River Yarrow	69	SD 5117
River Yarty	24	ST 2505
River Yealm	21	SX 6056
River Yeo (Avon)	33	ST 4463
River Yeo (Devon)	23	SS 7306
River Yeo (Devon)	23	SS 7726
River Yeo (Somer.)	25	ST 5223
River Ythan	121	NJ 8636
Rivington	69	SD 6214
Riv, The (sbk.)	139	HY 6847
Rivvalee (pt.)	143	HP 4805
Roade	51	SP 7551
Roadmeetings	95	NS 8649
Roadside	135	ND 1560
Roadside of Kinneff	119	NO 8476
Road, The (chan.)	18	SV 8912
Roadwater	32	ST 0238
Roag	122	NG 2744
Roa Island	76	SD 2364
Roana Bay	137	HY 5905
Roan Fell	89	NY 4592
Roan Head	136	ND 3896
Roath	41	ST 1978
Roberton (Borders)	89	NT 4314
Roberton (Strath.)	95	NS 9428
Roberton Law	95	NS 9129
Robertsbridge	29	TQ 7323
Roberttown	78	SE 1922
Robeston Cross	42	SM 8809
Robeston Wathen	42	SN 0815
Robin Hood's Bay	81	NZ 9505
Roborough	23	SS 5717
Rob Roy's Cave	100	NN 3310
Rob Roy's House	106	NN 1516
Roby Mill	69	SD 5106
Rocester	60	SK 1039
Roch	42	SM 8821
Rochdale	69	SD 8913
Rochdale Canal (Gtr Mches.)	70	SD 9518
Rochdale Canal (W Yorks.)	69	SD 9420
Roche	19	SW 9860
Roche Abbey (ant.)	71	SK 5489
Rochester (Kent)	30	TQ 7467
Rochester (Northum.)	90	NY 8397
Rochester Airport	30	TQ 7464
Rochford (Essex)	38	TQ 8790
Rochford (Here. and Worc.)	49	SO 6268
Rock (Corn.)	19	SW 9475
Rock (Here. and Worc.)	49	SO 7371
Rock (Northum.)	91	NU 2020
Rockbeare	24	SY 0195
Rockbourne	26	SU 1118
Rockbourne Down	26	SU 1020
Rockcliffe (Cumbr.)	89	NY 3561
Rockcliffe (Dumf. and Galwy.)	87	NX 8553
Rocken End	27	SZ 4875
Rock Ferry	68	SJ 3386
Rockfield (Gwent)	45	SO 4814
Rockfield (Highld.)	129	NH 9282
Rockham Bay	22	SS 4546
Rockhampton	46	ST 6593
Rockingham	52	SP 8691
Rockingham Forest	52	SP 9490
Rockland All Saints	64	TL 9896
Rockland St. Mary	65	TG 3104
Rockland St. Peter	64	TL 9897
Rockley	34	SU 1571
Rockwell End	36	SU 7988
Rodbourne	34	ST 9383
Rodd	48	SO 3162
Roddam	91	NU 0220
Rodden	25	SY 6184
Rode	33	ST 8053
Rode Heath (Ches.)	59	SJ 8056
Rodeheath (Ches.)	69	SJ 8766
Rodel	124	NG 0483
Roden	59	SJ 5716
Rodhuish	32	ST 0139
Rodings, The (dist.)	37	TL 5813
Rodington	59	SJ 5814
Rodley	46	SO 7411
Rodmarton	46	ST 9397
Rodmell	29	TQ 4106
Rodmersham	30	TQ 9261
Rodney Stoke	33	ST 4849
Rodono Hotel	95	NT 2321
Rodsley	60	SK 2040
Roecliffe	79	SE 3765
Roehampton	37	TQ 2373
Roe Ness	141	HU 3242
Roer Water	142	HU 3386
Roesound	141	HU 3465
Roewen	67	SH 7571
Roffey	28	TQ 1931
Rogan's Seat (mt.)	84	NY 9203
Rogart	129	NC 7303
Rogart Halt	129	NC 7202
Rogate	27	SU 8023
Roger Sand	63	TF 4841
Rogerstone	32	ST 2688
Rogerton	94	NS 6256
Rogiet	33	ST 4587
Roineabhal (mt.)	124	NG 0486
Roineval (Island of Skye) (mt.)	123	NG 4135
Roineval (Isle of Lewis) (mt.)	131	NB 2321
Roinn a' Bhuic	131	NB 4057
Rois-Bheinn	111	NM 7577
Roker	91	NZ 4059
Rollesby	65	TG 4415
Rolleston (Leic.)	61	SK 7300
Rolleston (Notts.)	61	SK 7452
Rolleston (Staffs.)	60	SK 2327
Rolston	75	TA 2145
Rolvenden	30	TQ 8431
Rolvenden Layne	30	TQ 8530
Romaldkirk	84	NY 9921
Romanby	85	SE 3693
Roman Gold Mines (ant.)	44	SN 6740
Romannobridge	95	NT 1547
Roman Ridge (ant.)	79	SE 4235
Roman River	39	TL 9920
Roman Road (ant.)	45	SO 4137
Romansleigh	23	SS 7220
Roman Steps	67	SH 6530
Rombalds Moor	78	SE 0845
Romford	37	TQ 5188
Romiley	69	SJ 9390
Romney Marsh	31	TR 0430
Romney Sands	31	TR 0823
Romsey	26	SU 3521
Romsley (Here. and Worc.)	50	SO 9679
Romsley (Shrops.)	49	SO 7883
Rona (is.)	130	HW 8132
Ronachan House	92	NR 7455
Ronachan Point	92	NR 7455
Ronague	76	SC 2472
Ronas Hill	142	HU 3083
Ronas Voe	142	HU 2881
Rona, The (chan.)	141	HU 3260
Ronay	124	NF 8955
Roneval (South Uist) (mt.)	112	NF 8114
Rooken Edge	90	NY 7895
Rookhope	84	NY 9342
Rookley	27	SZ 5084
Rooks Bridge	32	ST 3752
Roos	75	TA 2830
Roosebeck	76	SD 2568
Roos Wick	139	HY 6545
Rootpark	95	NS 9554
Ropley	27	SU 6431
Ropley Dean	27	SU 6331
Ropsley	62	SK 9834
Rora	121	NK 0650
Rora Head	136	ND 1799
Rora Moss	121	NK 0451
Rorandle	119	NJ 6518
Rorrington	58	SJ 3000
Rosall Point	77	SD 3147
Rosarie Forest	121	NJ 3548
Rose	18	SW 7754
Roseacre	77	SD 4336
Rose Ash	23	SS 7821
Rosebank	95	NS 8049
Rosebery Resr.	96	NT 3056
Rosebrough	97	NU 1326
Rose Cottage	111	NM 5369
Rosedale	80	SE 7295
Rosedale Abbey	80	SE 7296
Rosedale Moor	80	SE 7199
Roseden	97	NU 0321
Rosefield	129	NH 8552
Rosehaugh House	128	NH 6755
Rosehearty	121	NJ 9367
Rosehill	59	SJ 6630
Roseisle	129	NJ 1367
Roseisle Forest	129	NJ 1266
Rosemarket	42	SM 9508
Rosemarkie	129	NH 7357
Rosemarkie Bay	129	NH 7457
Rosemary Lane	24	ST 1514
Rosemount (Strath.)	93	NS 3729
Rosemount (Tays.)	108	NO 2043
Rosemullion Head	19	SW 7928
Rosenannon	19	SW 9566
Rose Ness	137	ND 5298
Rosewell	103	NT 2862
Roseworthy	18	SW 6139
Rosgill	83	NY 5316
Roshven	111	NM 7078
Rosinish (is.)	112	NL 6187
Roskhill	122	NG 2745
Rosley	82	NY 3245
Roslin	103	NT 2663
Rosliston	60	SK 2416
Rosneath	100	NS 2583
Rosneath Point	100	NS 2780
Ross (Dumf. and Galwy.)	87	NX 6444
Ross (Northum.)	97	NU 1336
Ross (Tays.)	107	NN 7621
Rossdhu House	101	NS 3689
Rossett	68	SJ 3657
Rossie Farm School	109	NO 6653
Rossie Moor	109	NO 6554
Rossie Ochill	102	NO 0812
Rossie Priory	108	NO 2830
Rossington	71	SK 6298
Rossinish	124	NF 8653
Rosskeen	128	NH 6869
Rossland	101	NS 4370
Ross of Mull (dist.)	105	NM 3919
Ross-on-Wye	45	SO 6024
Ross Priory	101	NS 4187
Roster	135	ND 2639
Rostherne	69	SJ 7483
Rosthwaite	82	NY 2514
Roston	60	SK 1241
Rosyth	102	NT 1183
Rothbury	91	NU 0601
Rothbury Forest	91	NU 0600
Rotherby	61	SK 6716
Rotherfield	29	TQ 5529
Rotherfield Greys	36	SU 7282
Rotherfield Peppard	36	SU 7081
Rotherham	71	SK 4492
Rother Levels	30	TQ 8725
Rothersthorpe	51	SP 7156
Rotherwick	35	SU 7156
Rothes	120	NJ 2749
Rothesay	100	NS 0864
Rothesay Bay	100	NS 0865
Rothiebrisbane	121	NJ 7437
Rothiemurchus	117	NH 9206
Rothienorman	121	NJ 7235
Rothiesholm	137	HY 6123
Rothiesholm Head	137	HY 6021
Rothley	61	SK 5812
Rothley Lakes	91	NZ 0490
Rothmaise	121	NJ 6832
Rothwell (Lincs.)	75	TF 1599
Rothwell (Northants.)	52	SP 8181
Rothwell (W Yorks.)	79	SE 3428
Rotsea	81	TA 0651
Rottal	109	NO 3769
Rottingdean	29	TQ 3702
Rottington	82	NX 9613
Roud	27	SZ 5280
Rougham	64	TF 8320
Rougham Green	54	TL 9061
Roughburn	115	NN 3781
Rough Close	59	SJ 9239
Rough Common	31	TR 1359
Rough Hill	93	NS 5445
Rough Island	87	NX 8453
Roughlee	78	SD 8440
Roughley	60	SP 1399
Rough Pike	90	NY 6285
Roughrigg Resr.	101	NS 8164
Roughsike	90	NY 5275
Roughton (Lincs.)	73	TF 2364
Roughton (Norf.)	65	TG 2136
Roughton (Shrops.)	59	SO 7594
Rough Tor (Corn.)	19	SX 1480
Rough Tor (Devon)	21	SX 6079
Rough Tower	55	TM 3928
Round Fell	87	NX 5372
Roundhay	79	SE 3235
Round Hill (Cumbr.)	83	NY 7336
Round Hill (Grampn.)	121	NJ 3427
Round Hill (N Yorks.)	78	SE 1253
Roundhill Resr.	78	SE 1476
Round Island	18	SV 9017
Round Loch of the Dungeon	87	NX 4684
Roundstreet Common	28	TQ 0528
Roundway	34	SU 0163
Roundway Hill	34	SU 0164
Rounton	85	NZ 4103
Rousay	138	HY 4030
Rousay Sound	136	HY 4529
Rousdon	24	SY 2990
Rous Lench	50	SP 0153
Routenburn	100	NS 1961
Routh	74	TA 0842
Row (Corn.)	19	SX 0976
Row (Cumbr.)	83	SD 4589
Rowallan Castle (ant.)	93	NS 4342
Rowanburn	89	NY 4177
Rowardennan Forest	101	NS 3896
Rowardennan Lodge	101	NS 3699
Rowde	34	ST 9762
Rowe Ditch (ant.)	45	SO 3859
Rowfoot	90	NY 6860
Row Head	136	HY 2218
Rowhedge	39	TM 0221
Rowhook	28	TQ 1234
Rowington	50	SP 2069
Rowland	70	SK 2072
Rowland's Castle	27	SU 7310
Rowland's Gill	91	NZ 1658
Rowledge	35	SU 8243
Rowley (Devon)	23	SS 7219
Rowley (Humbs.)	74	SE 9732
Rowley (Shrops.)	58	SJ 3006
Rowley Regis	50	SO 9787
Rowlstone	45	SO 3727
Rowly	28	TQ 0441
Rowney Green	50	SP 0471
Rownhams	26	SU 3816
Rowsham	36	SP 8518
Rowsley	71	SK 2566
Rowston	62	TF 0856
Rowton (Ches.)	68	SJ 4464
Rowton (Shrops.)	59	SJ 6119
Rowton Castle (ant.)	58	SJ 3712
Roxburgh	96	NT 6930
Roxby (Humbs.)	74	SE 9217
Roxby (N Yorks.)	85	NZ 7616
Roxby Beck	85	NZ 7415
Roxby High Moor	85	NZ 7512
Roxton	52	TL 1554
Roxwell	38	TL 6408
Royal British Legion Village	29	TQ 7257
Royal Forest	106	NN 2053
Royal Greenwich Observatory	29	TQ 6410
Royal Leamington Spa	50	SP 3166
Royal Military Canal	31	TR 0133
Royal Sovereign (lightship)	29	TV 7393
Royal Tunbridge Wells	29	TQ 5839
Roybridge	115	NN 2781
Roydon (Essex)	37	TL 4009
Roydon (Norf.)	64	TF 7022
Roydon (Norf.)	55	TM 0980
Royl Field (mt.)	141	HU 3928
Royston (Herts.)	53	TL 3541
Royston (S Yorks.)	71	SE 3611
Royton	69	SD 9207
Ruabon	58	SJ 3043
Ruabon Mountain	58	SJ 2446
Ruadh Sgeir	99	NR 7292
Ruadh-stac Mór	126	NG 9561
Ruaig	104	NM 0647
Ruan Lanihorne	19	SW 8942
Ruan Minor	18	SW 7115
Ruardean	45	SO 6117
Ruardean Woodside	45	SO 6216
Rubers Law	90	NT 5715
Rubery	50	SO 9777
Rubha a Ghraineig	110	NM 1555
Rubha Aird Druimnich	111	NM 5772
Rubha Airigh Bheirg	92	NR 8848
Rubha a'Mhail	98	NR 4872
Rubha a'Mharaiche	92	NR 5812
Rubha an Aird	110	NM 3855
Rubha an Daraich	123	NG 7909
Rubha an Dùine	124	NF 9771
Rubha an Fhasaidh	111	NM 4487
Rubha an Ridire	105	NM 7340
Rubha Ard Slisneach	123	NG 7409
Rubha Ardvule	112	NF 7029
Rubha Beag	126	NG 8997
Rubh' a'Bhacain	99	NR 7096
Rubh' a' Bhaid Bheithe	106	NN 0259
Rubh' a' Bhàigh Uaine	131	NB 4229
Rubh' a' Bhaile Fo Thuath	124	NF 9087
Rubh' a' Bhaird	125	NB 3101
Rubha Bhilidh	112	NF 8632
Rubh' a' Bhinnein	110	NM 2263
Rubh' a' Bhiogair	131	NB 3451
Rubha Bhlanisgaidh	131	NB 3755
Rubha Bhocaig	125	NG 1891
Rubha Bhoisnis	124	NF 8880
Rubha Bholsa	98	NR 3778
Rubha Bhrollum	125	NB 3202
Rubha Bolum	112	NF 8328
Rubha Buidhe	123	NG 7812
Rubha Cam nan Gall	124	NF 8847
Rubha Caol	131	NB 2447
Rubha Carrach	111	NM 4670
Rubh' a'Chàirn Bhàin	92	NR 6653
Rubh' a'Chamais	98	NR 5978
Rubh' a'Chaoil	104	NM 3346
Rubha Charn nan Cearc	111	NG 5503
Rubha Chlachan	92	NR 6106
Rubh' a'Chnaip	105	NM 7810
Rubh' a' Choin	132	NC 0314
Rubha Chràiginis	104	NL 9245
Rubh' a'Chrois-aoinidh	98	NR 5080
Rubha Chuaig	123	NG 6959
Rubha Còigeach	132	NB 9818
Rubha Crago	125	NG 2397
Rubha Creagan Dubha	92	NR 9352
Rubha Dubh (Colonsay)	98	NR 3991
Rubha Dubh (Island of Mull)	105	NM 5621
Rubha Dubh (Tiree)	104	NM 0948
Rubha Dubh Tighary	124	NF 7072
Rubha Dùin Bhàin	92	NR 5914
Rubha Fàsachd	110	NM 1652
Rubha Garbh àird	105	NM 8736
Rubha Garbh-ard	99	NR 7896
Rubh'a'Geodha	98	NR 4399
Rubha Ghlamraidh	98	NR 1758
Rubha Hellisdale	112	NF 8430
Rubha Hogh	110	NM 1759
Rubha Hunish	125	NG 4077
Rubha Iosal	131	NB 4216
Rubh' Aird an Fheidh	111	NM 6375
Rubh' Aird an t-Sionnaich	132	NC 1443
Rubh' Aird-mhicheil	112	NF 7233
Rubh' Aird na Sgitheich	98	NR 4779
Rubha Lamanais	98	NR 2068
Rubha Langanes	110	NG 2406
Rubha Leacach	124	NB 0107
Rubha Leathan	100	NR 9261
Rubha Leathann	131	NB 3654
Rubha Leumair	132	NC 0426
Rubha Màs a' Chnuic	124	NF 9794
Rubha Meall na Hoe	112	NF 8217
Rubh a'Mhail	98	NR 4279
Rubha Mhic Gille-mhicheil	124	NF 9363
Rubh' a' Mhill Dheirg	132	NC 0228
Rubh' a' Mhucard	132	NC 1637
Rubha Mór (Barra)	112	NL 6997
Rubha Mór (Coll, Strath.)	110	NM 2464
Rubha Mór (Highld.)	132	NB 9814
Rubha Mór (Highld.)	126	NG 8696
Rubha Mór (Highld.)	106	NM 9655
Rubha Mór (Island of Mull)	105	NM 5844
Rubha Mór (Islay)	98	NR 2948
Rubha na Brèige	132	NC 0519
Rubha na Crannaig	111	NM 4984
Rubha na Creige Móire (Isle of Lewis)	131	NB 4217
Rubha na Creige Móire (South Uist)	112	NF 8320
Rubha na Faing	98	NR 1553
Rubha na Faing Móire	111	NM 6477
Rubha na Fearn	123	NG 7261
Rubha na Gainmhich	98	NR 4346
Rubha na Greine	131	NB 5633
Rubha na h-Airde	99	NR 7083
Rubha na h-Airde Glaise	123	NG 5145
Rubha na h-Airde Uinnsinn	111	NM 8752
Rubha na h-Aiseig	123	NG 4476
Rubha na h-Easgainne	123	NG 5211
Rubha na h-Ordaig	112	NF 8414
Rubha na h-Uamha	105	NM 4028
Rubha na h-Uamha-sàile	98	NR 6094
Rubha na' Leac	123	NG 5938
Rubha na Leacaig	132	NC 2055
Rubha nam Bàirneach	131	NB 5531
Rubha nam Bàrr	99	NR 7491
Rubha nam Bràithrean	105	NM 4317
Rubha nam Brathairean	123	NG 5262
Rubha na Mèise Bàine	98	NR 3341
Rubha nam Faoilean	105	NM 6704
Rubha nam Maol Móra	104	NM 3316
Rubha nam Meirleach	110	NM 3691
Rubha nam Plèac	124	NF 9467
Rubha nan Cearc	104	NM 3225
Rubha nan Clach	122	NG 3033
Rubha nan Còsan	132	NC 0734
Rubha nan Crann	98	NR 6181
Rubha nan Eun	112	NF 7307
Rubha nan Gall (Island of Mull)	111	NM 5056
Rubha nan Gall (Ulva)	105	NM 4141
Rubha nan Leacan	98	NR 3140
Rubha nan Oirean	110	NM 3551
Rubha nan Sasan	126	NG 8192
Rubha nan Sgarbh (Highld.)	129	NH 7087
Rubha nan Sgarbh (Strath.)	92	NR 8033
Rubha nan Totag	124	NB 0303
Rubha nan Tri Chlach	111	NM 4989
Rubha na Rodagrich	124	NF 8953
Rubha na Roinne	111	NG 4200
Rubha na Seann Charraige	104	NM 0445
Rubha na Stròine	104	NM 3642
Rubha na Tràille	98	NR 5162
Rubh' an Dùnain (Island of Skye)	122	NG 3816
Rubh' an Dùnain (Isle of Lewis)	131	NB 2448
Rubha Nead a' Gheòidh	104	NM 0946
Rubh' an Fhir Léithe	132	NC 1863
Rubh' an Teampuill	124	NF 9791
Rubh' an Tòrra Mhóir	123	NG 5333
Rubh' an t-Sàilein	98	NR 5082
Rubh' an t-Suibhein	104	NM 3645
Rubh 'Aoineadh Mhéinis	105	NM 6521
Rubha Port Bhiosd	104	NL 9648
Rubha Port na Caranean	111	NM 4298
Rubha Port Scolpaig	124	NF 7068
Rubha Quidnish	125	NG 1086
Rubha Raonuill	111	NM 7399
Rubha Raouill	124	NF 7166
Rubh' Ardalanish	104	NM 3516
Rubh' Ard na Bà	126	NG 8584
Rubha Réidh	126	NG 7391
Rubha Righinn	105	NM 7002
Rubh' Arisaig	111	NM 6184
Rubha Rodha	132	NC 0523
Rubha Romagi	124	NG 0396
Rubha Rossel	112	NF 8734
Rubha Ruadh (Highld.)	132	NC 1651
Rubha Ruadh (Highld.)	111	NG 8208
Rubha Seanach	105	NM 8025
Rubha Sgeirigin	124	NF 9998
Rubha Sgorr an t-Snidhe	110	NM 3493

Rubha Shamhnan Insir ... 110 NG 3704
Rubha Suisnish ... 123 NG 5815
Rubha Thormaid ... 133 NC 5467
Rubha Tràigh an Dùin ... 104 NM 0343
Rubh' Dubh ... 131 NB 5229
Rubh Fiart ... 105 NM 7835
Ru Chorachan ... 122 NG 3761
Ruckcroft ... 83 NY 5344
Ruckinge ... 31 TR 0233
Ruckland ... 73 TF 3378
Ruckley ... 59 SJ 5300
Ruddington ... 61 SK 5733
Ruddons Point ... 103 NO 4500
Rudge ... 33 ST 8252
Rudgeway ... 33 ST 6286
Rudgwick ... 28 TQ 0934
Rudhall ... 45 SO 6225
Rudland Rigg ... 85 SE 6495
Rudloe ... 33 ST 8470
Rudry ... 41 ST 1986
Rudston ... 81 TA 0967
Rudyard ... 71 SJ 9557
Rudyard Resr. ... 69 SJ 9459
Rue Point ... 76 NX 4003
Rueval (mt.) ... 124 NF 8253
Rufford ... 68 SD 4515
Rufforth ... 79 SE 5251
Rufus Stone (ant.) ... 26 SU 2612
Rugby ... 51 SP 5075
Rugeley ... 60 SK 0418
Ruilick ... 128 NH 5046
Ruinsival (mt.) ... 110 NM 3594
Ruisgarry ... 124 NF 9282
Ruishton ... 24 ST 2624
Ruislip ... 36 TQ 0987
Ruislip Common ... 36 TQ 0789
Rumble (is.) ... 141 HU 6060
Rumbling Bridge ... 102 NT 0199
Rumblings (is.) ... 143 HP 6019
Rumburgh ... 55 TM 3581
Rumford ... 19 SW 8970
Rumley Point ... 136 ND 4894
Rumney ... 41 ST 2179
Rumps Point ... 19 SW 9381
Rumsdale Water ... 134 NC 9840
Rumster Forest ... 135 ND 2038
Runcorn ... 69 SJ 5182
Runcton ... 27 SU 8802
Runcton Holme ... 64 TF 6109
Runfold ... 35 SU 8747
Runhall ... 64 TG 0507
Runham ... 65 TG 4610
Runnel Stone ... 18 SW 3720
Runnington ... 24 ST 1121
Runswick ... 85 NZ 8016
Runtaleave ... 108 NO 2867
Runwell ... 38 TQ 7494
Ruperra Castle ... 41 ST 2186
Rushall (Here. and Worc.) ... 46 SO 6434
Rushall (Norf.) ... 55 TM 1982
Rushall (Wilts.) ... 34 SU 1255
Rushall (W Mids.) ... 60 SK 0201
Rushbrooke ... 54 TL 8961
Rushbury ... 48 SO 5191
Rushden (Herts.) ... 53 TL 3031
Rushden (Northants.) ... 52 SP 9566
Rushford ... 54 TL 9281
Rush Green ... 37 TQ 5187
Rushlake Green ... 29 TQ 6218
Rushmere ... 55 TM 4987
Rushmere St. Andrew ... 55 TM 2046
Rushmoor ... 26 SU 8740
Rushmore House ... 26 ST 9518
Rushock ... 49 SO 8871
Rusholme ... 69 SJ 8494
Rushton (Ches.) ... 69 SJ 5863
Rushton (Northants.) ... 52 SP 8483
Rushton (Shrops.) ... 59 SJ 6008
Rushton Spencer ... 69 SJ 9363
Rushwick ... 49 SO 8353
Rushyford ... 84 NZ 2828
Rushy Knowe ... 90 NY 9299
Rusk Holm ... 138 HY 5136
Ruskie ... 101 NN 6200
Ruskington ... 62 TF 0850
Rusland ... 77 SD 3488
Rusper ... 28 TQ 2037
Ruspidge ... 46 SO 6512
Russaness Hill ... 141 HU 3749
Russell's Water ... 28 TQ 0502
Ruston Parva ... 81 TA 0661
Ruswarp ... 81 NZ 8809
Rutherford ... 96 NT 6530
Rutherglen ... 101 NS 6161
Ruthernbridge ... 19 SX 0166
Ruthin ... 68 SJ 1257
Ruthrieston ... 119 NJ 9204
Ruthven (Gramp.) ... 121 NJ 5046
Ruthven (Highld.) ... 116 NH 8133
Ruthven (Tays.) ... 108 NO 2848
Ruthven Barracks ... 116 NN 7699
Ruthven House ... 108 NO 3048
Ruthvoes ... 19 SW 9360
Ruthwell ... 89 NY 1067
Rutland Water ... 62 SK 9307
Rutupiae (ant.) ... 31 TR 3060
Ruyton-XI-Towns ... 58 SJ 3922
Ryal ... 91 NZ 0174
Ryal Fold ... 78 SD 6621
Ryall ... 24 SY 4094
Ryarsh ... 30 TQ 6659
Rydal ... 82 NY 3606
Rydal Fell ... 82 NY 3609
Rydal Water ... 82 NY 3606
Ryde ... 27 SZ 5992
Ryde Roads ... 27 SZ 5894
Ryder's Hill ... 21 SX 6569
Rye ... 30 TQ 9220
Rye Bay ... 31 TQ 9617
Rye Dale ... 79 SE 5982
Rye Foreign ... 30 TQ 8822
Rye Harbour ... 30 TQ 9419
Rye Water ... 93 NS 2752
Ryhall ... 62 TF 0311
Ryhill ... 71 SE 3814
Ryhope ... 84 NZ 4152
Ryknild Street (Derby.) (ant.) ... 60 SK 2930
Ryknild Street (Derby.) (ant.) ... 60 SK 3848
Ryknild Street (Warw.) (ant.) ... 50 SP 0762
Rylstone ... 78 SD 9758
Ryme Intrinseca ... 25 ST 5810
Rysa Little (is.) ... 136 ND 3197
Ryther ... 79 SE 5539
Ryton (Glos.) ... 46 SO 7232
Ryton (N Yorks.) ... 80 SE 7975
Ryton (Shrops.) ... 59 SJ 7502
Ryton (Tyne and Wear) ... 91 NZ 1564
Ryton-on-Dunsmore ... 50 SP 3874

S

Sabden ... 78 SD 7737
Sabden Brook ... 78 SD 7535
Sàbhal Beag ... 132 NC 3742
Saccombe ... 37 TL 3419
Sacquoy Head ... 138 HY 3835
Sacriston ... 84 NZ 2447
Sadberge ... 85 NZ 3416
Saddell ... 92 NR 7832

Saddell Bay ... 92 NR 7931
Saddell Glen ... 92 NR 7832
Saddington ... 51 SP 6591
Saddington Resr. ... 51 SP 6691
Saddleback or Blencathra (ant.) ... 82 NY 3227
Saddle Bow ... 64 TF 6015
Saddle Hill ... 129 NA 7843
Saddle, The (Highld.) (mt.) ... 114 NG 9313
Saddle, The (Strath.) (mt.) ... 100 NS 2296
Saddleworth Moor ... 70 SE 0305
Saddle Yoke ... 89 NT 1412
Sadgill ... 83 NY 4805
Sae Breck (mt.) ... 142 HU 2178
Saffron Walden ... 53 TL 5438
Saham Toney ... 64 TF 9002
Saighton ... 68 SJ 4462
Sail Chalmadale ... 92 NR 9139
Sàil Mhòr (mt.) ... 126 NH 0388
St. Abbs ... 97 NT 9167
St. Abb's Head ... 97 NT 9169
St. Agnes (Corn.) ... 18 SW 7150
St. Agnes (Is. of Sc.) (is.) ... 18 SV 8807
St. Agnes Head ... 18 SW 6951
St. Albans ... 37 TL 1507
St. Alban's or St. Aldhelm's Head ... 26 SY 9675
St. Aldhelm's or St. Alban's Head ... 26 SY 9675
St. Allen ... 19 SW 8250
St. Andrews ... 109 NO 5016
St. Andrews Bay ... 109 NO 5318
St. Andrews Major ... 41 ST 1471
St. Anne's (Lancs.) ... 77 SD 3129
St. Ann's (Dumf. and Galwy.) ... 89 NY 0793
St. Ann's Chapel (Corn.) ... 20 SX 4170
St. Ann's Chapel (Devon) ... 21 SX 6647
St. Ann's Head ... 42 SM 8002
St. Anthony-in-Meneage ... 18 SW 7725
St. Arvans ... 45 ST 5196
St. Asaph (Lanelwy) ... 67 SJ 0374
St. Athan ... 41 ST 0168
St. Austell ... 19 SX 0152
St. Austell Bay ... 19 SX 0650
St. Baldred's Boat (pt.) ... 103 NT 6184
St. Baldred's Cradle (pt.) ... 103 NT 6381
St. Bees ... 82 NX 9611
St. Bees Head ... 82 NX 9314
St. Blazey ... 19 SX 0654
St. Boswells ... 96 NT 5930
St. Breock ... 19 SW 9771
St. Breock Downs ... 19 SW 9668
St. Breward ... 19 SX 0977
St. Briavels ... 45 SO 5504
St. Brides ... 42 SM 8010
St. Brides Bay ... 42 SM 7917
St. Bride's Major ... 41 SS 8974
St. Bride's Netherwent ... 33 ST 4289
St. Brides-super-Ely ... 41 ST 1078
St. Bride's Wentlooge ... 32 ST 2982
St. Budeaux ... 20 SX 4558
St. Buryan ... 18 SW 4025
St. Catherines ... 100 NN 1207
St. Catherine's Bay ... 137 HY 6226
St. Catherine's Dub (pt.) ... 121 NK 0428
St. Catherine's Point ... 27 SZ 4975
St. Clears ... 43 SN 2716
St. Cleer ... 19 SX 2468
St. Clement ... 18 SW 8443
St. Clement's Isle ... 18 SW 4726
St. Clether ... 20 SX 2084
St. Colmac ... 100 NS 0467
St. Colme House ... 102 NT 1884
St. Columb Major ... 19 SW 9163
St. Columb Minor ... 19 SW 8362
St. Columb Road ... 19 SW 9059
St. Combs ... 121 NK 0563
St. Cross South Elmham ... 55 TM 2984
St. Cyrus ... 109 NO 7464
St. David's (Dyfed) ... 42 SM 7525
St. Davids (Fife) ... 102 NT 1582
St. David's (Tays.) ... 108 NN 9420
St. David's Head ... 42 SM 7228
St. Day ... 18 SW 7242
St. Dennis ... 19 SW 9558
St. Devereux ... 45 SO 4431
St. Dogmaels ... 42 SN 1646
St. Dogwells ... 42 SM 9728
St. Dominick ... 20 SX 3967
St. Donats ... 41 SS 9368
St. Endellion ... 19 SW 9978
St. Enoder ... 19 SW 8956
St. Erme ... 18 SW 5435
St. Erth ... 18 SW 5535
St. Erth Praze ... 18 SW 5735
St. Ervan ... 19 SW 8870
St. Eval ... 19 SW 8769
St. Ewe ... 19 SW 9745
St. Fagans ... 41 ST 1177
St. Fergus ... 121 NK 0951
St. Fergus Moss ... 121 NK 0553
St. Fillans ... 107 NN 6924
St. Florence ... 42 SN 0801
St. Gennys ... 20 SX 1497
St. George (Clwyd) ... 67 SH 9775
St. George's (S Glam.) ... 41 ST 0976
St. George's or Looe Island ... 19 SX 2551
St. Germans ... 20 SX 3557
St. Giles in the Wood ... 23 SS 5318
St. Giles-on-the-Heath ... 20 SX 3590
St. Govan's Head ... 42 SR 9792
St. Gwynno Forest ... 41 ST 0396
St. Harmon ... 57 SN 9872
St. Helena ... 65 TG 1816
St. Helen Auckland ... 84 NZ 1826
St. Helens (I. of W.) ... 27 SZ 6288
St. Helen's (Is. of Sc.) (is.) ... 18 SV 9017
St. Helens (Mers.) ... 69 SJ 5095
St. Hilary (Corn.) ... 18 SW 5531
St. Hilary (S Glam.) ... 41 ST 0173
St. Illtyd ... 41 SO 2102
St. Ippollitts ... 52 TL 1927
St. Ishmael's ... 42 SM 8307
St. Issey ... 19 SW 9271
St. Ive (Corn.) ... 20 SX 3167
St. Ives (Cambs.) ... 53 TL 3171
St. Ives (Corn.) ... 18 SW 5140
St. Ives (Dorset) ... 26 SU 1203
St. Ives Bay ... 18 SW 5441
St. James South Elmham ... 55 TM 3281
St. John (Corn.) ... 20 SX 4053
St. John's (Durham) ... 84 NZ 0634
St. Johns (Here. and Worc.) ... 49 SO 8453
St. Johns (I. of M.) ... 76 SC 2781
St. John's Beck ... 82 NY 3123
St. John's Chapel ... 84 NY 8837
St. John's Fen End ... 63 TF 5311
St. John's Head ... 136 HY 1803
St. John's Highway ... 63 TF 5314
St. John's Loch ... 135 ND 2272
St. John's Point ... 135 ND 3175
St. John's Town of Dalry ... 88 NX 6281
St. Jude's ... 76 SC 3996
St. Just ... 18 SW 3631
St. Just in Roseland ... 19 SW 8435
St. Katherines ... 121 NJ 7834
St. Keverne ... 19 SW 7821
St. Kew ... 19 SX 0276
St. Kew Highway ... 19 SX 0375
St. Keyne ... 19 SX 2460
St. Lawrence (Corn.) ... 19 SX 0466

Saintbury ... 50 SP 1139
Saint Hill ... 29 TQ 3835
St. Lawrence (Essex) ... 39 TL 9604
St. Lawrence (I. of W.) ... 27 SZ 5476
St. Leonards (Bucks.) ... 36 SP 9006
St. Leonards (Dorset) ... 26 SU 1002
St. Leonards (E Susx) ... 30 TQ 8009
St. Leonard's Forest ... 28 TQ 2231
St. Levan ... 18 SW 3722
St. Lythans ... 41 ST 1073
St. Mabyn ... 19 SX 0373
St. Magnus Bay ... 142 HU 2568
St. Magnus Church (ant.) ... 138 HY 4630
St. Margarets ... 45 SO 3534
St. Margaret's at Cliffe ... 31 TR 3644
St. Margaret's Bay ... 31 TR 3744
St. Margaret's Hope (Fife) ... 102 NT 1181
St. Margaret's Hope (S. Ronaldsay) ... 136 ND 4493
St. Margaret South Elmham ... 55 TM 3183
St. Mark's ... 76 SC 2974
St. Martin ... 19 SW 7324
St. Martin (Corn.) ... 19 SX 2555
St. Martin's (Is. of Sc.) ... 18 SV 9215
St. Martin's (Shrops.) ... 58 SJ 3236
St. Martins (Tays.) ... 108 NO 1530
St. Mary Bourne ... 34 SU 4250
St. Mary Church ... 41 ST 0071
St. Mary Cray ... 37 TQ 4767
St. Mary Hill ... 41 SS 9678
St. Mary Hoo ... 30 TQ 8076
St. Mary in the Marsh ... 31 TR 0628
St. Mary's (Is. of Sc.) (is.) ... 18 SV 9111
St. Mary's (Orkney) ... 136 HY 4701
St. Mary's Bay ... 31 TR 0927
St. Mary's Grove ... 33 ST 4769
St. Mary's Isle ... 87 NX 6749
St. Mary's Loch ... 95 NT 2422
St. Mary's Marshes ... 38 TQ 8078
St. Mary's or Bait Island ... 91 NZ 3575
St. Mary's or Newton Haven ... 97 NU 2424
St. Mary's Sound ... 18 SV 8909
St. Mawes ... 19 SW 8433
St. Mawgan ... 19 SW 8765
St. Mellion ... 20 SX 3865
St. Mellons ... 41 ST 2281
St. Merryn ... 19 SW 8874
St. Mewan ... 19 SW 9951
St. Michael Caerhays ... 19 SW 9642
St. Michael Penkevil ... 19 SW 8542
St. Michaels (Here. and Worc.) ... 48 SO 5765
St. Michaels (Kent) ... 30 TQ 8835
St. Michael's Island ... 76 SC 2967
St. Michael's Mount ... 18 SW 5130
St. Michael's on Wyre ... 77 SD 4640
St. Michael South Elmham ... 55 TM 3483
St. Minver ... 19 SW 9677
St. Monance ... 103 NO 5201
St. Neot (Corn.) ... 19 SX 1867
St. Neots (Cambs.) ... 52 TL 1860
St. Newlyn East ... 19 SW 8356
St. Nicholas (Dyfed) ... 42 SM 9035
St. Nicholas (S Glam.) ... 41 ST 0874
St. Nicholas at Wade ... 31 TR 2666
St. Ninians ... 101 NS 7991
St. Ninian's Cave ... 87 NX 4236
St. Ninian's Chapel ... 87 NX 4836
St. Ninian's Isle ... 141 HU 3621
St. Ninian's Point ... 100 NS 0361
St. Osyth ... 39 TM 1215
St. Osyth Marsh ... 39 TM 1113
St. Owen's Cross ... 45 SO 5324
St. Pancras Station ... 37 TQ 2982
St. Patrick's Isle ... 76 SC 2484
St. Pauls Cray ... 37 TQ 4768
St. Paul's Walden ... 37 TL 1922
St. Peter's ... 31 TR 3668
St. Peter's Flat (sbk.) ... 39 TM 0408
St. Petrox ... 42 SR 9797
St. Pinnock ... 19 SX 2063
St. Quivox ... 93 NS 3723
St. Radegund's Abbey ... 31 TR 2471
St. Serf's Island ... 102 NO 1500
St. Stephen (Corn.) ... 19 SW 9453
St. Stephens (Corn.) ... 20 SX 3285
St. Stephen's (Corn.) ... 19 SX 4158
St. Teath ... 19 SX 0680
St. Tudwal's Islands ... 56 SH 3425
St. Tudwal's Road ... 56 SH 3328
St. Tudy ... 19 SX 0676
St. Twynnells ... 42 SR 9597
St. Vigeans ... 109 NO 6443
St. Wenn ... 19 SW 9664
St. Weonards ... 45 SO 4924
S. Winnow ... 19 SX 1157
S Airde Beinn ... 111 NM 4753
Salachan Glen ... 106 NM 9852
Salcey Forest ... 51 SP 7951
Salcombe ... 21 SX 7338
Salcombe Regis ... 24 SY 1488
Salcott ... 38 TL 9413
Sale ... 69 SJ 7990
Saleby ... 73 TF 4578
Sale Green ... 49 SO 9358
Salehurst ... 29 TQ 7424
Salem (Dyfed) ... 43 SN 6226
Salem (Dyfed) ... 57 SN 6684
Salem (Gwyn.) ... 66 SH 5456
Salen (Highld.) ... 111 NM 6864
Salen (Island of Mull) ... 105 NM 5743
Salen Forest (Strath.) ... 105 NM 5347
Salen Forest (Strath.) ... 105 NM 6739
Salesbury ... 77 SD 6732
Sales Point ... 39 TM 0209
Salford (Beds.) ... 52 SP 9339
Salford (Gtr Mches.) ... 69 SJ 7796
Salford (Oxon.) ... 47 SP 2828
Salford Priors ... 50 SP 0751
Salfords ... 29 TQ 2846
Salhouse ... 65 TG 3114
Saligo Bay ... 98 NR 2066
Saline ... 102 NT 0292
Salisbury ... 34 SU 1429
Salisbury Plain ... 34 SU 0645
Sallachan Point ... 106 NM 9961
Sallachy (Highld.) ... 128 NC 5408
Sallachy (Highld.) ... 114 NG 9130
Salle ... 65 TG 1024
Salmonby ... 73 TF 3273
Salmond's Muir ... 109 NO 5837
Salperton ... 46 SP 0720
Salph End ... 52 TL 0752
Salsburgh ... 101 NS 8262
Salt ... 60 SJ 9527
Saltash ... 20 SX 4259
Saltburn ... 129 NH 7269
Saltburn-by-the-Sea ... 85 NZ 6621
Saltby ... 62 SK 8526
Saltcoats ... 93 NS 2441
Saltdean ... 29 TQ 3802
Salter ... 78 SD 6073
Salterforth ... 78 SD 8845
Saltergate ... 80 SE 8594
Salter's Bank (sbk.) ... 77 SD 3126
Saltersbrook Bridge ... 70 SE 1300
Salterswall ... 69 SJ 6267
Saltfleet ... 73 TF 4593
Saltfleetby All Saints ... 73 TF 4590
Saltfleetby St. Clements ... 73 TF 4591
Saltfleetby St. Peter ... 73 TF 4389
Saltford ... 33 ST 6867
Salthaugh Grange ... 75 TA 2321

Salthouse ... 64 TG 0743
Salt Island ... 66 SH 2583
Saltmarshe ... 74 SE 7824
Saltney ... 68 SJ 3864
Saltom Bay ... 82 NX 9515
Salton ... 80 SE 7180
Salt Scar ... 85 NZ 6126
Saltwick ... 85 NZ 9211
Saltwood ... 31 TR 1536
Salum ... 104 NM 0648
Salwarpe ... 49 SO 8762
Salwayash ... 25 SY 4596
Salwick Station ... 77 SD 4632
Samala ... 124 NF 7962
Samalaman Island ... 111 NM 6678
Samalan Island ... 105 NM 4536
Sambourne ... 50 SP 0561
Sambrook ... 59 SJ 7124
Samlesbury ... 77 SD 5829
Samlesbury Aerodrome ... 77 SD 6230
Samlesbury Bottoms ... 77 SD 6229
Sampford Arundel ... 24 ST 1018
Sampford Brett ... 24 ST 0940
Sampford Courtenay ... 23 SS 6301
Sampford Peverell ... 24 ST 0214
Sampford Spiney ... 21 SX 5372
Samphrey (is.) ... 143 HU 4676
Samson (is.) ... 18 SV 8712
Samuelston ... 103 NT 4870
Sanaigmore ... 98 NR 2370
Sancreed ... 18 SW 4029
Sancton ... 74 SE 8939
Sand ... 141 HU 3447
Sandaig ... 111 NG 7102
Sandaig Bay ... 111 NG 7101
Sandaig Islands ... 123 NG 7614
Sanda Island ... 92 NR 7204
Sanda Stour (is.) ... 141 HU 3441
Sanday (Highld.) ... 110 NG 2704
Sanday (Orkney) ... 139 HY 6841
Sanday Aerodrome ... 139 HY 6740
Sanday Sound ... 139 HY 6634
Sandbach ... 69 SJ 7560
Sandbank ... 100 NS 1580
Sandbanks ... 26 SZ 0487
Sand Bay ... 32 ST 3264
Sandend ... 121 NJ 5566
Sandend Bay ... 121 NJ 5666
Sanderstead ... 37 TQ 3461
Sandford (Avon) ... 32 ST 4159
Sandford (Cumbr.) ... 83 NY 7216
Sandford (Devon) ... 23 SS 8202
Sandford (Dorset) ... 26 SY 9289
Sandford (Strath.) ... 94 NS 7143
Sandfordhill ... 121 NK 1141
Sandford-on-Thames ... 47 SP 5301
Sandford Orcas ... 25 ST 6220
Sandford St. Martin ... 47 SP 4226
Sandgarth ... 137 HY 5215
Sandgate ... 31 TR 2035
Sandhaven ... 121 NJ 9667
Sandhead ... 86 NX 0949
Sandholme (Humbs.) ... 74 SE 8230
Sandholme (Lincs.) ... 63 TF 3337
Sandhurst (Berks.) ... 36 SU 8361
Sandhurst (Glos.) ... 46 SO 8223
Sandhurst (Kent) ... 30 TQ 8028
Sandhutton (N Yorks.) ... 79 SE 3881
Sand Hutton (N Yorks.) ... 80 SE 6958
Sandiacre ... 61 SK 4736
Sandilands ... 73 TF 5280
Sandiway ... 69 SJ 6070
Sandleheath ... 26 SU 1214
Sandleigh ... 47 SP 4501
Sandling ... 30 TQ 7558
Sandness ... 141 HU 1957
Sandness Hill ... 140 HU 1955
Sandon (Essex) ... 38 TL 7404
Sandon (Herts.) ... 53 TL 3234
Sandon (Staffs.) ... 59 SJ 9429
Sandown ... 27 SZ 5984
Sandown Airport ... 27 SZ 5784
Sandown Bay ... 27 SZ 6083
Sandplace ... 19 SX 2457
Sand Point ... 32 ST 3165
Sandray (is.) ... 112 NL 6491
Sandridge ... 37 TL 1710
Sandringham ... 64 TF 6928
Sandsend ... 85 NZ 8512
Sand Side (Highld.) ... 134 NC 9606
Sandside Bay (Orkney) ... 137 HY 5906
Sandside Burn ... 134 NC 9661
Sandside House ... 134 NC 9565
Sands of Forvie ... 121 NK 0126
Sands of Nigg ... 129 NH 7670
Sandsound ... 141 HU 3548
Sandsound Voe ... 141 HU 3548
Sandtoft ... 74 SE 7408
Sand Water (Shetld.) ... 141 HU 4154
Sand Water (Shetld.) ... 143 HU 4274
Sandwich ... 31 TR 3358
Sandwich Bay ... 31 TR 3759
Sandwich Flats (sbk.) ... 31 TR 3540
Sandwick (Cumbr.) ... 83 NY 4219
Sandwick (Isle of Lewis) ... 131 NB 4432
Sandwick (Shetld.) ... 141 HU 4323
Sand Wick (Shetld.) ... 141 HU 4323
Sandwick (Shetld.) (dist.) ... 141 HU 3924
Sandwick (South Uist) ... 124 NF 8343
Sandwick (S. Ronaldsay) ... 136 ND 4388
Sandwick (S. Ronaldsay) ... 136 ND 4389
Sand Wick (Unst) ... 143 HP 6202
Sandwith ... 82 NX 9614
Sandwood Loch ... 132 NC 2364
Sandy ... 52 TL 1649
Sandycroft ... 68 SJ 3366
Sandy Edge ... 90 NT 5201
Sandygate ... 76 SC 3797
Sandy Lane ... 34 ST 9668
Sangobeg ... 133 NC 4266
Sanna ... 111 NM 4469
Sanna Bay ... 111 NM 4368
Sanna Point ... 111 NM 4370
Sannox Bay ... 92 NS 0145
Sanquhar ... 88 NS 7809
Santon ... 74 SE 9312
Santon Bridge ... 82 NY 1001
Santon Downham ... 54 TL 8187
Santon Head ... 76 SC 3370
Sapcote ... 61 SP 4893
Sapey Common ... 49 SO 7064
Sapiston ... 54 TL 9175
Sapperton (Glos.) ... 46 SO 9403
Sapperton (Lincs.) ... 62 TF 0133
Saracen's Head ... 63 TF 3427
Sarclet ... 135 ND 3443
Sarclet Head ... 135 ND 3543
Sarisbury ... 27 SU 5008
Sarkfoot Point ... 89 NY 3265
Sarn (Mid Glam.) ... 41 SS 9083
Sarn (Powys) ... 48 SO 2090
Sarnau (Dyfed) ... 43 SN 3151
Sarnau (Dyfed) ... 43 SN 3050
Sarnau (Gwyn.) ... 67 SH 9739
Sarnau (Powys) ... 58 SJ 2315
Sarn-bâch ... 56 SH 3026
Sarnesfield ... 45 SO 3750

Sarn Ilelen (Dyfcd) (ant.) ... 43 SN 6449
Sarn Helen (Gwyn.) (ant.) ... 67 SH 7229
Sarn Meyllteyrn ... 66 SH 2432
Saron (Dyfed) ... 43 SN 3738
Saron (Dyfed) ... 66 SN 6012
Sarratt ... 37 TQ 0499
Sarre ... 31 TR 2565
Sarsden ... 47 SP 2822
Sarsgrum ... 132 NC 3764
Satley ... 84 NZ 1143
Satterleigh ... 23 SS 6622
Satterthwaite ... 82 SD 3392
Sauchar Point ... 103 NT 4999
Sauchen ... 119 NJ 7010
Sauchie ... 108 NO 1933
Sauchieburn ... 60 NO 6669
Sauchie Law ... 89 NT 2910
Sauchrie ... 93 NS 3014
Saughall ... 68 SJ 3669
Saugh Hill ... 86 NX 2197
Saughtree ... 95 NY 5696
Saughtree Fell ... 90 NY 5599
Saul ... 46 SO 7409
Saundby ... 72 SK 7888
Saundersfoot ... 42 SN 1304
Saundersfoot Station ... 42 SN 1206
Saunderton ... 36 SP 7901
Saunderton Station ... 36 SU 8198
Saunton ... 22 SS 4537
Sausthorpe ... 73 TF 3869
Saval ... 128 NC 5908
Savary ... 105 NM 6346
Savernake Forest ... 34 SU 2266
Saviskaill Bay ... 138 HY 4133
Saviskaill Head ... 138 HY 4035
Sawbridgeworth ... 37 TL 4814
Sawdon ... 81 SE 9485
Sawley (Derby.) ... 61 SK 4731
Sawley (Lancs.) ... 78 SD 7746
Sawley (N Yorks.) ... 79 SE 2467
Sawrey ... 82 SD 3695
Sawston ... 53 TL 4849
Sawtry ... 52 TL 1683
Saxa Vord (mt.) ... 143 HP 6316
Saxby (Leic.) ... 62 SK 8220
Saxby (Lincs.) ... 72 TF 0086
Saxby All Saints ... 74 SE 9816
Saxelbye ... 62 SK 6921
Saxilby ... 72 SK 8875
Saxlingham ... 64 TG 0239
Saxlingham Nethergate ... 65 TM 2397
Saxmundham ... 55 TM 3863
Saxondale ... 61 SK 6840
Saxon Street ... 53 TL 6859
Saxtead ... 55 TM 2665
Saxtead Green ... 55 TM 2564
Saxthorpe ... 65 TG 1130
Saxton ... 79 SE 4736
Sayers Common ... 28 TQ 2618
Scabbacombe Head ... 21 SX 9351
Scackleton ... 79 SE 6472
Scad Head ... 136 HY 3430
Sca Fell ... 82 NY 2006
Scafell Pikes ... 82 NY 2107
Scaftworth ... 72 SK 6691
Scagglethorpe ... 80 SE 8372
Scaladale River ... 131 NB 1709
Scalasaig ... 98 NR 3894
Scalby (Humbs.) ... 74 SE 8329
Scalby (N Yorks.) ... 85 TA 0090
Scalby Ness Rocks ... 85 TA 0391
Scald Law ... 103 NT 1961
Scaldwell ... 51 SP 7672
Scaleby ... 90 NY 4563
Scaleby Hill ... 89 NY 4363
Scale Houses ... 83 NY 5845
Scales (Cumbr.) ... 82 NY 3426
Scales (Cumbr.) ... 77 SD 2772
Scales Moor ... 77 SD 7176
Scalford ... 61 SK 7624
Scaling ... 85 NZ 7413
Scaling Resr. ... 85 NZ 7412
Scalla Field (mt.) ... 141 HU 3857
Scallastle ... 105 NM 6938
Scallastle Bay ... 105 NM 6939
Scalloway ... 141 HU 4039
Scalpay (Harris, W Isles) ... 123 NG 2395
Scalpay (Island of Skye) ... 123 NG 6030
Scalpay House ... 123 NG 6328
Scalpsie Bay ... 100 NS 0558
Scalp, The (mt.) ... 33 SJ 3636
Scamblesby ... 73 TF 2778
Scammonden Resr. ... 70 SE 0416
Scamodale ... 111 NM 8473
Scampston ... 80 SE 8575
Scampton ... 72 SK 9479
Scapa ... 136 HY 4309
Scapa Bay ... 136 HY 4307
Scapa Flow (roadstead) ... 136 ND 3899
Scar ... 139 HY 6745
Scaraben (mt.) ... 135 ND 0626
Scarastavore ... 124 NG 0092
Scarba ... 105 NM 7004
Scarborough ... 81 TA 0388
Scarcliffe ... 71 SK 4968
Scarcroft ... 79 SE 3540
Scardroy ... 127 NH 2151
Scares (is.) ... 86 NX 2634
Scarff ... 142 HU 2480
Scarfskerry ... 135 ND 2673
Scarfskerry Point ... 135 ND 2674
Scargill ... 84 NZ 0510
Scargill High Moor ... 84 NZ 0009
Scargill Resr. ... 79 SE 2851
Scar Hill ... 121 NJ 4801
Scar House Reservoir ... 104 NM 0444
Scarinish ... 104 NM 0444
Scarisbrick ... 77 SD 3713
Scarning ... 64 TF 9512
Scarp (is.) ... 130 NA 9715
Scarrington ... 61 SK 7341
Scars, The ... 77 NZ 2993
Scarth Gap Pass ... 82 NY 1813
Scarth Hill ... 77 SD 4206
Scartho ... 75 TA 2606
Scarva Taing ... 137 HY 5708
Scar Water ... 88 NS 8195
Scarweather (lightship) ... 40 SS 6574
Scat Ness ... 141 HU 3909
Scatsta ... 143 HU 3972
Scaur Hill ... 95 NS 8830
Scaur or Kippford ... 87 NX 8355
Scawby ... 74 SE 9605
Scawton ... 79 SE 5483
Scayne's Hill ... 29 TQ 3723
Scethrog ... 44 SO 1025
Schiehallion (mt.) ... 107 NN 7154
Schil, The ... 97 NT 8722
Scholar Green ... 69 SJ 8357
Scholes (W Yorks.) ... 70 SE 1507
Scholes (W Yorks.) ... 79 SE 3736
Schooner Point ... 110 NM 3098
Scleddau ... 42 SM 9434
Scoat Fell ... 82 NY 1511
Scock Ness ... 138 HY 4532
Scole ... 55 TM 1579
Scolpaig ... 124 NF 7275
Scolton ... 42 SM 9922
Scolty ... 119 NO 6793
Sconce (pt.) ... 26 SZ 3389

Stane Street (Essex) (ant.) Sunderland Bank (sbk.)

Stane Street (Essex) (ant.) 37 TL 5421
Stane Street (Surrey) (ant.) 28 TQ 1439
Stanfield 64 TF 9320
Stanford (Beds.) 52 TL 1641
Stanford (Kent) 31 TR 1238
Stanford Bishop 49 SO 6851
Stanford Bridge 49 SO 7165
Stanford Dingley 35 SU 5771
Stanford in the Vale 47 SU 3493
Stanford le Hope 38 TQ 6882
Stanford on Avon 51 SP 5878
Stanford on Soar 61 SK 5422
Stanford on Teme 49 SO 7065
Stanford Rivers 37 TL 5301
Stanger Head 138 HY 5142
Stanghow 85 NZ 6715
Stanhoe 64 TF 8036
Stanhope 95 NT 1229
Stanhope 84 NY 9939
Stanhope Common 84 NY 9642
Stanion 52 SP 9187
Stanley (Derby.) 60 SK 4140
Stanley (Durham) 84 NZ 1953
Stanley (Staffs.) 59 SJ 9252
Stanley (Tays.) 108 NO 1033
Stanley (W Yorks.) 79 SE 3422
Stanley Force 82 SD 1699
Stanmer 29 TQ 3309
Stanmore (Berks.) 35 SU 4778
Stanmore (Gtr London) 37 TQ 1692
Stannery Knowe 93 NS 4912
Stannington (Northum.) 91 NZ 2179
Stannington (S Yorks.) 71 SK 2988
Stansbatch 48 SO 3461
Stansfield 54 TL 7852
Stansore Point 27 SZ 4698
Stanstead 54 TL 8449
Stanstead Abbotts 37 TL 3811
Stansted 30 TQ 6062
Stansted Airport 37 TL 5422
Stansted House 27 SU 7610
Stansted Mountfitchet 37 TL 5124
Stanton (Glos.) 46 SP 0634
Stanton (Northum.) 91 NZ 1390
Stanton (Staffs.) 60 SK 1246
Stanton (Suff.) 54 TL 9673
Stanton by Bridge 60 SK 3627
Stanton by Dale 61 SK 4637
Stanton Drew 33 ST 5963
Stanton Fitzwarren 34 SU 1790
Stanton Harcourt 47 SP 4105
Stanton Hill 71 SK 4860
Stanton in Peak 71 SK 2464
Stanton Lacy 48 SO 4978
Stanton Long 48 SO 5690
Stanton-on-the-Wolds 61 SK 6330
Stanton Prior 33 ST 6762
Stanton St. Bernard 34 SU 0962
Stanton St. John 47 SP 5709
Stanton St. Quintin 33 ST 9079
Stanton Street 54 TL 9566
Stanton under Bardon 61 SK 4610
Stanton upon Hine Heath 59 SJ 5624
Stanton Wick 33 ST 6162
Stanwardine in the Fields 58 SJ 4124
Stanway (Essex) 38 TL 9324
Stanway (Glos.) 46 SP 0532
Stanwell 36 TQ 0574
Stanwell Moor 36 TQ 0474
Stanwick 52 SP 9871
Stanydale 140 HU 2850
Stape 80 SE 7993
Stapehill 26 SU 0500
Stapeley 59 SJ 6749
Staple 31 TR 2756
Staplecross 30 TQ 7822
Staplefield 28 TQ 2728
Staple Fitzpaine 24 ST 2618
Stapleford (Cambs.) 53 TL 4751
Stapleford (Herts.) 37 TL 3117
Stapleford (Leic.) 61 SK 8018
Stapleford (Lincs.) 72 SK 8757
Stapleford (Notts.) 61 SK 4837
Stapleford (Wilts.) 26 SU 0637
Stapleford Abbotts 37 TQ 5095
Stapleford Aerodrome 37 TQ 4996
Stapleford Tawney 37 TQ 5098
Staplegrove 24 ST 2126
Staple Hill 24 ST 2416
Staplehurst 30 TQ 7843
Staplers 27 SZ 5189
Staple Sound 97 NU 2236
Stapleton (Avon) 33 ST 6175
Stapleton (Cumbr.) 89 NY 5071
Stapleton (Here. and Worc.) 48 SO 3265
Stapleton (Leic.) 60 SP 4398
Stapleton (N Yorks.) 84 NZ 2612
Stapleton (Shrops.) 58 SJ 4604
Stapleton (Somer.) 25 ST 4621
Stapley 24 ST 1813
Staploe 52 TL 1460
Star (Dyfed) 43 SN 2435
Star (Fife) 103 NO 3103
Star (Somer.) 33 ST 4358
Starbotton 78 SD 9574
Starcross 21 SX 9781
Starg Dam 108 NO 0438
Starston 55 TM 2384
Start Bay 21 SX 8444
Startforth 84 NZ 0416
Startley 34 ST 9482
Start Point (Corn.) 20 SX 0485
Start Point (Devon) 21 SX 8337
Start Point (Sanday, Orkney) 139 HY 7843
Startup Hill 95 NS 9729
Stathe 24 ST 3728
Stathern 61 SK 7731
Station Town 85 NZ 4036
Stattic Point 126 NG 9796
Staughton Highway 52 TL 1364
Staunton (Glos.) 45 SO 5412
Staunton (Glos.) 46 SO 7929
Staunton Harold Hall 60 SK 3721
Staunton Harold Reservoir 60 SK 3723
Staunton on Arrow 45 SO 3660
Staunton on Wye 45 SO 3645
Stava Ness 141 HU 5060
Staveley (Cumbr.) 83 SD 4698
Staveley (Derby.) 71 SK 4374
Staveley (N Yorks.) 79 SE 3662
Staveley-in-Cartmel 77 SD 3886
Staverton (Devon) 21 SX 7964
Staverton (Glos.) 46 SO 8923
Staverton (Northants.) 51 SP 5461
Staverton (Wilts.) 33 ST 8560
Stawell 32 ST 3638
Staxigoe 135 ND 3852
Staxton 81 TA 0179
Staylittle 57 SN 8892
Staythorpe 61 SK 7554
Stean 78 SE 0873
Stean Moor 78 SE 0770
Stearsby 79 SE 6171
Steart 32 ST 2745
Stebbing 38 TL 6624
Stedham 27 SU 8622
Steele Road 90 NY 5292
Steel's Knowe 102 NN 9607
Steen's Bridge 45 SO 5457
Steep 27 SU 7525
Steep Holm (is.) 32 ST 2260
Steeping River 73 TF 4661
Steeple (Dorset) 25 SY 9080
Steeple (Essex) 38 TL 9303
Steeple Ashton 33 ST 9056
Steeple Aston 47 SP 4725
Steeple Barton 47 SP 4424
Steeple Bumpstead 54 TL 6741
Steeple Claydon 51 SP 7027
Steeple Gidding 52 TL 1381
Steeple Langford 26 SU 0337
Steeple Morden 53 TL 2842
Steer Rig 97 NT 8524
Steeton 78 SE 0344
Steilston Hill 88 NX 8782
Steinacleit (ant.) 131 NB 3954
Steinmanhill 121 NJ 7642
Steisay 124 NF 8544
Stelling Minnis 31 TR 1446
Stemster 135 ND 1862
Stemster Hill 135 ND 1941
Stemster House 135 ND 1860
Stenalees 19 SX 0157
Stenbury Down 27 SZ 5378
Stenhousemuir 102 NS 8682
Stenhouse Resr. 103 NT 2187
Stenness 142 HU 2177
Stenton 103 NT 6274
Stepney 37 TQ 3581
Steppingley 52 TL 0135
Stepps 101 NS 6668
Sternfield 55 TM 3861
Stert 34 SU 0259
Stert Flats (sbk.) 32 ST 2647
Stetchworth 54 TL 6458
Stevenage 53 TL 2325
Stevenston 93 NS 2642
Steventon (Hants.) 35 SU 5547
Steventon (Oxon.) 35 SU 4691
Stevington 52 SP 9853
Stewartby 52 TL 0242
Stewarton 93 NS 4246
Stewkley 52 SP 8525
Stewton 73 TF 3687
Stey Fell 87 NX 5560
Steyning 28 TQ 1711
Steynton 42 SM 9108
Stibb 22 SS 2210
Stibbard 64 TF 9828
Stibb Cross 22 SS 4314
Stibb Green 34 SU 2262
Stibbington 62 TL 0898
Stichill 96 NT 7138
Sticker 19 SW 9750
Stickford 73 TF 3560
Sticklepath 21 SX 6394
Stickle Pike 82 SD 2192
Stickle Tarn 82 NY 2907
Stickney 63 TF 3456
Stiffkey 64 TF 9743
Stifford's Bridge 49 SO 7348
Stilligarry 112 NF 7638
Stillingfleet 79 SE 5940
Stillington (Cleve. - Durham) 85 NZ 3723
Stillington (N Yorks.) 79 SE 5867
Stilton 52 TL 1689
Stinchcombe 46 ST 7298
Stinsford 25 SY 7191
Stiperstones 58 SO 3699
Stirchley 59 SJ 6906
Stirkoke House 135 ND 3150
Stirling 101 NS 7993
Stisted 38 TL 8024
Stithians 18 SW 7336
Stivichall 50 SP 3376
Stixwould 73 TF 1765
Stoak 68 SJ 4273
Stob a'Choin 107 NN 4115
Stob a'Ghrianain 115 NN 0882
Stob an Aonaich Mhóir 107 NN 5469
Stob an Eas 100 NN 1807
Stob an t-Sluichd 117 NJ 1102
Stob Binnein 107 NN 4322
Stob Choire Claurigh 115 NN 2673
Stob Coir' an Albannaich 106 NN 1644
Stob Coire a' Chearcaill 106 NN 0172
Stob Coire Easain (Highld.) 106 NN 2372
Stob Coire Easain (Highld.) 106 NN 3072
Stob Dubh 106 NN 1648
Stob Ghabhar 106 NN 2345
Stobieside 94 NS 6239
Stob Law 95 NT 2333
Stob na Cruaiche 107 NN 3657
Stobo 95 NT 1837
Stoborough 25 SY 9286
Stoborough Green 25 SY 9184
Stock 38 TQ 6998
Stockay 124 NF 6663
Stockbridge 26 SU 3535
Stockbriggs 94 NS 7936
Stockbury 30 TQ 8461
Stockcross 34 SU 4368
Stockdalewath 83 NY 3845
Stockerston 62 SP 8397
Stock Gaylard House 25 ST 7212
Stock Green 50 SO 9859
Stockingford 50 SP 3391
Stocking Pelham 53 TL 4529
Stockinish Island 125 NG 1389
Stockland 24 ST 2404
Stockland Bristol 32 ST 2443
Stockleigh English 23 SS 8406
Stockleigh Pomeroy 23 SS 8703
Stockley 34 SU 0067
Stockport 69 SJ 8989
Stocksbridge 71 SK 2798
Stocksfield 91 NZ 0561
Stocks Resr. 77 SD 7256
Stockton (Here. and Worc.) 48 SO 5161
Stockton (Norf.) 65 TM 3894
Stockton (Shrops.) 59 SO 7299
Stockton (Warw.) 50 SP 4363
Stockton (Wilts.) 34 ST 9738
Stockton Heath 69 SJ 6185
Stockton-on-Tees 85 NZ 4419
Stockton on Teme 49 SO 7167
Stockton on the Forest 79 SE 6556
Stockwith 72 SK 7994
Stock Wood 50 SP 0058
Stodmarsh 31 TR 2160
Stody 64 TG 0535
Stoer 132 NC 0328
Stoford (Somer.) 25 ST 5613
Stoford (Wilts.) 26 SU 0835
Stogumber 24 ST 0937
Stogursey 32 ST 2042
Stoke (Devon) 22 SS 2324
Stoke (Hants.) 34 SU 4051
Stoke (Hants.) 27 SU 7202
Stoke (Kent) 30 TQ 8275
Stoke Abbott 25 ST 4500
Stoke Albany 51 SP 8088
Stoke Ash 55 TM 1170
Stoke Bardolph 61 SK 6441
Stoke Bliss 49 SO 6562
Stoke Bruerne 51 SP 7450
Stoke by Clare 54 TL 7443
Stoke-by-Nayland 54 TL 9836
Stoke Canon 21 SX 9397
Stoke Charity 35 SU 4839
Stoke Climsland 20 SX 3574
Stoke D'Abernon 37 TQ 1259
Stoke Doyle 52 TL 0286
Stoke Dry 62 SP 8597
Stoke Ferry 64 TF 7000
Stoke Fleming 21 SX 8648
Stokeford 25 SY 8787
Stoke Gabriel 21 SX 8457
Stoke Gifford 33 ST 6280
Stoke Golding 60 SP 3997
Stoke Goldington 52 SP 8348
Stokeham 72 SK 7876
Stoke Hammond 52 SP 8829
Stoke Holy Cross 65 TG 2301
Stokeinteignhead 21 SX 9170
Stoke Lacy 45 SO 6149
Stoke Lyne 47 SP 5628
Stoke Mandeville 36 SP 8310
Stokenchurch 36 SU 7596
Stoke Newington 37 TQ 3286
Stokenham 21 SX 8042
Stoke on Tern 59 SJ 6327
Stoke-on-Trent 59 SJ 8745
Stoke Orchard 46 SO 9128
Stoke Poges 36 SU 9884
Stoke Point 21 SX 5645
Stoke Prior (Here. and Worc.) 45 SO 5256
Stoke Prior (Here. and Worc.) 49 SO 9467
Stoke Rivers 23 SS 6335
Stoke Rochford 62 SK 9127
Stoke Row 36 SU 6883
Stokesay 48 SO 4381
Stokes Bay 27 SZ 5897
Stokesby 65 TG 4310
Stokesley 85 NZ 5208
Stoke St. Gregory 24 ST 3426
Stoke St. Mary 24 ST 2622
Stoke St. Michael 33 ST 6646
Stoke St. Milborough 48 SO 5682
Stoke sub Hamdon 25 ST 4717
Stoke Talmage 36 SU 6799
Stoke Trister 25 ST 7328
Stolford 32 ST 2245
Stondon Massey 37 TL 5800
Stone (Bucks.) 36 SP 7812
Stone (Glos.) 46 ST 6895
Stone (Here. and Worc.) 49 SO 8675
Stone (Kent) 37 TQ 5774
Stone (Staffs.) 59 SJ 9034
Stone Allerton 32 ST 3950
Ston Easton 33 ST 6253
Stonebroom 71 SK 4159
Stonechrubie 132 NC 2419
Stone Cross 29 TQ 6104
Stonefield 94 NS 6957
Stonefield Castle Hotel 99 NR 8671
Stonegate 29 TQ 6628
Stonegate Crofts 121 NK 0339
Stonegrave 79 SE 6577
Stonehaugh 90 NY 7976
Stonehaven 119 NO 8685
Stonehenge (ant.) 34 SU 1242
Stone House (Cumbr.) 78 SD 7785
Stonehouse (Glos.) 46 SO 8005
Stonehouse (Northum.) 90 NY 6958
Stonehouse (Strath.) 94 NS 7546
Stone-in-Oxney 30 TQ 9427
Stoneleigh 50 SP 3272
Stonely 52 TL 1067
Stonesby 62 SK 8224
Stonesdale Moor 84 NY 8804
Stonesfield 47 SP 3917
Stones Green 55 TM 1626
Stoneside Hill 82 SD 1489
Stone Street (Kent) (ant.) 31 TR 1350
Stone Street (Suff.) (ant.) 55 TM 3686
Stoneybridge 112 NF 7433
Stoneyburn 102 NS 9762
Stoney Cross 26 SU 2511
Stoneygate 61 SK 6102
Stoneyhills 38 TQ 9497
Stoneykirk 86 NX 0853
Stoney Middleton. 71 SK 2275
Stoney Stanton 61 SP 4894
Stoney Stratton 33 ST 6539
Stoney Stretton 58 SJ 3809
Stoneywood 119 NJ 8910
Stonga Banks 142 HU 2985
Stonganess 143 HP 5402
Stonham Aspal 55 TM 1359
Stonnall 60 SK 0603
Stonor 36 SU 7388
Stonton Wyville 61 SP 7395
Stonybreck 139 HZ 2071
Stonyfield 128 NH 6973
Stonyhurst College 77 SD 6838
Stony Stratford 51 SP 7840
Stood Hill 88 NS 8512
Stoodleigh 23 SS 9218
Stoodleigh Beacon 23 SS 8818
Stopham 28 TQ 0219
Stopsley 37 TL 1023
Storeton 68 SJ 3084
Stornoway 131 NB 4233
Stornoway Aerodrome 131 NB 4533
Storridge 49 SO 7448
Storrington 28 TQ 0814
Storrs 83 SD 3994
Storr, The (mt.) 123 NG 4954
Storth 77 SD 4780
Stotfold 52 TL 2136
Stottesdon 49 SO 6782
Stoughton (Leic.) 61 SK 6402
Stoughton (Surrey) 28 SU 9851
Stoughton (W Susx) 27 SU 8011
Stoul 111 NM 7594
Stoulton 49 SO 9049
Stourbridge 49 SO 8984
Stourbrough Hill 140 HU 2152
Stourhead 25 ST 7734
Stourpaine 25 ST 8509
Stourport-on-Severn 49 SO 8171
Stour Provost 25 ST 7921
Stour Row 25 ST 8220
Stourton (Here. and Worc.) 49 SO 8585
Stourton (Warw.) 50 SP 2936
Stourton (Wilts.) 25 ST 7733
Stourton Caundle 25 ST 7114
Stove 139 HY 6035
Stoven 55 TM 4481
Stow (Borders) 96 NT 4644
Stow (Lincs.) 72 SK 8781
Stow Bardolph 64 TF 6205
Stow Bardolph Fen 63 TF 5603
Stow Bedon 64 TL 9596
Stowbridge 64 TF 6007
Stow cum Quy 53 TL 5260
Stowe (Shrops.) 48 SO 3173
Stowe-by-Chartley 60 SK 0027
Stowell 25 ST 6822
Stowe School 51 SP 6737
Stowford 20 SX 4386
Stowlangtoft 54 TL 9568
Stow Longa 52 TL 1171
Stow Maries 38 TQ 8399
Stowmarket 54 TM 0458
Stow-on-the-Wold 47 SP 1925
Stowting 31 TR 1241
Stowupland 54 TM 0659
Straad 100 NS 0462
Strachan 119 NO 6792
Strachur 100 NN 0901
Strachur Bay 100 NN 0801
Stradbroke 55 TM 2373
Stradishall 54 TL 7452
Stradsett 64 TF 6605
Stragglethorpe 62 SK 9152
Strait of Dover 31 TR 3828
Straiton (Lothian) 103 NT 2766
Straiton (Strath.) 93 NS 3804
Straloch (Grampn.) 121 NJ 8621
Straloch (Tays.) 108 NO 0463
Stramshall 60 SK 0735
Strandburgh Ness 143 HU 6793
Strangend Currick 83 NY 8443
Stranraer 86 NX 0660
Strata Florida 57 SN 7465
Stratfield Mortimer 36 SU 6764
Stratfield Saye 36 SU 6961
Stratfield Turgis 36 SU 6959
Stratford St. Andrew 55 TM 3560
Stratford St. Mary 54 TM 0434
Stratford Tony 26 SU 0926
Stratford-upon-Avon 50 SP 2055
Stratford-upon-Avon Canal 50 SP 1764
Strath 126 NG 7978
Strathaird 123 NG 5419
Strathallan 101 NN 8307
Strathallan Castle 108 NN 9115
Strathan (Highld.) 132 NC 0821
Strathan (Highld.) 114 NM 9891
Strath an Lòin 133 NC 4416
Strathaven 94 NS 7044
Strath Avon 117 NJ 1525
Strath Beag 127 NH 1087
Strath Beg 134 NC 8531
Strath Blane (Central) 101 NS 5381
Strathblane (Central) 101 NS 5679
Strathblane Hills 101 NS 5581
Strath Bogie (Grampn.) 121 NJ 5237
Strathbogie (Grampn.) (dist.) 121 NJ 4937
Strathbraan 108 NN 9739
Strath Bran 127 NH 2460
Strath Brora 134 NC 7609
Strath Burn 135 ND 2450
Strathcarron (Highld.) 126 NG 9442
Strathcarron (Highld.) 128 NH 5591
Strathcoil 105 NM 6830
Strathconon 127 NH 4055
Strathconon Forest 127 NH 2347
Strath Cuileannach 128 NH 4393
Strathdearn 116 NH 7724
Strathdon 118 NJ 3513
Strath Dores 116 NH 6137
Strath Eachaig 100 NS 1484
Strath Earn 108 NN 8818
Stratherrick 116 NH 5017
Strath Fillan 107 NN 3628
Strath Finella 119 NO 6879
Strathfinella Hill 119 NO 6978
Strath Fleet 128 NC 6702
Strath Gartney 101 NN 4610
Strathgarve Forest 128 NH 4163
Strathglass 115 NH 3734
Strathgryfe 100 NS 3270
Strath Halladale 134 NC 8953
Strathhardle 108 NO 1153
Strath Isla 121 NJ 4451
Strath Kanaird (Highld.) 127 NC 1400
Strath Kanaird (Highld) 127 NC 1501
Strathkinness 109 NO 4516
Strathlachlan Forest 100 NS 0093
Strath Lungard 126 NG 9264
Strath Mashie 116 NN 5891
Strathmashie House 116 NN 5891
Strath Melness Burn 133 NC 5663
Strathmiglo 103 NO 2109
Strath More (Highld.) 133 NC 4545
Strath More (Highld.) 127 NH 1882
Strathmore (Tays.) (dist.) 109 NO 4353
Strathmore Lodge 135 ND 1047
Strathmore River 133 NC 4546
Strath Mulzie 127 NH 3193
Strathnairn 116 NH 6832
Strathnairn Forest 116 NH 6930
Strath nan Lùb 100 NS 0792
Strath na Sealga 127 NH 0680
Strathnasheallag Forest 127 NH 0483
Strathnaver 134 NC 7148
Strath of Appin 106 NM 9545
Strath of Kildonan or Strath Ullie 134 NC 8923
Strath of Orchy 106 NN 1627
Strathord Forest 108 NO 0631
Strath Oykel 128 NC 4300
Strathpeffer 128 NH 4858
Strath Rannoch (Highld.) 127 NH 3872
Strathrannoch (Highld.) 127 NH 3874
Strath Rory 128 NH 6976
Strath Rusdale 128 NH 5777
Strath Sgitheach 128 NH 5263
Strath Shinary 132 NC 2561
Strath Skinsdale 134 NC 7518
Strathspey 117 NJ 1536
Strath Stack 132 NC 2740
Strath Suardal 123 NG 6221
Strath Tay 108 NO 0043
Strath Tirry 133 NC 5319
Strath Ullie or Strath of Kildonan 134 NC 8923
Strath Vagastie 133 NC 5430
Strath Vaich 127 NH 3572
Strathvaich Forest 127 NH 3276
Strathvaich Lodge 127 NH 3474
Strathwhillan 92 NS 0235
Strathy 134 NC 8465
Strathy Bay 134 NC 8366
Strathy Forest (Highld.) 134 NC 8256
Strathy Forest (Highld.) 134 NC 8262
Strathy Point 134 NC 8269
Strathyre 107 NN 5617
Strathyre Forest 107 NN 5718
Stratton (Corn.) 22 SS 2306
Stratton (Dorset) 25 SY 6593
Stratton (Glos.) 46 SP 0103
Stratton Audley 47 SP 6026
Stratton-on-the-Fosse 33 ST 6550
Stratton St. Margaret 34 SU 1787
Stratton St. Michael 65 TM 2093
Stratton Strawless 65 TG 2220
Stravanan Bay 92 NS 0755
Stravithie 103 NO 5311
Strawarren Fell 86 NX 1679
Streat 29 TQ 3515
Streatham 37 TQ 2972
Streatlam Castle 84 NZ 0819
Streatley (Beds.) 52 TL 0728
Streatley (Berks.) 35 SU 5980
Streens 117 NH 8638
Street (Lancs.) 77 SD 5252
Street (N Yorks.) 80 NZ 7304
Street (Somer.) 25 ST 4836
Street End 27 SZ 8599
Streethay 60 SK 1410
Streetly 60 SP 0898
Strefford 48 SO 4485
Strem Ness 140 HT 9741
Strensall 79 SE 6360
Strensham 49 SO 9040
Stretcholt 32 ST 2943
Strete 21 SX 8447
Stretford 69 SJ 7894
Stretford Court 45 SO 4455
Strethall 53 TL 4939
Stretham 53 TL 5174
Strettington 27 SU 8807
Stretton (Ches.) 58 SJ 4452
Stretton (Ches.) 69 SJ 6182
Stretton (Derby.) 71 SK 3961
Stretton (Leic.) 62 SK 9415
Stretton (Staffs.) 59 SJ 8811
Stretton (Staffs.) 60 SK 2526
Stretton en le Field 60 SK 3012
Stretton Grandison 45 SO 6344
Stretton Heath 58 SJ 3610
Stretton-on-Dunsmore 50 SP 4072
Stretton-on-Fosse 50 SP 2238
Stretton under Fosse 51 SP 4581
Stretton Westwood 59 SO 5998
Strichen 121 NJ 9455
Strines Resr. 71 SK 2290
Stringston 32 ST 1742
String, The 136 HY 4714
Strixton 52 SP 9061
Stroan Loch 88 NX 6470
Stroat 45 ST 5798
Stròc-bheinn 123 NG 4539
Stroin Vuigh (pt.) 76 SC 2174
Stromeferry 123 NG 8634
Stromemore 123 NG 8635
Strom Ness (Muckle Roe) 140 HU 2965
Strom Ness (N. Ronaldsay) 139 HY 7651
Stromness (Orkney) 136 HY 2509
Strom Ness (Vaila) 140 HU 2245
Stromness Taing 136 HY 4425
Stronabo 115 NN 2084
Stronachlachar 101 NN 4010
Stronchreggan 106 NN 0772
Stronchrubie 132 NC 2419
Stronchullin Hill 100 NS 1686
Strond 124 NG 0384
Strone (Highld.) 116 NH 5228
Strone (Highld.) 115 NN 1481
Strone (Strath.) 100 NS 1880
Strone Glen 92 NR 6310
Stronend (mt.) 101 NS 6289
Strone Point (Strath.) 100 NS 0771
Strone Point (Strath.) 100 NS 1980
Strone Water 92 NR 6310
Stronmilchan 106 NN 1528
Stronsay 137 HY 6525
Stronsay Aerodrome 137 HY 6329
Stronsay Firth 137 HY 5722
Strontian 111 NM 8161
Strontian River 111 NM 8363
Stronuich Reservoir 107 NN 5042
Strood 30 TQ 7369
Stroud (Glos.) 46 SO 8504
Stroud (Hants.) 27 SU 7223
Struan 122 NG 3438
Struan Station 107 NN 8065
Strubby 73 TF 4582
Struie (mt.) 128 NH 6584
Strumble Head 42 SM 8941
Strumpshaw 65 TG 3507
Strutherhill 94 NS 7650
Struy 115 NH 4039
Struy Forest 115 NH 3737
Stuartfield 121 NJ 9745
Stubbington 27 SU 5503
Stubbins 69 SD 7918
Stubhampton 25 ST 9113
Stub Place 82 SD 0890
Stubton 62 SK 8748
Stuchd an Lochain 107 NN 4844
Stuckgowan 100 NN 3202
Stuckton 26 SU 1613
Stuc Scardan 100 NN 1114
Studham 36 TL 0215
Studland 26 SZ 0382
Studland Bay 26 SZ 0584
Studley (Warw.) 50 SP 0763
Studley (Wilts.) 34 ST 9671
Studley Roger 79 SE 2970
Stulaval (Isle of Lewis) (mt.) 131 NB 1312
Stulaval (South Uist) (mt.) 112 NF 8024
Stuley 112 NF 8323
Stump Cross 53 TL 5044
Stuntney 53 TL 5578
Sturbridge 59 SJ 8330
Sturdy Hill 119 NO 5977
Sturgate Airport 72 SK 8888
Sturmer 54 TL 6944
Sturminster Common 25 ST 7812
Sturminster Marshall 26 SY 9499
Sturminster Newton 25 ST 7813
Sturry 31 TR 1760
Sturton by Stow 72 SK 8980
Sturton le Steeple 72 SK 7884
Stuston 55 TM 1378
Stutton (N Yorks.) 79 SE 4741
Stutton (Suff.) 55 TM 1434
Styal 69 SJ 8383
Sty Head 82 NY 2109
Sty Wick 139 HY 6838
Suainaval (mt.) 130 NB 0730
Succoth 121 NJ 4235
Suckley 49 SO 7151
Suckley Hills 49 SO 7352
Sudborough 52 SP 9682
Sudbourne 55 TM 4153
Sudbrook 33 ST 5087
Sudbrooke 72 TF 0276
Sudbury (Derby.) 60 SK 1631
Sudbury (Suff.) 54 TL 8741
Suddie 128 NH 6654
Sudeley Castle (ant.) 46 SP 0327
Sudgrove 46 SO 9307
Sueno's Stone (ant.) 129 NJ 0459
Suffield 65 TG 2332
Sugar Loaf 45 SO 2718
Sugnall 59 SJ 7930
Suidh'a'Mhinn 123 NG 4068
Suidhe Ghuirmain (mt.) 115 NH 3826
Suie Hill 121 NJ 5523
Suilven (mt.) 132 NC 1517
Suisgill Burn 134 NC 8925
Suisnish Hill 123 NG 5634
Sula Sgeir (is.) 130 HW 6230
Sulby 76 SC 3994
Sulby Reservoir 51 SP 6581
Sulby River 76 SC 3890
Sule Skerry 132 HX 6224
Sulgrave 51 SP 5545
Sulham 36 SU 6474
Sulhamstead 36 SU 6368
Sullington 28 TQ 0913
Sullom 142 HU 3573
Sullom Voe 143 HU 3773
Sully 41 ST 1568
Sully Island 41 ST 1667
Sulma Water 140 HU 2555
Sumburgh 141 HU 4009
Sumburgh Airport 141 HU 3910
Sumburgh Head 141 HU 4007
Sumburgh Roost (chan.) 141 HU 4006
Summer Bridge 78 SE 1962
Summercourt 19 SW 8856
Summer Down 33 ST 9148
Summer Isles 126 NB 9706
Summerleaze 33 ST 4284
Summerseat 69 SD 7914
Summit 69 SD 9418
Sunadale 92 NR 8145
Sunart (dist.) 111 NM 7966
Sunbury 37 TQ 1069
Sunderland (Cumbr.) 82 NY 1735
Sunderland (Tyne and Wear) 85 NZ 3957
Sunderland Airport 91 NZ 3458
Sunderland Bank (sbk.) 77 SD 3956

Sunderland Bridge ... 84 NZ 2637
Sunderland Point ... 77 SD 4255
Sundhope ... 96 NT 3324
Sundon Park ... 52 TL 0525
Sundridge ... 29 TQ 4854
Sundrum (ant.) ... 93 NS 4121
Sunk (lightship) ... 39 TM 4623
Sunk Island ... 75 TA 2619
Sunk Island Sands ... 75 TA 3016
Sunk Sand ... 39 TM 3000
Sunningdale ... 36 SU 9567
Sunninghill ... 36 SU 9367
Sunningwell ... 47 SP 4900
Sunniside (Durham) ... 84 NZ 1438
Sunniside (Tyne and Wear) ... 91 NZ 2159
Sunny Bank ... 82 SD 2992
Sunnylaw ... 101 NS 7998
Sunnyside ... 29 TQ 3937
Surbiton ... 37 TQ 1867
Surfleet ... 63 TF 2528
Surfleet Seas End ... 63 TF 2628
Surlingham ... 65 TG 3106
Surrey Hill ... 36 SU 8863
Sursay ... 124 NF 9576
Sustead ... 65 TG 1837
Susworth ... 74 SE 8302
Sutcombe ... 22 SS 3411
Suton ... 65 TM 0999
Sutors of Cromarty ... 129 NH 8067
Sutterton ... 63 TF 2835
Sutton (Beds.) ... 53 TL 2247
Sutton (Cambs.) ... 53 TL 4479
Sutton (Gtr London) ... 37 TQ 2463
Sutton (Kent) ... 31 TR 3349
Sutton (Norf.) ... 65 TG 3823
Sutton (Northants.) ... 62 TL 0998
Sutton (Notts.) ... 71 SK 6784
Sutton (Notts.) ... 61 SK 7637
Sutton (Oxon.) ... 47 SP 4106
Sutton (Shrops.) ... 59 SJ 6631
Sutton (Shrops.) ... 48 SO 5082
Sutton (Shrops.) ... 49 SO 7286
Sutton (Staffs.) ... 59 SJ 7622
Sutton (Suff.) ... 55 TM 3046
Sutton (Surrey) ... 28 TQ 1046
Sutton (W Susx) ... 28 SU 9715
Sutton at Hone ... 37 TQ 5570
Sutton Basset ... 51 SP 7790
Sutton Benger ... 34 ST 9478
Sutton Bingham Resr. ... 25 ST 5410
Sutton Bonington ... 61 SK 5025
Sutton Bridge ... 63 TF 4821
Sutton Cheney ... 60 SK 4100
Sutton Coldfield ... 60 SP 1296
Sutton Courtenay ... 47 SU 5093
Sutton Crosses ... 63 TF 4321
Sutton Grange ... 84 SE 2874
Sutton Hoo Tumuli (ant.) ... 55 TM 2849
Sutton Howgrave ... 84 SE 3179
Sutton in Ashfield ... 71 SK 5058
Sutton-in-Craven ... 78 SE 0044
Sutton Lane Ends ... 69 SJ 9270
Sutton Leach ... 69 SJ 5393
Sutton Maddock ... 59 SJ 7201
Sutton Mallet ... 24 ST 3736
Sutton Mandeville ... 26 ST 9828
Sutton Montis ... 25 ST 6224
Sutton-on-Hull ... 75 TA 1132
Sutton on Sea ... 73 TF 5282
Sutton-on-the-Forest ... 79 SE 5864
Sutton on the Hill ... 60 SK 2333
Sutton on Trent ... 72 SK 7965
Sutton Park ... 60 SP 0996
Sutton Scotney ... 35 SU 4539
Sutton St. Edmund ... 63 TF 3613
Sutton St. James ... 63 TF 3918
Sutton St. Nicholas ... 45 SO 5345
Sutton-under-Brailes ... 50 SP 2937
Sutton-under-Whitestonecliffe ... 79 SE 4882
Sutton upon Derwent ... 74 SE 7046
Sutton Valence ... 30 TQ 8148
Sutton Veny ... 33 ST 9041
Sutton Waldron ... 25 ST 8615
Sutton Walls (ant.) ... 45 SO 5246
Sutton Weaver ... 69 SJ 5479
Swaby ... 73 TF 3877
Swadlincote ... 60 SK 3019
Swaffham ... 64 TF 8109
Swaffham Bulbeck ... 53 TL 5562
Swaffham Prior ... 53 TL 5764
Swafield ... 65 TG 2832
Swainbost ... 131 NB 5162
Swainby ... 85 NZ 4701
Swainshill ... 45 SO 4641
Swainsthorpe ... 65 TG 2101
Swainswick ... 33 ST 7568
Swalcliffe ... 50 SP 3738
Swalecliffe ... 31 TR 1367
Swaledale ... 84 SD 9598
Swale, The ... 31 TQ 9866
Swallow ... 75 TA 1703
Swallowcliffe ... 26 ST 9626
Swallow Falls ... 67 SH 7657
Swallowfield ... 36 SU 7264
Swanage ... 26 SZ 0278
Swanage Bay ... 26 SZ 0480
Swanbister Bay ... 136 HY 3604
Swanbister House ... 136 HY 3505
Swanbourne ... 51 SP 8027
Swanland ... 74 SE 9927
Swanley ... 37 TQ 5168
Swanmore ... 35 SU 5815
Swannington (Leic.) ... 60 SK 4116
Swannington (Norf.) ... 65 TG 1319
Swanscombe ... 30 TQ 6074
Swansea ... 40 SS 6593
Swansea Airport ... 40 SS 5691
Swansea Bay ... 40 SS 6888
Swansea Valley ... 41 SN 7506
Swanton Abbott ... 66 TG 2625
Swanton Morley ... 64 TG 0117
Swanton Novers ... 64 TG 0132
Swanwick (Derby.) ... 60 SK 4053
Swanwick (Hants.) ... 27 SU 5109
Swarbacks Head ... 140 HU 2861
Swarbacks Minn (chan.) ... 141 HU 3161
Swarby ... 62 TF 0440
Swardeston ... 65 TG 2002
Swarf, The ... 139 HY 6737
Swarkestone ... 60 SK 3728
Swarland ... 91 NU 1601
Swarland Estate ... 91 NU 1603
Swartz Geo ... 139 HZ 2170
Swaton ... 62 TF 1337
Swatte Fell ... 89 NT 1110
Swavesey ... 53 TL 3669
Sway ... 26 SZ 2798
Swayfield ... 62 SK 9822
Swaything ... 26 SU 4315
Sweetheart Abbey ... 88 NX 9566
Sweethope Hill ... 96 NT 6939
Sweethope Loughs ... 90 NY 9482
Sweffling ... 55 TM 3463
Swepstone ... 60 SK 3610
Swerford ... 47 SP 3731
Swettenham ... 69 SJ 8067
Sweyn Holm ... 136 HY 4522
Swffyd ... 41 ST 2198
Swilland ... 55 TM 1853
Swillington ... 79 SE 3830
Swimbridge ... 23 SS 6230
Swinbrook ... 47 SP 2812

Swindale Beck ... 83 NY 5112
Swinden Resrs. ... 78 SD 8933
Swinderby ... 72 SK 8662
Swindon (Glos.) ... 46 SO 9325
Swindon (Staffs.) ... 49 SO 8690
Swindon (Wilts.) ... 34 SU 1484
Swine ... 75 TA 1335
Swinefleet ... 74 SE 7621
Swineshead (Beds.) ... 52 TL 0565
Swineshead (Lincs.) ... 63 TF 2340
Swineshead Bridge ... 62 TF 2142
Swiney ... 135 ND 2335
Swinford (Leic.) ... 51 SP 5679
Swinford (Oxon.) ... 47 SP 4408
Swingfield Minnis ... 31 TR 2142
Swinhill ... 94 NS 7748
Swinhoe ... 97 NU 2028
Swinhope ... 73 TF 2196
Swining ... 141 HU 4566
Swining Voe ... 141 HU 4667
Swinister ... 143 HU 4472
Swinithwaite ... 84 SE 0489
Swinscoe ... 60 SK 1347
Swinside Hall ... 90 NT 7216
Swinstead ... 62 TF 0122
Swinsty Resr. ... 78 SE 1953
Swinton (Borders) ... 97 NT 8447
Swinton (Gtr Mches.) ... 69 SD 7701
Swinton (N Yorks.) ... 78 SE 2179
Swinton (N Yorks.) ... 80 SE 7573
Swinton (S Yorks.) ... 71 SK 4499
Swintonmill ... 97 NT 8145
Switha (is.) ... 136 ND 3690
Switha Sound ... 136 ND 3591
Swithland ... 61 SK 5413
Swithland Resr. ... 61 SK 5513
Swona (is.) ... 136 ND 3884
Swordale ... 128 NH 5765
Swordle ... 111 NM 7891
Swordland ... 134 NC 7363
Swordly ... 134 NC 7363
Sworton Heath ... 69 SJ 6784
Swyddffynnon ... 57 SN 6966
Swynnerton ... 59 SJ 8435
Swyre ... 25 SY 5288
Syde ... 46 SO 9411
Sydenham (Gtr London) ... 37 TQ 3571
Sydenham (Oxon.) ... 36 SP 7301
Sydenham Damerel ... 20 SX 4075
Syderstone ... 64 TF 8332
Sydling St. Nicholas ... 25 SY 6399
Sydmonton ... 35 SU 4857
Syerston ... 61 SK 7447
Syke ... 69 SD 8915
Sykehouse ... 71 SE 6216
Sykes ... 77 SD 6251
Sykes Fell ... 77 SD 6048
Sylen ... 43 SN 5107
Symbister ... 141 HU 5362
Symington (Strath.) ... 93 NS 3831
Symington (Strath.) ... 95 NS 9935
Symondsbury ... 25 SY 4493
Symonds Yat ... 45 SO 5516
Synod Inn ... 43 SN 4054
Syre ... 133 NC 6843
Syreford ... 46 SP 0320
Syresham ... 51 SP 6241
Syston (Leic.) ... 61 SK 6211
Syston (Lincs.) ... 62 SK 9240
Sytchampton ... 49 SO 8466
Sythe Harbour ... 124 NB 0203
Sywell ... 52 SP 8267
Sywell Resr. ... 52 SP 8365

T

Taberon Law ... 95 NT 1428
Tabhaidh Mhór (is.) ... 131 NB 4222
Tackley ... 47 SP 4720
Tacolneston ... 65 TM 1395
Tadcaster ... 79 SE 4843
Tadden ... 26 ST 9801
Taddington ... 70 SK 1471
Tadley ... 35 SU 6060
Tadlow ... 53 TL 2847
Tadmarton ... 50 SP 3937
Tadworth ... 28 TQ 2356
Tafarnaubach ... 41 SO 1110
Tafarn-y-Gelyn ... 68 SJ 1861
Taf Fechan ... 41 SO 0317
Taff's Well ... 41 ST 1283
Taff Vale ... 41 ST 0892
Tafolog ... 57 SH 8909
Tafolwern ... 57 SH 8902
Tafts Ness ... 139 HY 7647
Tahay ... 124 NF 9675
Tai-bach (Clwyd) ... 58 SJ 1528
Taibach (W Glam.) ... 41 SS 7789
Tailor's Leap (mt.) ... 106 NN 0027
Tain (Highld.) ... 135 ND 2266
Tain (Highld.) ... 129 NH 7782
Taing of Kelswick ... 143 HU 4969
Taing of Maywick ... 141 HU 3725
Taing, The (Orkney) ... 136 HY 4225
Taing, The (Shetld.) ... 141 HU 4011
Tai'n Lôn ... 66 SH 4450
Tai'r Bull ... 41 SN 9926
Tairlaw Ring ... 86 NX 4098
Takeley ... 37 TL 5521
Talachddu ... 44 SO 0733
Talacre ... 67 SJ 1083
Talaton ... 24 SY 0699
Talbenny ... 42 SM 8412
Talerddig ... 57 SH 9300
Talgarreg ... 43 SN 4251
Talgarth ... 41 SO 1534
Talhenbont (ant.) ... 66 SH 4639
Taliesin ... 57 SN 6591
Talisker ... 122 NG 3230
Talisker Bay ... 122 NG 3030
Talke ... 59 SJ 8253
Talkin ... 83 NY 5557
Talkin Tarn ... 90 NY 5458
Talla Bheith Forest ... 107 NN 5567
Talladale ... 126 NG 9270
Talla Linnfoots ... 89 NT 1320
Talland Bay ... 19 SX 2251
Tallaminnock ... 86 NX 4035
Tallantire ... 82 NY 1035
Talla Resr. ... 89 NT 1121
Talley ... 43 SN 6332
Tallington ... 62 TF 0908
Talmine ... 133 NC 5862
Talog ... 43 SN 3325
Talsarn ... 43 SN 5456
Talsarnau ... 66 SH 6135
Talskiddy ... 19 SW 9165
Talwrn ... 66 SH 4876
Talybont -(Dyfed) ... 57 SN 6589
Tal-y-bont (Gwyn.) ... 56 SH 5921
Tal-y-Bont (Gwyn.) ... 67 SH 7668
Talybont (Powys) ... 41 SO 1122
Talybont Reservoir ... 41 SO 0919
Tal-y-cafn ... 67 SH 7971
Tal y Fan ... 67 SH 7272
Tal-y-llyn (Gwyn.) ... 57 SH 7109
Talyllyn (Powys) ... 41 SO 1127
Talysarn ... 66 SH 4852
Talywern ... 57 SH 8200
Tamerton Foliot ... 20 SX 4761
Tamworth ... 60 SK 2004
Tandridge ... 29 TQ 3750

Tanera Beg (is.) ... 126 NB 9607
Tanera Mór (is.) ... 126 NB 9807
Tanfield ... 84 NZ 1855
Tangasdale ... 112 NF 6500
Tang Head (Highld.) ... 135 ND 2774
Tang Head (Highld.) ... 135 ND 3062
Tangley ... 34 SU 3352
Tangmere ... 27 SU 9006
Tangwick ... 142 HU 2377
Tangy Loch ... 92 NR 6927
Tan Hill (Durham-N Yorks.) ... 84 NY 8906
Tan Hill (Wilts.) ... 34 SU 0864
Tankerness ... 136 HY 5108
Tankersley ... 71 SK 3499
Tannach ... 135 ND 3247
Tannadice ... 109 NO 4758
Tannington ... 55 TM 2467
Tansley ... 71 SK 3259
Tansor ... 52 TL 0590
Tantallon Castle (ant.) ... 103 NT 5985
Tan, The ... 93 NS 1553
Tantobie ... 84 NZ 1754
Tanton ... 85 NZ 5210
Tanworth in Arden ... 50 SP 1170
Tan-y-fron ... 67 SH 9564
Tanygrisiau ... 67 SH 6845
Tan-y-groes ... 43 SN 2849
Tan-y-pistyll ... 67 SJ 0729
Taob ... 136 HY 5005
Tapeley ... 22 SS 4729
Taplow ... 36 SU 9182
Tap o' Noth (mt.) ... 121 NJ 4829
Tarain (mt.) ... 130 NB 0427
Taran Mór (mt.) ... 130 NB 0315
Taransay ... 124 NB 0201
Taransay Glorigs ... 124 NA 9606
Tarbat House ... 129 NH 7773
Tarbat Ness ... 129 NH 9487
Tarbert (Harris, W Isles) ... 125 NB 1500
Tarbert (Jura) ... 98 NR 6082
Tarbert (Strath.) ... 92 NR 6551
Tarbert (Strath.) ... 99 NR 8668
Tarbet (Highld.) ... 132 NC 1648
Tarbet (Highld.) ... 111 NM 7992
Tarbet (Strath.) ... 100 NN 3104
Tarbock Green ... 68 SJ 4687
Tarbolton ... 93 NS 4327
Tarbrax ... 95 NT 0255
Tarfessock (mt.) ... 86 NX 4088
Tarfside ... 118 NO 4979
Tarf Tail (pt.) ... 136 ND 3783
Tarf Water (Dumf. and Galwy.) ... 86 NX 2662
Tarf Water (Tays.) ... 117 NN 9080
Tarland ... 120 NJ 4804
Tarleton ... 82 SD 4420
Tarlogie ... 129 NH 7583
Tarlscough ... 68 SD 4313
Tarlshof (ant.) ... 141 HU 3909
Tarlton ... 46 SO 9599
Tarnbrook ... 77 SD 5855
Tarner Island ... 122 NG 2938
Tarporley ... 69 SJ 5562
Tarr ... 24 ST 1030
Tarrant Crawford ... 25 ST 9203
Tarrant Gunville ... 25 ST 9212
Tarrant Hinton ... 26 ST 9310
Tarrant Keynston ... 25 ST 9204
Tarrant Launceston ... 26 ST 9409
Tarrant Monkton ... 26 ST 9408
Tarrant Rawston ... 26 ST 9306
Tarrant Rushton ... 26 ST 9305
Tarras Water ... 89 NY 4086
Tarrenhendre ... 57 SH 6804
Tarring Neville ... 29 TQ 4404
Tarrington ... 45 SO 6140
Tarsappie ... 108 NO 1220
Tarskavaig ... 123 NG 5810
Tarskavaig Point ... 123 NG 5809
Tarty Burn ... 121 NJ 9325
Tarves ... 121 NJ 8631
Tarvie (Highld.) (dist.) ... 128 NH 4258
Tarvie (Tays.) ... 108 NO 0164
Tarvin ... 69 SJ 4867
Tasburgh ... 65 TM 2095
Tasley ... 59 SO 6994
Taston ... 47 SP 3521
Tatenhill ... 60 SK 2022
Tatham ... 77 SD 6069
Tatham Fells ... 77 SD 6763
Tathwell ... 73 TF 3282
Tatsfield ... 29 TQ 4156
Tattenhall ... 69 SJ 4858
Tattenham Corner Station ... 37 TQ 2258
Tatterford ... 64 TF 8628
Tattersett ... 64 TF 8429
Tattershall ... 73 TF 2157
Tattershall Bridge ... 62 TF 1956
Tattershall Thorpe ... 73 TF 2159
Tattingstone ... 55 TM 1337
Tatton Hall ... 69 SJ 7481
Tauchers ... 121 NJ 3749
Taunton ... 24 ST 2324
Taverham ... 65 TG 1513
Tavernspite ... 43 SN 1812
Tavistock ... 20 SX 4774
Tavool House ... 105 NM 4327
Taw Green ... 21 SS 6597
Tawstock ... 23 SS 5529
Taxal ... 70 SK 0079
Tay Bridge ... 109 NO 3827
Taymouth ... 108 NN 7846
Taynish ... 99 NR 7283
Taynton (Glos.) ... 46 SO 7221
Taynton (Oxon.) ... 47 SP 2313
Taynuilt ... 106 NN 0031
Tayport ... 109 NO 4528
Tay Road Bridge ... 109 NO 4129
Tayvallich ... 99 NR 7386
Tcohoval (mt.) ... 131 NB 1629
Tealby ... 73 TF 1590
Tealing ... 109 NO 4138
Teanamachar ... 124 NF 7762
Teangue ... 111 NG 6608
Teatle Water ... 106 NN 1324
Tebay ... 83 NY 6104
Tebworth ... 52 SP 9926
Tedburn St. Mary ... 21 SX 8194
Teddington (Glos.) ... 46 SO 9632
Teddington (Gtr London) ... 37 TQ 1671
Tedstone Delamere ... 49 SO 6958
Tedstone Wafre ... 49 SO 6759
Tees Bay ... 85 NZ 5727
Teesdale ... 84 NY 9227
Tees-side Airport ... 85 NZ 3813
Teeton ... 51 SP 6970
Teffont Evias ... 26 ST 9831
Teffont Magna ... 26 ST 9832
Tegryn ... 43 SN 2233
Teigh ... 62 SK 8616
Teigngrace ... 21 SX 8474
Teignmouth ... 21 SX 9473
Teindland ... 120 NJ 2755
Teindland Forest ... 120 NJ 2956
Telegraph Hill ... 21 SX 8570
Telford ... 59 SJ 6909
Tellisford ... 33 ST 8055
Telscombe ... 29 TQ 4003
Templand ... 89 NY 0886
Temple (Corn.) ... 19 SX 1473
Temple (Lothian) ... 103 NT 3158

Temple (Strath.) ... 101 NS 5469
Temple Bar ... 43 SN 5354
Temple Bruer ... 62 TF 0053
Temple Cloud ... 33 ST 6157
Templecombe ... 25 ST 7022
Temple Ewell ... 31 TR 2844
Temple Grafton ... 50 SP 1254
Temple Guiting ... 46 SP 0928
Temple Hirst ... 79 SE 6025
Temple Newsam (ant.) ... 79 SE 3532
Temple Normanton ... 71 SK 4167
Temple Sowerby ... 83 NY 6127
Templeton (Devon) ... 22 SS 8813
Templeton (Dyfed) ... 42 SN 1111
Tempsford ... 52 TL 1653
Tenbury Wells ... 49 SO 5968
Tenby ... 42 SN 1300
Tendring ... 39 TM 1424
Ten Mile Bank ... 64 TL 6097
Tenston ... 136 HY 2716
Tenterden ... 30 TQ 8833
Tentsmuir Forest ... 109 NO 4825
Terally Point ... 86 NX 1240
Terling ... 38 TL 7715
Ternhill ... 59 SJ 6332
Terregles ... 88 NX 9377
Terrington ... 79 SE 6670
Terrington Marsh ... 63 TF 5423
Terrington St. Clement ... 63 TF 5520
Terrington St. John ... 63 TF 5416
Teston ... 30 TQ 7053
Testwood ... 26 SU 3514
Tetbury ... 46 ST 8993
Tetbury Upton ... 46 ST 8795
Tetchill ... 58 SJ 3832
Tetcott ... 20 SX 3396
Tetford ... 73 TF 3374
Tetney ... 75 TA 3101
Tetney Lock ... 75 TA 3402
Tetsworth ... 36 SP 6802
Tettenhall ... 59 SO 8899
Teuchan ... 121 NK 0839
Teversal ... 71 SK 4661
Teversham ... 53 TL 4958
Teviot Dale ... 89 NT 4815
Teviothead ... 89 NT 4005
Tewin ... 37 TL 2714
Tewkesbury ... 46 SO 8932
Tewsgill Hill ... 95 NS 9523
Texa ... 98 NR 3943
Teynham ... 31 TQ 9663
Thakeham ... 28 TQ 1017
Thame ... 36 SP 7006
Thames Ditton ... 37 TQ 1567
Thames Haven ... 38 TQ 7581
Thamesmead ... 37 TQ 4779
Thaneston ... 119 NO 6374
Thanington ... 31 TR 1356
Thankerton ... 95 NS 9737
Tharston ... 65 TM 1894
Thatcham ... 35 SU 5167
Thatto Heath ... 68 SJ 5093
Thaxted ... 54 TL 6131
Theakston ... 78 SE 3085
Thealby ... 74 SE 8917
Theale (Berks.) ... 36 SU 6371
Theale (Somer.) ... 33 ST 4646
Thearne ... 74 TA 0736
Theberton ... 55 TM 4365
Thedden Grange ... 35 SU 6839
Theddingworth ... 51 SP 6685
Theddlethorpe All Saints ... 73 TF 4688
Theddlethorpe St. Helen ... 73 TF 4788
Thelbridge Barton ... 23 SS 7812
Thelnetham ... 54 TM 0178
Thelwall ... 69 SJ 6587
Themelthorpe ... 64 TG 0524
Thenford ... 51 SP 5141
Therfield ... 53 TL 3337
Thetford ... 54 TL 8783
Thetford Warren ... 54 TL 8383
Theydon Bois ... 37 TQ 4598
Thickwood ... 33 ST 8272
Thieves Holm ... 136 HY 4614
Thimbleby (Lincs.) ... 73 TF 2369
Thimbleby (N Yorks.) ... 85 SE 4495
Thirkleby ... 79 SE 4778
Thirlby ... 79 SE 4884
Thirlestane ... 96 NT 5647
Thirlestane Castle ... 96 NT 5347
Thirlmere ... 82 NY 3116
Thirl, The (pt.) ... 135 ND 1873
Thirlwall Castle (ant.) ... 90 NY 6566
Thirlwall Common ... 90 NY 6669
Thirn ... 78 SE 2185
Thirsk ... 79 SE 4282
Thirstane Hill ... 88 NS 8709
Thistleton ... 61 SK 9118
Thistley Green ... 54 TL 6776
Thixendale ... 80 SE 8461
Thockrington ... 90 NY 9579
Tholomas Drove ... 63 TF 4006
Tholthorpe ... 79 SE 4766
Thomas Chapel ... 42 SN 1008
Thomastown ... 121 NJ 5737
Thompson ... 64 TL 9296
Thomshill ... 120 NJ 2157
Thong ... 30 TQ 6770
Thoralby ... 78 SE 0086
Thoresby ... 71 SK 6371
Thoresthorpe ... 73 TF 4617
Thoresway ... 73 TF 1696
Thorganby (Lincs.) ... 73 TF 2097
Thorganby (N Yorks.) ... 74 SE 6841
Thorgill ... 80 SE 7096
Thorington ... 55 TM 4274
Thorington Street ... 54 TM 0135
Thorlby ... 78 SD 9652
Thorley ... 37 TL 4719
Thormanby ... 79 SE 4974
Thornaby-on-Tees ... 85 NZ 4518
Thornage ... 64 TG 0436
Thornborough (Bucks.) ... 51 SP 7433
Thornborough (N Yorks.) ... 79 SE 2979
Thornbury (Avon) ... 33 ST 6390
Thornbury (Devon) ... 22 SS 4008
Thornbury (Here. and Worc.) ... 45 SO 6359
Thorncliffe ... 70 SK 0158
Thorncombe ... 24 ST 3703
Thorncombe Street ... 28 TQ 0042
Thorndon ... 55 TM 1469
Thorne ... 74 SE 6813
Thorne Moors or Waste ... 74 SE 7315
Thorner ... 79 SE 3740
Thorness Bay ... 27 SZ 4493
Thorne St. Margaret ... 24 ST 0920
Thorne Waste or Moors ... 74 SE 7315
Thorney (Cambs.) ... 63 TF 2804
Thorney (Notts.) ... 72 SK 8572
Thorney Hill ... 26 SZ 2099
Thorney Island ... 27 SU 7503
Thornfalcon ... 24 ST 2723
Thorngumbald ... 75 TA 2026
Thornham ... 64 TF 7343
Thornham Magna ... 55 TM 1071
Thornham Parva ... 55 TM 1072
Thornhaugh ... 62 TF 0600
Thornhill (Central) ... 101 NS 6699
Thornhill (Derby.) ... 70 SK 1983
Thornhill (Dumf. and Galwy.) ... 88 NX 8795

Thornhill (Mid Glam.) ... 41 ST 1584
Thornhill (W Yorks.) ... 78 SE 2418
Thornicombe ... 25 ST 8703
Thornley (Durham) ... 84 NZ 1137
Thornley (Durham) ... 85 NZ 3639
Thornliebank ... 101 NS 5459
Thorns ... 54 TL 7455
Thornthwaite (Cumbr.) ... 82 NY 2225
Thornthwaite (N Yorks.) ... 78 SE 1858
Thornton (Bucks.) ... 51 SP 7535
Thornton (Fife) ... 103 NT 2897
Thornton (Humbs.) ... 74 SE 7545
Thornton (Lancs.) ... 77 SD 3342
Thornton (Leic.) ... 61 SK 4607
Thornton (Lincs.) ... 73 TF 2467
Thornton (Mers.) ... 68 SD 3300
Thornton (Northum.) ... 97 NT 9547
Thornton (Tays.) ... 109 NO 3946
Thornton (W Yorks.) ... 78 SE 1032
Thornton Beck ... 80 SE 8381
Thornton Castle ... 109 NO 6871
Thornton Curtis ... 74 TA 0817
Thornton Dale ... 80 SE 8383
Thorntonhall ... 94 NS 5955
Thornton Hough ... 68 SJ 3080
Thornton-in-Craven ... 78 SD 9048
Thornton Junction ... 103 NT 3097
Thornton-le-Beans ... 78 SE 3990
Thornton-le-Clay ... 80 SE 6865
Thornton-le-Moor (Lincs.) ... 72 TF 0496
Thornton-le-Moor (N Yorks.) ... 78 SE 3988
Thornton-le-Moors ... 68 SJ 4474
Thorntonloch ... 96 NT 7574
Thornton Moor Reservoir ... 78 SE 0334
Thorntonpark ... 97 NT 9448
Thornton Resr. (Leic.) ... 61 SK 4707
Thornton Rust ... 78 SD 9788
Thornton Steward ... 78 SE 1787
Thornton Watlass ... 78 SE 2385
Thornwood Common ... 37 TL 4705
Thorny Hill ... 87 NX 5388
Thornyhive Bay ... 119 NO 8882
Thoroton ... 61 SK 7642
Thorp Arch ... 79 SE 4346
Thorpe (Derby.) ... 60 SK 1550
Thorpe (Lincs.) ... 73 TF 4982
Thorpe (Norf.) ... 65 TM 4398
Thorpe (Notts.) ... 61 SK 7649
Thorpe (N Yorks.) ... 78 SE 0161
Thorpe (Surrey) ... 36 TQ 0268
Thorpe Abbotts ... 55 TM 1979
Thorpe Acre ... 61 SK 5120
Thorpe Arnold ... 61 SK 7620
Thorpe Audlin ... 71 SE 4715
Thorpe Bassett ... 80 SE 8573
Thorpe Bay ... 38 TQ 9284
Thorpe by Water ... 51 SP 8996
Thorpe Constantine ... 60 SK 2608
Thorpe End Garden Village ... 65 TG 2811
Thorpe Green ... 54 TL 9354
Thorpe Hall ... 78 SE 5776
Thorpe Hesley ... 71 SK 3796
Thorpe in Balne ... 71 SE 5910
Thorpe Langton ... 51 SP 7492
Thorpe Larches ... 85 NZ 3826
Thorpe le Fallows ... 72 SK 9180
Thorpe-le-Soken ... 39 TM 1822
Thorpe Malsor ... 52 SP 8379
Thorpe Mandeville ... 51 SP 5345
Thorpe Market ... 65 TG 2436
Thorpe Morieux ... 54 TL 9453
Thorpeness ... 55 TM 4759
Thorpe on the Hill ... 72 SK 9065
Thorpe Salvin ... 71 SK 5281
Thorpe Satchville ... 61 SK 7311
Thorpe St. Andrew ... 65 TG 2609
Thorpe St. Peter ... 73 TF 4861
Thorpe Thewless ... 85 NZ 4023
Thorpe Underwood ... 79 SE 4658
Thorpe Waterville ... 52 TL 0281
Thorpe Willoughby ... 79 SE 5731
Thorrington ... 39 TM 0920
Thorverton ... 23 SS 9202
Thrandeston ... 55 TM 1176
Thrapston ... 52 SP 9978
Threapland ... 82 SD 9860
Threapwood ... 58 SJ 4345
Threave Castle (ant.) ... 88 NX 7362
Three Bridges ... 29 TQ 2837
Three Cocks ... 45 SO 1737
Three Crosses ... 40 SS 5794
Three Holes ... 63 TF 5000
Three Hundreds of Aylesbury, The (dist.) ... 36 SP 8607
Threekingham ... 62 TF 0836
Three Leg Cross ... 29 TQ 6831
Three Legged Cross ... 26 SU 0806
Three Mile Cross ... 36 SU 7168
Threemilestone ... 19 SW 7844
Three Pikes (mt.) ... 83 NY 8334
Threipmuir Reservoir ... 102 NT 1764
Threlkeld ... 82 NY 3225
Threshfield ... 78 SD 9863
Thrigby ... 65 TG 4512
Thringarth ... 83 NY 9323
Thringstone ... 60 SK 4217
Thrintoft ... 78 SE 3293
Thriplow ... 53 TL 4446
Throcking ... 53 TL 3330
Throckley ... 91 NZ 1567
Throckmorton ... 50 SO 9749
Throphill ... 91 NZ 1385
Thropton ... 91 NU 0202
Throsk ... 102 NS 8690
Throwleigh ... 21 SX 6690
Throwley ... 31 TQ 9955
Thrumpton ... 61 SK 5131
Thrumster ... 135 ND 3345
Thrunton ... 91 NU 0810
Thrupp (Glos.) ... 46 SO 8603
Thrupp (Oxon.) ... 47 SP 4715
Thruscross Resr. ... 78 SE 1557
Thrussington ... 61 SK 6416
Thruxton (Hants.) ... 34 SU 2845
Thruxton (Here. and Worc.) ... 45 SO 4334
Thruxton Aerodrome ... 34 SU 2845
Thrybergh ... 71 SK 4694
Thundersley ... 38 TQ 7788
Thurcaston ... 61 SK 5610
Thurcroft ... 71 SK 4988
Thurgarton (Norf.) ... 65 TG 1835
Thurgarton (Notts.) ... 61 SK 6949
Thurgoland ... 71 SE 2801
Thurlaston (Leic.) ... 61 SP 5099
Thurlaston (Warw.) ... 51 SP 4671
Thurlby (Lincs.) ... 62 SK 9061
Thurlby (Lincs.) ... 62 TF 1017
Thurleigh ... 52 TL 0558
Thurlestone ... 21 SX 6742
Thurloxton ... 24 ST 2730
Thurlow ... 54 TL 6750
Thurlstone ... 71 SE 2303
Thurlton ... 65 TM 4198
Thurmaston ... 61 SK 6109
Thurnby ... 61 SK 6404
Thurne ... 65 TG 4015
Thurnham (Kent) ... 30 TQ 8057

203

Name	Page	Grid
Thurnham (Lancs.)	77	SD 4554
Thurning (Norf.)	64	TG 0729
Thurning (Northants.)	52	TL 0883
Thurnscoe	71	SE 4605
Thursby	82	NY 3250
Thursford	64	TF 9833
Thursley	35	SU 9039
Thurso	135	ND 1168
Thurso Bay	135	ND 1169
Thurstaston	68	SJ 2483
Thurston	54	TL 9365
Thurstonfield	82	NY 3156
Thurstonland	70	SE 1610
Thurton	65	TG 3200
Thuruaston	50	SK 2437
Thuxton	64	TG 0307
Thwaite (N Yorks.)	84	SD 8998
Thwaite (Suff.)	55	TM 1168
Thwaite St. Mary	65	TM 3395
Thwing	81	TA 0570
Tianavaig Bay	123	NG 5138
Tibbermore	108	NO 0523
Tibberton (Glos.)	46	SO 7521
Tibberton (Here. and Worc.)	49	SO 9057
Tibberton (Shrops.)	59	SJ 6720
Tibbie Sheils Inn	89	NT 2320
Tibenham	55	TM 1389
Tibshelf	71	SK 4360
Tibthorpe	81	SE 9555
Ticehurst	29	TQ 6930
Tichborne	27	SU 5630
Tickencote	62	SK 9809
Tickenham	33	ST 4571
Tick Fen	53	TL 3384
Tickhill	71	SK 5993
Ticklerton	48	SO 4890
Ticknall	60	SK 3524
Tickton	74	TA 0641
Tidbury Ring (ant.)	35	SU 4642
Tidcombe	34	SU 2858
Tiddington (Oxon.)	36	SP 6404
Tiddington (Warw.)	50	SP 2256
Tidebrook	29	TQ 6130
Tideford	20	SX 3459
Tidenham	45	ST 5596
Tidenham Chase	45	ST 5598
Tideswell	70	SK 1575
Tidmarsh	36	SU 6374
Tidmington	50	SP 2538
Tidpit	26	SU 0718
Tiers Cross	42	SM 9010
Tiffield	51	SP 6951
Tifty	121	NJ 7740
Tigerton	109	NO 5364
Tigharry	124	NF 7171
Tigh na Blair	107	NN 7716
Tighnabruaich	100	NR 9772
Tighnafiline	126	NG 8789
Tighvein (mt.)	92	NR 9927
Tigley	21	SX 7560
Tilbrook	52	TL 0769
Tilbury	30	TQ 6376
Tile Cross	50	SP 1687
Tile Hill	50	SP 2777
Tilehurst	36	SU 6673
Tilford	35	SU 8743
Tillathrowie	121	NJ 4634
Tillicoultry	102	NS 9197
Tillingham	39	TL 9903
Tillington (Here. and Worc.)	45	SO 4645
Tillington (W Susx.)	28	SU 9621
Tillington Common	45	SO 4546
Tillyarblet	109	NO 5267
Tillycorthie	121	NJ 9123
Tillydrine House	119	NO 6098
Tillyfourie	119	NJ 6412
Tillygarmond	119	NO 6393
Tillygreig	121	NJ 8823
Tilly Whim Caves	26	SZ 0377
Tilmanstone	31	TR 3051
Tilney All Saints	63	TF 5618
Tilney High End	63	TF 5617
Tilney St. Lawrence	63	TF 5414
Tilshead	34	SU 0347
Tilstock	59	SJ 5337
Tilston	58	SJ 4551
Tilstone Fearnall	69	SJ 5660
Tilsworth	36	SP 9724
Tilton on the Hill	61	SK 7405
Timberland	72	TF 1158
Timberland Delph	73	TF 1559
Timbersbrook	69	SJ 8962
Timberscombe	23	SS 9542
Timble	78	SE 1752
Timperley	69	SJ 7988
Timsbury (Avon)	33	ST 6658
Timsbury (Hants.)	26	SU 3424
Timsgarry	130	NB 0533
Timworth Green	54	TL 8669
Tincleton	25	SY 7691
Tindale	90	NY 6159
Tindale Fells	83	NY 6157
Tindale Tarn	90	NY 6058
Tind, The (pt.)	143	HU 6790
Tingewick	51	SP 6533
Tingley	79	SE 2826
Tingrith	52	TL 0032
Tinhay	20	SX 4085
Tinnis Castle (ant.)	95	NT 1434
Tinnis Hill	89	NY 4385
Tinshill	79	SE 2540
Tinsley	71	SK 3990
Tintagel	18	SX 0588
Tintagel Head	20	SX 0489
Tintern Abbey (ant.)	45	SO 5300
Tintern Parva	45	SO 5200
Tintinhull	25	ST 5019
Tinto	95	NS 9534
Tinto Hills	95	NS 9534
Tintwistle	70	SK 0297
Tinwald	88	NY 0081
Tinwell	62	TF 0006
Tipperty	121	NJ 9627
Tipperweir (mt.)	119	NO 6885
Tipton	50	SO 9592
Tipton St. John	24	SY 0991
Tiptree	38	TL 8916
Tirabad	44	SN 8741
Tiree (is.)	104	NM 0045
Tiree Aerodrome	104	NM 0045
Tirfergus Hill	92	NR 6617
Tirga Mòr (mt.)	124	NB 0511
Tirley	46	SO 8328
Tirphil	41	SO 1303
Tir Rhiwiog	57	SH 9216
Tirril	83	NY 5026
Tir y mynach	57	SH 9302
Tisbury	26	ST 9429
Tissington	60	SK 1752
Titchberry	22	SS 2427
Titchfield	27	SU 5305
Titchmarsh	52	TL 0279
Titchwell	64	TF 7543
Tithby	61	SK 6936
Titley	45	SO 3260
Titlington	91	NU 1015
Tittensor	59	SJ 8738
Titterstone Clee Hill	49	SO 5978
Tittesworth Resr.	70	SJ 9959
Tittleshall	64	TF 8920
Tiumpan Head	131	NB 5737
Tiverton (Ches.)	69	SJ 5560
Tiverton (Devon)	23	SS 9512
Tiverton Junction Station	24	ST 0311
Tivetshall St. Margaret	55	TM 1787
Tivetshall St. Mary	55	TM 1686
Tixall	60	SJ 9722
Tixover	62	SK 9700
Toab (Orkney)	136	HY 5106
Toab (Shetld.)	141	HU 3811
Toa Galson	131	NB 4560
Tobermory	111	NM 5055
Toberonochy	105	NM 7408
Tobson	131	NB 1438
Tocher	121	NJ 6932
Tockenham	34	SU 0379
Tockenham Wick	34	SU 0381
Tockholes	77	SD 6623
Tockington	33	ST 6186
Tockwith	79	SE 4652
Todber	25	ST 7919
Toddington (Beds.)	52	TL 0129
Toddington (Glos.)	46	SP 0432
Toddun (mt.)	125	NB 2102
Todenham	50	SP 2436
Todhead Point	119	NO 8676
Tod Hill	92	NR 7212
Todhills	89	NY 3663
Tod Law	94	NS 7735
Todmorden	78	SD 9324
Todwick	71	SK 4984
Toe Head	124	NF 9594
Toes (is.)	42	SR 8994
Toft (Cambs.)	53	TL 3655
Toft (Ches.)	69	SJ 7676
Toft (Lincs.)	62	TF 0617
Toft Monks	65	TM 4295
Toft Newton Resr.	72	TF 0488
Toft next Newton	72	TF 0488
Toftrees	64	TF 8927
Toft Sand	63	TF 4441
Tofts Voe	143	HU 4375
Toftwood	64	TF 9811
Togston	91	NU 2401
Tokavaig	123	NG 6011
Tokers Green	36	SU 7077
Tolland	23	ST 1032
Tollard Royal	26	ST 9417
Toll Creagach	115	NH 1928
Toller Fratrum	25	SY 5797
Toller Porcorum	25	SY 5697
Tollerton (Notts.)	61	SK 6134
Tollerton (N Yorks.)	79	SE 5164
Tollesbury	38	TL 9510
Tolleshunt D'Arcy	38	TL 9312
Tolleshunt Major	38	TL 9011
Toll of Birness	121	NK 0034
Tollomuick Forest	117	NH 3380
Tolmount	117	NO 2079
Tolob	141	HU 3811
Tolpuddle	25	SY 7994
Tolquhon Castle (ant.)	121	NJ 8728
Tolsta Chaolais	131	NB 1938
Tolsta Head	131	NB 5647
Tolworth	37	TQ 1965
Tom a'Choinich	115	NH 1627
Tom an t-Saighdeir	106	NM 9715
Tom ant-Suidhe Mhòir	117	NJ 1018
Tomatin	116	NH 8028
Tom Bailgeann (mt.)	116	NH 5829
Tombane Burn	108	NN 9241
Tombreck	116	NH 6934
Tomchrasky	115	NH 2512
Tomdoun	115	NH 1501
Tomich (Highld.)	115	NH 3127
Tomich (Highld.)	128	NH 5348
Tomich (Highld.)	129	NH 7071
Tomintoul (Grampn.)	117	NJ 1618
Tomintoul (Grampn.)	117	NO 1490
Tomlachlan Burn	117	NH 9337
Tom na h-Iolaire	100	NR 9485
Tomnaven	121	NJ 4033
Tomnavoukin	117	NJ 2026
Tomont End	100	NS 1759
Tom's Cairn	119	NO 6194
Tomsléibhe	105	NM 6137
Tom Soilleir	105	NM 8409
Tomtain (mt.)	101	NS 7181
Tonbridge	29	TQ 5845
Tondu	41	SS 8984
Tong (Isle of Lewis)	131	NB 4536
Tong (Shrops.)	59	SJ 7907
Tonga	143	HP 5814
Tonge	60	SK 4123
Tongham	35	SU 8848
Tongland	87	NX 6953
Tongue	133	NC 5957
Tongue (lightship)	39	TR 3485
Tongue Bay	133	NC 6061
Tongue House	133	NC 5958
Tongwynlais	41	ST 1581
Tòn Mhòr	98	NR 2371
Tonna	41	SS 7798
Ton-Teg	41	ST 0986
Tòn Tire (pt.)	105	NM 6019
Tonwell	37	TL 3317
Tonypandy	41	SS 9992
Tonyrefail	41	ST 0188
Toot Baldon	47	SP 5600
Toot Hill (Essex)	37	TL 5102
Toot Hill (Hants.)	26	SU 3718
Topcliffe	79	SE 3976
Topcroft	65	TM 2693
Topcroft Street	55	TM 2692
Toppesfield	54	TL 7337
Toppings	69	SD 7213
Topsham	24	SX 9788
Torbay	21	SX 8962
Tor Bay	21	SX 9259
Torbeg	92	NR 8929
Torboll Farm	129	NH 7598
Torbreck Burn	128	NC 6907
Torbryan	21	SX 8266
Torcastle	115	NN 1378
Torcross	21	SX 8242
Tore	116	NH 6052
Tore Hill	117	NH 9817
Torfichen Hill	96	NT 3353
Torhousemuir	86	NX 3957
Torksey	72	SK 8378
Torlum (Benbecula)	124	NF 7850
Torlum (Tays.)	107	NN 8219
Torlum Wood	107	NN 8218
Torlundy	115	NN 1477
Tormarton	33	ST 7678
Tormisdale	98	NR 1958
Tormitchell	86	NX 2394
Tormore	92	NR 8932
Tornagrain	129	NH 7649
Tornahaish	117	NJ 2908
Tornashean Forest	118	NJ 3710
Tornaveen	119	NJ 6106
Torness (Highld.)	116	NH 5727
Torness (Hoy, Orkney)	136	ND 2588
Tor Ness (N. Ronaldsay)	139	HY 7555
Tor Ness (Orkney)	136	HY 4219
Tor Ness (Stronsay)	139	HY 6520
Torogay	124	NF 9178
Torosay Castle	105	NM 7335
Torpantau	41	SO 0418
Torpenhow	82	NY 2039
Torphichen	102	NS 9672
Torphins	119	NJ 6202
Torpoint	20	SX 4355
Torquay	21	SX 9164
Torquhan	96	NT 4447
Torrachilty Forest	128	NH 4455
Torran (Island of Raasay)	123	NG 5949
Torran (Strath.)	105	NM 8704
Torrance	101	NS 6174
Torran Rocks	104	NM 2713
Torran Tùrach (mt.)	100	NS 0070
Torran Water	127	ND 0554
Torrent Walk	57	SH 7518
Torridon	126	NG 9056
Torridon Forest	126	NG 9158
Torridon House	126	NG 8757
Torrie Forest	101	NN 6403
Torrin	123	NG 5720
Torrisholme	77	NC 6761
Torrisdale (Highld.)	133	NC 6761
Torrisdale (Strath.)	92	NR 7737
Torrisdale Bay	133	NC 6863
Torrisdale Castle	92	NR 7936
Torrisdale Water	92	NR 7636
Torrish	134	NC 9718
Torrisholme	77	SD 4464
Torr Meadhonach	92	NR 9551
Torr Mòr	92	NS 1053
Torr Nead an Eoin	92	NR 9549
Torroble	128	NC 5904
Torrs Warren	86	NX 1455
Torr, The	92	NR 9225
Torry (Grampn.)	121	NJ 4339
Torry (Grampn.)	121	NJ 9404
Torry Bay	102	NT 0185
Torryburn	102	NT 0286
Torrylin	92	NR 9621
Torrylinwater Foot	92	NR 9520
Torsay Island	105	NM 7613
Torside Reservoir	70	SK 0698
Torterston	121	NK 0747
Torthorwald	89	NY 0378
Tortington	28	TQ 0005
Tortworth	33	ST 6992
Torvaig	123	NG 4944
Torver	82	SD 2894
Torwood	101	NS 8484
Torworth	71	SK 6586
Toscaig	123	NG 7138
Toseland	53	TL 2362
Tosside	78	SD 7655
Tosside Beck	78	SD 7853
Tosson Hill	91	NZ 0098
Tostock	54	TL 9563
Totaig	122	NG 2050
Tote	123	NG 4149
Totegan	134	NC 8268
Totland	26	SZ 3286
Totland Bay	26	SZ 3186
Totley	71	SK 3179
Totnes	21	SX 8060
Toton	61	SK 5034
Totronald	110	NM 1656
Totscore	122	NG 3866
Tottenham	37	TQ 3491
Tottenhill	64	TF 6310
Totteridge	37	TQ 2494
Totternhoe	36	SP 9921
Tottiford Resr.	21	SX 8183
Tottington	69	SD 7712
Totton	26	SU 3513
Touch Hills	101	NS 7291
Tournaig	126	NG 8783
Toux (Grampn.)	121	NJ 5458
Toux (Grampn.)	121	NJ 9850
Tovil	29	TQ 7554
Toward	100	NS 1368
Toward Point	100	NS 1367
Towcester	51	SP 6948
Towednack	18	SW 4838
Tower Hill Station	20	SX 3690
Tower Point	42	SM 7911
Towersey	36	SP 7305
Towie	118	NJ 4412
Towiemore	121	NJ 3845
Tow Law	84	NZ 1139
Towneley Hall (ant.)	78	SD 8530
Town End (Cambs.)	63	TL 4195
Town End (Cumbr.)	77	SD 4483
Townhead	87	NX 6946
Townhead of Greenlaw	88	NX 7465
Townhill	102	NT 1089
Townshend	18	SW 5932
Town Yetholm	97	NT 8228
Towthorpe	79	SE 6258
Towton	79	SE 4839
Towy Forest	44	SN 8350
Towyn (Clwyd)	67	SH 9779
Towyn (Gwyn.)	56	SH 5800
Toynton All Saints	73	TF 3964
Toynton Fen Side	73	TF 3961
Toynton St. Peter	73	TF 4063
Toy's Hill	29	TQ 4751
Trabboch	93	NS 4321
Trabbochburn	93	NS 4621
Traboe	18	SW 7421
Tradespark (Highld.)	129	NH 8656
Tradespark (Orkney)	136	HY 4408
Traeth Bach	66	SH 5735
Trafford Park	69	SJ 7996
Trahenna Hill	95	NT 1337
Traigh House	111	NM 6590
Traigh Mhòr	112	NF 7005
Trallong	41	SN 9629
Tranent	103	NT 4072
Trannon	57	SN 9096
Trantlemore	134	NC 8853
Tranwell	91	NZ 1883
Trapp	43	SN 6519
Traprain	103	NT 5975
Traprain Law (ant.)	103	NT 5874
Traquair	96	NT 3334
Trawden	78	SD 9138
Trawsallt	57	SN 7870
Trawsfynydd	57	SH 7035
Trawsfynydd Lake (Resr.)	67	SH 6936
Trealaval (mt.)	131	NB 2623
Trealaw	41	SS 9992
Treales	77	SD 4432
Trearddur Bay	66	SH 2478
Treaslane	123	NG 3953
Trebartha	20	SX 2677
Trebetherick	19	SW 9377
Treborough	23	ST 0036
Trebudannon	19	SW 8961
Treburley	20	SX 3477
Trecastle	41	SN 8729
Trecwn	42	SM 9632
Trecynon	41	SN 9903
Tredavoe	18	SW 4528
Tre-ddiog	42	SM 8928
Tredegar	41	SO 1409
Tredington	50	SP 2543
Tredinnick	19	SW 9270
Tredomen	41	SO 1231
Tredrizzick	19	SW 9577
Tredunnock	45	ST 3795
Treen	18	SW 3923
Treeton	71	SK 4387
Trefdraeth	66	SH 4070
Trefeca	41	SO 1431
Trefeglwys	57	SN 9690
Trefenter	43	SN 6068
Treffgarne	42	SM 9523
Treffynnon	42	SM 8428
Trefil	41	SO 1212
Trefilan	43	SN 5457
Trefnanney	58	SJ 2015
Trefnant	67	SJ 0570
Trefonen	58	SJ 2526
Trefor	66	SH 3779
Treforest Industrial Estate	41	ST 1186
Trefriw	67	SH 7763
Tregadillett	20	SX 2983
Tregaian	66	SH 4579
Tregaron	44	SN 6759
Tregarth	66	SH 6067
Tregeare	20	SX 2486
Tregeare Rounds (ant.)	19	SX 0379
Tregeiriog	58	SJ 1733
Tregele	66	SH 3592
Tregidden	18	SW 7523
Treglemais	42	SM 8229
Tregole	20	SX 1998
Tregonetha	19	SW 9563
Tregony	19	SW 9244
Tregonning Hill	18	SW 6029
Tregoyd	45	SO 1937
Tre-groes	43	SN 4044
Tregurrian	19	SW 8465
Tregynon	57	SO 0999
Trehafod	41	ST 0491
Treharris	41	ST 1097
Treherbert	41	SS 9398
Treknow	20	SX 0586
Trelan	18	SW 7418
Trelawnyd	67	SJ 0879
Trelech	43	SN 2830
Trelech a'r Betws	43	SN 3026
Treleddyd-fawr	42	SM 7528
Trelewis	41	ST 1197
Treligga	20	SX 0584
Trelights	19	SW 9879
Trelill	19	SX 0477
Trelissick	19	SW 8339
Trelleck	45	SO 5005
Trelleck Grange	45	SO 4901
Trelogan	68	SJ 1180
Trelowarren (ant.)	18	SW 7124
Trelystan	58	SJ 2603
Tremadog	66	SH 5640
Tremadog Bay	66	SH 5234
Tremail	20	SX 1686
Tremain	43	SN 2348
Tremaine	20	SX 2388
Tremar	19	SX 2568
Trematon	20	SX 3959
Tremeirchion	67	SJ 0773
Trenance	19	SW 8567
Trenarren	19	SX 0348
Trench	59	SJ 6913
Trenchford Resr.	21	SX 8082
Trendrine Hill	18	SW 4838
Treneglos	20	SX 2088
Trenewan	19	SX 1753
Trent	25	ST 5918
Trent and Mersey Canal (Ches.)	69	SJ 7263
Trent and Mersey Canal (Derby)	60	SK 3529
Trentham	59	SJ 8640
Trentishoe	23	SS 6448
Trent Valley	61	SK 0120
Treoes	41	SS 9478
Treorchy	41	SS 9596
Tre'r Ceiri (ant.)	66	SH 3744
Tre-r-ddôl	57	SN 6592
Tre'r gaer (Tregare)	45	SO 4110
Tresaith	43	SN 2751
Tresco	18	SV 8914
Trescott	59	SO 8497
Trescowe	18	SW 5731
Tresham	33	ST 7991
Treshnish Isles	104	NM 2741
Treshnish Point	104	NM 3348
Tresillian	19	SW 8646
Tresinwen	42	SM 9040
Tresmeer	20	SX 2387
Tres Ness	139	HY 7137
Tressait	107	NN 8160
Tresta (Fetlar)	143	HU 6190
Tresta (Shetld.)	141	HU 3651
Treswell	72	SK 7779
Trethewey	18	SW 3823
Trethomas	41	ST 1889
Trethurgy	19	SX 0355
Tretio	42	SM 7829
Tretire	45	SO 5124
Tretower	41	SO 1821
Tretower Court (ant.)	41	SO 1821
Treuddyn	68	SJ 2458
Trevalga	20	SX 0889
Trevanson	19	SW 9772
Trevarren	19	SW 9160
Trevarrick	19	SW 9843
Trevellas	18	SW 7452
Treverva	18	SW 7631
Trevethin	45	SO 2802
Trevigro	20	SX 3369
Trevine	42	SM 8432
Treviscoe	19	SW 9455
Trevone	19	SW 8975
Trevor	66	SH 3746
Trevose Head	19	SW 8576
Trewarmett	20	SX 0686
Trewarthenick	19	SW 9044
Trewassa	20	SX 1486
Trewavas Head	18	SW 5926
Trewellard	18	SW 3733
Trewen	20	SX 2583
Trewent Point	42	SS 0297
Trewidland	20	SX 2560
Trewint	20	SX 1897
Trewithian	19	SW 8737
Trewoon	19	SW 9952
Treyarnon Bay	19	SW 8673
Treyford	27	SU 8218
Triangular Lodge (ant.)	52	SP 8383
Trichrug	40	ST 7023
Trickett's Cross	26	SU 0801
Trigon Hill	25	SY 8989
Trimdon	85	NZ 3634
Trimdon Colliery	85	NZ 3835
Trimdon Grange	85	NZ 3735
Trimingham	65	TG 2738
Trimley St. Martin	55	TM 2737
Trimley St. Mary	55	TM 2737
Trimpley	49	SO 7978
Trimpley Resr.	49	SO 7779
Trimsaran	43	SN 4504
Trimstone	23	SS 5043
Trinant	41	SO 2000
Tring	36	SP 9211
Trinity	109	NO 6061
Trislaig	115	NN 0874
Trispen	19	SW 8450
Tritlington	91	NZ 2092
Triuirebheinn	112	NF 8121
Trochry	108	NN 9740
Troedyraur	43	SN 3245
Troedyrhiw	41	SO 0702
Trofarth	67	SH 8571
Troisgeach (mt.)	106	NN 2819
Trondra (is.)	141	HU 3936
Troon (Corn.)	18	SW 6638
Troon (Strath.)	93	NS 3230
Trossachs, The (dist.)	101	NN 4907
Troston	54	TL 8972
Troswick Ness	141	HU 4117
Trotternish (dist.)	123	NG 4552
Trottiscliffe	30	TQ 6460
Trotton	28	SU 8322
Troughend Common	90	NY 8490
Troup Head	121	NJ 8267
Troutbeck	83	NY 4103
Troutbeck Bridge	83	NY 4000
Trowbridge	33	ST 8557
Trow Green	45	SO 5706
Trowell	60	SK 4839
Trowie Glen	136	ND 2499
Trowle Common	33	ST 8358
Trows	96	NT 6932
Trowse Newton	65	TG 2406
Trudoxhill	33	ST 7443
Trull	24	ST 2122
Truman	41	SN 7420
Trumau (mt.)	57	SN 8567
Trum Gelli	57	SH 6501
Trumisgarry	124	NF 8674
Trumland House	136	HY 4227
Trumpan	122	NG 2261
Trumpet	49	SO 6539
Trumpington	53	TL 4455
Trunch	65	TG 2834
Trundle, The (ant.)	27	SU 8711
Truro	19	SW 8244
Trusham	21	SX 8582
Trusley	60	SK 2535
Trusthorpe	73	TF 5183
Trwyn Cilan	56	SH 2923
Trwyn Llanbedrog (pt.)	66	SH 3330
Trwyn Maen Dylan	66	SH 4252
Trwyn-y-bwa	42	SN 0542
Trwyn y Gorlech	66	SH 3445
Trwyn yr Wylfa	56	SH 3224
Trysull	59	SO 8494
Tuarie Burn	134	NC 8120
Tubney	47	SU 4498
Tuckenhay	21	SX 8156
Tuddenham (Suff.)	54	TL 7371
Tuddenham (Suff.)	55	TM 1948
Tudeley	29	TQ 6245
Tudhoe	84	NZ 2635
Tudhope Hill	89	NY 4399
Tudweiliog	66	SH 2336
Tuffley	46	SO 8315
Tugby	61	SK 7601
Tugford	48	SO 5587
Tulach Hill	108	NN 8664
Tulliallan Castle	102	NS 9388
Tulliallan Forest	102	NS 9588
Tullibody	102	NS 8595
Tullibole Castle (ant.)	102	NO 0500
Tullich (Highld.)	129	NH 8576
Tullich (Strath.)	106	NN 0815
Tullich Hill	107	NN 7036
Tullich Muir	129	NH 7373
Tulliemet	108	NN 9952
Tulliemet House	108	NN 9954
Tulloch (Grampn.)	109	NO 7671
Tulloch (Highld.)	128	NH 6192
Tulloch (Highld.) (dist.)	117	NN 9914
Tulloch Castle	128	NH 5460
Tullochcoy	117	NO 2394
Tullochgorm	100	NR 9695
Tulloch Station	115	NN 3580
Tulloes	109	NO 5145
Tullo Hill	109	NO 4964
Tullybannocher	107	NN 7521
Tullybeagles Lodge	108	NO 0136
Tullybothy Craigs	103	NO 6310
Tullyfergus	108	NO 2149
Tullymurdoch	108	NO 1952
Tullynessle	119	NJ 5519
Tulm Bay	123	NG 4075
Tumble	43	SN 5411
Tumby	73	TF 2359
Tumby Woodside	73	TF 2657
Tummel Bridge	107	NN 7659
Tummel Hill Scar	76	SD 1767
Tumpa, The (mt.)	41	SO 2235
Tungadal River	123	NG 4238
Tunstall (Humbs.)	74	TA 3032
Tunstall (Kent)	30	TQ 8961
Tunstall (Lancs.)	80	SD 6073
Tunstall (Norf.)	65	TG 4107
Tunstall (N Yorks.)	84	SE 2195
Tunstall (Staffs.)	59	SJ 8551
Tunstall (Suff.)	55	TM 3655
Tunstall Forest	55	TM 3854
Tunstall Resr.	84	NZ 0641
Tunstead	65	TG 2921
Tunworth	35	SU 6748
Tupsley	45	SO 5340
Turgis Green	36	SU 6959
Turin	109	NO 5352
Turin Hill	109	NO 5153
Turkdean	46	SP 1017
Tur Langton	61	SP 7194
Turls Head	142	HU 2886
Turnastone	45	SO 3536
Turnberry	93	NS 2005
Turnberry Bay	93	NS 1905
Turnditch	60	SK 2946
Turner's Hill	29	TQ 3435
Turners Puddle	25	SY 8293
Turnworth	25	ST 8107
Turra Field Aerodrome	143	HU 6191
Turriff	121	NJ 7249
Turton Bottoms	69	SD 7315
Turton Moor	69	SD 6818
Turves	63	TL 3396
Turvey	52	SP 9452
Turville	36	SU 7691
Turville Heath	36	SU 7391
Turweston	51	SP 6037
Tushielaw Inn	89	NT 3017
Tusker Rock	41	SS 8474
Tutbury	60	SK 2129
Tutnall	50	SO 9870
Tutshill	45	ST 5394
Tuttington	65	TG 2227
Tuxford	72	SK 7370
Twa Havens	121	NK 1036
Twatt (Orkney)	136	HY 2624
Twatt (Shetld.)	141	HU 3253
Twechar	101	NS 6975
Tweedmouth	97	NT 9952
Tweedsmuir	88	NT 1024
Tweed's Well (Source of River Tweed)	89	NT 0514
Twelveheads	18	SW 7642
Twenty	62	TF 1520
Twenty Foot River	63	TL 3397
Twerton	33	ST 7263
Twickenham	37	TQ 1473
Twigworth	46	SO 8421
Twineham	29	TQ 2519
Twiness	138	HY 4941
Twinhoe	33	ST 7359
Twinlaw Cairns (ant.)	96	NT 6254
Twinstead	54	TL 8637
Twiness	139	HY 5422
Twiss Green	69	SJ 6595
Twitchen (Devon)	23	SS 7830
Twitchen (Shrops.)	48	SO 3678
Twizell House	97	NU 1328
Two Bridges	21	SX 6075
Two Dales	71	SK 2762
Two Gates	60	SK 2101

Twopenny Knowe....94 NS 6332
Twr-gwyn (ant.)....57 SN 9195
Twycross....60 SK 3305
Twyford (Berks.)....36 SU 7975
Twyford (Bucks.)....51 SP 6626
Twyford (Hants.)....27 SU 4724
Twyford (Leic.)....61 SK 7210
Twyford (Norf.)....64 TG 0124
Twyford Common....45 SO 5135
Twyn-du....41 SO 0820
Twynholm....87 NX 6654
Twyning....49 SO 8936
Twyning Green....49 SO 9037
Twynllanan....41 SN 7524
Twyn Rhyd-car....44 SN 9642
Twyn-y-Sheriff....45 SO 4005
Twywell....45 SP 9578
Tyberton....45 SO 3739
Tyburn....50 SP 1490
Tycroes....43 SN 6010
Ty Croes Station....66 SH 3472
Tycrwyn....57 SJ 1018
Tydd Gote....63 TF 4518
Tydd St. Giles....63 TF 4216
Tydd St. Giles Fen....63 TF 3914
Tydd St. Mary....63 TF 4418
Ty-hen....66 SH 1731
Tyldesley....42 SD 6902
Tyler Hill....31 TR 1460
Tylers Green....36 SU 9094
Tylorstown....41 ST 0195
Tylwch....57 SN 9780
Ty-mawr....67 SH 9047
Ty-nant (Clwyd)....67 SH 9944
Ty-nant (Gwyn.)....57 SH 9026
Tyndrum....106 NN 3330
Tyndwr Hall....58 SJ 2241
Tyneham....25 SY 8880
Tynehead....103 NT 3959
Tyne Mouth (Lothian)....103 NT 6480
Tynemouth (Tyne and Wear)....91 NZ 3468
Tyne Water....103 NT 3863
Tynewydd....41 SS 9399
Tyninghame....103 NT 6179
Tynribbie....106 NM 9446
Tynron....88 NX 8093
Tyn-y-ffridd....58 SJ 1230
Tyn-y-graig....57 SH 7771
Ty'n-y-groes....67 SH 7771
Tyrebagger Hill....119 NJ 8412
Ty Rhiw....41 ST 1283
Tyringham....52 SP 8547
Tythegston....41 SS 8578
Tytherington (Avon)....33 ST 6788
Tytherington (Ches.)....69 SJ 9175
Tytherington (Somer.)....33 ST 7744
Tytherington (Wilts.)....33 ST 9140
Tytherleigh....24 ST 3203
Ty-uchaf....57 SH 9900
Tywardreath....19 SX 0854
Tywyn....56 SH 5901
Tywyn....67 SH 7878
Tywyn Trewan....66 SH 3175

U

Uachdar....124 NF 7955
Uags....123 NG 7235
Uair, The....134 NC 8252
Uamh Bheag....108 NN 6911
Ubbeston Green....55 TM 3271
Ubley....33 ST 5257
Uchd a' Chlàrsair....116 NN 8181
Uckerby....84 NZ 2402
Uckfield....29 TQ 4721
Uckington....46 SO 9224
Udairn....123 NG 5142
Udale Bay....129 NH 7166
Uddingston....101 NS 6960
Uddington....95 NS 8633
Udimore....30 TQ 8718
Udny Green....121 NJ 8726
Udstonhead....94 NS 7047
Uffcott....34 SU 1277
Uffculme....24 ST 0612
Uffington (Lincs.)....62 TF 0608
Uffington (Oxon.)....34 SU 3089
Uffington (Shrops.)....59 SJ 5313
Uffington Castle (ant.)....34 SU 2986
Ufford (Northants.)....62 TF 0904
Ufford (Suff.)....55 TM 2953
Ufton....50 SP 3762
Ufton Nervet....36 SU 6367
Ugadale....92 NR 7828
Ugadale Point....92 NR 7828
Ugborough....21 SX 6755
Ugborough Beacon....21 SX 6659
Ugborough Moor....21 SX 6462
Uggeshall....55 TM 4580
Ugglebarnby....81 NZ 8707
Ugley....53 TL 5128
Ugley Green....53 TL 5227
Ugthorpe....85 NZ 7911
Uig (Island of Skye)....122 NG 1952
Uig (Island of Skye)....123 NG 3963
Uig Bay....122 NG 3862
Uigshader....123 NG 4246
Uinessan (is.)....112 NL 6695
Uisenis (is.)....125 NB 3306
Uisge Labhair....107 NN 4370
Uisge Misgeach....115 NH 1837
Uisge Toll a' Mhadaidh....126 NG 9784
Uisgnaval Mór (mt.)....125 NB 1208
Uisken....104 NM 3819
Ukna Skerry....141 HU 3531
Ulbster....135 ND 3241
Ulceby (Humbs.)....75 TA 1014
Ulceby (Lincs.)....73 TF 4272
Ulcombe....30 TQ 8449
Uldale....82 NY 2536
Uldale Head (mt.)....83 NY 6300
Uldale House....83 SD 7396
Uley....46 ST 7898
Ulfhart Point....123 NG 4716
Ulgham....91 NZ 2392
Ulladale River....130 NB 0714
Ullapool....127 NH 1294
Ullapool River....127 NH 1495
Ullaval (mt.)....131 NB 0811
Ullenhall....50 SP 1267
Ullenwood....46 SO 9416
Ulleskelf....79 SE 5140
Ullesthorpe....51 SP 5087
Ulley....71 SK 4687
Ullingswick....45 SO 5950
Ullinish....122 NG 3238
Ullock....82 NY 0724
Ullswater....83 NY 4220
Ulpha....82 SD 1993
Ulpha Fell....82 SD 1695
Ulpha Park....82 SD 1990
Ulrome....81 TA 1656
Ulsta....143 HU 4680
Ulva (is.)....105 NM 4040
Ulva House....105 NM 4439
Ulverston....77 SD 2878
Ulzieside....88 NS 7708
Umberleigh....23 SS 6023
Unapool....132 NC 2332

Underbarrow....83 SD 4692
Undercliff, The (I. of W.)....26 SZ 3883
Undercliff, The (I. of W.)....27 SZ 5375
Underhoull....143 HP 5704
Underriver....29 TQ 5552
Underwood (Gwent)....33 ST 3889
Underwood (Notts.)....61 SK 4750
Undy....33 ST 4386
Unifirth....140 HU 2856
Union Canal....102 NT 1171
Union Cottage....119 NO 8290
Union Mills....76 SC 3578
Unst (is.)....143 HP 6009
Unstone....71 SK 3777
Unthank....83 NY 4536
Upavon....34 SU 1354
Up Cerne....25 ST 6502
Upchurch....30 TQ 8467
Upcott....45 SO 3250
Upend....54 TL 7058
Up Exe....23 SS 9302
Uphall....102 NT 0571
Uphall Station....102 NT 0670
Upham (Devon)....23 SS 8808
Upham (Hants.)....27 SU 5320
Up Hatherley....46 SO 9120
Uphill (Avon)....32 ST 3158
Up Hill (Kent)....31 TR 2140
Up Holland....69 SD 5105
Uplawmoor....93 NS 4355
Upleadon....46 SO 7527
Upleatham....85 NZ 6319
Uplees....31 TQ 9964
Uplowman....23 ST 0115
Uplyme....24 SY 3293
Upminster....37 TQ 5686
Up Nately....35 SU 6951
Upnor....30 TQ 7470
Upottery....27 ST 2007
Uppark....27 SU 7717
Upper Affcot....48 SO 4486
Upper Ardchronie....128 NH 6188
Upper Arley....49 SO 7680
Upper Astrop....51 SP 5137
Upper Basildon....35 SU 5976
Upper Beeding....28 TQ 1910
Upper Benefield....52 SP 9789
Upper Boddington....51 SP 4853
Upper Borth....56 SN 6088
Upper Breinton....45 SO 4640
Upper Broughton....61 SK 6826
Upper Brow Top....77 SD 5258
Upper Bucklebury....35 SU 5368
Upper Burnhaugh....119 NO 8394
Upper Caldecote....52 TL 1645
Upper Chapel....44 SO 0040
Upper Chute....34 SU 2953
Upper Clatford....34 SU 3543
Upper Clynnog....66 SH 4746
Upper Cokeham....28 TQ 1605
Upper Coll....131 NB 4539
Upper Cwmtwrch....44 SN 7611
Upper Dallachy....127 NJ 3662
Upper Dean....52 TL 0467
Upper Denby....71 SE 2207
Upper Derraid....117 NJ 0233
Upper Dicker....29 TQ 5510
Upper Elkstone....70 SK 0559
Upper End....70 SK 0876
Upper Ethie....129 NH 7663
Upper Farringdon....27 SU 7135
Upper Framilode....46 SO 7510
Upper Froyle....35 SU 7542
Upper Glenfintaig....115 NN 2588
Upper Gravenhurst....52 TL 1136
Upper Green....34 SU 3663
Upper Hackney....71 SK 2961
Upper Hale....35 SU 8448
Upper Hambleton....62 SK 8907
Upper Hardres Court....31 TR 1550
Upper Hartfield....29 TQ 4634
Upper Heath....48 SO 5685
Upper Helmsley....80 SE 6956
Upper Heyford....47 SP 4926
Upper Hill....45 SO 4753
Upper Hopton....70 SE 1918
Upper Hulme....70 SK 0160
Upper Icknield Way (ant.)....36 SP 9212
Upper Inglesham....47 SU 2096
Upper Killay....40 SS 5892
Upper Knockando....129 NJ 1843
Upper Lambourn....34 SU 3180
Upper Langwith....71 SK 5169
Upper Lochton....119 NO 6997
Upper Loch Torridon....126 NG 8556
Upper Longdon....60 SK 0614
Upper Longwood....59 SJ 6007
Upper Longwood....59 SJ 6015
Upper Maes-coed....45 SO 3335
Uppermill....70 SD 9906
Upper Minety....34 SU 0091
Upper North Dean....36 SU 8598
Upper Poppleton....79 SE 5554
Upper Quinton....50 SP 1746
Upper Sanday....137 HY 5303
Upper Sapey....49 SO 6863
Upper Scoulag....100 NS 1059
Upper Seagry....33 ST 9580
Upper Shelton....52 SP 9943
Upper Sheringham....65 TG 1441
Upper Skelmorlie....100 NS 1968
Upper Slaughter....47 SP 1523
Upper Soudley....46 SO 6610
Upper Stondon....52 TL 1535
Upper Stowe....51 SP 6456
Upper Street (Hants.)....26 SU 1418
Upper Street (Norf.)....65 TG 3016
Upper Sundon....52 TL 0527
Upper Swell....47 SP 1726
Upper Tamar Lake Reservoir....22 SS 2811
Upper Tean....60 SK 0139
Upperthong....70 SE 1208
Upper Tillyrie....102 NO 1006
Upperton....28 SU 9522
Upper Tooting....37 TQ 2772
Upper Town (Avon)....33 ST 5265
Uppertown (Island of Stroma)....135 ND 3576
Upper Tysoe....50 SP 3343
Upper Upham....34 SU 2277
Upper Wardington....51 SP 4946
Upper Weald....51 SP 8037
Upper Weedon....51 SP 6258
Upper Wield....35 SU 6238
Upper Winchendon....36 SP 7414
Upper Woodford....26 SU 1237
Uppingham....62 SP 8699
Uppington....59 SJ 5909
Upsall....79 SE 4587
Upshire....37 TL 4100
Up Somborne....26 SU 3932
Upstreet....31 TR 2262
Up Sydling....25 ST 6201
Upton (Berks.)....36 SU 9879
Upton (Bucks.)....36 SP 7711
Upton (Cambs.)....52 TL 1778
Upton (Ches.)....68 SJ 4069
Upton (Dorset)....26 SY 9893
Upton (Hants.)....34 SU 3555
Upton (Hants.)....26 SU 3716
Upton (Leic.)....60 SP 3699
Upton (Lincs.)....72 SK 8686
Upton (Mers.)....68 SJ 2687

Upton (Norf.)....65 TG 3912
Upton (Northants.)....51 SP 7160
Upton (Northants.)....62 TF 1000
Upton (Notts.)....71 SK 7354
Upton (Notts.)....72 SK 7476
Upton (Oxon.)....35 SU 5186
Upton (Somer.)....23 SS 9928
Upton (W Yorks.)....71 SE 4713
Upton Bishop....46 SO 6427
Upton Cheyney....33 ST 6969
Upton Cressett....50 SO 6592
Upton Cross....20 SX 2872
Upton Grey....35 SU 6948
Upton Hellions....23 SS 8303
Upton Lovell....34 ST 9440
Upton Magna....59 SJ 5512
Upton Noble....33 ST 7139
Upton Pyne....23 SX 9197
Upton Scudamore....33 ST 8647
Upton Snodsbury....49 SO 9454
Upton St. Leonards....46 SO 8615
Upton upon Severn....49 SO 8540
Upton Warren....49 SO 9267
Upwaltham....28 SU 9413
Upware....53 TL 5370
Upwell....63 TF 5002
Upwell Fen (Cambs.)....63 TL 4795
Upwell Fen (Norf.)....63 TL 5499
Upwey....25 SY 6684
Upwood....52 TL 2582
Uradale....141 HU 4137
Ura Firth (Shetld.)....142 HU 2977
Urafirth (Shetld.)....142 HU 3078
Urchal....129 NH 7544
Urchfont....34 SU 0356
Urdimarsh....45 SO 5249
Ure....63 HU 2280
Urgha....125 NG 1799
Urie Lingey....143 HU 5995
Urie Ness....143 HU 5994
Urishay Common....45 SO 3137
Urit Hill....125 NS 7626
Urlar Burn....107 NN 8345
Urlay Nook....85 NZ 4014
Urmston....69 SJ 7695
Urquhart....129 NJ 2863
Urquhart Bay....116 NH 5229
Urquhart Castle (ant.)....116 NH 5328
Urra....85 NZ 5702
Urrall Fell....78 NX 2870
Urray....128 NH 5053
Urray Forest....128 NH 4850
Urr Water....88 NX 7670
Urswick....76 SD 2674
Urvaig (pt.)....110 NM 0850
Ushaw Moor....84 NZ 2342
Usinish....112 NF 8635
Usk....45 SO 3701
Uskie Geo....143 HU 2047
Usk Resr.....41 SN 8128
Usselby....73 TF 0993
Usta Ness....140 HU 3841
Usway Burn....90 NT 8713
Utley....78 SE 0542
Uton....21 SX 8298
Utterby....73 TF 3093
Uttoxeter....60 SK 0933
Uwchmynydd (Gwyn.)....66 SH 1425
Uwch-mynydd (Gwyn.)....57 SH 9634
Uxbridge....36 TQ 0583
Uyea (Shetld.) (is.)....142 HU 3192
Uyea (Unst) (is.)....143 HU 6098
Uyeasound (Unst)....143 HP 5901
Uyea Sound (Unst)....143 HU 5899
Uynarey (is.)....143 HU 6493
Uzmaston....42 SM 9714

V

Vacsay....131 NB 1136
Vaila (is.)....140 HU 2346
Vaila Hall....140 HU 2246
Vaila Sound....140 HU 2347
Vaitam (is.)....124 NF 9380
Vale of Belvoir....61 SK 7838
Vale of Berkeley....46 ST 6897
Vale of Catmose....62 SK 8709
Vale of Clwyd....67 SJ 0668
Vale of Conwy....67 SH 7867
Vale of Evesham....50 SP 0943
Vale of Gloucester....46 SO 8421
Vale of Mawgan or Lanherne....19 SW 8964
Vale of Neath....41 SN 8303
Vale of Pewsey....34 SU 1259
Vale of Taunton Deane....24 ST 1727
Vale of White Horse....34 SU 3291
Valla Field (dist.)....143 HP 5807
Vallay (Harris, W Isles)....124 NG 0582
Vallay (North Uist)....124 NF 7776
Vallay Strand....124 NF 7875
Valley....66 SH 2979
Valley Airfield....66 SH 3075
Valleyfield....102 NT 0086
Valsgarth....143 HP 6413
Valtos (Island of Skye)....123 NG 5163
Valtos (Isle of Lewis)....131 NB 0936
Vange....38 TQ 7287
Vardre....40 SN 6902
Varne (lightship)....31 TR 3020
Varragill River....123 NG 4737
Varteg....45 SO 2605
Vatersay (W Isles)....112 NL 6394
Vatersay (W Isles)....112 NL 6396
Vatersay Bay....112 NL 6495
Vatisker Point....131 NB 4939
Vatten....122 NG 2843
Vaul....104 NM 0448
Vaul Bay....110 NM 0549
Vauld, The....45 SO 5349
Vaynol Hall....66 SH 5369
Vaynor....41 SO 0410
Vaynor Park....58 SJ 1700
Veantrow Bay....136 HY 5020
Veensgarth....141 HU 4244
Veilish Point....124 NF 8178
Velindre (Dyfed)....42 SN 1039
Velindre (Dyfed)....43 SN 3538
Velindre (Powys)....45 SO 1836
Vellan Head....18 SW 6615
Vementry (is.)....140 HU 2960
Veness (Eday)....137 HY 5729
Ve Ness (Orkney)....136 HY 3705
Venford Resr.....21 SX 6870
Vennington....58 SJ 3309
Venn Ottery....24 SY 0791
Venta (Gwent) (ant.)....33 ST 4790
Venta (Hants.) (ant.)....27 SU 4829
Ventnor....27 SZ 5677
Vercovicium (ant.)....90 NY 7868
Vere, The....143 HP 6403
Vermuden's or Forty Foot Drain....53 TL 3888
Vernham Dean....34 SU 3356
Vernham Street....34 SU 3457
Vernolds Common....48 SO 4780
Verran Island....112 NF 7234
Verulamium (ant.)....37 TL 1307
Verwig....43 SN 1849
Verwood....26 SU 0908
Veryan....19 SW 9139
Veryan Bay....19 SW 9640

Ve Skerries....140 HU 1065
Vestra Fiold (mt.)....136 HY 2322
Vicarage....24 SY 2088
Vickerstown....76 SD 1868
Victoria....19 SW 9961
Victoria Station....37 TQ 2979
Vidlin....141 HU 4765
Vidlin Voe....141 HU 4866
Viewing Hill....83 NY 7833
Viewpark....101 NS 7161
Villavin....23 SS 5816
Vindovala (ant.)....91 NZ 1067
Vinehall Street....29 TQ 7520
Vine's Cross....29 TQ 5917
Virda Field (mt.)....140 HU 1561
Virginia Water....36 SU 9967
Virginstow....20 SX 3792
Virley Channel....39 TM 0011
Vironcium (ant.)....59 SJ 5608
Vobster....33 ST 7048
Voe (Shetld.)....141 HU 3381
Voe (Shetld.)....141 HU 4015
Voe (Shetld.)....141 HU 4063
Voe of Cullingsburgh....141 HU 5242
Voe of Dale....140 HU 1752
Voe of Snarraness....140 HU 2356
Vord Hill....143 HU 6293
Vorogay....124 NF 7864
Vowchurch....45 SO 3636
Voxter....143 HU 3770
Voy....136 HY 2515
Vuia Beag (is.)....131 NB 1233
Vuia Mór (is.)....131 NB 1234

W

Waberthwaite....82 SD 1093
Wackerfield....84 NZ 1522
Wacton....55 TM 1891
Wadbister Voe....141 HU 4450
Wadborough....49 SO 8947
Waddesdon....36 SP 7416
Waddingham....73 SK 9896
Waddington (Lancs.)....77 SD 7243
Waddington (Lincs.)....72 SK 9764
Wadebridge....19 SW 9972
Wadeford....24 ST 3110
Wadenhoe....52 TL 0083
Wadesmill....37 TL 3517
Wadhurst....29 TQ 6431
Wadshelf....71 SK 3171
Wadsworth Moor....78 SD 9634
Wadworth....71 SK 5697
Waen Fach....58 SJ 2017
Wag....135 ND 0126
Wainfleet All Saints....73 TF 4959
Wainfleet Bank....73 TF 4759
Wainfleet Sand....73 TF 5455
Wainhope....90 NY 6793
Wainhouse Corner....22 SX 1895
Wainscott....30 TQ 7471
Wainstalls....78 SE 0428
Waitby....83 NY 7507
Wakefield....79 SE 3320
Wakerley....62 SP 9599
Wakes Colne....54 TL 8928
Walberswick....55 TM 4974
Walberton....28 SU 9705
Walbury Hill....34 SU 3761
Walcot (Lincs.)....62 TF 0535
Walcot (Lincs.)....73 SJ 5912
Walcot (Shrops.)....48 SO 3485
Walcot (Warw.)....50 SP 1258
Walcote....51 SP 5683
Walcott (Lincs.)....62 TF 1256
Walcott (Norf.)....65 TG 3632
Walden....78 SE 0082
Walden Head....78 SD 9880
Walden Stubbs....71 SE 5516
Waldersey....63 TF 4304
Waldershare Park....31 TR 2948
Walderslade....30 TQ 7563
Walderton....28 SU 7910
Walditch....24 SY 4892
Waldridge....84 NZ 2549
Waldringfield....55 TM 2844
Waldron....29 TQ 5419
Wales....73 SK 4782
Walesby (Lincs.)....73 TF 1392
Walesby (Notts.)....71 SK 6870
Walford (Here. and Worc.)....48 SO 3872
Walford (Here. and Worc.)....45 SO 5820
Walford (Shrops.)....58 SJ 4320
Walgherton....59 SJ 6948
Walgrave....51 SP 8071
Walker....91 NZ 2864
Walkerburn....95 NT 3637
Walker Fold....77 SD 6742
Walkeringham....72 SK 7692
Walkerith....72 SK 7892
Walkern....53 TL 2926
Walker's Green....45 SO 5248
Walkerton....103 NO 2301
Walkerwood Resr.....70 SJ 9999
Walkhampton....21 SX 5369
Walkington....74 SE 9936
Walk Mill....77 SD 8629
Wall (Northum.)....90 NY 9168
Wall (Staffs.)....60 SK 0906
Wallace's Hill....96 NT 3035
Wallacetown....93 NS 3422
Walland Marsh....31 TQ 9922
Wallasey....68 SJ 2992
Wall Bank....48 SO 5092
Wallbury (ant.)....37 TL 4918
Wallend....30 TQ 8775
Waller's Haven....29 TQ 6607
Wall Hill....87 NX 7244
Wall Hills (ant.)....45 SO 6359
Walling Fen....74 SE 8829
Wallingford....35 SU 6089
Wallington (Gtr London)....37 TQ 2863
Wallington (Hants.)....27 SU 5806
Wallington (Herts.)....53 TL 2933
Wallington Hall (ant.)....64 TF 6207
Wallis....42 SN 0125
Walliswood....28 TQ 1138
Walls....140 HU 2449
Wallsend....91 NZ 2766
Walls, The (ant.)....59 SO 3671
Wallyford....103 NT 3671
Walmer....31 TR 3750
Walmer Bridge....77 SD 4724
Walmersley....69 SD 8013
Walmley....60 SP 1393
Walney Airfield....76 SD 1770
Walpole....55 TM 3674
Walpole Highway....63 TF 5113
Walpole St. Andrew....63 TF 5017
Walpole St. Peter....63 TF 5016
Walsall....60 SP 0198
Walsall Wood....60 SK 0403
Walsden....78 SD 9322
Walsgrave on Sowe....50 SP 3781
Walsham le Willows....54 TM 0071
Walshaw Dean Resrs.....78 SD 9634
Walsoken....63 TF 4710
Walston....95 NT 0545
Walter's Ash....36 SU 8398

Walterstone....45 SO 3425
Waltham (Humbs.)....75 TA 2503
Waltham (Kent)....31 TR 1148
Waltham Abbey....37 TL 3800
Waltham Chase....27 SU 5614
Waltham on the Wolds....61 SK 8025
Waltham St. Lawrence....36 SU 8276
Walthamstow....37 TQ 3788
Walton (Bucks.)....52 SP 8936
Walton (Cumbr.)....90 NY 5264
Walton (Derby.)....71 SK 3569
Walton (Leic.)....51 SP 5987
Walton (Powys)....45 SO 2559
Walton (Shrops.)....59 SJ 5818
Walton (Somer.)....25 ST 4636
Walton (Suff.)....55 TM 2935
Walton (Warw.)....50 SP 2853
Walton (W Yorks.)....71 SE 3516
Walton (W Yorks.)....79 SE 4447
Walton Cardiff....46 SO 9032
Walton East....42 SN 0123
Walton Highway....63 TF 4912
Walton-in-Gordano....33 ST 4273
Walton-le-Dale....77 SD 5627
Walton-on-Thames....37 TQ 1066
Walton-on-the-Hill (Staffs.)....60 SJ 9520
Walton on the Hill (Surrey)....37 TQ 2255
Walton-on-the-Naze....39 TM 2521
Walton on the Wolds....61 SK 5919
Walton-on-Trent....60 SK 2118
Walton West....42 SM 8711
Walworth....84 NZ 2218
Walwyn's Castle....42 SM 8711
Wambrook....24 ST 2907
Wamphray Water....89 NY 1398
Wanborough....34 SU 2082
Wandleby (ant.)....53 TL 4953
Wandsworth....37 TQ 2673
Wangford....55 TM 4679
Wangford Fen....54 TL 7483
Wangford Warren....54 TL 7782
Wanlip....61 SK 5910
Wanlockhead....88 NS 8712
Wansdyke (Avon) (ant.)....33 ST 6763
Wansdyke (Wilts.) (ant.)....34 SU 1264
Wansford (Cambs.)....62 TL 0799
Wansford (Humbs.)....81 TA 0656
Wanstead....37 TQ 4088
Wanstrow....33 ST 7141
Wanswell....46 SO 6801
Wantage....34 SU 4087
Wapley....33 ST 7179
Wappenbury....51 SP 3769
Wappenham....51 SP 6245
Warbleton....29 TQ 6018
Warborough....47 SU 6093
Warboys....53 TL 3080
Warbstow....20 SX 2090
Warburton....69 SJ 7089
Warcop....83 NY 7415
Warcop Fell....83 NY 7920
Warden....31 TR 0271
Warden Point....31 TR 0272
Ward Green....54 TM 0564
Ward Hill (Eday)....138 HY 5530
Ward Hill (Hoy, Orkney)....136 HY 2202
Ward Hill (Orkney)....136 HY 3308
Ward Hill (S. Ronaldsay)....136 ND 4588
Wardington....51 SP 4946
Wardlaw Hill....94 NS 6822
Wardle (Ches.)....69 SJ 6057
Wardle (Gtr Mches.)....69 SD 9116
Wardley....62 SK 8300
Wardlow....70 SK 1874
Ward of Bressay (mt.)....141 HU 5038
Ward of Culswick (mt.)....140 HU 2645
Ward of Redland (mt.)....136 HY 3617
Ward of Scousburgh (mt.)....141 HU 3818
Ward of Veester (mt.)....141 HU 4126
War Ness....137 HY 5528
Ward's Stone....77 SD 5858
Wardy Hill....53 TL 4782
Ware....37 TL 3614
Wareham....25 SY 8892
Wareham Forest....25 SY 8892
Warehorne....31 TQ 9832
Warenford....97 NU 1328
Waren Mill....97 NU 1534
Warenton....97 NU 1030
Wareside....53 TL 3915
Waresley....53 TL 2454
Warfield....36 SU 8872
Wargrave....36 SU 7878
Warham....64 TF 9441
Wark (Northum.)....90 NT 8238
Wark (Northum.)....90 NY 8576
Wark Forest....90 NY 7478
Warkleigh....23 SS 6422
Warks Burn....90 NY 8077
Warkton....52 SP 8980
Warkworth....91 NU 2406
Warlaby....85 SE 3591
Warland....78 SD 9419
Warland Resr.....78 SD 9521
Warlegan....20 SX 1569
Warley Moor Resr.....78 SE 0331
Warlingham....37 TQ 3658
Warmfield....79 SE 3720
Warmingham....69 SJ 7161
Warmington (Northants.)....52 TL 0791
Warmington (Warw.)....51 SP 4147
Warminster....33 ST 8644
Warmsworth....71 SE 5400
Warmwell....25 SY 7585
Warndon....49 SO 8856
War Ness....137 HY 5528
Warnford....27 SU 6223
Warnham....28 TQ 1633
Warningcamp....28 TQ 0307
Warninglid....28 TQ 2526
Warren (Ches.)....69 SJ 8870
Warren (Dyfed)....42 SR 9397
Warren Row....36 SU 8180
Warren Street....30 TQ 9253
Warrington (Bucks.)....52 SP 8954
Warrington (Ches.)....69 SJ 6088
Warsash....27 SU 4905
Warslow....70 SK 0858
Warsop....71 SK 5667
Warter....80 SE 8750
Warth Hill (Cumbr.)....77 SD 5684
Warth Hill (Highld.)....135 ND 3770
Warthill....80 SE 6755
Wart Holm....138 HY 4838
Wartling....29 TQ 6509
Wartnaby....61 SK 7123
Warton (Lancs.)....83 SD 4028
Warton (Lancs.)....77 SD 4972
Warton (Northum.)....91 NU 0002
Warton (Warw.)....60 SK 2803
Warton Aerodrome....77 SD 4127
Warton Sands....77 SD 4675
Wart, The (Sanday, Orkney) (mt.)....139 HY 6337
Wart, The (S. Ronaldsay) (mt.)....136 ND 4393
Warwick (Cumbr.)....83 NY 4656
Warwick (Warw.)....50 SP 2865
Warwick Bridge....83 NY 4756
Wasbister....137 HY 3932
Wasdale Head (mt.)....82 NY 1808
Washaway....19 SX 0369
Washbourne....21 SX 7954
Washfield....23 SS 9315

Washfold Whiddon Down

Washfold 84 NZ 0502
Washford 32 ST 0441
Washford Pyne 23 SS 8111
Washingborough 72 TF 0170
Washington (Tyne and Wear) 84 NZ 3356
Washington (W Susx) 28 TQ 1212
Wash, The (Dyfed) (pt.) 42 SR 9194
Wash, The (Lincs. - Norf.) 63 TF 5342
Wasing 35 SU 5764
Waskerley 84 NZ 0545
Waskerley Resr. 84 NZ 0244
Wasperton 50 SP 2659
Wass 79 SE 5579
Wass Wick 136 HY 4122
Waste or Thorne Moors 74 SE 7315
Wast Water 82 NY 1505
Watchet 32 ST 0743
Watchfield (Oxon.) 34 SU 2490
Watchfield (Somer.) 32 ST 3446
Watchgate 83 SD 5399
Watch Hill (Borders - Dumf. and Galwy.) 89 NY 4390
Watch Hill (Cumbr.) 83 NY 6246
Watch Water Resr. 96 NT 6556
Watendlath 82 NY 2615
Water 78 SD 8425
Waterbeach 53 TL 4965
Waterbeck 89 NY 2477
Waterden 64 TF 8835
Water End (Herts.) 36 TL 0310
Water End (Herts.) 37 TL 2304
Waterfall 60 SK 0851
Waterfoot (Lancs.) 78 SD 8321
Waterfoot (Strath.) 94 NS 5654
Waterford 37 TL 3114
Watergate Bay 19 SW 8264
Watergrove Resr. 69 SD 9017
Waterhead (Cumbr.) 83 NY 3703
Waterhead (Strath.) 93 NS 5411
Waterhead Hill 88 NS 5700
Waterhead Moor 100 NS 2562
Waterheads 95 NT 2451
Waterhouses (Durham) 84 NZ 1841
Waterhouses (Staffs.) 60 SK 0850
Wateringbury 29 TQ 6853
Wateringhouse 136 ND 3090
Waterloo (Dorset) 26 SZ 0194
Waterloo (Mers.) 68 SJ 3297
Waterloo (Norf.) 65 TG 2219
Waterloo (Strath.) 95 NS 8153
Waterloo (Tays.) 108 NO 0636
Waterloo Station 37 TQ 3179
Waterlooville 27 SU 6809
Water Meetings 88 NS 9513
Watermillock 83 NY 4322
Water Newton 62 TL 1097
Waternish (dist.) 122 NG 2658
Waternish Point 122 NG 2367
Water of Ae 88 NY 0186
Water of Ailnack 117 NJ 1314
Water of App 86 NX 0774
Water of Aven 119 NO 5988
Water of Buchat 118 NJ 3517
Water of Caiplich 117 NJ 0709
Water of Charr 119 NO 6180
Water of Coyle 93 NS 4613
Water of Deugh 93 NS 5502
Water of Dye 119 NO 6485
Water of Feugh 119 NO 6191
Water of Girvan 93 NS 3004
Water of Ken 88 NX 6494
Water of Leith 102 NT 1163
Water of Luce 86 NX 1762
Water of Mark 118 NO 3883
Water of May 102 NO 0309
Water of Milk 89 NY 1681
Water of Minnoch 86 NX 3684
Water of Nevis 106 NN 1668
Water of Nochty 118 NJ 3115
Water of Ruchill 107 NN 7217
Water of Saughs 118 NO 4274
Water of Tanar 118 NO 4392
Water of Tarf 118 NO 4883
Water of Tig 86 NX 1382
Water of Tulla 106 NN 3546
Water of Unich 118 NO 3478
Water Orton 50 SP 1791
Waterperry 36 SP 6206
Waterrow 24 ST 0525
Watersfield 28 TQ 0115
Waterside (Strath.) 93 NS 4308
Waterside (Strath.) 93 NS 4843
Waterside (Strath.) 101 NS 5160
Waterside (Strath.) 101 NS 6773
Water Sound 136 ND 4695
Waterstein Head 122 NG 1447
Waterstock 36 SP 6305
Waterston 42 SM 9306
Water Stratford 51 SP 6534
Waters Upton 59 SJ 6319
Water Yeat 82 SD 2889
Watford (Herts.) 37 TQ 1196
Watford (Northants.) 51 SP 6069
Wath (N Yorks.) 78 SE 1467
Wath (N Yorks.) 79 SE 3277
Wath Upon Dearne 71 SE 4300
Watling Street (Gtr London) (ant.) 37 TQ 1792
Watling Street (Herts.) (ant.) 37 TL 1110
Watling Street (Leic.) (ant.) 51 SP 4490
Watling Street (Staffs.) (ant.) 59 SJ 8311
Watlington (Norf.) 64 TF 6211
Watlington (Oxon.) 36 SU 6994
Watnall 61 SK 4946
Wat's Dyke (ant.) 58 SJ 3144
Wats Ness 140 HU 1750
Watten 135 ND 2454
Wattisfield 54 TM 0174
Wattisham 54 TM 0151
Watton (Humbs.) 81 TA 0150
Watton (Norf.) 64 TF 9100
Watton at Stone 37 TL 3019
Watton Beck 81 TA 0349
Wattston 101 NS 7770
Wattstown 41 ST 0194
Watty Bell's Cairn 90 NT 8901
Wauchope Forest 90 NT 6104
Waulkmill Bay 136 HY 3806
Waunarlwydd 40 SS 6095
Waun Fâch 41 SO 2129
Waunfawr 66 SH 5259
Waun Lysiog 41 SO 0215
Waun-oer 57 SH 7814
Wavendon 52 SP 9137
Waverley Abbey (ant.) 35 SU 8645
Waverton (Ches.) 68 SJ 4663
Waverton (Cumbr.) 82 NY 2247
Wawne 74 TA 0836
Waxham 65 TG 4326
Waxholme 75 TA 3229
Wayford 24 ST 4006
Wayland's Smithy (ant.) 34 SU 2885
Way Village 23 SS 8810
Wealdstone 37 TQ 1689
Weald, The (dist.) 31 TQ 6035
Weardale 84 NY 8838
Weare 32 ST 4152
Weare Giffard 22 SS 4721
Weasenham All Saints 64 TF 8421
Weasenham St. Peter 64 TF 8522
Weather Ness 138 HY 5240
Weaverham 69 SJ 6173
Weaver Hills 60 SK 0946
Weaver's Point 124 NF 9569
Weaverthorpe 81 SE 9670
Webheath 50 SP 0266
Weddel Sound 136 ND 3394
Wedder Dod (mt.) 88 NS 8215
Wedder Holm 143 HU 6197
Wedderlairs 121 NJ 8532
Wedder Law 88 NS 9302
Weddington 60 SP 3693
Wedhampton 34 SU 0557
Wedholme Flow 82 NY 2252
Wedmore 33 ST 4347
Wednesbury 60 SP 0095
Wednesfield 59 SJ 9400
Weedon 36 SP 8118
Weedon Bec 51 SP 6259
Weedon Lois 51 SP 6047
Weeford 60 SK 1404
Week 23 SS 7316
Weekley 52 SP 8880
Week St. Mary 20 SX 2397
Weeley 39 TM 1422
Weeley Heath 39 TM 1520
Weem 107 NN 8449
Weem Hill 107 NN 8251
Weeping Cross 59 SJ 9421
Wee Queensberry (mt.) 88 NX 9897
Weeting 54 TL 7788
Weeton (Lancs.) 77 SD 3834
Weeton (W Yorks.) 79 SE 2846
Weets Hill 78 SD 8544
Weetwood Hall 97 NU 0129
Weir 78 SD 8724
Weir Dike 74 SE 9714
Weir Wood Reservoir 29 TQ 3934
Weisdale (dist.) 141 HU 3953
Weisdale Voe 141 HU 3848
Welbeck Abbey 71 SK 5674
Welborne 64 TG 0610
Welbourn 62 SK 9654
Welburn 80 SE 7168
Welbury 85 NZ 3902
Welby 62 SK 9738
Welches Dam 53 TL 4786
Welcombe 22 SS 2218
Weldon 52 SP 9289
Weldon Bridge 91 NZ 1398
Welford (Berks.) 34 SU 4073
Welford (Northants.) 51 SP 6480
Welford-on-Avon 50 SP 1552
Welham 51 SP 7692
Welham Green 37 TL 2305
Well (Hants.) 35 SU 7646
Well (Lincs.) 73 TF 4473
Well (N Yorks.) 78 SE 2682
Welland 49 SO 7940
Wellesbourne 50 SP 2755
Wellgrain Dod (mt.) 88 NS 9018
Well Hill (Dumf. and Galwy.) 88 NS 9106
Well Hill (Kent) 37 TQ 4963
Welling 37 TQ 4575
Wellingborough 52 SP 8968
Wellingham 64 TF 8722
Wellingore 62 SK 9856
Wellington (Here. and Worc.) 45 SO 4948
Wellington (Shrops.) 59 SJ 6411
Wellington (Somer.) 24 ST 1320
Wellington Heath 49 SO 7140
Well of Kildinguie 137 HY 6527
Wellow (Avon) 33 ST 7358
Wellow (I. of W.) 26 SZ 3887
Wellow (Notts.) 71 SK 6666
Wells 33 ST 5445
Wellsborough 60 SK 3602
Wells-Next-The-Sea 64 TF 9143
Wells of Ythan 121 NJ 6338
Wellwood 102 NT 0888
Welney 63 TL 5294
Welshampton 58 SJ 4334
Welsh Bicknor 45 SO 5917
Welsh Channel 67 SJ 0985
Welsh End 59 SJ 5035
Welsh Frankton 58 SJ 3633
Welsh Grounds (sbk.) 33 ST 4582
Welsh Hook 42 SM 9327
Welsh Newton 45 SO 4918
Welshpool (Trallwng) 58 SJ 2207
Welsh St. Donats 41 ST 0276
Welton (Cumbr.) 82 NY 3544
Welton (Humbs.) 74 SE 9527
Welton (Lincs.) 72 TF 0079
Welton (Northants.) 51 SP 5865
Welton le Marsh 73 TF 4768
Welton le Wold 73 TF 2787
Welwick 75 TA 3421
Welwyn 37 TL 2316
Welwyn Garden City 37 TL 2412
Wem 59 SJ 5129
Wembdon 24 ST 2837
Wembley 37 TQ 1985
Wembury 20 SX 5148
Wembury Bay 20 SX 5147
Wembworthy 23 SS 6609
Wemyss Bay 100 NS 1869
Wenallt 67 SH 9842
Wendens Ambo 53 TL 5136
Wendlebury 47 SP 5519
Wendling 64 TF 9213
Wendover 36 SP 8708
Wendron 18 SW 6731
Wendy 53 TL 3247
Wenhaston 55 TM 4275
Wenlock Edge (mt.) 48 SO 5089
Wennington (Cambs.) 53 TL 2379
Wennington (Essex) 37 TQ 5381
Wennington (Lancs.) 77 SD 6169
Wensley (Derby.) 71 SK 2661
Wensley (N Yorks.) 84 SE 0989
Wensleydale 78 SD 9988
Wentbridge 71 SE 4817
Wentnor 48 SO 3892
Wentwood 45 ST 4194
Wentworth (Cambs.) 53 TL 4878
Wentworth (S Yorks.) 71 SK 3898
Wentworth Castle 71 SE 3103
Wenvoe 41 ST 1272
Weobley 45 SO 4051
Weobley Marsh 45 SO 4151
Wereham 64 TF 6801
Wergs 59 SJ 8601
Wernrheolydd 45 SO 3913
Werrington (Devon) 20 SX 3287
Werrington (Northants.) 62 TF 1703
Werrington (Staffs.) 60 SJ 9647
Wervin 68 SJ 4171
Wesham 77 SD 4132
Wessington 71 SK 3757
West Acre 64 TF 7715
West Allerdean 97 NT 9646
West Alvington 21 SX 7243
West Anstey 23 SS 8527
West Ashby 73 TF 2672
West Ashling 27 SU 8007
West Ashton 33 ST 8755
West Auckland 84 NZ 1826
West Bagborough 24 ST 1633
West Barns 103 NT 6578
West Barsham 64 TF 9033
West Baugh Fell 83 SD 7295
West Bay (Dorset) 25 SY 4690
West Bay (Dorset) 25 SY 6773
West Beckham 65 TG 1339
Westbere 31 TR 1961
West Bergholt 54 TL 9527
West Bexington 25 SY 5386
West Bilney 64 TF 7115
West Blatchington 28 TQ 2706
Westborough 62 SK 8544
Westbourne (Dorset) 26 SZ 0690
Westbourne (W Susx) 27 SU 7507
West Bradford 77 SD 7444
West Bradley 25 ST 5536
West Bretton 71 SE 2813
West Bridgford 61 SK 5837
West Bromwich 50 SP 0091
West Buckland (Devon) 23 SS 6531
West Buckland (Somer.) 24 ST 1720
West Burra (is.) 141 HU 3632
West Burrafirth 140 HU 2657
West Burton (N Yorks.) 78 SE 0186
West Burton (W Susx) 28 TQ 0014
Westbury (Bucks.) 51 SP 6235
Westbury (Shrops.) 58 SJ 3509
Westbury (Wilts.) 33 ST 8751
Westbury Leigh 33 ST 8649
Westbury-on-Severn 46 SO 7114
Westbury-sub-Mendip 33 ST 5049
Westby 77 SD 3731
West Caister 65 TG 5011
West Calder 102 NT 0163
West Camel 25 ST 5724
West Challow 34 SU 3688
West Charleton 21 SX 7542
West Chelborough 25 ST 5405
West Chevington 91 NZ 2297
West Chiltington 28 TQ 0918
West Clandon 28 TQ 0452
West Cliffe 31 TR 3445
Westcliff-on-Sea 38 TQ 8685
West Clyne 129 NC 8906
West Coker 25 ST 5113
Westcombe 33 ST 6739
West Compton (Dorset) 25 SY 5694
West Compton (Somer.) 33 ST 5942
Westcote 47 SP 2120
Westcott (Bucks.) 36 SP 7117
Westcott (Devon) 24 ST 0104
Westcott (Surrey) 28 TQ 1348
Westcott Barton 47 SP 4224
West Cross 40 SS 6189
West Curry 20 SX 2893
West Curthwaite 82 NY 3248
West Dart River 21 SX 6373
Westdean (E Susx) 29 TV 5299
West Dean (Wilts.) 26 SU 2526
West Dean (W Susx) 27 SU 8512
West Deeping 62 TF 1009
West Derby 68 SJ 3993
West Dereham 64 TF 6500
West Ditchburn 91 NU 1320
West Down (Devon) 22 SS 5142
West Down (Wilts.) 34 SU 0548
West Drayton (Gtr London) 36 TQ 0679
West Drayton (Notts.) 72 SK 7074
West End (Avon) 33 ST 4469
West End (Beds.) 52 SP 9853
West End (Hants.) 27 SU 4614
West End (Norf.) 65 TG 4911
West End (N Yorks.) 78 SE 1457
West End (Oxon.) 47 SP 4204
West End (Surrey) 36 SU 9461
West End Green 36 SU 6661
Westenhanger (ant.) 31 TR 1237
Wester Culbeuchly Crofts 121 NJ 6562
Westerdale (Highld.) 135 ND 1251
Westerdale (N Yorks.) 85 NZ 6605
Westerdale Moor 85 NZ 6502
Wester Denoon 109 NO 3543
Wester Fearn Burn 128 NH 5985
Westerfield (Shetld.) 141 HU 3551
Westerfield (Suff.) 55 TM 1747
Wester Fintray 119 NJ 8116
Westergate 28 SU 9305
Wester Gruinards 128 NH 5292
Westerham 29 TQ 4454
Wester Hoevdi (pt.) 140 HT 9338
Wester Lealty 128 NH 6073
Westerleigh 33 ST 6979
Wester Lonvine 129 NH 7172
Western Cleddau 42 SM 9418
Wester Newburn 103 NO 4405
Westernhope Moor 84 NY 9233
Western Isles or Hebrides 124 NG 0040
Western Isles or Hebrides 131 NG 0239
Western Rocks 18 SV 8406
Wester Ross (dist.) 127 NH 0562
Wester Skeld 140 HU 2943
Westerton 109 NO 6654
Wester Wick (Shetld.) 140 HU 2842
Westerwick (Shetld.) 140 HU 2843
West Farleigh 29 TQ 7152
West Fell 83 NY 6602
West Felton 58 SJ 3425
West Fen (Cambs.) 53 TL 5182
West Fen (Isle of Ely) (Cambs.) 63 TL 3698
West Fen (Lincs.) 63 TF 3053
Westfield (E Susx) 30 TQ 8115
Westfield (Highld.) 135 ND 0564
Westfield (Lothian) 102 NS 9372
Westfield (Norf.) 64 TF 9909
West Firle 29 TQ 4707
West Fleetham 97 NU 1928
Westgate (Durham) 84 NY 9038
Westgate (Humbs.) 74 SE 7707
Westgate (Norf.) 64 TF 9740
Westgate on Sea 31 TR 3270
West Gerinish 124 NF 7741
West Ginge 34 SU 4386
West Glen River 62 TF 0022
West Grafton 34 SU 2460
West Green 35 SU 7456
West Grimstead 26 SU 2026
West Grinstead 28 TQ 1721
West Haddlesey 79 SE 5526
West Haddon 51 SP 6371
West Hagbourne 35 SU 5187
Westhall (Cumbr.) 90 NY 5667
Westhall (Grampn.) (ant.) 121 NJ 6726
Westhall (Suff.) 55 TM 4280
West Hallam 60 SK 4341
West Halton 74 SE 9020
Westham (E Susx) 29 TQ 6404
West Ham (Gtr London) 37 TQ 4081
Westham (Somer.) 32 ST 4046
Westhampnett 27 SU 8706
West Handley 71 SK 3977
West Hanney 34 SU 4092
West Hanningfield 38 TQ 7399
West Hardwick 71 SE 4118
West Harptree 33 ST 5556
West Hatch 24 ST 2820
Westhay 33 ST 4342
Westhead 68 SD 4407
West Heath 35 SU 8556
West Helmsdale 135 ND 0114
West Hendred 35 SU 4488
West Heslerton 81 SE 9175
Westhide 45 SO 5844
Westhill 119 NJ 8307
West Hill 24 SY 0694
West Hoathly 29 TQ 3632
West Holme 25 SY 8885
Westhope (Here. and Worc.) 45 SO 4651
Westhope (Shrops.) 48 SO 4786
West Horndon 38 TQ 6288
Westhorpe (Lincs.) 62 TF 2131
Westhorpe (Suff.) 54 TM 0469
West Horrington 33 ST 5747
West Horsley 28 TQ 0753
West Hougham 31 TR 2640
Westhoughton 69 SD 6505
Westhouse 77 SD 6673
Westhouses 71 SK 4257
West Hoyle Bank (sbk.) 67 SJ 1088
Westhumble 28 TQ 1652
West Hyde 36 TQ 0391
West Ilsley 35 SU 4682
Westing 143 HP 5705
West Itchenor 27 SU 7900
West Kame (mt.) 141 HU 3959
West Kennet 34 SU 1167
West Kilbride 93 NS 2048
West Kingsdown 37 TQ 5762
West Kington 33 ST 8077
West Kirby 68 SJ 2186
West Knighton 25 SY 7387
West Knock 118 NO 4775
West Knoyle 25 ST 8532
Westlake 21 SX 6253
West Langdon 31 TR 3247
West Langwell 133 NC 6909
West Lavington (Wilts.) 34 SU 0052
West Lavington (W Susx) 27 SU 8920
West Lavington Down 34 ST 9949
West Layton 84 NZ 1409
West Leake 61 SK 5226
Westleigh (Devon) 22 SS 4628
Westleigh (Devon) 24 ST 0517
Westleton 55 TM 4469
West Lexham 64 TF 8417
Westley (Shrops.) 58 SJ 3507
Westley (Suff.) 54 TL 8264
Westley Waterless 54 TL 6256
West Lilling 79 SE 6465
West Linga (is.) 141 HU 5364
Westlington 36 SP 7610
West Linton (Borders) 95 NT 1551
Westlinton (Cumbr.) 89 NY 3964
West Littleton 33 ST 7575
West Loch Roag 131 NB 0939
West Loch Tarbert (Harris, W Isles) 125 NB 0803
West Loch Tarbert (Strath.) 99 NR 8062
West Lomond (mt.) 103 NO 1906
West Lulworth 25 SY 8280
West Lutton 81 SE 9269
West Lynn 64 TF 6120
West Mains 95 NS 9550
West Malling 29 TQ 6857
West Malvern 49 SO 7646
West Marden 27 SU 7613
West Markham 72 SK 7272
Westmarsh 31 TR 2761
West Marton 78 SD 8850
West Meon 27 SU 6424
West Mersea 39 TM 0112
Westmeston 29 TQ 3313
Westmill 53 TL 3627
West Milton 25 SY 5096
Westminster 37 TQ 2979
West Monar Forest 127 NH 0842
West Monkton 24 ST 2528
West Moors 26 SU 0802
West Moulie Geo 140 HU 2940
West Mouse (is.) 66 SH 3094
Westmuir (Tays.) 109 NO 3652
West Muir (Tays.) 109 NO 5661
West Ness (Fife) 103 NO 6106
Westness (Rousay) 136 HY 3829
Westnewton (Cumbr.) 82 NY 1344
West Newton (Humbs.) 75 TA 1037
West Newton (Norf.) 64 TF 6927
West Norwood 37 TQ 3171
West Ogwell 21 SX 8170
Weston (Avon) 33 ST 7266
Weston (Berks.) 34 SU 3973
Weston (Ches.) 69 SJ 5080
Weston (Ches.) 59 SJ 7252
Weston (Dorset) 25 SY 6870
Weston (Hants.) 27 SU 7221
Weston (Herts.) 53 TL 2630
Weston (Lincs.) 63 TF 2925
Weston (Northants.) 51 SP 5847
Weston (Notts.) 72 SK 7767
Weston (Shrops.) 59 SJ 5628
Weston (Shrops.) 48 SO 5993
Weston (Staffs.) 60 SJ 9727
Weston (W Yorks.) 78 SE 1747
Weston Airport 32 ST 3460
Weston Bay 32 ST 3060
Weston Beggard 45 SO 5841
Weston by Welland 51 SP 7791
Weston Colville 54 TL 6153
Weston Favell 51 SP 7862
Weston Green 54 TL 6252
Weston Heath 59 SJ 7813
Weston Hill 48 SO 5582
Weston Hills 63 TF 2821
Westoning 52 TL 0332
Weston-in-Gordano 33 ST 4474
Weston Jones 59 SJ 7524
Weston Longville 65 TG 1116
Weston Lullingfields 58 SJ 4224
Weston-on-the-Green 47 SP 5318
Weston-on-Trent 60 SK 4027
Weston Patrick 35 SU 6946
Weston Rhyn 58 SJ 2835
Weston Subedge 50 SP 1240
Weston-super-Mare 32 ST 3261
Weston Turville 36 SP 8511
Weston-under-Lizard 59 SJ 8010
Weston under Penyard 45 SO 6323
Weston under Wetherley 50 SP 3569
Weston Underwood (Bucks.) 52 SP 8650
Weston Underwood (Derby.) 60 SK 2942
Westonzoyland 24 ST 3534
West Overton 34 SU 1367
Westow 80 SE 7565
West Parley 26 SZ 0997
West Peckham 29 TQ 6452
West Pennard 33 ST 5438
West Pentire 18 SW 7760
Westport 24 ST 3819
West Putford 22 SS 3515
West Quantoxhead 32 ST 1141
West Rainton 84 NZ 3246
West Rasen 72 TF 0589
Westray 138 HY 4546
Westray Aerodrome 138 HY 4652
Westray Firth 138 HY 4437
West Raynham 64 TF 8725
West Reef 104 NM 2313
Westrigg 102 NS 9067
West Road 31 TR 0016
West Row 54 TL 6775
West Rudham 64 TF 8127
West Runton 65 TG 1842
Westruther 96 NT 6349
Westry 63 TL 3998
West Saltoun 103 NT 4667
West Sandwick 143 HU 4588
West Scar 85 NZ 5926
West Scrafton 78 SE 0783
West Sedge Moor 24 ST 3525
Westside 138 HY 3730
West Somerset Railway 24 ST 1435
West Stafford 25 SY 7289
West Stoke 27 SU 8208
West Stonesdale 84 NY 8802
West Stoughton 32 ST 4149
West Stour 25 ST 7822
West Stourmouth 31 TR 2562
West Stow 54 TL 8170
West Stowell 34 SU 1362
West Street 30 TQ 9054
West Tanfield 79 SE 2778
West Tarbert 99 NR 8467
West Tarbert Bay 92 NR 6453
West Thorney 27 SU 7602
West Thurrock 37 TQ 5877
West Tilbury 30 TQ 6677
West Tisted 27 SU 6429
West Tofts 108 NO 1134
West Torrington 73 TF 1381
West Town 33 ST 4767
West Tytherley 26 SU 2730
West Tytherton 34 ST 9474
West Voe 141 HU 3630
West Voe of Sumburgh 141 HU 3909
West Walton 63 TF 4713
Westward 82 NY 2744
Westward Ho! 22 SS 4329
West Water 109 NO 5170
West Water Resr. 95 NT 1152
Westwell (Kent) 31 TQ 9947
Westwell (Oxon.) 47 SP 2210
Westwell Leacon 31 TQ 9647
West Wellow 26 SU 2818
West Wemyss 103 NT 3294
West Wick (Avon) 32 ST 3661
Westwick (Cambs.) 53 TL 4265
Westwick (Norf.) 65 TG 2727
West Wickham (Cambs.) 54 TL 6149
West Wickham (Gtr London) 37 TQ 3866
West Winch 64 TF 6316
West Winterslow 26 SU 2232
West Wittering 27 SZ 7999
West Witton 78 SE 0688
Westwood (Devon) 24 SY 0199
Westwood (Wilts.) 33 ST 8158
West Woodburn 90 NY 8986
West Woodhay 34 SU 3962
West Woodlands 33 ST 7743
Westwoodside 74 SK 7499
West Worldham 27 SU 7436
West Wratting 54 TL 6052
West Wycombe 36 SU 8394
West Yell 143 HU 4582
Wetheral 83 NY 4654
Wetherby 79 SE 4048
Wether Cairn 90 NT 9411
Wetherden 54 TM 0062
Wether Fell 78 SD 8786
Wether Hill (Dumf. and Galwy.) 88 NX 6994
Wether Hill (Grampn.) 88 NX 7087
Wether Hill (Tays.) 102 NN 9205
Wetheringsett 55 TM 1266
Wether Lair (mt.) 90 NY 7096
Wether Law 95 NT 1948
Wethersfield 54 TL 7131
Wethersta 141 HU 3665
Wetherup Street 55 TM 1464
Wetley Rocks 60 SJ 9649
Wet Sleddale Resr. 83 NY 5511
Wettenhall 69 SJ 6261
Wetton 60 SK 1055
Wetwang 81 SE 9359
Wetwood 59 SJ 7733
Wexcombe 34 SU 2758
Weybourne 65 TG 1143
Weybread 55 TM 2480
Weybridge 36 TQ 0764
Weydale 135 ND 1464
Weyhill 34 SU 3146
Weymouth 25 SY 6778
Weymouth Bay 25 SY 6980
Whaddon (Bucks.) 51 SP 8034
Whaddon (Cambs.) 53 TL 3546
Whaddon (Glos.) 46 SO 8313
Whaddon (Wilts.) 26 SU 1926
Whaddon Chase 51 SP 7932
Whale 83 NY 5221
Whale Chine 27 SZ 4678
Whale Firth 143 HU 4694
Whale Geo 143 HU 4493
Whale Island 27 SU 6302
Whaley 71 SK 5171
Whaley Bridge 70 SK 0181
Whaligoe 135 ND 3240
Whalley 77 SD 7335
Whalsay 141 HU 5663
Whalton 91 NZ 1281
Whalwick Taing 142 HU 2381
Wham 78 SD 7762
Whaness 136 HY 2502
Whaplode 63 TF 3224
Whaplode Drove 63 TF 3113
Whaplode Fen 63 TF 3220
Whaplode River 63 TF 3429
Wharfe 78 SD 7869
Wharfedale 78 SE 0653
Wharles 77 SD 4435
Wharncliffe Side 71 SK 2994
Wharram le Street 80 SE 8666
Wharton (Ches.) 69 SJ 6666
Wharton (Here. and Worc.) 45 SO 5055
Whashton 84 NZ 1406
Whatcombe 25 ST 8301
Whatcote 50 SP 2944
Whatfield 54 TM 0246
Whatley 33 ST 7347
Whatlington 29 TQ 7618
Whatstandwell 60 SK 3354
Whatton 61 SK 7439
Whauphill 86 NX 4049
Whaw 84 NY 9804
Wheatacre 65 TM 4594
Wheathampstead 37 TL 1713
Wheatley (Hants.) 35 SU 7840
Wheatley (Notts.) 72 SK 7685
Wheatley (Oxon.) 47 SP 5905
Wheatley Hill 85 NZ 3839
Wheatley Lane 78 SD 8337
Wheaton Aston 59 SJ 8412
Wheat Stack 97 NT 8670
Wheddon Cross 23 SS 9238
Wheedlemont 121 NJ 4726
Wheeldale Moor 80 SE 7997
Wheelerstreet 28 SU 9440
Wheelock 69 SJ 7458
Wheelton 77 SD 6021
Wheen 109 NO 3670
Wheldrake 79 SE 6744
Whelford 47 SU 1698
Whelpley Hill 36 TL 0004
Whenby 79 SE 6369
Whepstead 54 TL 8358
Whernside (mt.) 77 SD 7381
Wherstead 55 TM 1540
Wherwell 34 SU 3840
Wheston 70 SK 1376
Whetsted 29 TQ 6546
Whetstone 61 SP 5597
Whicham 76 SD 1382
Whichford 47 SP 3134
Whickham 91 NZ 2061
Whiddon Down 21 SX 6992

Whigstreet	109	NO 4844
Whillan Beck	82	NY 1701
Whilton	51	SP 6364
Whimple	24	SY 0497
Whimpwell Green	65	TG 3829
Whinburgh	64	TG 0009
Whinfell Beacon	83	NY 5700
Whinlatter Pass	121	NY 1924
Whinnyfold	121	NK 0733
Whins Brow	77	SD 6353
Whippingham	27	SZ 5193
Whipsnade	36	TL 0117
Whipsnade Park Zoo	36	TL 0017
Whipton	21	SX 9493
Whissendine	62	SK 8214
Whissonsett	64	TF 9123
Whistley Green	35	SU 7974
Whiston (Mers.)	69	SJ 4791
Whiston (Northants.)	51	SP 8560
Whiston (Staffs.)	60	SJ 8914
Whiston (Staffs.)	60	SK 0347
Whiston (S Yorks.)	71	SK 4489
Whitaloo Point	136	HY 2628
Whitbeck	76	SD 1184
Whitbourne	49	SO 7156
Whitburn (Lothian)	102	NS 9464
Whitburn (Tyne and Wear)	91	NZ 4061
Whitby (Ches.)	68	SJ 4075
Whitby (N Yorks.)	81	NZ 8911
Whitchurch (Avon)	33	ST 6167
Whitchurch (Bucks.)	36	SP 8020
Whitchurch (Devon)	20	SX 4972
Whitchurch (Dyfed)	42	SM 8025
Whitchurch (Hants.)	35	SU 4648
Whitchurch (Here. and Worc.)	45	SO 5417
Whitchurch (Oxon.)	36	SU 6377
Whitchurch (S Glam.)	41	ST 1680
Whitchurch (Shrops.)	59	SJ 5441
Whitchurch Canonicorum	24	SY 3995
Whitchurch Hill	36	SU 6478
Whitcott Keysett	48	SO 2782
Whiteacen	120	NJ 2646
Whiteadder Resr.	103	NT 6563
Whiteadder Water (Borders)	97	NT 8555
Whiteadder Water (Lothian)	103	NT 6267
Whiteash Hill Wood	121	NJ 3657
Whitebrook	45	SO 5306
Whitecairns	119	NJ 9218
White Cart Water	101	NS 5263
White Castle (ant.)	45	SO 3716
White Caterthun (mt.)	109	NO 5465
White Chapel	77	SD 5542
Whitchurch	42	SN 1436
Whitcliff Bay	27	SZ 6485
White Coomb	89	NT 1614
White Coppice	69	SD 6119
Whitecraig (Lothian)	103	NT 3570
Whitecraig (Strath.) (mt.)	95	NT 0753
Whitecroft	45	SO 6106
Whitecross	102	NS 9676
White Esk	89	NY 2499
Whiteface	129	NH 7089
Whitefarland Point	92	NR 8642
Whitefauld Hill	88	NY 0293
White Fen	53	TL 3492
Whitefield (Gtr Mches.)	69	SD 8005
Whitefield (Tays.)	108	NO 1734
Whitefield Loch	86	NX 2355
Whiteford	121	NJ 7126
Whiteford Point	40	SS 4496
Whitehall	137	HY 6528
Whitehaugh Forest	121	NJ 5822
Whitehaven	82	NX 9718
White Hill (Borders)	90	NT 5211
White Hill (Grampn.)	119	NO 5388
Whitehill (Hants.)	27	SU 7934
White Hill (Lancs.)	77	SD 6758
White Hill (Strath.)	93	NS 2656
White Hill (Strath.)	88	NS 8519
White Hill (Tays.)	109	NO 4072
Whitehills	121	NJ 6565
White Hope Edge	89	NY 3397
Whitehope Law	96	NT 3344
Whitehorse Hill	34	SU 2986
Whitehouse (Grampn.)	119	NJ 6214
Whitehouse (Strath.)	99	NR 8161
White Island	18	SV 9217
Whitekirk	103	NT 5981
White Knowes	88	NS 6104
White Lackington	25	SY 7198
White Ladies Aston	49	SO 9252
White Law	97	NT 8526
Whitelaw Hill (Borders)	95	NT 1935
Whitelaw Hill (Lothian)	103	NT 5771
Whitelee Hill	93	NS 5442
Whiteley Village	36	TQ 0962
White Loch	86	NX 1060
White Lyne	90	NY 5373
Whitemans Green	29	TQ 3025
White Meldon	95	NT 2242
Whitemill Bay	139	HY 6944
Whitemill Point	139	HY 7046
Whitemire	129	NH 9754
Whitemoor	19	SW 9757
Whitemoor Reservoir	78	SD 8743
White Mounth	117	NO 2384
White Ness (Kent)	31	TR 4070
White Ness (Shetld.)	141	HU 3844
Whiteness (Shetld.) (dist.)	141	HU 4147
Whiteness Head	129	NH 8058
Whiteness Sands	129	NH 8386
Whiteness Voe	141	HU 3943
Whiten Head or An Ceann Geal	133	NC 4968
White Notley	38	TL 7818
Whiteparish	26	SU 2423
White Preston	90	NY 5977
Whiterashes	121	NJ 8523
White Roding or White Roothing	37	TL 5613
White Roothing or White Roding	37	TL 5613
Whiterow	135	ND 3548
Whitesand Bay (Corn.)	18	SW 3427
Whitesand Bay or Porth-mawr (Dyfed)	42	SM 7227
White Sands	68	SJ 2771
White Shank (mt.)	89	NT 2006
White Sheet Castle (ant.)	25	ST 8034
White Sheet Hill (Wilts.)	25	ST 8034
White Sheet Hill (Wilts.)	26	ST 9424
Whiteshill	46	SO 8307
Whiteshoot Hill	26	SU 2833
Whiteside (Lothian)	102	NS 9663
Whiteside (Northum.)	90	NY 7069
Whitesmith	29	TQ 5214
Whitestaunton	24	ST 2810
Whitestone	21	SX 8694
Whitestone Hill	90	NT 8014
White Top of Culreoch	88	NX 5963
White Waltham	36	SU 8577
Whiteway	46	SO 9110
Whiteway House	21	SX 8783
Whitewell	77	SD 6546
Whiteworks	21	SX 6071
Whitewreath	120	NJ 2356
Whitfell	82	SD 1592
Whitfield (Glos.)	33	ST 6791
Whitfield (Kent)	31	TR 3146
Whitfield (Northants.)	51	SP 6039
Whitfield (Northum.)	90	NY 7758
Whitfield Moor	83	NY 7454
Whitford	68	SJ 1477
Whitgift	74	SE 8022
Whitgreave	59	SJ 8928
Whithorn	87	NX 4440
Whiting Bay (Island of Arran)	92	NS 0425
Whiting Bay (Island of Arran)	92	NS 0526
Whitland	43	SN 1916
Whitletts	93	NS 3622
Whitley (Berks.)	36	SU 7170
Whitley (Ches.)	69	SJ 6178
Whitley (N Yorks.)	79	SE 5521
Whitley Bay	91	NZ 3572
Whitley Chapel	84	NY 9257
Whitley Row	29	TQ 5052
Whitlock's End	50	SP 1076
Whitminster	46	SO 7708
Whit Moor	77	SD 5864
Whitmore	59	SJ 8041
Whitnage	24	ST 0215
Whitnash	50	SP 3263
Whitney	45	SO 2647
Whitrigg (Cumbr.)	82	NY 2038
Whitrigg (Cumbr.)	82	NY 2257
Whitsand Bay	26	SX 3751
Whitsbury	26	SU 1218
Whitsome	97	NT 8650
Whitson	32	ST 3783
Whitstable	31	TR 1166
Whitstone	26	SX 2698
Whittingham	91	NU 0611
Whittingslow	48	SO 4288
Whittington (Derby.)	71	SK 3975
Whittington (Glos.)	46	SP 0120
Whittington (Here. and Worc.)	49	SO 8582
Whittington (Here. and Worc.)	49	SO 8757
Whittington (Lancs.)	77	SD 5976
Whittington (Norf.)	64	TL 7199
Whittington (Shrops.)	58	SJ 3230
Whittington (Staffs.)	51	SK 1508
Whittington (Staffs.)	51	SP 4843
Whittle-le-Woods	77	SD 5822
Whittlesey	63	TL 2797
Whittlesey Mere	53	TL 2290
Whittlesford	53	TL 4748
Whittlewood Forest	51	SP 7243
Whitton (Cleve.)	85	NZ 3822
Whitton (Humbs.)	74	SE 9024
Whitton (Northum.)	91	NU 0501
Whitton (Powys)	48	SO 2667
Whitton (Shrops.)	48	SO 5772
Whitton (Suff.)	55	TM 1447
Whittonditch	34	SU 2872
Whittonstall	84	NZ 0757
Whitwell (Derby.)	71	SK 5276
Whitwell (Herts.)	52	TL 1821
Whitwell (I. of W.)	27	SZ 5277
Whitwell (Leic.)	62	SK 9208
Whitwell (N Yorks.)	84	SE 2899
Whitwell-on-the-Hill	80	SE 7265
Whitwick	60	SK 4316
Whitwood	79	SE 4124
Whitworth	69	SD 8818
Whixall	59	SJ 5034
Whixley	79	SE 4457
Whorlton (Durham)	84	NZ 1014
Whorlton (N Yorks.)	85	NZ 4802
Whorlton Moor	85	SE 4998
Whygate	90	NY 7675
Whyle	45	SO 5560
Whyteleafe	37	TQ 3358
Wiay (Benbecula)	124	NF 8746
Wiay (Island of Skye)	122	NG 2936
Wibdon	45	ST 5797
Wibtoft	51	SP 4787
Wichenford	49	SO 7860
Wichling	30	TQ 9256
Wick (Avon)	33	ST 6972
Wick (Dorset)	26	SZ 1591
Wick (Here. and Worc.)	50	SO 9645
Wick (Highld.)	135	ND 3650
Wick (S Glam.)	41	SS 9272
Wick (Shetld.)	141	HU 4439
Wick (Unst)	143	HP 5603
Wick (Wilts.)	26	SU 1621
Wick (W Susx)	28	TQ 0203
Wick Airport	135	ND 3652
Wick Bay	135	ND 3750
Wick Down	26	SU 1321
Wicken (Cambs.)	53	TL 5770
Wicken (Northants.)	51	SP 7439
Wicken Bonhunt	53	TL 5033
Wickenby	72	TF 0882
Wickenby Airport	73	TF 1081
Wickersley	71	SK 4891
Wickford	38	TQ 7593
Wickham (Berks.)	34	SU 3971
Wickham (Hants.)	27	SU 5711
Wickham Bishops	38	TL 8412
Wickhambreaux	31	TR 2158
Wickhambrook	54	TL 7454
Wickhamford	50	SP 0642
Wickham Market	55	TM 3056
Wickhampton	65	TG 4205
Wickham Skeith	55	TM 0969
Wickham St. Paul	54	TL 8336
Wickham Street (Suff.)	54	TL 7554
Wickham Street (Suff.)	55	TM 0869
Wick Hill	36	SU 8064
Wicklewood	64	TG 0702
Wickmere	65	TG 1633
Wick of Breakon	143	HP 5205
Wick of Gruting	143	HU 6592
Wick of Mucklabrek	140	HT 9428
Wick of Sandsayre	141	HU 4323
Wick of Shunni	141	HU 3515
Wick of Tresta	143	HU 6388
Wick River	135	ND 2953
Wick St. Lawrence	32	ST 3665
Wickwar	33	ST 7288
Widdale Fell	78	SD 8088
Widdington	53	TL 5331
Widdop Resr.	78	SD 9332
Widdrington	91	NZ 2595
Widdrington Station	91	NZ 2494
Widdybank Fell	83	NY 8230
Widecombe In the Moor	21	SX 7176
Wide Firth	136	HY 4316
Wideford Hill	136	HY 4111
Widegates	19	SX 2857
Widemouth Bay	22	SS 2002
Wide Open	91	NZ 2472
Widewall	136	ND 4391
Widewall Bay	136	ND 4292
Widford (Essex)	38	TL 6905
Widford (Herts.)	37	TL 4115
Widmerpool	61	SK 6327
Widnes	69	SJ 5185
Wife Geo	135	ND 3969
Wigan	69	SD 5805
Wiggaton	24	SY 1093
Wiggenhall St. Germans	64	TF 5914
Wiggenhall St. Mary Magdalen	64	TF 5911
Wiggenhall St. Mary the Virgin	63	TF 5814
Wigginton (N Yorks.)	79	SE 5958
Wigginton (Herts.)	36	SP 9410
Wigginton (Oxon.)	47	SP 3833
Wigginton (Staffs.)	60	SK 2106
Wigglesworth	78	SD 8056
Wiggonby	82	NY 2953
Wiggonholt	28	TQ 0616
Wighill	79	SE 4746
Wighton	64	TF 9339
Wigmore (Here. and Worc.)	48	SO 4169
Wigmore (Kent)	30	TQ 8063
Wigsley	72	SK 8570
Wigsthorpe	52	TL 0482
Wigston	51	SP 6099
Wig, The (roadstead)	86	NX 0467
Wigtoft	73	TF 2636
Wigton	82	NY 2548
Wigtown	87	NX 4355
Wigtown Bay	87	NX 5249
Wigtown Sands	87	NX 4556
Wilbarston	51	SP 8188
Wilberfoss	80	SE 7350
Wilburton	53	TL 4875
Wilby (Norf.)	54	TM 0389
Wilby (Northants.)	51	SP 8666
Wilby (Suff.)	55	TM 2472
Wilcot	34	SU 1461
Wildboarclough	70	SJ 9868
Wilden	52	TL 0955
Wilden	34	SU 3550
Wildmore Fen	63	TF 2551
Wildsworth	72	SK 8097
Wiley Sike	90	NY 6369
Wilford	61	SK 5637
Wilkesley	59	SJ 6241
Wilkhaven	129	NH 9486
Wilkieston	102	NT 1168
Willand	23	ST 0310
Willaston (Ches.)	68	SJ 3277
Willaston (Ches.)	59	SJ 6752
Willen	52	SP 8741
Willenhall (W Mids.)	50	SO 9698
Willenhall (W Mids.)	50	SP 3676
Willerby (Humbs.)	74	TA 0230
Willerby (N Yorks.)	81	TA 0079
Willersey	50	SP 1039
Willersley	45	SO 3147
Willesborough	31	TR 0441
Willesden	37	TQ 2284
Willett	24	ST 1033
Willey (Shrops.)	59	SO 6799
Willey (Warw.)	51	SP 4984
William Law	96	NT 4839
Williamscot	47	SP 4745
Willian	53	TL 2230
Willimontswick	90	NY 7763
Willingale	38	TL 5907
Willingdon	29	TQ 5902
Willingdon Hill	29	TQ 5600
Willingham (Cambs.)	53	TL 4070
Willingham by Stow	72	SK 8784
Willington (Beds.)	52	TL 1150
Willington (Derby.)	60	SK 2928
Willington (Durham)	84	NZ 1935
Willington (Tyne and Wear)	91	NZ 3167
Willington (Warw.)	50	SP 2638
Willington Corner	69	SJ 5367
Williton	24	ST 0740
Willoughby (Lincs.)	73	TF 4772
Willoughby (Warw.)	51	SP 5167
Willoughby-on-the-Wolds	61	SK 6325
Willoughby Waterleys	51	SP 5792
Willoughton	72	SK 9293
Willy Howe (ant.)	81	TA 0672
Wilmcote	50	SP 1658
Wilmington (Devon)	24	SY 2199
Wilmington (E Susx)	29	TQ 5404
Wilmington (Kent)	37	TQ 5372
Wilmslow	69	SJ 8480
Wilnecote	50	SK 2201
Wilpshire	77	SD 6832
Wilsden	78	SE 0935
Wilsford (Lincs.)	62	TF 0043
Wilsford (Wilts.)	34	SU 1339
Wilsill	78	SE 1864
Wilson	60	SK 4024
Wilson's Pike	90	NY 5589
Wilsthorpe	52	TF 0913
Wilstone	36	SP 9014
Wilstone Reservoir	36	SP 9013
Wilton (Cleve.)	85	NZ 5819
Wilton (N Yorks.)	80	SE 8582
Wilton (Wilts.)	26	SU 0931
Wilton (Wilts.)	34	SU 2661
Wilton Dean	90	NT 4914
Wilton House (ant.)	26	SU 0831
Wimbish	53	TL 5936
Wimbish Green	54	TL 6035
Wimbleball Reservoir	23	SS 9730
Wimbledon	37	TQ 2470
Wimbledon Park	37	TQ 2472
Wimblington	53	TL 4192
Wimblington Fen	53	TL 4589
Wimborne Minster	26	SZ 0199
Wimborne St. Giles	26	SU 0212
Wimbotsham	64	TF 6205
Wimpole Hall (ant.)	53	TL 3351
Wimpstone	50	SP 2148
Wincanton	25	ST 7128
Wincham	69	SJ 6675
Winchburgh	102	NT 0874
Winchcombe	46	SP 0228
Winchelsea	30	TQ 9017
Winchelsea Beach	30	TQ 9115
Winchester	27	SU 4829
Winchfield	27	SU 7654
Winchmore Hill (Bucks.)	36	SU 9395
Winchmore Hill (Gtr London)	37	TQ 3195
Wincle	70	SJ 9565
Windbury Point	22	SS 2926
Winderton	47	SP 3240
Windermere (Cumbr.)	83	SD 3995
Windermere (Cumbr.)	83	SD 4198
Windlesham Reservoirs	70	SE 1501
Windlesham	36	SU 9363
Windlestraw Law	96	NT 3743
Windley	71	SK 3045
Windmill Hill (E Susx)	29	TQ 6412
Windmill Hill (Somer.)	24	ST 3116
Windrush	47	SP 1913
Windsor	36	SU 9676
Windsor Forest	36	SU 9373
Windsor Great Park	36	SU 9572
Wind Wick	136	ND 4587
Windy Crag	90	NT 7705
Windygates	103	NO 3400
Windy Gyle	90	NT 8614
Windyheads Hill	121	NJ 8561
Windy Standard (Dumf. and Galwy) (mt.)	88	NS 6101
Windy Standard (Strath.) (mt.)	93	NS 5204
Wineham	28	TQ 2320
Winestead	75	TA 2924
Winfarthing	55	TM 1085
Winford	33	ST 5364
Winforton	45	SO 2947
Winfrith Newburgh	25	SY 8084
Wing (Bucks.)	36	SP 8822
Wing (Leic.)	62	SK 8903
Wingate (Durham)	85	NZ 4036
Wingates (Gtr Mches.)	69	SD 6507
Wingates (Northum.)	91	NZ 0995
Wingerworth	71	SK 3867
Wingfield (Beds.)	52	SP 9926
Wingfield (Suff.)	55	TM 2276
Wingfield (Wilts.)	33	ST 8256
Wingham	31	TR 2457
Wingrave	36	SP 8719
Win Green	25	ST 9220
Winkburn	72	SK 7158
Winkfield	36	SU 9072
Winkfield Row	36	SU 9071
Winkhill	60	SK 0651
Winklebury (ant.)	26	ST 9521
Winkleigh	23	SS 6308
Winksley	79	SE 2471
Winless	135	ND 3054
Winmarleigh	77	SD 4748
Winna Ness	143	HU 6098
Winnersh	36	SU 7870
Winscales	82	NY 0226
Winscombe	32	SE 1502
Winsford (Ches.)	69	SJ 6566
Winsford (Somer.)	23	SS 9034
Winsford Hill	23	SS 8734
Winsham	24	ST 3706
Winshill	60	SK 2623
Winskill	83	NY 5835
Winslade	35	SU 6547
Winsley	33	ST 7960
Winslow	36	SP 7627
Winson	46	SP 0908
Winster (Cumbr.)	83	SD 4193
Winster (Derby.)	71	SK 2460
Winston (Durham)	84	NZ 1416
Winston (Suff.)	55	TM 1861
Winstone	46	SO 9609
Winswell	22	SS 4913
Winterborne Abbas	25	SY 6190
Winterborne Clenston	25	ST 8302
Winterborne Herringston	25	SY 6887
Winterborne Houghton	25	ST 8104
Winterborne Kingston	25	SY 8697
Winterborne Monkton (Dorset)	25	SY 6787
Winterborne Steepleton	25	SY 6289
Winterborne Stickland	25	ST 8304
Winterborne Whitechurch	25	SY 8399
Winterborne Zelston	25	SY 8997
Winterbourne	33	ST 6480
Winterbourne Bassett	34	SU 1074
Winterbourne Dauntsey	26	SU 1734
Winterbourne Earls	26	SU 1633
Winterbourne Gunner	26	SU 1735
Winterbourne Monkton (Wilts.)	34	SU 0972
Winterbourne Stoke	34	SU 0740
Winterburn	78	SD 9358
Winterburn Resr.	78	SD 9460
Wintercleuch Fell	88	NS 9910
Winter Hill	69	SD 6614
Winterhope Reservoir	89	NY 2782
Winteringham	74	SE 9222
Winterley	59	SJ 7457
Wintersett	71	SE 3815
Winterton	74	SE 9218
Winterton-on-Sea	65	TG 4919
Winthorpe (Lincs.)	73	TF 5665
Winthorpe (Notts.)	62	SK 8156
Winton (Cumbr.)	84	NY 7810
Winton (Dorset)	26	SZ 0894
Winton Fell	84	NY 8307
Wintringham	81	SE 8873
Winwick (Cambs.)	52	TL 1080
Winwick (Ches.)	69	SJ 6092
Winwick (Northants.)	51	SP 6273
Wirksworth	60	SK 2854
Wirral	68	SJ 3181
Wirswall	59	SJ 5444
Wisbech	63	TF 4609
Wisbech St. Mary	63	TF 4208
Wisborough Green	28	TQ 0526
Wiseton	72	SK 7189
Wishaw (Strath.)	94	NS 7954
Wishaw (Warw.)	50	SP 1794
Wisp Hill	89	NY 3899
Wispington	73	TF 2071
Wissett	55	TM 3679
Wiss, The (mt.)	117	NT 2620
Wistanstow	48	SO 4385
Wistanswick	59	SJ 6629
Wistaston	59	SJ 6853
Wiston (Dyfed)	42	SN 0218
Wiston (Strath.)	95	NS 9531
Wiston (W Susx)	28	TQ 1512
Wistow (Cambs.)	53	TL 2781
Wistow (N Yorks.)	79	SE 5835
Wiswell	77	SD 7437
Witcham	53	TL 4680
Witchampton	26	ST 9806
Witchford	53	TL 5078
Witham	38	TL 8114
Witham Friary	33	ST 7440
Witham on the Hill	62	TF 0516
Withens Clough Resr.	78	SD 9822
Witherenden Hill	29	TQ 6426
Witheridge	23	SS 8014
Witherley	60	SP 3297
Withern	73	TF 4382
Withernsea	75	TA 3328
Withernwick	75	TA 1940
Withersdale Street	55	TM 2781
Withersfield	54	TL 6547
Witherslack	83	SD 4384
Witherslack Hall	83	SD 4386
Withiel	19	SW 9965
Withiel Florey	23	SS 9832
Withington (Ches.)	69	SJ 8170
Withington (Glos.)	46	SP 0315
Withington (Gtr Mches.)	69	SJ 8392
Withington (Here. and Worc.)	45	SO 5643
Withington (Shrops.)	59	SJ 5713
Withington Green	69	SJ 8031
Withleigh	23	SS 9012
Withnell	77	SD 6322
Withybrook	51	SP 4384
Withy Bush Aerodrome	42	SM 9519
Withycombe	23	ST 0141
Withyham	29	TQ 4935
Withypool	23	SS 8435
Withypool Common	23	SS 8135
Witley	28	SU 9439
Witnesham	55	TM 1850
Witney	47	SP 3509
Wittering	52	TF 0502
Wittersham	30	TQ 8927
Witton	65	TG 3331
Witton Gilbert	84	NZ 2345
Witton-le-Wear	84	NZ 1431
Witton Park	84	NZ 1730
Wiveliscombe	23	ST 0827
Wivelsfield	29	TQ 3420
Wivelsfield Green	29	TQ 3519
Wivelsfield Station	29	TQ 3420
Wivenhoe	39	TM 0321
Wiveton	64	TG 0343
Wix	55	TM 1628
Wixford	50	SP 0854
Wixoe	54	TL 7142
Woburn	52	SP 9433
Woburn Abbey	52	SP 9632
Woburn Sands	52	SP 9235
Woden Law	90	NT 7612
Wokefield Park	35	SU 6765
Woking	36	TQ 0058
Wokingham	36	SU 8068
Wold Fell	78	SD 7885
Woldingham	29	TQ 3755
Wold Newton (Humbs.)	81	TA 0473
Wold Newton (Humbs.)	73	TF 2496
Wolds, The (Humbs.)	81	SE 9762
Wolds, The (Lincs.) (dist.)	64	TF 2585
Wolferlow	49	SO 6661
Wolferton	64	TF 6528
Wolfhill	108	NO 1533
Wolfhole Crag	77	SD 6257
Wolf Rock	18	SW 2612
Wolf's Castle	42	SM 9667
Wolfsdale	42	SM 9321
Woll	96	NT 4622
Wollaston (Northants.)	52	SP 9062
Wollaston (Shrops.)	58	SJ 3212
Wollerton	59	SJ 6229
Wolsingham	84	NZ 0737
Wolsingham Park Moor	84	NZ 0340
Wolston	50	SP 4175
Wolvercote	47	SP 4809
Wolverhampton	59	SO 9198
Wolverley (Here. and Worc.)	49	SO 8279
Wolverley (Shrops.)	58	SJ 4631
Wolverton (Bucks.)	52	SP 8141
Wolverton (Hants.)	35	SU 5557
Wolverton (Warw.)	50	SP 2062
Wolvey	50	SP 4387
Wolviston	85	NZ 4525
Wombleton	79	SE 6683
Wombourne	59	SO 8793
Wombwell	71	SE 3902
Womenswold	31	TR 2250
Womersley	71	SE 5319
Wonastow	45	SO 4811
Wonersh	28	TQ 0145
Wonston	35	SU 4739
Wooburn	36	SU 9187
Wooburn Green	36	SU 9188
Woodale	78	SE 0279
Woodbastwick	65	TG 3315
Woodbeck	72	SK 7777
Woodborough (Notts.)	61	SK 6347
Woodborough (Wilts.)	34	SU 1059
Woodbridge	55	TM 2749
Woodbury	21	SY 0087
Woodbury Hill (ant.)	49	SO 7464
Woodbury Salterton	24	SY 0189
Woodchester	46	SO 8302
Woodchurch	30	TQ 9434
Woodcote (Oxon.)	36	SU 6481
Woodcote (Shrops.)	59	SJ 7715
Woodcroft	45	ST 5495
Wood Dalling	65	TG 0927
Woodditton	54	TL 6559
Woodeaton	47	SP 5311
Woodend (Cumbr.)	82	SD 1696
Wood End (Herts.)	53	TL 3225
Woodend (Northants.)	51	SP 6149
Wood End (Warw.)	50	SP 1071
Woodend (W Susx)	27	SU 8108
Wood Enderby	73	TF 2764
Woodfalls	26	SU 1920
Woodford (Corn.)	22	SS 2113
Woodford (Devon)	21	SX 7950
Woodford (Gtr London)	37	TQ 4090
Woodford (Gtr Mches.)	69	SJ 8982
Woodford (Northants.)	52	SP 9676
Woodford (Wilts.)	26	SU 1136
Woodford Aerodrome	69	SJ 8982
Woodford Bridge	37	TQ 4291
Woodford Green	37	TQ 4192
Woodford Halse	51	SP 5452
Woodgate (Here. and Worc.)	50	SO 9666
Woodgate (Norf.)	64	TG 0215
Woodgate (W Mids.)	50	SO 9982
Woodgate (W Susx)	28	SU 9304
Wood Green (Gtr London)	37	TQ 3191
Woodgreen (Hants.)	26	SU 1717
Woodhall	84	SD 9790
Woodhall Loch	87	NX 6867
Woodhall Spa	73	TF 1963
Woodham	36	TQ 0261
Woodham Ferrers	38	TQ 7999
Woodham Mortimer	38	TL 8104
Woodham Walter	38	TL 8006
Woodhaven	109	NO 4127
Woodhead (Grampn.)	121	NJ 7938
Woodhead (Grampn.)	121	NJ 9061
Woodhenge (ant.)	34	SU 1543
Woodhill	59	SO 7384
Woodhouse (Leic.)	61	SK 5315
Woodhouse (S Yorks.)	71	SK 4184
Woodhouse Eaves	61	SK 5214
Woodhouselee	103	NT 2364
Woodhurst	53	TL 3176
Woodingdean	29	TQ 3605
Woodland (Devon)	21	SX 7968
Woodland (Durham)	84	NZ 0726
Woodland Bay	86	NX 1795
Woodland Fell (Cumbr.)	82	SD 2589
Woodland Fell (Durham)	84	NZ 0326
Woodlands	32	SJ 3253
Woodlands (Dorset)	26	SU 0508
Woodlands (Grampn.)	119	NO 7895
Woodlands (Hants.)	26	SU 3111
Woodlands Park	36	SU 8578
Woodleigh	21	SX 7348
Woodlesford	79	SE 3629
Woodmancote (Glos.)	46	SP 0008
Woodmancote (W Susx)	27	SU 7707
Woodmancott	35	SU 5642
Woodmansey	74	TA 0537
Woodmansterne	37	TQ 2760
Woodminton	26	SU 0122
Woodnesborough	31	TR 3156
Woodnewton	52	TL 0394
Wood Norton	64	TG 0128
Wood of Ordiequish	121	NJ 3555
Woodplumpton	77	SD 4934
Woodrising	64	TF 9803
Woodseaves (Shrops.)	59	SJ 6830
Woodseaves (Staffs.)	59	SJ 7925
Woodsend	34	SU 2275
Woodsetts	71	SK 5483
Woodsford	25	SY 7690
Woodside (Berks.)	36	SU 9371
Woodside (Herts.)	37	TL 2506
Woodside (Tays.)	108	NO 2037
Woodstock	47	SP 4416
Wood Street	49	SU 9551
Woodthorpe (Derby.)	71	SK 4574
Woodthorpe (Leic.)	61	SK 5417
Woodtown	22	SS 4926
Woodville	60	SK 3119
Woodwalton	52	TL 2180
Wood Yates	136	HY 3923
Woody Bay	22	SS 6849
Woofferton	48	SO 5168
Wookey	32	ST 5145
Wookey Hole	33	ST 5347
Wool	25	SY 8486
Woolacombe	22	SS 4543
Woolaston	45	ST 5999
Woolbeding	27	SU 8722
Wooler	97	NT 9928
Woolfardisworthy (Devon)	22	SS 3321
Woolfardisworthy (Devon)	23	SS 8208

Woolfords Cottages ... 95 NT 0057
Woolhampton ... 35 SU 5766
Woolhope ... 45 SO 6135
Woollage Green ... 31 TR 2449
Woolland ... 25 ST 7706
Woolley (Cambs.) ... 52 TL 1474
Woolley (W Yorks.) ... 71 SE 3113
Woolley House ... 34 SU 4179
Woolmer Green ... 37 TL 2518
Woolpit ... 54 TL 9762
Woolscott ... 51 SP 4968
Woolsington ... 91 NZ 1969
Woolstaston ... 58 SO 4498
Woolsthorpe ... 62 SK 8334
Woolston (Ches.) ... 69 SJ 6589
Woolston (Devon) ... 21 SX 7141
Woolston (Hants.) ... 27 SU 4410
Woolston (Shrops.) ... 58 SJ 3224
Woolston (Shrops.) ... 48 SJ 4287
Woolstone (Bucks.) ... 52 SP 8738
Woolstone (Oxon.) ... 34 SU 2987
Woolston Green ... 21 SX 7766
Wooltack Point ... 42 SM 7509
Woolton ... 68 SJ 4286
Woolton Hill ... 34 SU 4261
Woolverstone ... 55 TM 1838
Woolverton ... 33 ST 7853
Woolwich ... 37 TQ 4478
Wooperton ... 91 NU 0420
Woore ... 59 SJ 7242
Wootton (Beds.) ... 52 TL 0045
Wootton (Hants.) ... 26 SZ 2498
Wootton (Humbs.) ... 74 TA 0815
Wootton (Kent) ... 31 TR 2246
Wootton (Northants.) ... 51 SP 7656
Wootton (Oxon.) ... 47 SU 4319
Wootton (Oxon.) ... 47 SP 4701
Wootton (Staffs.) ... 59 SJ 8227
Wootton (Staffs.) ... 60 SK 1045
Wootton Bassett ... 34 SU 0682
Wootton Bridge ... 27 SZ 5491
Wootton Common ... 27 SZ 5390
Wootton Courtenay ... 23 SS 9343
Wootton Fitzpaine ... 24 SY 3695
Wootton Rivers ... 34 SU 1962
Wootton St. Lawrence ... 35 SU 5953
Wootton Wawen ... 50 SP 1563
Worbarrow Bay ... 25 SY 8579
Worcester ... 49 SO 8555
Worcester and Birmingham Canal ... 49 SO 9465
Wordsley ... 49 SO 8887
Worfield ... 59 SO 7595
Work ... 136 HY 4713
Workington ... 82 NX 9928
Worksop ... 71 SK 5879
Worlaby ... 74 TA 0113
World's End (Berks.) ... 35 SU 4876
World's End (Clwyd) ... 58 SJ 2347
Worle ... 32 ST 3562
Worlebury (ant.) ... 32 ST 3262
Worleston ... 59 SJ 6856
Worlingham ... 55 TM 4489
Worlington (Devon) ... 23 SS 7713
Worlington (Suff.) ... 54 TL 6973
Worlingworth ... 55 TM 2368
Wormbridge ... 45 SO 4230
Wormegay ... 64 TF 6611
Wormelow Tump ... 45 SO 4930
Wormhill ... 70 SK 1274
Wormiehills ... 109 NO 6239
Wormingford ... 54 TL 9332

Worminghall ... 36 SP 6408
Wormington ... 50 SP 0336
Worminster ... 33 ST 5742
Wormit ... 109 NO 3925
Wormleighton ... 51 SP 4453
Wormley ... 37 TL 3605
Wormley West End ... 37 TL 3306
Worms Head ... 40 SS 3887
Wormshill ... 30 TQ 8857
Wormsley ... 45 SO 4248
Worplesdon ... 28 SU 9753
Worrall ... 71 SK 3092
Worsbrough ... 71 SE 3503
Worsley ... 69 SD 7400
Worstead ... 65 TG 3026
Worsthorne ... 78 SD 8732
Worston ... 78 SD 7642
Worswell ... 21 SX 5347
Worth (Kent) ... 31 TR 3356
Worth (W Susx) ... 29 TQ 3036
Worth Abbey ... 29 TQ 3134
Wortham ... 54 TM 0777
Worthen ... 58 SJ 3204
Worthenbury ... 58 SJ 4146
Worthing (Norf.) ... 64 TF 9919
Worthing (W Susx) ... 28 TQ 1402
Worthington ... 60 SK 4020
Worth Matravers ... 26 SY 9777
Worthy Down ... 27 SU 4635
Wortley ... 71 SK 3099
Worton ... 34 ST 9757
Wortwell ... 55 TM 2784
Wotherton ... 58 SJ 2800
Wotter ... 21 SX 5561
Wotton ... 28 TQ 1348
Wotton Under Edge ... 46 ST 7593
Wotton Underwood ... 36 SP 6815
Woughton on the Green ... 52 SP 8737
Wouldham ... 30 TQ 7164
Wrabness ... 55 TM 1731
Wragby ... 73 TF 1378
Wrakendike (ant.) ... 91 NZ 3162
Wramplingham ... 65 TG 1106
Wrangham ... 121 NJ 6331
Wrangle ... 63 TF 4250
Wrangway ... 24 ST 1217
Wrantage ... 24 ST 3022
Wrawby ... 74 TA 0108
Wraxall (Avon) ... 33 ST 4872
Wraxall (Somer.) ... 25 ST 5936
Wray ... 77 SD 6067
Wray Castle ... 83 NY 3700
Wraysbury ... 36 TQ 0173
Wrea Green ... 77 SD 3931
Wreay (Cumbr.) ... 83 NY 4349
Wreay (Cumbr.) ... 83 NY 4423
Wrekenton ... 91 NZ 2758
Wrekin, The ... 59 SJ 6208
Wrelton ... 80 SE 7686
Wrenbury ... 59 SJ 5947
Wreningham ... 65 TM 1699
Wrentham ... 55 TM 4982
Wressle ... 74 SE 7031
Wrestlingworth ... 53 TL 2547
Wretton ... 64 TF 6800
Wrexham ... 58 SJ 3349
Wrexham Industrial Estate ... 58 SJ 3849
Wribbenhall ... 49 SO 7975
Wrightington Bar ... 69 SD 5313
Wrightington Hall (ant.) ... 69 SD 5310
Wrinehill ... 59 SJ 7546
Wrington ... 33 ST 4662
Writtle ... 38 TL 6606

Wrockwardine ... 59 SJ 6212
Wroot ... 74 SE 7102
Wrotham ... 30 TQ 6159
Wrotham Heath ... 30 TQ 6258
Wrotham Park ... 37 TQ 2599
Wroughton ... 34 SU 1480
Wroxall (I. of W.) ... 27 SZ 5579
Wroxall (Warw.) ... 50 SP 2271
Wroxeter ... 59 SJ 5608
Wroxham ... 65 TG 3017
Wroxton ... 50 SP 4141
Wryde Croft ... 63 TF 3107
Wrynose Pass ... 82 NY 2702
Wyaston ... 60 SK 1842
Wyberton ... 63 TF 3240
Wyboston ... 52 TL 1656
Wybunbury ... 59 SJ 6949
Wychbold ... 49 SO 9166
Wych Cross ... 29 TQ 4231
Wyche ... 49 SO 7643
Wyck ... 35 SU 7539
Wyck Rissington ... 47 SP 1821
Wycombe Marsh ... 36 SU 8992
Wyddial ... 53 TL 3731
Wye ... 31 TR 0546
Wyke (Dorset.) ... 25 ST 7926
Wyke (Shrops.) ... 59 SJ 6402
Wyke (W Yorks.) ... 78 SE 1526
Wykeham (N Yorks.) ... 80 SE 9675
Wykeham (N Yorks.) ... 81 SE 9683
Wyke Regis ... 25 SY 6677
Wyke, The (N Yorks.) (pt.) ... 81 TA 0983
Wyke, The (Shrops.) ... 59 SJ 7306
Wykey ... 58 SJ 3925
Wylam ... 91 NZ 1164
Wylde Green ... 50 SP 1293
Wylfa Power Sta. ... 66 SH 3594
Wylye ... 26 SU 0037
Wylye Valley ... 26 SU 0037
Wymering ... 27 SU 6405
Wymeswold ... 61 SK 6023
Wymington ... 52 SP 9564
Wymondham (Leic.) ... 62 SK 8518
Wymondham (Norf.) ... 65 TG 1101
Wymondley ... 52 TL 2128
Wyndburgh Hill ... 90 NT 5504
Wyndham ... 41 SS 9391
Wynford Eagle ... 25 SY 5895
Wyre ... 136 HY 4426
Wyre Forest ... 49 SO 7576
Wyre Piddle ... 50 SO 9647
Wyresdale Tower (ruin) ... 77 SD 6054
Wyre Sound ... 136 HY 4226
Wysall ... 61 SK 6027
Wytch Heath ... 26 SY 9784
Wythall ... 50 SP 0775
Wytham ... 47 SP 4708
Wythburn Fells ... 82 NY 3212
Wyverstone ... 54 TM 0468
Wyverstone Street ... 54 TM 0367
Wyvis Lodge ... 128 NH 4873

Y

Yaddlethorpe ... 74 SE 8806
Yafford ... 27 SZ 4581
Yafforth ... 85 SE 3494
Yair Hill Forest ... 96 NT 4333
Yalding ... 29 TQ 7050
Yantlet Dredged Channel ... 38 TQ 9180
Yanworth ... 46 SP 0713

Yapham ... 80 SE 7851
Yapton ... 28 SU 9703
Yarburgh ... 73 TF 3493
Yarcombe ... 24 ST 2408
Yardley ... 50 SP 1385
Yardley Chase ... 52 SP 8455
Yardley Gobion ... 51 SP 7644
Yardley Hastings ... 52 SP 8656
Yardro ... 45 SO 2258
Yarkhill ... 45 SO 6042
Yarlet ... 59 SJ 9129
Yarlington ... 25 ST 6529
Yarm ... 85 NZ 4111
Yarmouth ... 26 SZ 3589
Yarmouth Roads ... 65 TG 5507
Yarnbury Castle (ant.) ... 34 SU 0340
Yarnfield ... 59 SJ 8632
Yarnscombe ... 23 SS 5523
Yarnton ... 47 SP 4711
Yarpole ... 48 SO 4665
Yarrow ... 96 NT 3527
Yarrow Feus ... 96 NT 3325
Yarrow Water ... 96 NT 3728
Yarsop ... 45 SO 4047
Yarwell ... 62 TL 0697
Yate ... 33 ST 7082
Yateley ... 36 SU 8160
Yatesbury ... 34 SU 0671
Yattendon ... 35 SU 5474
Yatton (Avon) ... 33 ST 4265
Yatton (Here. and Worc.) ... 48 SO 4367
Yatton Keynell ... 33 ST 8676
Yaverland ... 27 SZ 6185
Yaxham ... 64 TG 0010
Yaxley (Cambs.) ... 52 TL 1892
Yaxley (Suff.) ... 55 TM 1173
Yazor ... 45 SO 4046
Y Bwlchcau ... 41 SS 888
Y Clogydd ... 57 SJ 0628
Y Cribau (mt.) ... 67 SH 6753
Y Drum ... 44 SN 7358
Yeading ... 37 TQ 1182
Yeadon ... 78 SE 2040
Yealand Conyers ... 77 SD 5074
Yealand Redmayne ... 77 SD 5075
Yealmpton ... 21 SX 5751
Yearsley ... 58 SE 5874
Yeaton ... 58 SJ 4319
Yeaveley ... 60 SK 1840
Yeavering Bell ... 97 NT 9329
Yedingham ... 81 SE 8979
Yelden ... 52 TL 0167
Yelford ... 47 SP 3504
Yell (is.) ... 143 HU 4890
Yelling ... 53 TL 2562
Yell Sound ... 143 HU 4087
Yelvertoft ... 51 SP 5975
Yelverton (Devon) ... 21 SX 5267
Yelverton (Norf.) ... 65 TG 2901
Yenston ... 25 ST 7120
Yeoford ... 21 SX 7898
Yeolmbridge ... 20 SX 3187
Yeoman Wharf (sbk.) ... 77 SD 3563
Yeovil ... 25 ST 5515
Yeovil Airfield ... 25 ST 5315
Yeovil Junction Station ... 25 ST 5713
Yeovil Marsh ... 25 ST 5418
Yeovilton ... 25 ST 5422
Yerbeston ... 42 SN 0609
Yesnaby ... 136 HY 2215
Yester Castle ... 103 NT 5566
Yester Ho. ... 103 NT 5467
Yes Tor ... 21 SX 5890

Yetlington ... 91 NU 0209
Yetminster ... 25 ST 5910
Yettington ... 24 SY 0585
Yetts o'Muckhart ... 102 NO 0001
Y Fan ... 57 SN 9487
Y Ffôr ... 66 SH 3939
Y Foel ... 57 SN 8484
Y Gaer (Powys) (ant.) ... 41 SO 0029
Y Gaer (S Glam.) (ant.) ... 41 ST 0674
Y Gamlas ... 66 SH 3432
Y Garn ... 57 SH 7023
Y Gribin ... 57 SH 8417
Yieldshields ... 95 NS 8750
Yiewsley ... 36 TQ 0680
Y Llethr ... 57 SH 6625
Ynysboeth ... 41 ST 0696
Ynysddu ... 41 ST 1892
Ynysdeullyn ... 42 SM 8434
Ynys Dulas ... 66 SH 5090
Ynys Gwylan-fawr ... 56 SH 1824
Ynyshir ... 41 ST 0292
Ynyslas ... 56 SN 6092
Ynys-Lochtyn (pt.) ... 43 SN 3155
Ynysybwl ... 41 ST 0594
Yockenthwaite ... 78 SD 9079
Yockleton ... 58 SJ 3910
Yokefleet ... 74 SE 8124
Yoker ... 101 NS 5168
Yonder Bognie ... 121 NJ 5946
York ... 79 SE 6052
Yorkletts ... 31 TR 0963
Yorkley ... 45 SO 6306
Yorton ... 59 SJ 4923
Youlgreave ... 70 SK 2164
Youlstone ... 22 SS 2715
Youlthorpe ... 80 SE 7655
Youlton ... 79 SE 4863
Young's End ... 38 TL 7319
Yoxall ... 60 SK 1419
Yoxford ... 55 TM 3968
Y Pigwn ... 41 SN 8131
Yr Allt (Dyfed) ... 57 SN 8376
Yr Allt (Powys) ... 41 SN 9129
Yr Aran ... 66 SH 6051
Yr Arddu ... 67 SH 675i
Yr Eifl (mt.) ... 66 SH 3544
Y Rhiw ... 56 SH 2228
Ysbyty Ifan ... 67 SH 8448
Ysbyty Ystwyth ... 57 SN 7371
Ysceifiog ... 68 SJ 1571
Ysgubor-y-coed ... 57 SN 6895
Ysgyryd Fawr ... 45 SO 3318
Ystalyfera ... 41 SN 7608
Ystrad ... 41 SS 9796
Ystrad Aeron ... 43 SN 5256
Ystradfellte ... 41 SN 9313
Ystradfellte Resr. ... 41 SN 9417
Ystradffin ... 44 SN 7846
Ystradgynlais ... 41 SN 7910
Ystrad Meurig ... 57 SN 7067
Ystrad Mynach ... 41 ST 1493
Ystradowen (Dyfed) ... 41 SN 7512
Ystradowen (S Glam.) ... 41 ST 0177
Ythanbank ... 121 NJ 9034
Ythsie ... 121 NJ 8830

Z

Zeal Monachorum ... 23 SS 7103
Zeals ... 25 ST 7731
Zelah ... 19 SW 8051
Zennor ... 18 SW 4538
Zone Point ... 19 SW 8431

SIGNS GIVING ORDERS

These signs are mostly circular and those with red circles are mostly prohibitive

Maximum speed

National speed limit applies

Stop and Give Way

Give way to traffic on major road

Manually operated temporary 'STOP' sign

School crossing patrol

School crossing patrol

No entry for vehicular traffic

No vehicles

No motor vehicles

No motor vehicles except solo motorcycles, scooters or mopeds

No vehicles with over 12 seats except regular scheduled, school and works buses

No vehicle or combination of vehicles over length shown

No goods vehicles over maximum gross weight shown in tonnes

No vehicles over axle weight shown in tonnes

No vehicles, including load, over weight shown (total weight limit in tonnes)

No vehicles over height shown

No vehicles over width shown

No cycling

No pedestrians

No overtaking

No stopping (Clearway)

Give priority to vehicles from opposite direction

No right turn

No left turn

No U turns

URBAN CLEARWAY
Monday to Friday
am 8 9 30   pm 4 30 6 30

No stopping during times shown except for up to 2 mins. to set down or pick up passengers

Meter ZONE
Entrance to controlled parking zone

Zone ENDS
End of controlled parking zone

Plates below some signs qualify their message

End — End of restriction

Except for loading — Exception for loading/unloading goods and access to off-street garaging

Except buses and coaches — Exception for vehicles with over 12 seats

Except buses — Exception for stage and scheduled express carriages, school and works buses

Except for access — Exception for access to premises and land adjacent to the road where there is no alternative route

With-flow bus lane

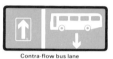
Contra-flow bus lane

Signs with blue circles but no red border are mostly compulsory

Ahead only

Turn left ahead (right if symbol reversed)

Turn left (right if symbol reversed)

Keep left (right if symbol reversed)

Vehicles may pass either side to reach same destination

Route to be used by pedal cyclists only

Minimum speed

End of minimum speed

Mini-roundabout (roundabout circulation – give way to vehicles from the immediate right)

One-way traffic (Compare circular "Ahead only" sign)

WARNING SIGNS

Mostly triangular

Roundabout

Cross roads

Side road

T junction

Staggered junction

Dual carriageway ends

Road narrows on both sides

Road narrows on right (left if symbol reversed)

School
Children going to or from school

Patrol
School crossing patrol ahead (Some signs have amber lights which flash when patrol is operating)

Pedestrian crossing

Slippery road

Two-way traffic straight ahead

Two-way traffic crosses one-way road

Traffic merges from left

Traffic merges from right

Double bend first to left (may be reversed)

Bend to right (or left if symbol reversed)

Single file traffic
Single file in each direction

10% — Steep hill downwards
20% — Steep hill upwards
Gradients may be shown as a ratio i.e. 20% = 1:5

Hump bridge

Uneven road

Traffic signals

Road works

Right-hand lane closed (symbols may be varied)

Change to opposite carriageway (may be reversed)

Single track road
Road wide enough for only one line of traffic

Safe height 16'-6"
Overhead electric cable; plate indicates maximum height of vehicles which can pass safely

Low-flying aircraft or sudden aircraft noise

Loose chippings

Ford
Worded warning sign

Cattle

Wild animals

Wild horses or ponies

Accompanied horses or ponies crossing the road ahead

Falling or fallen rocks

Fallen tree
Other danger; plate indicates nature of danger

14'-6"
Height limit (e.g. low bridge)

14'-6"
Available width of headroom indicated

Opening or swing bridge ahead

Quayside or river bank

REDUCE SPEED NOW
Plate below some signs

Sharp deviation of route to left (or right if chevrons reversed)

STOP 100 yds
Distance to "Stop" line ahead

1 mile
Distance to hazard

For 2 miles
Distance over which hazard extends

AUTOMATIC BARRIERS STOP when lights show
Plate to indicate a level crossing equipped with automatic barriers and flashing lights

Level crossing with barrier or gate ahead

Level crossing without barrier or gate ahead

Location of level crossing without barrier or gate

"Count-down" markers approaching concealed level crossing (each bar represents ⅓ the distance from the first warning sign to the crossing)

GIVE WAY 50 yds
Distance to "Give Way" line ahead